EXPLORING MICROSOFT® POWERPOINT FOR WINDOWS® 95

VERSION 7.0

EXPLORING MICROSOFT® POWERPOINT FOR WINDOWS® 95

VERSION 7.0

Robert T. Grauer / Maryann Barber

University of Miami

Prentice Hall, Upper Saddle River, New Jersey 07458

Library of Congress Cataloging in Publication Data

Grauer, Robert T. [date]
Exploring Microsoft PowerPoint for Windows 95, version 7.0 /
Robert T. Grauer, Maryann Barber.
p. cm.
Includes index.
ISBN 0-13-503328-4
1. Microsoft PowerPoint. 2. Presentation Software.
I. Barber, Maryann M. II. Title.
HF5548.4.M523G72 1996
005.369—dc20 95-12937
CIP

Acquisitions editor: Carolyn Henderson
Editorial/production supervisor: Greg Hubit Bookworks
Interior and cover design: Suzanne Behnke
Manufacturing buyer: Paul Smolenski
Managing editor: Nicholas Radhuber
Editorial assistant: Audrey Regan
Production coordinator: Renée Pelletier

Printed in the United States of America
10 9 8 7 6 5 4

ISBN 0-13-503328-4

Prentice Hall International (UK) Limited, *London*
Prentice Hall of Australia Pty. Limited, *Sydney*
Prentice Hall of Canada Inc., *Toronto*
Prentice Hall Hispanoamericano, S.A., *Mexico*
Prentice Hall of India Private Limited, *New Delhi*
Prentice Hall of Japan, Inc., *Tokyo*
Simon & Schuster Asia Pte. Ltd., *Singapore*
Editora Prentice Hall do Brasil, Ltda., *Rio de Janeiro*

CONTENTS

2

Creating a Presentation: Content, Formatting, and Animation 47

3

Adding Impact: Object Linking and Embedding 93

PREFACE

Exploring Microsoft PowerPoint for Windows 95 Version 7.0 is one of several books in the *Exploring Windows* series. Other series titles include: *Exploring Windows 95 and Essential Computing Concepts, Exploring Microsoft Word Version 7.0, Exploring Microsoft Excel Version 7.0, Exploring Microsoft Access Version 7.0,* and *Exploring the Internet.* We have also created *Exploring Microsoft Office Professional—Volume I* by taking selected chapters from the individual books. And finally, there is *Exploring Microsoft Office Professional—Volume II,* which consists of advanced chapters and appendices from the individual books that were not included in Volume I.

The *Exploring Windows* series is different from other books, both in its scope and in the way in which material is presented. Students learn by doing. Concepts are stressed and memorization is minimized. Shortcuts and other important information are consistently highlighted in the many tips that appear throughout the series. Every chapter contains an average of three guided exercises to be completed at the computer.

Each book in the *Exploring Windows* series is accompanied by a comprehensive Instructor's Resource Manual with tests, PowerPoint lectures, and student/instructor resource disks. (The Instructor's Resource Manual for the entire series is also available on a single CD-ROM.) Instructors can also use the Prentice Hall Computerized Online Testing System to prepare customized tests for their courses and may obtain Interactive Multimedia courseware as a further supplement. The *Exploring Windows* series is part of the Prentice Hall custom binding program.

What's New

Exploring Microsoft PowerPoint for Windows 95 Version 7.0 is a revision of our existing text, *Exploring PowerPoint 4.0.* In addition to updating our book to reflect changes in Windows 95, we sought to add topics that were previously omitted and have included a 20-page appendix on multimedia. Object Linking and Embedding is stressed in Chapter 3, where the student learns how to incorporate objects from other applications into a PowerPoint presentation. We have added an introductory section on Microsoft Office that emphasizes the common user interface and shows how knowledge of one Office application helps in learning another. We have also included a supplement on Windows 95 to introduce the reader to the essentials of the new operating system.

We believe, however, that our most important improvement is the expanded end-of-chapter material, which provides a wide variety of student assignments. Every chapter contains *15 multiple-choice questions* (with answers) so that students can test themselves quickly and objectively. Every chapter has *four conceptual problems* that do not require participation at the computer. Every chapter also has *four computer-based practice exercises* to build student proficiency. And finally, every chapter ends with *four case studies* in which the student is given little guidance in the means of the solution. This unique *15-four-by-four-by-four* format provides substantial opportunity for students to master the material while simultaneously giving instructors considerable flexibility in student assignments. Instructors may also assign the hands-on exercises within each chapter to ensure further practice on the part of their students.

FEATURES AND BENEFITS

Exploring Microsoft PowerPoint Version 7.0 is written for the computer novice and assumes no previous knowledge about Windows 95. A detailed supplement introduces the reader to the operating system and emphasizes the file operations he or she will need.

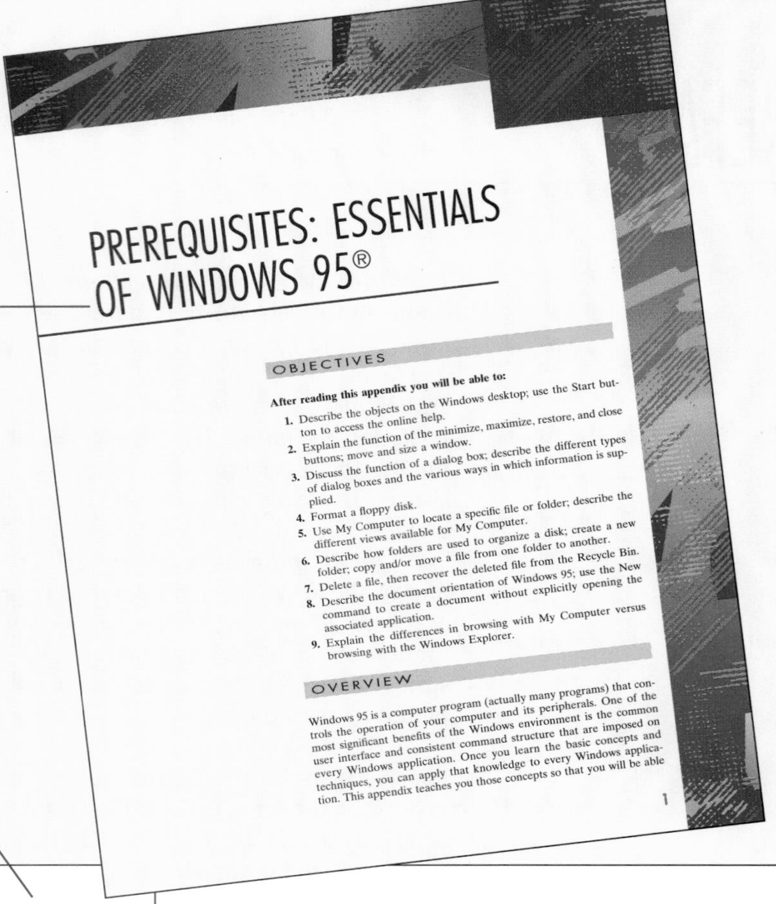

PREREQUISITES: ESSENTIALS OF WINDOWS 95®

OBJECTIVES

After reading this appendix you will be able to:

1. Describe the objects on the Windows desktop; use the Start button to access the online help.
2. Explain the function of the minimize, maximize, restore, and close buttons; move and size a window.
3. Discuss the function of a dialog box; describe the different types of dialog boxes and the various ways in which information is supplied.
4. Format a floppy disk.
5. Use My Computer to locate a specific file or folder; describe the different views available for My Computer.
6. Describe how folders are used to organize a disk; create a new folder; copy and/or move a file from one folder to another.
7. Delete a file, then recover the deleted file from the Recycle Bin.
8. Describe the document orientation of Windows 95; use the New command to create a document without explicitly opening the associated application.
9. Explain the differences in browsing with My Computer versus browsing with the Windows Explorer.

OVERVIEW

Windows 95 is a computer program (actually many programs) that controls the operation of your computer and its peripherals. One of the most significant benefits of the Windows environment is the common user interface and consistent command structure that are imposed on every Windows application. Once you learn the basic concepts and techniques, you can apply that knowledge to every Windows application. This appendix teaches you those concepts so that you will be able

1

An introductory section on the Microsoft Office emphasizes the benefits of the common user interface. Although the text assumes no previous knowledge, some users may already be acquainted with another Office application, in which case they can take advantage of what they already know.

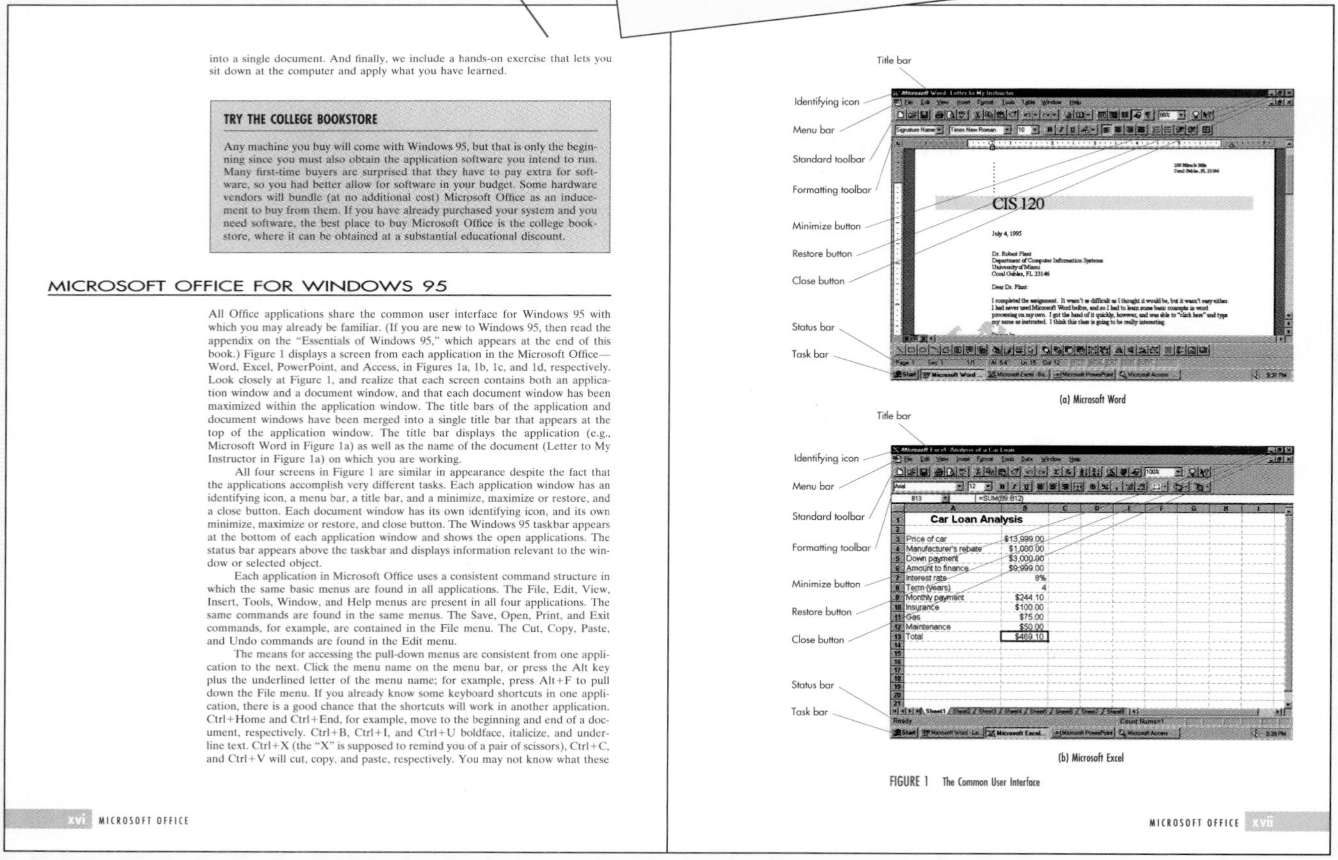

into a single document. And finally, we include a hands-on exercise that lets you sit down at the computer and apply what you have learned.

TRY THE COLLEGE BOOKSTORE

Any machine you buy will come with Windows 95, but that is only the beginning since you must also obtain the application software you intend to run. Many first-time buyers are surprised that they have to pay extra for software, so you had better allow for software in your budget. Some hardware vendors will bundle (at no additional cost) Microsoft Office as an inducement to buy from them. If you have already purchased your system and you need software, the best place to buy Microsoft Office is the college bookstore, where it can be obtained at a substantial educational discount.

MICROSOFT OFFICE FOR WINDOWS 95

All Office applications share the common user interface for Windows 95 with which you may already be familiar. (If you are new to Windows 95, then read the appendix on the "Essentials of Windows 95," which appears at the end of this book.) Figure 1 displays a screen from each application in the Microsoft Office—Word, Excel, PowerPoint, and Access, in Figures 1a, 1b, 1c, and 1d, respectively. Look closely at Figure 1, and realize that each screen contains both an application window and a document window, and that each document window has been maximized within the application window. The title bars of the application and document windows have been merged into a single title bar that appears at the top of the application window. The title bar displays the application (e.g., Microsoft Word in Figure 1a) as well as the name of the document (Letter to My Instructor in Figure 1a) on which you are working.

All four screens in Figure 1 are similar in appearance despite the fact that the applications accomplish very different tasks. Each application window has an identifying icon, a menu bar, a title bar, and a minimize, maximize or restore, and a close button. Each document window has its own identifying icon, and its own minimize, maximize or restore, and close button. The Windows 95 taskbar appears at the bottom of each application window and shows the open applications. The status bar appears above the taskbar and displays information relevant to the window or selected object.

Each application in Microsoft Office uses a consistent command structure in which the same basic menus are found in all applications. The File, Edit, View, Insert, Tools, Window, and Help menus are present in all four applications. The same commands are found in the same menus. The Save, Open, Print, and Exit commands, for example, are contained in the File menu. The Cut, Copy, Paste, and Undo commands are found in the Edit menu.

The means for accessing the pull-down menus are consistent from one application to the next. Click the menu name on the menu bar, or press the Alt key plus the underlined letter of the menu name; for example, press Alt+F to pull down the File menu. If you already know some keyboard shortcuts in one application, there is a good chance that the shortcuts will work in another application. Ctrl+Home and Ctrl+End, for example, move to the beginning and end of a document, respectively. Ctrl+B, Ctrl+I, and Ctrl+U boldface, italicize, and underline text. Ctrl+X (the "X" is supposed to remind you of a pair of scissors), Ctrl+C, and Ctrl+V will cut, copy, and paste, respectively. You may not know what these

Title bar
Identifying icon
Menu bar
Standard toolbar
Formatting toolbar
Minimize button
Restore button
Close button
Status bar
Task bar
CIS 120

(a) Microsoft Word

Title bar
Identifying icon
Menu bar
Standard toolbar
Formatting toolbar
Minimize button
Restore button
Close button
Status bar
Task bar
Car Loan Analysis
Price of car $13,999.00
Manufacturer's rebate $1,000.00
Down payment $3,000.00
Amount to finance $9,999.00
Interest rate 8%
Term (years) 4
Monthly payment $244.10
Insurance $100.00
Gas $75.00
Maintenance $50.00
Total $469.10

(b) Microsoft Excel

FIGURE 1 The Common User Interface

xvi MICROSOFT OFFICE

MICROSOFT OFFICE xvii

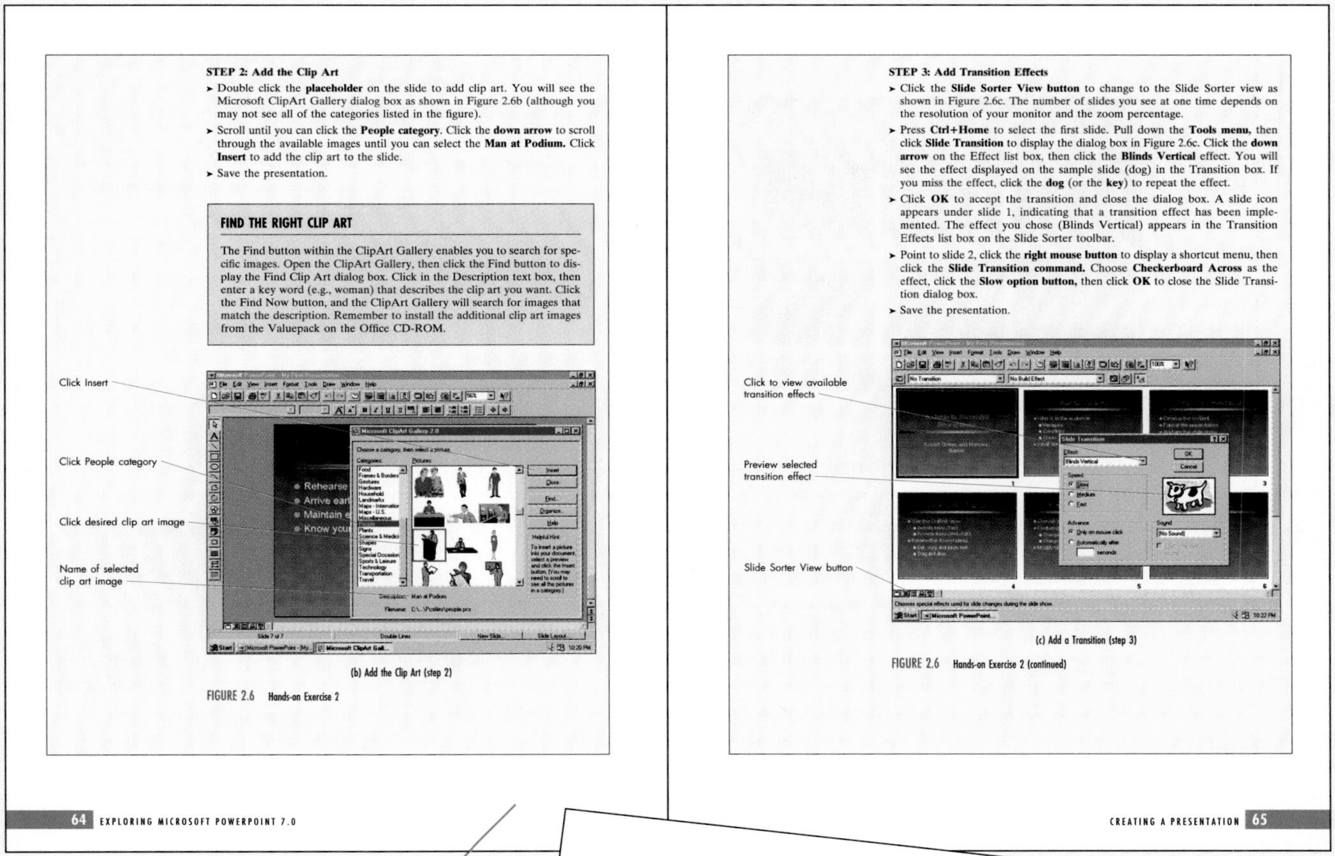

STEP 2: Add the Clip Art

- Double click the **placeholder** on the slide to add clip art. You will see the Microsoft ClipArt Gallery dialog box as shown in Figure 2.6b (although you may not see all of the categories listed in the figure).
- Scroll until you can click the **People category**. Click the **down arrow** to scroll through the available images until you can select the **Man at Podium.** Click **Insert** to add the clip art to the slide.
- Save the presentation.

FIND THE RIGHT CLIP ART

The Find button within the ClipArt Gallery enables you to search for specific images. Open the ClipArt Gallery, then click the Find button to display the Find Clip Art dialog box. Click in the Description text box, then enter a key word (e.g., woman) that describes the clip art you want. Click the Find Now button, and the ClipArt Gallery will search for images that match the description. Remember to install the additional clip art images from the Valuepack on the Office CD-ROM.

Click Insert
Click People category
Click desired clip art image
Name of selected clip art image

(b) Add the Clip Art (step 2)

FIGURE 2.6 Hands-on Exercise 2

64 EXPLORING MICROSOFT POWERPOINT 7.0

STEP 3: Add Transition Effects

- Click the **Slide Sorter View button** to change to the Slide Sorter view as shown in Figure 2.6c. The number of slides you see at one time depends on the resolution of your monitor and the zoom percentage.
- Press **Ctrl+Home** to select the first slide. Pull down the **Tools menu,** then click **Slide Transition** to display the dialog box in Figure 2.6c. Click the **down arrow** on the Effect list box, then click the **Blinds Vertical** effect. You will see the effect displayed on the sample slide (dog) in the Transition box. If you miss the effect, click the **dog** (or the **key**) to repeat the effect.
- Click **OK** to accept the transition and close the dialog box. A slide icon appears under slide 1, indicating that a transition effect has been implemented. The effect you chose (Blinds Vertical) appears in the Transition Effects list box on the Slide Sorter toolbar.
- Point to slide 2, click the **right mouse button** to display a shortcut menu, then click the **Slide Transition command.** Choose **Checkerboard Across** as the effect, click the **Slow option button,** then click **OK** to close the Slide Transition dialog box.
- Save the presentation.

Click to view available transition effects
Preview selected transition effect
Slide Sorter View button

(c) Add a Transition (step 3)

FIGURE 2.6 Hands-on Exercise 2 (continued)

CREATING A PRESENTATION 65

A total of 12 in-depth tutorials (hands-on exercises) guide the reader at the computer. Each tutorial is illustrated with large, full-color screen captures that are clear and easy to read. Each tutorial is accompanied by numerous tips that present different ways to accomplish a given task, but in a logical and relaxed fashion.

The Original Clip Art
Flip Vertically
Copy and Flip Horizontally
Change Colors
Ungroup and Resize
Get Your Ducks in a Row

FIGURE 3.3 What You Can Do with Clip Art

ADDING IMPACT 105

You don't have to be an artist to use the drawing tools within PowerPoint. Chapter 3 shows how to modify existing clip art to create new drawings to enliven your presentations.

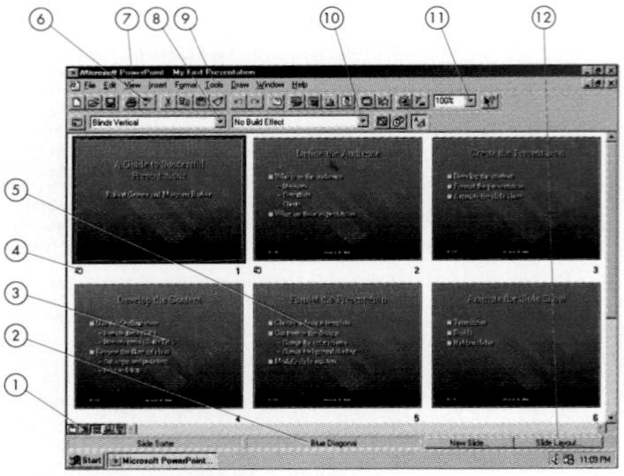
FIGURE 2.11 Screen for Problem 1

Action	Result
a. Click at 1	____ Choose a new template
b. Double click at 2	____ Spell check the presentation
c. Click at 4	____ Switch to the Outline view
d. Click at 5, click at 10	____ Run the Style Checker
e. Click at 3, click at 8	____ Create a build for slide 5
f. Click at 6	____ Change the AutoLayout for the current slide
g. Click at 7	____ Preview the transition for the first slide
h. Click at 9	____ Create a transition for slide 4
i. Click at 11	____ Modify the slide master
j. Click at 12	____ Change the zoom in effect

2. The Answer Wizard functions identically in PowerPoint as it does in the other Office applications. Accordingly, use what you know about Microsoft Office, or explore on your own, to answer the following with respect to Figure 2.12:
   a. How do you display the dialog box in Figure 2.12? Is this type of help information available in the other Office applications?
   b. What is the difference between the Contents, Index, Find, and Answer Wizard tabs? Which tab is currently selected?

84 EXPLORING MICROSOFT POWERPOINT 7.0

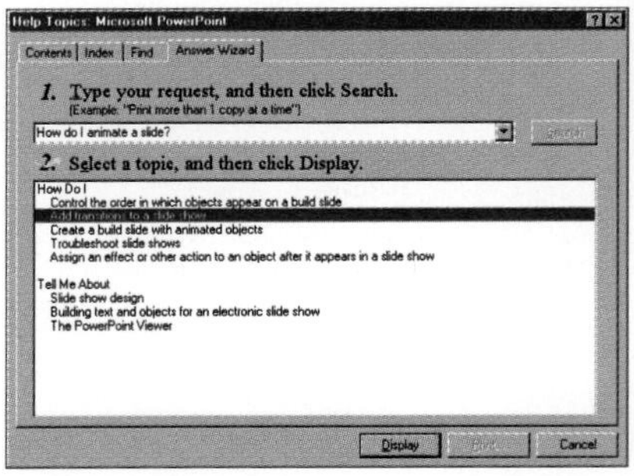
FIGURE 2.12 Screen for Problem 2

   c. What did the user enter once the dialog box appeared? What was displayed in response to the user's input?
   d. What would be the effect of clicking the Display command button?
3. Answer the following with respect to the dialog box in Figure 2.13:
   a. What command(s) displayed the dialog box?
   b. What is the difference between the Presentation Designs tab and the Presentations tab? Which one is currently selected?

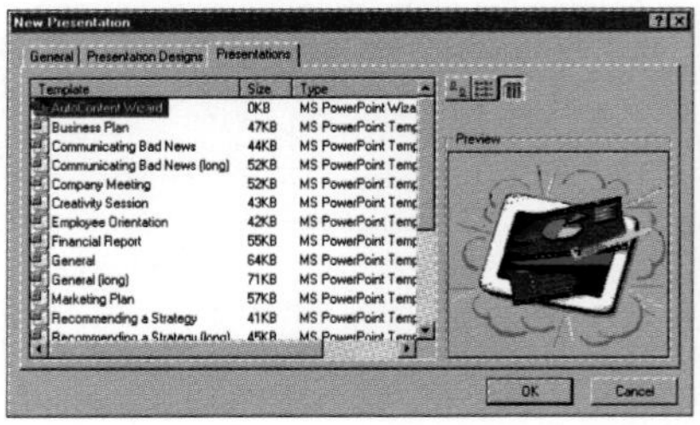
FIGURE 2.13 Screen for Problem 3

ING A PRESENTATION 85

At the end of every chapter are abundant and thought-provoking exercises to review and extend the material. There are objective multiple-choice questions, conceptual problems that do not require interaction with the computer, guided computer exercises, as well as less structured case studies.

Object Linking and Embedding (OLE) is stressed throughout the series. Students learn how to branch within a presentation and how to link or embed objects from other applications.

BRANCHING WITHIN A PRESENTATION

The most effective public speakers are sensitive to their audiences and are able to adapt their presentations to specific situations. Thus far all of the presentations in our text have been designed to be viewed sequentially, starting with the first slide and ending with the last slide. Figure 3.10 introduces *branching* into a presenta-

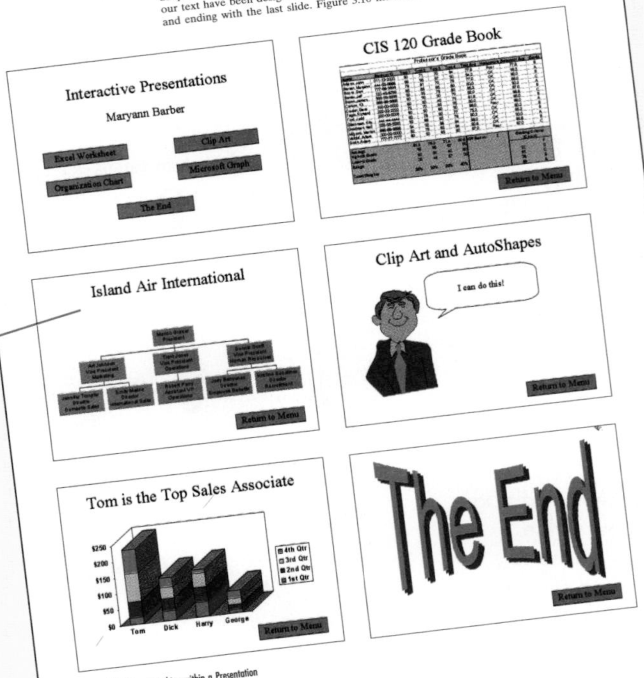

Interactive Presentations
Maryann Barber
Excel Worksheet
Clip Art
Organization Chart
Microsoft Graph
The End
CIS 120 Grade Book
Return to Menu
Island Air International
Return to Menu
Clip Art and AutoShapes
I can do this!
Return to Menu
Tom is the Top Sales Associate
Tom
Dick
Harry
George
Return to Menu
The End
Return to Menu

FIGURE 3.10 Branching within a Presentation

132 EXPLORING MICROSOFT POWERPOINT 7.0

Appendix B on multimedia shows students how to animate a presentation and incorporate sound and video files. The reader is also introduced to the multimedia resources available on the CD-ROM version of Microsoft Office.

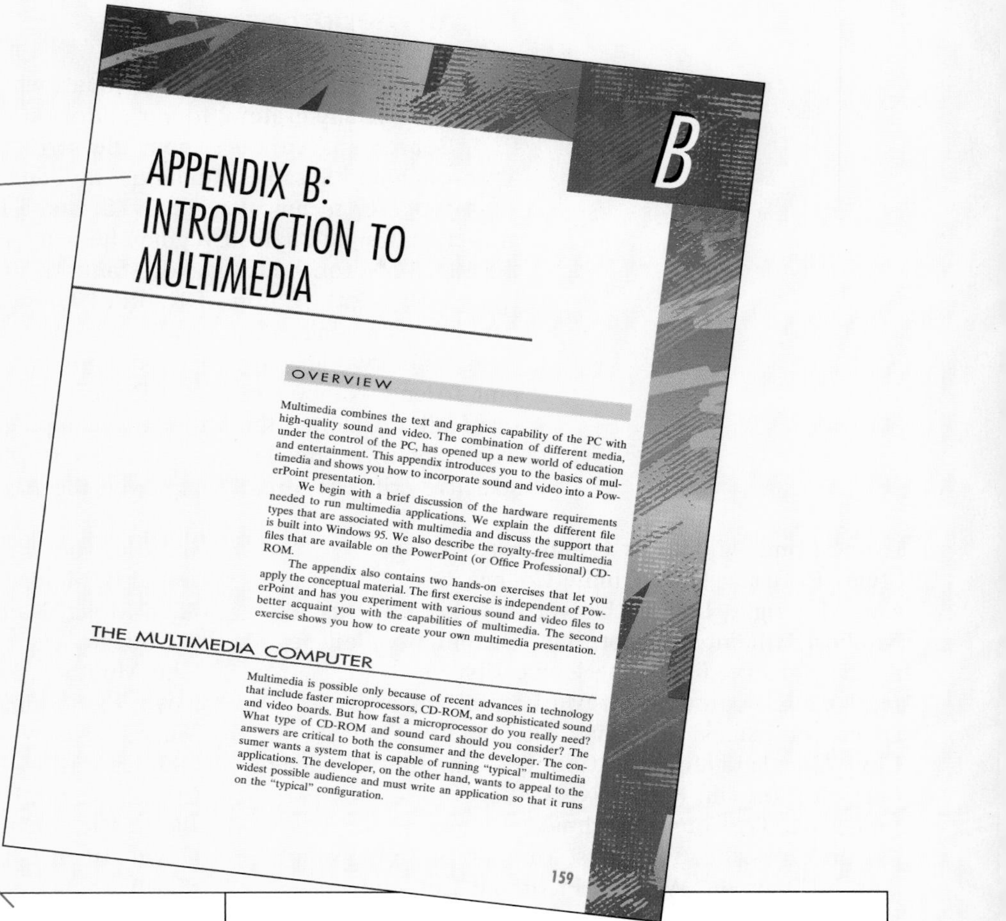

B

APPENDIX B: INTRODUCTION TO MULTIMEDIA

OVERVIEW

Multimedia combines the text and graphics capability of the PC with high-quality sound and video. The combination of different media, under the control of the PC, has opened up a new world of education and entertainment. This appendix introduces you to the basics of multimedia and shows you how to incorporate sound and video into a PowerPoint presentation.

We begin with a brief discussion of the hardware requirements needed to run multimedia applications. We explain the different file types that are associated with multimedia and discuss the support that is built into Windows 95. We also describe the royalty-free multimedia files that are available on the PowerPoint (or Office Professional) CD-ROM.

The appendix also contains two hands-on exercises that let you apply the conceptual material. The first exercise is independent of PowerPoint and has you experiment with various sound and video files to better acquaint you with the capabilities of multimedia. The second exercise shows you how to create your own multimedia presentation.

THE MULTIMEDIA COMPUTER

Multimedia is possible only because of recent advances in technology that include faster microprocessors, CD-ROM, and sophisticated sound and video boards. But how fast a microprocessor do you really need? What type of CD-ROM and sound card should you consider? The answers are critical to both the consumer and the developer. The consumer wants a system that is capable of running "typical" multimedia applications. The developer, on the other hand, wants to appeal to the widest possible audience and must write an application so that it runs on the "typical" configuration.

159

Concepts are emphasized so that the reader appreciates the theory behind the application. Students are not just taught what to do, but are provided with the rationale for why they are doing it, and are able to extend the information to additional learning on their own.

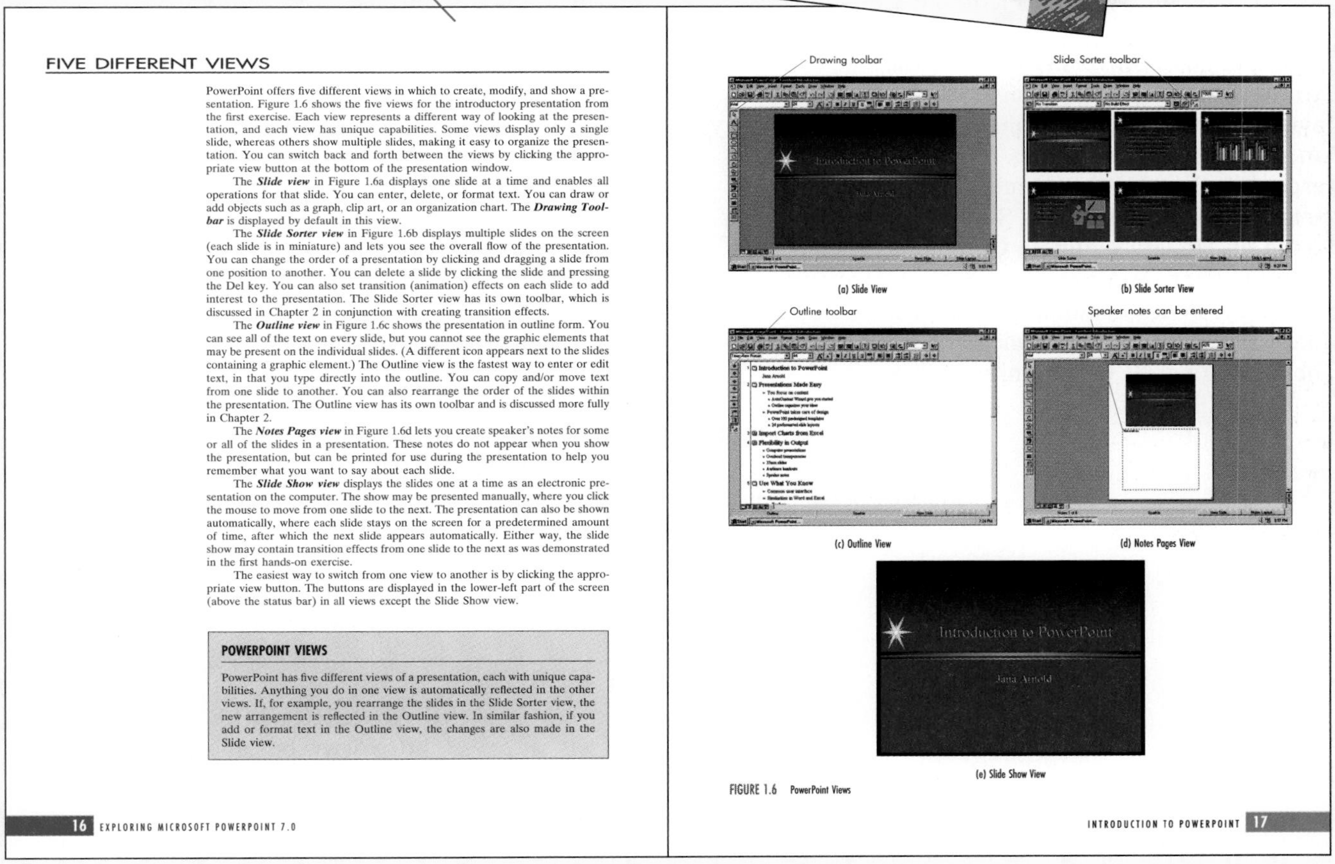

FIVE DIFFERENT VIEWS

PowerPoint offers five different views in which to create, modify, and show a presentation. Figure 1.6 shows the five views for the introductory presentation from the first exercise. Each view represents a different way of looking at the presentation, and each view has unique capabilities. Some views display only a single slide, whereas others show multiple slides, making it easy to organize the presentation. You can switch back and forth between the views by clicking the appropriate view button at the bottom of the presentation window.

The ***Slide view*** in Figure 1.6a displays one slide at a time and enables all operations for that slide. You can enter, delete, or format text. You can draw or add objects such as a graph, clip art, or an organization chart. The ***Drawing Toolbar*** is displayed by default in this view.

The ***Slide Sorter view*** in Figure 1.6b displays multiple slides on the screen (each slide is in miniature) and lets you see the overall flow of the presentation. You can change the order of a presentation by clicking and dragging a slide from one position to another. You can delete a slide by clicking the slide and pressing the Del key. You can also set transition (animation) effects on each slide to add interest to the presentation. The Slide Sorter view has its own toolbar, which is discussed in Chapter 2 in conjunction with creating transition effects.

The ***Outline view*** in Figure 1.6c shows the presentation in outline form. You can see all of the text on every slide, but you cannot see the graphic elements that may be present on the individual slides. (A different icon appears next to the slides containing a graphic element.) The Outline view is the fastest way to enter or edit text, in that you type directly into the outline. You can copy and/or move text from one slide to another. You can also rearrange the order of the slides within the presentation. The Outline view has its own toolbar and is discussed more fully in Chapter 2.

The ***Notes Pages view*** in Figure 1.6d lets you create speaker's notes for some or all of the slides in a presentation. These notes do not appear when you show the presentation, but can be printed for use during the presentation to help you remember what you want to say about each slide.

The ***Slide Show view*** displays the slides one at a time as an electronic presentation on the computer. The show may be presented manually, where you click the mouse to move from one slide to the next. The presentation can also be shown automatically, where each slide stays on the screen for a predetermined amount of time, after which the next slide appears automatically. Either way, the slide show may contain transition effects from one slide to the next as was demonstrated in the first hands-on exercise.

The easiest way to switch from one view to another is by clicking the appropriate view button. The buttons are displayed in the lower-left part of the screen (above the status bar) in all views except the Slide Show view.

POWERPOINT VIEWS

PowerPoint has five different views of a presentation, each with unique capabilities. Anything you do in one view is automatically reflected in the other views. If, for example, you rearrange the slides in the Slide Sorter view, the new arrangement is reflected in the Outline view. In similar fashion, if you add or format text in the Outline view, the changes are also made in the Slide view.

16 EXPLORING MICROSOFT POWERPOINT 7.0

Drawing toolbar
Slide Sorter toolbar
Introduction to PowerPoint
(a) Slide View
(b) Slide Sorter View
Outline toolbar
Speaker notes can be entered
(c) Outline View
(d) Notes Pages View
Introduction to PowerPoint
Jana Arnold
(e) Slide Show View

FIGURE 1.6 PowerPoint Views

INTRODUCTION TO POWERPOINT 17

Acknowledgments

We want to thank the many individuals who helped bring this project to fruition. We are especially grateful to our editors at Prentice Hall, Carolyn Henderson and P. J. Boardman, without whom the series would not have been possible. Cecil Yarbrough and Susan Hoffman did an outstanding job in checking the manuscript and proofs for technical accuracy. Suzanne Behnke developed the innovative and attractive design. Phyllis Bregman helped us to go online. Grace Walkus produced the CD-ROM for the Instructor Manuals, and Gretchen Marx of Saint Joseph College and Carlotta Eaton of Radford University wrote the text. Nicholas Radhuber was managing editor. Paul Smolenski was senior manufacturing supervisor. Greg Hubit was in charge of production and kept the project on target from beginning to end. Nancy Evans and Deborah Emry, our marketing managers at Prentice Hall, developed the innovative campaigns that made the series a success. We also want to acknowledge our reviewers who, through their comments and constructive criticism, greatly improved the *Exploring Windows* series.

Lynne Band, Middlesex Community College
Stuart P. Brian, Holy Family College
Carl M. Briggs, Indiana University School of Business
Kimberly Chambers, Scottsdale Community College
Alok Charturvedi, Purdue University
Jerry Chin, Southwest Missouri State University
Dean Combellick, Scottsdale Community College
Cody Copeland, Johnson County Community College
Larry S. Corman, Fort Lewis College
Janis Cox, Tri-County Technical College
Martin Crossland, Southwest Missouri State University
Paul E. Daurelle, Western Piedmont Community College
David Douglas, University of Arkansas
Carlotta Eaton, Radford University
Raymond Frost, Central Connecticut State University
James Gips, Boston College
Vernon Griffin, Austin Community College
Michael Hassett, Fort Hays State University
Wanda D. Heller, Seminole Community College
Bonnie Homan, San Francisco State University
Ernie Ivey, Polk Community College
Mike Kelly, Community College of Rhode Island
Jane King, Everett Community College
John Lesson, University of Central Florida
David B. Meinert, Southwest Missouri State University
Alan Moltz, Naugatuck Valley Technical Community College
Kim Montney, Kellogg Community College
Kevin Pauli, University of Nebraska
Mary McKenry Percival, University of Miami
Delores Pusins, Hillsborough Community College
Gale E. Rand, College Misericordia
Judith Rice, Santa Fe Community College
David Rinehard, Lansing Community College
Marilyn Salas, Scottsdale Community College
John Shepherd, Duquesne University
Helen Stoloff, Hudson Valley Community College
Mike Thomas, Indiana University School of Business
Suzanne Tomlinson, Iowa State University
Karen Tracey, Central Connecticut State University
Sally Visci, Lorain County Community College
David Weiner, University of San Francisco
Connie Wells, Georgia State University
Wallace John Whistance-Smith, Ryerson Polytechnic University
Jack Zeller, Kirkwood Community College

A final word of thanks to the unnamed students at the University of Miami who make it all worthwhile. And most of all, thanks to you, our readers, for choosing this book. Please feel free to contact us with any comments and suggestions.

Robert T. Grauer
RGRAUER@UMIAMI.MIAMI.EDU
http://www.bus.miami.edu/~rgrauer

Maryann Barber
MBARBER@UMIAMI.MIAMI.EDU
http://www.bus.miami.edu/~mbarber

EXPLORING MICROSOFT® POWERPOINT FOR WINDOWS® 95

VERSION 7.0

MICROSOFT OFFICE FOR WINDOWS 95: FOUR APPLICATIONS IN ONE

OVERVIEW

Word processing, spreadsheets, and data management have always been significant microcomputer applications. The early days of the PC saw these applications emerge from different vendors with radically different user interfaces. WordPerfect, Lotus, and dBASE, for example, were dominant applications in their respective areas, and each was developed by a different company. The applications were totally dissimilar, and knowledge of one application did not help in learning another.

The widespread acceptance of Windows 3.1 promoted the concept of a common user interface, which required all applications to follow a consistent set of conventions. This meant that all applications worked essentially the same way, and it provided a sense of familiarity when you learned a new application, since every application presented the same user interface. The development of a suite of applications from a single vendor extended this concept by imposing additional similarities on all applications within the suite.

This introduction will acquaint you with the ***Microsoft Office for Windows 95*** and its four major applications—Word, Excel, PowerPoint, and Access. Our primary purpose is to emphasize the similarities between these applications and to help you extend your knowledge from one application to the next. You will find the same commands in the same menus. You will also recognize familiar toolbars and will be able to take advantage of similar keyboard shortcuts. Our goal is to show you how much you already know and to get you up and running as quickly as possible.

The introduction also introduces you to Schedule+, and to shared applications and utilities such as the ClipArt Gallery and WordArt, which are included within Microsoft Office. We discuss the Office Shortcut Bar and describe how to start an application and open a new or existing document. We also introduce you to Object Linking and Embedding, which enables you to combine data from multiple applications into a single document.

TRY THE COLLEGE BOOKSTORE

Any machine you buy will come with Windows 95, but that is only the beginning since you must also obtain the application software you intend to run. Many first-time buyers are surprised that they have to pay extra for software, so you had better allow for software in your budget. Some hardware vendors will bundle (at no additional cost) Microsoft Office as an inducement to buy from them. If you have already purchased your system and you need software, the best place to buy Microsoft Office is the college bookstore, where it can be obtained at a substantial educational discount.

MICROSOFT OFFICE FOR WINDOWS 95

All Office applications share the common user interface for Windows 95 with which you may already be familiar. (If you are new to Windows 95, then read the appendix on the "Essentials of Windows 95," which appears at the end of this book.) Figure 1 displays a screen from each application in the Microsoft Office—Word, Excel, PowerPoint, and Access, in Figures 1a, 1b, 1c, and 1d, respectively. Look closely at Figure 1, and realize that each screen contains both an application window and a document window, and that each document window has been maximized within the application window. The title bars of the application and document windows have been merged into a single title bar that appears at the top of the application window. The title bar displays the application (e.g., Microsoft Word in Figure 1a) as well as the name of the document (Letter to My Instructor in Figure 1a) on which you are working.

All four screens in Figure 1 are similar in appearance despite the fact that the applications accomplish very different tasks. Each application window has an identifying icon, a menu bar, a title bar, and a minimize, maximize or restore, and a close button. Each document window has its own identifying icon, and its own minimize, maximize or restore, and close button. The Windows 95 taskbar appears at the bottom of each application window and shows the open applications. The status bar appears above the taskbar and displays information relevant to the window or selected object.

Each application in Microsoft Office uses a consistent command structure in which the same basic menus are found in all applications. The File, Edit, View, Insert, Tools, Window, and Help menus are present in all four applications. The same commands are found in the same menus. The Save, Open, Print, and Exit commands, for example, are contained in the File menu. The Cut, Copy, Paste, and Undo commands are found in the Edit menu.

The means for accessing the pull-down menus are consistent from one application to the next. Click the menu name on the menu bar, or press the Alt key plus the underlined letter of the menu name; for example, press Alt+F to pull down the File menu. If you already know some keyboard shortcuts in one application, there is a good chance that the shortcuts will work in another application. Ctrl+Home and Ctrl+End, for example, move to the beginning and end of a document, respectively. Ctrl+B, Ctrl+I, and Ctrl+U boldface, italicize, and underline text. Ctrl+X (the "X" is supposed to remind you of a pair of scissors), Ctrl+C, and Ctrl+V will cut, copy, and paste, respectively. You may not know what these commands do now, but once you learn how they work in one application, you will intuitively know how they work in the others.

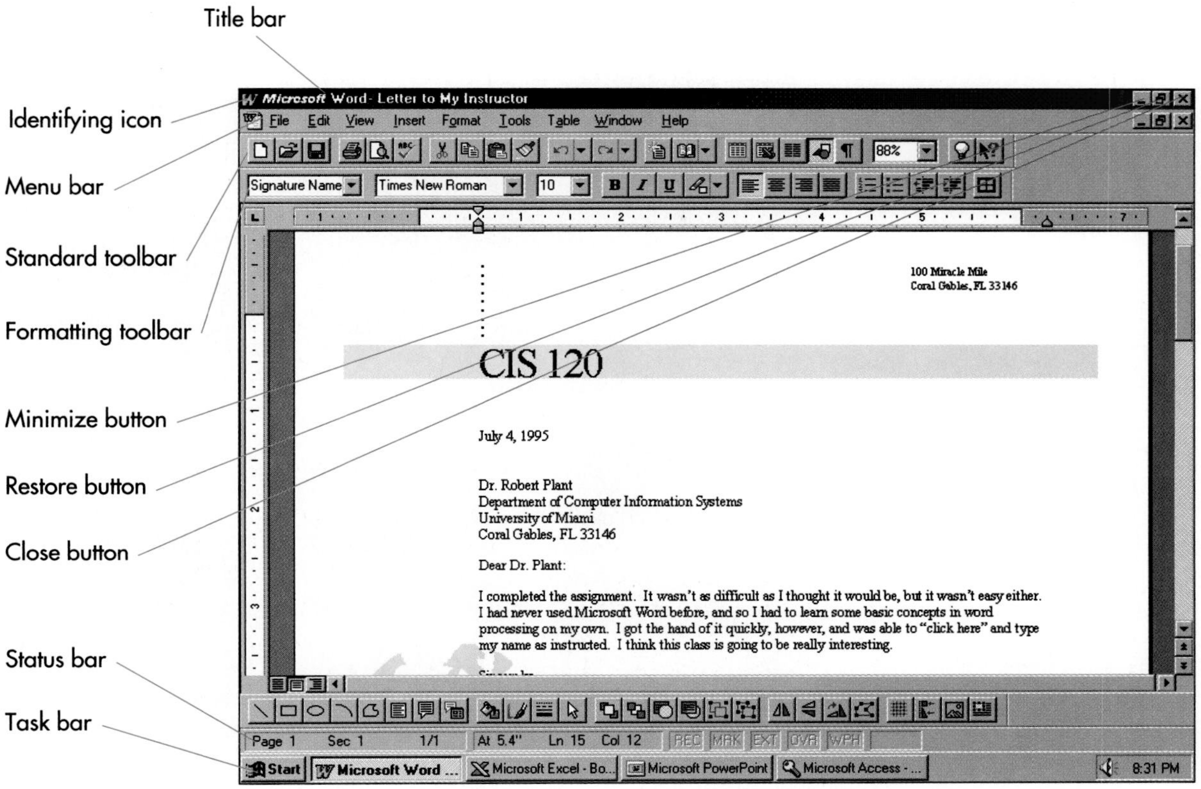
Title bar
Identifying icon
Menu bar
Standard toolbar
Formatting toolbar
Minimize button
Restore button
Close button
Status bar
Task bar
Microsoft Word - Letter to My Instructor
100 Miracle Mile
Coral Gables, FL 33146
CIS 120
July 4, 1995
Dr. Robert Plant
Department of Computer Information Systems
University of Miami
Coral Gables, FL 33146
Dear Dr. Plant:
I completed the assignment. It wasn't as difficult as I thought it would be, but it wasn't easy either. I had never used Microsoft Word before, and so I had to learn some basic concepts in word processing on my own. I got the hand of it quickly, however, and was able to "click here" and type my name as instructed. I think this class is going to be really interesting.

(a) Microsoft Word

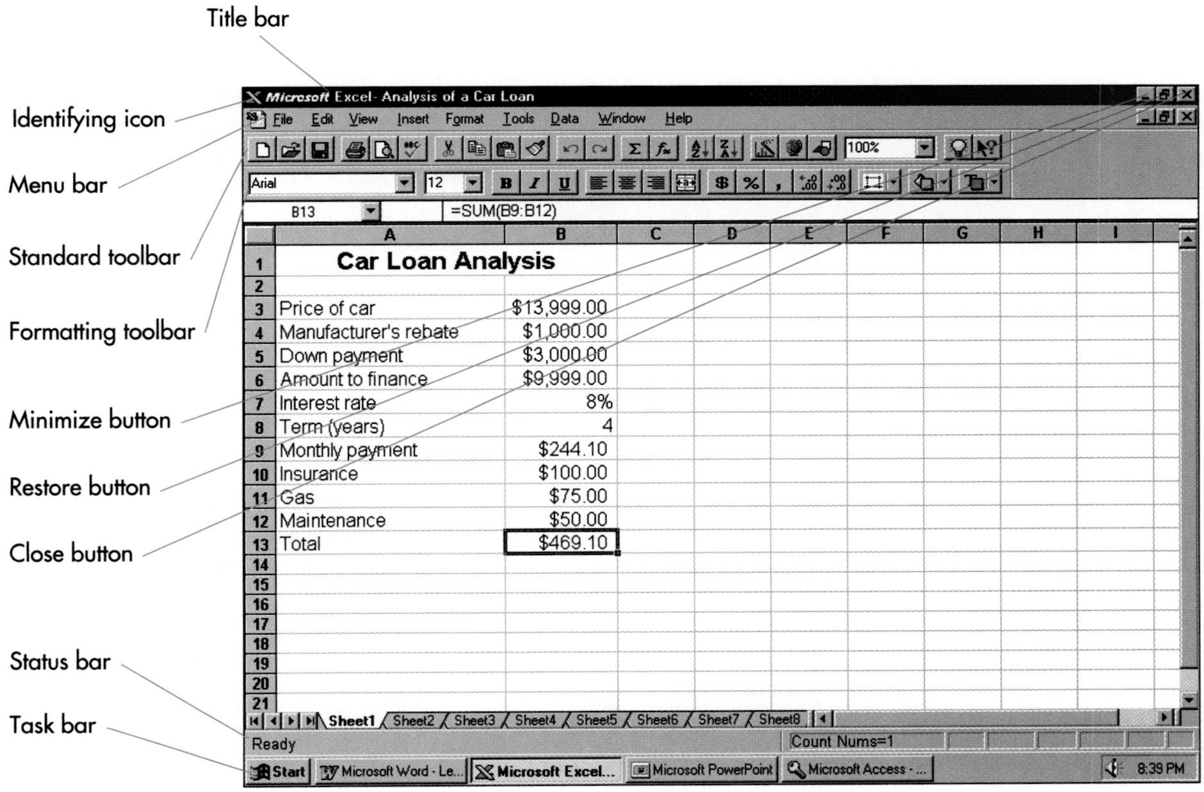
Title bar
Identifying icon
Menu bar
Standard toolbar
Formatting toolbar
Minimize button
Restore button
Close button
Status bar
Task bar
Microsoft Excel - Analysis of a Car Loan
=SUM(B9:B12)
Car Loan Analysis
Price of car $13,999.00
Manufacturer's rebate $1,000.00
Down payment $3,000.00
Amount to finance $9,999.00
Interest rate 8%
Term (years) 4
Monthly payment $244.10
Insurance $100.00
Gas $75.00
Maintenance $50.00
Total $469.10

(b) Microsoft Excel

FIGURE 1 The Common User Interface

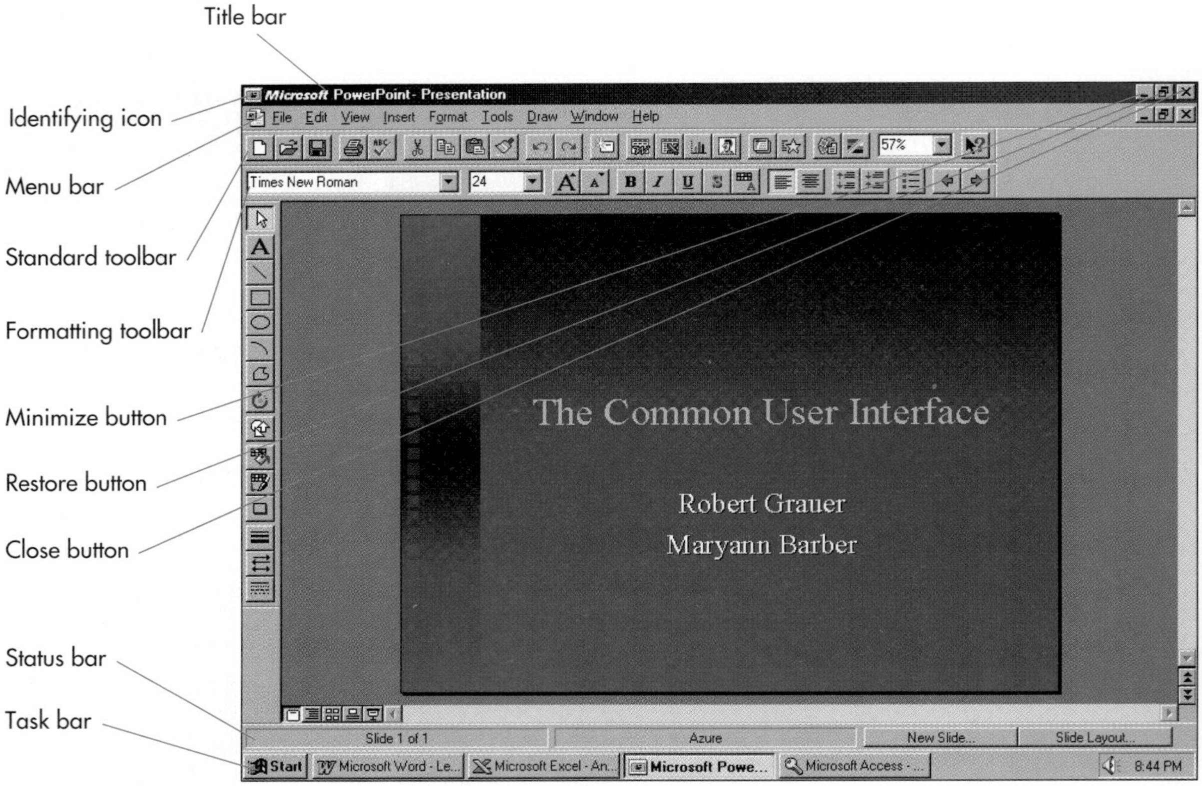
Title bar
Identifying icon
Menu bar
Standard toolbar
Formatting toolbar
Minimize button
Restore button
Close button
Status bar
Task bar
Microsoft PowerPoint - Presentation
File Edit View Insert Format Tools Draw Window Help
Times New Roman
24
57%
The Common User Interface
Robert Grauer
Maryann Barber
Slide 1 of 1
Azure
New Slide...
Slide Layout...
Start
Microsoft Word - Le...
Microsoft Excel - An...
Microsoft Powe...
Microsoft Access - ...
8:44 PM

(c) Microsoft PowerPoint

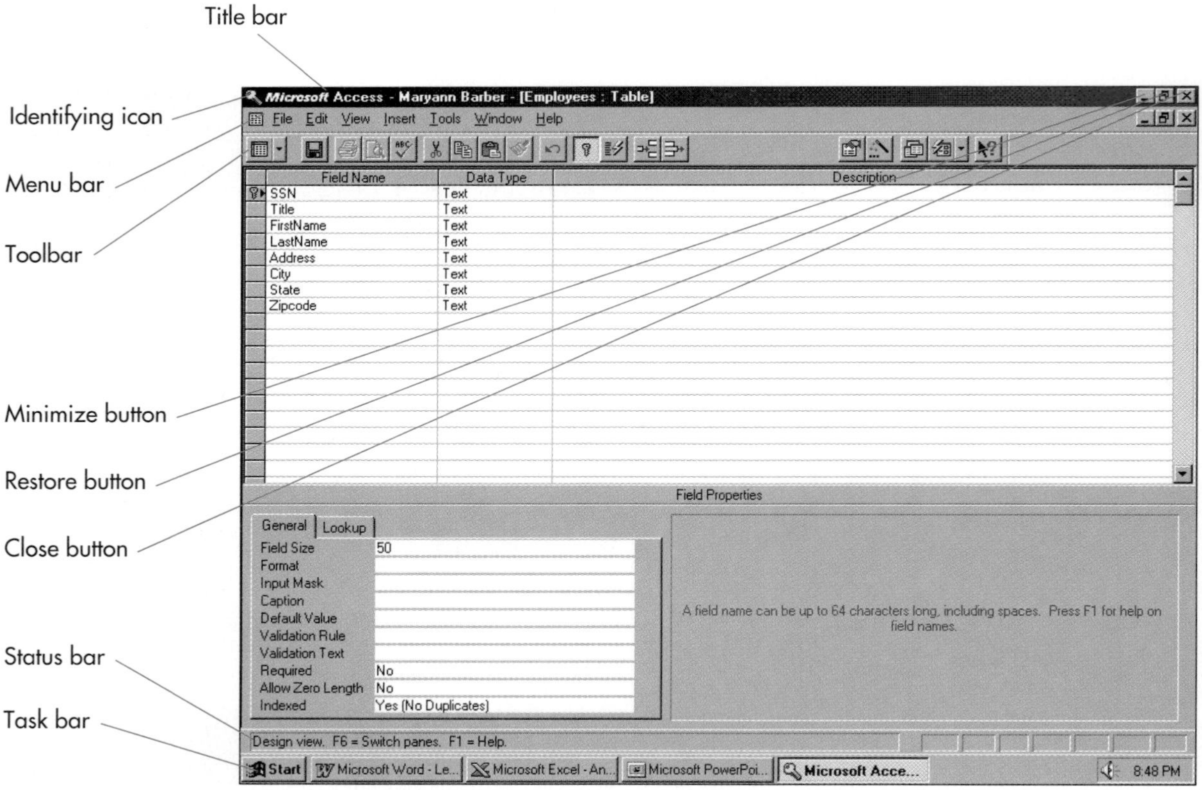
Title bar
Identifying icon
Menu bar
Toolbar
Minimize button
Restore button
Close button
Status bar
Task bar
Microsoft Access - Maryann Barber - [Employees : Table]
File Edit View Insert Tools Window Help
Field Name
Data Type
Description
SSN
Title
FirstName
LastName
Address
City
State
Zipcode
Text
Field Properties
General
Lookup
Field Size
50
Format
Input Mask
Caption
Default Value
Validation Rule
Validation Text
Required
No
Allow Zero Length
No
Indexed
Yes (No Duplicates)
A field name can be up to 64 characters long, including spaces. Press F1 for help on field names.
Design view. F6 = Switch panes. F1 = Help.
Start
Microsoft Word - Le...
Microsoft Excel - An...
Microsoft PowerPoi...
Microsoft Acce...
8:48 PM

(d) Microsoft Access

FIGURE 1 The Common User Interface (continued)

All four applications use consistent (and often identical) dialog boxes. The dialog boxes to open and close a file, for example, are identical in every application. All four applications also share a common dictionary. The AutoCorrect feature (to correct common spelling mistakes) works identically in all four applications. The help feature also functions identically.

There are, of course, differences between the applications. Each application has its own unique menus and associated toolbars. Nevertheless, the Standard and Formatting toolbars in all applications contain many of the same tools (especially the first several tools on the left of each toolbar). The ***Standard toolbar*** contains buttons for basic commands such as Open, Save, or Print. It also contains buttons to cut, copy, and paste, and all of these buttons are identical in all four applications. The ***Formatting toolbar*** provides access to common formatting operations such as boldface, italics, or underlining, or changing the font or point size, and again, these buttons are identical in all four applications. ToolTips are present in all applications. Suffice it to say, therefore, that once you know one Office application, you have a tremendous head start in learning another.

MICROSOFT OFFICE VERSUS OFFICE PROFESSIONAL

Microsoft distributes two versions of the Office Suite: Standard Office and Office Professional. Both versions include Word, Excel, and PowerPoint. The Office Professional also has Microsoft Access. The difference is important when you are shopping and comparing prices from different sources. Be sure to purchase the version that is appropriate for your needs.

Online Help

Each application in the Microsoft Office has the extensive ***online help*** facility as shown in Figure 2. Help is available at any time, and is accessed from the application's Help menu. (The Help screens in Figure 2 pertain to Microsoft Office, as opposed to a specific application, and were accessed through the Answer Wizard button on the Office Shortcut Bar.)

The ***Contents tab*** in Figure 2a is similar to the table of contents in an ordinary book. The major topics are represented by books, each of which can be opened to display additional topics. Each open book displays one or more topics, which may be viewed and/or printed to provide the indicated information.

The ***Index tab*** in Figure 2b is analogous to the index of an ordinary book. Type the first several letters of the topic to look up, such as "he" in Figure 2b. Help then returns all of the topics beginning with the letters you entered. Select the topic you want, then display the topic for immediate viewing, or print it for later reference.

The ***Answer Wizard*** in Figure 2c lets you ask questions in your own words, then it returns the relevant help topics. The Help screen in Figure 2d was accessed from the selections provided by the Answer Wizard, and it, in turn, will lead you to new features in the individual applications.

Office Shortcut Bar

The ***Microsoft Office Shortcut Bar*** provides immediate access to each application within Microsoft Office. It consists of a row of buttons and can be placed anywhere on the screen. The Shortcut Bar is anchored by default on the right side of the desktop, but you can position it along any edge, or have it "float" in the middle of the desktop. You can even hide it from view when it is not in use.

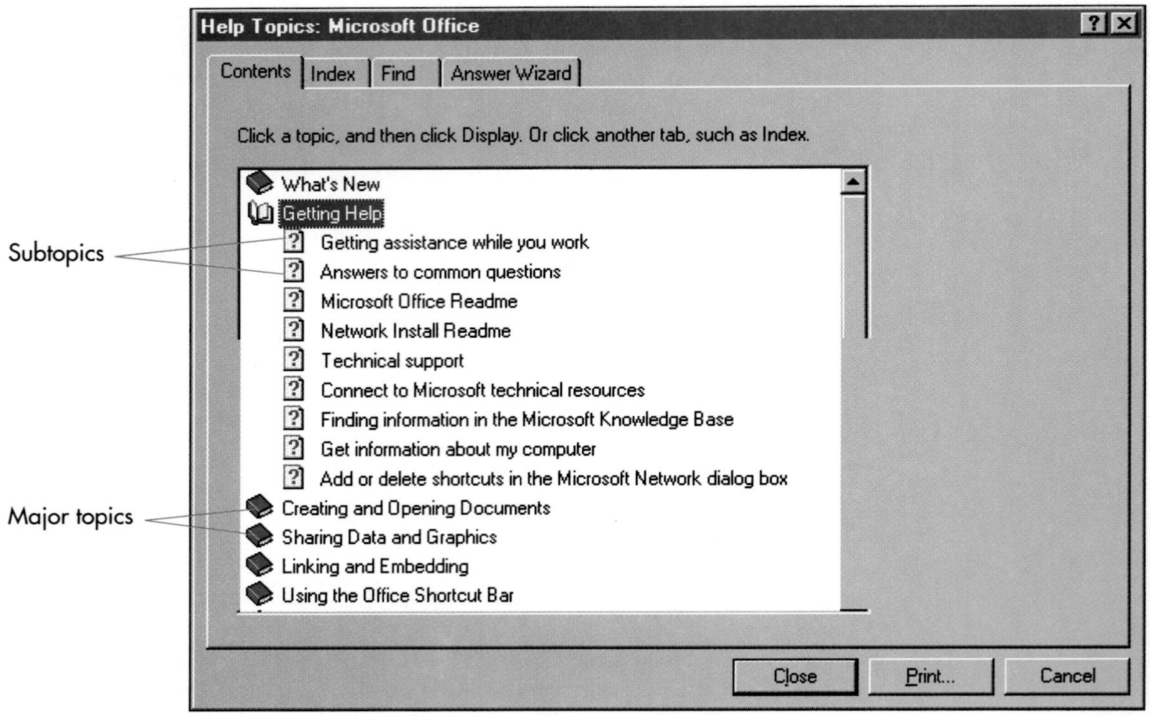
Help Topics: Microsoft Office
Contents
Index
Find
Answer Wizard
Click a topic, and then click Display. Or click another tab, such as Index.
What's New
Getting Help
Getting assistance while you work
Answers to common questions
Microsoft Office Readme
Network Install Readme
Technical support
Connect to Microsoft technical resources
Finding information in the Microsoft Knowledge Base
Get information about my computer
Add or delete shortcuts in the Microsoft Network dialog box
Creating and Opening Documents
Sharing Data and Graphics
Linking and Embedding
Using the Office Shortcut Bar
Close
Print...
Cancel
Subtopics
Major topics

(a) Contents Tab

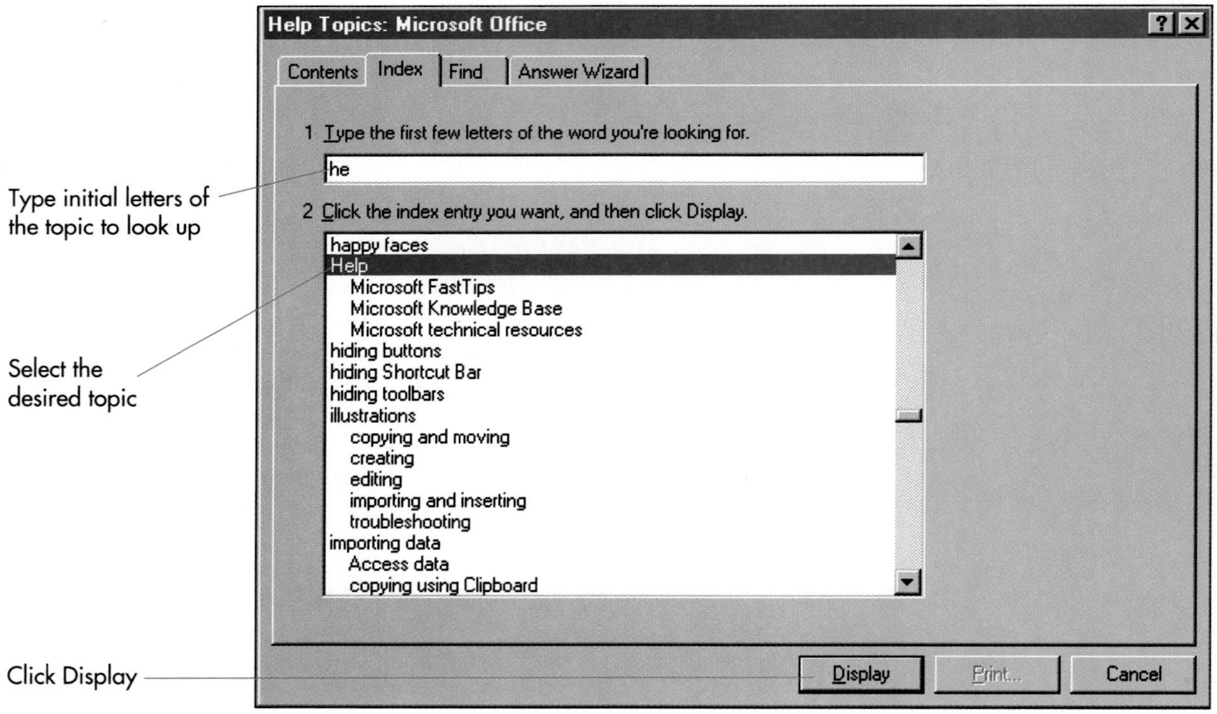
Help Topics: Microsoft Office
Contents
Index
Find
Answer Wizard
1 Type the first few letters of the word you're looking for.
he
2 Click the index entry you want, and then click Display.
happy faces
Help
Microsoft FastTips
Microsoft Knowledge Base
Microsoft technical resources
hiding buttons
hiding Shortcut Bar
hiding toolbars
illustrations
copying and moving
creating
editing
importing and inserting
troubleshooting
importing data
Access data
copying using Clipboard
Display
Print...
Cancel
Type initial letters of the topic to look up
Select the desired topic
Click Display

(b) Index Tab

FIGURE 2 Online Help

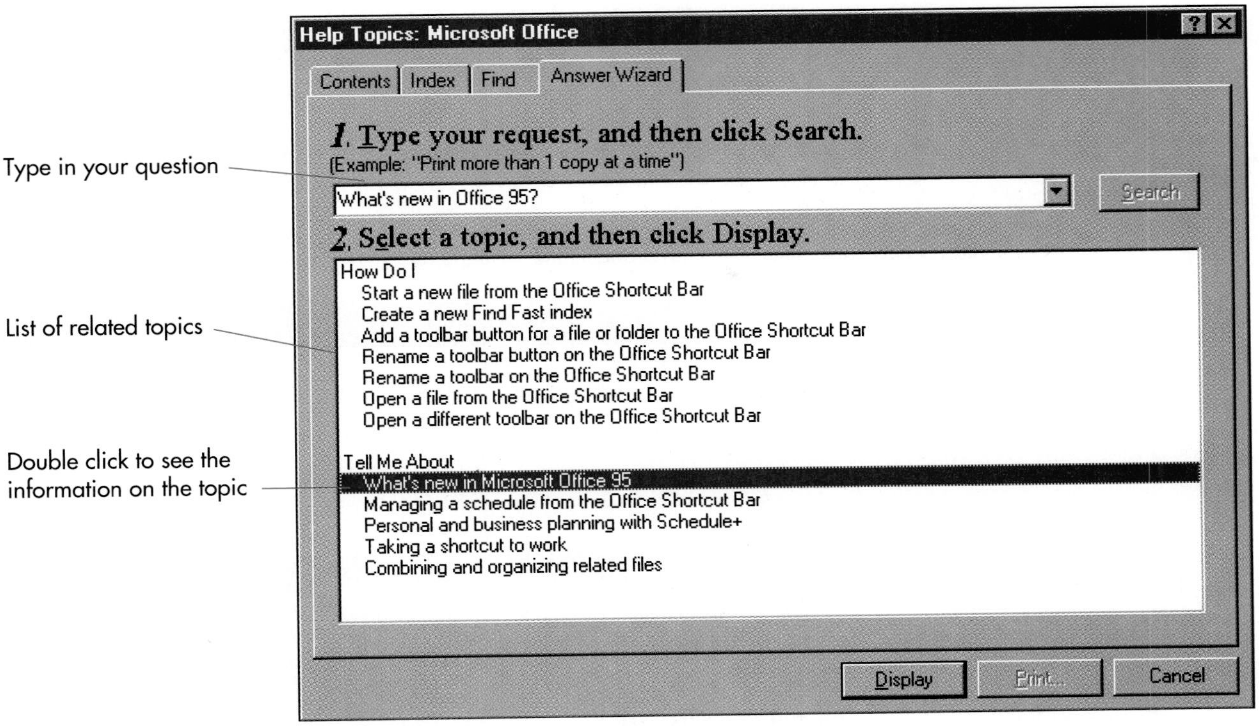
Type in your question
List of related topics
Double click to see the information on the topic
Help Topics: Microsoft Office
Contents
Index
Find
Answer Wizard
1. Type your request, and then click Search.
(Example: "Print more than 1 copy at a time")
What's new in Office 95?
Search
2. Select a topic, and then click Display.
How Do I
Start a new file from the Office Shortcut Bar
Create a new Find Fast index
Add a toolbar button for a file or folder to the Office Shortcut Bar
Rename a toolbar button on the Office Shortcut Bar
Rename a toolbar on the Office Shortcut Bar
Open a file from the Office Shortcut Bar
Open a different toolbar on the Office Shortcut Bar
Tell Me About
What's new in Microsoft Office 95
Managing a schedule from the Office Shortcut Bar
Personal and business planning with Schedule+
Taking a shortcut to work
Combining and organizing related files
Display
Print...
Cancel

(c) Answer Wizard

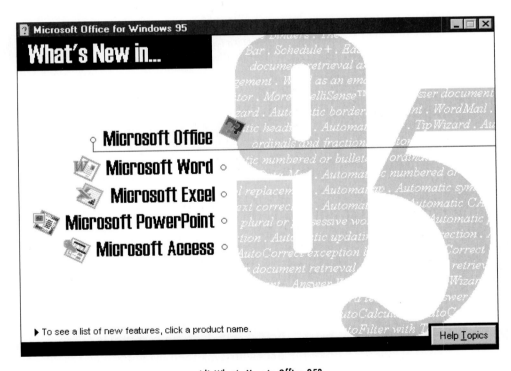
Microsoft Office for Windows 95
What's New in...
Microsoft Office
Microsoft Word
Microsoft Excel
Microsoft PowerPoint
Microsoft Access
To see a list of new features, click a product name.
Help Topics

(d) What's New in Office 95?

FIGURE 2 Online Help (continued)

Figure 3a displays the Shortcut Bar as it appears on our desktop. The buttons that are displayed (and the order in which they appear) are established through the Customize dialog box in Figure 3b. (We show you how to customize the Shortcut Bar in the hands-on exercise that follows shortly.) Our Shortcut Bar contains a button for each Office application, a button for the Windows Explorer, and a button to access help.

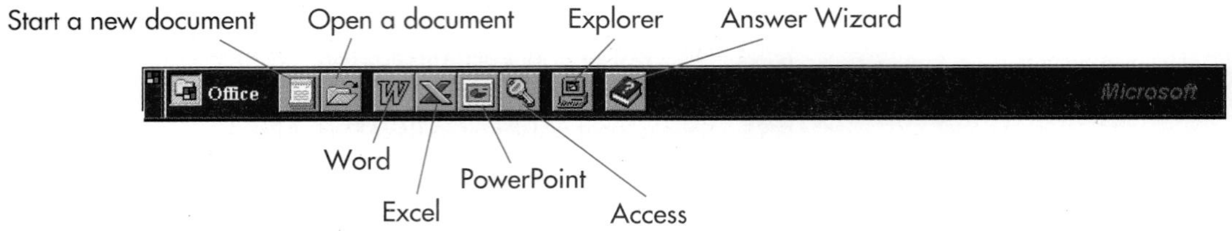

Start a new document
Open a document
Explorer
Answer Wizard
Office
Microsoft
Word
Excel
PowerPoint
Access

(a) Office Shortcut Bar

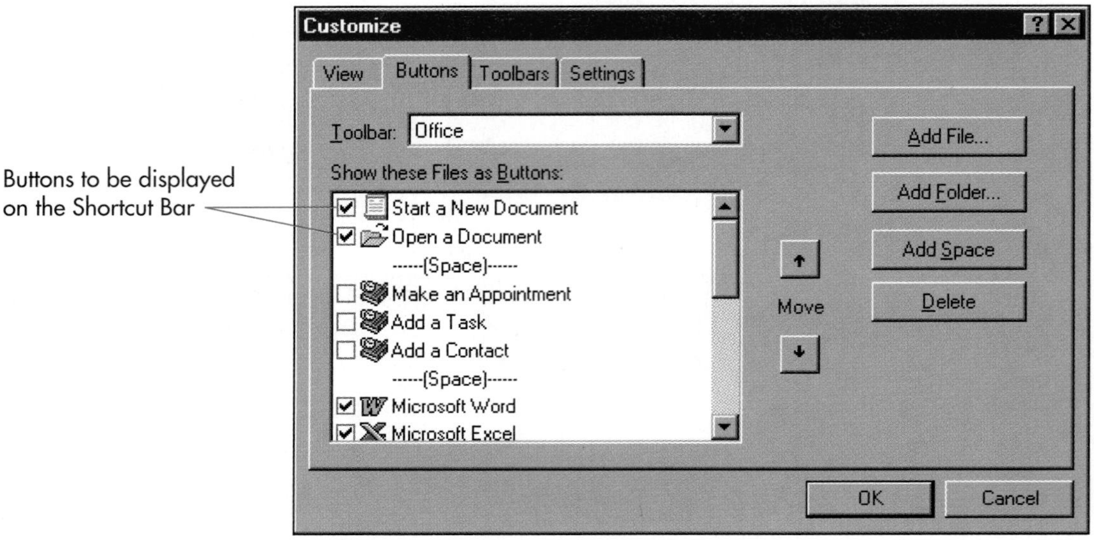

Buttons to be displayed on the Shortcut Bar
Customize
View
Buttons
Toolbars
Settings
Toolbar: Office
Show these Files as Buttons:
Start a New Document
Open a Document
------(Space)------
Make an Appointment
Add a Task
Add a Contact
------(Space)------
Microsoft Word
Microsoft Excel
Move
Add File...
Add Folder...
Add Space
Delete
OK
Cancel

(b) Customize Dialog Box

FIGURE 3 Office Shortcut Bar

Docucentric Orientation

Our Shortcut Bar contains two additional buttons: to open an existing document and to start a new document. These buttons are very useful and take advantage of the "docucentric" orientation of Microsoft Office, which lets you think in terms of a document rather than the associated application. You can still open a document in traditional fashion, by starting the application (e.g., clicking its button on the Shortcut Bar), then using the File Open command to open the document. It's easier, however, to locate the document, then double click its icon, which automatically loads the associated program.

Consider, for example, the Open dialog box in Figure 4a, which is displayed by clicking the Open a Document button on the Shortcut Bar. The Open dialog box is common to all Office applications, and it works identically in each application. The My Documents folder is selected in Figure 4a, and it contains four documents of various file types. The documents are displayed in the Details view,

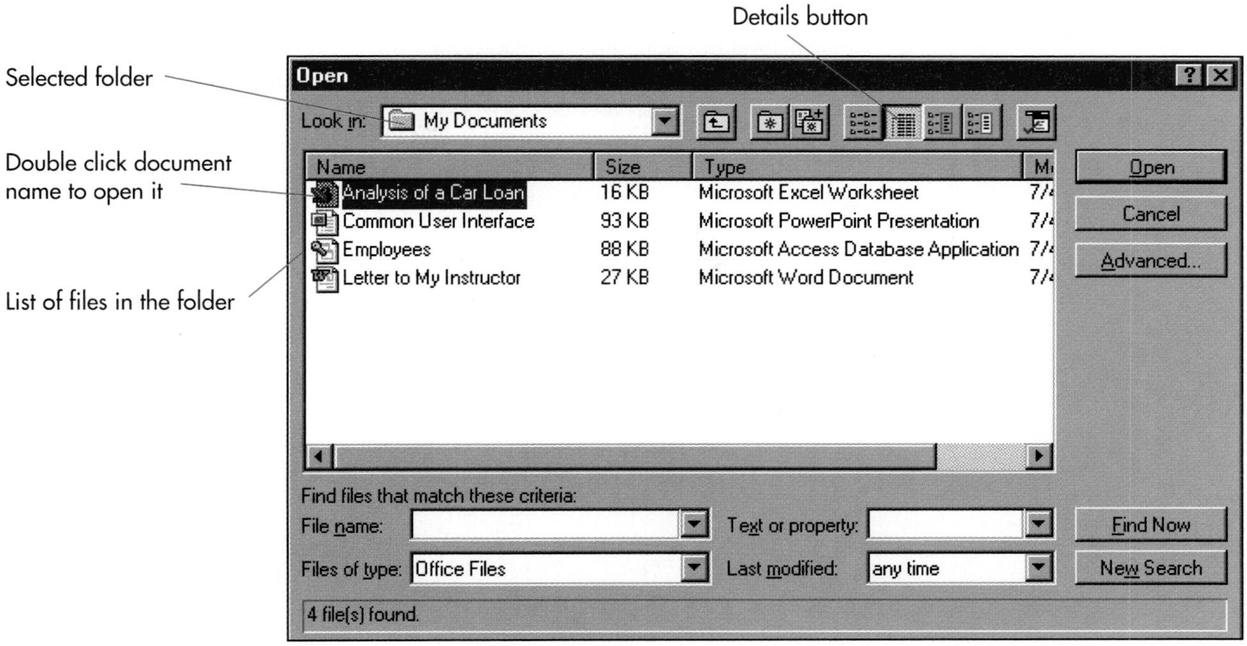
Details button
Selected folder
Double click document name to open it
List of files in the folder
Open
Look in: My Documents
Name
Size
Type
Analysis of a Car Loan
16 KB
Microsoft Excel Worksheet
Common User Interface
93 KB
Microsoft PowerPoint Presentation
Employees
88 KB
Microsoft Access Database Application
Letter to My Instructor
27 KB
Microsoft Word Document
Open
Cancel
Advanced...
Find files that match these criteria:
File name:
Text or property:
Files of type: Office Files
Last modified: any time
Find Now
New Search
4 file(s) found.

(a) Open an Existing Document

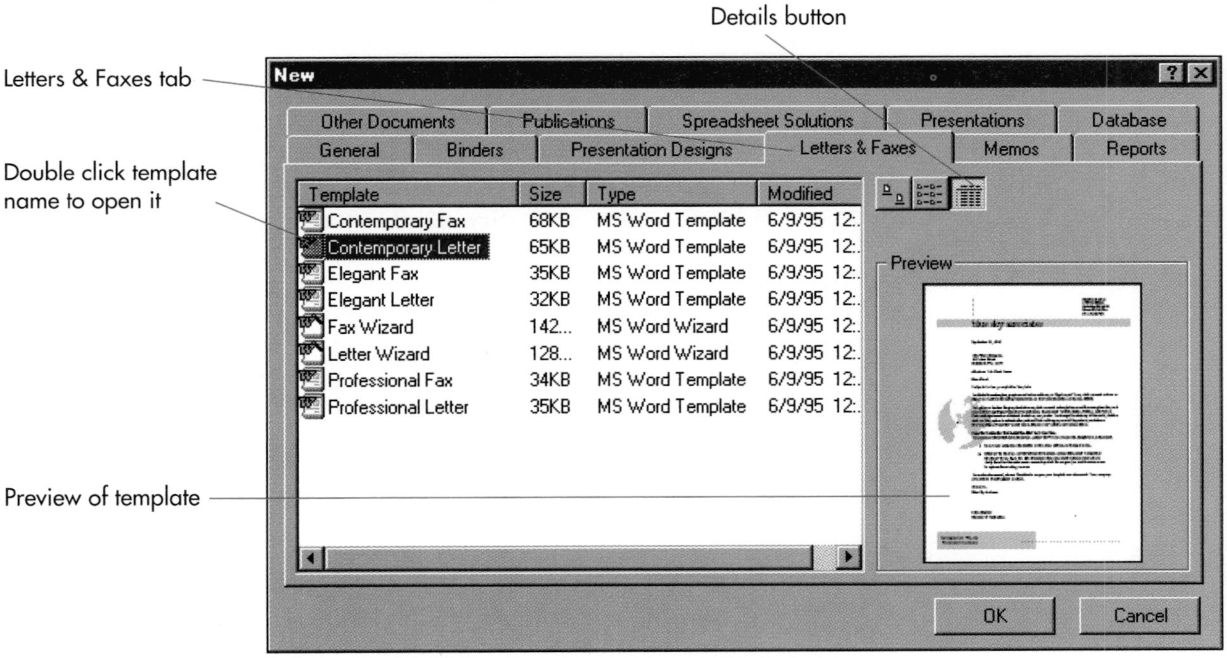
Details button
Letters & Faxes tab
Double click template name to open it
Preview of template
New
Other Documents
Publications
Spreadsheet Solutions
Presentations
Database
General
Binders
Presentation Designs
Letters & Faxes
Memos
Reports
Template
Size
Type
Modified
Contemporary Fax
68KB
MS Word Template
Contemporary Letter
65KB
Elegant Fax
35KB
Elegant Letter
32KB
Fax Wizard
142...
MS Word Wizard
Letter Wizard
128...
Professional Fax
34KB
Professional Letter
35KB
Preview
OK
Cancel

(b) Start a New Document

FIGURE 4 Document Orientation

which shows the document name, size, file type, and date and time the document was last modified. To open any document—for example, "Analysis of a Car Loan"—just double click its name or icon. The associated application (Microsoft Excel in this example) will be started automatically; and it, in turn, will open the selected workbook.

The "docucentric" orientation also applies to new documents. Click the Start a New Document button on the Office Shortcut Bar, and you display the New dialog box in Figure 4b. Click the tab corresponding to the type of document you want to create, such as Letters & Faxes in Figure 4b. Change to the Preview view, then click (select) various templates so that you can choose the one most appropriate for your purpose. Double click the desired template to start the application, which opens the template and enables you to create the document.

CHANGE THE VIEW

The toolbar in the Open dialog box displays the documents within the selected folder in one of several views. Click the Details button to switch to the Details view and see the date and time the file was last modified, as well as its size and type. Click the List button to display an icon representing the associated application, enabling you to see many more files than in the Details view. The Preview button lets you see a document before you open it. The Properties button displays information about the document, including the number of revisions.

SHARED APPLICATIONS AND UTILITIES

Microsoft Office includes a fifth application, Schedule+, as well as several smaller applications and shared utilities. ***Schedule+*** can be started from the Office Shortcut Bar or from the submenu for Microsoft Office, which is accessed through the Programs command on the Start button. Figure 6a displays one screen from Schedule+, providing some indication of what the application can do.

In essence, Schedule+ is a personal information manager that helps you schedule (and keep) appointments. It will display your schedule on a daily, weekly, or monthly basis. It will beep to remind you of appointments. It will also maintain a list of important phone numbers and contacts. Schedule+ is beyond the scope of our text, but it is an easy application to learn since it follows the common user interface and has a detailed help facility.

The other applications (or applets as they are sometimes known) are easy to miss because they do not appear as buttons on the Shortcut Bar. Nor do they appear as options on any menu. Instead, these applications are loaded from within one of the major applications, typically through the Insert Object command. Two of the more popular applications, the ***ClipArt Gallery*** and ***WordArt,*** are illustrated in Figures 6b and 6c, respectively.

The ClipArt Gallery contains more than 1,100 clip art images in 26 different categories. Select a category such as Cartoons, select an image such as the duck smashing a computer, then click the Insert command button to insert the clip art into a document. Once an object is inserted into a document (regardless of whether it is a Word document, an Excel worksheet, a PowerPoint presentation, or an Access form or report), it can be moved and sized like any other Windows object.

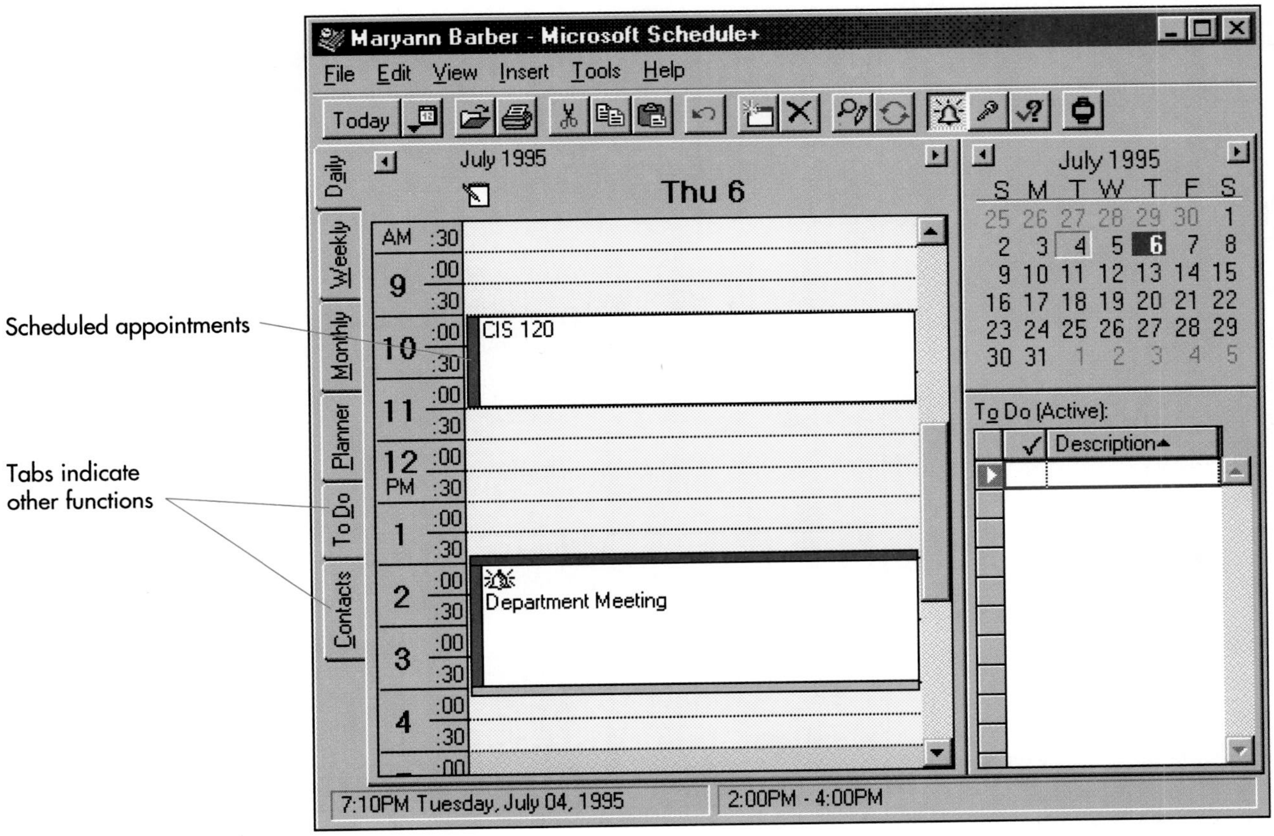
Maryann Barber - Microsoft Schedule+
File Edit View Insert Tools Help
Today
July 1995
Thu 6
Daily
Weekly
Monthly
Planner
To Do
Contacts
CIS 120
Department Meeting
July 1995
S M T W T F S
To Do (Active):
Description
7:10PM Tuesday, July 04, 1995
2:00PM - 4:00PM
Scheduled appointments
Tabs indicate other functions

(a) Microsoft Schedule+

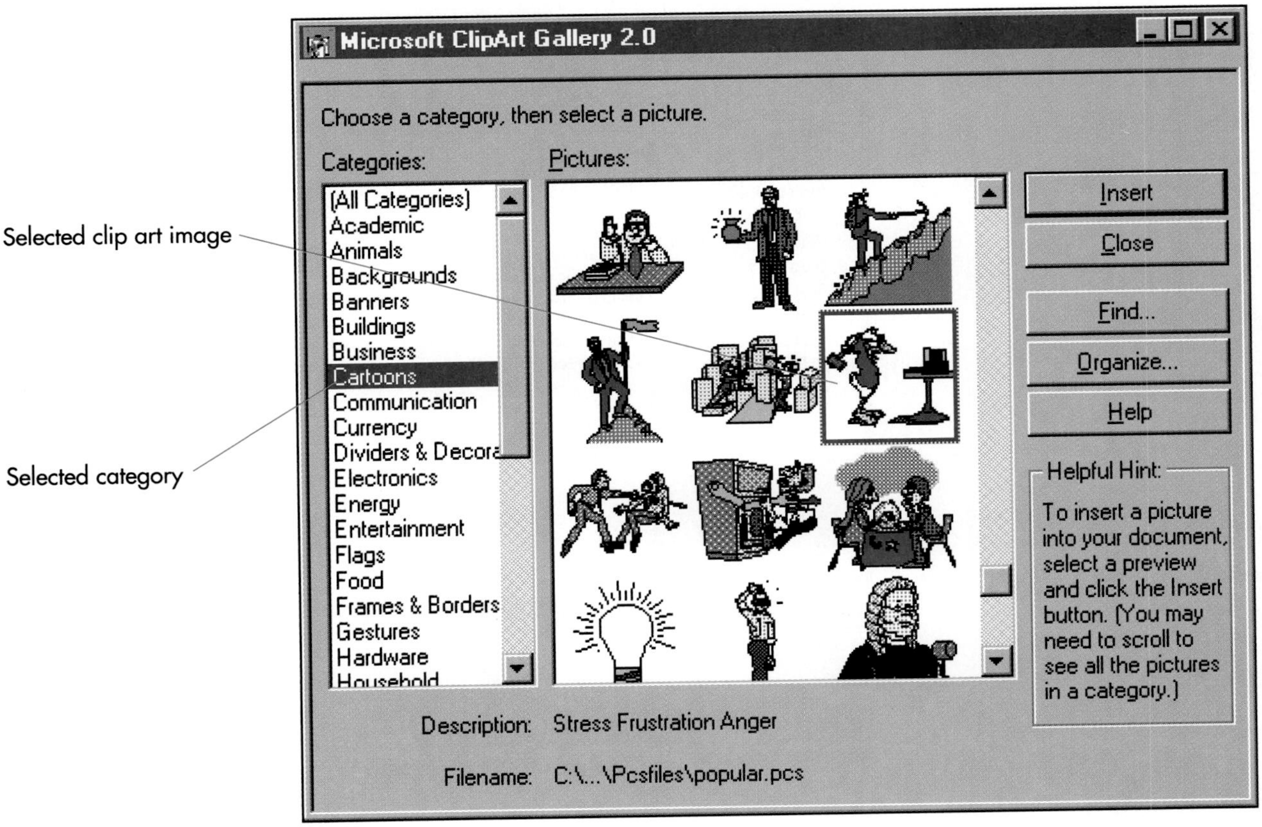
Microsoft ClipArt Gallery 2.0
Choose a category, then select a picture.
Categories:
Pictures:
(All Categories)
Academic
Animals
Backgrounds
Banners
Buildings
Business
Cartoons
Communication
Currency
Dividers & Decora
Electronics
Energy
Entertainment
Flags
Food
Frames & Borders
Gestures
Hardware
Household
Insert
Close
Find...
Organize...
Help
Helpful Hint:
To insert a picture into your document, select a preview and click the Insert button. (You may need to scroll to see all the pictures in a category.)
Description: Stress Frustration Anger
Filename: C:\...\Pcsfiles\popular.pcs
Selected clip art image
Selected category

(b) ClipArt Gallery

FIGURE 6 Shared Applications

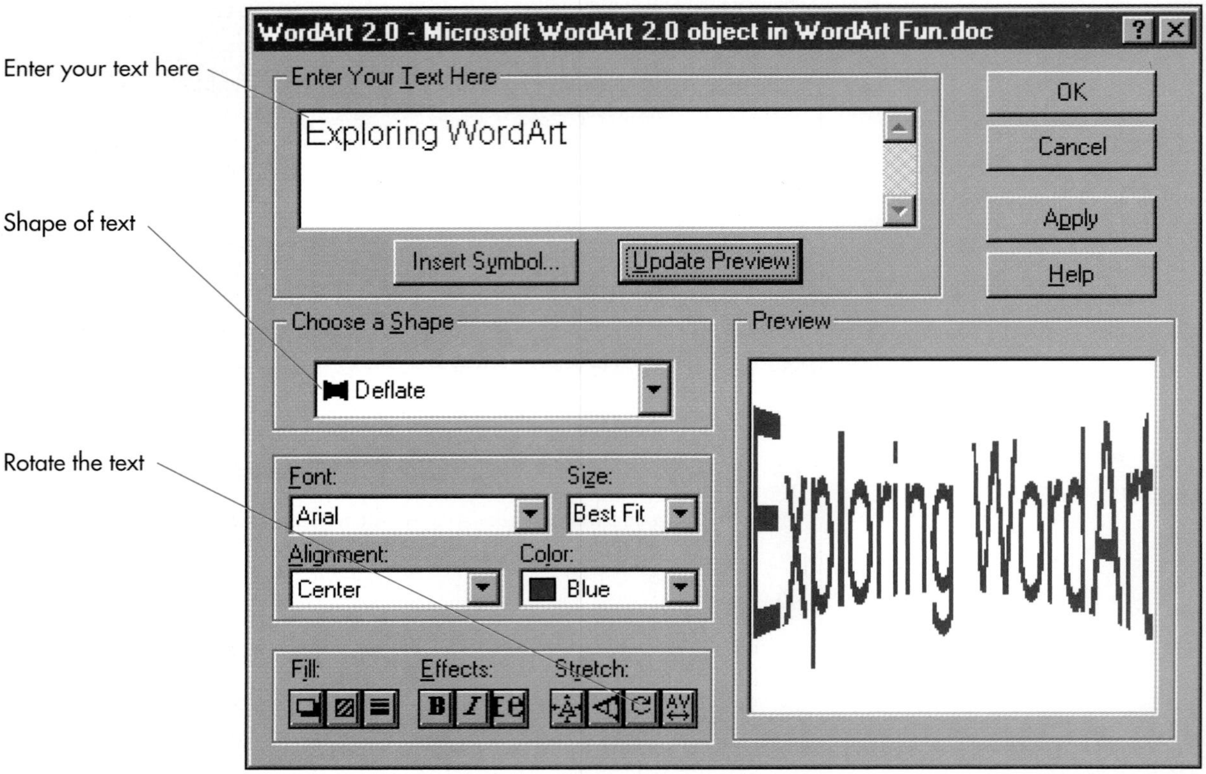
Enter your text here
Shape of text
Rotate the text
WordArt 2.0 - Microsoft WordArt 2.0 object in WordArt Fun.doc
Enter Your Text Here
Exploring WordArt
OK
Cancel
Apply
Help
Insert Symbol...
Update Preview
Choose a Shape
Deflate
Preview
Font:
Arial
Size:
Best Fit
Alignment:
Center
Color:
Blue
Fill:
Effects:
Stretch:

(c) WordArt

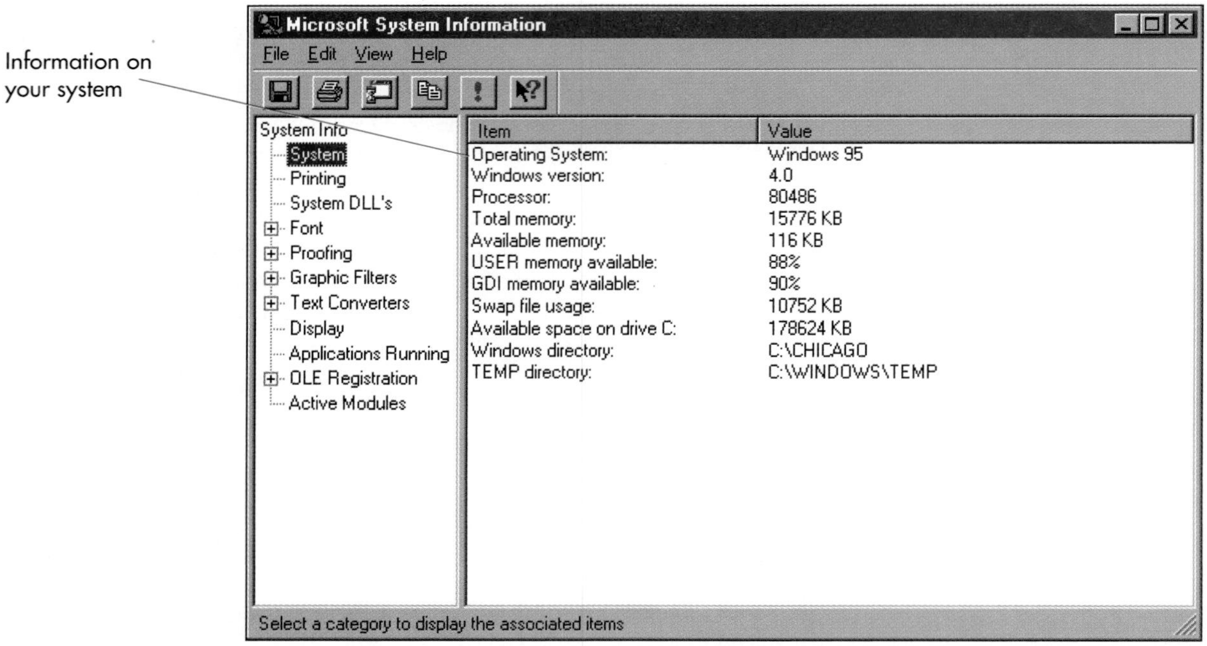
Information on your system
Microsoft System Information
File Edit View Help
System Info
System
Printing
System DLL's
Font
Proofing
Graphic Filters
Text Converters
Display
Applications Running
OLE Registration
Active Modules
Item
Value
Operating System: Windows 95
Windows version: 4.0
Processor: 80486
Total memory: 15776 KB
Available memory: 116 KB
USER memory available: 88%
GDI memory available: 90%
Swap file usage: 10752 KB
Available space on drive C: 178624 KB
Windows directory: C:\CHICAGO
TEMP directory: C:\WINDOWS\TEMP
Select a category to display the associated items

(d) Microsoft System Information

FIGURE 6 Shared Applications (continued)

WordArt enables you to create special effects with text. It lets you rotate and/or flip text, shade it, slant it, arch it, or even print it upside down. WordArt is intuitively easy to use. In essence, you enter the text in the dialog box of Figure 6c, choose a shape from the drop-down list box, then choose a font and point size. You can boldface or italicize the text or add special effects such as stretching or shadows.

The ***System Information Utility*** in Figure 6d is accessed from any major application by pulling down the Help menu, clicking the About button, then clicking the System Info command button. The utility provides detailed information about all aspects of your system. The information may prove to be invaluable should problems arise on your system and you need to supply technical details to support personnel.

THE OTHER SHARED APPLICATIONS

Microsoft Office includes several additional applications whose functions can be inferred from their names. The Equation Editor, Organization Chart, Data Map, and Graph utilities are accessed through the Insert Object command. All of these applications are straightforward and easy to use as they follow the common user interface and provide online help.

OBJECT LINKING AND EMBEDDING

The applications in Microsoft Office are thoroughly integrated with one another. They look alike and they work in consistent fashion. Equally important, they share information through a technology known as ***Object Linking and Embedding*** (OLE), which enables you to create a ***compound document*** containing data (objects) from multiple applications.

The compound document in Figure 7 was created in Word, and it contains objects (a worksheet and a chart) that were created in Excel. The letterhead uses a logo that was taken from the ClipArt Gallery, while the name and address of the recipient were drawn from an Access database. The various objects were inserted into the compound document through linking or embedding, which are actually two very different techniques. Both operations, however, are much more sophisticated than simply pasting an object, because with either linking or embedding, you can edit the object by using the tools of the original application.

The difference between linking and embedding depends on whether the object is stored within the compound document (***embedding***) or in its own file (***linking***). An *embedded object* is stored in the compound document, which in turn becomes the only user (client) of that object. A *linked object* is stored in its own file, and the compound document is one of many potential clients of that object. The compound document does not contain the linked object per se, but only a representation of the object as well as a pointer (link) to the file containing the object. The advantage of linking is that the document is updated automatically if the object changes.

The choice between linking and embedding depends on how the object will be used. Linking is preferable if the object is likely to change and the compound document requires the latest version. Linking should also be used when the same object is placed in many documents so that any change to the object has to be made in only one place. Embedding should be used if you need to take the object with you—for example, if you intend to edit the document on a different computer.

Office of Residential Living

University of Miami • P.O. Box 243984 • Coral Gables, FL 33124

September 25, 1995

Mr. Jeffrey Redmond, President
Dynamic Dining Services
4329 Palmetto Lane
Miami, FL 33157

Dear Jeff,

As per our earlier conversation, occupancy is up in all of the dorms for the 1995 - 1996 school year. I have enclosed a spreadsheet and chart that show our occupancy rates for the 1992 - 1995 school years. Please realize, however, that the 1995 figures are projections, as the Fall 1995 numbers are still incomplete. The final 1995 numbers should be confirmed within the next two weeks. I hope that this helps with your planning. If you need further information, please contact me at the above address.

Dorm Occupancy

	1992	1993	1994	1995
Beatty	330	285	270	310
Broward	620	580	520	565
Graham	450	397	352	393
Rawlings	435	375	326	372
Tolbert	615	554	524	581

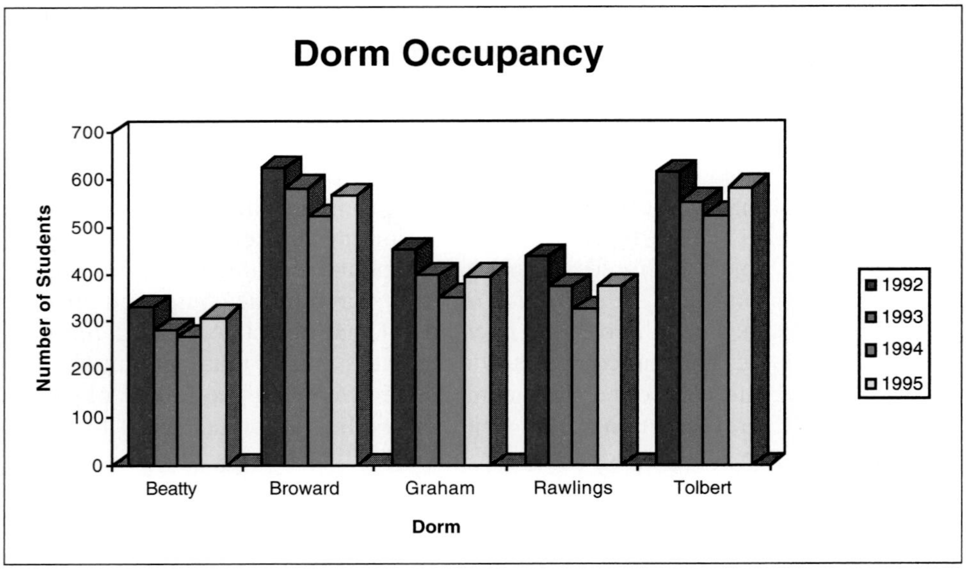
Dorm Occupancy
Number of Students
700
600
500
400
300
200
100
0
Beatty
Broward
Graham
Rawlings
Tolbert
Dorm
1992
1993
1994
1995

FIGURE 7 A Compound Document

OBJECT LINKING AND EMBEDDING

Object Linking and Embedding (OLE) enables you to create a compound document containing objects (data) from multiple Windows applications. OLE is one of the major benefits of working in the Windows environment, but it would be impossible to illustrate all of the techniques in a single exercise. Accordingly, we have created the icon at the left to help you identify the many examples of object linking and embedding that appear throughout the Exploring Windows series.

SUMMARY

The common user interface requires every Windows application to follow a consistent set of conventions and ensures that all applications work basically the same way. The development of a suite of applications from a single vendor extends this concept by imposing additional similarities on all applications within the suite.

Microsoft distributes two versions of the Office Suite: Standard Office and Office Professional. Both versions include Word, Excel, and PowerPoint. The Office Professional also has Microsoft Access. Both versions also include a fifth application, Schedule+, as well as several smaller applications and shared utilities.

The Microsoft Office Shortcut Bar provides immediate access to each application in Microsoft Office. The Shortcut Bar is fully customizable with respect to the buttons it displays, its appearance, and its position on the desktop. The Open a Document and Start a New Document buttons enable you to think in terms of a document rather than the associated application.

Object Linking and Embedding (OLE) enables you to create a compound document containing data (objects) from multiple applications. Linking and embedding are different operations. The difference between the two depends on whether the object is stored within the compound document (embedding) or in its own file (linking).

KEY WORDS AND CONCEPTS

- Answer Wizard
- ClipArt Gallery
- Compound document
- Common user interface
- Contents tab
- Embedding
- Formatting toolbar
- Index tab
- Linking
- Microsoft Access
- Microsoft Excel
- Microsoft Office Professional
- Microsoft PowerPoint
- Microsoft Standard Office
- Microsoft Word
- Object Linking and Embedding (OLE)
- Microsoft Office Shortcut Bar
- Online help
- Schedule+
- Standard toolbar
- System Information Utility
- WordArt

1

INTRODUCTION TO POWERPOINT: PRESENTATIONS MADE EASY

OBJECTIVES

After reading this chapter you will be able to:

1. Describe the common user interface; give several examples of how PowerPoint follows the same conventions as other Microsoft applications.
2. Start PowerPoint; open, modify, and view an existing presentation.
3. Describe the different ways to print a presentation.
4. List the different views in PowerPoint; describe the unique features of each view.
5. Use the Outline view to add slides to, and/or delete slides from, an existing presentation and/or to modify the text on an existing slide.
6. Add clip art to an existing slide.
7. Use the Rehearse Timings feature to time a presentation.
8. Describe the Meeting Minder, Slide Navigator, and Pen; explain how these tools are used to enhance a presentation.

OVERVIEW

This chapter introduces you to PowerPoint, one of the four major applications in the Professional version of Microsoft Office (Microsoft Word, Microsoft Excel, and Microsoft Access are the other three). In essence, PowerPoint helps you to create a professional presentation without relying on others. It enables you to deliver a presentation on the computer (or via 35-mm slides or overhead transparencies) and to print that presentation in a variety of formats.

PowerPoint is easy to learn because it is a Windows application and follows all of the conventions associated with the common user interface. Thus, if you already use one Windows application, it is that much easier to learn PowerPoint because you can apply much of what you know. It's even easier if you use Microsoft Word, Excel, or Access, since there are over 100 commands that are common to the Microsoft Office.

The chapter begins by showing you an actual PowerPoint presentation so that you can better appreciate what you will be able to do. We describe the five different PowerPoint views and the unique capabilities of each view. We show you how to add slides to, and delete slides from, an existing presentation, how to modify the text of a presentation; and how to add clip art. (We will show you how to create your own presentation in Chapter 2.) We also provide three hands-on exercises, in which you apply the conceptual material at the computer. The exercises are essential to the learn-by-doing philosophy we follow throughout the text, and it is through the exercises that you will truly master the material.

One final point, before we begin, is that while PowerPoint can help you create attractive presentations, the content and delivery are still up to you. It is important that you express yourself clearly and that you deliver the presentation effectively. The chapter ends with several suggestions to help you in this regard.

A POWERPOINT PRESENTATION

A PowerPoint presentation consists of a series of slides such as those in Figure 1.1. Each slide contains different elements, including text, clip art, and/or a chart. Nevertheless, the presentation has a consistent look from slide to slide with respect to its overall design and color scheme.

You might think that creating a presentation such as Figure 1.1 is difficult, but it isn't. It is remarkably easy, and that is the beauty of PowerPoint. In essence, PowerPoint allows you to concentrate on the *content* of a presentation without worrying about its *appearance.* You supply the text and supporting elements and leave the formatting to PowerPoint.

In addition to helping you create the presentation, PowerPoint provides a variety of ways to deliver it. You can show the presentation on a computer using animated transition effects as you move from one slide to the next. You can include sound in the presentation, provided your system has a sound card and speakers. You can also automate the presentation and distribute it on a disk for display at a convention booth or kiosk. If you cannot show the presentation on a computer, you can convert it to 35-mm slides or overhead transparencies.

PowerPoint gives you the ability to print the presentation in various ways to distribute to your audience. You can print one slide per page, or you can print miniature versions of each slide and can choose between two, three, or six slides per page. You can prepare speaker notes for yourself, consisting of a picture of each slide together with notes for its delivery. You can also print the entire presentation in outline form. Giving the audience a copy of the presentation (in any format) enables them to follow it more closely, and to take it home when the session is over.

INTRODUCTION TO POWERPOINT

The desktop in Figure 1.2 should look somewhat familiar, even if you have never used PowerPoint, because PowerPoint shares the common user interface that is present in every Windows application. You should recognize, therefore, the two open windows in Figure 1.2—the application window for PowerPoint and the document window for the current presentation.

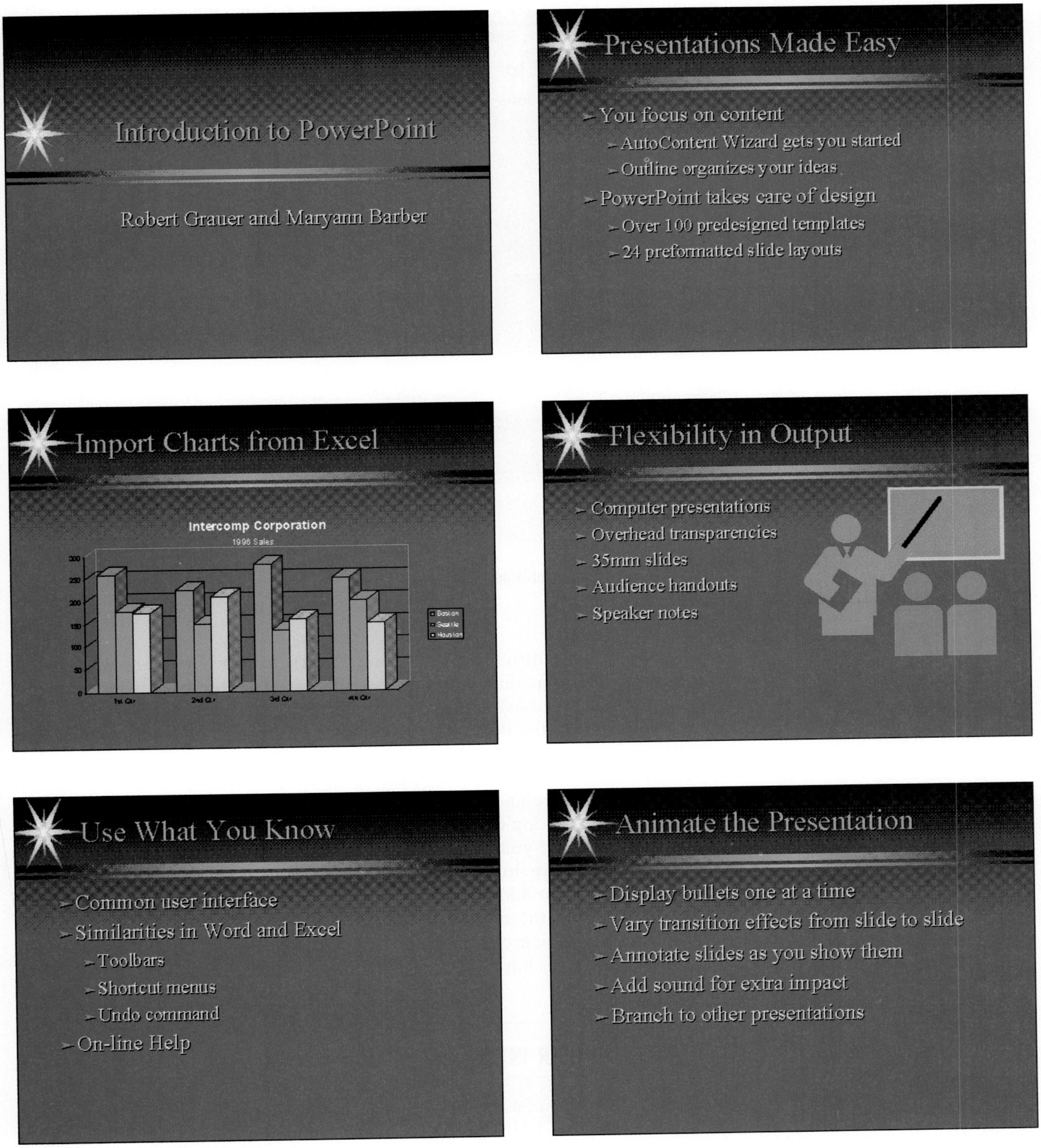

Introduction to PowerPoint
Robert Grauer and Maryann Barber
Presentations Made Easy
You focus on content
AutoContent Wizard gets you started
Outline organizes your ideas
PowerPoint takes care of design
Over 100 predesigned templates
24 preformatted slide layouts
Import Charts from Excel
Intercomp Corporation
1996 Sales
Flexibility in Output
Computer presentations
Overhead transparencies
35mm slides
Audience handouts
Speaker notes
Use What You Know
Common user interface
Similarities in Word and Excel
Toolbars
Shortcut menus
Undo command
On-line Help
Animate the Presentation
Display bullets one at a time
Vary transition effects from slide to slide
Annotate slides as you show them
Add sound for extra impact
Branch to other presentations

FIGURE 1.1 A PowerPoint Presentation

Each window has its own Minimize, Maximize (or Restore), and Close buttons. Both windows have been maximized, and thus the title bars have been merged into a single title bar that appears at the top of the application window. The title bar indicates the application (Microsoft PowerPoint) as well as the name

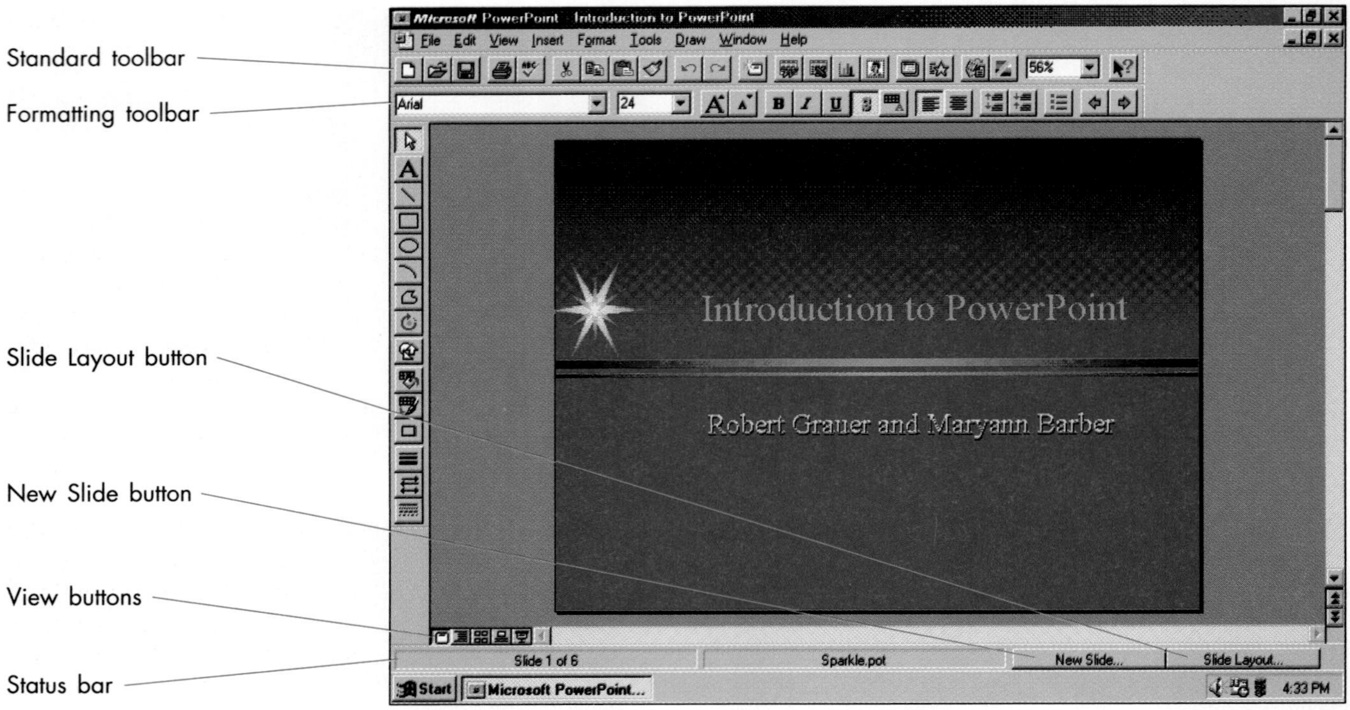
Standard toolbar
Formatting toolbar
Slide Layout button
New Slide button
View buttons
Status bar
Microsoft PowerPoint - Introduction to PowerPoint
File Edit View Insert Format Tools Draw Window Help
Arial
24
56%
Introduction to PowerPoint
Robert Grauer and Maryann Barber
Slide 1 of 6
Sparkle.pot
New Slide...
Slide Layout...
Start
Microsoft PowerPoint...
4:33 PM

FIGURE 1.2 The PowerPoint Window

of the presentation (Introduction to PowerPoint) on which you are working. A ***menu bar*** appears immediately below the title bar. Two toolbars (which are discussed in the next section) appear below the menu bar. A ***scroll bar*** appears at the right (bottom) of the document window. The Windows 95 taskbar appears at the bottom of the screen and shows the open applications.

The ***status bar*** at the bottom of the application window displays information about what you are seeing and doing as you work on a presentation. It indicates the slide you are working on (e.g., Slide 1 in Figure 1.2), or it provides information about a command you have selected. The shortcut buttons on the right side of the status bar provide immediate access to two additional commands. The ***New Slide button*** is used to add a slide to the presentation. The ***Slide Layout button*** changes the layout of the current slide.

The ***view buttons*** are located to the left of the horizontal scroll bar immediately above the status bar and are used to switch between the five different views

THE COMMON USER INTERFACE

One of the most significant benefits of the Windows environment is the ***common user interface,*** which provides a sense of familiarity when you begin to learn a new application. In other words, once you know one Windows application, it will be that much easier for you to learn PowerPoint, because all applications work basically the same way. The benefits are magnified if you use other applications in Microsoft Office; indeed, if you use either Word or Excel, you already know more than 100 commands in PowerPoint.

of a presentation. (The Slide view is displayed in Figure 1.2.) Each view offers a different way of looking at a presentation and has unique capabilities. PowerPoint views are discussed later in the chapter.

Toolbars

The Standard and Formatting toolbars are similar to those in Word and Excel, and you may recognize several buttons from those applications. The ***Standard toolbar*** appears immediately below the menu bar and contains buttons for the most basic commands in PowerPoint—for example, opening, saving, and printing a presentation. The ***Formatting toolbar,*** under the Standard toolbar, provides access to formatting operations such as boldface, italics, and underlining.

As with all other Microsoft applications, you can point to any button on any toolbar and PowerPoint will display the name of the button, which indicates its function. You can also gain an overall appreciation for the toolbars by considering the buttons in groups, as shown in Figure 1.3.

Remember, too, that while PowerPoint is designed for a mouse, it provides keyboard equivalents for almost every command. The shortcut buttons on the status bar offer still other ways to accomplish two of the most frequent operations. You may at first wonder why there are so many different ways to do the same thing, but you will come to recognize the many options as part of PowerPoint's charm. The most appropriate technique depends on personal preference, as well as the specific situation.

If, for example, your hands are already on the keyboard, it is faster to use the keyboard equivalent. Other times, your hand will be on the mouse and that will be the fastest way. It is not necessary to memorize anything, nor should you even try; just be flexible and willing to experiment. The more you do, the easier it will be!

The File Menu

The ***File menu*** is a critically important menu in virtually every Windows application. It contains the ***Save command*** to save a presentation to disk and the ***Open command*** to retrieve (open) the presentation at a later time. The File menu also contains the ***Print command*** to print a presentation, the ***Close command*** to close the current presentation but continue working in PowerPoint, and the ***Exit command*** to quit PowerPoint altogether.

The Save command copies the presentation that is currently being edited (i.e., the presentation in memory) to disk. The File Save dialog box appears the first time a presentation is saved so that you can specify the file name and other required information. All subsequent executions of the Save command save the presentation under the assigned name, replacing the previously saved version with the new version.

The File Save dialog box requires a file name (e.g., *My First Presentation* in Figure 1.4a), which can be up to 255 characters in length and may contain both spaces and commas. The dialog box also requires the drive (and folder) in which the file is to be saved, as well as the file type, which determines the application the file is associated with. (Long-time DOS users will remember the three-character extension at the end of a file name, such as PPT to indicate a PowerPoint presentation. The extension is generally hidden in Windows 95, according to options set through the View menu in My Computer. See page 30 in the Windows appendix.)

The Open command brings a copy of a previously saved presentation into memory, enabling you to show, edit, and/or print the presentation. The Open command displays the Open dialog box in which you specify the file to retrieve. You

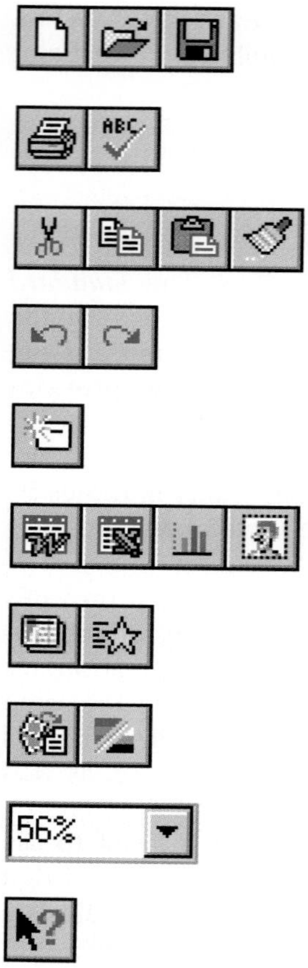
56%

- Starts a new document, opens an existing document, or saves the document to disk
- Prints the document or checks the spelling in the document
- Cuts or copies the selection to the clipboard; pastes the clipboard contents; copies the format of the selected text
- Undoes or redoes a previously executed command
- Inserts a new slide
- Inserts a Microsoft Word table, a Microsoft Excel worksheet, a graph, or a ClipArt image
- Applies a design template or an animation effect
- Exports a PowerPoint outline to Microsoft Word; changes the display to black and white
- Changes the zoom percentage
- Accesses online help

(a) Standard Toolbar

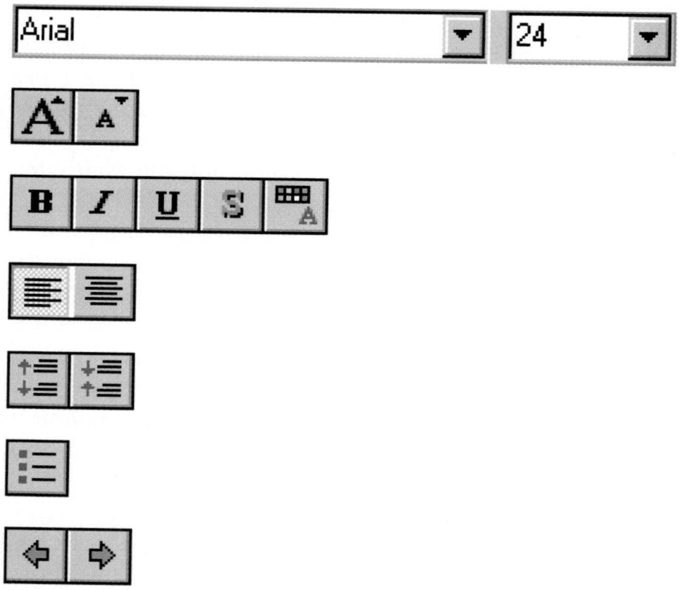
Arial
24

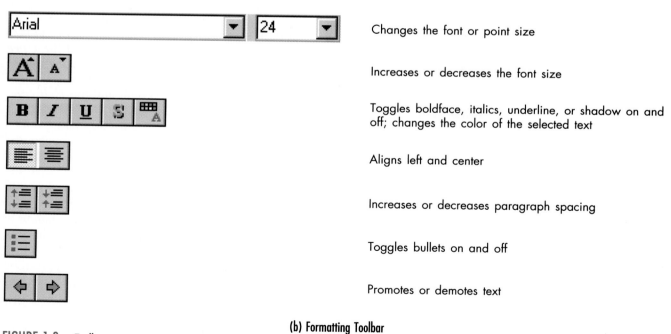

- Changes the font or point size
- Increases or decreases the font size
- Toggles boldface, italics, underline, or shadow on and off; changes the color of the selected text
- Aligns left and center
- Increases or decreases paragraph spacing
- Toggles bullets on and off
- Promotes or demotes text

(b) Formatting Toolbar

FIGURE 1.3 Toolbars

indicate the drive (and the folder) that contains the file, as well as the type of file you want to retrieve. PowerPoint will then list all files of that type on the designated drive (and folder), enabling you to open the file you want.

The Save and Open commands work in conjunction with one another. The File Save dialog box in Figure 1.4a, for example, saves the file *My First Presentation* onto the disk in drive A. The Open dialog box in Figure 1.4b brings that file back into memory so that you can work with the file, after which you can save the revised file for use at a later time.

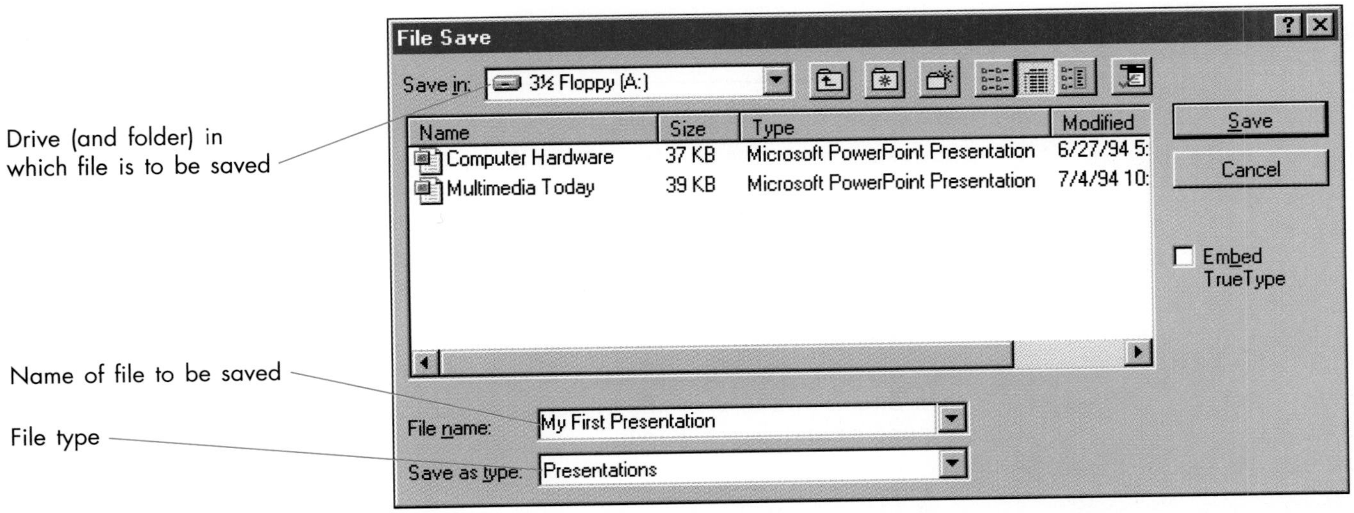
Drive (and folder) in which file is to be saved
Name of file to be saved
File type
File Save
Save in: 3½ Floppy (A:)
Name
Size
Type
Modified
Computer Hardware
37 KB
Microsoft PowerPoint Presentation
6/27/94 5:
Multimedia Today
39 KB
Microsoft PowerPoint Presentation
7/4/94 10:
Save
Cancel
Embed TrueType
File name:
My First Presentation
Save as type:
Presentations

(a) File Save Dialog Box

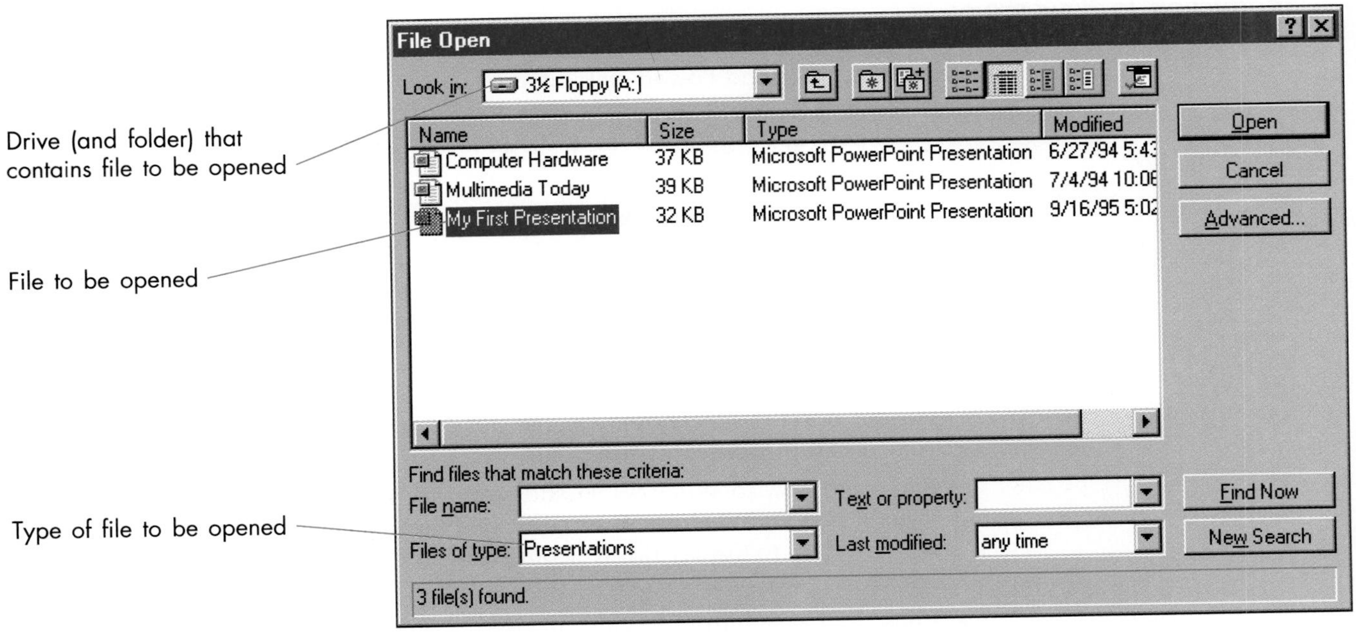
Drive (and folder) that contains file to be opened
File to be opened
Type of file to be opened
File Open
Look in: 3½ Floppy (A:)
Name
Size
Type
Modified
Computer Hardware
37 KB
Microsoft PowerPoint Presentation
6/27/94 5:4
Multimedia Today
39 KB
Microsoft PowerPoint Presentation
7/4/94 10:0
My First Presentation
32 KB
Microsoft PowerPoint Presentation
9/16/95 5:0
Open
Cancel
Advanced...
Find files that match these criteria:
File name:
Text or property:
Find Now
Files of type:
Presentations
Last modified:
any time
New Search
3 file(s) found.

(b) File Open Dialog Box

FIGURE 1.4 The Save and Open Commands

THE SAVE AS COMMAND

The Save As command saves a presentation under a different name, and is useful when you want to retain a copy of the original presentation prior to making any changes. The original (unmodified) presentation is kept on disk under its original name. A second copy of the presentation is saved under a new name and remains in memory. All subsequent editing is done on the new presentation.

LEARNING BY DOING

We believe strongly in learning by doing, and thus there comes a point where you must sit down at the computer if the discussion is to have real meaning. The exercise introduces you to the data disk that is available from your instructor. The data disk contains the presentations referenced in the hands-on exercises throughout the text and can also be used to store the presentations you create. (Alternatively, you can store the presentations on a hard disk if you have access to your own computer.)

The following exercise has you retrieve the presentation of Figure 1.1 from the data disk. The exercise has you change the title slide to include your name, then directs you to view the presentation on the computer and to print the corresponding audience handouts.

HANDS-ON EXERCISE 1

Introduction to PowerPoint

Objective: To load PowerPoint, open an existing presentation, and modify the text on an existing slide. To show an existing presentation and print handouts of its slides. Use Figure 1.5 as a guide in the exercise.

STEP 1: Welcome to Windows 95

- ➤ Turn on the computer and all of its peripherals. The floppy drive should be empty prior to starting your machine. This ensures that the system starts by reading from the hard disk, which contains the Windows files, as opposed to a floppy disk, which does not.
- ➤ Your system will take a minute or so to get started, after which you should see the desktop in Figure 1.5a. Do not be concerned if the appearance of your desktop is different from ours.
- ➤ If you are new to Windows 95 and you want a quick introduction, click the **What's New** or **Windows Tour command button.** (Follow the instructions in the boxed tip to display the Welcome dialog box if it does not appear on your system.)
- ➤ Click the **Close button** to close the Welcome window and continue with the exercise.

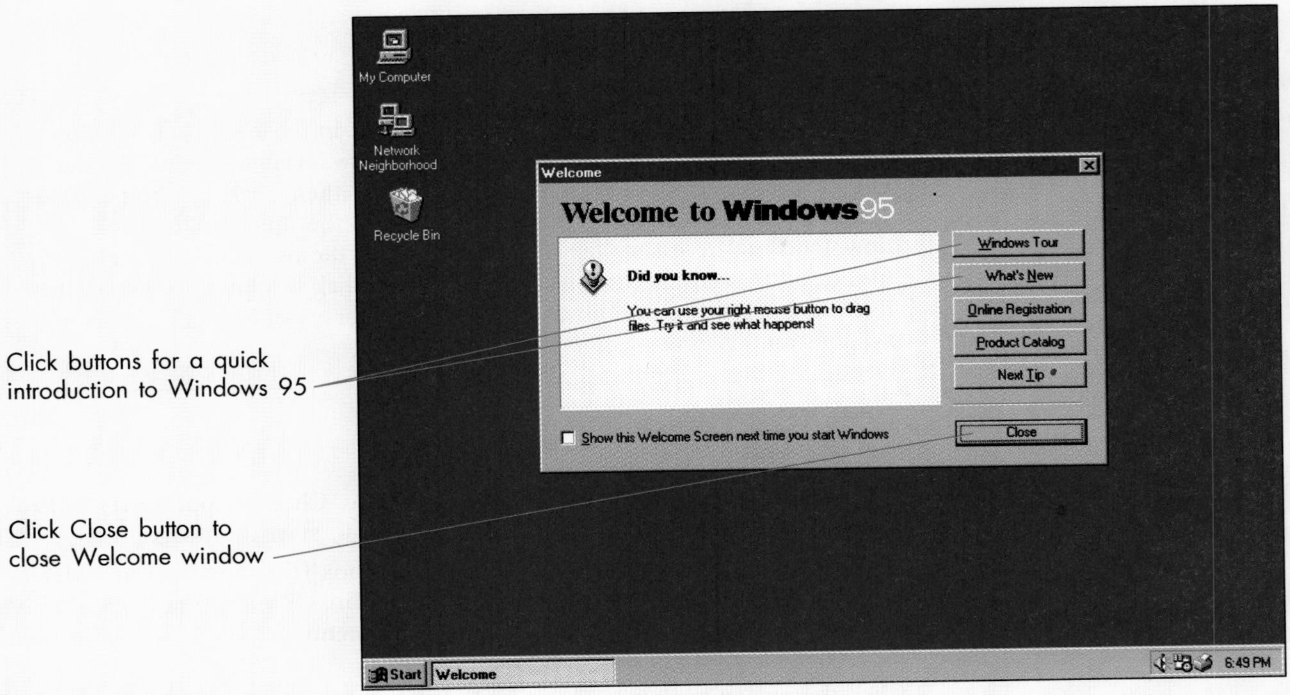
Click buttons for a quick introduction to Windows 95
Click Close button to close Welcome window
My Computer
Network Neighborhood
Recycle Bin
Welcome
Welcome to Windows95
Did you know...
You can use your right mouse button to drag files. Try it and see what happens!
Windows Tour
What's New
Online Registration
Product Catalog
Next Tip
Show this Welcome Screen next time you start Windows
Close
Start
Welcome
6:49 PM

(a) Welcome to Windows 95 (step 1)

FIGURE 1.5 Hands-on Exercise 1

TAKE THE WINDOWS 95 TOUR

Windows 95 greets you with a Welcome window that contains a command button to take you on a 10-minute tour of Windows 95. Click the command button and enjoy the show. You might also try the What's New command button for a quick overview of changes from Windows 3.1. If you do not see the Welcome window when you start Windows 95, click the Start button, click Run, type C:\WINDOWS\WELCOME in the Open text box, and press enter.

STEP 2: Install the Data Disk

- Your instructor will make the files referenced on the data disk available to you in different ways. For example:
  - The files may be on a network drive, in which case you can use the Windows Explorer to copy the files from the network to a floppy disk.
  - There may be an actual "data disk" that you are to check out from the lab in order to use the Copy Disk command to duplicate the disk.
- Alternatively, you can download the data disk from the lab at school, or from home if you have access to the Internet and World Wide Web. Ask your instructor for any additional instructions that pertain to your school.

DOWNLOAD THE DATA DISK

You can download the data disk for any book in the *Exploring Windows* series from Bob Grauer's home page (http://www.bus.miami.edu/~rgrauer). Use any Web browser to get to Bob's page, then click the link to the *Exploring Windows* series, where you choose the appropriate book and download the necessary file. (Be sure to read the associated "Read Me" file for additional instructions.) You can also click the link to CIS120, the microcomputer applications course at the University of Miami to see Bob's syllabus and current assignment.

STEP 3: Start PowerPoint

- Click the **Start button** to display the Start menu. Click (or point to) the **Programs menu,** then click **Microsoft PowerPoint** to start the program.
- Click **OK** to close the Tip of the Day dialog box (if it appears) in order to display the PowerPoint dialog box in Figure 1.5b. (If you do not see a tip of the day, and you want to, pull down the **Help menu** and click **Tip of the Day,** then check the box to **Show Tips at Startup.**)
- Click the **option button** to **Open an Existing Presentation,** then click **OK.** (If you do not see the PowerPoint dialog box, pull down the **File menu** and click **Open,** or click the **Open button** on the Standard toolbar.)

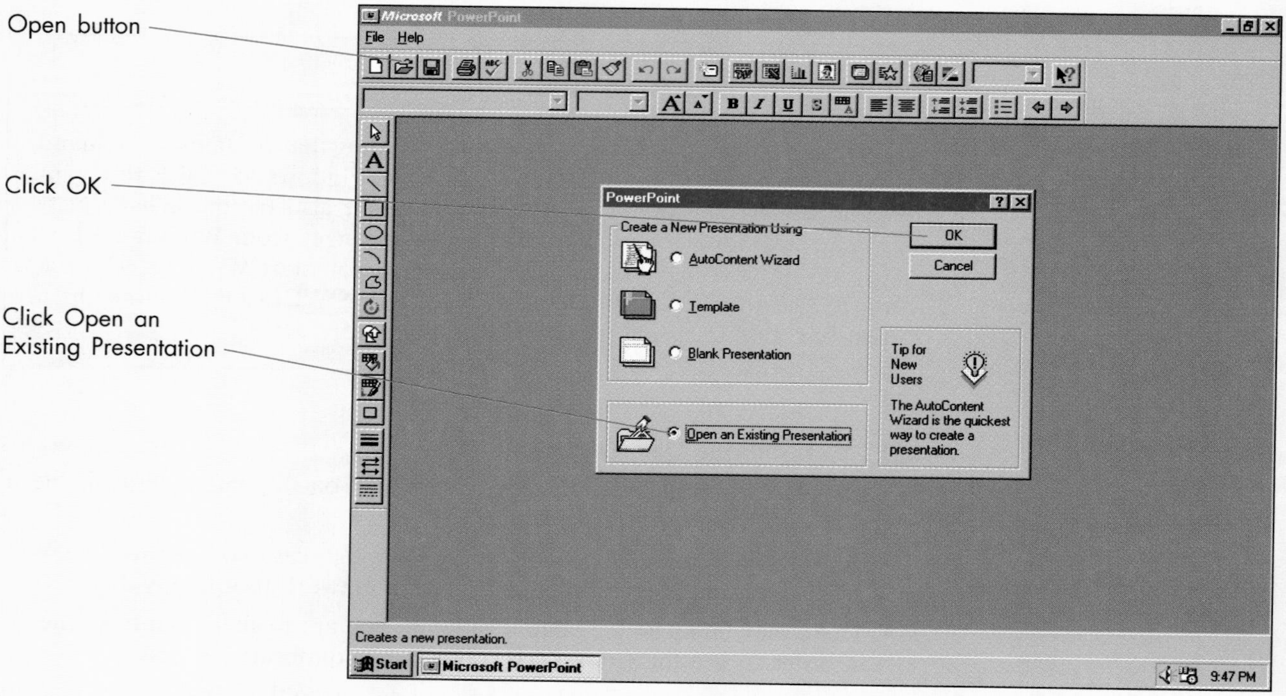

Open button
Click OK
Click Open an Existing Presentation
Microsoft PowerPoint
File Help
PowerPoint
Create a New Presentation Using
AutoContent Wizard
Template
Blank Presentation
Open an Existing Presentation
OK
Cancel
Tip for New Users
The AutoContent Wizard is the quickest way to create a presentation.
Creates a new presentation.
Start
Microsoft PowerPoint
9:47 PM

(b) Start PowerPoint (step 3)

FIGURE 1.5 Hands-on Exercise 1 (continued)

POINT AND SLIDE

Click the Start button, then slowly slide the mouse pointer over the various menu options. Notice that each time you point to a submenu, its items are displayed. Point to (don't click) the Programs menu, then click the Microsoft PowerPoint item to open the program. In other words, you don't have to click a submenu—you can just point and slide!

STEP 4: Open a Presentation

- You should see a File Open dialog box similar to the one in Figure 1.5c. Click the **Details button** to change to the Details view. If necessary, click and drag the vertical border between columns to increase (or decrease) the size of a column.
- Click the **drop-down arrow** on the Look In list box. Click the appropriate drive, drive C or drive A, depending on the location of your data. Double click the **Exploring PowerPoint folder** to make it the active folder (the folder from which you will retrieve and into which you will save the presentation).
- Click **Introduction to PowerPoint** to select the presentation. Click the **Open button** to open the presentation and begin the exercise.

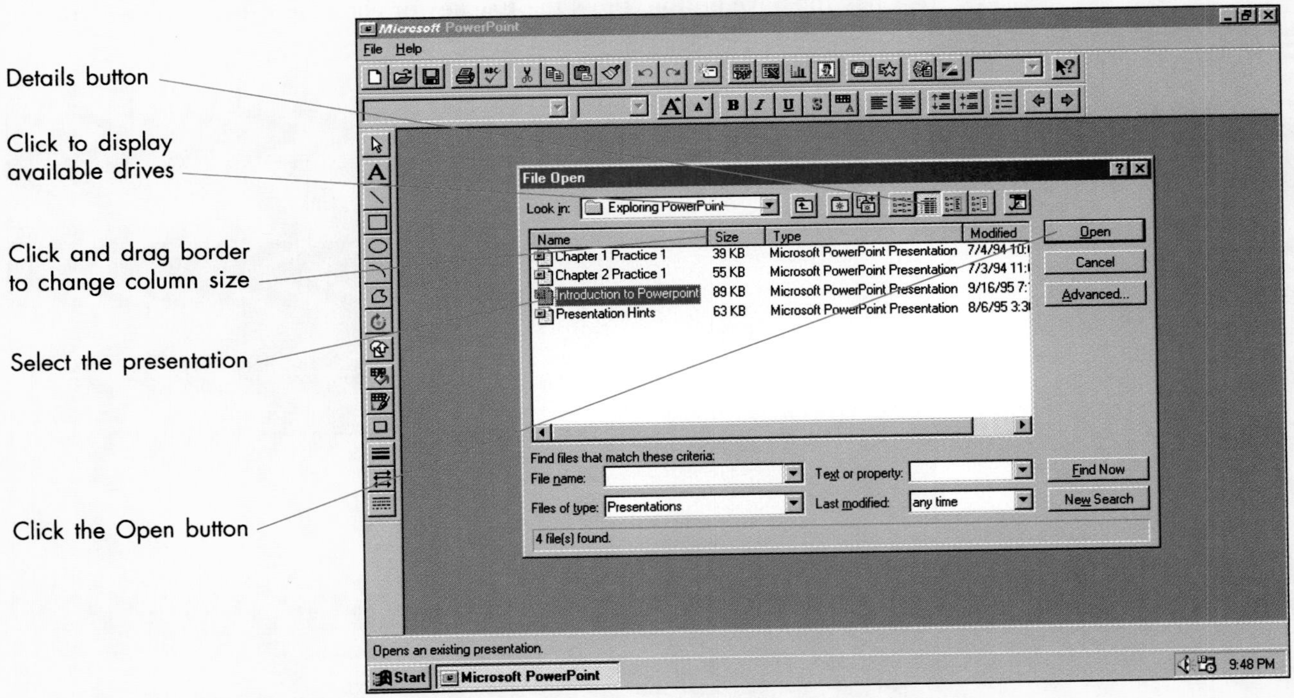
Details button
Click to display available drives
Click and drag border to change column size
Select the presentation
Click the Open button
Microsoft PowerPoint
File Help
File Open
Look in: Exploring PowerPoint
Name
Size
Type
Modified
Chapter 1 Practice 1
Chapter 2 Practice 1
Introduction to Powerpoint
Presentation Hints
Open
Cancel
Advanced...
Find files that match these criteria:
File name:
Files of type: Presentations
Text or property:
Last modified: any time
Find Now
New Search
4 file(s) found.
Opens an existing presentation.
Start
Microsoft PowerPoint
9:48 PM

(c) Open an Existing Presentation (step 4)

FIGURE 1.5 Hands-on Exercise 1 (continued)

A VERY USEFUL TOOLBAR

The File Open and File Save dialog boxes display similar toolbars with several common buttons. Click the Details button to switch to the Details view and see the date and time the file was last modified, as well as its size. Click the List button to display an icon for each file, enabling you to see many more files at the same time than in the Details view. The Preview button (available only in the File Open dialog box) lets you see a presentation before you open it. The Properties button displays information about the presentation, including the author's name and number of revisions.

STEP 5: The Save As Command

- If necessary, click the **Maximize button** in the application window so that PowerPoint takes the entire desktop. Click the **Maximize button** in the document window (if necessary) so that the document window is as large as possible.
- Pull down the **File menu.** Click **Save As** to display the dialog box shown in Figure 1.5d. Enter **Finished Introduction** as the name of the new presentation. (A file name may contain up to 255 characters; blanks are permitted.)
- Click the **Save button.** Press the **Esc key** or click the **Close button** if you see a Properties dialog box.

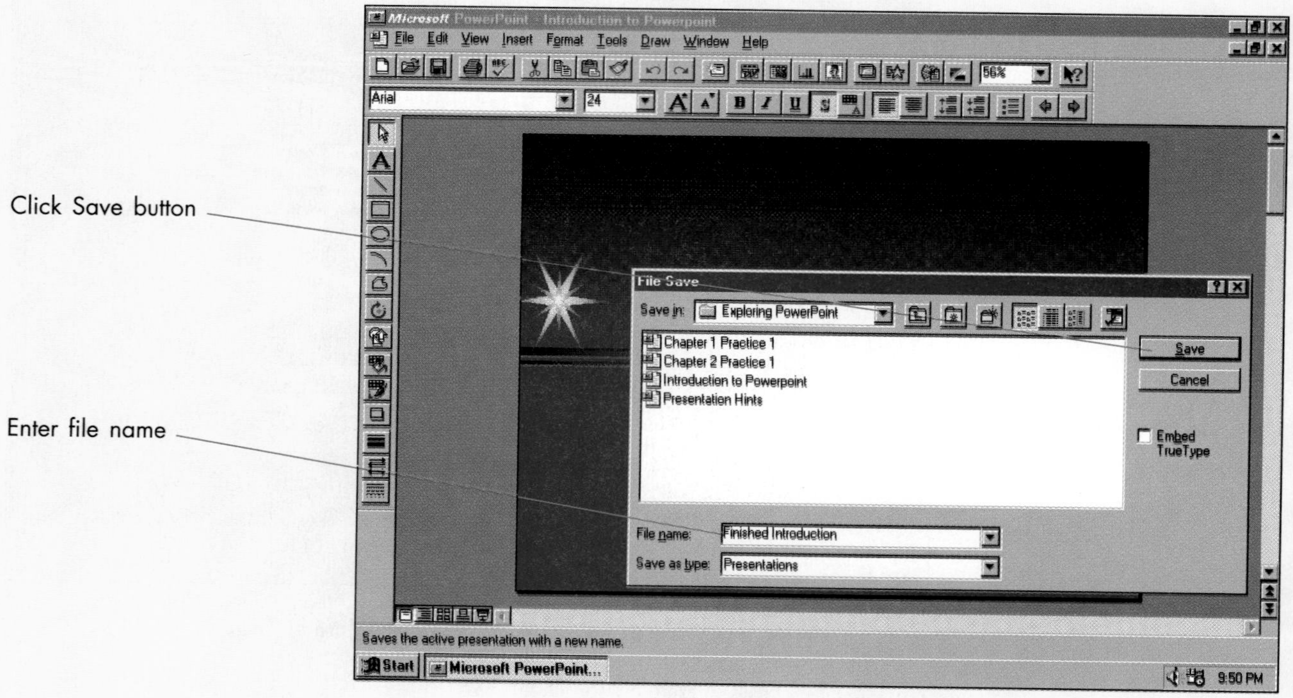
Click Save button
Enter file name
File Save
Save in: Exploring PowerPoint
Chapter 1 Practice 1
Chapter 2 Practice 1
Introduction to Powerpoint
Presentation Hints
Save
Cancel
Embed TrueType
File name: Finished Introduction
Save as type: Presentations
Saves the active presentation with a new name.
Start
Microsoft PowerPoint...
9:50 PM

(d) The Save As Command (step 5)

FIGURE 1.5 Hands-on Exercise 1 (continued)

➤ There are now two identical copies of the file on disk: "Introduction to PowerPoint," which is the original presentation that we supplied, and "Finished Introduction," which you just created. The title bar shows the latter name, as it is the presentation currently in memory.

FILE PROPERTIES

PowerPoint automatically stores summary information and other properties for each presentation you create, and prompts for that information when the presentation is saved initially. The information is interesting, but is typically not used by beginners, and hence we suggest you suppress the prompt for this information. Pull down the Tools menu, click Options, click the General tab, then clear the box to Prompt for File Properties. You can view (edit) the properties of any presentation by clicking the Properties command in the File menu.

STEP 6: Modify a Slide

➤ Press and hold the left mouse button as you drag the mouse over the presenters' names (Robert Grauer and Maryann Barber). Release the mouse.

➤ The names should be highlighted (selected) as shown in Figure 1.5e. The selected text is the text that will be affected by the next command.

➤ Type your name, which automatically replaces the selected text. Click outside the placeholder to deselect it.

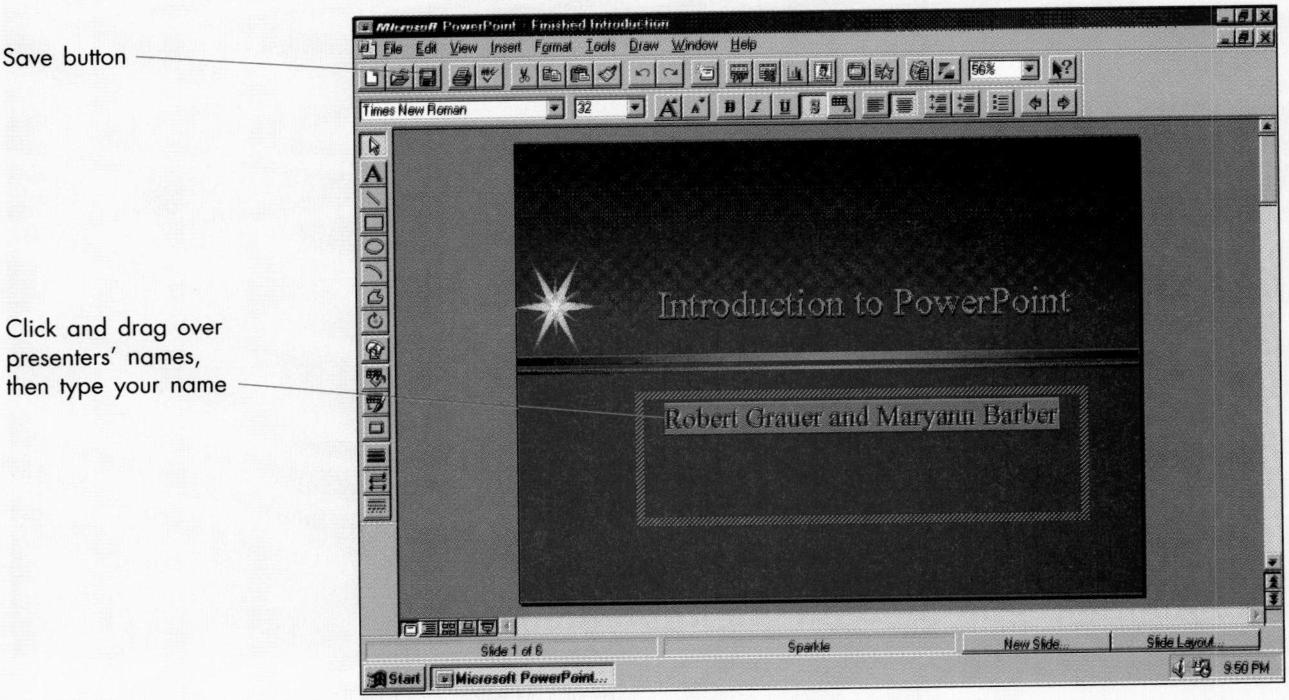
Save button
Click and drag over presenters' names, then type your name
Microsoft PowerPoint - Finished Introduction
File Edit View Insert Format Tools Draw Window Help
Times New Roman
32
56%
Introduction to PowerPoint
Robert Grauer and Maryann Barber
Slide 1 of 6
Sparkle
New Slide...
Slide Layout...
Start
Microsoft PowerPoint...
9:50 PM

(e) Modify a Slide (step 6)

FIGURE 1.5 Hands-on Exercise 1 (continued)

➤ Pull down the **File menu** and click **Save** (or click the **Save button** on the Standard toolbar).

THE HELP BUTTON

Click the Help button on the Standard toolbar (the mouse pointer changes to include a large question mark), then click any other toolbar button to display a help screen with information about that button. Click anywhere to close the help screen and continue working.

STEP 7: Show the Presentation

➤ Pull down the **View menu** and click **Slide Show** to produce the Slide Show dialog box:
- The **All option button** should be selected under Slides.
- The **Manual Advance option button** should be selected under Advance.
- Click the **Show command button** to begin the presentation.

➤ The presentation will begin with the first slide as shown in Figure 1.5f. You should see your name on the slide because of the modification you made in the previous step.

➤ Click the mouse to move to the second slide, which comes into the presentation from the left side of your monitor. (This is one of several transition

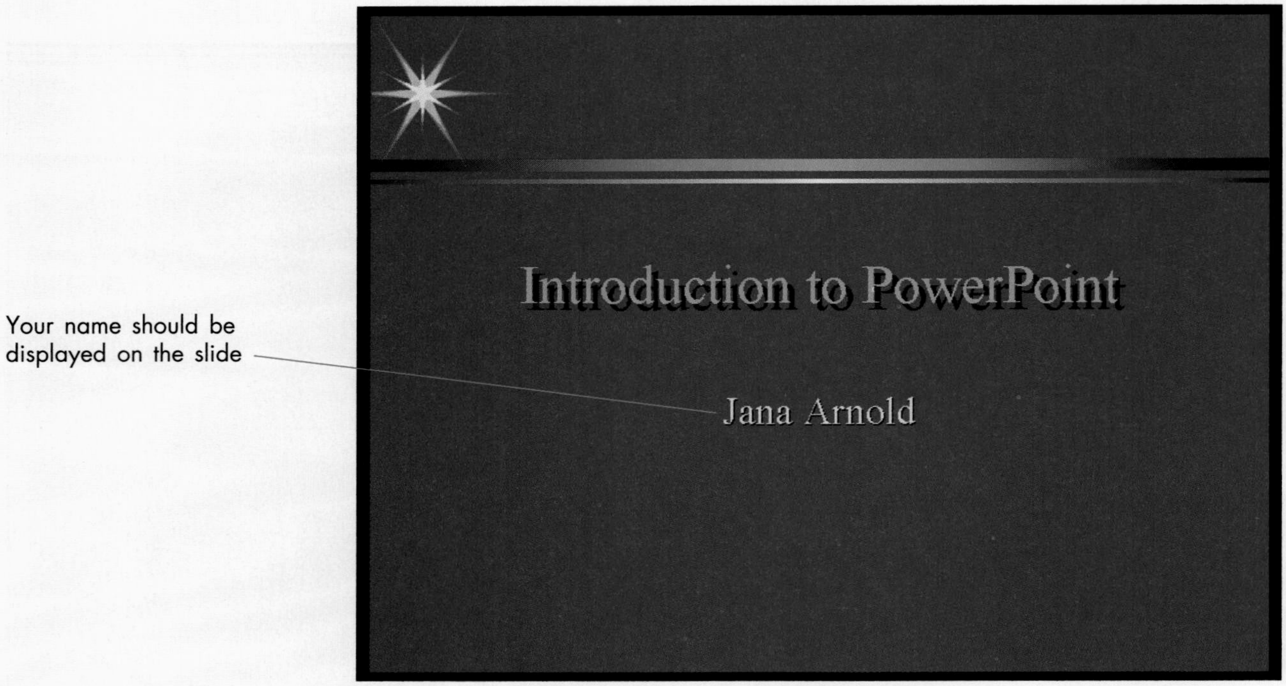
Your name should be displayed on the slide
Introduction to PowerPoint
Jana Arnold

(f) View the Presentation (step 7)

FIGURE 1.5 Hands-on Exercise 1 (continued)

effects available to add interest to a presentation.) Click the mouse again to move to the next (third) slide, which also comes in from the left.

➤ Continue to view the show until you come to the end of the presentation:

- You can press the **Esc key** at any time to cancel the show and return to the PowerPoint window.
- The last slide (Animate the Presentation) utilizes a build effect, which requires you to click the mouse to display each bullet on the slide.

➤ Click the left mouse button a final time to return to the regular PowerPoint window.

STEP 8: Print the Presentation

➤ Pull down the **File menu.** Click **Print** to produce the Print dialog box in Figure 1.5g.

- Click the **down arrow** in the **Print What** drop-down list box.
- Scroll to, then click, **Handouts (6 slides per page)** as shown in Figure 1.5g.
- Check the box to **Frame Slides.**
- Check that the **All option button** is selected under Print range.

➤ Click the **OK command button** to print the handouts for the presentation.

STEP 9: Exit PowerPoint

➤ Pull down the **File menu.** Click **Close** to close the presentation but remain in PowerPoint. Click **Yes** when asked whether to save the changes.

➤ Pull down the **File menu.** Click **Exit** to exit PowerPoint if you do not want to continue with the next exercise at this time.

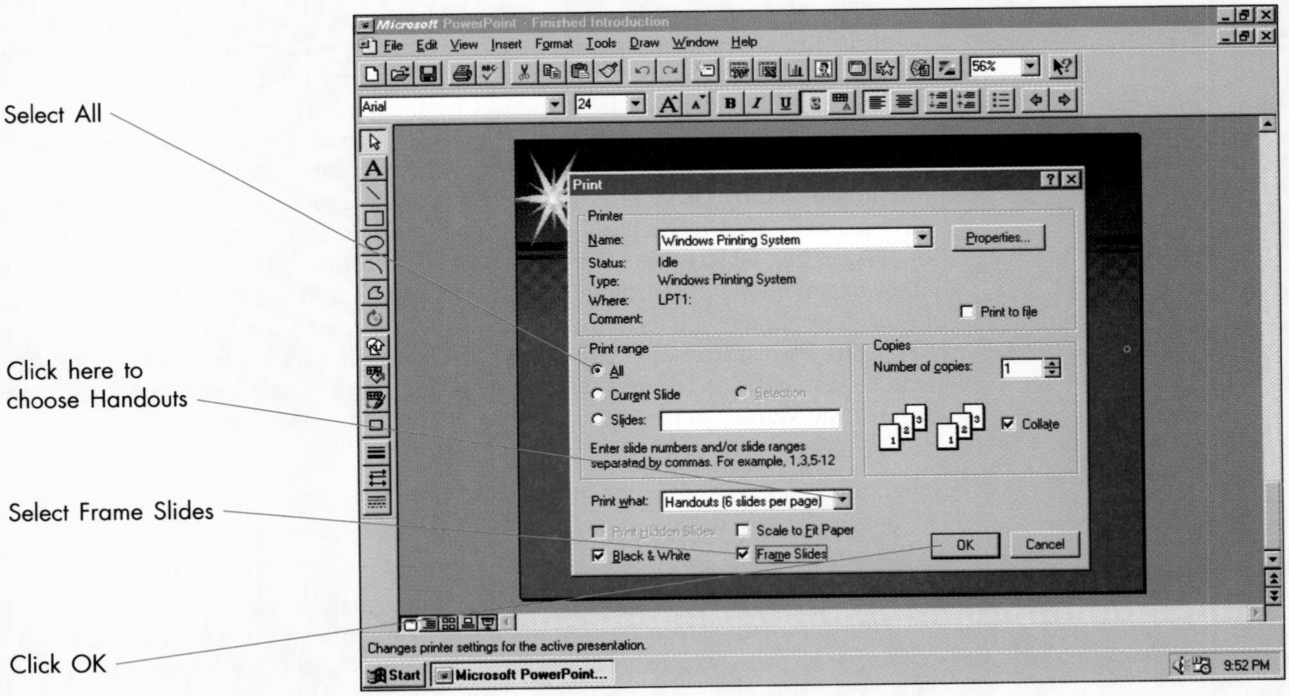

Select All
Click here to choose Handouts
Select Frame Slides
Click OK
Microsoft PowerPoint - Finished Introduction
File Edit View Insert Format Tools Draw Window Help
Print
Printer
Name: Windows Printing System
Properties...
Status: Idle
Type: Windows Printing System
Where: LPT1:
Comment:
Print to file
Print range
All
Current Slide
Selection
Slides:
Enter slide numbers and/or slide ranges separated by commas. For example, 1,3,5-12
Copies
Number of copies: 1
Collate
Print what: Handouts (6 slides per page)
Print Hidden Slides
Scale to Fit Paper
Black & White
Frame Slides
OK
Cancel
Changes printer settings for the active presentation.
Start
Microsoft PowerPoint...
9:52 PM

(g) Print the Presentation (step 8)

FIGURE 1.5 Hands-on Exercise 1 (continued)

FIVE DIFFERENT VIEWS

PowerPoint offers five different views in which to create, modify, and show a presentation. Figure 1.6 shows the five views for the introductory presentation from the first exercise. Each view represents a different way of looking at the presentation, and each view has unique capabilities. Some views display only a single slide, whereas others show multiple slides, making it easy to organize the presentation. You can switch back and forth between the views by clicking the appropriate view button at the bottom of the presentation window.

The ***Slide view*** in Figure 1.6a displays one slide at a time and enables all operations for that slide. You can enter, delete, or format text. You can draw or add objects such as a graph, clip art, or an organization chart. The ***Drawing Toolbar*** is displayed by default in this view.

The ***Slide Sorter view*** in Figure 1.6b displays multiple slides on the screen (each slide is in miniature) and lets you see the overall flow of the presentation. You can change the order of a presentation by clicking and dragging a slide from one position to another. You can delete a slide by clicking the slide and pressing the Del key. You can also set transition (animation) effects on each slide to add interest to the presentation. The Slide Sorter view has its own toolbar, which is discussed in Chapter 2 in conjunction with creating transition effects.

The ***Outline view*** in Figure 1.6c shows the presentation in outline form. You can see all of the text on every slide, but you cannot see the graphic elements that may be present on the individual slides. (A different icon appears next to the slides containing a graphic element.) The Outline view is the fastest way to enter or edit text, in that you type directly into the outline. You can copy and/or move text from one slide to another. You can also rearrange the order of the slides within the presentation. The Outline view has its own toolbar and is discussed more fully in Chapter 2.

The ***Notes Pages view*** in Figure 1.6d lets you create speaker's notes for some or all of the slides in a presentation. These notes do not appear when you show the presentation, but can be printed for use during the presentation to help you remember what you want to say about each slide.

The ***Slide Show view*** displays the slides one at a time as an electronic presentation on the computer. The show may be presented manually, where you click the mouse to move from one slide to the next. The presentation can also be shown automatically, where each slide stays on the screen for a predetermined amount of time, after which the next slide appears automatically. Either way, the slide show may contain transition effects from one slide to the next as was demonstrated in the first hands-on exercise.

The easiest way to switch from one view to another is by clicking the appropriate view button. The buttons are displayed in the lower-left part of the screen (above the status bar) in all views except the Slide Show view.

POWERPOINT VIEWS

PowerPoint has five different views of a presentation, each with unique capabilities. Anything you do in one view is automatically reflected in the other views. If, for example, you rearrange the slides in the Slide Sorter view, the new arrangement is reflected in the Outline view. In similar fashion, if you add or format text in the Outline view, the changes are also made in the Slide view.

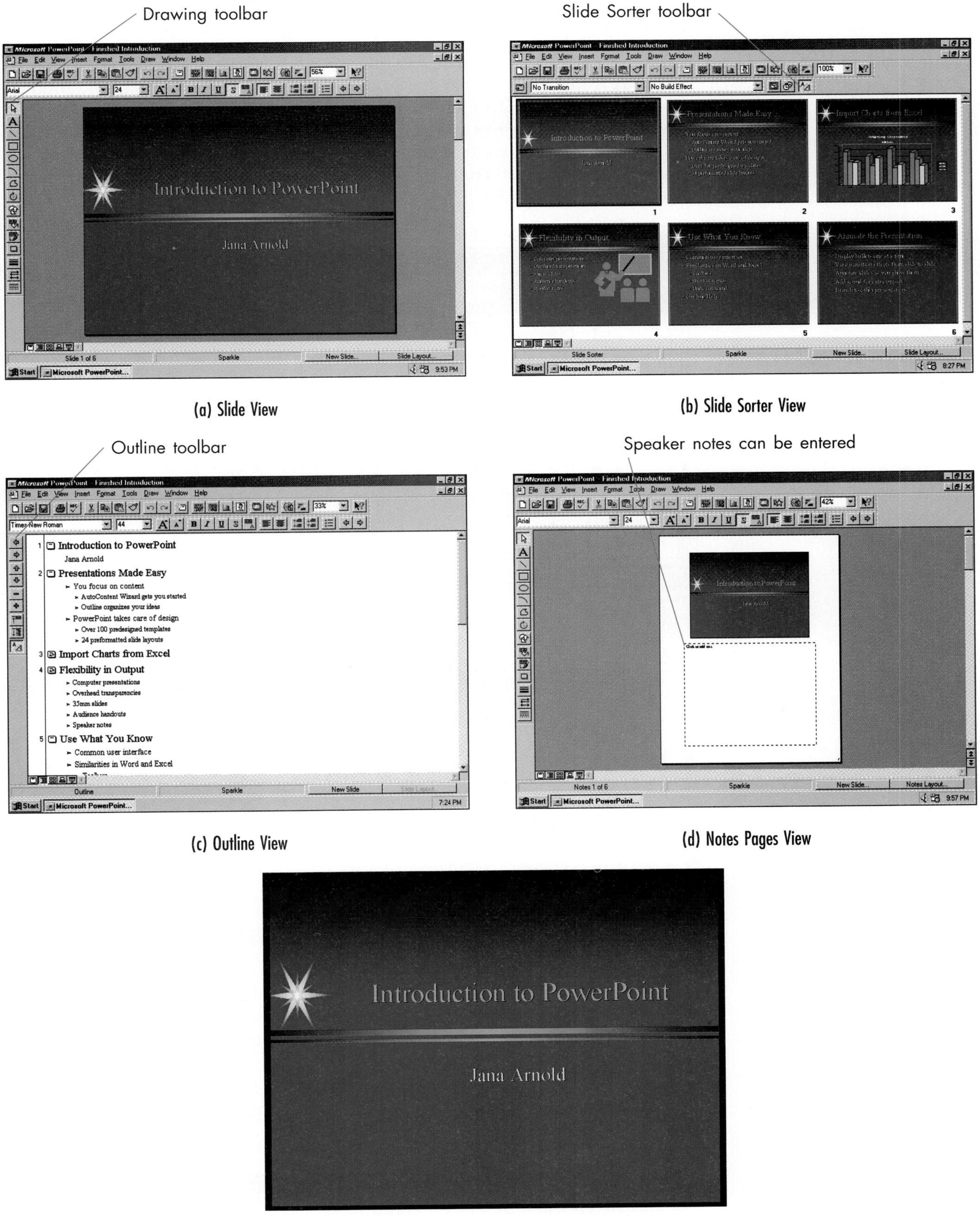

Drawing toolbar
Slide Sorter toolbar
(a) Slide View
(b) Slide Sorter View
Outline toolbar
Speaker notes can be entered
(c) Outline View
(d) Notes Pages View
Introduction to PowerPoint
Jana Arnold
Presentations Made Easy
You focus on content
AutoContent Wizard gets you started
Outline organizes your ideas
PowerPoint takes care of design
Over 100 predesigned templates
24 preformatted slide layouts
Import Charts from Excel
Flexibility in Output
Computer presentations
Overhead transparencies
35mm slides
Audience handouts
Speaker notes
Use What You Know
Common user interface
Similarities in Word and Excel
(e) Slide Show View

FIGURE 1.6 PowerPoint Views

ADDING AND DELETING SLIDES

Slides are added to a presentation by using one of 24 predefined slide formats known as ***AutoLayouts.*** Click the New Slide button on the status bar to produce the dialog box in Figure 1.7a, then choose the type of slide you want. (The slide will be added to the presentation immediately after the current slide.)

Figure 1.7a depicts the addition of a bulleted slide with clip art. The user chooses the desired layout, then clicks the OK command button to switch to the slide view in Figure 1.7b. The AutoLayout contains ***placeholders*** for the various

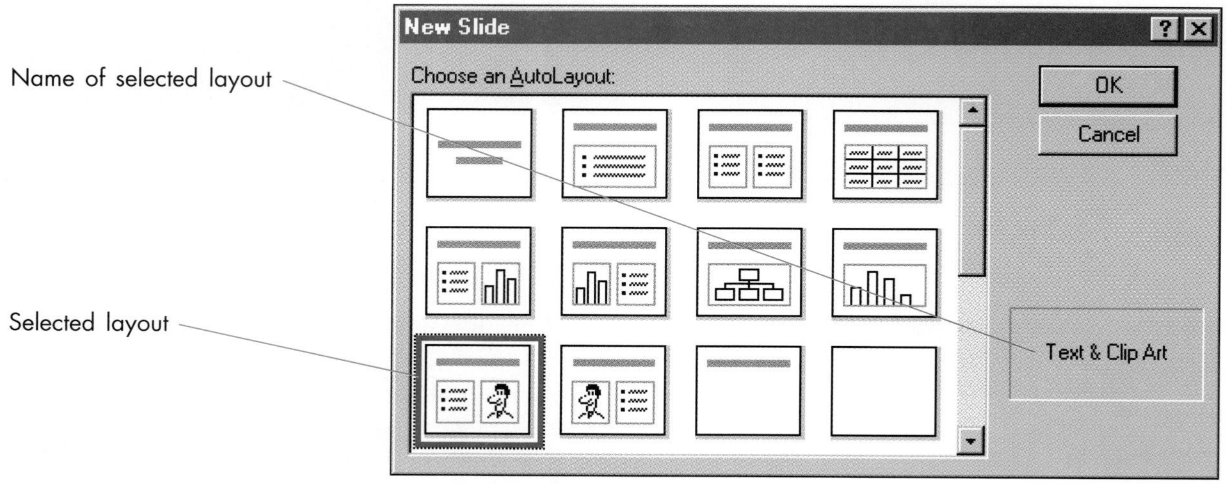
Name of selected layout
Selected layout
New Slide
Choose an AutoLayout:
OK
Cancel
Text & Clip Art

(a) AutoLayout

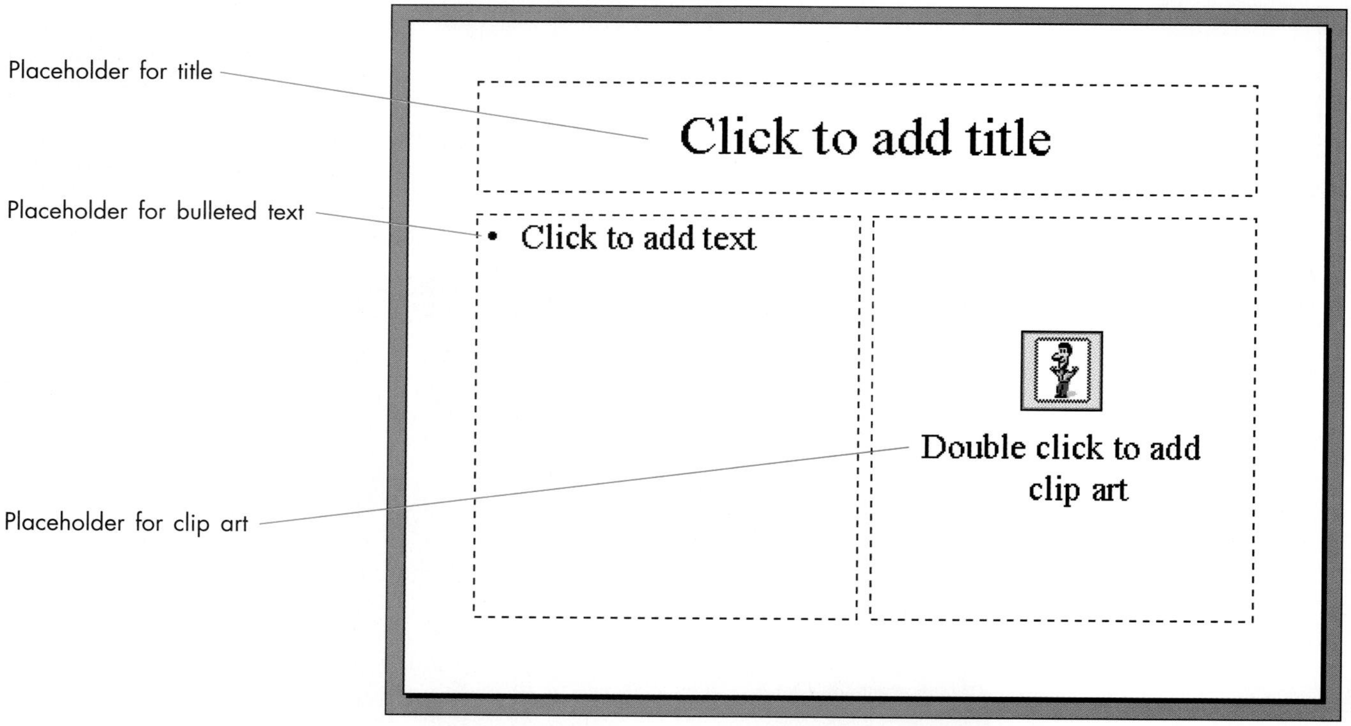
Placeholder for title
Placeholder for bulleted text
Placeholder for clip art
Click to add title
• Click to add text
Double click to add clip art

(b) Placeholders

FIGURE 1.7 Adding a Slide

objects on the slide that position the object on the slide. There are three placeholders in Figure 1.7b—one for the title, one for the bulleted text, and one for the clip art. Just follow the directions on the slide by clicking the appropriate place to add the title or text, or double clicking to add the clip art. It's that easy, as you will see in the exercise that follows shortly.

You can delete a slide from any view except the Slide Show view. To delete a slide from the Slide or Notes Pages view, select the slide by making it the current slide, pull down the Edit menu, and choose the Delete Slide command. To delete a slide from the Slide Sorter or Outline view, select the slide, then press the Del key.

HANDS-ON EXERCISE 2

PowerPoint Views

Objective: To switch between the different views while modifying a presentation; to use the ClipArt Gallery and add clip art to a slide; to add a slide to an existing presentation. Use Figure 1.8 as a guide in the exercise.

STEP 1: Add a New Slide

➤ Start PowerPoint. Follow the instructions from step 4 in the previous exercise to open the **Finished Introduction** presentation.

➤ Pull down the **Insert menu** and click **New slide** (or click the **New Slide command button** on the status bar). You will see the New Slide dialog box in Figure 1.8a.

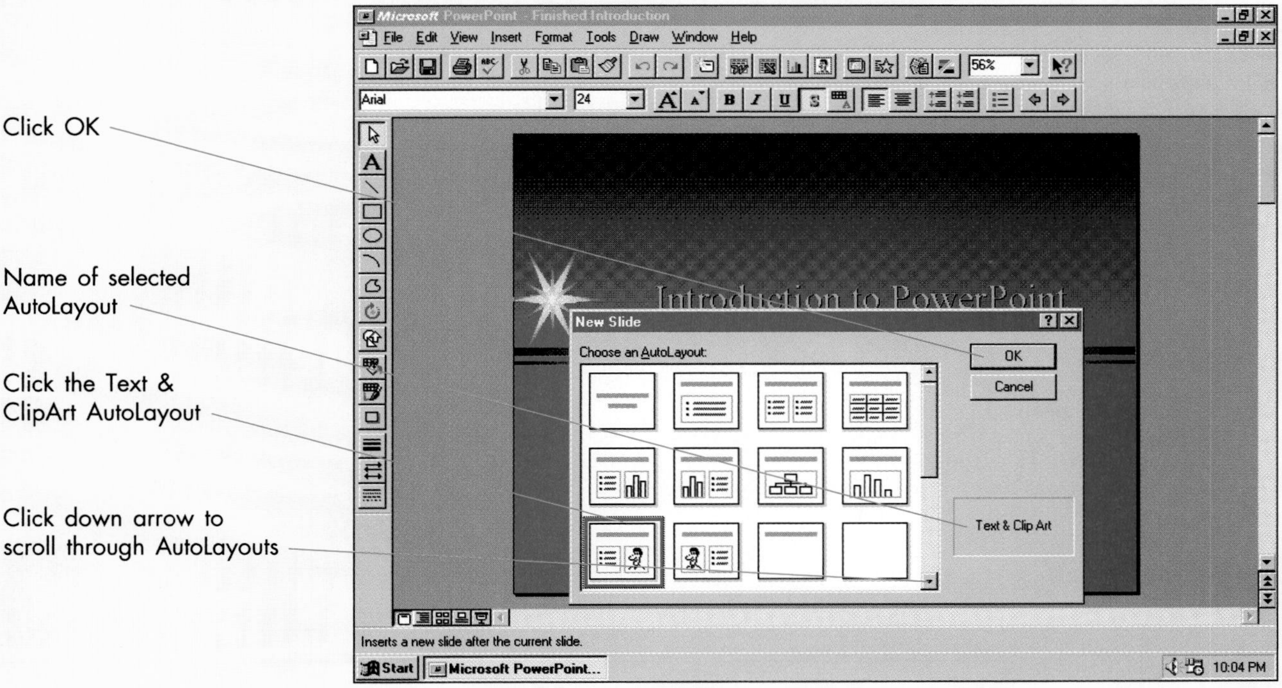

Click OK
Name of selected AutoLayout
Click the Text & ClipArt AutoLayout
Click down arrow to scroll through AutoLayouts
Microsoft PowerPoint - Finished Introduction
File Edit View Insert Format Tools Draw Window Help
Introduction to PowerPoint
New Slide
Choose an AutoLayout:
OK
Cancel
Text & Clip Art
Inserts a new slide after the current slide.
Start
Microsoft PowerPoint...
10:04 PM

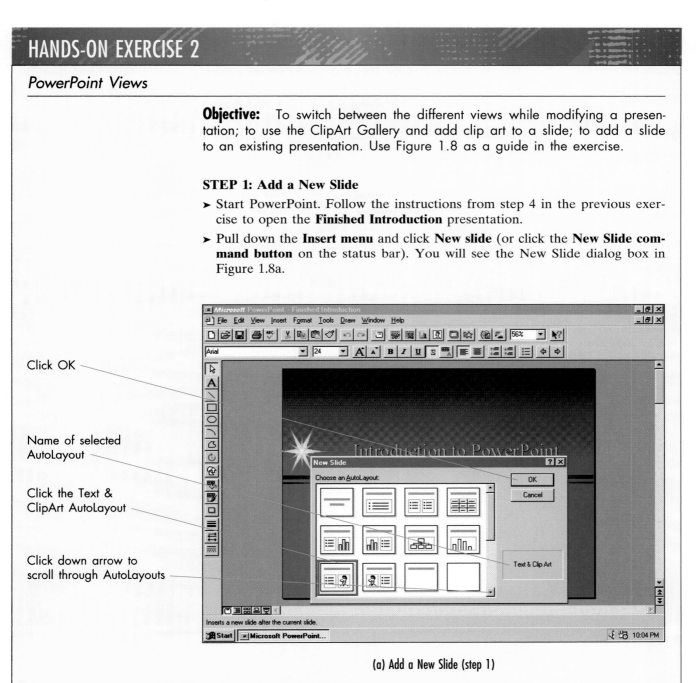

(a) Add a New Slide (step 1)

FIGURE 1.8 Hands-on Exercise 2

➤ Click the **down arrow** on the vertical scroll bar to scroll through AutoLayouts within PowerPoint.

➤ Select (click) the **Text & Clip Art layout** as shown in the figure. (The name of the selected layout appears in the lower-right corner of the dialog box.) Click the **OK command button.**

THE MOST RECENTLY OPENED FILE LIST

The easiest way to open a recently used presentation is to select the presentation directly from the File menu. Pull down the File menu, but instead of clicking the Open command, check to see if the presentation appears on the list of the most recently opened presentations located at the bottom of the menu. If so, you can click the presentation name rather than having to make the appropriate selections through the Open dialog box.

STEP 2: Click Here

➤ Click the **placeholder** where it says **Click to add title** in Figure 1.8b. Type **The ClipArt Gallery** as the title of the slide.

➤ Click the **placeholder** where it indicates **Click to add text.** Type **Choose from many different categories** as the first bullet. Press **enter** to move to the next bullet.

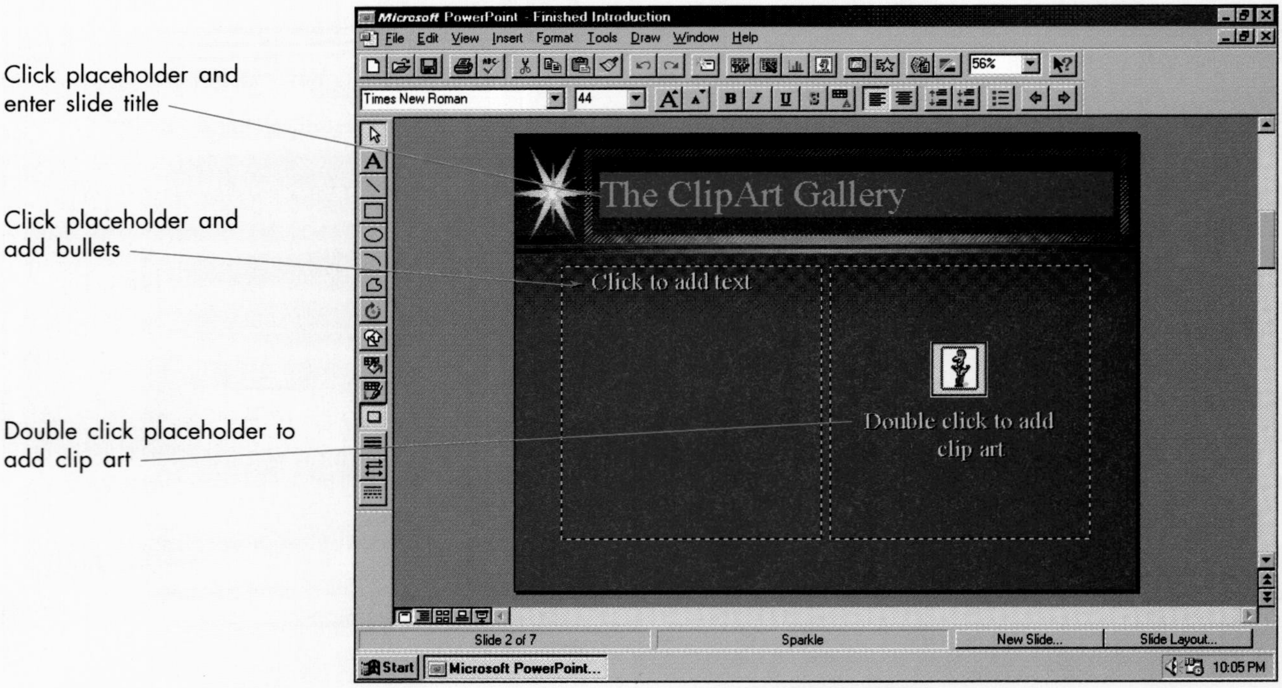
Click placeholder and enter slide title
Click placeholder and add bullets
Double click placeholder to add clip art
Microsoft PowerPoint - Finished Introduction
File Edit View Insert Format Tools Draw Window Help
Times New Roman
44
56%
The ClipArt Gallery
Click to add text
Double click to add clip art
Slide 2 of 7
Sparkle
New Slide...
Slide Layout...
Start
Microsoft PowerPoint...
10:05 PM

(b) Click Here (step 2)

FIGURE 1.8 Hands-on Exercise 2 (continued)

- Press **Tab** to indent the next bullet one level. Type **Cartoons.** Press **enter** to move to the next bullet.
- You do *not* have to press the Tab key because PowerPoint automatically aligns each succeeding bullet under the previous bullet. Type **Maps.** Press **enter** to move to the next bullet.
- Type **People.** Press **enter** to move to the next bullet.

➤ Press **Shift+Tab** to move the new bullet one level to the left. Enter **Valuepack on CD contains more than 1,000 images** as the final bullet. Do *not* press the enter key or else you will create another bullet.

BULLETS AND THE TAB (SHIFT+TAB) KEY

Bullets are entered one after another simply by typing the text of a bullet and pressing the enter key. A new bullet appears automatically under the previous bullet. Press the Tab key to indent the new bullet or press Shift+Tab to move the bullet back one level to the left.

STEP 3: Add Clip Art

➤ Double click the **placeholder** for the **clip art.** You will see the ClipArt Gallery dialog box shown in Figure 1.8c (although you may not see all of the categories listed in the figure).

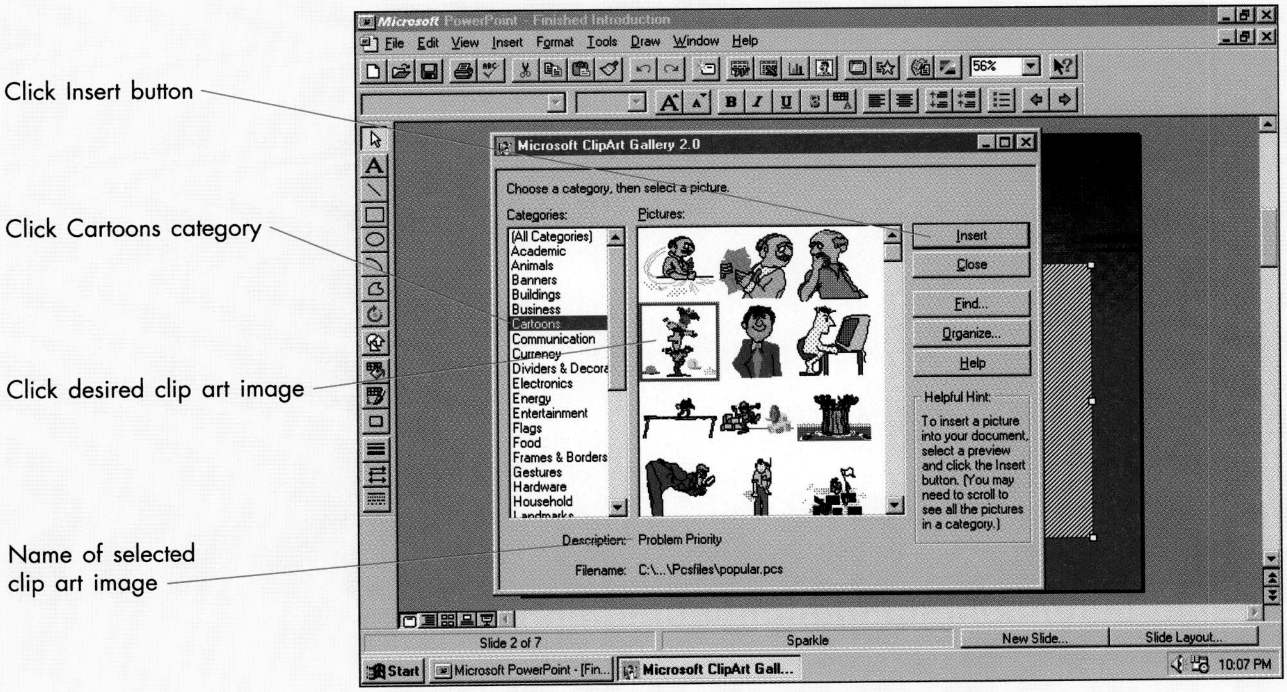
Click Insert button
Click Cartoons category
Click desired clip art image
Name of selected clip art image
Microsoft ClipArt Gallery 2.0
Choose a category, then select a picture.
Categories:
Pictures:
Insert
Close
Find...
Organize...
Help
Helpful Hint:
To insert a picture into your document, select a preview and click the Insert button. (You may need to scroll to see all the pictures in a category.)
Description: Problem Priority
Filename: C:\...\Pcsfiles\popular.pcs
Slide 2 of 7
Sparkle
New Slide...
Slide Layout...

(c) The ClipArt Gallery (step 3)

FIGURE 1.8 Hands-on Exercise 2 (continued)

- ➤ Click the **Cartoons** category. If necessary, click the **down arrow** on the scroll bar to scroll through the available cartoons until you see the image you want.
- ➤ Select (click) the **Problem Priority** cartoon as shown in Figure 1.8c. Click the **Insert button** to insert the clip art onto the slide.

> **MISSING CLIP ART—MS OFFICE VALUEPACK**
>
> The default installation of PowerPoint includes only a limited number of clip art images and hence you may not see all of the images we display. Additional clip art is available from several sources, including the CD-ROM version of Microsoft Office, which has a Valuepack containing more than 1,000 images (see case study on page 46). To add clip art, click the Insert Clip Art button on the Standard toolbar, click Organize, then click Add Pictures. Select the folder containing the clip art (e.g., the Clip Art folder in the Valuepack), then click Open to add the clip art.

STEP 4: Select-Then-Do

- ➤ You should see the completed slide in Figure 1.8d. Click and drag to select the number 1,000.
  - Click the **Bold button** on the Formatting toolbar to boldface the selected text.

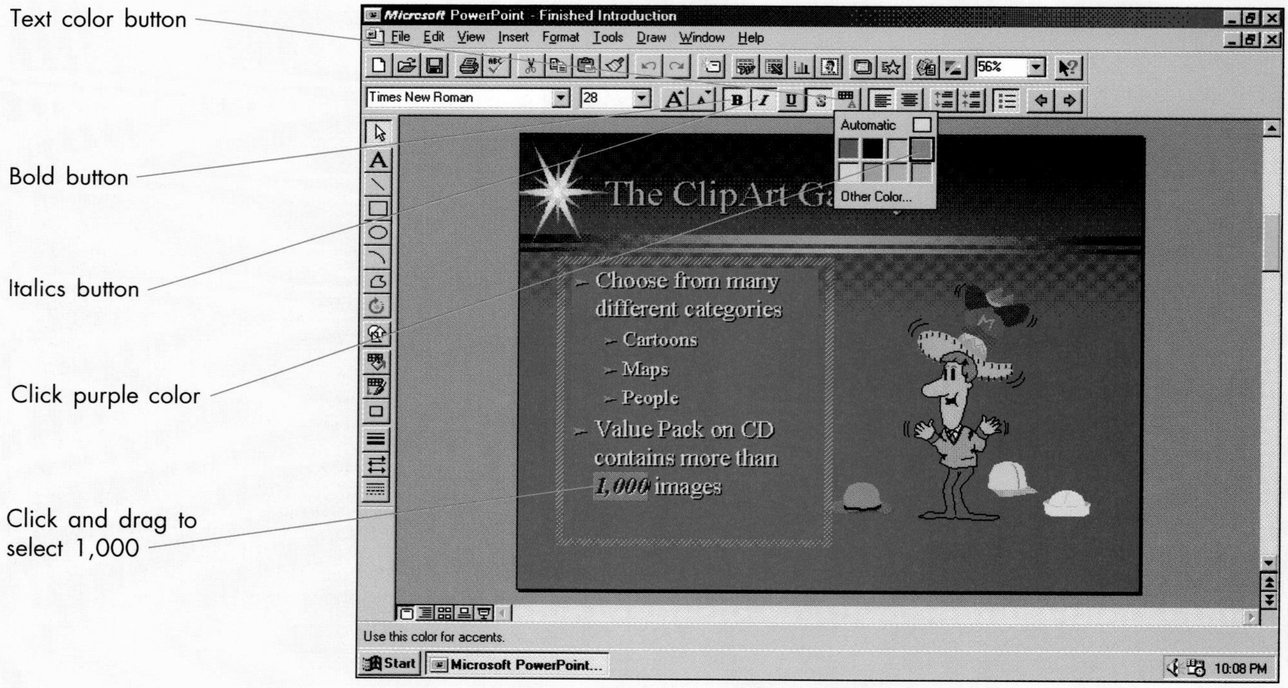

Text color button
Bold button
Italics button
Click purple color
Click and drag to select 1,000
Microsoft PowerPoint - Finished Introduction
File Edit View Insert Format Tools Draw Window Help
56%
Times New Roman
28
Automatic
Other Color...
The ClipArt Ga
Choose from many different categories
Cartoons
Maps
People
Value Pack on CD contains more than 1,000 images
Use this color for accents.
Start
Microsoft PowerPoint...
10:08 PM

(d) Select-Then-Do (step 4)

FIGURE 1.8 Hands-on Exercise 2 (continued)

- Click the **Italic button** on the Formatting toolbar to italicize the selected text.
- Click the **Text color button** on the Formatting toolbar to display the available text colors. Click **purple** (or any other color).

➤ Click outside the text area to deselect the text to see the results. Save the presentation.

> **SELECT-THEN-DO**
>
> All editing and formatting operations take place within the context of select-then-do; that is, you select a block of text, then you execute the command to operate on that text. Selected text is affected by any subsequent operation; for example, clicking the Boldface or Italic button changes the selected text to boldface or italics, respectively. In similar fashion, pressing the Del key deletes the selected text. And finally, the fastest way to replace existing text is to select the text, then type a new entry while the text is still selected. Selected text remains highlighted until you click elsewhere on the slide.

STEP 5: The Slide Sorter View

➤ Pull down the **View menu** and click **Slide Sorter** (or click the **Slide Sorter View button** on the status bar). This changes to the Slide Sorter view in Figure 1.8e.

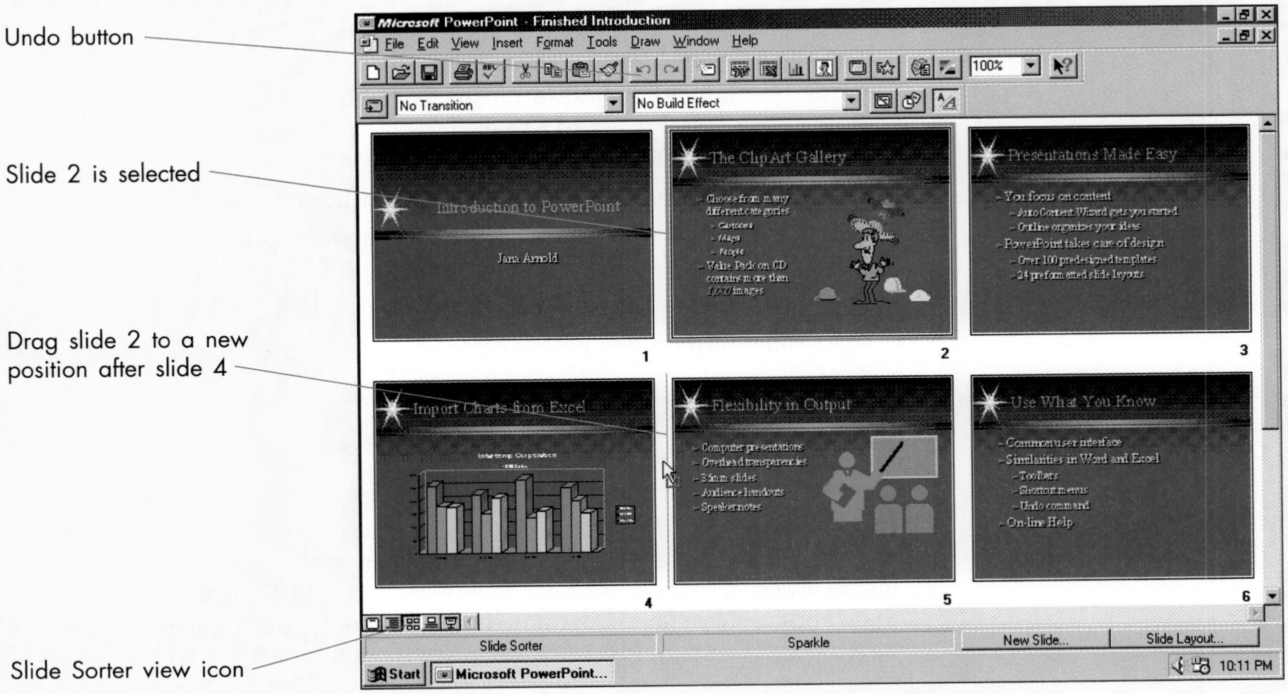

Undo button
Slide 2 is selected
Drag slide 2 to a new position after slide 4
Slide Sorter view icon
Microsoft PowerPoint - Finished Introduction
File Edit View Insert Format Tools Draw Window Help
100%
No Transition
No Build Effect
Introduction to PowerPoint
Jana Arnold
The ClipArt Gallery
Presentations Made Easy
Import Charts from Excel
Flexibility in Output
Use What You Know
1
2
3
4
5
6
Slide Sorter
Sparkle
New Slide...
Slide Layout...
Start
Microsoft PowerPoint...
10:11 PM

(e) Slide Sorter View (step 5)

FIGURE 1.8 Hands-on Exercise 2 (continued)

- ➤ Slide 2 (the slide you just created) is already selected as indicated by the heavy border around the slide.
- ➤ Click and drag slide 2 and move it after slide 4. (A vertical line appears in the presentation as you drag the slide to indicate where it will be placed.)
- ➤ Release the mouse. The existing slides are automatically renumbered to reflect the new sequence.
- ➤ Pull down the **Edit menu** and click **Undo Move** (or click the **Undo button** on the Standard toolbar). The slide containing the clip art goes back to its original position.
- ➤ Click and drag slide 2 and move it after slide 4.
- ➤ Save the presentation.

MULTIPLE LEVEL UNDO

The Undo command reverses (undoes) the most recent command. The command is executed from the Edit menu or more easily by clicking the Undo button on the Standard toolbar. Each click of the Undo button reverses one command; that is, click the Undo button and you reverse the last command. Click the Undo button a second time and you reverse the previous command. The Redo command works in reverse and undoes the most recent Undo command (i.e., it redoes the command you just undid). The maximum number of Undo commands (the default is 20) is set through the Tools menu. Pull down the Tools menu, click Options, click the Advanced tab, then enter the desired number.

STEP 6: The Outline View

- ➤ Click the **Outline View button** on the status bar to change to the Outline view in Figure 1.8f. Press **Ctrl+End** to move to the end of the outline where you will enter the next slide:
  - Type **Five Different Views** (the title of the slide). Press **enter.**
  - Press the **Tab key** to indent one level. Type **Slide view** as shown in Figure 1.8f. Press **enter** to move to the next bullet.
  - Type **Outline view.** Press **enter.**
  - Type **Slide Sorter view.** Press **enter.**

MOVING WITHIN THE PRESENTATION

Ctrl+Home and Ctrl+End are universal Windows shortcuts that move to the beginning or end of a document, respectively. Not only do the techniques work in PowerPoint, but they work in four of the five views (the Slide Show view is the exception). The shortcuts are quite valuable as you develop a presentation because you often need to move to the first or last slide.

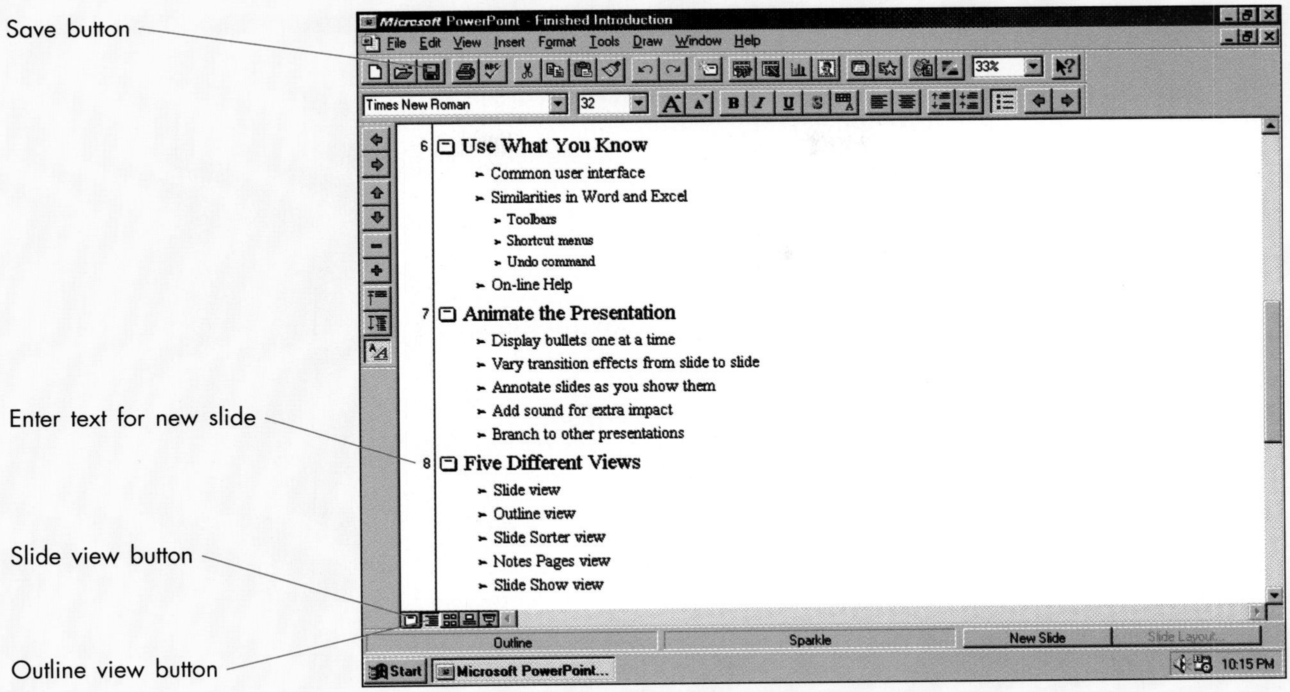
Save button
Enter text for new slide
Slide view button
Outline view button
Microsoft PowerPoint - Finished Introduction
File Edit View Insert Format Tools Draw Window Help
Times New Roman
32
33%
6 Use What You Know
Common user interface
Similarities in Word and Excel
Toolbars
Shortcut menus
Undo command
On-line Help
7 Animate the Presentation
Display bullets one at a time
Vary transition effects from slide to slide
Annotate slides as you show them
Add sound for extra impact
Branch to other presentations
8 Five Different Views
Slide view
Outline view
Slide Sorter view
Notes Pages view
Slide Show view
Outline
Sparkle
New Slide
Slide Layout
Start
Microsoft PowerPoint...
10:15 PM

(f) Outline View (step 6)

FIGURE 1.8 Hands-on Exercise 2 (continued)

- Type **Notes Pages view.** Press **enter.**
- Type **Slide Show view.**

➤ The slide is complete. Click the **Save button** on the Standard toolbar to save the presentation.

STEP 7: The Slide View

➤ Click the **Slide View button** to change to the Slide view as shown in Figure 1.8g. You should see the Slide view of the slide created in the previous step.

➤ Click the **Previous Slide button** on the vertical scroll bar (or press the **PgUp key**) to move to the previous slide (slide 7) in the presentation.

➤ Click the **Next Slide button** on the vertical scroll bar (or press the **PgDn key**) to move to the next slide (slide 8).

THE SLIDE ELEVATOR

PowerPoint uses the scroll box (common to all Windows applications) in the vertical scroll bar as an elevator to move up and down within the presentation. Click and drag the elevator to go to a specific slide; as you drag, you will see a ToolTip indicating the slide you are about to display. Release the mouse when you see the number (title) of the slide you want.

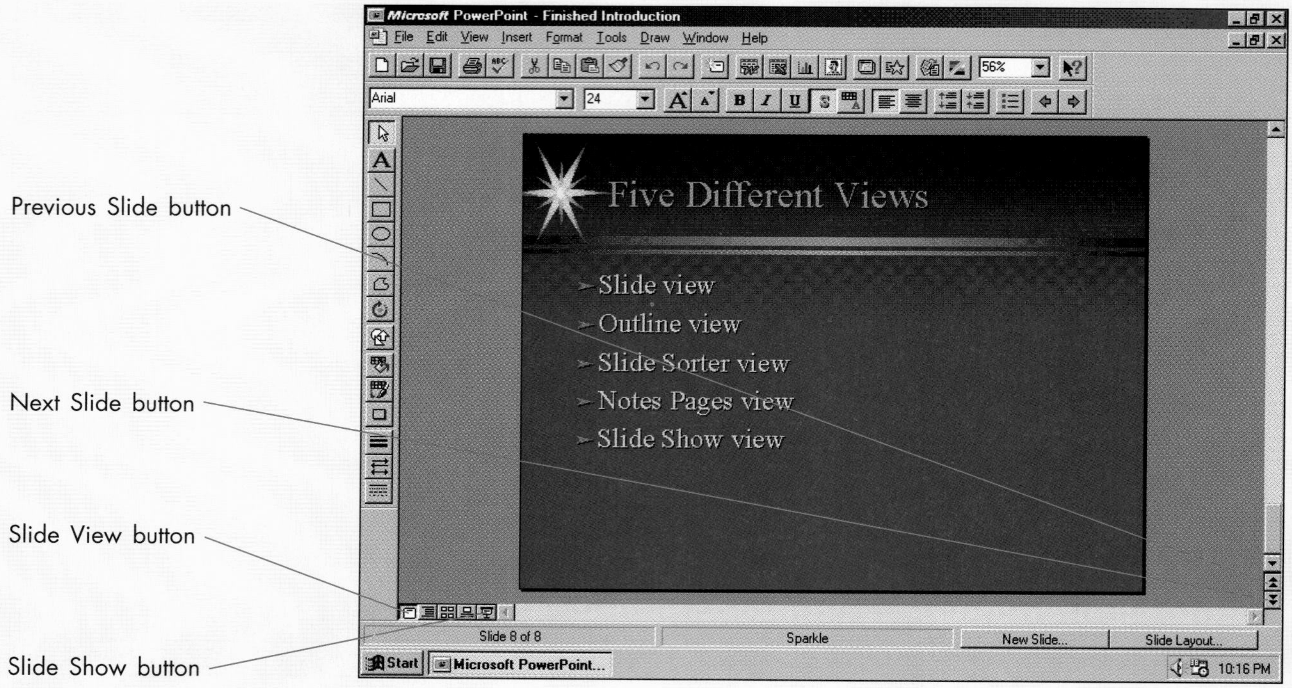
Previous Slide button
Next Slide button
Slide View button
Slide Show button
Microsoft PowerPoint - Finished Introduction
File Edit View Insert Format Tools Draw Window Help
Five Different Views
Slide view
Outline view
Slide Sorter view
Notes Pages view
Slide Show view
Slide 8 of 8
Sparkle
New Slide...
Slide Layout...
Start
Microsoft PowerPoint...
10:16 PM

(g) Slide View (step 7)

FIGURE 1.8 Hands-on Exercise 2 (continued)

STEP 8: The Slide Show View

➤ Press **Ctrl+Home** to move to the beginning of the presentation. Click the **Slide Show button** to view the presentation as follows:

- Click the **left mouse button** (or press the **PgDn key**) to move forward in the presentation. Continue to click the left mouse button to move from one slide to the next.
- Click the **right mouse button** and click **Previous** from the shortcut menu (or press the **PgUp key**) to move backward in the presentation.
- Press the **Esc key** at any time to quit the presentation and return to the Slide view.

TRANSITIONS AND BUILDS

Transitions add interest and variety to a presentation by changing the way in which you progress from one slide to the next. Slides may move onto the screen from the left or right, be uncovered by horizontal or vertical blinds, fade, dissolve, etc. Transitions may also be applied to individual bullets to display the bullets one at a time. Transitions and builds are further described in Chapter 2.

STEP 9: The Notes Pages View

- Press **Ctrl+Home** to move to the beginning of the presentation. Click the **Notes Pages View button** to change to this view, as shown in Figure 1.8h. (If necessary, click the **down arrow** on the Zoom Control box to change to **100%** magnification so that you will be able to see what you are typing.)
- Click in the **notes placeholder,** then enter the text in Figure 1.8h. (The information is for the presenter rather than the audience.) Click outside the placeholder to deselect it. Save the presentation.
- Pull down the **File menu.** Click **Print** to produce the Print dialog box.
- Click the **down arrow** in the **Print What** drop-down list box. Scroll so that you can click **Notes Pages.** Click the **Current Slide option button** to print just this slide. Click **OK.**
- Pull down the **File menu.** Click **Close** to close the presentation but remain in PowerPoint. Click **Yes** if asked whether to save the changes.
- Pull down the **File menu** a second time (or click the **Close button**) to exit PowerPoint if you do not want to continue with the next exercise at this time.

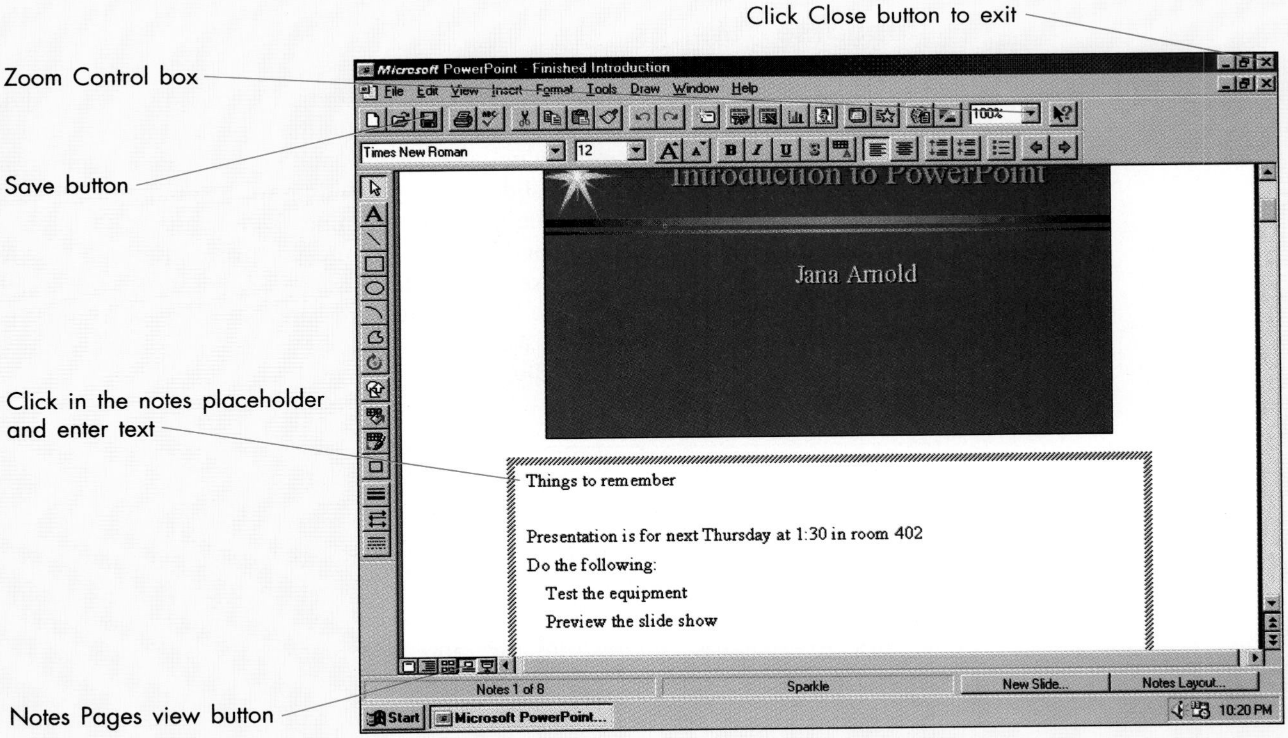
Click Close button to exit
Zoom Control box
Save button
Click in the notes placeholder and enter text
Notes Pages view button
Microsoft PowerPoint - Finished Introduction
File Edit View Insert Format Tools Draw Window Help
100%
Times New Roman
12
Introduction to PowerPoint
Jana Arnold
Things to remember
Presentation is for next Thursday at 1:30 in room 402
Do the following:
Test the equipment
Preview the slide show
Notes 1 of 8
Sparkle
New Slide...
Notes Layout...
Start
Microsoft PowerPoint...
10:20 PM

(h) Notes Pages View (step 9)

FIGURE 1.8 Hands-on Exercise 2 (continued)

PowerPoint can help you create an attractive presentation, but it is up to you to deliver the presentation effectively. Accordingly, PowerPoint provides a series of Slide Show tools to help you accomplish this goal. The tools can be accessed from any slide during the slide show by clicking the right mouse button to display a shortcut menu. The tools are discussed briefly in conjunction with the presentation in Figure 1.9, then illustrated in detail in a hands-on exercise.

POLISH YOUR DELIVERY

The speaker is still the most important part of any presentation, and a poor delivery will kill even the best presentation. Look at the audience as you speak to open communication and gain credibility. Don't read from a prepared script. Speak clearly and try to vary your delivery. Pause to emphasize key points and be sure the person in the last row can hear you.

Rehearse Timings

The Slide Show view in Figure 1.9a displays a presentation consisting of five slides. It is similar to the Slide Show view shown earlier in the chapter, but with one significant difference. Look carefully under the slides and you will see a number preceded by a colon (e.g., :30 under slide 1) corresponding to the amount of time the presenter intends to devote to the slide. The timings were entered through the ***Rehearse Timings*** feature that enables you to time your presentation. This feature is extremely valuable because it provides a sense of timing as you practice your presentation. (The Rehearse Timings feature can also be used to automate a presentation so that each slide will be shown for the set time, after which the next slide will appear automatically.)

PRACTICE MAKES PERFECT

You have worked hard to gain the opportunity to present your ideas. Be prepared! You cannot bluff your way through a presentation. Practice aloud several times, preferably under the same conditions as the actual presentation. Everyone is nervous, but the more you practice, the more confident you will be.

Action Items

Questions arise during any presentation, suggestions are given, and action items are developed. The ***Meeting Minder*** enables you to keep track of these items as they occur and to summarize them at the end of the presentation. The slide in Figure 1.9b, for example, is not part of the original presentation (it does not appear in the Slide Sorter view) but will be created *during* the presentation, as explained in the hands-on exercise.

Note, too, the annotation that has been added to the Action Items slide. The mouse pointer has changed from an arrow to a pencil, changing the effect of the

Time allotted to slide with Rehearse Timings feature

Icon indicates a hidden slide

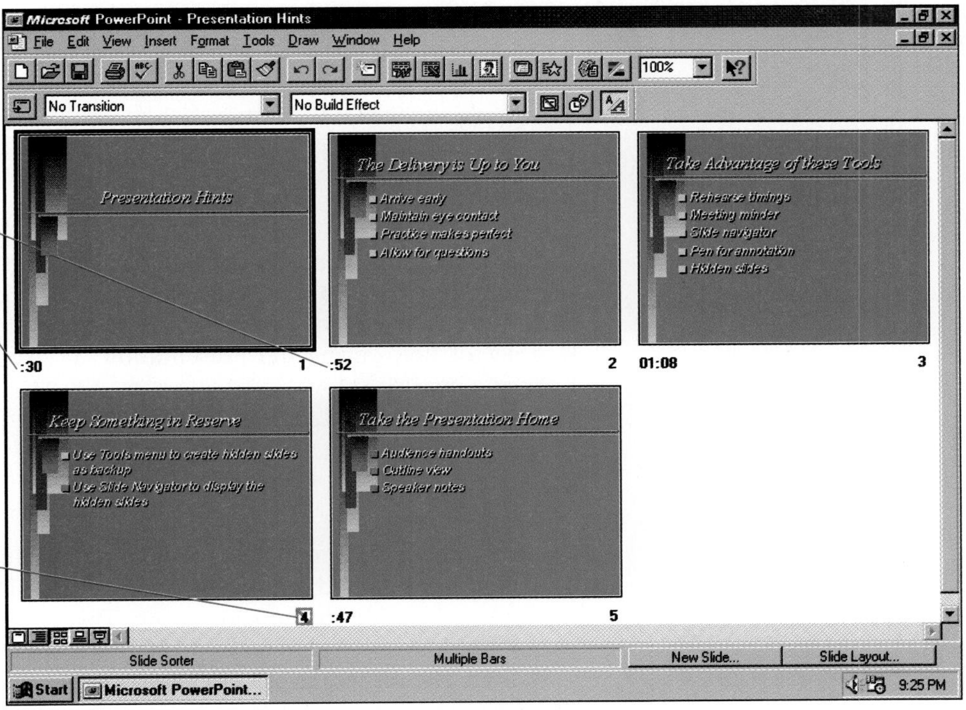
Microsoft PowerPoint - Presentation Hints
File Edit View Insert Format Tools Draw Window Help
100%
No Transition
No Build Effect
Presentation Hints
The Delivery is Up to You
Arrive early
Maintain eye contact
Practice makes perfect
Allow for questions
Take Advantage of these Tools
Rehearse timings
Meeting minder
Slide navigator
Pen for annotation
Hidden slides
:30
1
:52
2
01:08
3
Keep Something in Reserve
Use Tools menu to create hidden slides as backup
Use Slide Navigator to display the hidden slides
Take the Presentation Home
Audience handouts
Outline view
Speaker notes
4
:47
5
Slide Sorter
Multiple Bars
New Slide...
Slide Layout...
Start
Microsoft PowerPoint...
9:25 PM

(a) Timings and Hidden Slides

Action Items slide created during presentation through Meeting Minder

Annotation added to slide

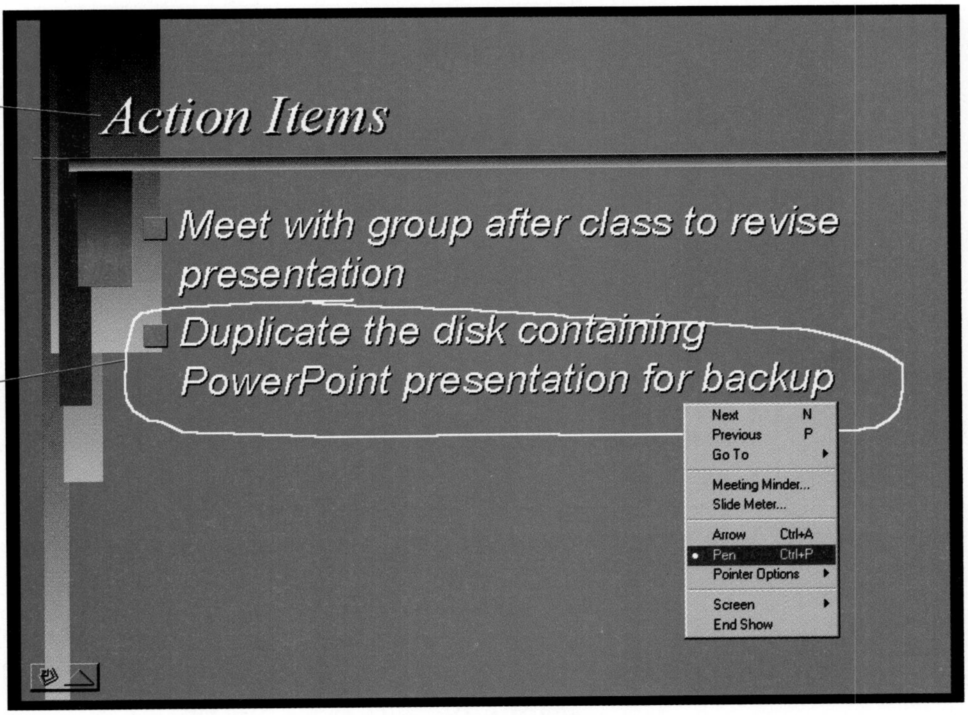
Action Items
Meet with group after class to revise presentation
Duplicate the disk containing PowerPoint presentation for backup
Next N
Previous P
Go To
Meeting Minder...
Slide Meter...
Arrow Ctrl+A
Pen Ctrl+P
Pointer Options
Screen
End Show

(b) Action Items and Annotation

FIGURE 1.9 Slide Show

mouse to an annotation tool. This enables you to click anywhere on the slide in order to ***annotate the slide*** as shown in Figure 1.9b. The ***Pen*** is a wonderful addition to any presentation.

ARRIVE EARLY

You will need plenty of time to gather your thoughts and set up the presentation. Start PowerPoint and open the presentation prior to beginning. Be sure your notes are with you or on the podium. Check that water is available for you during the presentation. Try to relax. Greet the audience as they come in.

Hidden Slides

The icon under slide number 4 in Figure 1.9a indicates that it is a ***hidden slide.*** The slide is contained within the presentation, but the presenter has elected not to display the slide in the slide show. This is a common practice among experienced speakers who anticipate probing questions that may arise during the presentation. The presenter prefers not to address the topic initially and elects to hide the slide. The presenter can, however, access the slide during the show (through the ***Slide Navigator***) should it become necessary.

BE FLEXIBLE

Every presentation begins with its slides in a specific order. Each audience is different, however, and you may find it necessary to change the order, to jump to a later slide, or to return to an earlier slide. You may also find it necessary to display a hidden slide, a slide that you kept in reserve for a specific question, if that question arises. Be flexible and use the Slide Navigator to respond appropriately to questions from the audience.

HANDS-ON EXERCISE 3

Slide Show Tools

Objective: To use the Rehearse Timings feature to time a presentation; to hide a slide, then use the Slide Navigator to display that slide on demand; to use the Meeting Minder to create a list of action items during a presentation; and to annotate a slide for emphasis. Use Figure 1.10 as a guide in the exercise.

STEP 1: Open the Existing Presentation

- Start PowerPoint. Open **Presentation Hints** in the **Exploring PowerPoint folder** as shown in Figure 1.10a. Click where indicated to add your name to the title slide.
- Pull down the **File menu,** click the **Save As command** to display the File Save dialog box, then save the presentation as **Finished Presentation Hints.** (Press

Click to add your name to the slide

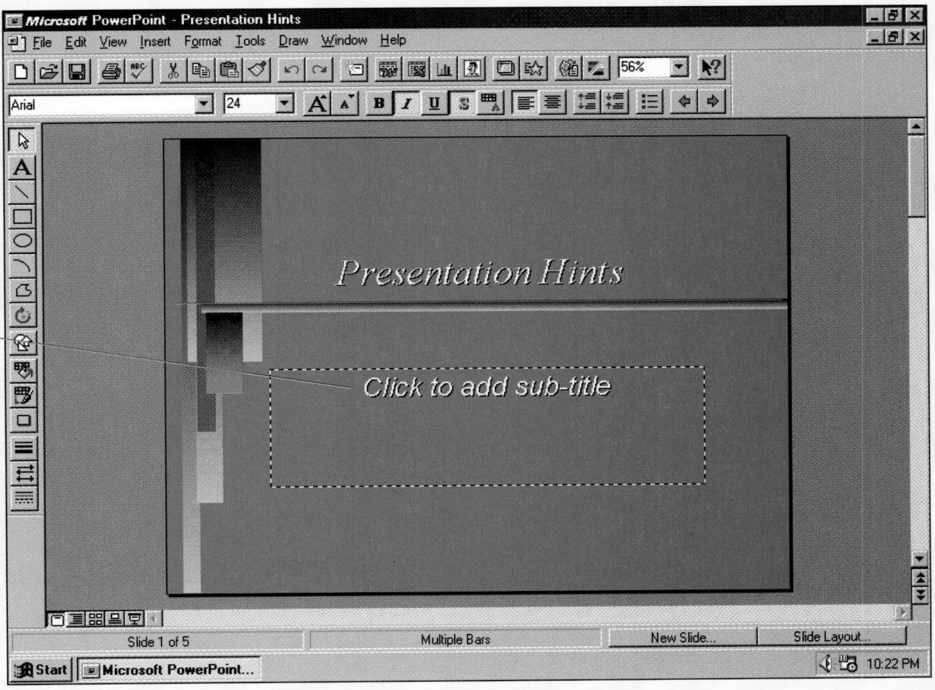
Microsoft PowerPoint - Presentation Hints
File Edit View Insert Format Tools Draw Window Help
Presentation Hints
Click to add sub-title
Slide 1 of 5
Multiple Bars
New Slide...
Slide Layout...
Start
Microsoft PowerPoint...
10:22 PM

(a) Open the Presentation (step 1)

FIGURE 1.10 Hands-on Exercise 3

the **Esc key** or click the **Close button** if you see a Properties dialog box after saving the file.)

CHANGE THE DEFAULT FOLDER

The default folder is the folder where PowerPoint retrieves (saves) presentations unless it is otherwise instructed. To change the default folder, pull down the Tools menu, click Options, click the Advanced tab, then enter the name of the default folder (for example, C:\Exploring PowerPoint) in the Default File Location text box. Click OK. The next time you execute the Open command, PowerPoint will automatically look in this folder.

STEP 2: Hide a Slide

- Click the **Slide Sorter View button** to change to this view as shown in Figure 1.10b. If necessary, click the **down arrow** on the Zoom Control box to zoom to 100%. The slides are larger and easier to read.
- Point to slide 4 (Keep Something in Reserve), then click the **right mouse button** to select the slide and simultaneously display a shortcut menu.
- Click **Hide Slide** as shown in Figure 1.10b. The menu closes and a hidden slide icon is displayed under slide 4. The slide remains in the presentation,

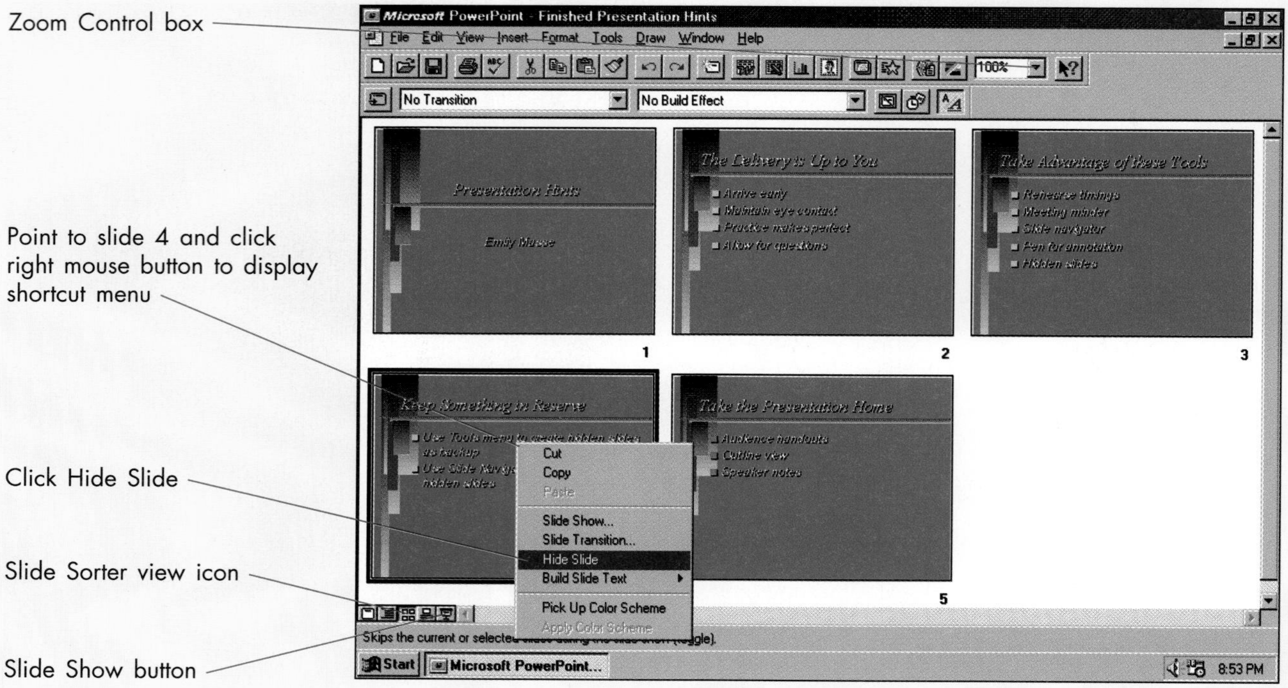
Zoom Control box
Point to slide 4 and click right mouse button to display shortcut menu
Click Hide Slide
Slide Sorter view icon
Slide Show button
Microsoft PowerPoint - Finished Presentation Hints
File Edit View Insert Format Tools Draw Window Help
No Transition
No Build Effect
100%
Presentation Hints
The Delivery is Up to You
Take Advantage of these Tools
Keep Something in Reserve
Take the Presentation Home
Cut
Copy
Paste
Slide Show...
Slide Transition...
Hide Slide
Build Slide Text
Pick Up Color Scheme
Apply Color Scheme
Start
Microsoft PowerPoint...
8:53 PM

(b) Hide a Slide (step 2)

FIGURE 1.10 Hands-on Exercise 3 (continued)

but it will *not* be displayed during the slide show. (The Hide Slide command functions as a toggle switch. Click it once and the slide is hidden. Click the command a second time and the slide is no longer hidden.)

➤ Save the presentation. Press **Ctrl+Home,** then click the **Slide Show button** to move quickly through the presentation. You will not see the slide titled Keep Something in Reserve because it has been hidden. (You can still access this slide through the Slide Navigator as described in step 5.)

STEP 3: Rehearse the Presentation

➤ Press **Ctrl+Home** to return to the first slide. Pull down the **View menu** and click **Slide Show** to display the Slide Show dialog box. Click the **option button** to **Rehearse New Timings,** then click the **Show button.**

➤ The first slide appears in the Slide Show view, and the Rehearsal dialog box is displayed in the lower-right corner of the screen. Speak as though you were presenting the slide, then click the mouse to register the elapsed time for that slide and move to the next slide.

➤ The second slide in the presentation should appear as shown in Figure 1.10c. Speak as though you were presenting the slide and note the times that appear in the dialog box. The cumulative time appears on the left (1 minute and 6 seconds). The time for this specific slide (39 seconds) is shown at the right.

- Click the **Repeat button** to redo the timing for the slide.
- Click the **Pause button** to (temporarily) stop the clock. Click the **Pause button** a second time to resume the clock.
- Click the **Next Slide button** to record the timing and move to the next slide.

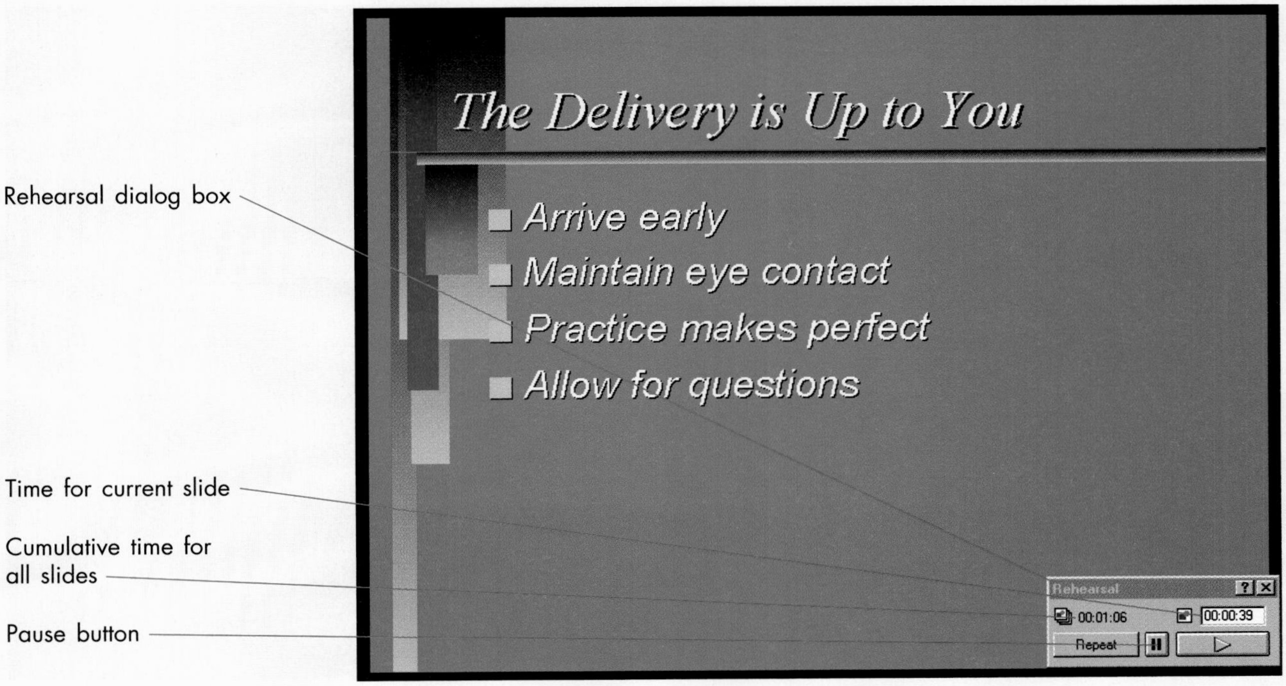
Rehearsal dialog box
Time for current slide
Cumulative time for all slides
Pause button
The Delivery is Up to You
Arrive early
Maintain eye contact
Practice makes perfect
Allow for questions
Rehearsal
00:01:06
00:00:39
Repeat

(c) Rehearse Timings (step 3)

FIGURE 1.10 Hands-on Exercise 3 (continued)

- Continue rehearsing the show until you reach the end of the presentation. (You will not see the hidden slide from the previous step.)
- You should see a dialog box at the end of the presentation that indicates the total time of the slide show. Click **Yes** when asked whether you want to record the new timings.
- PowerPoint returns to the Slide Sorter view and records the timings under each slide (except for the hidden slide). Note, too, the hidden icon under the fourth slide.

STEP 4: The Meeting Minder

- Click the **first slide** (or press **Ctrl+Home**) to move to the beginning of the presentation. Click the **Slide Show button** to show the presentation.
- You should see the title slide with your name as shown in Figure 1.10d. Point anywhere on the slide and click the **right mouse button** to display a shortcut menu containing the various slide show tools.
- Click **Meeting Minder** to display the Meeting Minder dialog box, then click the **Action Items tab** as shown in Figure 1.10d.
- Click in the work area of the dialog box and enter the first action item in Figure 1.10d. Press **enter,** then enter the second item. Click **OK** to close the dialog box and continue viewing the presentation.
- Click the **mouse button** to move from one slide to the next (you can enter an action item from any slide) until you reach the end of the presentation (the slide titled Action Items). A new slide has been created containing the action items you just supplied. Leave this slide on the screen (i.e., do not end the show at this time).

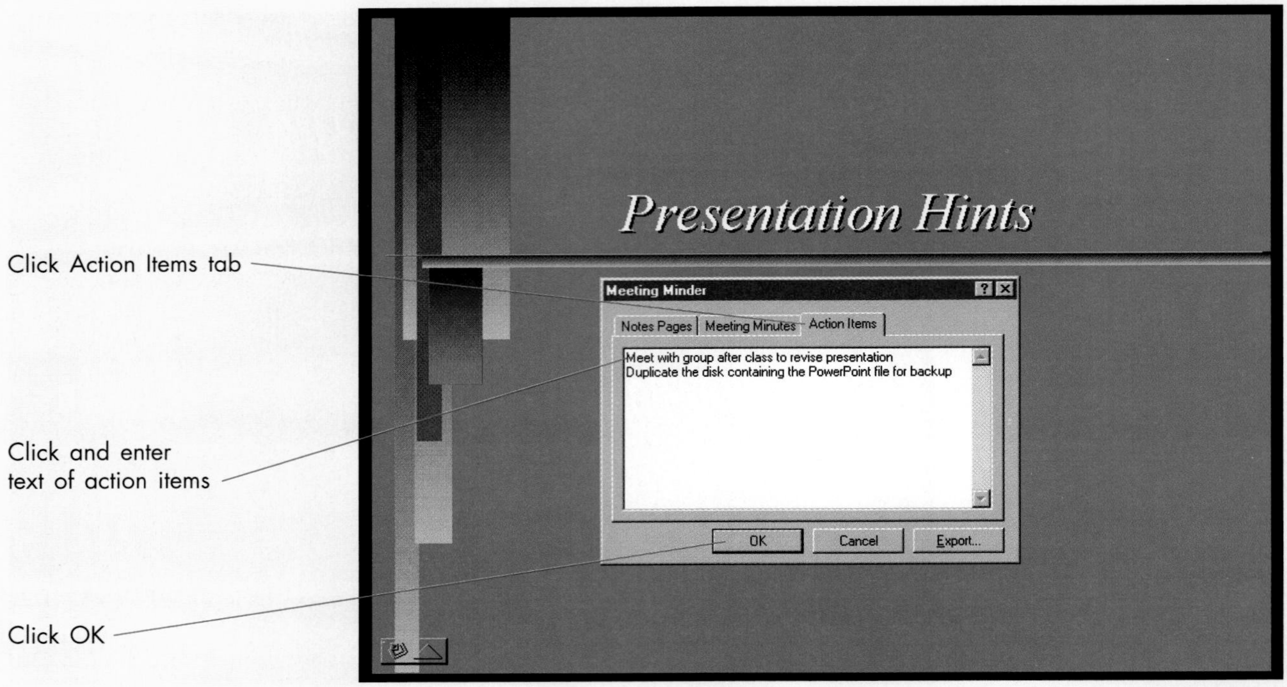
Presentation Hints
Meeting Minder
Notes Pages
Meeting Minutes
Action Items
Meet with group after class to revise presentation
Duplicate the disk containing the PowerPoint file for backup
OK
Cancel
Export...
Click Action Items tab
Click and enter text of action items
Click OK

(d) Meeting Minder (step 4)

FIGURE 1.10 Hands-on Exercise 3 (continued)

BACK UP IMPORTANT FILES

We cannot overemphasize the importance of adequate backup. Hard disks die, files are accidentally deleted or lost, and viruses may infect a system. It takes only a few minutes to copy your data files to a floppy disk, so do it now. (See the Windows appendix for information on My Computer and the Windows Explorer to learn how to back up your files.) You will thank us when (not if) you lose an important file and wish you had another copy.

STEP 5: The Slide Navigator

- You should be positioned on the last slide (Action Items). Click the **right mouse button** to display a shortcut menu, click **Go to,** then click **Slide Navigator** to display the Slide Navigator dialog box as shown in Figure 1.10e.
- The titles of all slides (including the hidden slide) are displayed in the Slide Navigator dialog box. The number of the hidden slide, however, is enclosed in parentheses to indicate it is a hidden slide.
- Select (click) the **hidden slide,** then click the **Go To button** to display this slide.

Click Go To

Select the hidden slide

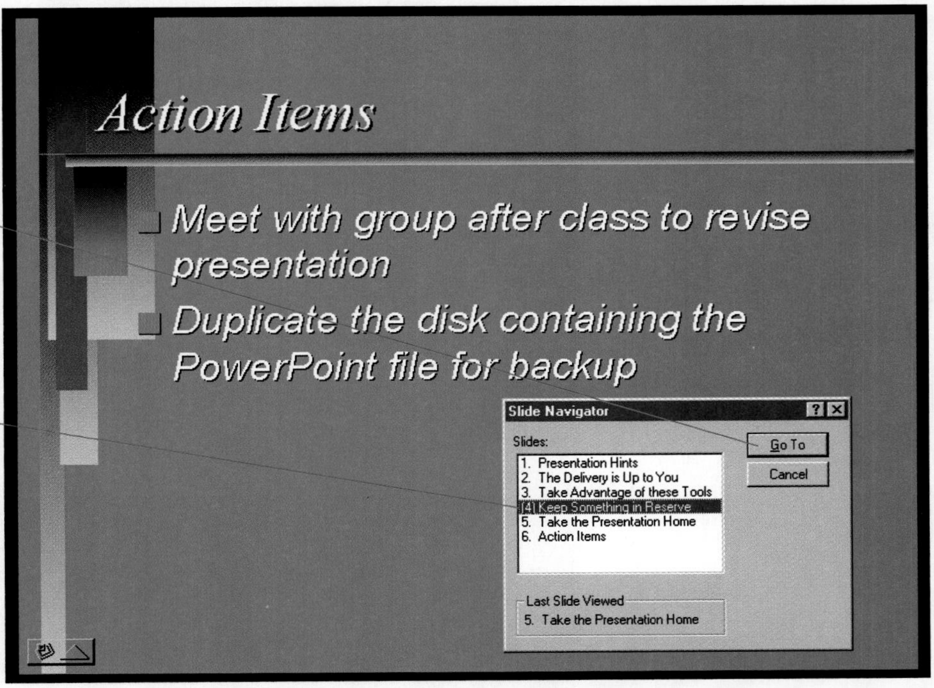
Action Items
Meet with group after class to revise presentation
Duplicate the disk containing the PowerPoint file for backup
Slide Navigator
Slides:
1. Presentation Hints
2. The Delivery is Up to You
3. Take Advantage of these Tools
(4) Keep Something in Reserve
5. Take the Presentation Home
6. Action Items
Go To
Cancel
Last Slide Viewed
5. Take the Presentation Home

(e) Slide Navigator (step 5)

FIGURE 1.10 Hands-on Exercise 3 (continued)

QUESTIONS AND ANSWERS (Q & A))

Indicate at the beginning of your talk whether you will take questions during the presentation or collectively at the end. Announce the length of time that will be allocated to questions. Rephrase all questions so the audience can hear, then use the Slide Navigator to return to the appropriate slide in order to answer the question. Rephrase hostile questions in a neutral way and try to disarm the challenger by paying a compliment. If you don't know the answer, say so.

STEP 6: Annotate a Slide

- You should see the slide in Figure 1.10f. Click the **right mouse button** to display the shortcut menu containing the Slide Show tools. Click **Pen.** The mouse pointer changes from an arrow to a pencil.
- Click and drag on the slide to annotate the slide as shown in Figure 1.10f. The annotation is temporary and will be visible only as long as you display the slide.
- Press **N** (or the **PgDn key**) to move to the next slide, then press **P** (or the **PgUp key**) to return to the previous (i.e., this) slide. The annotation is gone.
- Click the **right mouse button,** point to (or click) **Pointer Options,** point to (or click) **Pen Color,** then choose (click) a different color. The mouse pointer automatically changes to the pen, and you can annotate the slide in the new color.

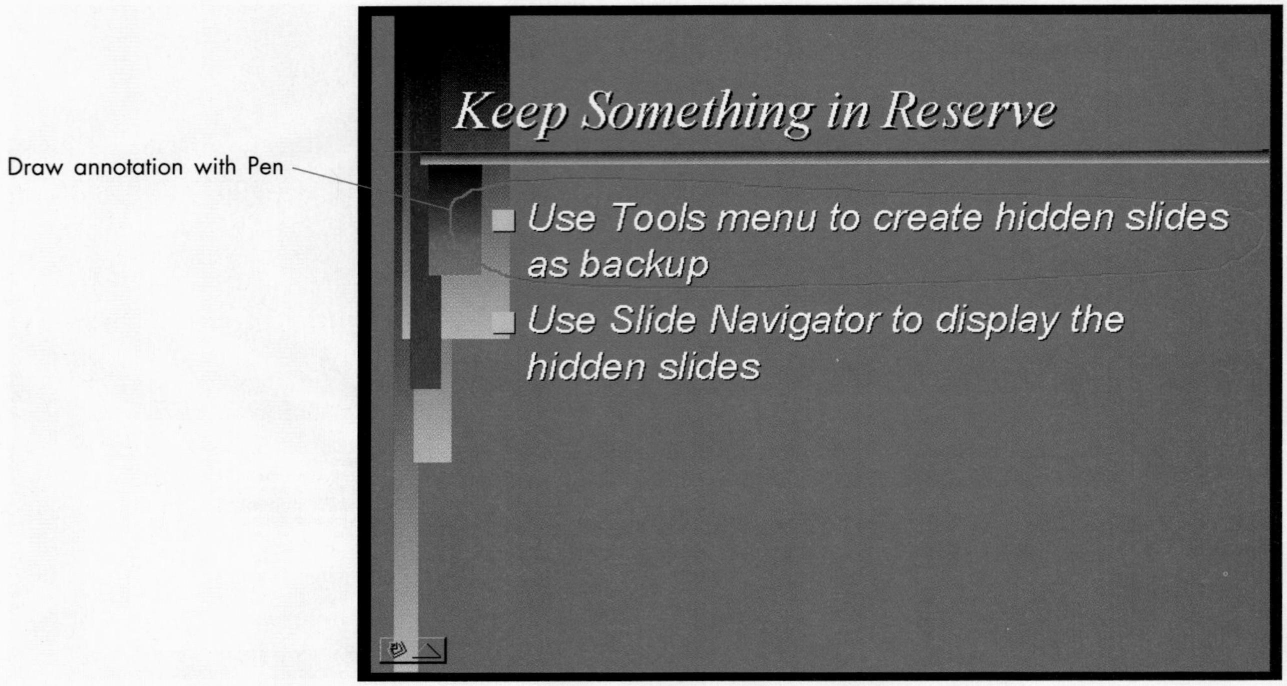
Draw annotation with Pen
Keep Something in Reserve
Use Tools menu to create hidden slides as backup
Use Slide Navigator to display the hidden slides

(f) Annotate a Slide (step 6)

FIGURE 1.10 Hands-on Exercise 3 (continued)

THE PEN AND THE ARROW

The shortcut menu can be used to toggle the mouse pointer between the Pen and the arrow, but we find various other shortcuts easier. For example, press Ctrl+P or Ctrl+A at any time to change to the pencil or an arrow, respectively. You can also press the Esc key to return the mouse to a pointer after using it as a Pen. And finally, you can use the keyboard to move to a different slide, which automatically resets the mouse to the pointer.

STEP 7: End the Show

- Click the **right mouse button** to display the shortcut menu, then click **End Show** to end the presentation.
- Pull down the **File menu.** Click **Print** to produce the Print dialog box. Click the **arrow** in the **Print What** drop-down list box. Click **Handouts (6 slides per page).** Check the boxes for **Frame Slides** and **Print Hidden Slides.**
- Check that the **All option button** is selected under Print Range. You will print every slide in the presentation, including the hidden slide and the slide containing the action items. Click **OK.**
- Pull down the **File menu** and click **Exit** to leave PowerPoint. Click **Yes** when asked whether to save the changes to the presentation.

SUMMARY

A PowerPoint presentation consists of a series of slides with a consistent design and color scheme. A PowerPoint presentation may be delivered on a computer, via overhead transparencies or 35-mm slides, and/or printed in a variety of formats.

The PowerPoint window contains the basic elements of any Windows application. The benefits of the common user interface are magnified further if you are familiar with other applications in the Microsoft Office such as Word or Excel. PowerPoint is designed for a mouse, but it provides keyboard equivalents for almost every command. Toolbars provide still another way to execute the most frequent operations.

PowerPoint has five different views, each with unique capabilities. The Slide view displays one slide at a time and enables all operations on that slide. The Slide Sorter view displays multiple slides on one screen (each slide is in miniature) and lets you see the overall flow of the presentation. The Outline view shows the presentation text in outline form and is the fastest way to enter or edit text. The Notes Pages view enables you to create speaker's notes for use in giving the presentation. The Slide Show view displays the slides one at a time with transition effects for added interest.

Slides are added to a presentation using one of 24 predefined slide formats known as AutoLayouts. Each AutoLayout contains placeholders for the different objects on the slide. A slide may be deleted from a presentation in any view except the Slide Show view.

PowerPoint includes several slide show tools to help you enliven a presentation. The Rehearse Timings feature enables you to time and/or automate a presentation. The Slide Navigator enables you to branch directly to any slide, including hidden slides. The Pen lets you annotate a slide for added emphasis. The Meeting Minder enables you to create a list of action items.

Although PowerPoint helps to create attractive presentations, you are still the most important element in delivering the presentation. The chapter ended with several hints on how to rehearse and present presentations effectively.

KEY WORDS AND CONCEPTS

Annotating a slide
AutoLayout
Clip art
Close command
Common user interface
Drawing toolbar
Elevator
Exit command
File menu
Formatting toolbar
Hidden slide
Meeting Minder
Menu bar
New Slide button
Notes Pages view
Open command
Outline view
Pen
Placeholders
Print Command
Redo command
Rehearse Timings
Save command
Scroll bar
Slide Layout button
Slide Navigator
Slide Show view
Slide Sorter view
Slide view
Standard toolbar
Status bar
ToolTip
Transition effects
Undo command
View buttons

MULTIPLE CHOICE

1. How do you save changes to a PowerPoint presentation?
   (a) Pull down the File menu and click the Save command
   (b) Click the Save button on the Standard toolbar
   (c) Both (a) and (b)
   (d) Neither (a) nor (b)
2. Which toolbars are displayed by default in all views?
   (a) The Standard toolbar
   (b) The Formatting toolbar
   (c) Both (a) and (b)
   (d) Neither (a) nor (b)
3. Which view displays multiple slides on a single screen?
   (a) Outline view
   (b) Slide Sorter view
   (c) Both (a) and (b)
   (d) Neither (a) nor (b)
4. Which view displays multiple slides and also shows the graphical elements in each slide?
   (a) Outline view
   (b) Slide Sorter view
   (c) Both (a) and (b)
   (d) Neither (a) nor (b)
5. Which view lets you delete a slide?
   (a) Outline view
   (b) Slide Sorter view
   (c) Both (a) and (b)
   (d) Neither (a) nor (b)
6. Which of the following can be printed in support of a PowerPoint presentation?
   (a) Audience handouts
   (b) Speaker's notes
   (c) An outline
   (d) All of the above
7. Which menu contains the Undo command?
   (a) File menu
   (b) Edit menu
   (c) Tools menu
   (d) Format menu
8. Ctrl+Home and Ctrl+End are keyboard shortcuts that move to the beginning or end of the presentation in the:
   (a) Outline view
   (b) Slide Sorter view
   (c) Slide view
   (d) All of the above

9. The predefined slide formats in PowerPoint are known as:
   (a) Views
   (b) AutoLayouts
   (c) Audience handouts
   (d) Speaker notes

10. Which menu contains the commands to save the current presentation, or to open a previously saved presentation?
   (a) The Tools menu
   (b) The File menu
   (c) The View menu
   (d) The Edit menu

11. The Open command:
   (a) Brings a presentation from disk into memory
   (b) Brings a presentation from disk into memory, then erases the presentation on disk
   (c) Stores the presentation in memory on disk
   (d) Stores the presentation in memory on disk, then erases the presentation from memory

12. The Save command:
   (a) Brings a presentation from disk into memory
   (b) Brings a presentation from disk into memory, then erases the presentation on disk
   (c) Stores the presentation in memory on disk
   (d) Stores the presentation in memory on disk, then erases the presentation from memory

13. Which of the following is true about hidden slides?
   (a) Hidden slides are invisible in every view
   (b) Hidden slides cannot be accessed during a slide show
   (c) Both (a) and (b)
   (d) Neither (a) nor (b)

14. Which view displays timings for individual slides after the timings have been established by rehearsing the presentation?
   (a) Slide view
   (b) Outline view
   (c) Slide Sorter view
   (d) All of the above

15. Which of the following is true about annotating a slide?
   (a) The annotations are permanent; that is, once entered on a slide, they cannot be erased
   (b) The annotations are entered by using the pen during the slide show
   (c) Both (a) and (b)
   (d) Neither (a) nor (b)

ANSWERS

1. c	**3.** c	**5.** c
2. c	**4.** b	**6.** d

7. b	**10.** b	**13.** d
8. d	**11.** a	**14.** c
9. b	**12.** c	**15.** b

EXPLORING MICROSOFT POWERPOINT 7.0

1. Use Figure 1.11 to match each action with its result. A given action may be used more than once or not at all. Some results can be achieved by more than one action.

Action	**Result**
a. Click at 1	_____ Open an existing presentation
b. Click at 2	_____ Save the current presentation
c. Click at 3	_____ Change to the Outline view
d. Click at 4	_____ Change to the Slide Sorter view
e. Click at 5	_____ Insert a new slide
f. Click at 6	_____ Move to slide 2
g. Click at 7	_____ Print the current presentation
h. Click at 8	_____ Run (show) the current presentation
i. Click at 9	_____ Exit PowerPoint
j. Click at 10	_____ Access online help

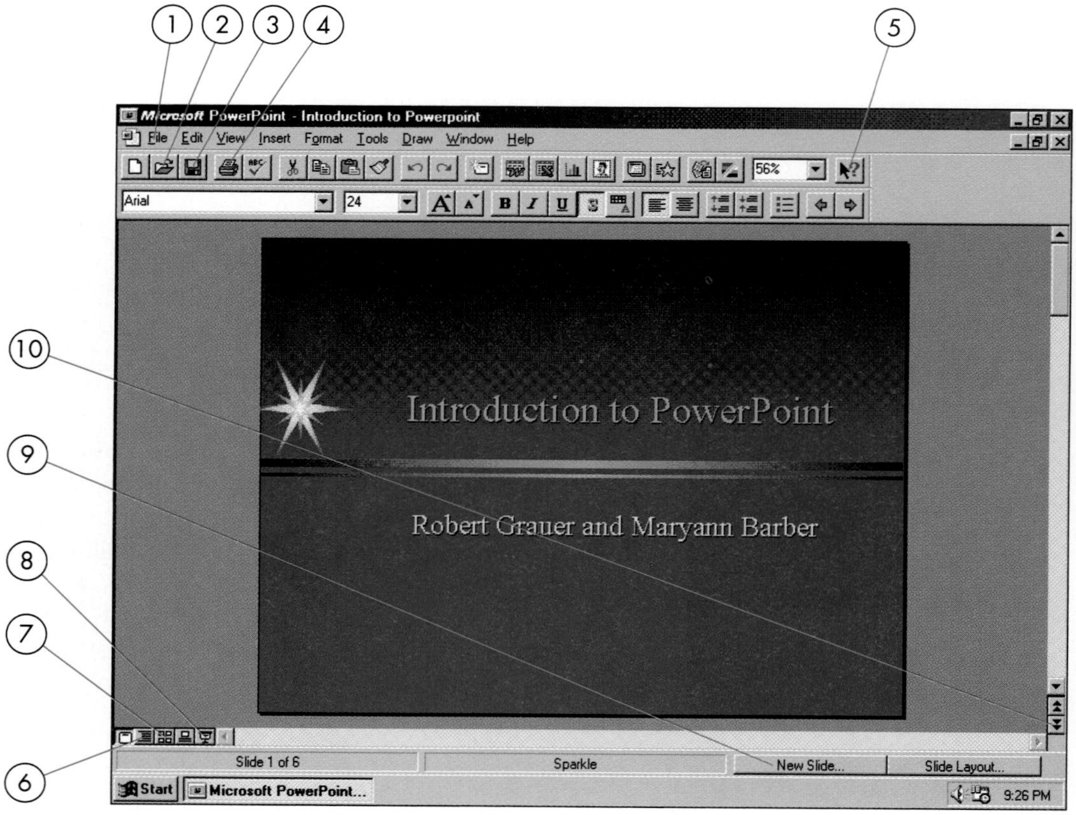
1
2
3
4
5
6
7
8
9
10
Microsoft PowerPoint - Introduction to Powerpoint
File Edit View Insert Format Tools Draw Window Help
56%
Arial
24
Introduction to PowerPoint
Robert Grauer and Maryann Barber
Slide 1 of 6
Sparkle
New Slide...
Slide Layout...
Start
Microsoft PowerPoint...
9:26 PM

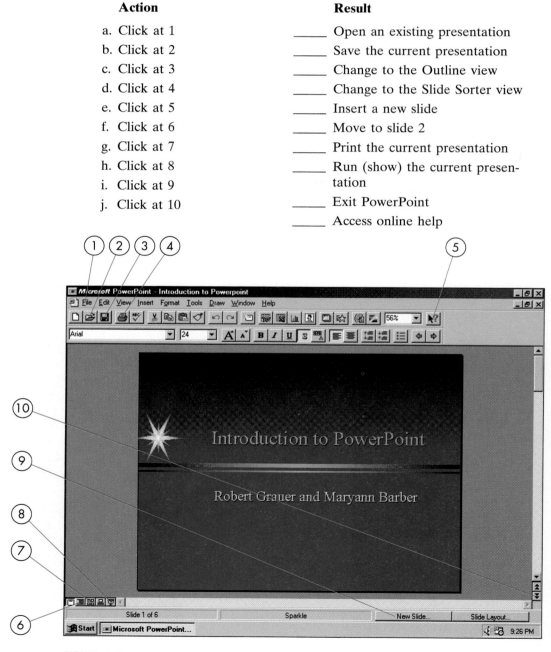

FIGURE 1.11 Screen for Problem 1

2. PowerPoint uses the same commands and follows the same conventions as other applications in Microsoft Office. This means that you can apply what you already know about basic operations in Word or Excel to PowerPoint. Answer the questions below, realizing that in every instance the answer is the same for PowerPoint, Word, and Excel.
   a. Which button on which toolbar saves a PowerPoint presentation? a Word document? an Excel spreadsheet?
   b. How do you print a PowerPoint presentation? a Word document? an Excel spreadsheet?
   c. How do you boldface or italicize existing text?
   d. Which keystroke combination moves immediately to the beginning (end) of a PowerPoint presentation? a Word document? an Excel spreadsheet?
   e. How do you access online help?
   f. What happens if you point to a button on a toolbar? What happens if you click the Help button, then point to a different toolbar button?
3. Answer the following with respect to the presentation shown in Figure 1.12:
   a. What is the name of the presentation?
   b. Are the Standard and Formatting toolbars both visible? How do you display the missing toolbar?
   c. What would be the effect of typing *Quotations,* given the selected text shown on the screen?
   d. How do you save the presentation after making the change in part c?
   e. In which view is the slide displayed? How would you change to the Outline view? to the Slide Sorter view?
   f. Which slide is selected? How would you move to the first slide in the presentation? to the last slide?
   g. How would you add a new slide at the end of the presentation?

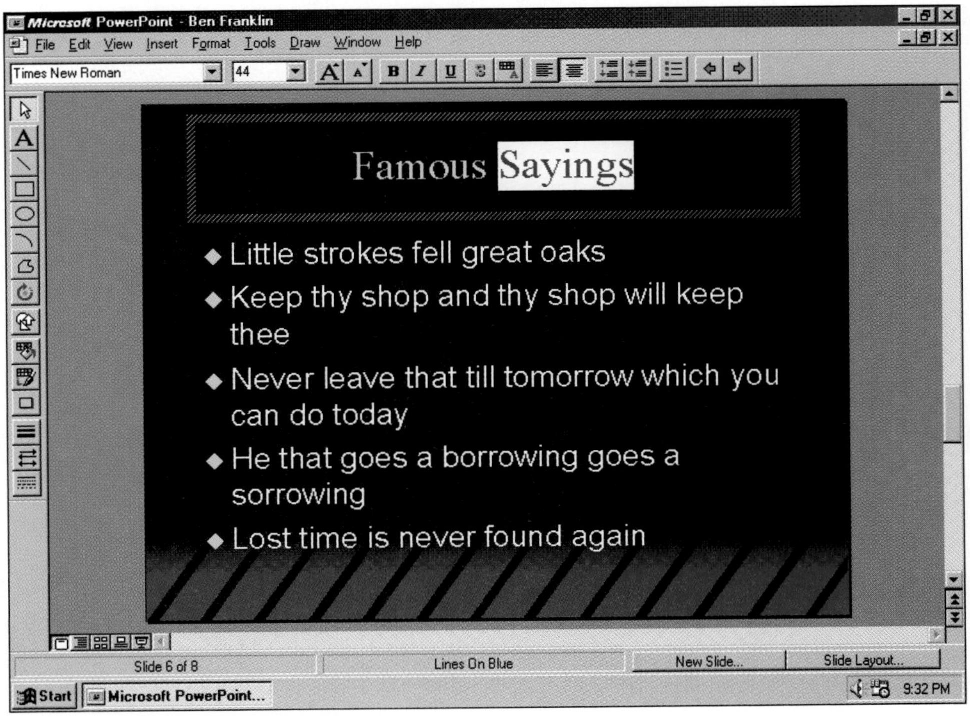
Microsoft PowerPoint - Ben Franklin
File Edit View Insert Format Tools Draw Window Help
Times New Roman
44
Famous Sayings
Little strokes fell great oaks
Keep thy shop and thy shop will keep thee
Never leave that till tomorrow which you can do today
He that goes a borrowing goes a sorrowing
Lost time is never found again
Slide 6 of 8
Lines On Blue
New Slide...
Slide Layout...
Start
Microsoft PowerPoint...
9:32 PM

FIGURE 1.12 Screen for Problem 3

4. Online help functions identically in PowerPoint as it does in the other Office applications. Accordingly, use what you know about Microsoft Office, or explore on your own, to answer the following questions with respect to the dialog box in Figure 1.13:
   a. How do you display the dialog box in Figure 1.13?
   b. What is the difference between the Contents and Index tabs? Which tab is currently selected? How do you select a different tab?
   c. Which books are open in the figure? Which books are closed? How do you open a closed book? How do you close an open book?
   d. What is the Answer Wizard?
   e. How is the dialog box in Figure 1.13 similar to the corresponding dialog boxes in other Office applications?

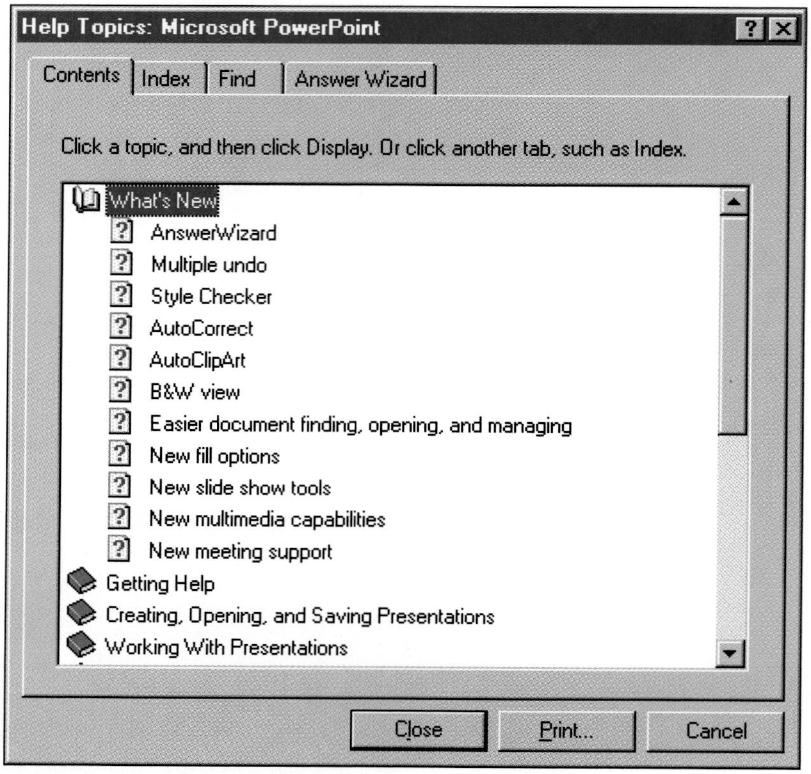
Help Topics: Microsoft PowerPoint
Contents
Index
Find
Answer Wizard
Click a topic, and then click Display. Or click another tab, such as Index.
What's New
AnswerWizard
Multiple undo
Style Checker
AutoCorrect
AutoClipArt
B&W view
Easier document finding, opening, and managing
New fill options
New slide show tools
New multimedia capabilities
New meeting support
Getting Help
Creating, Opening, and Saving Presentations
Working With Presentations
Close
Print...
Cancel

FIGURE 1.13 Screen for Problem 4

PRACTICE WITH MICROSOFT POWERPOINT 7.0

1. Figure 1.14 displays the Slide Sorter view of a presentation that was created by one of our students in a successful job search. Open the presentation as it exists on the data disk (it is found in the Exploring PowerPoint folder), then modify the presentation to reflect your personal data. Print the revised audience handouts (six per page) and submit them to your instructor.

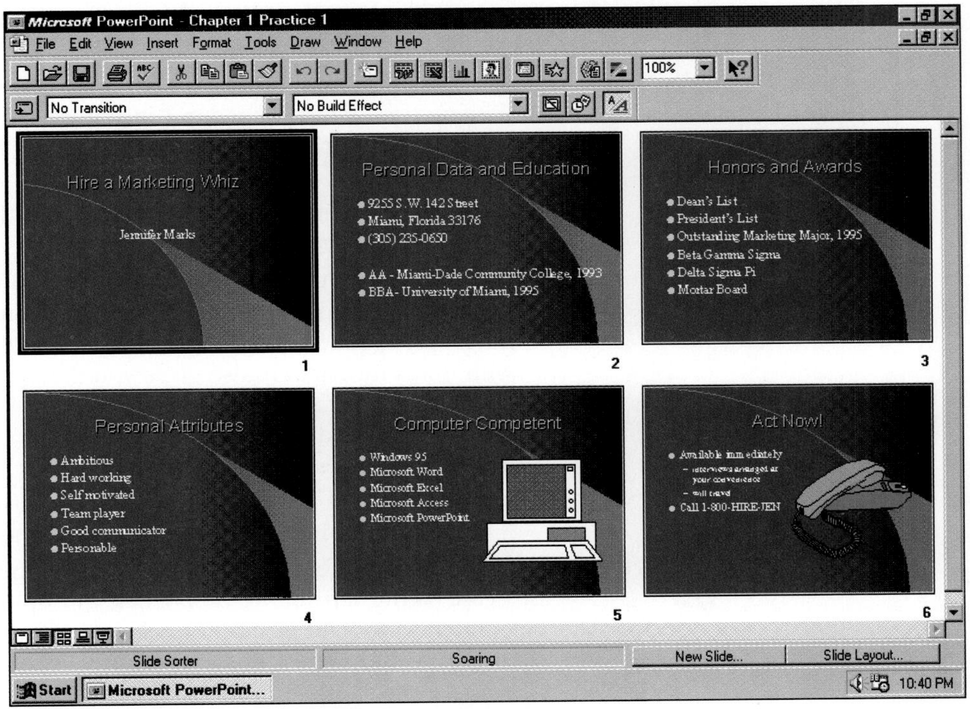

Microsoft PowerPoint - Chapter 1 Practice 1
File Edit View Insert Format Tools Draw Window Help
No Transition
No Build Effect
100%
Hire a Marketing Whiz
Jennifer Marks
Personal Data and Education
9255 S.W. 142 Street
Miami, Florida 33176
(305) 235-0650
AA - Miami-Dade Community College, 1993
BBA - University of Miami, 1995
Honors and Awards
Dean's List
President's List
Outstanding Marketing Major, 1995
Beta Gamma Sigma
Delta Sigma Pi
Mortar Board
Personal Attributes
Ambitious
Hard working
Self motivated
Team player
Good communicator
Personable
Computer Competent
Windows 95
Microsoft Word
Microsoft Excel
Microsoft Access
Microsoft PowerPoint
Act Now!
Available immediately
Call 1-800-HIRE-JEN
Slide Sorter
Soaring
New Slide...
Slide Layout...
Start
Microsoft PowerPoint...
10:40 PM

FIGURE 1.14 Screen for Practice Exercise 1

2. Ready-made presentations: The most difficult part of a presentation is getting started. PowerPoint anticipates the problem and provides general outlines on a variety of topics as shown in Figure 1.15.
   a. Pull down the File menu, click New, click the Presentations tab (if necessary), then click the Details button so that your screen matches Figure 1.15.

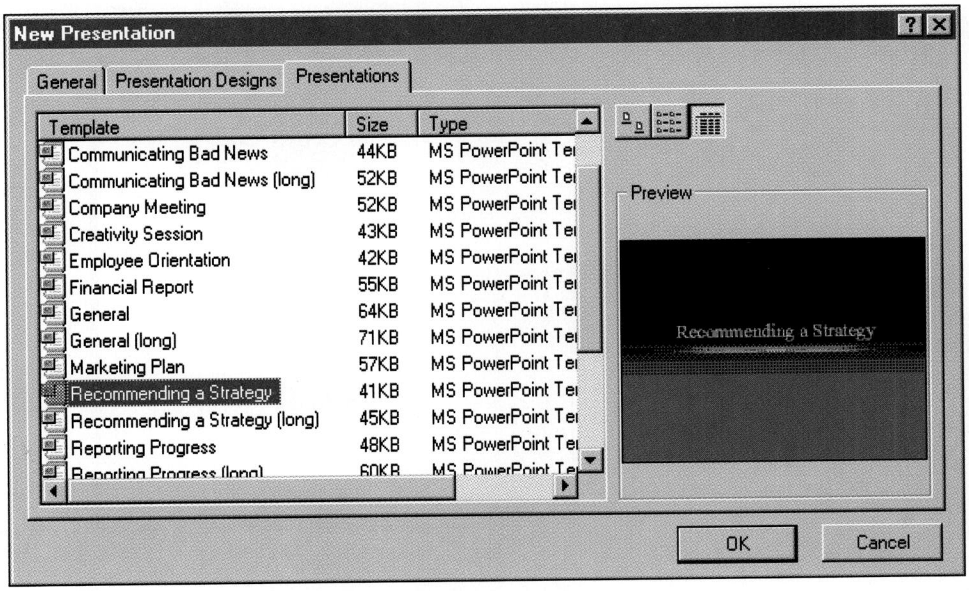

New Presentation
General
Presentation Designs
Presentations
Template
Size
Type
Communicating Bad News 44KB MS PowerPoint Te
Communicating Bad News (long) 52KB MS PowerPoint Te
Company Meeting 52KB MS PowerPoint Te
Creativity Session 43KB MS PowerPoint Te
Employee Orientation 42KB MS PowerPoint Te
Financial Report 55KB MS PowerPoint Te
General 64KB MS PowerPoint Te
General (long) 71KB MS PowerPoint Te
Marketing Plan 57KB MS PowerPoint Te
Recommending a Strategy 41KB MS PowerPoint Te
Recommending a Strategy (long) 45KB MS PowerPoint Te
Reporting Progress 48KB MS PowerPoint Te
Preview
Recommending a Strategy
OK
Cancel

FIGURE 1.15 Screen for Practice Exercise 2

b. Select Recommending a Strategy as shown in Figure 1.15. Click OK to open the presentation.

c. Change to the Outline view so that you can see the text of the overall presentation, which is general in nature and intended for any type of strategy. Modify the presentation to develop a strategy for doing well in this class.

d. Add your name to the title page. Print the presentation in miniature and submit it to your instructor.

3. The PowerPoint Write-Up command imports a presentation into a Word document as shown in Figure 1.16. The command combines audience handouts with speaker notes, enabling you to display several slides on one page with notes for each. It also gives you the option to link the slides to the Word document, so that if a slide changes, the Word document is updated automatically. (The document is not, however, updated to reflect the insertion or deletion of slides.)

a. Do Hands-on Exercises 1 and 2 as described in the chapter, then retrieve the Finished Introduction presentation as the basis of this problem.

b. Pull down the Tools menu and click the Write-Up command to display the Write-Up dialog box. Click the option button for the type of document you want (e.g., Notes Next to Slide so that you will create Figure 1.16 at the end of this exercise).

c. Click the option button to Paste Link the slides to a Word document, then click OK. PowerPoint will create a document similar to the one in Figure 1.16. Be patient, for this step takes time, especially on a non-Pentium machine.

d. Change to the Page Layout view in Word and zoom to Two Pages. Click in the cell next to each slide (the Word document is a table) and enter an appropriate comment.

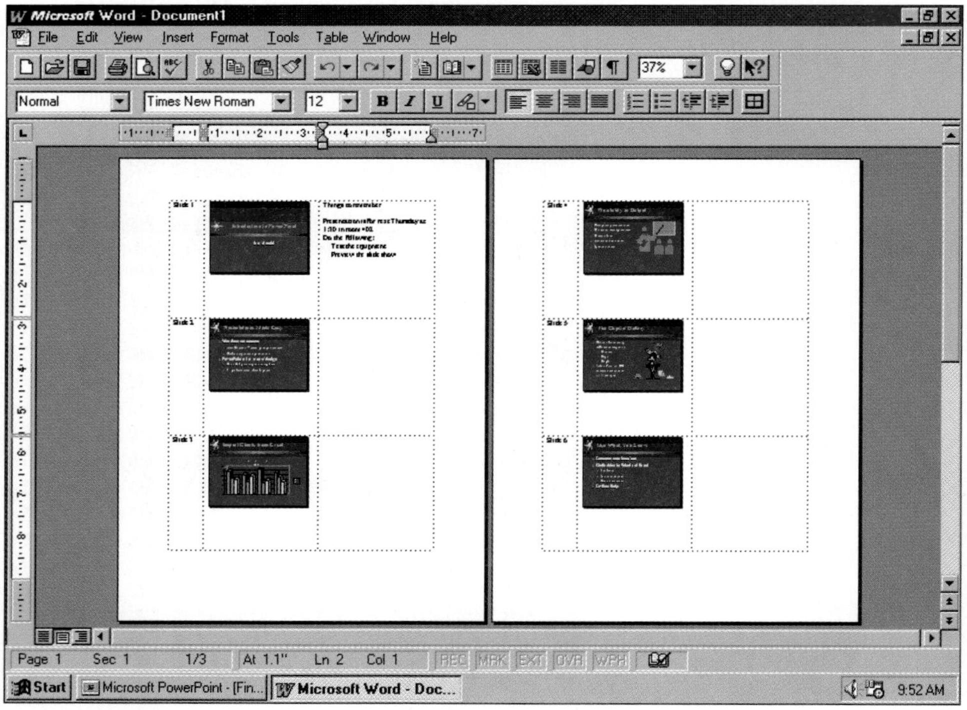
Microsoft Word - Document1
File Edit View Insert Format Tools Table Window Help
37%
Normal
Times New Roman
12
Page 1 Sec 1 1/3 At 1.1" Ln 2 Col 1
Start
Microsoft PowerPoint - [Fin...
Microsoft Word - Doc...
9:52 AM

FIGURE 1.16 Screen for Practice Exercise 3

e. Save and print the document just as you would any other Word document. Submit the finished document to your instructor as proof that you did this exercise.

4. Adding Sound: The presentation in Figure 1.17 is one of many presentations included on the CD-ROM version of Microsoft Office. (See the Valuepack case study for additional information.)

   a. Start PowerPoint, pull down the File menu, and click Open. Select the CD-ROM drive in the Look In box, then scroll until you can open (double click) the Valuepack folder. Open the Audio folder, open the Network folder, and finally double click the Netmusic presentation.

   b. Be sure that you are on the first slide in the presentation, click the Slide Show button, and enjoy the show.

   c. Print the audience handouts (six per page) and submit the document to your instructor as proof that you did the exercise.

   d. A different sound presentation (from another company) is found in the Cambium folder within the Audio folder. If you enjoyed this exercise, you might be interested in viewing (hearing) that presentation as well.

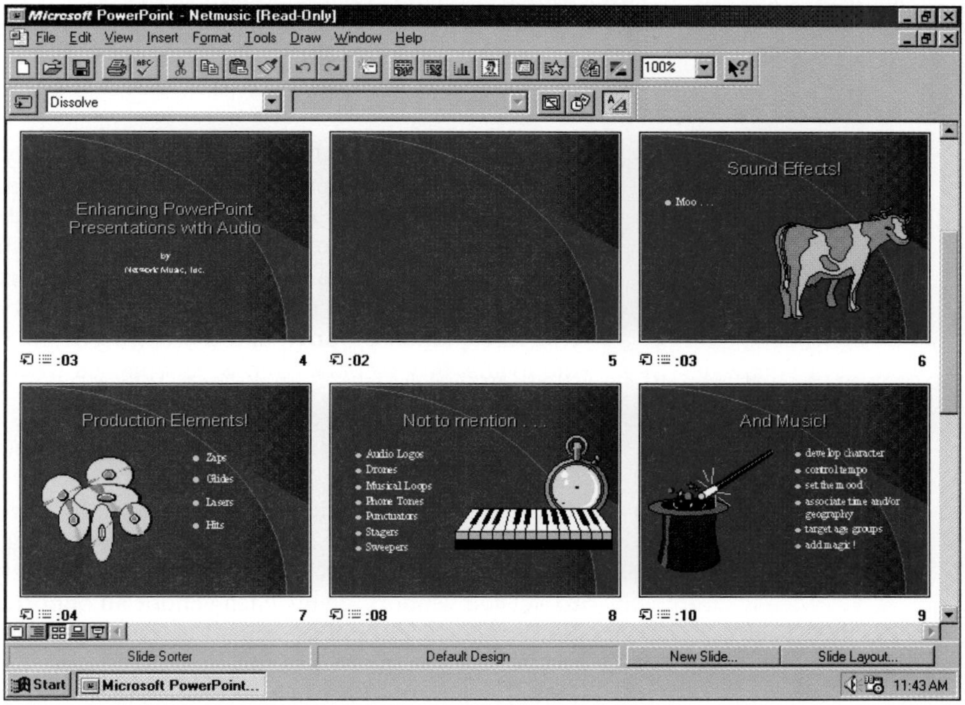

Microsoft PowerPoint - Netmusic [Read-Only]
File Edit View Insert Format Tools Draw Window Help
100%
Dissolve
Enhancing PowerPoint Presentations with Audio
Sound Effects!
Moo . . .
:03 4
:02 5
:03 6
Production Elements!
Zaps
Glides
Lasers
Hits
Not to mention . . .
Audio Logos
Drones
Musical Loops
Phone Tones
Punctuators
Stagers
Sweepers
And Music!
:04 7
:08 8
:10 9
Slide Sorter
Default Design
New Slide...
Slide Layout...
Start
Microsoft PowerPoint...
11:43 AM

FIGURE 1.17 Screen for Practice Exercise 4

CASE STUDIES

Planning for Disaster

This case has nothing to do with presentations per se, but it is perhaps the most important case of all, as it deals with the question of backup. Do you have a backup strategy? Do you even know what a backup strategy is? This is a good time to learn, because sooner or later you will need to recover a file. The problem always seems to occur the night before an assignment is due. You accidentally erased a file, are unable to read from a floppy disk, or worse yet, suffer a hardware failure in which you are unable to access the hard drive. The ultimate disaster is the disappearance of your computer, by theft or natural disaster (e.g., Hurricane Andrew, the floods in the Midwest, or the Los Angeles earthquake). Describe in 250 or fewer words the backup strategy you plan to implement in conjunction with your work in this class.

Slides to Go

You have created the perfect presentation and are scheduled for delivery next week. The presentation looks great on your PC, but you have to deliver the presentation without the aid of a computer. How do you create 35-mm slides or overhead transparencies as an alternative to the slide show? It's much easier than you think as PowerPoint provides access to the Genigraphics Corporation through the File menu. Use the Genigraphics Wizard to determine what can be done, then call the company (an 800 number is provided) to determine the exact costs for a 20-slide presentation. Summarize your findings in a one-page report to your instructor.

Clip Art

Clip art—you see it all the time, but where do you get it, and how much does it cost? A limited number of images are installed automatically with PowerPoint, but you will quickly grow tired of this selection. Additional clip art is available on the Valuepack (see the next case study), and we recommend that you install this clip art to your hard drive (assuming you have the space). Scan the computer magazines and find at least two sources for additional clip art. Return to class with specific information on price and the nature of the clip art. You might also research the availability of photographs, as opposed to clip art.

PowerPoint Valuepack

The CD version of Microsoft Office contains a Valuepack with more than 200MB of multimedia files for PowerPoint. You will find clip art, sound bites, photographs, video files, and so on. Microsoft did not create these elements, but instead went to outside vendors, giving each vendor an opportunity to advertise its product. Use the Windows 95 Find command to search on the PPT extension (enter *.PPT) in the Names list box to search for all presentations contained on the CD-ROM. Double click the icon of any presentation that seems interesting to start PowerPoint and load that presentation. Add a slide(s) to the presentation (immediately after the title page) with your impression of that presentation. Print the modified presentation (six slides per page) and submit it to your instructor.

2

CREATING A PRESENTATION: CONTENT, FORMATTING, AND ANIMATION

OBJECTIVES

After reading this chapter you will be able to:

1. Use the Outline view to create and edit a presentation; display and hide text within the Outline view.
2. Check the spelling in a presentation.
3. Apply a design template to a presentation.
4. Add transition effects to the slides in a presentation; apply build effects to the bullets and graphical objects in a specific slide.
5. Modify the template of an existing presentation by changing its color scheme and/or background shading.
6. Explain the role of masters in formatting a presentation; modify the slide master to include a company name.
7. Use the Style Checker to ensure consistent formatting in a presentation.

OVERVIEW

There are in essence two independent steps to creating a PowerPoint presentation. You must develop the content, and you must format the presentation. PowerPoint lets you do the steps in either order, but we suggest you start with the content. Both steps are iterative in nature, and you are likely to go back and forth many times before you are finished.

We begin the chapter by showing you how to enter the text of a presentation in the Outline view. We show you how to move and copy text within a slide (or from one slide to another) and how to rearrange the order of the slides within the presentation. We illustrate the use of the Spell Check and AutoCorrect features that are common to all Office applications. We also introduce the Style Checker to ensure consistent formatting from one slide to the next.

The chapter also shows you how to format a presentation using one of many professionally designed templates that are supplied with PowerPoint. The templates control every aspect of a presentation, from the formatting of the text to the color scheme of the slides. We describe how to change the template and/or how to vary a color scheme. We show you how to add transition and build effects to individual slides to enhance a presentation as it is given on a computer. The chapter also shows you how to fine-tune a presentation by changing the slide master to include a corporate logo (or other text) on every slide.

> **CRYSTALLIZE YOUR MESSAGE**
>
> Every presentation exists to deliver a message, whether it's to sell a product, present an idea, or provide instruction. Decide on the message you want to deliver, then write the text for the presentation. Edit the text to be sure it is consistent with your objective. Then, and only then, should you think about formatting, but always keep the message foremost in your mind.

CREATING A PRESENTATION

The text of a presentation can be developed in the Slide view or the Outline view or a combination of the two. You can begin in the Outline view, switch to the Slide view to see how a particular slide will look, return to the Outline view to enter the text for additional slides, and so on. We prefer the Outline view because it displays the text for many slides at once. It also enables you to change the order of slides and to move and copy text from one slide to another.

The Outline View

Figure 2.1 displays the outline of the presentation we will develop in this chapter. The outline shows the title of each slide, followed by the text on that slide. (Graphic elements such as clip art and charts are not visible in the Outline view.) Each slide is numbered, and the numbers adjust automatically for the insertion or deletion of slides as you edit the presentation.

A ***slide icon*** appears between the number and title of the slide. The icon is subtly different, depending on the slide layout. In Figure 2.1, for example, the same icon appears next to slides 1 through 6 and indicates the slides contain only text. A different icon appears next to slide 7 and indicates the presence of a graphic element, such as clip art.

Each slide begins with a title, followed by bulleted items, which are indented one to five levels corresponding to the importance of the item. The main points appear on level one. Subsidiary items are indented below the main point to which they apply. Any item can be ***promoted*** to a higher level or ***demoted*** to a lower level, either before or after the text is entered.

Consider, for example, slide 4 in Figure 2.1a. The title of the slide, *Develop the Content*, appears immediately after the slide number and icon. The first bullet, *Use the Outline view,* is indented one level under the title, and it in turn has two subsidiary bullets. The next main bullet, *Review the flow of ideas,* is moved back to level one, and it, too, has two subsidiary bullets.

The outline is (to us) the ideal way to create and edit the presentation. The ***insertion point*** marks the place where new text is entered; this is established by

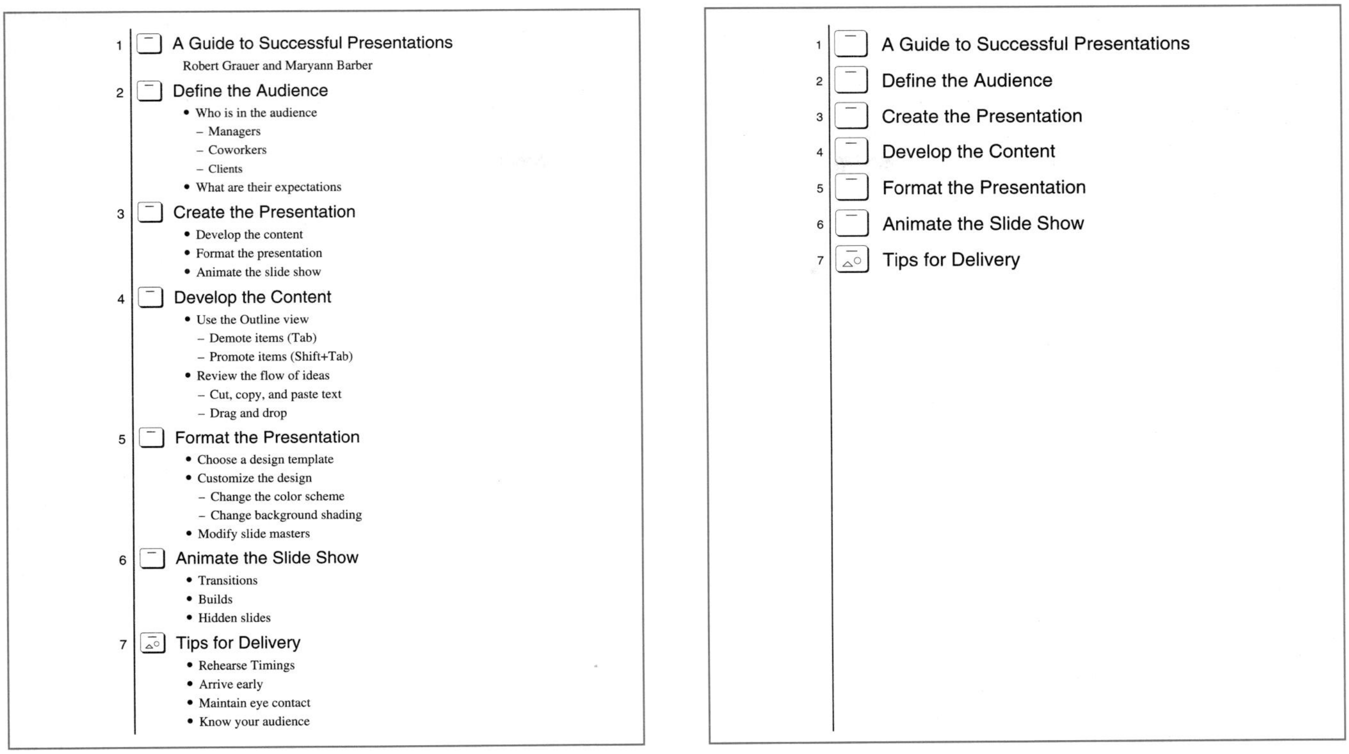
1 A Guide to Successful Presentations
Robert Grauer and Maryann Barber
2 Define the Audience
• Who is in the audience
– Managers
– Coworkers
– Clients
• What are their expectations
3 Create the Presentation
• Develop the content
• Format the presentation
• Animate the slide show
4 Develop the Content
• Use the Outline view
– Demote items (Tab)
– Promote items (Shift+Tab)
• Review the flow of ideas
– Cut, copy, and paste text
– Drag and drop
5 Format the Presentation
• Choose a design template
• Customize the design
– Change the color scheme
– Change background shading
• Modify slide masters
6 Animate the Slide Show
• Transitions
• Builds
• Hidden slides
7 Tips for Delivery
• Rehearse Timings
• Arrive early
• Maintain eye contact
• Know your audience
1 A Guide to Successful Presentations
2 Define the Audience
3 Create the Presentation
4 Develop the Content
5 Format the Presentation
6 Animate the Slide Show
7 Tips for Delivery

(a) The Expanded Outline

(b) The Collapsed Outline

FIGURE 2.1 The Outline View

clicking anywhere in the outline. (The insertion point is automatically placed at the title of the first slide in a new presentation.) To enter text, click in the outline to establish the insertion point, then start typing. Press enter after typing the title of a slide or after entering the text of a bulleted item, which starts a new slide or bullet, respectively. The new item may then be promoted (by pressing **Shift+Tab**) or demoted (by pressing **Tab**) as necessary.

Editing is accomplished through the same techniques used in other Windows applications. For example, you can use the Cut, Copy, and Paste commands in the Edit menu (or the corresponding buttons on the Standard toolbar) to move and copy selected text, or you can simply drag and drop text from one place to another.

Figure 2.1b displays a collapsed view of the outline, which displays only the title of each slide. The advantage to this view is that you see more slides on the screen at the same time, making it easier to move slides within the presentation. The slides are expanded or collapsed by using the appropriate tool on the Outline toolbar as described in a hands-on exercise. (The ***Outline toolbar*** appears

SPELLING COUNTS

You are in the midst of giving your presentation when all of a sudden someone in the audience points out a misspelling in the title of a crucial slide. Take it from us, nothing takes more away from a presentation than a misspelled word. You've lost your audience, and it didn't have to happen. PowerPoint provides a full-featured spelling checker. Use it!

automatically when you switch to the Outline view. As with the Standard and Formatting toolbars in Chapter 1, a ToolTip will appear when you point to a button to describe its function.)

Text is formatted by using the select-then-do approach common to Word and Excel; that is, you select the text, then you execute the appropriate command or click the appropriate button. The selected text remains highlighted and is affected by all subsequent commands until you click elsewhere in the outline.

The AutoContent Wizard

Outline or not, one of the hardest things about creating a presentation is getting started. You have a general idea of what you want to say, but the words do not come to you. The ***AutoContent Wizard*** helps you begin. It is accessed through the New command in the File menu and is illustrated in Figure 2.2.

The AutoContent Wizard asks you a series of questions, then uses your answers to create a presentation. The Wizard asks for your name and other information to create the title slide, as shown in Figure 2.2a. It prompts for the type of presentation you intend to give in Figure 2.2b, and for the visual style and duration in Figure 2.2c. The Wizard selects a template for you according to the requested style (e.g., Professional), and it ends by displaying the title slide in Figure 2.2d.

The real benefit of the Wizard, however, is the suggested outline shown in Figure 2.2e, which corresponds to the topic you selected earlier (Selling a Product, Service, or Idea). The outline is very general, as it must be, but it provides the essential topics to include in your presentation. You simply replace the general topic with the specific information unique to your presentation.

You work with the outline provided by the AutoContent Wizard just as you would with any other outline. You can type over existing text, add or delete slides, move slides around, promote or demote items, and so on. In short, you don't use the AutoContent outline exactly as it is presented; instead, you use the outline as a starting point, then modify it to fit the needs of your presentation.

SUGGESTED PRESENTATIONS

PowerPoint provides a total of 21 suggested presentations covering a wide range of topics. You will find a presentation to create a business or a marketing plan as well as a presentation to prepare a financial report. There is a Top Ten Presentation with animation effects built in. There is even a presentation to communicate bad news. All of these presentations can be accessed through the AutoContent Wizard, or alternatively, through the New command in the File menu. (Select the Presentations tab from the New Presentation dialog box.)

TEMPLATES

PowerPoint enables you to concentrate on the content of a presentation without concern for its appearance. You focus on what you are going to say, and trust in PowerPoint to format the presentation attractively. The formatting is implemented automatically by selecting one of the more than 100 templates that are supplied with PowerPoint.

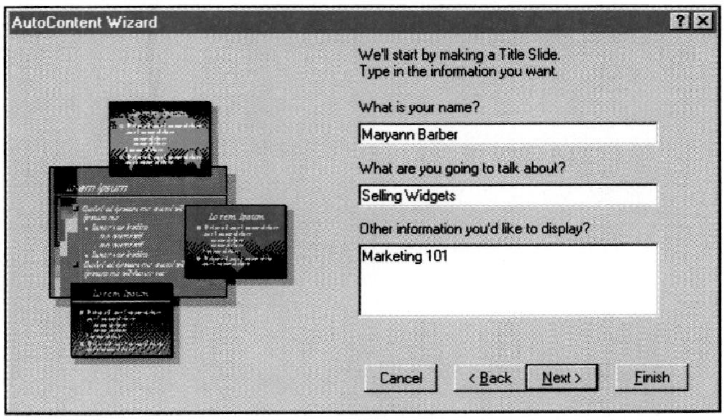
AutoContent Wizard
We'll start by making a Title Slide.
Type in the information you want.
What is your name?
Maryann Barber
What are you going to talk about?
Selling Widgets
Other information you'd like to display?
Marketing 101
Cancel
< Back
Next >
Finish

(a) Information for the Title Slide

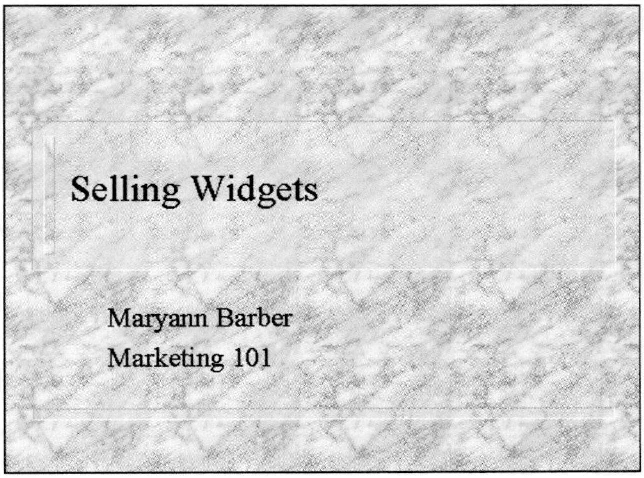
Selling Widgets
Maryann Barber
Marketing 101

(d) Title Slide

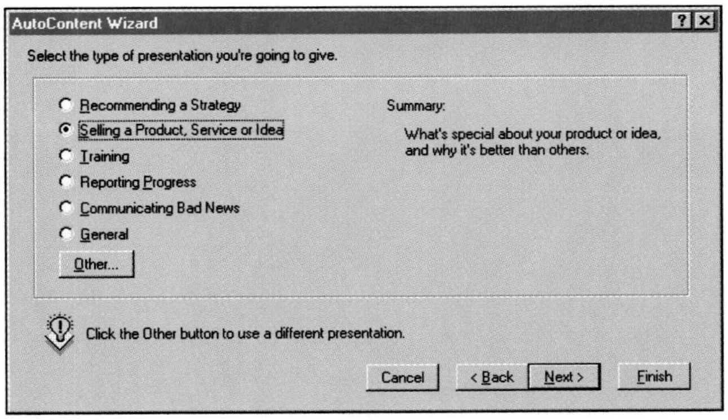
AutoContent Wizard
Select the type of presentation you're going to give.
Recommending a Strategy
Selling a Product, Service or Idea
Training
Reporting Progress
Communicating Bad News
General
Other...
Summary:
What's special about your product or idea, and why it's better than others.
Click the Other button to use a different presentation.
Cancel
< Back
Next >
Finish

(b) Select the Topic

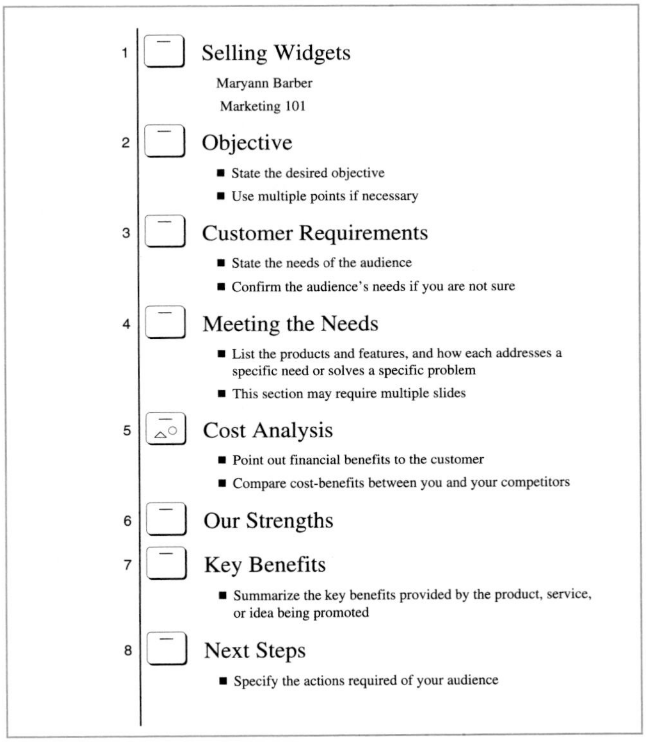
1
Selling Widgets
Maryann Barber
Marketing 101
2
Objective
State the desired objective
Use multiple points if necessary
3
Customer Requirements
State the needs of the audience
Confirm the audience's needs if you are not sure
4
Meeting the Needs
List the products and features, and how each addresses a specific need or solves a specific problem
This section may require multiple slides
5
Cost Analysis
Point out financial benefits to the customer
Compare cost-benefits between you and your competitors
6
Our Strengths
7
Key Benefits
Summarize the key benefits provided by the product, service, or idea being promoted
8
Next Steps
Specify the actions required of your audience

(e) Suggested Outline

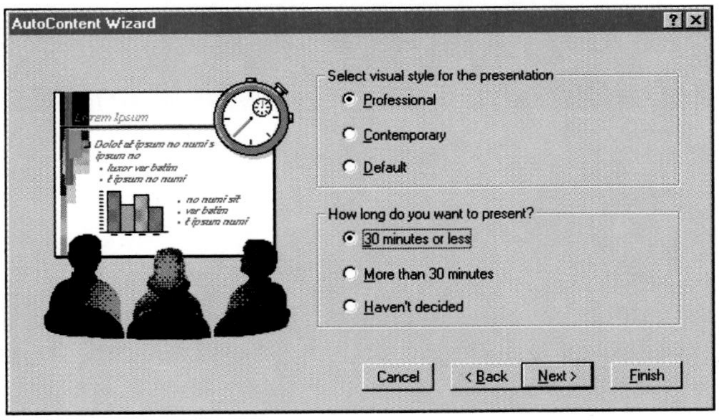
AutoContent Wizard
Select visual style for the presentation
Professional
Contemporary
Default
How long do you want to present?
30 minutes or less
More than 30 minutes
Haven't decided
Cancel
< Back
Next >
Finish

(c) Additional Information

FIGURE 2.2 The AutoContent Wizard

A ***template*** is a design specification that controls every element in a presentation. It specifies the color scheme for the slides and the arrangement of the different elements (placeholders) on each slide. It determines the formatting of the text, the fonts that are used, and the design, size, and placement of the bulleted text.

Figure 2.3 displays the title slide of a presentation in four different templates. Just choose the template you like, and PowerPoint formats the entire presentation

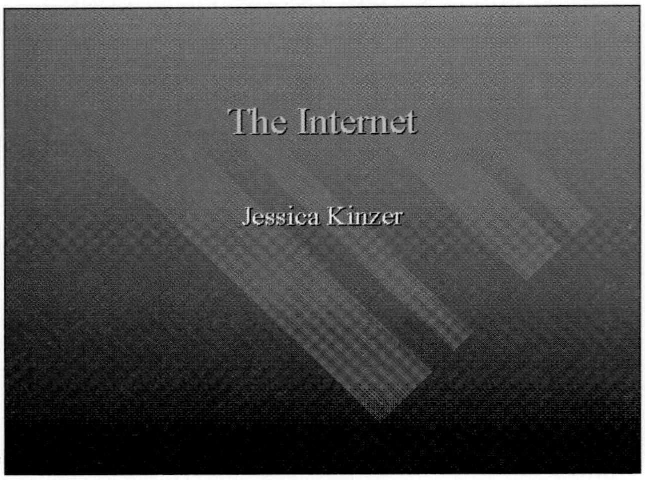
The Internet
Jessica Kinzer

(a) Blue Diagonal Template

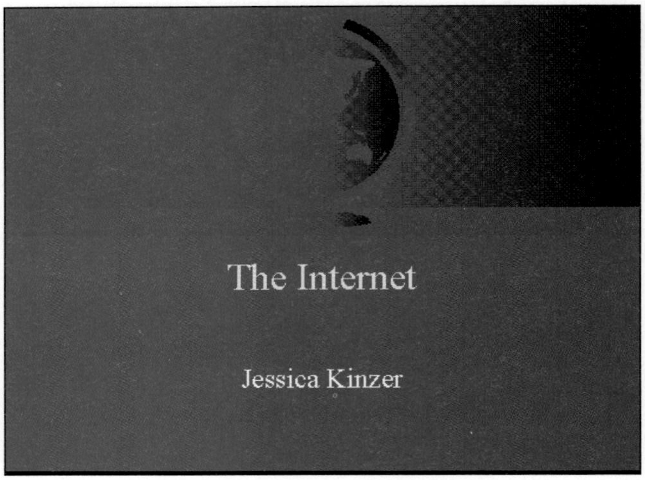
The Internet
Jessica Kinzer

(b) International Template

The Internet
Jessica Kinzer

(c) Blue Green Template

The Internet
Jessica Kinzer

(d) Bevel Template

FIGURE 2.3 Templates

according to that template. And don't be afraid to change your mind. You can use the Format menu at any time to select a different template and change the look of your presentation.

CHOOSE AN APPROPRIATE TEMPLATE

A template should enhance a presentation without calling attention to itself. It should be consistent with your message, and as authoritative or informal as the situation demands. Choosing the right template requires common sense and good taste. What works in one instance will not necessarily work in another. You wouldn't, for example, use the same template to proclaim a year-end bonus as you would to announce a fourth-quarter loss and impending layoffs.

HANDS-ON EXERCISE 1

Creating a Presentation

Objective: To create a presentation by entering text in the Outline view; to check a presentation for spelling errors, and to apply a design template to a presentation. Use Figure 2.4 as a guide in the exercise.

STEP 1: Create a New Presentation

- Start PowerPoint. Click **OK** to close the Tip of the Day dialog box, which in turn displays the PowerPoint dialog box.
- Click the **option button** to create a new presentation using a **Blank Presentation**. Click **OK**. You should see the **New Slide** dialog box in Figure 2.4a with the AutoLayout for the title slide already selected. Click **OK** to create a title slide and simultaneously close the New Slide dialog box.
- If necessary, click the **Maximize buttons** in both the application and document windows so that PowerPoint takes the entire desktop and the current presentation is as large as possible. Both Maximize buttons will be replaced with Restore buttons as shown in Figure 2.4a.

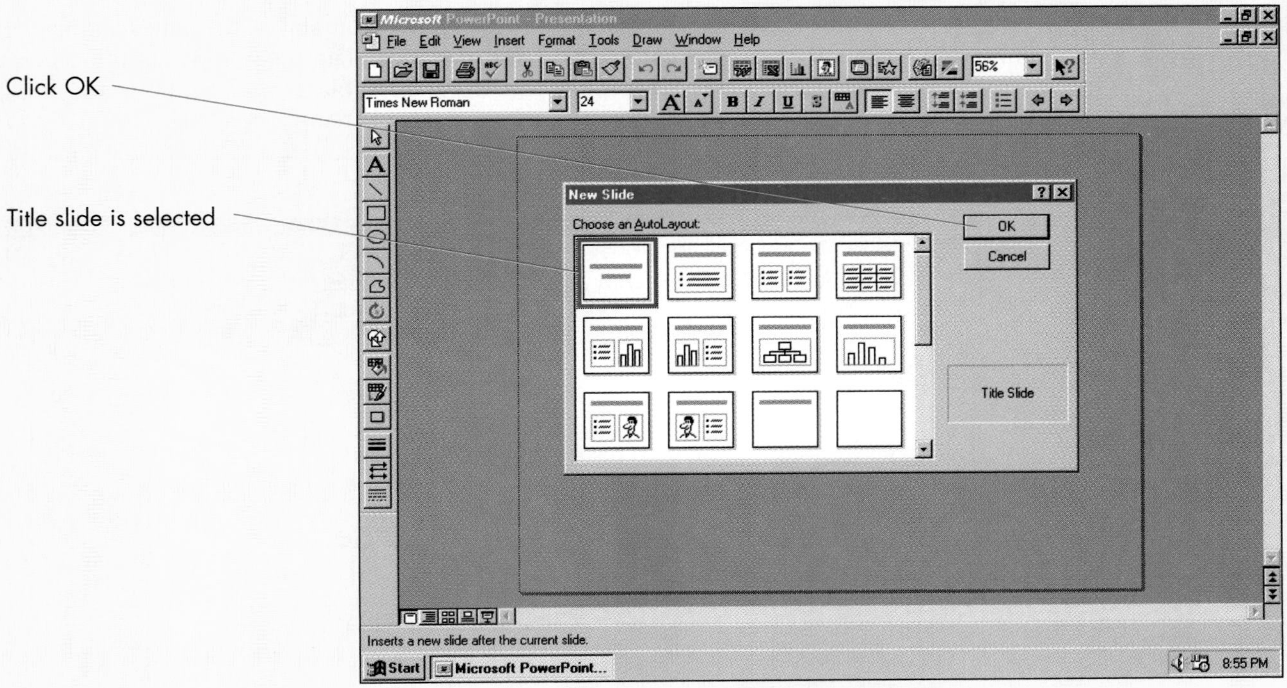
Click OK
Title slide is selected
Microsoft PowerPoint - Presentation
File Edit View Insert Format Tools Draw Window Help
Times New Roman
24
56%
New Slide
Choose an AutoLayout:
OK
Cancel
Title Slide
Inserts a new slide after the current slide.
Start
Microsoft PowerPoint...
8:55 PM

(a) Start PowerPoint (step 1)

FIGURE 2.4 Hands-on Exercise 1

CONTENT, CONTENT, AND CONTENT

It is much more important to focus on the content of the presentation than to worry about how it will look. Start with the AutoContent Wizard or with a blank presentation in the Outline view. Save the formatting for last. Otherwise you will spend too much time changing templates and too little time developing the text.

STEP 2: Create the Title Slide

- Click anywhere in the box containing **Click to add title**, then type the title **A Guide to Successful Presentations** as shown in Figure 2.4b. The title will automatically wrap to a second line.
- Click anywhere in the box containing **Click to add sub-title** and enter your name. Click outside the sub-title area when you have completed your name.

THE DEFAULT PRESENTATION

PowerPoint supplies a default presentation containing the specifications for color, text formatting, and AutoLayouts. The default presentation is selected automatically when you work on a blank presentation, and it remains in effect until you choose a different template.

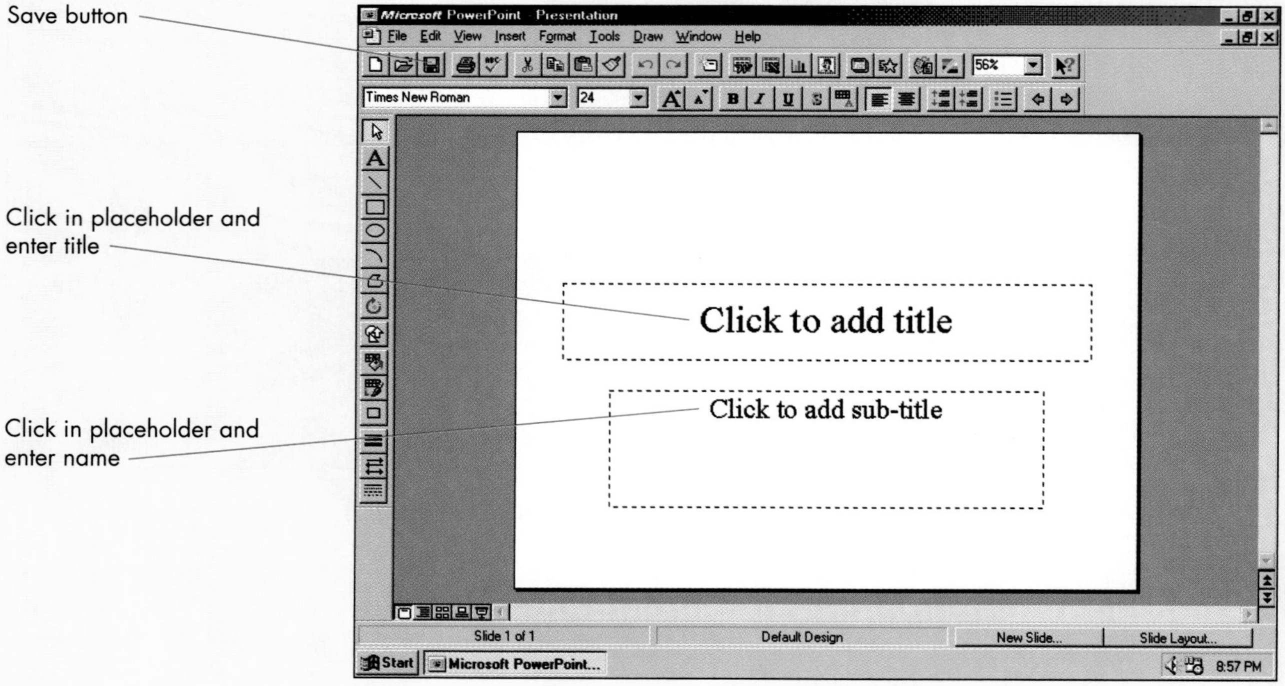
Save button
Click in placeholder and enter title
Click in placeholder and enter name
Microsoft PowerPoint - Presentation
File Edit View Insert Format Tools Draw Window Help
56%
Times New Roman
24
Click to add title
Click to add sub-title
Slide 1 of 1
Default Design
New Slide...
Slide Layout...
Start
Microsoft PowerPoint...
8:57 PM

(b) Create the Title Slide (step 2)

FIGURE 2.4 Hands-on Exercise 1 (continued)

STEP 3: Save the Presentation

- Pull down the **File menu** and click **Save** (or click the **Save button** on the Standard toolbar). You should see the File Save dialog box in Figure 2.4c. If necessary, click the **List button** so that the display on your monitor more closely matches our figure.
- To save the file:
  - Click the **drop-down arrow** on the Save In list box.
  - Click the appropriate drive, drive C or drive A, depending on whether or not you installed the data disk on your hard drive.
  - Double click the **Exploring PowerPoint folder,** to make it the active folder (the folder in which you will save the document).
  - Enter **My First Presentation** as the name of the presentation.
  - Click **Save** or press the **enter key.** Click **Cancel** or press the **Esc key** if you see the Properties dialog box. The title bar changes to reflect the name of the presentation.

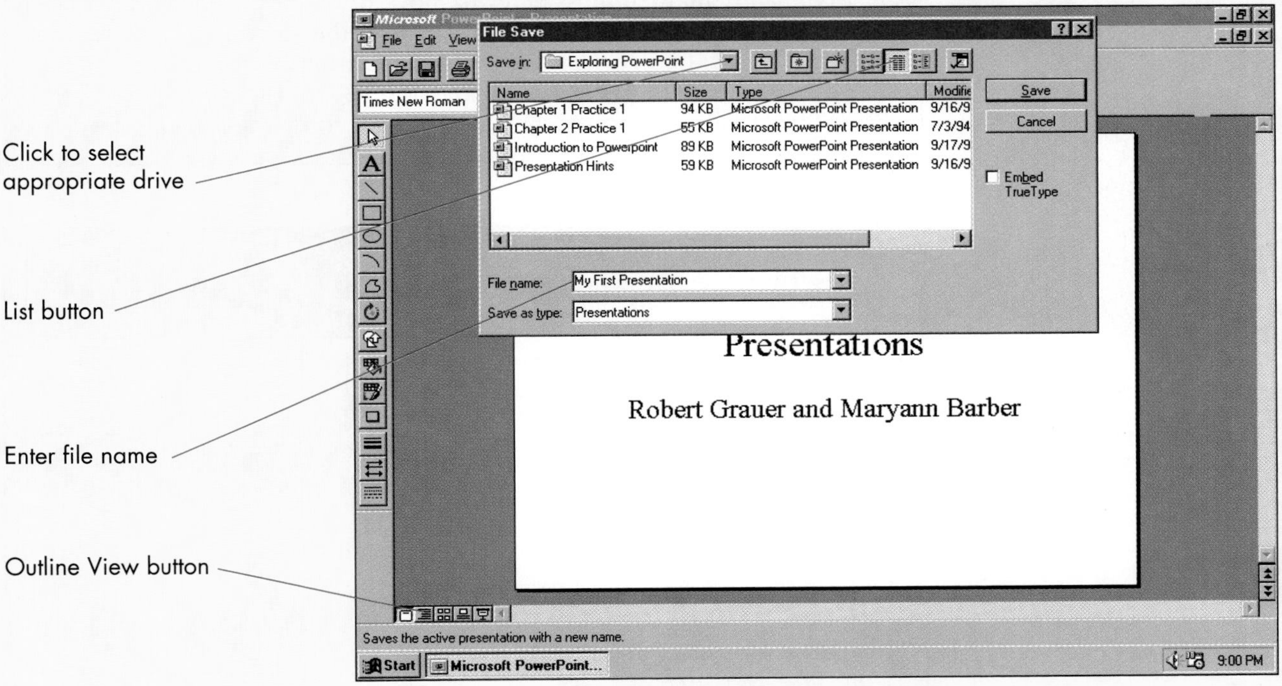
Click to select appropriate drive
List button
Enter file name
Outline View button
File Save
Save in:
Exploring PowerPoint
Name
Size
Type
Chapter 1 Practice 1
94 KB
Microsoft PowerPoint Presentation
Chapter 2 Practice 1
55 KB
Introduction to Powerpoint
89 KB
Presentation Hints
59 KB
Save
Cancel
Embed TrueType
File name:
My First Presentation
Save as type:
Presentations
Times New Roman
Presentations
Robert Grauer and Maryann Barber
Saves the active presentation with a new name.
Start
Microsoft PowerPoint...
9:00 PM

(c) The Save Command (step 3)

FIGURE 2.4 Hands-on Exercise 1 (continued)

STEP 4: Create the Presentation

- Click the **Outline view button** above the status bar to change to the Outline view. Your presentation at this point contains only the title slide with your name.
- Click the **New Slide button** on the status bar. The icon for slide 2 will appear in the outline. Type **Define the Audience** as the title of the slide and press **enter.**
- Press the **Tab key** (or click the **Demote button** on the Outline toolbar) to enter the first bullet. Type **Who is in the audience** and press **enter.**

➤ Press the **Tab key** (or click the **Demote button** on the Outline toolbar) to enter the second-level bullets.

- Type **Managers.** Press **enter.**
- Type **Coworkers.** Press **enter.**
- Type **Clients.** Press **enter.**

➤ Press **Shift+Tab** (or click the **Promote button** on the Outline toolbar) to return to the first-level bullets.

- Type **What are their expectations.** Press **enter.**

➤ Press **Shift+Tab** to enter the title of the third slide. Type **Tips for Delivery.** Add the remaining text for this slide and for slide 4 as shown in Figure 2.4d.

JUST KEEP TYPING

The easiest way to enter the text for a presentation is in the Outline view. Just type an item, then press enter to move to the next item. You will be automatically positioned at the next item on the same level, where you can type the next entry. Continue to enter text in this manner. Press the Tab key as necessary to demote an item (move it to the next lower level). Press Shift+Tab to promote an item (move it to the next higher level).

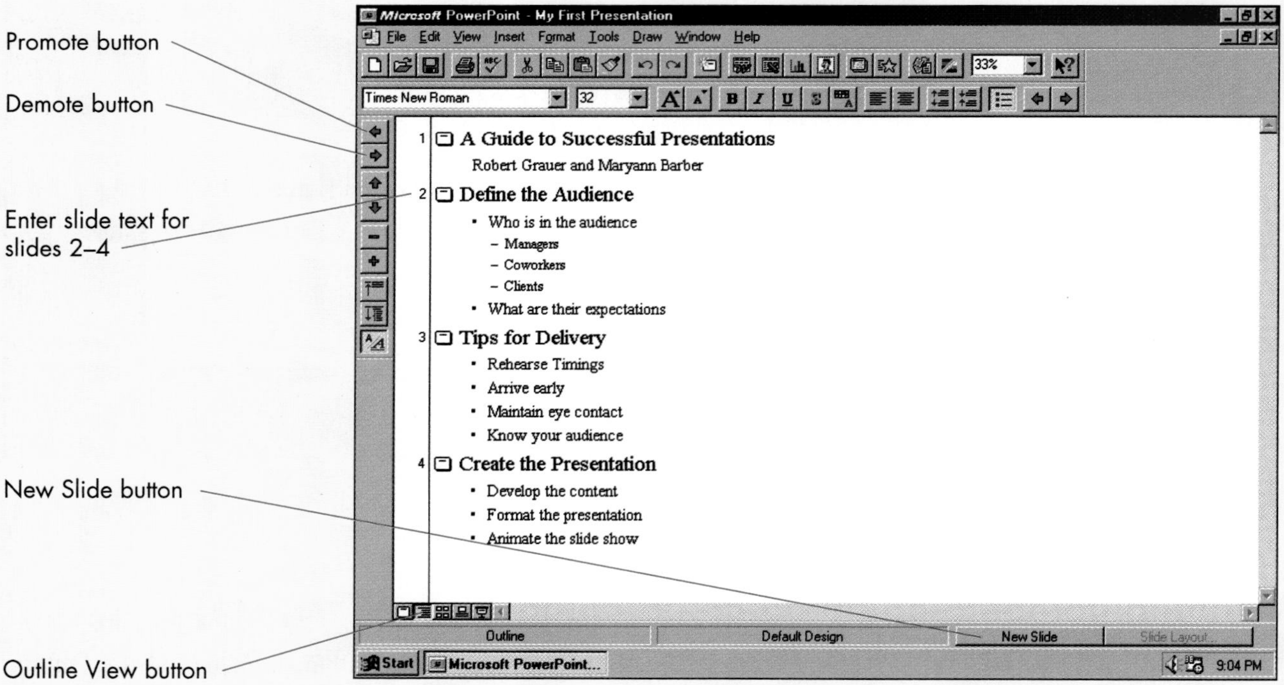

Promote button
Demote button
Enter slide text for slides 2–4
New Slide button
Outline View button
Microsoft PowerPoint - My First Presentation
File Edit View Insert Format Tools Draw Window Help
Times New Roman
32
33%
1 A Guide to Successful Presentations
Robert Grauer and Maryann Barber
2 Define the Audience
Who is in the audience
– Managers
– Coworkers
– Clients
What are their expectations
3 Tips for Delivery
Rehearse Timings
Arrive early
Maintain eye contact
Know your audience
4 Create the Presentation
Develop the content
Format the presentation
Animate the slide show
Outline
Default Design
New Slide
Slide Layout...
Start
Microsoft PowerPoint...
9:04 PM

(d) Create the Presentation (step 4)

FIGURE 2.4 Hands-on Exercise 1 (continued)

STEP 5: The Spell Check

- Enter the title of the fifth slide as **Develop teh Content** (deliberately misspelling the word "the"). Try to look at the monitor as you type to see the AutoCorrect feature (common to all Office applications) in action. PowerPoint will correct the misspelling and change *teh* to *the.*
- If you did not see the correction being made, click the arrow next to the Undo button on the Standard toolbar and undo the last several actions. Click the arrow next to the Redo button and redo the corrections in order to see the error and subsequent auto correction.
- Enter the text of the remaining slides as shown in Figure 2.4e. Do *not* press enter after entering the last bullet on the last slide or else you will add a blank slide at the end of your presentation.
- Click the **Spelling button** on the Standard toolbar to check the presentation for spelling:
  - The result of the Spell Check will depend on how accurately you entered the text of the presentation. We deliberately misspelled the word "Transitions" in the last slide.
  - Continue to check the document for spelling errors. Click **OK** when PowerPoint indicates it has checked the entire presentation.
- Click the **Save button** on the Standard toolbar to save the presentation.

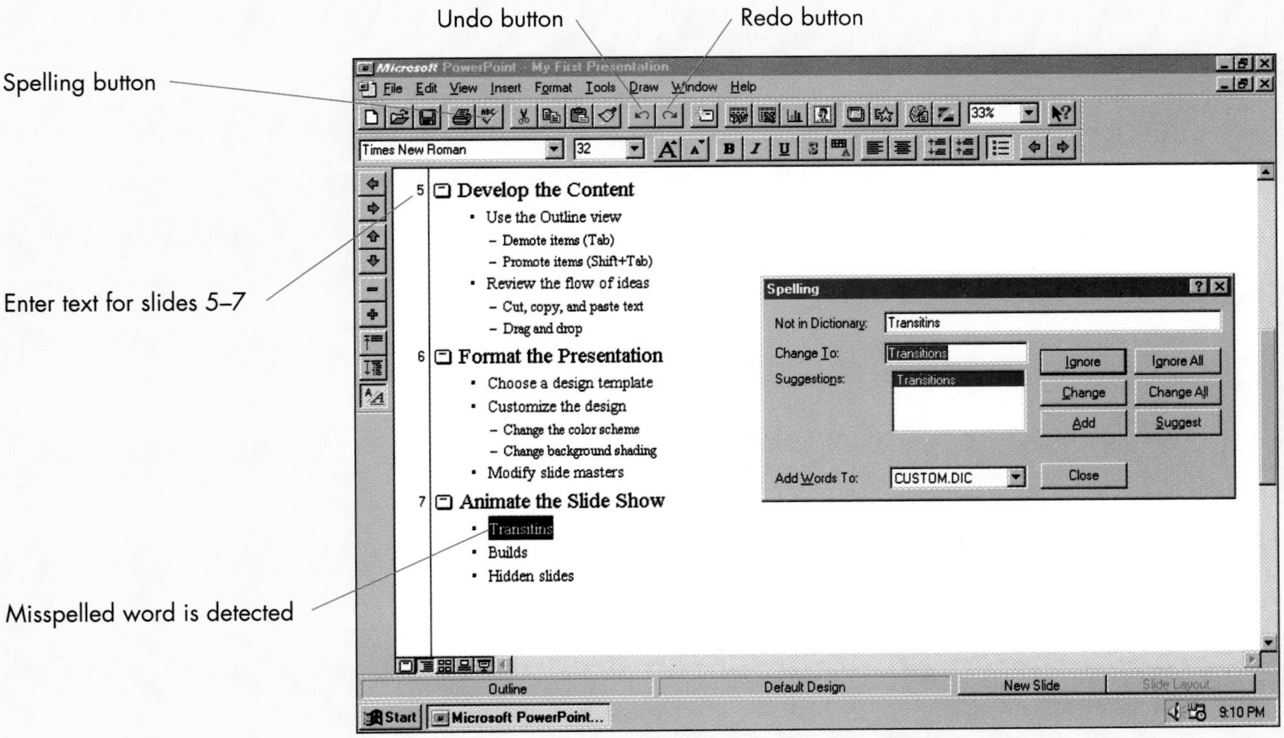
Undo button
Redo button
Spelling button
Enter text for slides 5–7
Misspelled word is detected
File Edit View Insert Format Tools Draw Window Help
Times New Roman
32
33%
5 Develop the Content
Use the Outline view
Demote items (Tab)
Promote items (Shift+Tab)
Review the flow of ideas
Cut, copy, and paste text
Drag and drop
6 Format the Presentation
Choose a design template
Customize the design
Change the color scheme
Change background shading
Modify slide masters
7 Animate the Slide Show
Transitins
Builds
Hidden slides
Spelling
Not in Dictionary: Transitins
Change To: Transitions
Suggestions: Transitions
Ignore
Ignore All
Change
Change All
Add
Suggest
Add Words To: CUSTOM.DIC
Close
Outline
Default Design
New Slide
Slide Layout...
Start
Microsoft PowerPoint...
9:10 PM

(e) The Spell Check (step 5)

FIGURE 2.4 Hands-on Exercise 1 (continued)

CREATE YOUR OWN SHORTHAND

Use the AutoCorrect feature, which is common to all Office applications, to expand abbreviations such as "usa" for United States of America. Pull down the Tools menu, click AutoCorrect, then type the abbreviation in the Replace text box and the expanded entry in the With text box. Click the Add command button, then click OK to exit the dialog box and return to the document. The next time you type usa in a presentation, it will automatically be expanded to United States of America.

STEP 6: Drag and Drop

- Press **Ctrl+Home** to move to the beginning of the presentation. Click the **Show Titles button** on the Outline toolbar to collapse the outline as shown in Figure 2.4f.
- Click the **icon** for **slide 3** (Tips for Delivery). The slide is selected and its title is highlighted. Point to the **slide icon** (the mouse pointer changes to a four-headed arrow), then click and drag to move the slide to the end of the presentation. Release the mouse.
- All of the slides have been renumbered. The slide titled Tips for Delivery has been moved to the end of the presentation and appears as slide 7. Click the **Show All button** to display the contents of each slide. Click anywhere in the presentation to deselect the last slide.
- Click the **Save button** on the Standard toolbar to save the presentation.

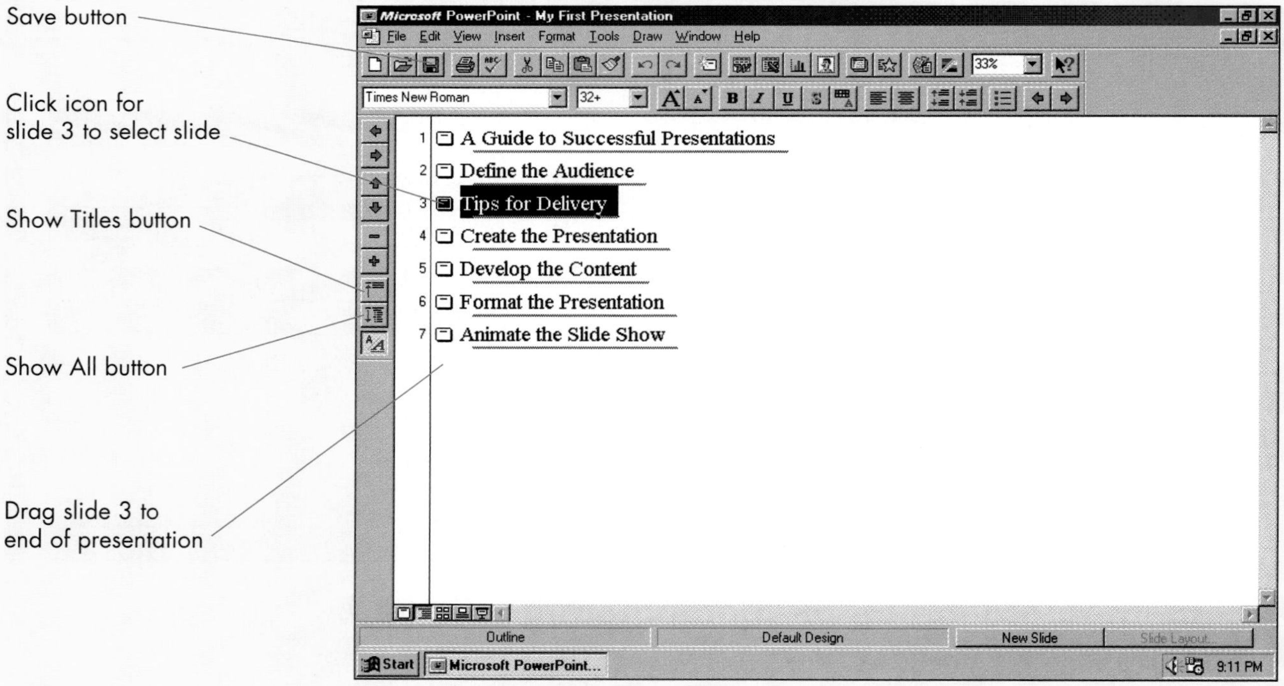

Save button
Click icon for slide 3 to select slide
Show Titles button
Show All button
Drag slide 3 to end of presentation
Microsoft PowerPoint - My First Presentation
File Edit View Insert Format Tools Draw Window Help
33%
Times New Roman
32+
1 A Guide to Successful Presentations
2 Define the Audience
3 Tips for Delivery
4 Create the Presentation
5 Develop the Content
6 Format the Presentation
7 Animate the Slide Show
Outline
Default Design
New Slide
Slide Layout...
Start
Microsoft PowerPoint...
9:11 PM

(f) Drag and Drop (step 6)

FIGURE 2.4 Hands-on Exercise 1 (continued)

SELECTING SLIDES IN THE OUTLINE VIEW

Click the slide icon or the slide number next to the slide title to select the slide. PowerPoint will select the entire slide (including its title, text, and any other objects that are not visible in the Outline view). Press and hold the Shift key, then click the beginning and ending slides to select a group of sequential slides. Press Ctrl+A to select the entire outline. You can use these techniques to select multiple slides regardless of whether the outline is collapsed or expanded. The selected slides can be copied, moved, or deleted as a unit.

STEP 7: Choose a Design Template

➤ Pull down the **Format menu.** Click **Apply Design Template** to display the dialog box in Figure 2.4g:

- The **Presentation Designs folder** should appear automatically in the List box. If it doesn't, change to this folder, which is contained within the Templates folder within the MSOffice folder.
- **Presentation Templates** should be selected in the Files of Type list box. If it isn't, click the **drop-down arrow** to change this file type.
- The **Preview view** should be selected. If it isn't, click the **Preview button** so that you can preview the selected template.
- Scroll through the available designs to select (click) the **Double Lines template** as shown in Figure 2.4g. Click **Apply** to apply the template to your presentation and close the dialog box.

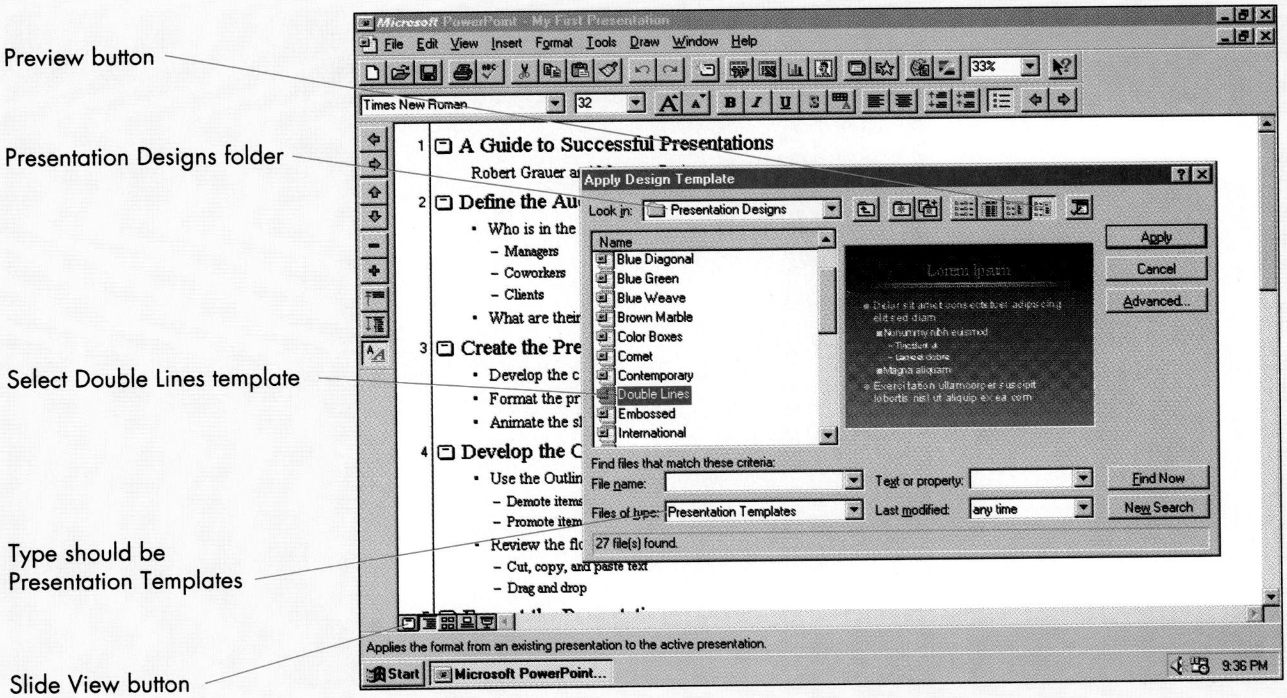
Preview button
Presentation Designs folder
Select Double Lines template
Type should be Presentation Templates
Slide View button
Microsoft PowerPoint - My First Presentation
Apply Design Template
Look in: Presentation Designs
Blue Diagonal
Blue Green
Blue Weave
Brown Marble
Color Boxes
Comet
Contemporary
Double Lines
Embossed
International
Apply
Cancel
Advanced...
Files of type: Presentation Templates
27 file(s) found.
Applies the format from an existing presentation to the active presentation.

(g) Apply a Design Template (step 7)

FIGURE 2.4 Hands-on Exercise 1 (continued)

- You are still in the Outline view, which does not show the selected template. Click the **Slide View button** to change to the Slide view to see that the template has been applied.
- Save the presentation.

STEP 8: View the Presentation

- Press **Ctrl+Home** to move to the beginning of the presentation. Click the **Slide Show button** on the status bar to view the presentation as shown in Figure 2.4h.
  - To move to the next slide: Click the **left mouse button,** type the letter **N,** or press the **PgDn key.**
  - To move to the previous slide: Type the letter **P,** or press the **PgUp key.**
- Continue to move from one slide to the next until you come to the end of the presentation and are returned to the Slide view.
- Pull down the **File menu** and click **Exit** if you do not want to continue with the next exercise at this time.

THE SLIDE NAVIGATOR

The Slide Navigator enables you to branch directly to a specific slide and provides the utmost in flexibility during a presentation. Click the right mouse button at any time to display a shortcut menu, click Go To, click Slide Navigator to display a list of all the slides in the presentation, then double click the desired slide to move directly to that slide.

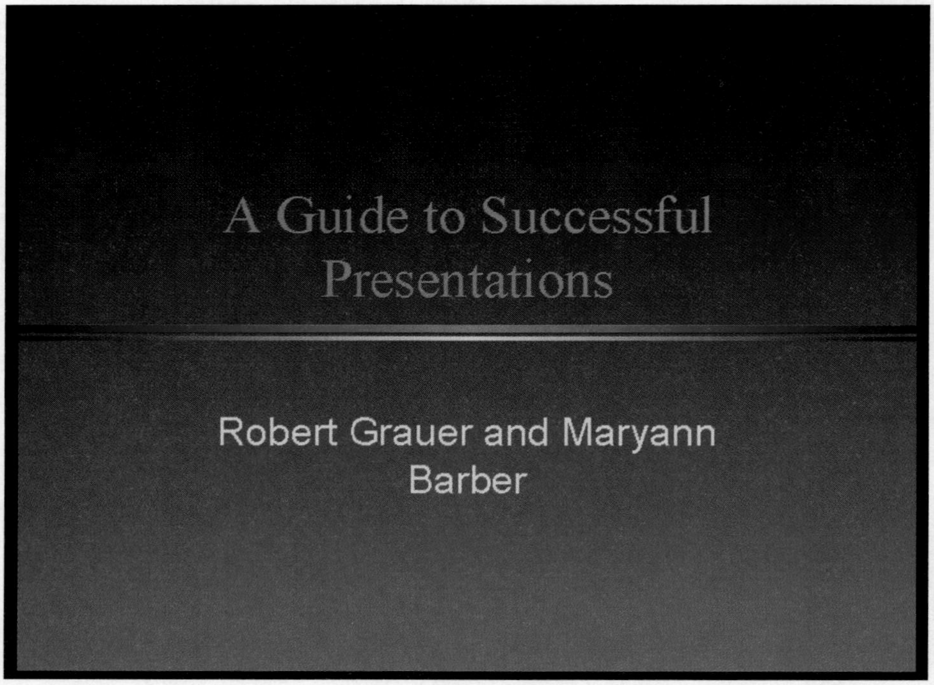
A Guide to Successful Presentations
Robert Grauer and Maryann Barber

(h) View the Presentation (step 8)

FIGURE 2.4 Hands-on Exercise 1 (continued)

CREATING A SLIDE SHOW

You develop the content of a presentation, then you format it attractively using a PowerPoint template. The most important step is yet to come—the delivery of the presentation to an audience, which is best accomplished through a computerized slide show (as opposed to using overhead transparencies or 35-mm slides). The computer becomes the equivalent of a slide projector, and the presentation is called a slide show.

PowerPoint can help you add interest to the slide show in two ways, transitions and builds. ***Transitions*** control the way in which one slide moves off the screen and the next slide appears. ***Builds*** are used to vary the display of the elements on a single slide.

Transitions are created through the Slide Transition command in the Tools menu, which displays the dialog box in Figure 2.5a. The drop-down list box enables you to choose the transition effect. Slides may move on to the screen from the left or right, be uncovered by horizontal or vertical blinds, fade, dissolve, and so on. The dialog box also enables you to set the speed of the transition and/or to preview the effect.

A build displays the bulleted items one at a time with each successive mouse click. It is created through the Build Slide Text command in the Tools menu, which displays the Animation Settings dialog box of Figure 2.5b. Each bullet can appear with its own transition effect. You can make the bullets appear one word or one letter at a time. You can specify that the bullets appear in reverse order (i.e., the bottom bullet first), and you can dim each bullet as the next one appears. You can even add sound and make the bullets appear in conjunction with a round of applause.

Transitions and builds can also be created from the Slide Sorter toolbar as shown in Figure 2.5c. As with the other toolbars, a ToolTip is displayed when you point to a button on the toolbar.

ANIMATE THE OTHER OBJECTS

A build can be applied to any object on a slide although it is used most frequently with bulleted text. You can create a special effect by animating another object, such as a piece of clip art or a chart. Point to the object, click the right mouse button to display a shortcut menu, then click Animation Settings to display a dialog box in which you choose the build effect(s).

AUTOLAYOUTS

Every slide in a presentation is created according to one of 24 predefined slide formats known as AutoLayouts. The AutoLayout determines the objects that will appear on a slide (e.g., text, clip art, a chart, or other object) and specifies the placement for those objects. You can choose the AutoLayout explicitly, or you can have PowerPoint do it for you. Any text entered through the Outline view, for example, is automatically formatted according to the Bullet List AutoLayout.

What if, however, you want to add a graphic element, such as clip art or a chart, to a bulleted slide that was created initially from the Outline view? The easiest way to do this is to change to the Slide view, then change the AutoLayout of the slide from a Bulleted List to one containing text and clip art. This procedure is illustrated in steps 1 and 2 of the next hands-on exercise.

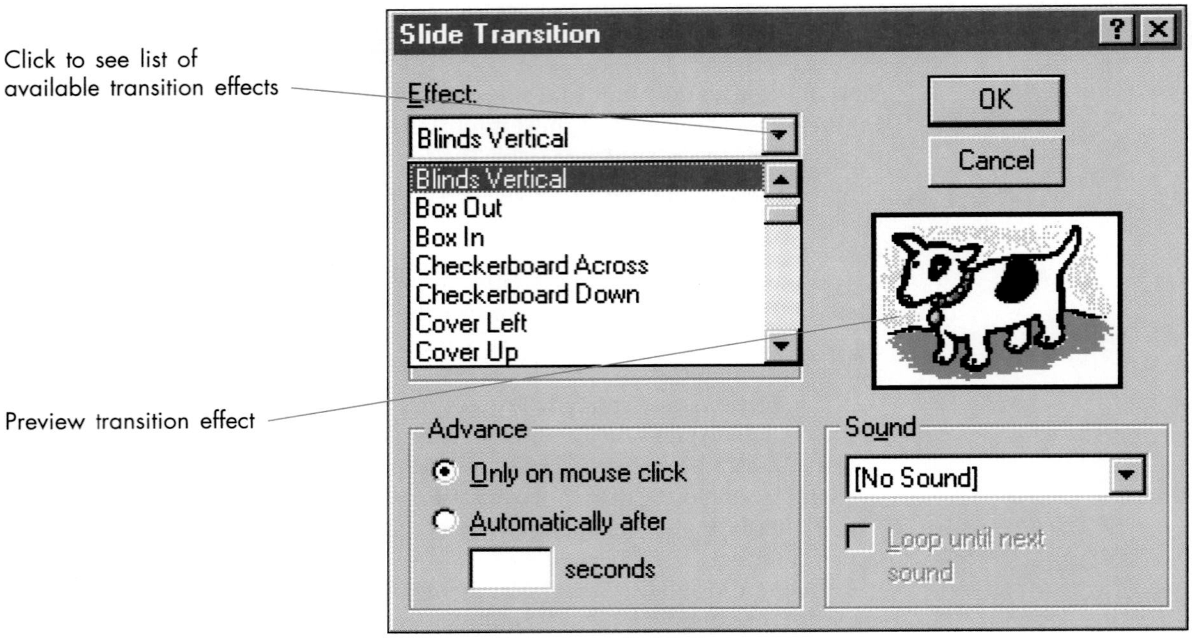
Click to see list of available transition effects
Preview transition effect
Slide Transition
Effect:
Blinds Vertical
Blinds Vertical
Box Out
Box In
Checkerboard Across
Checkerboard Down
Cover Left
Cover Up
OK
Cancel
Advance
Only on mouse click
Automatically after
seconds
Sound
[No Sound]
Loop until next sound

(a) Transitions

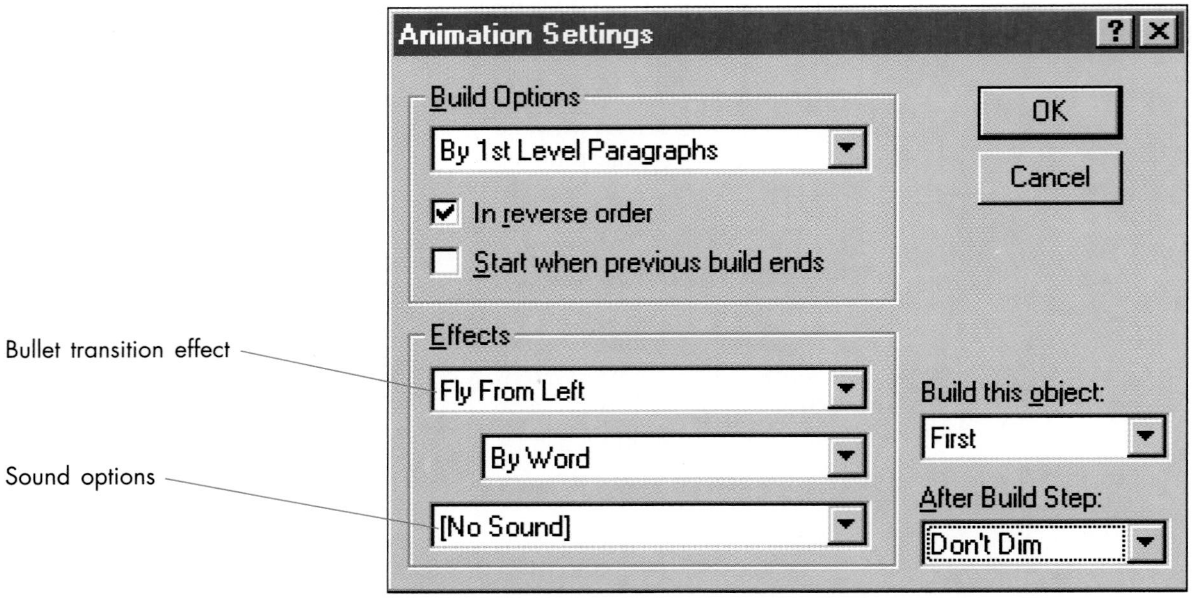
Bullet transition effect
Sound options
Animation Settings
Build Options
By 1st Level Paragraphs
In reverse order
Start when previous build ends
Effects
Fly From Left
By Word
[No Sound]
OK
Cancel
Build this object:
First
After Build Step:
Don't Dim

(b) Builds

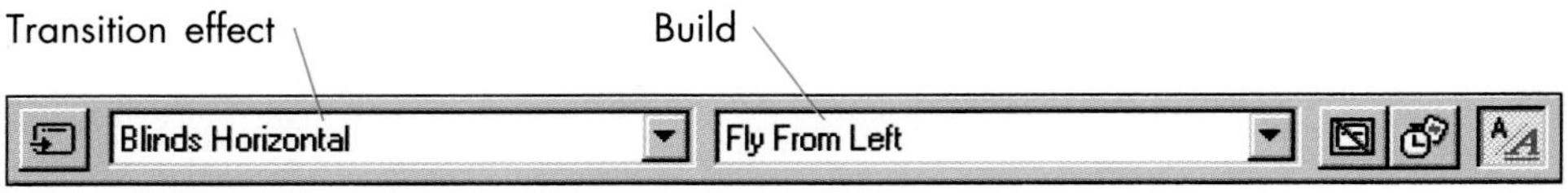
Transition effect
Build
Blinds Horizontal
Fly From Left

(c) Slide Sorter Toolbar

FIGURE 2.5 Transitions and Builds

HANDS-ON EXERCISE 2

Animating the Presentation

Objective: To change the layout of an existing slide; to establish transition and build effects. Use Figure 2.6 as a guide in the exercise.

STEP 1: Change the AutoLayout

- Start PowerPoint and open **My First Presentation** from the previous exercise. If necessary, switch to the Slide view, then press **Ctrl+End** to move to the last slide as shown in Figure 2.6a, which is currently a bulleted list.
- Pull down the **Format menu** and click **Slide Layout** (or click the **Slide Layout button** on the status bar).
- Choose the **Text and Clip Art layout** as shown in Figure 2.6a. Click the **Apply command button** to change the slide layout.

ADDING CLIP ART

The easiest way to add clip art to a bulleted list is to change to the Slide view, then change the AutoLayout of the slide. Click the Slide Layout button on the status bar, choose the AutoLayout with Text and Clip Art, and click the Apply command button. Double click the clip art placeholder on the slide, then select the desired image from the ClipArt Gallery in the usual fashion.

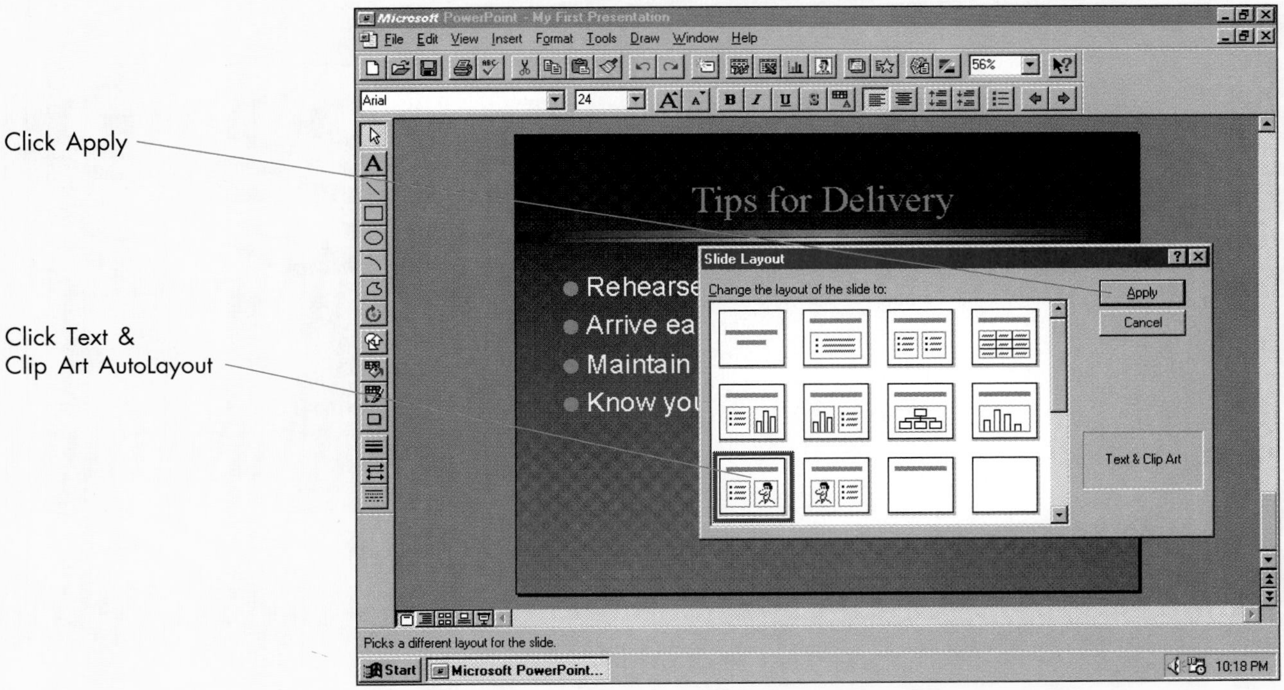

Click Apply
Click Text & Clip Art AutoLayout
Microsoft PowerPoint - My First Presentation
File Edit View Insert Format Tools Draw Window Help
56%
Arial
24
Tips for Delivery
Rehearse
Arrive ea
Maintain
Know yo
Slide Layout
Change the layout of the slide to:
Apply
Cancel
Text & Clip Art
Picks a different layout for the slide.
Start
Microsoft PowerPoint...
10:18 PM

(a) Change the AutoLayout (step 1)

FIGURE 2.6 Hands-on Exercise 2

STEP 2: Add the Clip Art

- Double click the **placeholder** on the slide to add clip art. You will see the Microsoft ClipArt Gallery dialog box as shown in Figure 2.6b (although you may not see all of the categories listed in the figure).
- Scroll until you can click the **People category**. Click the **down arrow** to scroll through the available images until you can select the **Man at Podium.** Click **Insert** to add the clip art to the slide.
- Save the presentation.

FIND THE RIGHT CLIP ART

The Find button within the ClipArt Gallery enables you to search for specific images. Open the ClipArt Gallery, then click the Find button to display the Find Clip Art dialog box. Click in the Description text box, then enter a key word (e.g., woman) that describes the clip art you want. Click the Find Now button, and the ClipArt Gallery will search for images that match the description. Remember to install the additional clip art images from the Valuepack on the Office CD-ROM.

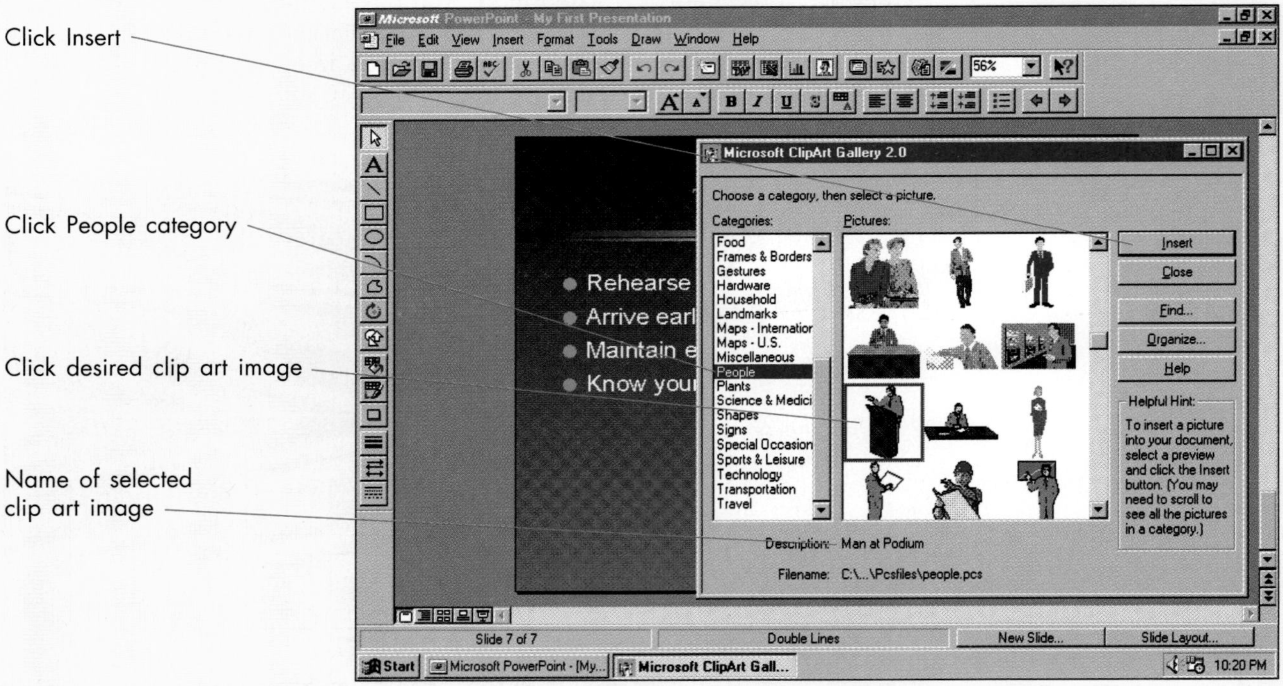
Click Insert
Click People category
Click desired clip art image
Name of selected clip art image
Microsoft PowerPoint - My First Presentation
File Edit View Insert Format Tools Draw Window Help
Microsoft ClipArt Gallery 2.0
Choose a category, then select a picture.
Categories:
Pictures:
Food
Frames & Borders
Gestures
Hardware
Household
Landmarks
Maps - Internatior
Maps - U.S.
Miscellaneous
People
Plants
Science & Medici
Shapes
Signs
Special Occasion
Sports & Leisure
Technology
Transportation
Travel
Insert
Close
Find...
Organize...
Help
Helpful Hint:
To insert a picture into your document, select a preview and click the Insert button. (You may need to scroll to see all the pictures in a category.)
Description: Man at Podium
Filename: C:\...\Pcsfiles\people.pcs
Rehearse
Arrive earl
Maintain e
Know you
Slide 7 of 7
Double Lines
New Slide...
Slide Layout...
Start
Microsoft PowerPoint - [My...
Microsoft ClipArt Gall...
10:20 PM

(b) Add the Clip Art (step 2)

FIGURE 2.6 Hands-on Exercise 2

STEP 3: Add Transition Effects

- Click the **Slide Sorter View button** to change to the Slide Sorter view as shown in Figure 2.6c. The number of slides you see at one time depends on the resolution of your monitor and the zoom percentage.
- Press **Ctrl+Home** to select the first slide. Pull down the **Tools menu,** then click **Slide Transition** to display the dialog box in Figure 2.6c. Click the **down arrow** on the Effect list box, then click the **Blinds Vertical** effect. You will see the effect displayed on the sample slide (dog) in the Transition box. If you miss the effect, click the **dog** (or the **key**) to repeat the effect.
- Click **OK** to accept the transition and close the dialog box. A slide icon appears under slide 1, indicating that a transition effect has been implemented. The effect you chose (Blinds Vertical) appears in the Transition Effects list box on the Slide Sorter toolbar.
- Point to slide 2, click the **right mouse button** to display a shortcut menu, then click the **Slide Transition command.** Choose **Checkerboard Across** as the effect, click the **Slow option button,** then click **OK** to close the Slide Transition dialog box.
- Save the presentation.

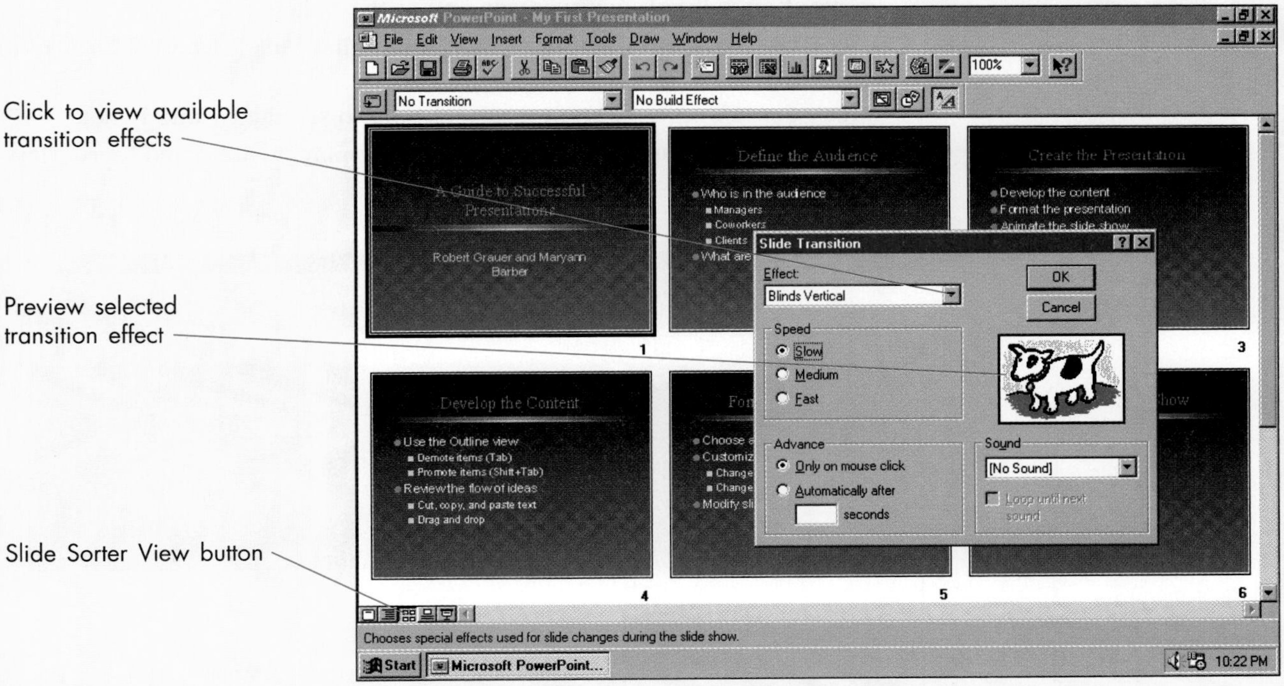
Click to view available transition effects
Preview selected transition effect
Slide Sorter View button
Microsoft PowerPoint - My First Presentation
File Edit View Insert Format Tools Draw Window Help
100%
No Transition
No Build Effect
A Guide to Successful Presentations
Robert Grauer and Maryann Barber
Define the Audience
Who is in the audience
Managers
Coworkers
Clients
What are
Create the Presentation
Develop the content
Format the presentation
Animate the slide show
Slide Transition
Effect:
Blinds Vertical
OK
Cancel
Speed
Slow
Medium
Fast
Advance
Only on mouse click
Automatically after
seconds
Sound
[No Sound]
Loop until next sound
Develop the Content
Use the Outline view
Demote items (Tab)
Promote items (Shift+Tab)
Review the flow of ideas
Cut, copy, and paste text
Drag and drop
Choose
Customiz
Change
Change
Modify sl
1
3
4
5
6
Chooses special effects used for slide changes during the slide show.
Start
Microsoft PowerPoint...
10:22 PM

(c) Add a Transition (step 3)

FIGURE 2.6 Hands-on Exercise 2 (continued)

CHANGE THE MAGNIFICATION

Click the down arrow on the Zoom Control box to change the display magnification, which in turn controls the size of individual slides. The higher the magnification, the easier it is to read the text of an individual slide, but the fewer slides you see at one time. Conversely, changing to a smaller magnification decreases the size of the individual slides, but enables you to see more of the presentation. Use whatever magnification appeals to you.

STEP 4: Create a Build

- Press **Ctrl+End** to move to the last slide (the slide containing the clip art image). Point to the slide, and click the **right mouse button** to display a shortcut menu as shown in Figure 2.6d.
- Click or point to **Build Slide Text,** then click **Fly From Left** as shown in the figure.
- Click the **Slide Show button.** You will see the title of the slide as well as the clip art. You will not, however, see any of the bullets.
  - Click the **left mouse button** to display the first bullet, which flies in from the left.
  - Click the **left mouse button** a second time to see the second bullet.
  - Click the **left mouse button** twice more to display the third and fourth (last) bullets.

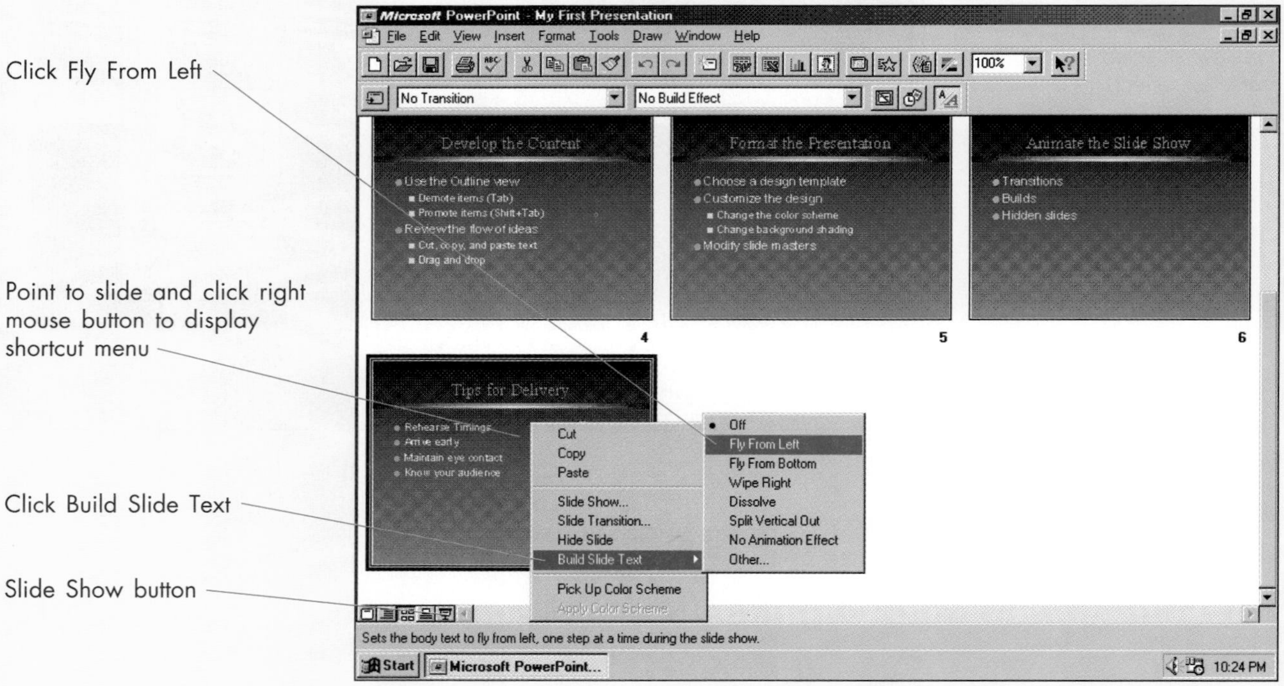
Click Fly From Left
Point to slide and click right mouse button to display shortcut menu
Click Build Slide Text
Slide Show button
Microsoft PowerPoint - My First Presentation
File Edit View Insert Format Tools Draw Window Help
100%
No Transition
No Build Effect
Develop the Content
Use the Outline view
Demote items (Tab)
Promote items (Shift+Tab)
Review the flow of ideas
Cut, copy, and paste text
Drag and drop
Format the Presentation
Choose a design template
Customize the design
Change the color scheme
Change background shading
Modify slide masters
Animate the Slide Show
Transitions
Builds
Hidden slides
4
5
6
Tips for Delivery
Rehearse Timings
Arrive early
Maintain eye contact
Know your audience
Cut
Copy
Paste
Slide Show...
Slide Transition...
Hide Slide
Build Slide Text
Pick Up Color Scheme
Apply Color Scheme
Off
Fly From Left
Fly From Bottom
Wipe Right
Dissolve
Split Vertical Out
No Animation Effect
Other...
Sets the body text to fly from left, one step at a time during the slide show.
Start
Microsoft PowerPoint...
10:24 PM

(d) Add a Build (step 4)

FIGURE 2.6 Hands-on Exercise 2 (continued)

➤ Press the **Esc key** to end the show and return to the Slide Sorter view.

➤ Save the presentation.

ANIMATION SETTINGS

Add additional interest to a build by displaying the bullets a letter or a word at a time. Select the slide to which you want to add the build, pull down the Tools menu, click Build Slide Text, then click Other to display the Animation Settings dialog box. Click the down arrow on the Build Options dialog box to choose how you want the build to occur (e.g., by first- or second-level bullets). Click the down arrow on the various list boxes to choose the special effects. Click OK to accept the settings and close the dialog box. Click the Slide Show button on the status bar to view the build effect (click the left mouse button to display each bullet).

STEP 5: Animation Settings (clip art)

➤ Be sure that the last slide is still selected, then change to the Slide view. Point to the clip art object, click the **right mouse button** to display a shortcut menu, then click **Animation Settings** to display the dialog box in Figure 2.6e:

- Click the **down arrow** on the Build Options list box. Click **Build.**
- Click the **down arrow** on the first Effects list box. Click **Fly From Top.**

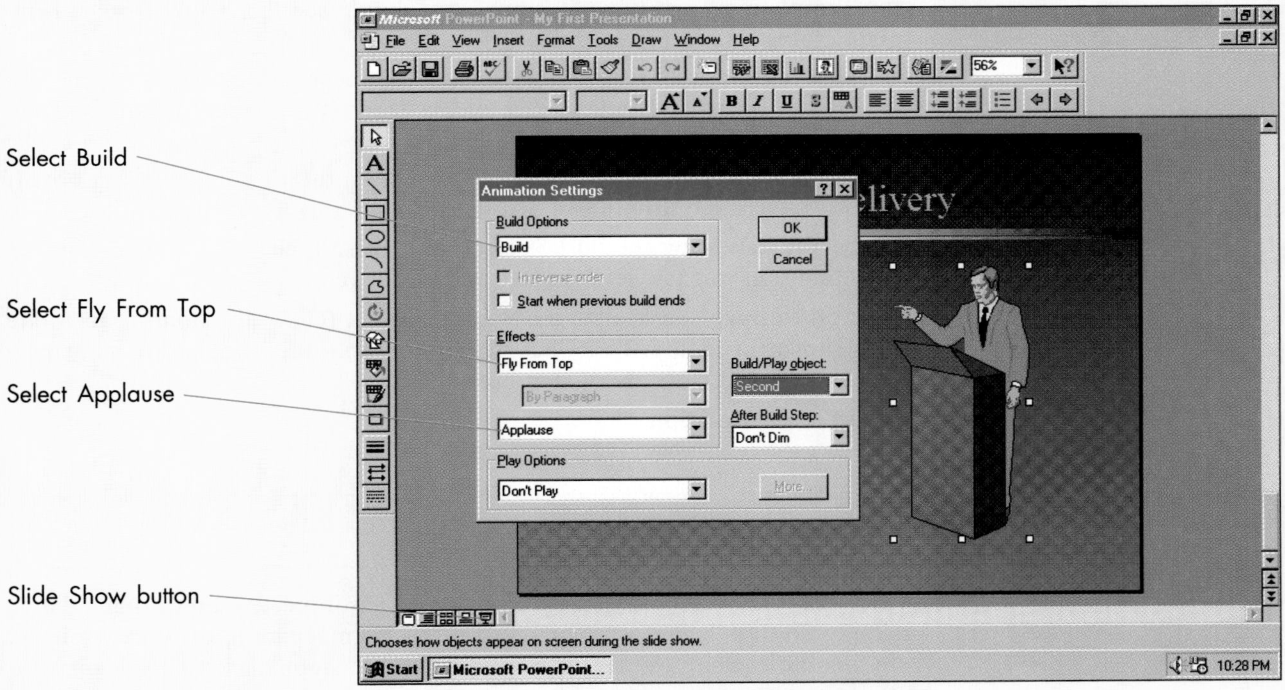
Select Build
Select Fly From Top
Select Applause
Slide Show button
Microsoft PowerPoint - My First Presentation
File Edit View Insert Format Tools Draw Window Help
56%
Animation Settings
Build Options
Build
In reverse order
Start when previous build ends
OK
Cancel
Effects
Fly From Top
By Paragraph
Applause
Build/Play object:
Second
After Build Step:
Don't Dim
Play Options
Don't Play
More...
elivery
Chooses how objects appear on screen during the slide show.
Start
Microsoft PowerPoint...
10:28 PM

(e) Animation Settings (step 5)

FIGURE 2.6 Hands-on Exercise 2 (continued)

- Click the **down arrow** on the last Effects list box. Click **Applause** (you need a sound card to hear the effect).
- Click the **down arrow** on the Build/Play object list box to select **Second.**
- Click **OK** to accept the settings and close the dialog box.

➤ Click the **Slide Show button** to view the animation effects for this slide. Click the **mouse** several times to see the bullets fly in from the left. Click the **mouse** one additional time (after the last bullet) to watch the clip art fly in from the top to the sound of applause.

➤ Press **Esc** to leave the show and continue building the presentation.

SELECTING MULTIPLE SLIDES

You can apply the same transition or build effect to multiple slides with a single command. Change to the Slide Sorter view, then press and hold the Shift key as you click multiple slides to select the slides. Use the Tools menu or the Slide Sorter toolbar to select the desired transition or build effect when all the slides have been selected. (You can select every slide by choosing the Select All command in the Edit menu.) Click anywhere in the Slide Sorter view to deselect the slides and continue working.

STEP 6: Change the Template

➤ Pull down the **Format menu** and click **Apply Design Template** or double click the Template area of the status bar. You should see the Apply Design Template dialog box in Figure 2.6f.

- The **Presentation Designs folder** should appear automatically in the List box. If it doesn't, change to this folder, which is contained within the Templates folder within the MSOffice folder.
- **Presentation Templates** should be selected in the Files of Type list box. If it isn't, click the **drop-down arrow** to change this file type.
- The **Preview view** should be selected. If it isn't, click the **Preview button** so that you can preview the selected template.
- Scroll through the available designs to select (click) the **Soaring template** as shown in Figure 2.6f. Click **Apply** to apply the template to your presentation and close the dialog box.

➤ Save the presentation.

CHANGE THE TEMPLATE

You can change the Design Template at any time, either through the Apply Design Template command in the Format menu, or more easily by double clicking the template portion of the status bar, which displays the name of the current template. Either way you will see the Apply Design Template dialog box from which you can select a new template.

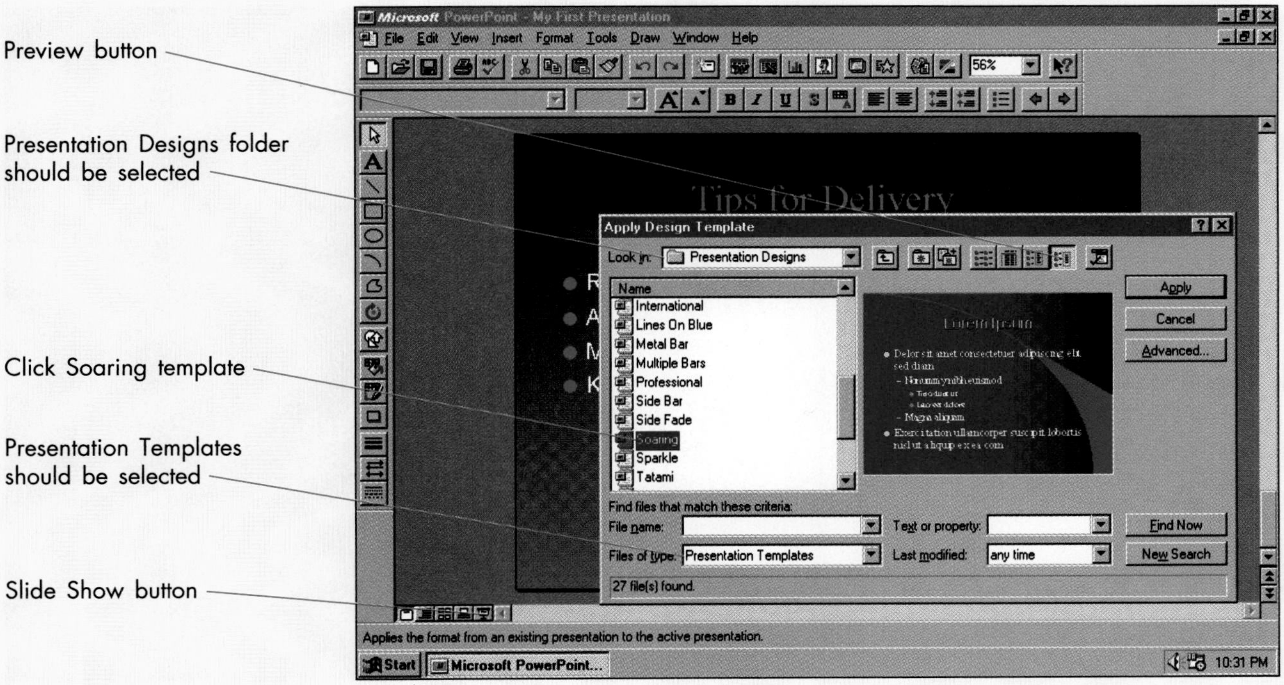
Preview button
Presentation Designs folder should be selected
Click Soaring template
Presentation Templates should be selected
Slide Show button
Microsoft PowerPoint - My First Presentation
File Edit View Insert Format Tools Draw Window Help
56%
Tips for Delivery
Apply Design Template
Look in: Presentation Designs
Name
International
Lines On Blue
Metal Bar
Multiple Bars
Professional
Side Bar
Side Fade
Soaring
Sparkle
Tatami
Apply
Cancel
Advanced...
Find files that match these criteria:
File name:
Text or property:
Find Now
Files of type: Presentation Templates
Last modified: any time
New Search
27 file(s) found.
Applies the format from an existing presentation to the active presentation.
Start
Microsoft PowerPoint...
10:31 PM

(f) Change the Design Template (step 6)

FIGURE 2.6 Hands-on Exercise 2 (continued)

STEP 7: Show the Presentation

- Press **Ctrl+Home** to return to the first slide, then click the **Slide Show button** to view the presentation. You should see the slide in Figure 2.6g.
- Click the **left mouse button** (or press the **PgDn key** or the letter **N**) to move to the next slide (or to the next bullet on the current slide when a build is in effect).
- Press the **PgUp key** (or the letter **P**) to return to the previous slide (or to the previous bullet on the current slide when a build is in effect).
- Continue to view the presentation until you come to the end. Click the left mouse button a final time to return to the Slide view.

THE MEETING MINDER

The Meeting Minder enables you to keep track of action items as they occur and to summarize them at the end of the presentation. Click the right mouse button at any time to display a shortcut menu, click Meeting Minder, then click the Action Items tab in the Meeting Minder dialog box. Enter the action item(s) and click OK to close the dialog box, then continue through the slide show. An Action Items slide will appear at the end of the presentation with the items you added during the show.

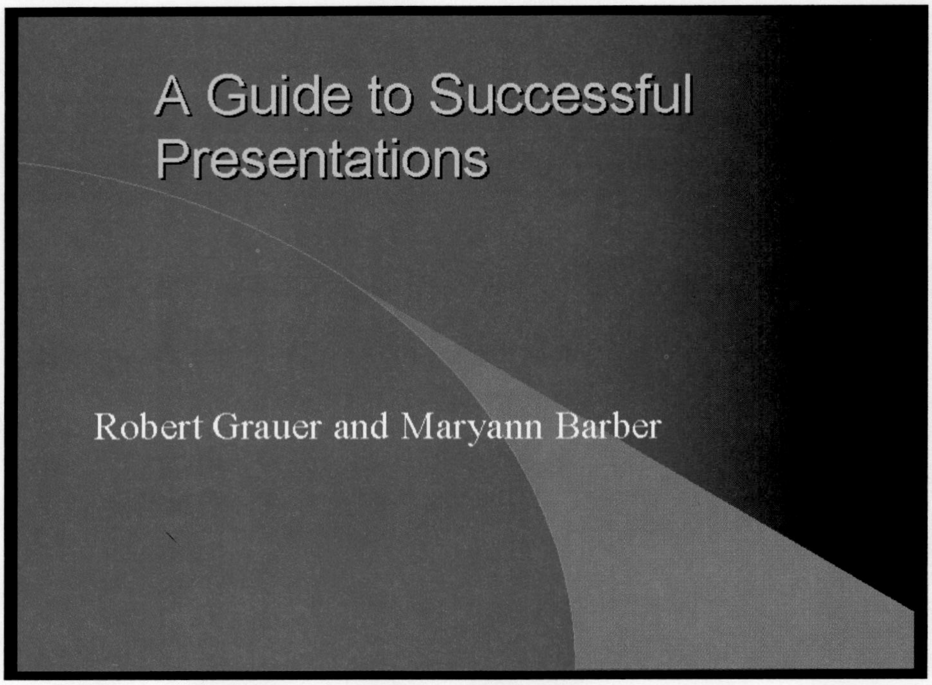
A Guide to Successful Presentations
Robert Grauer and Maryann Barber

(g) The Completed Presentation

FIGURE 2.6 Hands-on Exercise 2 (continued)

STEP 8: Exit PowerPoint

- Exit PowerPoint if you do not want to continue with the next exercise at this time.

FINE-TUNING A PRESENTATION

A template is a design specification that controls every aspect of a presentation. It specifies the formatting of the text, the fonts and colors that are used, and the design, size, and placement of the bullets. You can change the look of a presentation at any time by applying a different template. Changing from the Double Lines to the Soaring template (as you did in the previous exercise) changes the appearance of the presentation in every way.

What if, however, you want to make subtle changes to the template? In other words, you are content with the overall design, but you want to change one or more of its elements. You don't want a radical change, but you want to fine-tune the presentation by modifying its color scheme and/or ***background shading.*** Or perhaps you want to add a consistent element to every slide, such as a corporate name or logo.

The Color Scheme

A ***color scheme*** is a set of eight balanced colors that is associated with a template. It consists of a background color, a color for the title of each slide, a color for lines and text, and five additional colors to provide accents to different elements, such as shadows and fill colors. Each template has a default color scheme, which is applied when the template is selected. Each template also has a set of alternate color schemes from which to choose.

Figure 2.7a displays the title slide of our presentation at the end of the second exercise. The Soaring template has just been selected and the default (blue) color scheme is in effect. Figure 2.7b displays the Color Scheme dialog box (which is accessed through the Format menu) with the suggested color schemes for this template. To choose one of the other color schemes (e.g., green), select the color scheme, then click the Apply All command button to apply the new color scheme to the entire presentation.

You have additional flexibility in that you can change any of the individual colors within a color scheme. Select the desired color scheme, click the Custom tab, select the color you wish to change (e.g., the color of the Title Text), then click the Change Color command button as shown in Figure 2.7c. Figure 2.7d

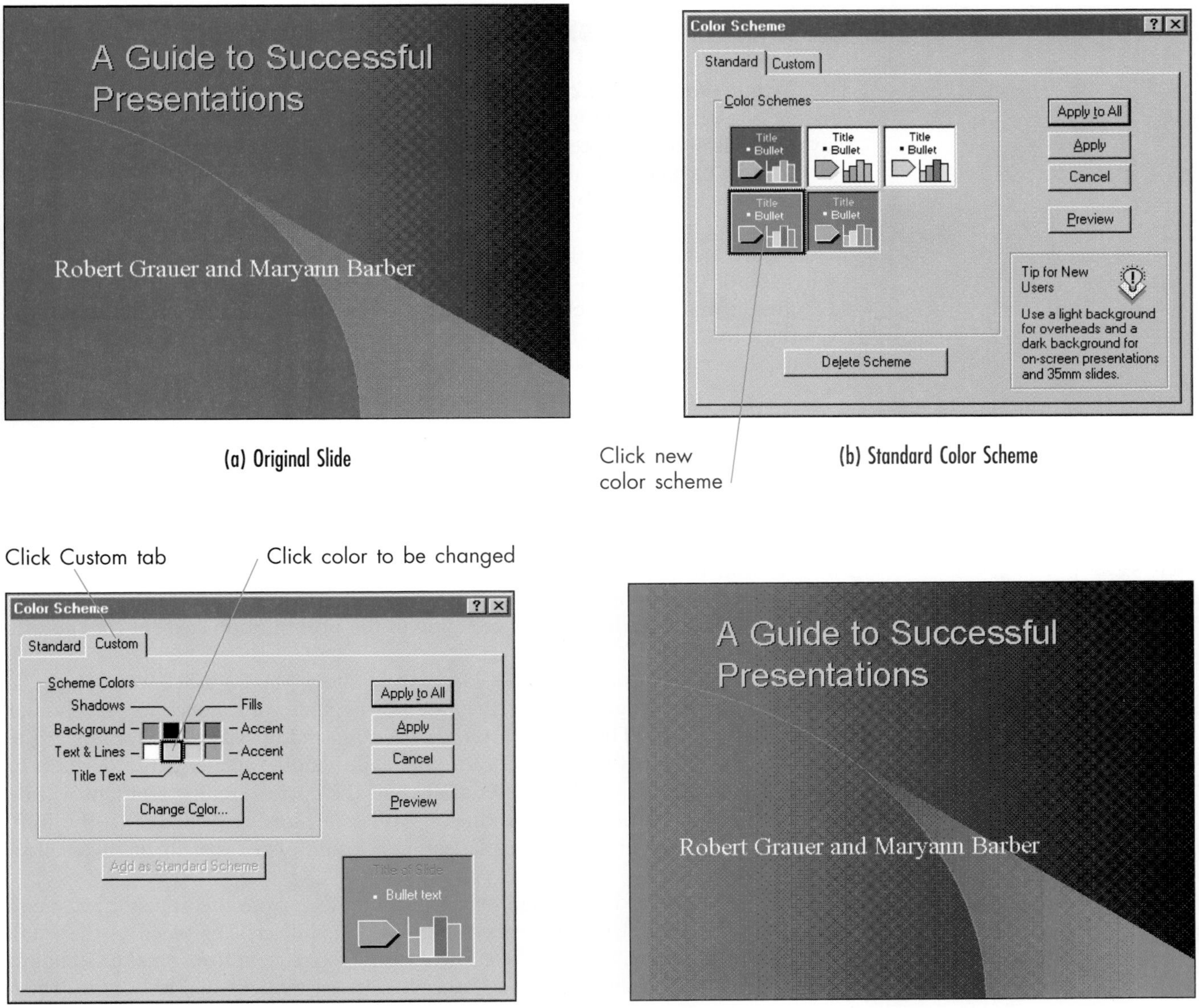

A Guide to Successful Presentations
Robert Grauer and Maryann Barber
Color Scheme
Standard
Custom
Color Schemes
Title
• Bullet
Apply to All
Apply
Cancel
Preview
Tip for New Users
Use a light background for overheads and a dark background for on-screen presentations and 35mm slides.
Delete Scheme
Click new color scheme
Click Custom tab
Click color to be changed
Scheme Colors
Shadows
Fills
Background
Accent
Text & Lines
Accent
Title Text
Accent
Change Color...
Add as Standard Scheme
Title of Slide
• Bullet text
A Guide to Successful Presentations
Robert Grauer and Maryann Barber

(a) Original Slide

(b) Standard Color Scheme

(c) Custom Colors

(d) Modified Slide

FIGURE 2.7 Changing the Color Scheme

displays the title slide after the color scheme has been changed to green, then further customized by changing the color of the title text to bright yellow.

> **SLIDES VERSUS TRANSPARENCIES**
>
> Choose the color scheme in conjunction with the means of delivery. Light backgrounds work best for overhead transparencies, whereas dark backgrounds are preferable for computer presentations and 35-mm slides. This suggestion is presented in the Color Scheme dialog box itself (as can be seen in Figure 2.7a). We urge you to look for similar tips as you use other PowerPoint features.

The Background Shading

The ***Custom Background command*** in the Format menu changes the background shading of a slide, enabling you to truly fine-tune a presentation. Figure 2.8a displays the title slide of a presentation using the International template. This design incorporates background shading that goes from blue to black in the top half of the slide. The shading is built into the template according to the Shaded Fill dialog box in Figure 2.8b.

Figure 2.8c changes the parameters within the Shaded Fill dialog box to use a single color (blue) and a horizontal shading pattern. Again, you have additional flexibility in that you can change the variation in color by dragging the scroll box from dark to light. You can also choose from one of four variations of horizontal shading. The modified title slide is shown in Figure 2.8d.

PowerPoint Masters

One of the best ways to customize a presentation is to add a unifying element to each slide, such as a corporate name or logo. You could add the element to every slide, but that would be unnecessarily tedious. It is much easier to use the View menu to add the element to the ***slide master,*** which defines the formatting and other elements that appear on the individual slides. Any change to the slide master is automatically reflected in every slide in the presentation (except for the title slide.)

Consider, for example, the slide master shown in Figure 2.9 on page 74, which contains a placeholder for the title of the slide and a second placeholder for the bulleted text. The slide master also contains additional placeholders at the bottom of the slide for the date, footer, and slide number. Change the position of any of these elements on the master slide, and the corresponding element will be changed throughout the presentation. In similar fashion, any change to the font, point size, or alignment within a placeholder would also carry through to all of the individual slides.

The slide master is modified by using commands from the appropriate menu or toolbar. The easiest way to place a logo on the slide master (such as the small computer in Figure 2.9), is to click the Insert Clip Art button on the Standard toolbar. This in turn displays the Microsoft ClipArt Gallery dialog box, in which you select the desired clip art. Once the clip art has been added to the slide master, you can click and drag its sizing handles to move and size the clip art like any other Windows object. Every slide in the presentation will contain the clip art image that was added to the slide master.

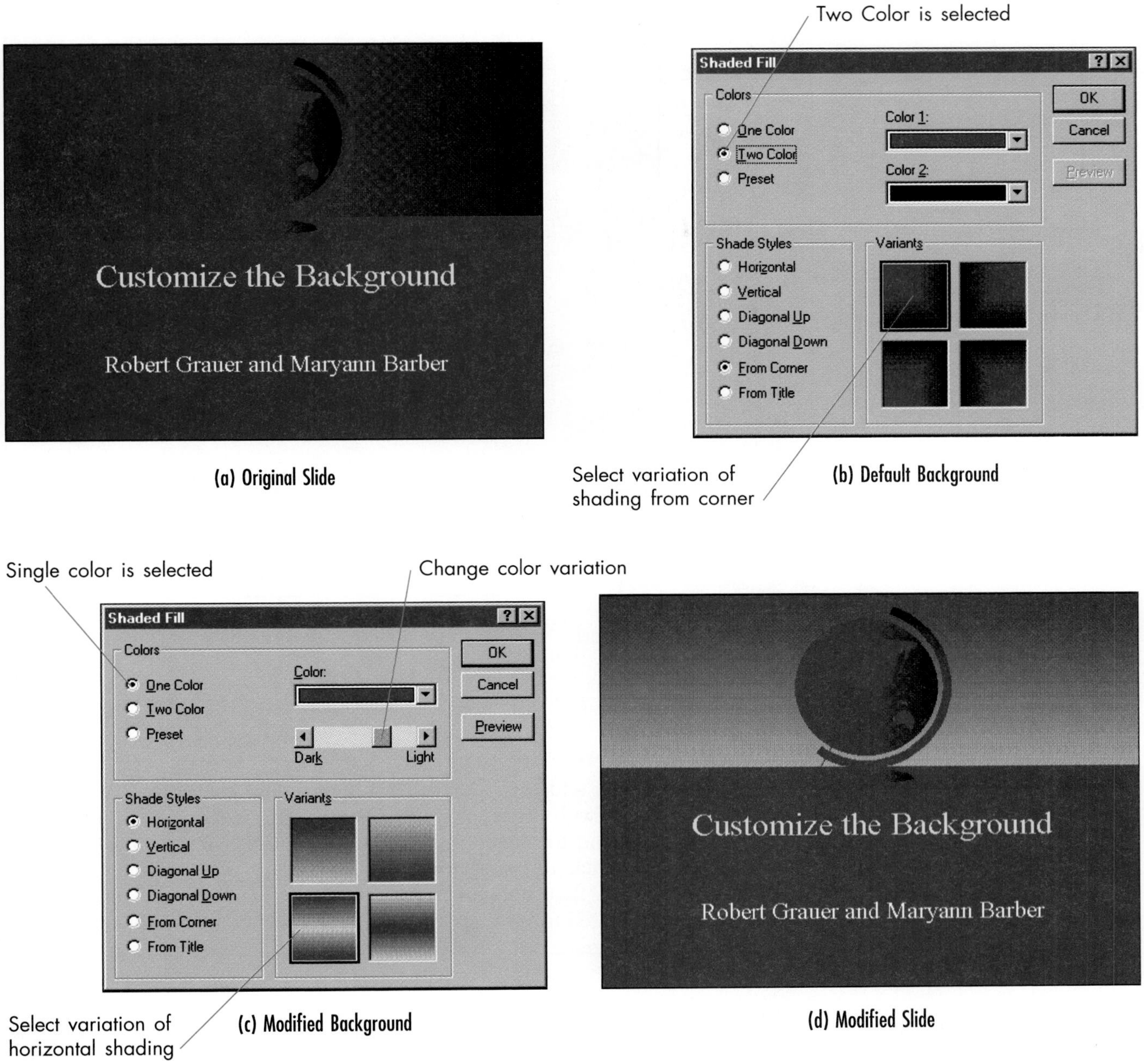
Two Color is selected
Customize the Background
Robert Grauer and Maryann Barber
Shaded Fill
Colors
One Color
Two Color
Preset
Color 1:
Color 2:
OK
Cancel
Preview
Shade Styles
Horizontal
Vertical
Diagonal Up
Diagonal Down
From Corner
From Title
Variants
(a) Original Slide
Select variation of shading from corner
(b) Default Background
Single color is selected
Change color variation
Shaded Fill
Colors
One Color
Two Color
Preset
Color:
Dark
Light
OK
Cancel
Preview
Shade Styles
Horizontal
Vertical
Diagonal Up
Diagonal Down
From Corner
From Title
Variants
Customize the Background
Robert Grauer and Maryann Barber
Select variation of horizontal shading
(c) Modified Background
(d) Modified Slide

FIGURE 2.8 Customize the Background

Style Checker

Are you conscious of the subtle uses of style that occur when you create a presentation? For example, do you use all uppercase letters for each word in the title of your slides, or do you begin each word with an uppercase letter? Do you place periods at the end of each title or each bullet? Is there a uniform look from one slide to the next with respect to punctuation and capitalization? Perhaps you never thought about the appearance of your slides in such detail, but it takes only a few minutes to ensure uniform style throughout a presentation.

The ***Style Checker*** checks the slides in a presentation for consistency in punctuation and capitalization. It is similar in concept to the ***Spell Check*** and is illustrated in steps 1 and 2 in the following hands-on exercise.

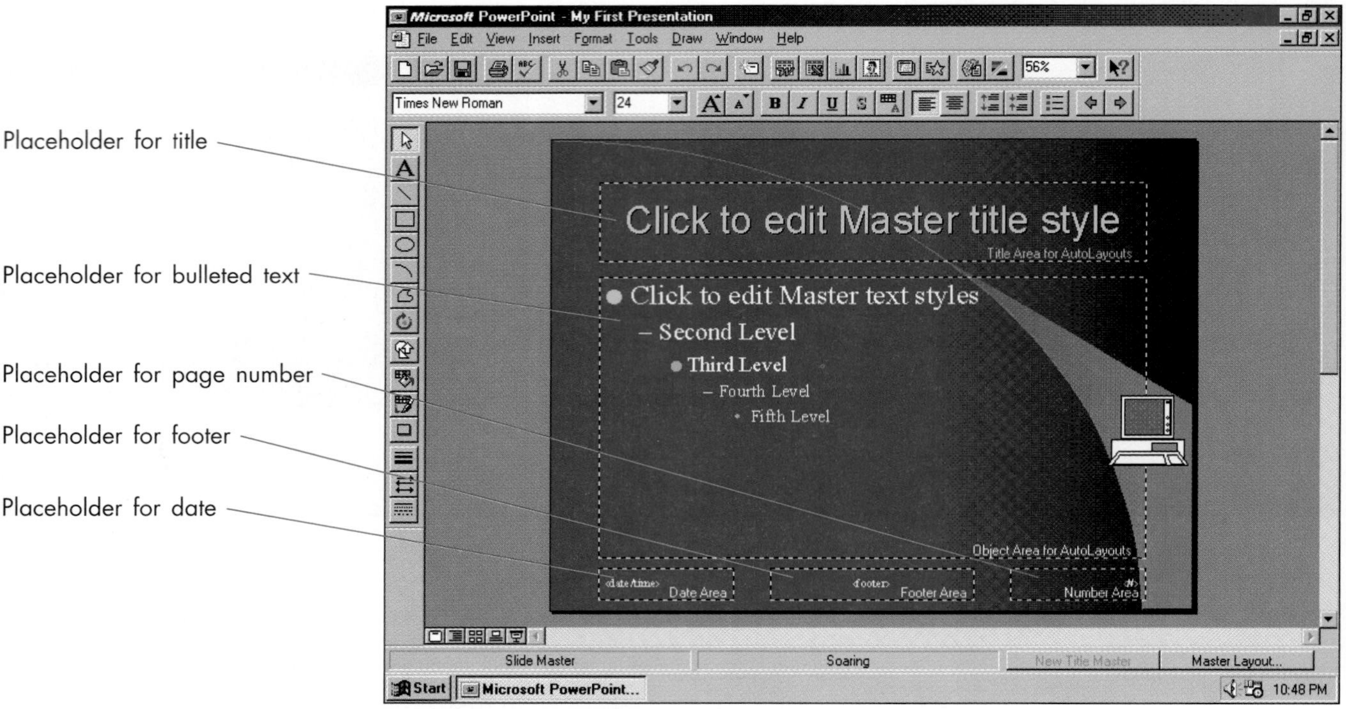
Placeholder for title
Placeholder for bulleted text
Placeholder for page number
Placeholder for footer
Placeholder for date
Microsoft PowerPoint - My First Presentation
File Edit View Insert Format Tools Draw Window Help
Times New Roman
24
56%
Click to edit Master title style
Title Area for AutoLayouts
Click to edit Master text styles
– Second Level
Third Level
– Fourth Level
Fifth Level
Object Area for AutoLayouts
Date Area
Footer Area
Number Area
Slide Master
Soaring
New Title Master
Master Layout...
Start
Microsoft PowerPoint...
10:48 PM

FIGURE 2.9 The Slide Master

SET A TIME LIMIT

We warn you—it's addictive and it can be very time consuming. Yes, it's fun to experiment with different color schemes and backgrounds, but it is all too easy to spend too much time fine-tuning the design by changing its color scheme or background shading. Concentrate on the content of your presentation rather than its appearance. Impose a limit on the amount of time you will spend on formatting. End the session when the limit is reached.

HANDS-ON EXERCISE 3

Fine-Tuning a Presentation

Objective: To use the Style Checker to check for consistency in punctuation and capitalization; to experiment with different color schemes and custom backgrounds. Use Figure 2.10 as a guide in the exercise.

STEP 1: Open the Presentation

- Start PowerPoint and open **My First Presentation** from the previous exercise. Change to the **Outline view** as shown in Figure 2.10a.
- Change the title of the first slide so that it appears in lowercase. Change the title of the second slide to uppercase. Add a period at the end of both titles.

Change title slide to lower-case and add a period

Change title to upper-case and add a period

Click Start

Click Outline view

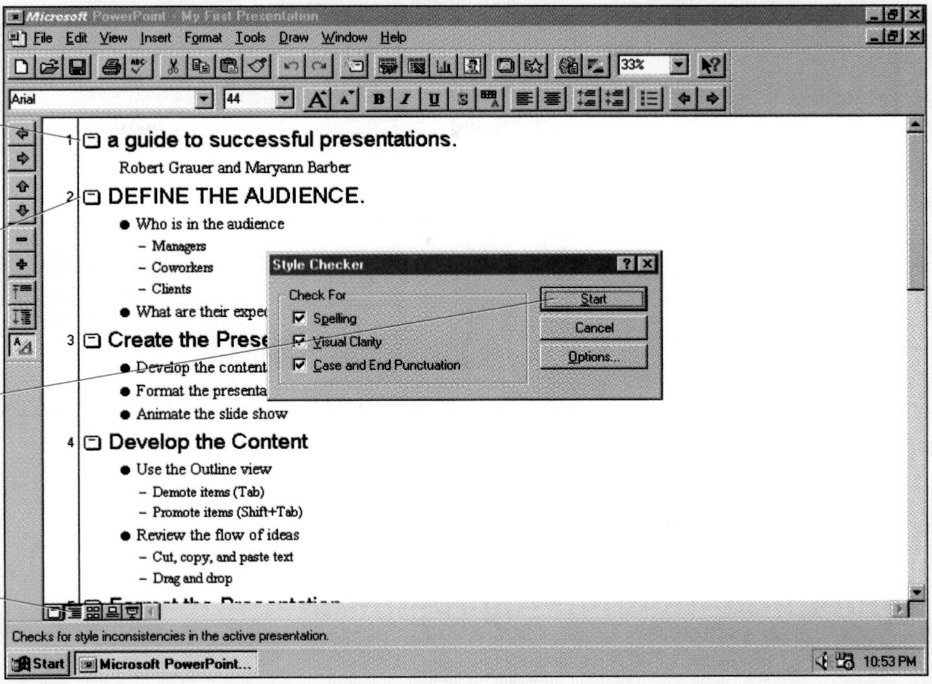
Microsoft PowerPoint - My First Presentation
File Edit View Insert Format Tools Draw Window Help
a guide to successful presentations.
Robert Grauer and Maryann Barber
DEFINE THE AUDIENCE.
Who is in the audience
Managers
Coworkers
Clients
Create the Prese
Develop the content
Format the presenta
Animate the slide show
Develop the Content
Use the Outline view
Demote items (Tab)
Promote items (Shift+Tab)
Review the flow of ideas
Cut, copy, and paste text
Drag and drop
Style Checker
Check For
Spelling
Visual Clarity
Case and End Punctuation
Start
Cancel
Options...
Checks for style inconsistencies in the active presentation.
Start
Microsoft PowerPoint...
10:53 PM

(a) The Style Checker (step 1)

FIGURE 2.10 Hands-on Exercise 3

➤ Press **Ctrl+Home** to return to the beginning of the presentation. Pull down the **Tools menu.** Click **Style Checker** to display the Style Checker dialog box in Figure 2.10a. Click **Start** to begin checking the document.

THE DOCUMENTS SUBMENU

One of the fastest ways to get to a recently used document, regardless of the application, is through the Windows 95 Start menu, which includes a Documents submenu containing the last 15 documents that were opened. Click the Start button, click (or point to) the Documents submenu, then click the document you wish to open (e.g., My First Presentation) if it appears on the submenu.

STEP 2: The Style Checker

➤ The Style Checker goes through the document looking for various errors. Some mistakes are fixed automatically (e.g., a change in case), whereas others require confirmation from you.

➤ Click the **Change button** to remove the period at the end of the title as shown in Figure 2.10b. Click the **Change button** a second time when asked to remove the period at the end of the second slide.

➤ Continue to check the presentation until PowerPoint indicates it has finished, then click **OK** to exit the Style Checker.

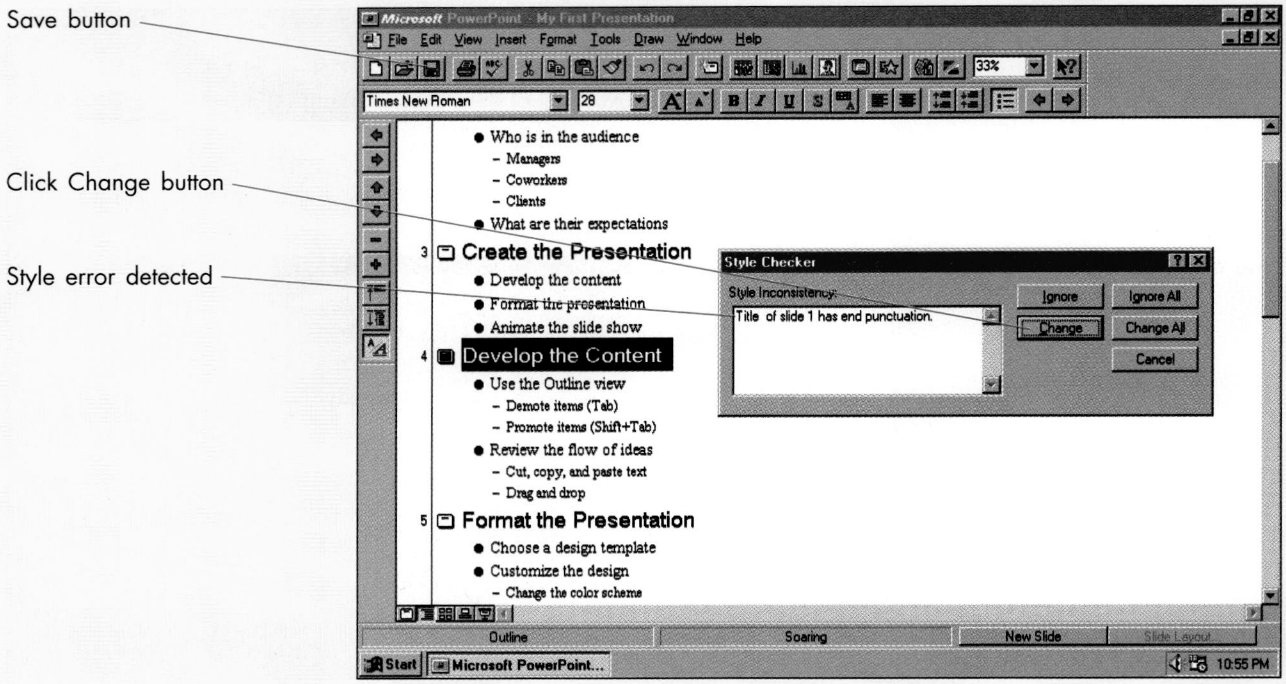
Save button
Click Change button
Style error detected
Microsoft PowerPoint - My First Presentation
File Edit View Insert Format Tools Draw Window Help
Times New Roman
28
33%
Who is in the audience
Managers
Coworkers
Clients
What are their expectations
Create the Presentation
Develop the content
Format the presentation
Animate the slide show
Develop the Content
Use the Outline view
Demote items (Tab)
Promote items (Shift+Tab)
Review the flow of ideas
Cut, copy, and paste text
Drag and drop
Format the Presentation
Choose a design template
Customize the design
Change the color scheme
Style Checker
Style Inconsistency:
Title of slide 1 has end punctuation.
Ignore
Ignore All
Change
Change All
Cancel
Outline
Soaring
New Slide
Slide Layout...
Start
Microsoft PowerPoint...
10:55 PM

(b) The Style Checker Continued (step 2)

FIGURE 2.10 Hands-on Exercise 3 (continued)

➤ Look carefully at the text of the presentation and note the consistency imposed by the Style Checker:

- The titles for slides 1 and 2 have been restored to title case (from lower- and uppercase, respectively).
- The periods at the end of the titles in slides 1 and 2 have been removed.

➤ Click the **Save button** on the Standard toolbar to save the presentation.

CUSTOMIZE THE STYLE CHECKER

The Style Checker enables you to ensure consistency throughout a presentation with respect to capitalization, punctuation, and formatting. The standards are your own, and you can change the default options to meet your personal preferences. Pull down the Tools menu, click Style Checker, then click the Options command button to display a dialog box in which you customize the Style Checker. Select the desired settings under both the Visual Clarity and Case and End Punctuation tabs, click OK to accept the new settings, then click Start to check the presentation for conformity to your standards.

STEP 3: Change the Slide Master

- Pull down the **View menu,** click **Master,** then click **Slide Master** to display the slide master as shown in Figure 2.10c. (The Header and Footer dialog box is not yet visible.)
- Click the **dashed lines** surrounding the number area at the bottom right of the slide to select this element. Press the **Del key** to delete this element.
- Click the **dashed lines** surrounding the footer area in the center of the slide, then click and drag the footer to the right side of the slide as shown in Figure 2.10c.
- Pull down the **View menu.** Click **Header and Footer** to display the Header and Footer dialog box:
  - Select the Date and Time check box. Click the **option button** to Update Automatically.
  - Select the Footer check box, then enter the name of your school as shown in Figure 2.10c.
  - Check the box to suppress the display on the title slide.
  - Click the **Apply to All command button** to accept these settings and close the dialog box.
- Click the **Slide view button** on the status bar, then press the **PgDn key** once or twice to move from slide to slide. You should see today's date and the name of your school at the bottom of each slide except for the title slide. (Press **Ctrl+Home** to view the title slide.)
- Save the presentation.

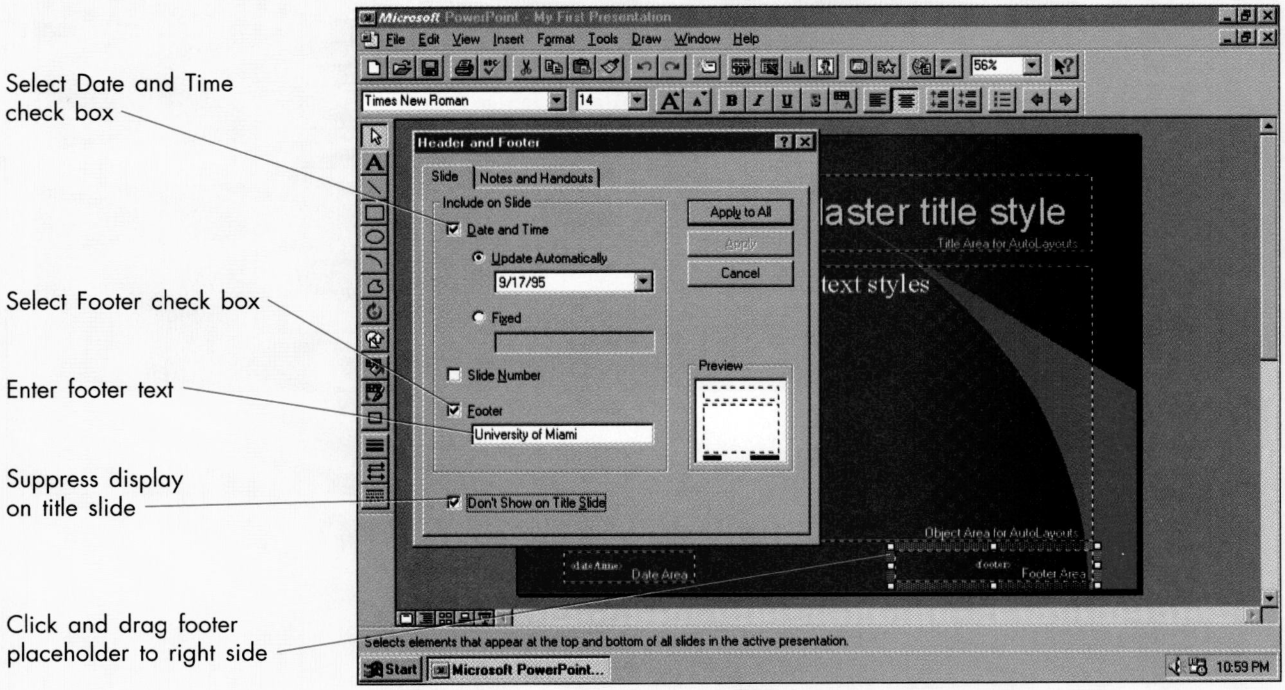

Select Date and Time check box
Select Footer check box
Enter footer text
Suppress display on title slide
Click and drag footer placeholder to right side
Microsoft PowerPoint - My First Presentation
File Edit View Insert Format Tools Draw Window Help
Times New Roman
14
56%
Header and Footer
Slide
Notes and Handouts
Include on Slide
Date and Time
Update Automatically
9/17/95
Fixed
Slide Number
Footer
University of Miami
Don't Show on Title Slide
Apply to All
Apply
Cancel
Preview
Master title style
Title Area for AutoLayouts
text styles
Object Area for AutoLayouts
Date Area
Footer Area
Selects elements that appear at the top and bottom of all slides in the active presentation.
Start
Microsoft PowerPoint...
10:59 PM

(c) Modify the Slide Master (step 3)

FIGURE 2.10 Hands-on Exercise 3 (continued)

THE VIEW BUTTONS AND THE SHIFT KEY

The Slide View button provides the fastest way to change to the slide master. Select any slide other than the title slide, then press and hold the Shift key as you click the Slide View button above the status bar to display the slide master. You can also press and hold the Shift key as you click the Slide Sorter or Outline View buttons to customize the handouts master for slide miniatures and outline handouts.

STEP 4: Change the Color Scheme

- Change to the **Slide Sorter view.** You should see a footer (containing the name of your school) on every slide except the title slide, as shown in Figure 2.10d.
- Pull down the **Format menu.** Click **Slide Color Scheme** to display the Color Scheme dialog box. Select a different color scheme (e.g., green), then click the **Apply to All button** to change the color scheme of every slide.

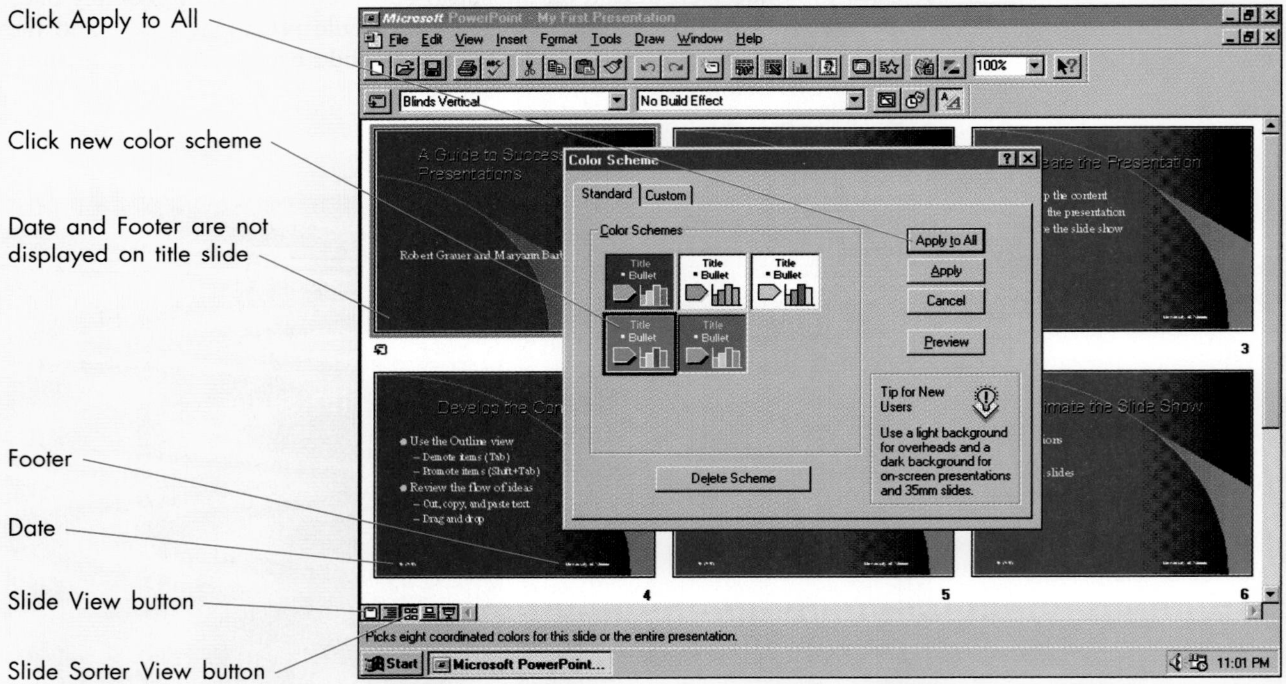

Click Apply to All
Click new color scheme
Date and Footer are not displayed on title slide
Footer
Date
Slide View button
Slide Sorter View button
Microsoft PowerPoint - My First Presentation
File Edit View Insert Format Tools Draw Window Help
Blinds Vertical
No Build Effect
Color Scheme
Standard
Custom
Color Schemes
Apply to All
Apply
Cancel
Preview
Tip for New Users
Use a light background for overheads and a dark background for on-screen presentations and 35mm slides.
Delete Scheme
Picks eight coordinated colors for this slide or the entire presentation.
Start
Microsoft PowerPoint...
11:01 PM

(d) Change the Color Scheme (step 4)

FIGURE 2.10 Hands-on Exercise 3 (continued)

STEP 5: Customize the Background

- Pull down the **Format menu.** Click **Custom Background** to display the Custom Background dialog box in Figure 2.10e.
- Click the **drop-down arrow** to display the various types of backgrounds (which are not shown in Figure 2.10e). Click **Shaded** to display the Shaded Fill dialog box.

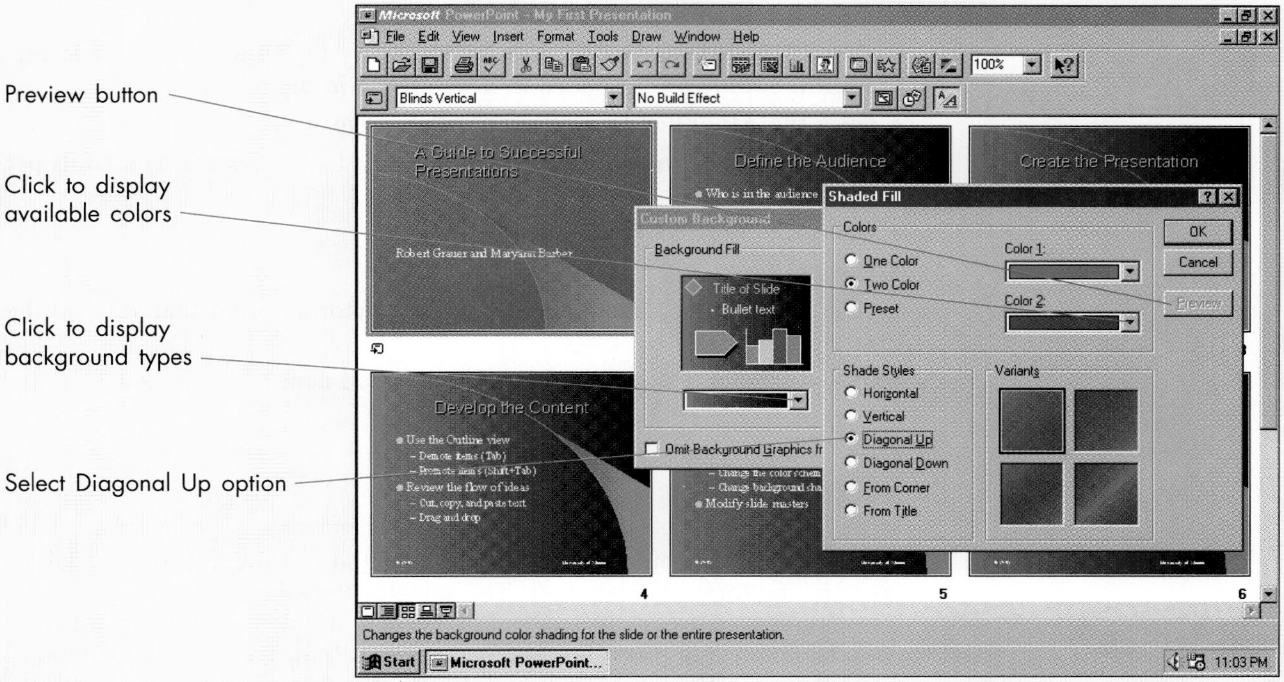
Preview button
Click to display available colors
Click to display background types
Select Diagonal Up option
Microsoft PowerPoint - My First Presentation
File Edit View Insert Format Tools Draw Window Help
Blinds Vertical
No Build Effect
A Guide to Successful Presentations
Robert Grauer and Maryann Barber
Define the Audience
Create the Presentation
Custom Background
Background Fill
Title of Slide
Bullet text
Omit Background Graphics fr
Shaded Fill
Colors
One Color
Two Color
Preset
Color 1:
Color 2:
OK
Cancel
Preview
Shade Styles
Horizontal
Vertical
Diagonal Up
Diagonal Down
From Corner
From Title
Variants
Develop the Content
Changes the background color shading for the slide or the entire presentation.
Start
Microsoft PowerPoint...
11:03 PM

(e) Customize the Background (step 5)

FIGURE 2.10 Hands-on Exercise 3 (continued)

- Click the **drop-down arrow** on the Color 2 list box. Select a different color (e.g., blue). Click the **Diagonal Up option button** as the Shade style.
- Click the **Preview button** to see the effect of these changes on the currently selected slide (slide 1 in Figure 2.10e). Experiment with additional changes, then click **OK** to accept the changes and close the Shaded Fill dialog box.
- Click **Apply to All** to apply the changes to all slides and close the Custom Background dialog box. Use the Undo command to return to the initial design if you are disappointed with your modification.

MULTIPLE LEVEL UNDO COMMAND

The Undo command reverses (undoes) the most recent command. The command is executed from the Edit menu or more easily by clicking the Undo button on the Standard toolbar. Each click of the Undo button reverses one command; that is, click the Undo button and you reverse the last command. Click the Undo button a second time and you reverse the previous command. The Redo button works in reverse and undoes the most recent Undo command (i.e., it redoes the command you just undid). The maximum number of Undo commands (the default is 20) is set through the Tools menu. Pull down the Tools menu, click Options, click the Advanced tab, then enter the desired number.

STEP 6: Print the Audience Handouts

➤ Pull down the **File menu.** Click **Print** to display the Print dialog box in Figure 2.10f. Set the print options to match those in the figure:

- Click the **All option button** as the print range.
- Click the **down arrow** on the Print What list box to select **6 Handouts per page.**
- Check the box to **Frame Slides.**
- Click **OK**.

➤ Submit the audience handouts to your instructor as proof that you did the exercise.

➤ Exit PowerPoint. Congratulations on a job well done.

PRINT THE OUTLINE

You can print the outline of a presentation and distribute it to the audience in the form of a handout. This enables the audience to follow the presentation as it is delivered and gives them an ideal vehicle on which to take notes. Pull down the File menu, click Print, then choose Outline view from the Print What list box. Be sure you know the expected size of the audience so that you will have an adequate number of handouts.

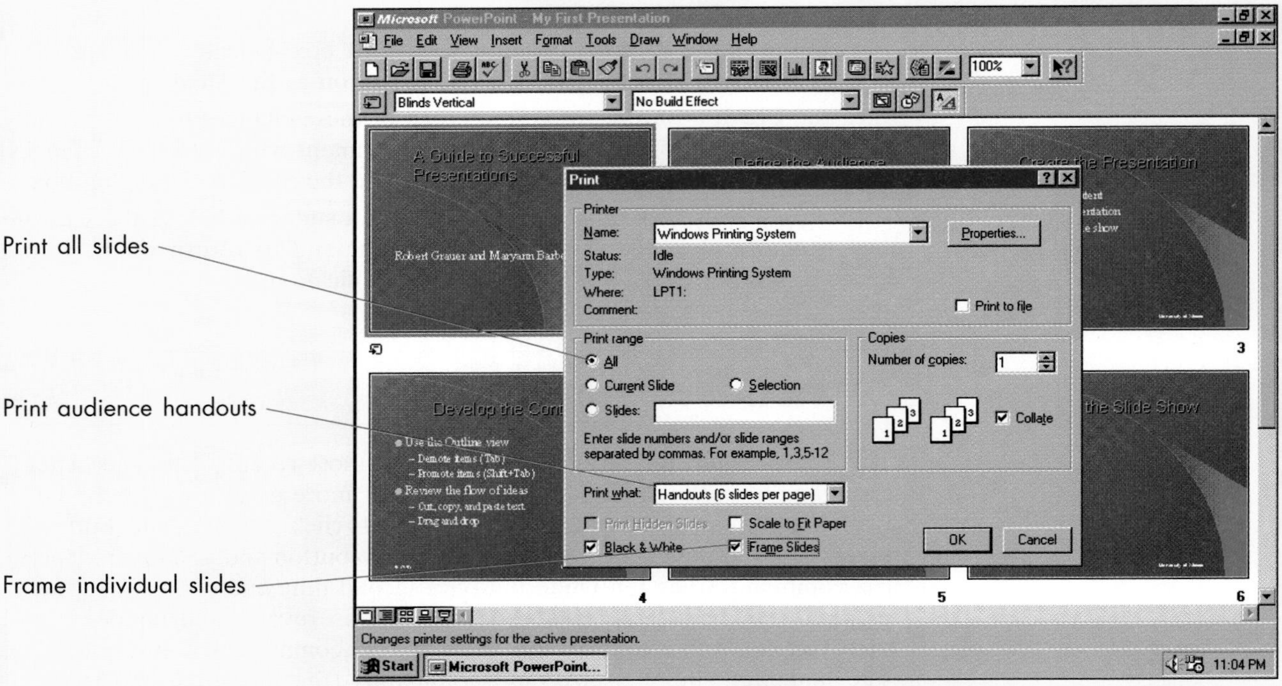

Print all slides
Print audience handouts
Frame individual slides
Microsoft PowerPoint - My First Presentation
File Edit View Insert Format Tools Draw Window Help
100%
Blinds Vertical
No Build Effect
Print
Printer
Name: Windows Printing System
Properties...
Status: Idle
Type: Windows Printing System
Where: LPT1:
Comment:
Print to file
Print range
All
Current Slide
Selection
Slides:
Enter slide numbers and/or slide ranges separated by commas. For example, 1,3,5-12
Copies
Number of copies: 1
Collate
Print what: Handouts (6 slides per page)
Print Hidden Slides
Scale to Fit Paper
Black & White
Frame Slides
OK
Cancel
Changes printer settings for the active presentation.
Start
Microsoft PowerPoint...
11:04 PM

(f) Prepare the Audience Handouts (step 6)

FIGURE 2.10 Hands-on Exercise 3 (continued)

SUMMARY

There are in essence two independent steps to creating a PowerPoint presentation. You must develop the content, and you must format the presentation. Both steps are iterative in nature, and you are likely to go back and forth many times before you are finished.

The text of a presentation can be developed from the Slide view or the Outline view or a combination of the two. The Outline view is easier because it displays the contents of many slides at once, enabling you to see the overall flow of your ideas. You can change the order of the slides and/or move text from one slide to another as necessary. Text can be entered continually in the outline, then promoted or demoted so that it appears on the proper level in the slide.

The AutoContent Wizard asks you questions about the type of presentation you are planning to give, then creates an outline for you. The outline is based on one of many predefined outlines and is a good starting point.

A template is a design specification that controls every aspect of a presentation. It specifies the formatting of the text, the fonts and colors that are used, and the design, size, and placement of the bullets.

Transitions and builds can be added to a presentation for additional interest. Transitions control the way in which one slide moves off the screen and the next slide appears. Builds are used to display the individual elements on a single slide.

The design of a presentation can be customized by modifying its color scheme or background shading. The slide master enables you to add a unifying element to every slide, such as a corporate name or logo.

Every presentation should be checked for spelling. The Style Checker ensures consistency throughout a presentation with respect to capitalization and punctuation.

KEY WORDS AND CONCEPTS

AutoContent Wizard
AutoCorrect
Background color
Background shading
Build
Color scheme
Custom Background command
Demote
Insertion point
Outline toolbar
Promote
Slide icon
Slide master
Slide Sorter toolbar
Spell Check
Style Checker
Template
Transition

MULTIPLE CHOICE

1. Which view displays multiple slides while letting you change the text in a slide?
(a) Outline view
(b) Slide Sorter view
(c) Both (a) and (b)
(d) Neither (a) nor (b)

2. **Where** will the insertion point be after you complete the text for a bullet in the Outline view and press the enter key?
   (a) On the next bullet at the same level of indentation
   (b) On the next bullet at a higher level of indentation
   (c) On the next bullet at a lower level of indentation
   (d) Impossible to determine

3. Which of the following is true?
   (a) Shift+Tab promotes an item to the next higher level
   (b) Tab demotes an item to the next lower level
   (c) Both (a) and (b)
   (d) Neither (a) nor (b)

4. Which of the following is true about the Outline view?
   (a) The position of a slide may be changed by dragging its icon
   (b) All slides display the identical icon regardless of content
   (c) Both (a) and (b)
   (d) Neither (a) nor (b)

5. What advantage, if any, is there to collapsing the Outline view so that only the slide titles are visible?
   (a) More slides are displayed at one time, making it easier to rearrange the slides in the presentation
   (b) Transition and build effects can be added
   (c) Graphic objects become visible
   (d) All of the above

6. Which of the following is true regarding transition and build effects?
   (a) Every slide must have the same transition effect
   (b) Every bullet must have the same build effect
   (c) Both (a) and (b)
   (d) Neither (a) nor (b)

7. The AutoContent Wizard provides suggested presentations for:
   (a) Communicating bad news
   (b) Selling a product, service, or idea
   (c) Both (a) and (b)
   (d) Neither (a) nor (b)

8. Which of the following is true?
   (a) Slides can be added to a presentation after a template has been chosen
   (b) The template can be changed after all of the slides have been created
   (c) Both (a) and (b)
   (d) Neither (a) nor (b)

9. What is the easiest way to add a corporate name to every slide (except the title slide) in the presentation?
   (a) Add the information to the handout master
   (b) Add the information to the slide master
   (c) Both (a) and (b)
   (d) Neither (a) nor (b)

10. Which of the following can be changed after a slide has been created?
    (a) Its layout and transition effect
    (b) Its position within the presentation
    (c) Both (a) and (b)
    (d) Neither (a) nor (b)

11. Which view enables you to select multiple slides?
    (a) Outline view
    (b) Slide sorter view
    (c) Both (a) and (b)
    (d) Neither (a) nor (b)

12. Which applications in Microsoft Office support the AutoCorrect feature?
    (a) PowerPoint
    (b) Word
    (c) Excel
    (d) All of the above

13. How do you move to the next slide during a slide show?
    (a) Click the left mouse button
    (b) Type the letter N
    (c) Press the PgDn key
    (d) All of the above

14. Which of the following can be corrected using the Style Checker?
    (a) Inconsistent use of capitalization
    (b) Inconsistent punctuation at the end of bulleted items
    (c) Both (a) and (b)
    (d) Neither (a) nor (b)

15. Which of the following can be changed without changing the template?
    (a) The color scheme and background shading
    (b) The slide master
    (c) Both (a) and (b)
    (d) Neither (a) nor (b)

ANSWERS

1. a	**6.** d	**11.** c
2. a	**7.** c	**12.** d
3. c	**8.** c	**13.** d
4. a	**9.** b	**14.** c
5. a	**10.** c	**15.** c

EXPLORING MICROSOFT POWERPOINT 7.0

1. Use Figure 2.11 to match each action with its result; a given action may be used more than once or not at all.

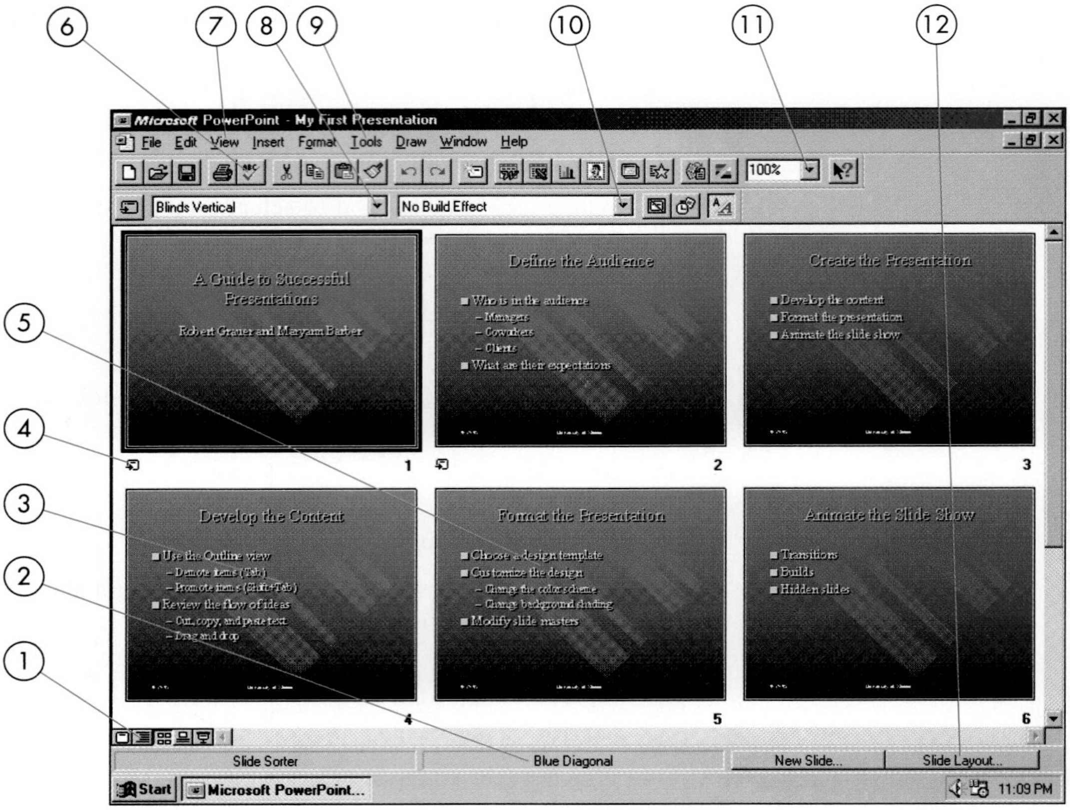

6
7
8
9
10
11
12
5
4
3
2
1
Microsoft PowerPoint - My First Presentation
File Edit View Insert Format Tools Draw Window Help
100%
Blinds Vertical
No Build Effect
A Guide to Successful Presentations
Robert Grauer and Maryann Barber
Define the Audience
Who is in the audience
Create the Presentation
Develop the content
Format the presentation
Animate the slide show
Develop the Content
Format the Presentation
Animate the Slide Show
Transitions
Builds
Hidden slides
Slide Sorter
Blue Diagonal
New Slide...
Slide Layout...
Start
Microsoft PowerPoint...
11:09 PM

FIGURE 2.11 Screen for Problem 1

Action	Result
a. Click at 1	_____ Choose a new template
b. Double click at 2	_____ Spell check the presentation
c. Click at 4	_____ Switch to the Outline view
d. Click at 5, click at 10	_____ Run the Style Checker
e. Click at 3, click at 8	_____ Create a build for slide 5
f. Click at 6	_____ Change the AutoLayout for the current slide
g. Click at 7	_____ Preview the transition for the first slide
h. Click at 9	_____ Create a transition for slide 4
i. Click at 11	_____ Modify the slide master
j. Click at 12	_____ Change the zoom in effect

2. The Answer Wizard functions identically in PowerPoint as it does in the other Office applications. Accordingly, use what you know about Microsoft Office, or explore on your own, to answer the following with respect to Figure 2.12:

a. How do you display the dialog box in Figure 2.12? Is this type of help information available in the other Office applications?

b. What is the difference between the Contents, Index, Find, and Answer Wizard tabs? Which tab is currently selected?

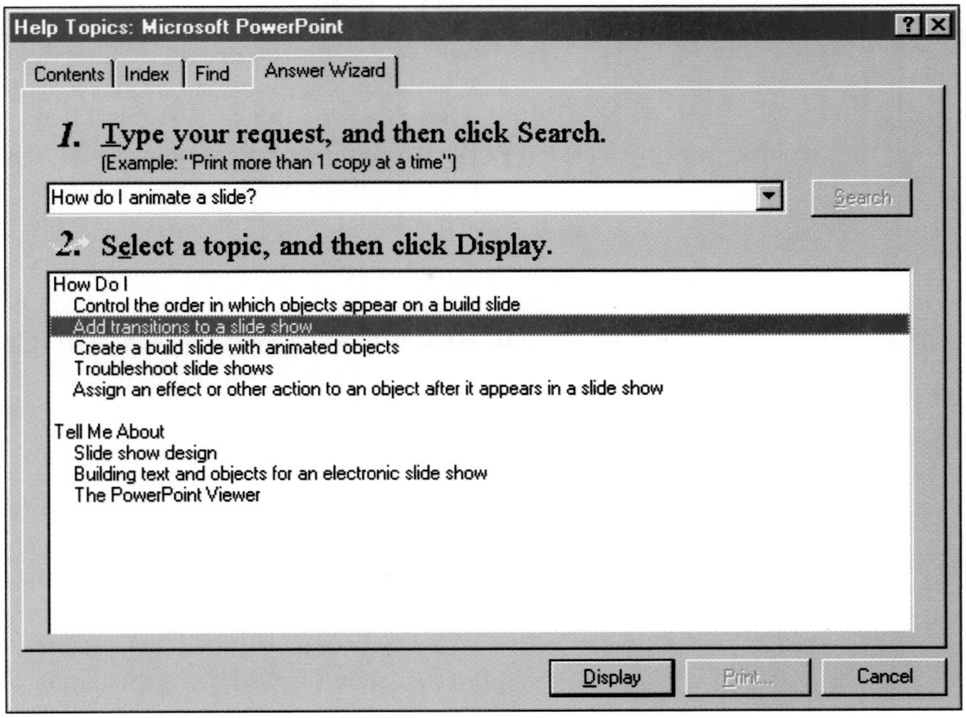
Help Topics: Microsoft PowerPoint
Contents
Index
Find
Answer Wizard
1. Type your request, and then click Search.
(Example: "Print more than 1 copy at a time")
How do I animate a slide?
Search
2. Select a topic, and then click Display.
How Do I
Control the order in which objects appear on a build slide
Add transitions to a slide show
Create a build slide with animated objects
Troubleshoot slide shows
Assign an effect or other action to an object after it appears in a slide show
Tell Me About
Slide show design
Building text and objects for an electronic slide show
The PowerPoint Viewer
Display
Print...
Cancel

FIGURE 2.12 Screen for Problem 2

c. What did the user enter once the dialog box appeared? What was displayed in response to the user's input?
d. What would be the effect of clicking the Display command button?

3. Answer the following with respect to the dialog box in Figure 2.13:
   a. What command(s) displayed the dialog box?
   b. What is the difference between the Presentation Designs tab and the Presentations tab? Which one is currently selected?

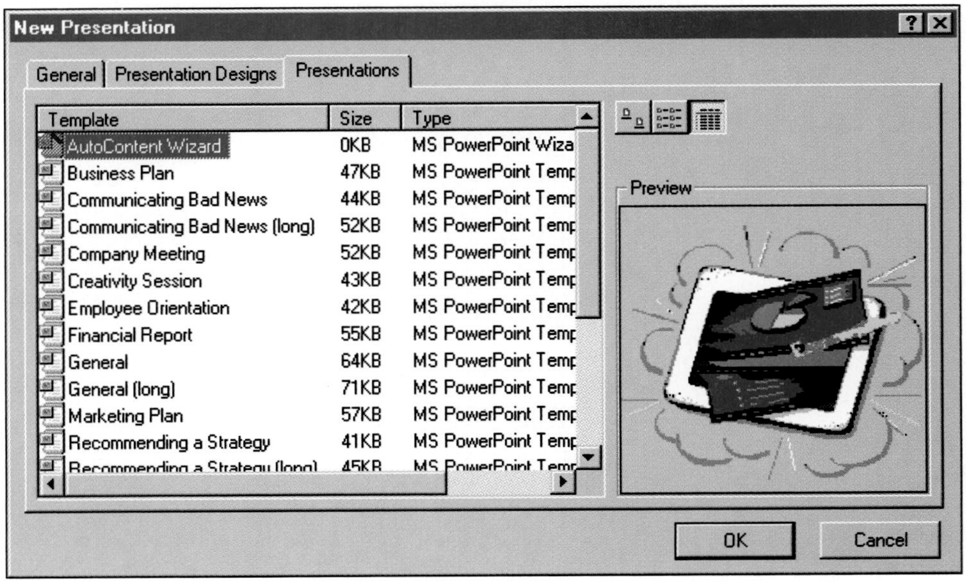
New Presentation
General
Presentation Designs
Presentations
Template
Size
Type
AutoContent Wizard
0KB
MS PowerPoint Wiza
Business Plan
47KB
Communicating Bad News
44KB
Communicating Bad News (long)
52KB
Company Meeting
52KB
Creativity Session
43KB
Employee Orientation
42KB
Financial Report
55KB
General
64KB
General (long)
71KB
Marketing Plan
57KB
Recommending a Strategy
41KB
Preview
OK
Cancel

FIGURE 2.13 Screen for Problem 3

c. What is the function of the three buttons that appear toward the upper right side of the dialog box? Which of these buttons is currently in effect?
d. What additional information would you expect to see if you clicked the down arrow on the vertical scroll bar?
e. What additional information would you expect to see if you clicked the right arrow on the horizontal scroll bar?
f. What would happen if you clicked the OK button? The Cancel button?

4. Answer the following with respect to the dialog boxes in Figure 2.14:
a. Which command displayed the dialog box in Figure 2.14a?
b. What date will appear on each slide in the presentation? Will this date be updated automatically in the future?
c. Will the specified options appear on the title slide?
d. What footer (if any) will appear on each slide? How do you change the contents of the footer?
e. Which command produced the dialog box in Figure 2.14b?
f. What is the difference between Title Case and Sentence case? What are the other options available for capitalization?
g. Will periods be added to or removed from the slide titles? Will they be added to or removed from bulleted text?
h. Is it possible to check for punctuation other than periods?
i. What additional capability is provided through the Visual Clarity tab?

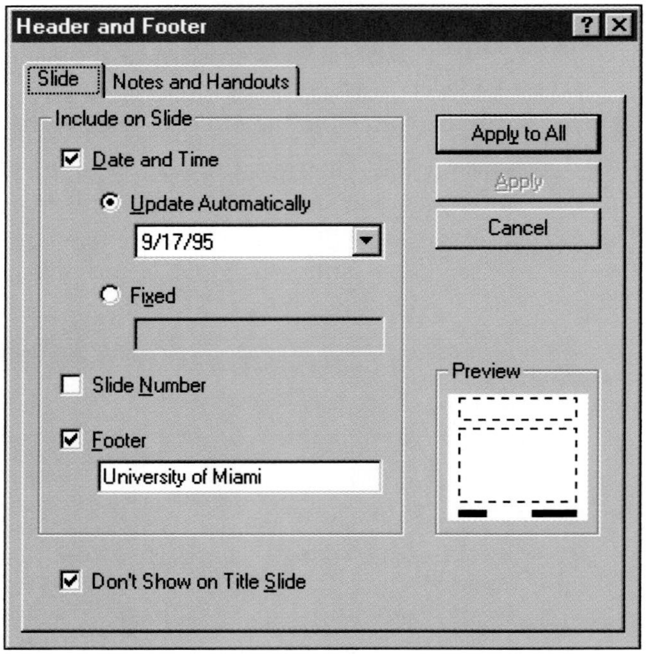
Header and Footer
Slide
Notes and Handouts
Include on Slide
Date and Time
Update Automatically
9/17/95
Fixed
Slide Number
Footer
University of Miami
Don't Show on Title Slide
Apply to All
Apply
Cancel
Preview

(a) Dialog Box 1

FIGURE 2.14 Screen for Problem 4

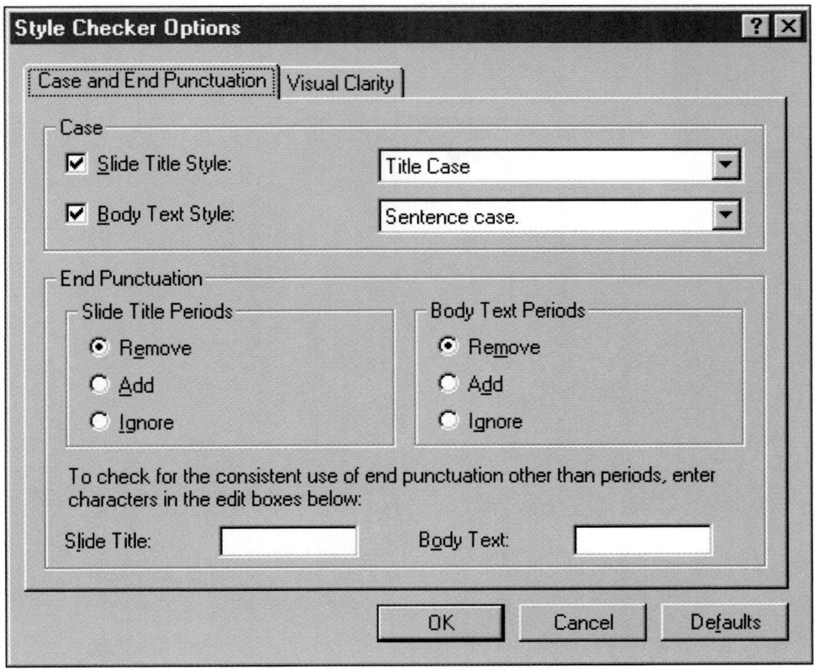
Style Checker Options
Case and End Punctuation
Visual Clarity
Case
Slide Title Style:
Title Case
Body Text Style:
Sentence case.
End Punctuation
Slide Title Periods
Remove
Add
Ignore
Body Text Periods
Remove
Add
Ignore
To check for the consistent use of end punctuation other than periods, enter characters in the edit boxes below:
Slide Title:
Body Text:
OK
Cancel
Defaults

(b) Dialog Box 2

FIGURE 2.14 Screen for Problem 4 (continued)

PRACTICE WITH MICROSOFT POWERPOINT 7.0

1. Figure 2.15 displays the title slide of a presentation that can be found in the Exploring PowerPoint folder on the data disk. Much of the presentation has been created for you, but there are several finishing touches:
   a. Open the existing presentation titled Chapter 2 Practice 1, then save it as Finished Chapter 2 Practice 1 so that you can return to the original presentation if necessary.
   b. Add your name to the title slide.
   c. Move the slide that describes printers after the slide about video.
   d. Delete the slide that describes the bus.
   e. Add a slide at the end of the presentation to consider mail-order purchase. Enter the names and phone numbers of three such companies.
   f. Change the layout of slide 2 to include clip art. Use any image you think is appropriate.
   g. Change the template to Comet.
   h. Print the completed presentation in both outline and handout form. Submit both to your instructor.
2. Figure 2.16 displays a very general outline for a presentation. The outline can be accessed through the AutoContent Wizard or directly through the File New command.
   a. Pull down the File menu, click New to display the New Presentation dialog box, click the Presentations tab, then double click the General presentation.

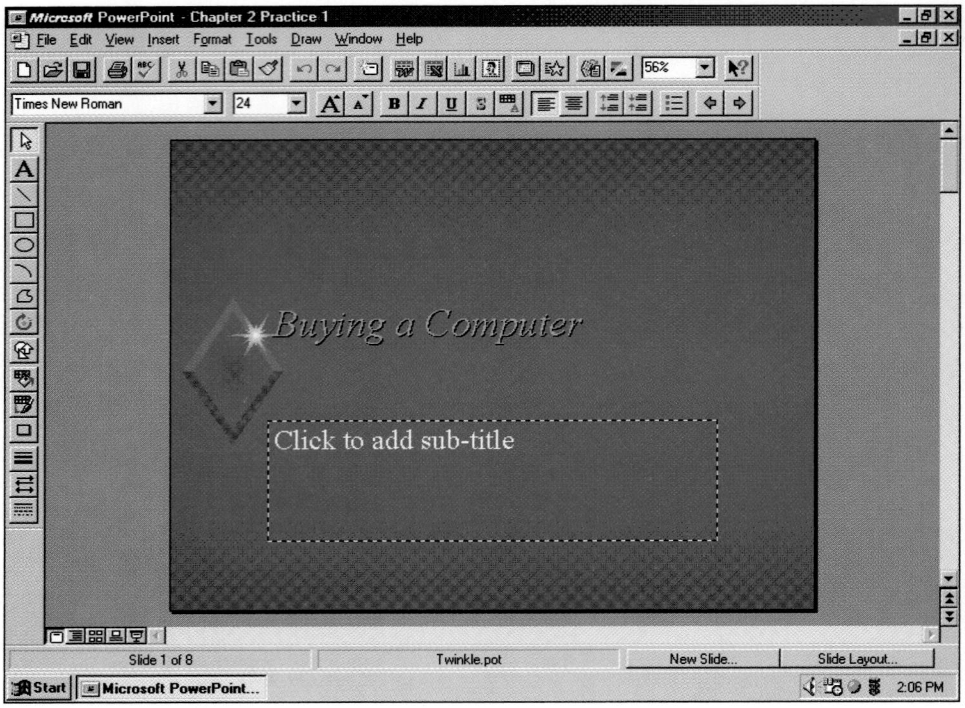
Microsoft PowerPoint - Chapter 2 Practice 1
File Edit View Insert Format Tools Draw Window Help
Times New Roman
24
Buying a Computer
Click to add sub-title
Slide 1 of 8
Twinkle.pot
New Slide...
Slide Layout...
Start
Microsoft PowerPoint...
2:06 PM

FIGURE 2.15 Screen for Practice Exercise 1

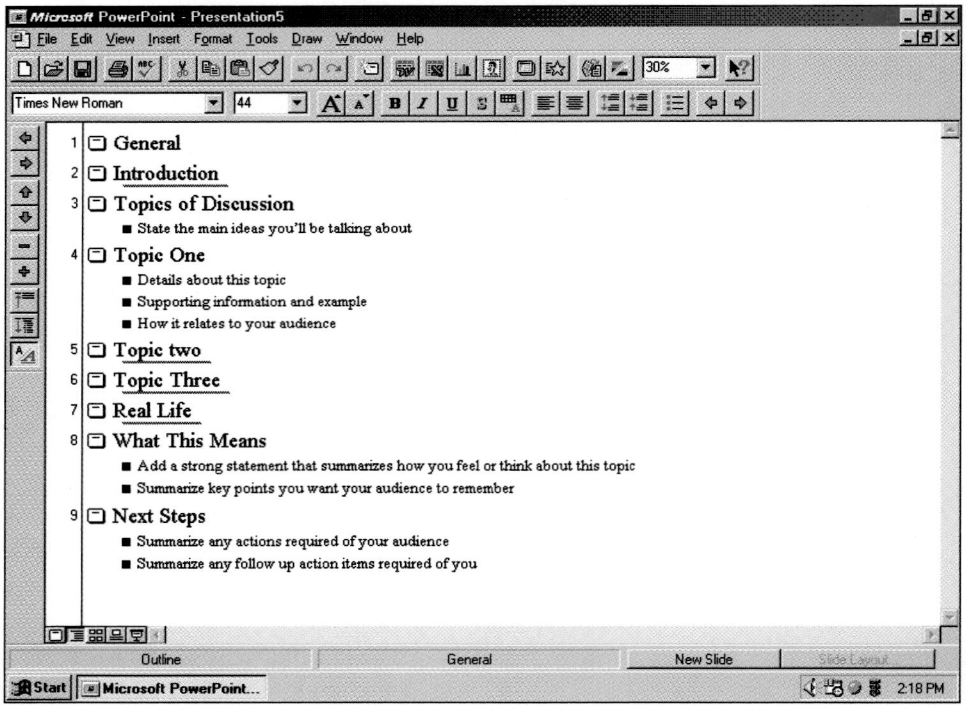
Microsoft PowerPoint - Presentation5
File Edit View Insert Format Tools Draw Window Help
Times New Roman
44
1 General
2 Introduction
3 Topics of Discussion
State the main ideas you'll be talking about
4 Topic One
Details about this topic
Supporting information and example
How it relates to your audience
5 Topic two
6 Topic Three
7 Real Life
8 What This Means
Add a strong statement that summarizes how you feel or think about this topic
Summarize key points you want your audience to remember
9 Next Steps
Summarize any actions required of your audience
Summarize any follow up action items required of you
Outline
General
New Slide
Slide Layout...
Start
Microsoft PowerPoint...
2:18 PM

FIGURE 2.16 Screen for Practice Exercise 2

b. Change to the Outline view to display the presentation in Figure 2.16. (Some slides have been collapsed in our outline as can be seen by the underlined slide titles.)

c. Choose any topic you like, then prepare a presentation on that topic using the outline provided. You need not follow the outline exactly, but it should provide a good beginning. The completed presentation should contain from six to ten slides.

d. Apply a new (different) design template to the completed presentation.

e. Use the Style Checker to check for spelling, punctuation, and consistent capitalization throughout the presentation.

f. Print the completed presentation in both outline and miniature slide form. Submit both handouts to your instructor.

3. It began with David Letterman, but today almost everyone has a list of the top ten reasons for something, and PowerPoint is no exception. Use the AutoContent Wizard (or the File New command as described in the previous exercise) to select the Top Ten List template shown in Figure 2.17.

a. Complete the presentation by entering your top 10 list in either the Slide or Outline view.

b. Press Ctrl+Home to return to the first slide, change to the Slide Show view, then sit back and enjoy the show. (The template includes transition and build effects as can be seen by the tiny icons under each slide in the Slide Sorter view of Figure 2.17.)

c. Prove to your instructor that you have done the exercise by providing a hard copy of the completed presentation. Print the presentation in Slide view, but be sure to print the slides without builds so that you conserve paper.

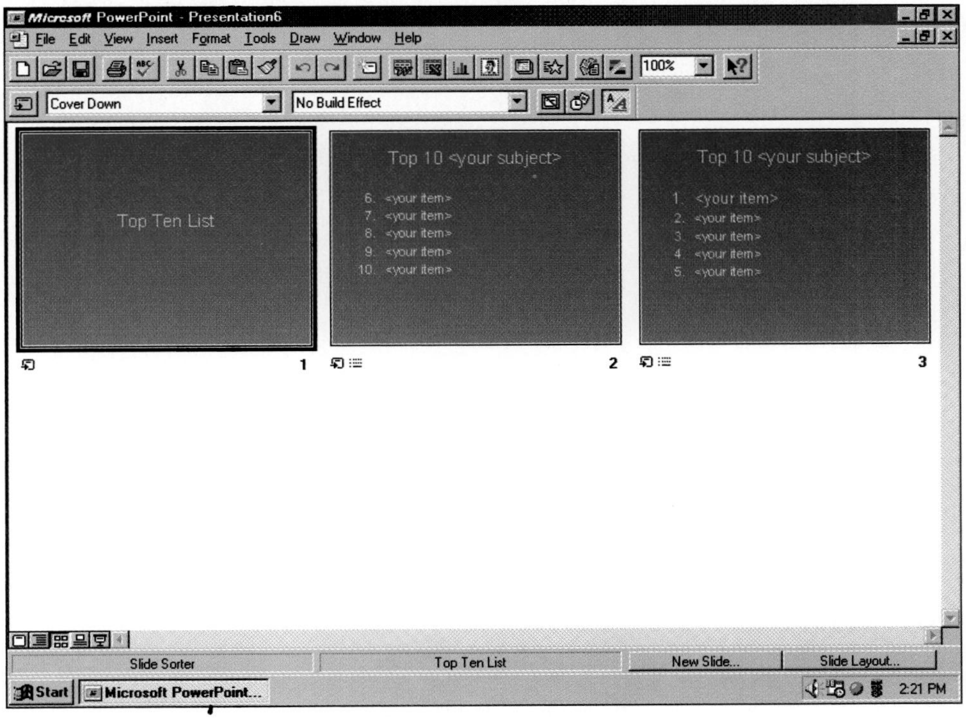
Microsoft PowerPoint - Presentation6
File Edit View Insert Format Tools Draw Window Help
100%
Cover Down
No Build Effect
Top Ten List
Top 10 <your subject>
6. <your item>
7. <your item>
8. <your item>
9. <your item>
10. <your item>
Top 10 <your subject>
1. <your item>
2. <your item>
3. <your item>
4. <your item>
5. <your item>
1
2
3
Slide Sorter
Top Ten List
New Slide...
Slide Layout...
Start
Microsoft PowerPoint...
2:21 PM

FIGURE 2.17 Screen for Practice Exercise 3

4. Figure 2.18 displays the Slide Sorter view of the Reporting Progress template that is accessed through the AutoContent Wizard or the File New command. (Six of the nine slides are visible.)
   a. Change the title of the presentation to reflect your progress in this course (e.g., CIS120 as shown in Figure 2.18).
   b. Modify the slides to reflect your progress in the class to date. You can add or delete slides as appropriate. You can also change the slide layout and content. Be as accurate and as honest as you can to provide feedback to your instructor on how the course is going.
   c. Use the Header and Footer command in the View menu to print today's date on every slide except the title slide.
   d. Modify the slide master to include a piece of clip art in the lower-right corner of each slide except the title slide.
   e. Use the Style Checker to check for spelling, punctuation, and consistent capitalization throughout the presentation.
   f. Print the completed presentation in miniature slide form and submit the printout to your instructor.

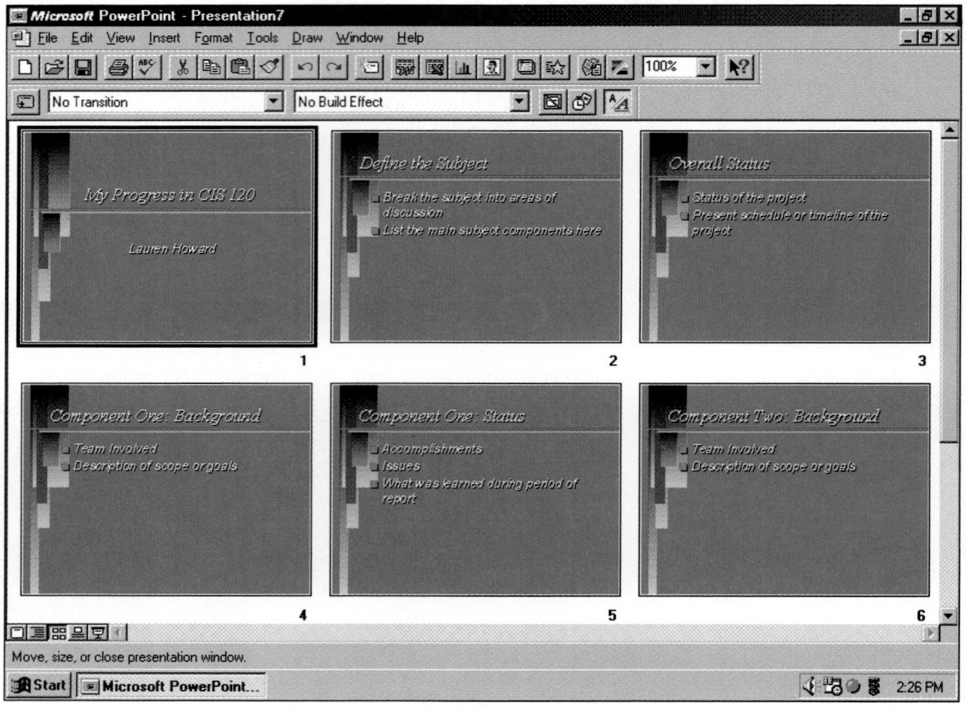
Microsoft PowerPoint - Presentation7
File Edit View Insert Format Tools Draw Window Help
100%
No Transition
No Build Effect
My Progress in CIS 120
Lauren Howard
1
Define the Subject
Break the subject into areas of discussion
List the main subject components here
2
Overall Status
Status of the project
Present schedule or timeline of the project
3
Component One: Background
Team Involved
Description of scope or goals
4
Component One: Status
Accomplishments
Issues
What was learned during period of report
5
Component Two: Background
Team Involved
Description of scope or goals
6
Move, size, or close presentation window.
Start
Microsoft PowerPoint...
2:26 PM

FIGURE 2.18 Screen for Practice Exercise 4

CASE STUDIES

Be Creative

One interesting way of exploring the potential of presentation graphics is to imagine it might have been used by historical figures had it been available. Choose any historical figure or current personality and create at least a six-slide presentation.

You could, for example, show how Columbus might have used PowerPoint to request funding from Queen Isabella, or how Elvis Presley might have pleaded for his first recording contract. The content of your presentation should be reasonable, but you don't have to spend an inordinate amount of time on research. Just be creative and use your imagination. Use clip art as appropriate, but don't overdo it. Place your name on the title slide as technical adviser.

The Annual Report

Corporate America spends a small fortune to produce its annual reports, which are readily available to the public. Choose any company and obtain a copy of its most recent annual report. Use your imagination on how best to obtain the data. You might try a stockbroker, the 800 directory, or even the Internet. Use the information in the annual report as the basis for a PowerPoint presentation. PowerPoint is one step ahead of you and offers a suggested financial report through the AutoContent Wizard.

Director of Marketing

Congratulations on your appointment as Director of Marketing. The company into which you have been hired has 50 sales representatives across the United States. Laptop computers have just been ordered for the entire sales staff and will be delivered at next week's annual sales meeting. Your job is to prepare a PowerPoint presentation that can be used by the sales staff in future sales calls. It's short notice, but it is a critical assignment. Use the Selling a Product template provided by the AutoContent Wizard as the basis for your presentation.

Take it on the Road

Your presentation looks great on the desktop, but you have to deliver it to a crowd of 50, too many people to crowd around your machine. Fortunately, however, you have a notebook computer and a generous budget. What equipment do you need to show the presentation from your notebook computer? How much will the equipment cost to buy? Can you rent the equipment instead, and if so, from whom?

3

ADDING IMPACT: OBJECT LINKING AND EMBEDDING

OBJECTIVES

After reading this chapter you will be able to:

1. Use Microsoft Graph to create and edit a graph within a presentation.
2. Use the Drawing and Drawing+ toolbars to modify existing clip art; describe the function of at least four different drawing tools.
3. Use Microsoft Organization Chart to embed an organization chart into a presentation.
4. Use Microsoft WordArt to embed a WordArt object into a presentation.
5. Link an Excel worksheet to a PowerPoint presentation.
6. Distinguish between linking and embedding; explain how in-place editing is used to modify an embedded object.
7. Embed a sound file into a PowerPoint presentation.
8. Use the Interactive Settings command to introduce branching into a presentation.

OVERVIEW

Thus far we have focused on presentations that consisted largely of text. PowerPoint also enables you to include a variety of visual elements that add impact to your presentation. You can add clip art from within PowerPoint through the ClipArt Gallery, or you can include clip art from other sources. You can use the supplementary applications that are included with Microsoft Office to add graphs, organization charts, and WordArt. You can also insert objects created in other applications, such as a worksheet from Microsoft Excel or a table from Microsoft Word.

We begin by introducing Microsoft Graph, an application that creates (and modifies) a graph based on data in an associated datasheet.

We show you how to use the Drawing and Drawing+ toolbars to modify existing clip art and/or develop original images, even if you are not artistic by nature. We describe how to create special text effects through WordArt and how to create organization charts. We show you how to embed a sound file, and we discuss Object Linking and Embedding, which incorporates objects from other applications. We also show you how to use the Interactive Settings command to allow branching in the presentation, so that you can view the slides in any order.

We think you will enjoy this chapter and be impressed with what you can do. As always, the hands-on exercises are essential to our learn-by-doing philosophy.

MICROSOFT GRAPH

The Microsoft Office suite includes a supplementary application called ***Microsoft Graph,*** which enables you to insert a graph into a presentation in support of numeric data. The program is called from within PowerPoint by choosing an AutoLayout containing a graph placeholder, then double clicking the placeholder to start Microsoft Graph. You create the graph using commands within Microsoft Graph, then you exit Microsoft Graph and return to your presentation.

Figure 3.1 illustrates the basics of the Microsoft Graph program as it will be used in a hands-on exercise later in the chapter. The program has many of the same commands and capabilities as the charting component of Microsoft Excel. (See Grauer and Barber, *Exploring Microsoft Excel for Windows 95 Version 7.0,* pages 139–185, Prentice Hall, 1996, for additional information on graphs and charting.)

The ***datasheet*** in Figure 3.1a displays the quarterly sales for each of three salesmen: Tom, Dick, and Harry. The datasheet contains 12 ***data points*** (four quarterly values for each of three salesmen). The data points are grouped into ***data series,*** which appear as rows or columns in the datasheet.

The graph in Figure 3.1b plots the data by row so that you can see the relative performance of each salesman in each quarter. There are three data series (Sales for Tom, Sales for Dick, and Sales for Harry), each with four data points (1st Qtr, 2nd Qtr, 3rd Qtr, and 4th Qtr). The text entries in the first row of the datasheet appear on the X axis as the category names. The text entries in the first column of the datasheet appear as a legend to indicate the name associated with each series.

Figure 3.1c, on the other hand, plots the data by column, making it easy to see the progress of each salesman over the course of the year. This time there are four data series (Sales for 1st Qtr, Sales for 2nd Qtr, Sales for 3rd Qtr, and Sales for 4th Qtr), each with three data points (one each for Tom, Dick, and Harry). The text entries in the first column of the datasheet appear on the X axis as the category names. The text entries in the first row of the datasheet appear in the legend to indicate the name associated with each series.

Figure 3.1d also displays the data series in columns, but uses a different graph type, a stacked column rather than side-by-side columns as in Figure 3.1c. The choice between the two types of graphs depends on your message. If, for example, you want your audience to see each individual's sales in each quarter, the side-by-side graph is more appropriate. If, on the other hand, you want to emphasize the total sales for each salesperson, the stacked column graph is preferable. Note, too, the different scale on the Y axis in the two graphs. The side-by-side graph in Figure 3.1c shows the sales in each quarter and so the Y axis goes only to $90,000. The stacked bars in Figure 3.1d, however, reflect the total sales for each salesperson and thus the scale goes to $250,000.

All three graphs contain the same number of data points (12 in all) but plot them differently to emphasize different information. All three graphs are equally correct, and the choice depends on the message you want to convey.

EMPHASIZE YOUR MESSAGE

A graph exists to deliver a message, and you want that message to be as clear as possible. One way to help put your point across is to choose a title that leads the audience. A neutral title such as *Revenue by Quarter* does nothing and requires the audience to reach its own conclusion. A better title might be *Tom Is the Leading Sales Associate* if the objective were to emphasize Tom's contribution. A well-chosen title emphasizes your message.

My Chart - Datasheet

		A	B	C	D	E
		1st Qtr	2nd Qtr	3rd Qtr	4th Qtr	
1	Tom	20.4	50	90	75	
2	Dick	30.6	38.6	34.6	31.6	
3	Harry	45.9	46.9	45	12	
4						

(a) The Datasheet (sales in thousands)

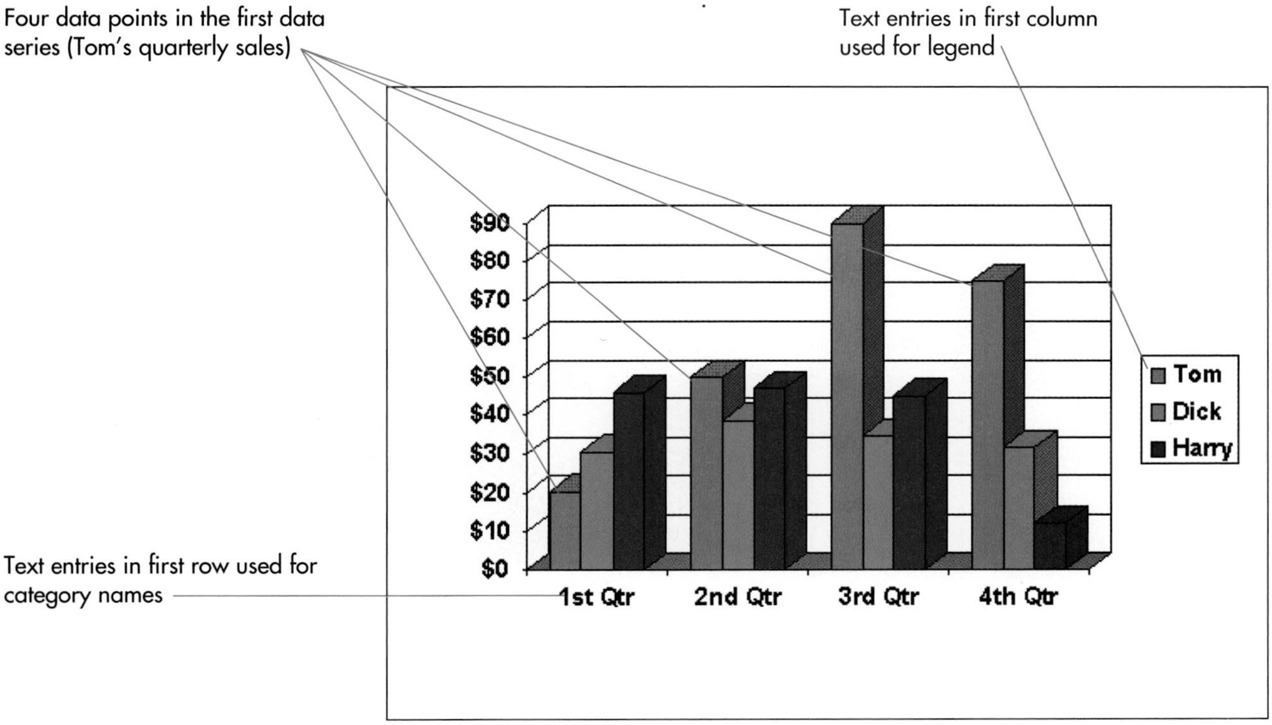

Four data points in the first data series (Tom's quarterly sales)
Text entries in first column used for legend
Text entries in first row used for category names
$90
$80
$70
$60
$50
$40
$30
$20
$10
$0
1st Qtr
2nd Qtr
3rd Qtr
4th Qtr
Tom
Dick
Harry

(b) Data Series in Rows (sales in thousands)

FIGURE 3.1 Microsoft Graph

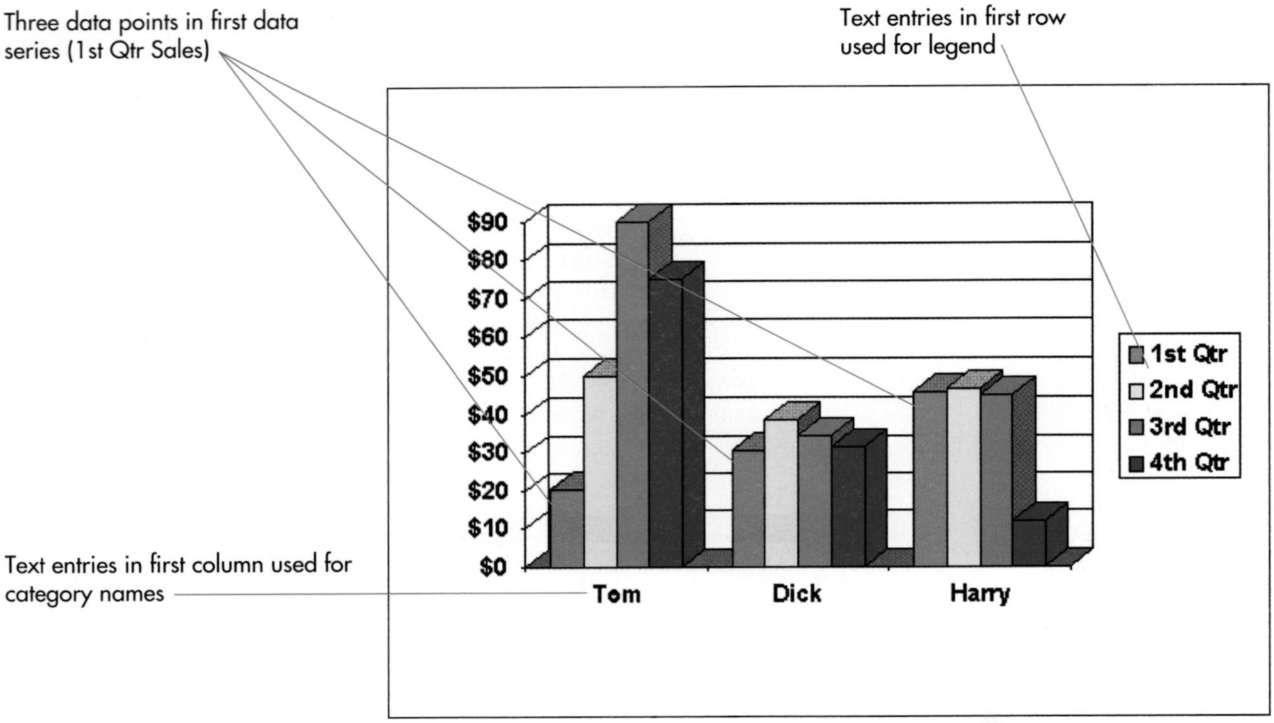

Three data points in first data series (1st Qtr Sales)
Text entries in first row used for legend
$90
$80
$70
$60
$50
$40
$30
$20
$10
$0
Tom
Dick
Harry
1st Qtr
2nd Qtr
3rd Qtr
4th Qtr
Text entries in first column used for category names

(c) Data Series in Columns (sales in thousands)

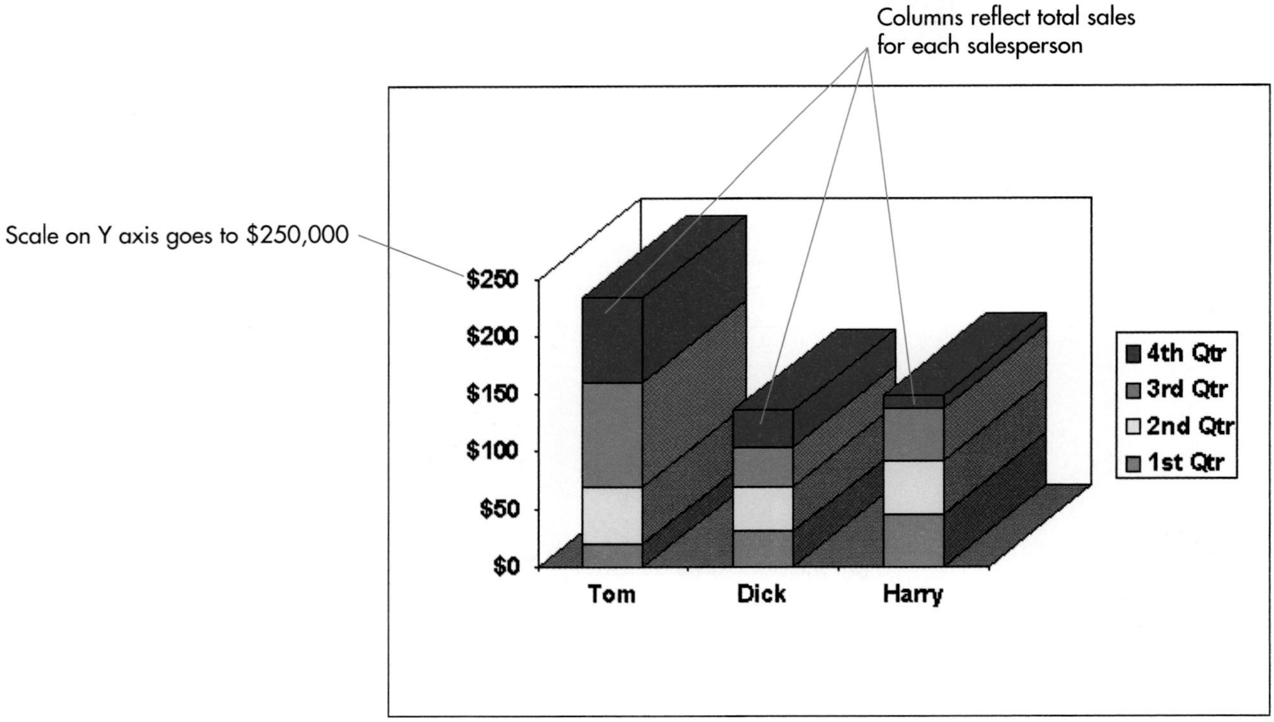

Columns reflect total sales for each salesperson
Scale on Y axis goes to $250,000
$250
$200
$150
$100
$50
$0
Tom
Dick
Harry
4th Qtr
3rd Qtr
2nd Qtr
1st Qtr

(d) Stacked Column Chart (sales in thousands)

FIGURE 3.1 Microsoft Graph (continued)

HANDS-ON EXERCISE 1

Microsoft Graph

Objective: Use Microsoft Graph to insert a graph into a presentation; modify the graph to display the data in rows or columns; change the graph format and underlying data. Use Figure 3.2 as a guide in the exercise.

STEP 1: Start Microsoft Graph

- Start PowerPoint. Click the option button to create a new presentation using a **Blank Presentation.** Click **OK.** You should see the New Slide dialog box.
- Select (click) the AutoLayout for a graph (it is the AutoLayout at the end of the second row), then click **OK** to add the slide as shown in Figure 3.2a. If necessary, maximize the document window.

INSERTING A GRAPH

There are several different ways to insert a graph into a presentation. You can choose one of three AutoLayouts containing a placeholder for a graph. You can also pull down the Insert menu and select Microsoft Graph, or you can click the Insert Graph button on the Standard toolbar. You can also insert a graph created in another application by executing the Insert Object command and selecting the appropriate object, such as a Microsoft Excel chart.

Double click placeholder to start Microsoft Graph

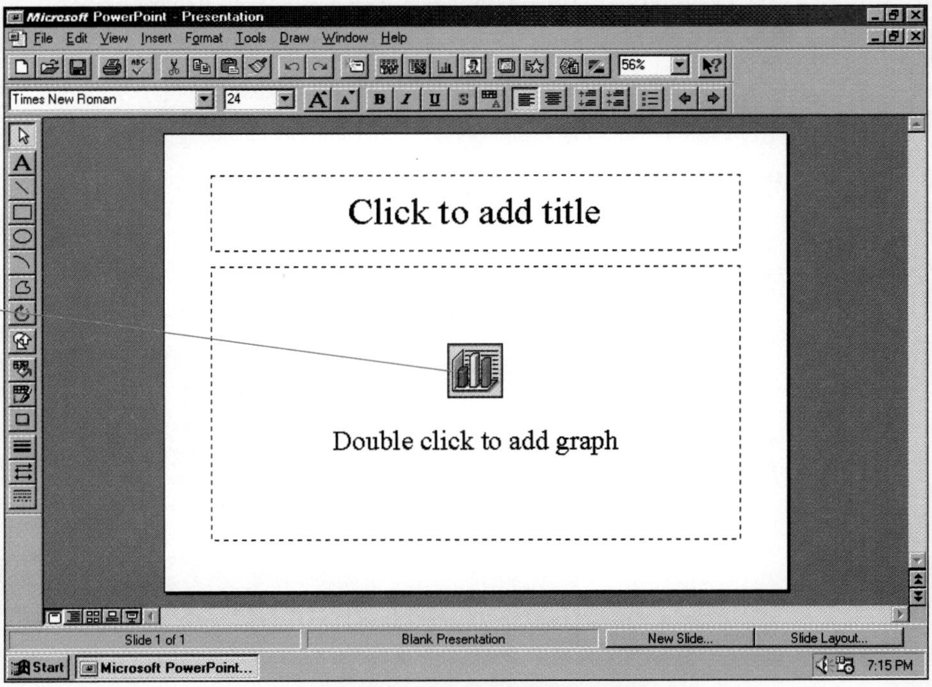

Microsoft PowerPoint - Presentation
File Edit View Insert Format Tools Draw Window Help
56%
Times New Roman
24
Click to add title
Double click to add graph
Slide 1 of 1
Blank Presentation
New Slide...
Slide Layout...
Start
Microsoft PowerPoint...
7:15 PM

(a) Start Microsoft Graph (step 1)

FIGURE 3.2 Hands-on Exercise 1

➤ Double click the placeholder to add a graph, which starts the Microsoft Graph application.

STEP 2: The Default Graph

➤ The default datasheet and graph should be displayed on your monitor, as shown in Figure 3.2b. The menus and toolbar have changed to reflect the Microsoft Graph application.

➤ Do not be concerned if the numbers in your datasheet are different from those in the figure. (You can create your own graph simply by editing the text and numeric values, as will be described in the next step.)

➤ Click and drag the **title bar** of the datasheet so that you can see more of the graph, as in the figure.

IN-PLACE EDITING

Microsoft Graph enables in-place editing as you create and/or modify a graph; that is, you remain in PowerPoint, but the toolbar and pull-down menus are those of Microsoft Graph. The File and Window menus are exceptions, however, and contain PowerPoint commands (so that you can save the presentation and/or view multiple presentations). In-place editing requires that both applications support the Microsoft specification for Object Linking and Embedding 2.0.

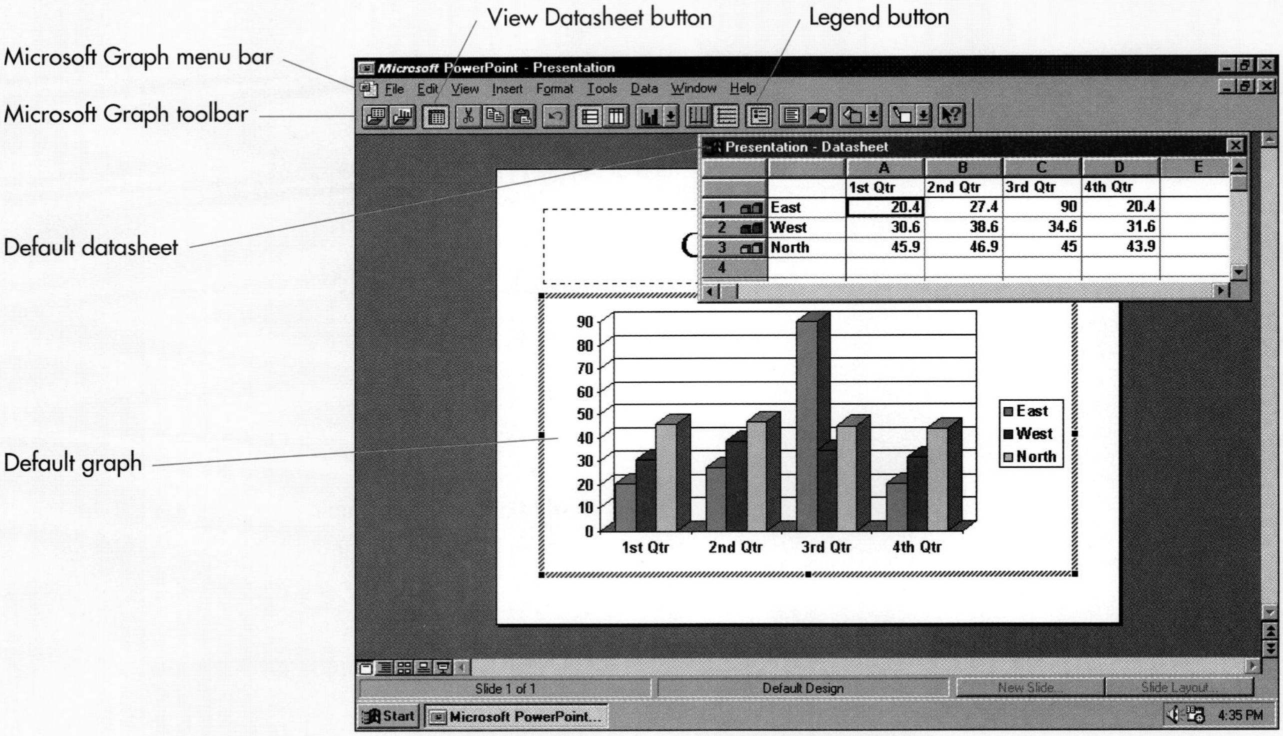
View Datasheet button
Legend button
Microsoft Graph menu bar
Microsoft Graph toolbar
Default datasheet
Default graph
Microsoft PowerPoint - Presentation
File Edit View Insert Format Tools Data Window Help
Presentation - Datasheet
A B C D E
1st Qtr 2nd Qtr 3rd Qtr 4th Qtr
1 East 20.4 27.4 90 20.4
2 West 30.6 38.6 34.6 31.6
3 North 45.9 46.9 45 43.9
East
West
North
1st Qtr 2nd Qtr 3rd Qtr 4th Qtr
Slide 1 of 1
Default Design
Start
Microsoft PowerPoint...
4:35 PM

(b) The Default Graph (step 2)

FIGURE 3.2 Hands-on Exercise 1 (continued)

- Click the **View Datasheet button** on the (Microsoft Graph) Standard toolbar to close the datasheet. Click the **View Datasheet button** a second time to open the datasheet.
- Click the **Legend button** on the Standard toolbar to suppress the legend on the graph. Click the **Legend button** a second time to display the legend.

STEP 3: Change the Data

- Click in **cell B1** of the datasheet (the value for East in the 2nd Quarter). Type **50** and press **enter.** The graph changes automatically to reflect the new data.
- Change the values of the following cells as follows:
  - Click in **cell D1.** Type **75.**
  - Click in **cell D3.** Type **12.**
  - Click in the cell containing **East.** Type **Tom.**
  - Press the **down arrow key** to move to the cell containing **West.** Type **Dick.**
  - Press the **down arrow key** to move to the cell containing **North.** Type **Harry.**
- Check that all of the values in your datasheet match those in Figure 3.2c. Click the **Close button** to close the datasheet.

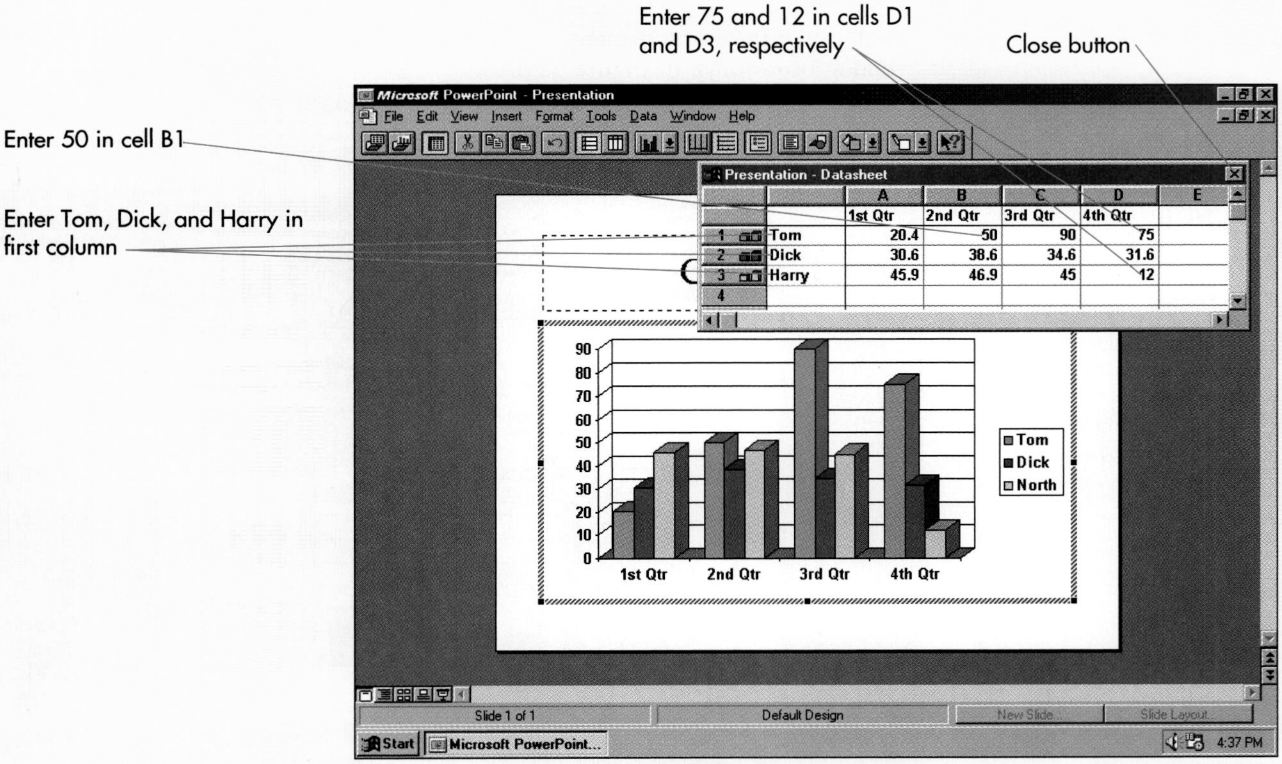

Enter 75 and 12 in cells D1 and D3, respectively
Close button
Enter 50 in cell B1
Enter Tom, Dick, and Harry in first column
Microsoft PowerPoint - Presentation
File Edit View Insert Format Tools Data Window Help
Presentation - Datasheet
A B C D E
1st Qtr 2nd Qtr 3rd Qtr 4th Qtr
1 Tom 20.4 50 90 75
2 Dick 30.6 38.6 34.6 31.6
3 Harry 45.9 46.9 45 12
4
90 80 70 60 50 40 30 20 10 0
1st Qtr 2nd Qtr 3rd Qtr 4th Qtr
Tom
Dick
North
Slide 1 of 1
Default Design
New Slide...
Slide Layout...
Start
Microsoft PowerPoint...
4:37 PM

(c) Change the Data (step 3)

FIGURE 3.2 Hands-on Exercise 1 (continued)

IMPORT THE DATA

Microsoft Graph enables you to import data from another application (e.g., Microsoft Excel) and use that data as the basis for the graph. Click in the upper-left cell (the cell above row 1 and to the left of column A) to select the entire datasheet. Click the Import Data button on the Microsoft Graph toolbar to produce an Import Data dialog box. Select the appropriate drive and directory containing the file you want to import, select the file, then click the OK command button.

STEP 4: Change the Orientation and Graph Type

- Click the **By Column button** on the Standard toolbar to change the data series from rows to columns as shown in Figure 3.2d. The X axis changes to display the names of the salespersons, and the legend indicates the quarter.
- Click the **By Row button** on the Standard toolbar to change the data series back to rows.
- Click the **By Column button** a second time to match the orientation in Figure 3.2d.
- Pull down the **Format menu.** Click **AutoFormat** to produce the AutoFormat dialog box shown in Figure 3.2d.

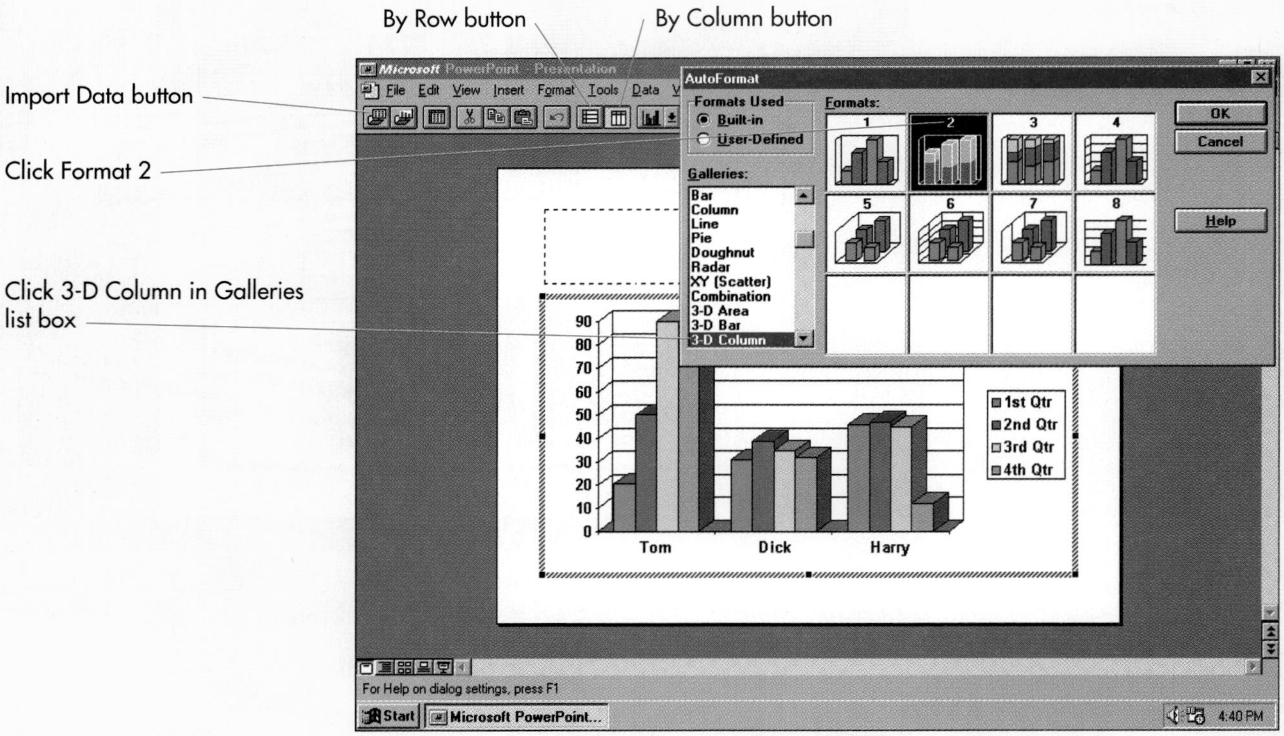

By Row button
By Column button
Import Data button
Click Format 2
Click 3-D Column in Galleries list box
AutoFormat
Formats Used
Built-in
User-Defined
Formats:
Galleries:
Bar
Column
Line
Pie
Doughnut
Radar
XY (Scatter)
Combination
3-D Area
3-D Bar
3-D Column
OK
Cancel
Help
Tom
Dick
Harry
1st Qtr
2nd Qtr
3rd Qtr
4th Qtr
For Help on dialog settings, press F1
Start
Microsoft PowerPoint...
4:40 PM

(d) Change the Orientation and Format (step 4)

FIGURE 3.2 Hands-on Exercise 1 (continued)

➤ If necessary, click **3-D Column** in the Galleries list box. Click **Format 2,** then click **OK** to create a stacked bar graph.

> **DON'T FORGET HELP**
>
> Microsoft Graph includes its own Help system, which functions identically to the Help in any other application. Pull down the Help menu and search on any topic for which you want additional information. Remember, too, that you can print the contents of a Help screen by pulling down the File menu and selecting the Print Topic command.

STEP 5: Return to PowerPoint

➤ Click outside the chart (and datasheet) to exit Microsoft Graph and return to PowerPoint. You should see the stacked column graph in Figure 3.2e.

➤ Click outside the graph to deselect it. The sizing handles disappear.

➤ Click inside the graph, and the sizing handles reappear to indicate the graph is selected. Click and drag a corner sizing handle to increase (decrease) the size of the graph within the slide.

➤ Click the **title placeholder,** which deselects the graph and positions the insertion point to enter the title. Type **Tom is the Top Sales Associate.**

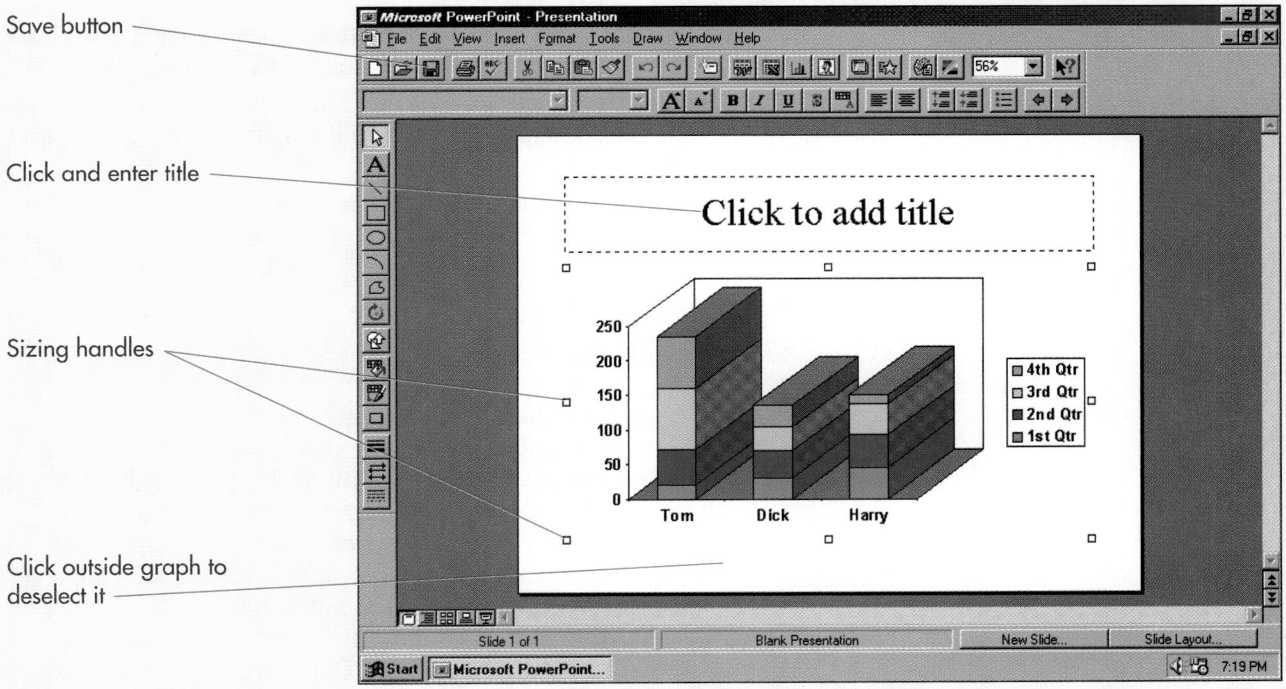
Save button
Click and enter title
Sizing handles
Click outside graph to deselect it
Microsoft PowerPoint - Presentation
File Edit View Insert Format Tools Draw Window Help
56%
Click to add title
250
200
150
100
50
0
Tom
Dick
Harry
4th Qtr
3rd Qtr
2nd Qtr
1st Qtr
Slide 1 of 1
Blank Presentation
New Slide...
Slide Layout...
Start
Microsoft PowerPoint...
7:19 PM

(e) Return to PowerPoint (step 5)

FIGURE 3.2 Hands-on Exercise 1 (continued)

➤ Pull down the **File menu** and click **Save** (or click the **Save button** on the Standard toolbar). Save the presentation as **My Chart** in the **Exploring PowerPoint folder.**

TO CLICK OR DOUBLE CLICK

Once you create a graph and return to your presentation, the graph becomes an embedded object, which retains its connection to Microsoft Graph for easy editing. You can click the graph to select it, then move or size the graph just as you would any other Windows object. You can also double click the graph to restart Microsoft Graph (the application that created the graph) and then edit it using the tools of the original application.

STEP 6: Add a Data Series

➤ Point to the graph and click the **right mouse button** to display a shortcut menu, then click **Edit Chart Object.** (You can also double click the graph as described in the previous tip.) Once again you are in Microsoft Graph, and the menus and toolbar have changed to reflect this application.

➤ Click the **View Datasheet button** to reopen the datasheet. If necessary, click and drag the title bar of the datasheet so you can see more of the graph.

➤ Add an additional data series as follows:

- Click in the cell under Harry. Type **George,** then press the **right arrow key** to move to cell A4. George appears as a category name on the X axis.
- Enter **10, 15, 20,** and **25** in cells A4, B4, C4, and D4, respectively. Notice that as you complete each entry, the graph adjusts automatically to reflect the value you just entered.

➤ The data for George is plotted automatically as shown in Figure 3.2f. Close the datasheet.

REMOVING A DATA SERIES

To delete a data series, open the datasheet, then click the row number or column header of the data series you want to delete, and press the Del key. The data series will disappear from both the datasheet and the associated graph. Alternatively, you can leave the data series in the datasheet but exclude it from the graph. (This enables you to subsequently include the data in the graph without having to reenter it.) Click the row number or column header to select the data series, pull down the Data menu, and select the Exclude Row/Column command. To restore the data series in the graph, select the series, pull down the Data menu, and select the Include Row/Column command.

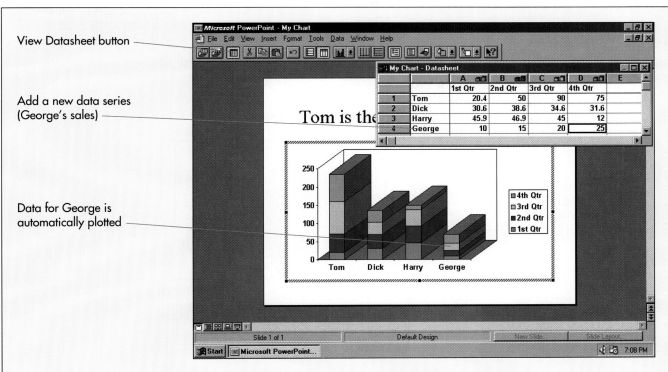

View Datasheet button

Add a new data series (George's sales)

Data for George is automatically plotted

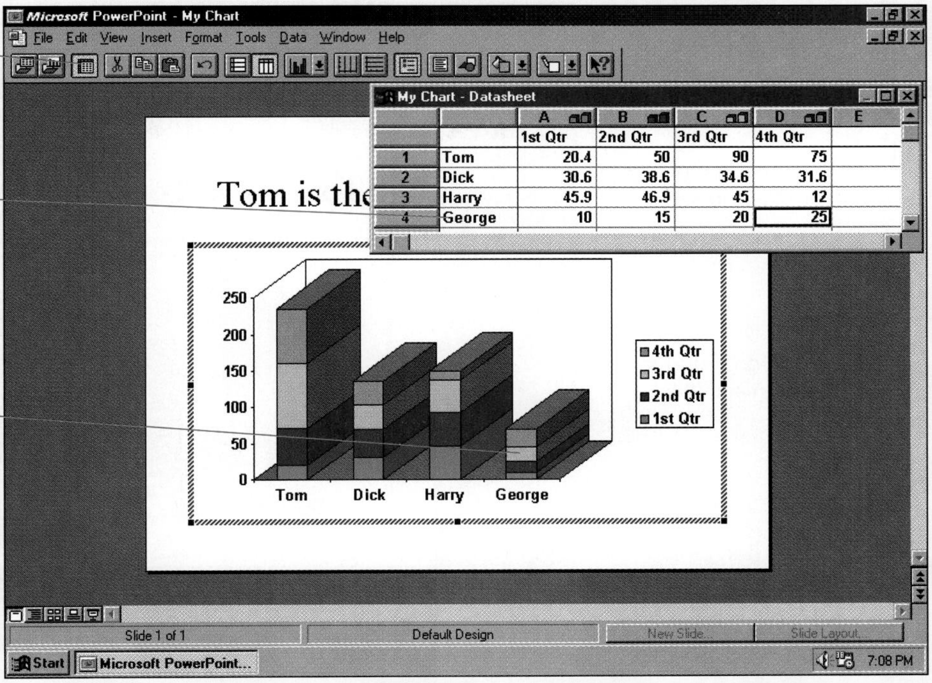
Microsoft PowerPoint - My Chart
File Edit View Insert Format Tools Data Window Help
My Chart - Datasheet
Tom is the
Tom
Dick
Harry
George
1st Qtr
2nd Qtr
3rd Qtr
4th Qtr
Slide 1 of 1
Default Design
New Slide...
Slide Layout...
Start
Microsoft PowerPoint...
7:08 PM

		A	B	C	D	E
		1st Qtr	2nd Qtr	3rd Qtr	4th Qtr	
1	Tom	20.4	50	90	75	
2	Dick	30.6	38.6	34.6	31.6	
3	Harry	45.9	46.9	45	12	
4	George	10	15	20	25	

(f) Add a Data Series (step 6)

FIGURE 3.2 Hands-on Exercise 1 (continued)

STEP 7: The Finishing Touches

- You can customize every object within a chart (the legend, axis, plot area, and so on) by pointing to the object and clicking the right mouse button to display a shortcut menu.
- Point to the gray section (4th Qtr Sales) of any column and click the **right mouse button** to display a shortcut menu. Click **Format Data Series.**
- Click the **Patterns tab** (if necessary) in the Format Data Series dialog box and click **red** as the new color. Click **OK** to close the dialog box. The data series for the fourth quarter has been changed to red as shown in Figure 3.2g.
- Point to any value on the vertical axis, then click the **right mouse button** to display the shortcut menu in Figure 3.2g. Click **Format Axis.**
- Click the **Number tab** in the Format Number dialog box, then scroll within the Category list box until you can select the **Currency format.** Click **OK.** The format of the axis has been changed to include the dollar sign.

STEP 8: Save the Presentation

- Click outside the chart to exit Microsoft Graph and return to PowerPoint. Save the presentation.
- Pull down the **File menu** and click **Print** (or click the **Print button**). Click **OK** to print the slide.
- Exit PowerPoint if you do not want to continue with the next exercise at this time. Click **Yes** if prompted to save the changes to the presentation.

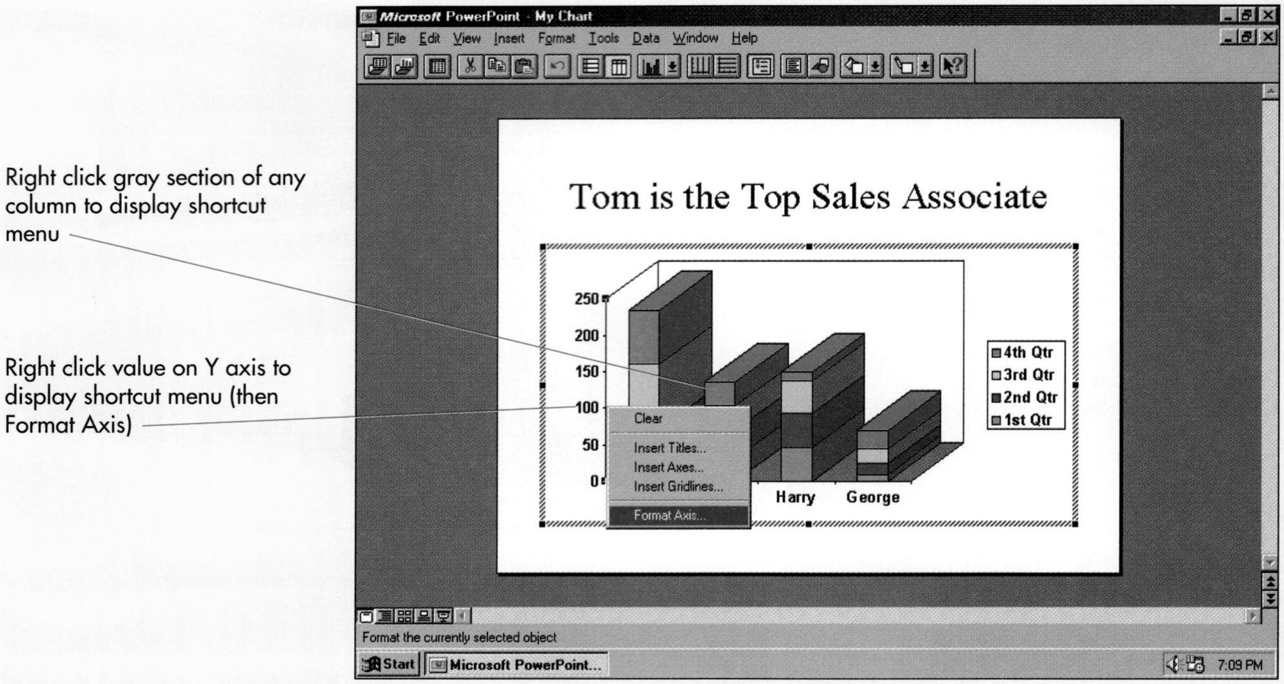
Right click gray section of any column to display shortcut menu
Right click value on Y axis to display shortcut menu (then Format Axis)
Microsoft PowerPoint - My Chart
File Edit View Insert Format Tools Data Window Help
Tom is the Top Sales Associate
250
200
150
100
50
0
Clear
Insert Titles...
Insert Axes...
Insert Gridlines...
Format Axis...
Harry
George
4th Qtr
3rd Qtr
2nd Qtr
1st Qtr
Format the currently selected object
Start
Microsoft PowerPoint...
7:09 PM

(g) The Finishing Touches (step 7)

FIGURE 3.2 Hands-on Exercise 1 (continued)

THE 3-D VIEW COMMAND

The 3-D View command enables you to fine-tune the appearance of a graph by controlling the rotation, elevation, and other parameters found within its dialog box. The rotation controls the rotation around the vertical axis and determines how much of the stacked bars you see. The elevation controls the height at which you view the graph. Pull down the Format menu, select the 3-D View command, then set these parameters as you see fit.

DRAWING IN POWERPOINT

PowerPoint provides a set of drawing tools to develop virtually any type of illustration. Even if you are not an artist, you can use these tools to modify existing clip art and thus create new and very different illustrations. Consider, for example, Figure 3.3, which contains an original piece of clip art and five variations. (The clip art was taken from the Cartoons category of the Microsoft ClipArt Gallery.)

We are not artistic by nature, and there is no way that we could have created the original duck. We did, however, create all of the variations, and you will too, in the hands-on exercise that follows. All it took was a little imagination and a sense of what can be done. The modifications were done with tools on the Drawing and Drawing+ toolbars.

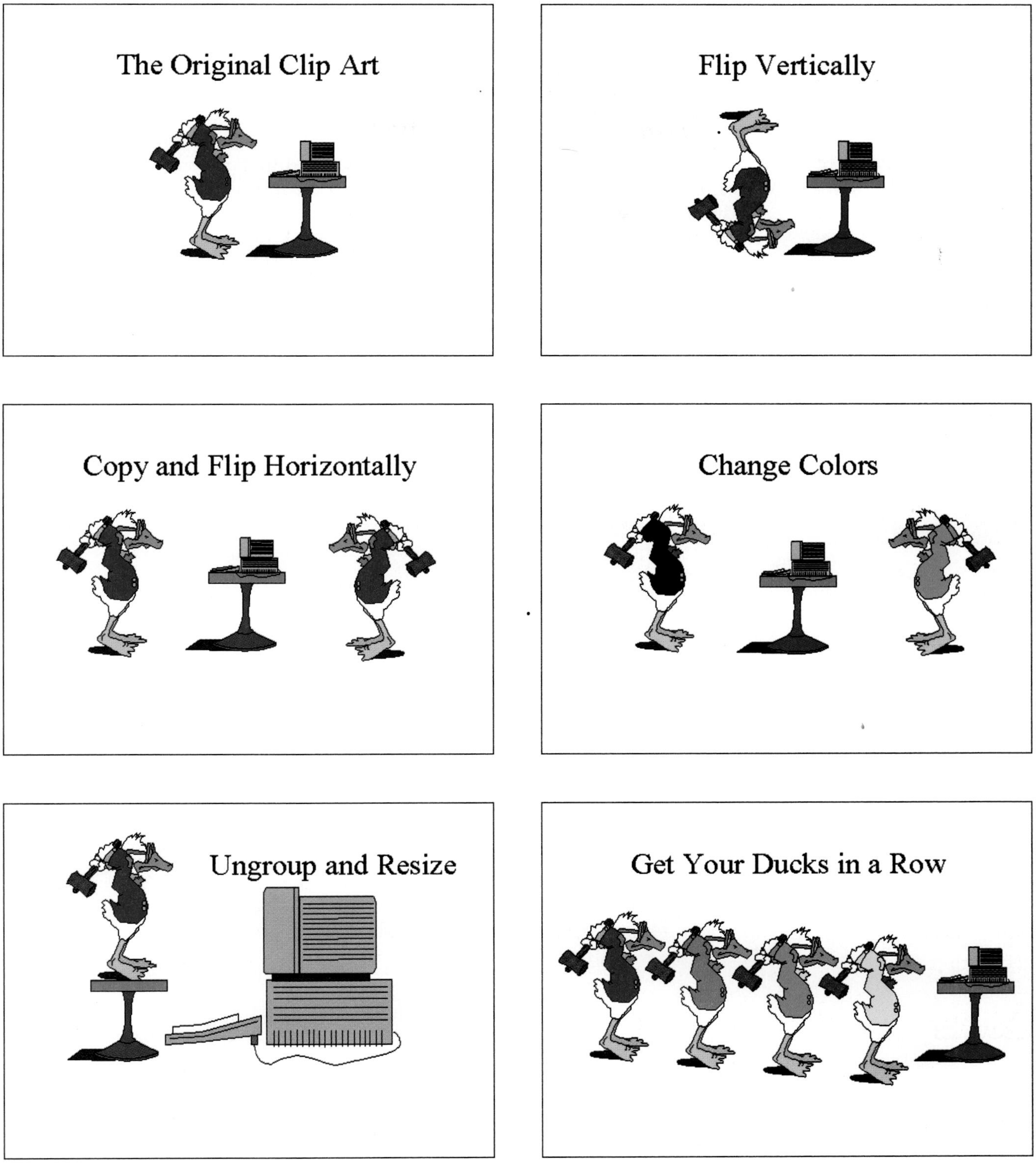
The Original Clip Art
Flip Vertically
Copy and Flip Horizontally
Change Colors
Ungroup and Resize
Get Your Ducks in a Row

FIGURE 3.3 What You Can Do with Clip Art

The Drawing and Drawing+ Toolbars

The Drawing and Drawing+ toolbars are displayed in Figures 3.4a and 3.4b, respectively. The ***Drawing toolbar*** is displayed by default in the Slide view. The ***Drawing+ toolbar*** is displayed through the View menu or by pointing to any visible toolbar and clicking the right mouse button to display a shortcut menu.

As with the other toolbars, there is no need to memorize what the individual buttons do. You can, however, gain a better appreciation for their function by viewing the tools in groups as is done in Figure 3.4. And, as with all toolbars, you can point to any tool and PowerPoint will display the name of the tool. Finally, you can access the online help facility for detailed information on a specific tool.

An ***object*** is anything you put on a slide. The Drawing and Drawing+ toolbars are used to create objects such as a line, a shape, or text. Select a tool—for example, the Line tool on the Drawing toolbar—then click and drag in the slide to create the object. Objects are the building blocks of a drawing, in that any draw-

Selects an object

A
Creates a text box, line, rectangle, ellipse, arc, or freeform object; rotates an object

Displays the AutoShapes toolbar

Changes the fill color or line color; toggles a shadow on and off

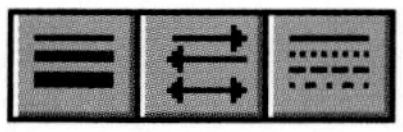
Changes the line thickness, arrowhead style, or line style

(a) The Drawing Toolbar

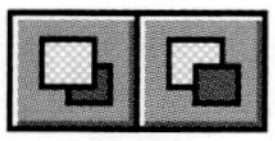
Brings object forward or sends object to back

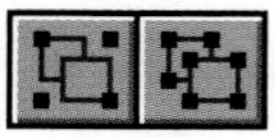
Groups or ungroups an object

Rotates an object left or right

Flips object horizontally or vertically

(b) The Drawing+ Toolbar

FIGURE 3.4 The Drawing Toolbars

ing can be broken down into a series of lines and shapes, each of which is considered an object.

As you create a drawing, you often work with many objects at the same time in order to apply the same command to those objects. The ***Group command*** combines individual objects so that you can work with them at the same time. The ***Ungroup (Disassemble Picture) command*** does the opposite, and breaks up an object into smaller objects so you can work with each object on an individual basis.

The exercise that follows has you insert a insert a clip art image into a presentation, then modify that image using various tools on the Drawing and Drawing+ toolbars. Be flexible and willing to experiment. Try, and try again, and don't be discouraged if you don't succeed initially. Just keep trying, and you will amaze yourself at what you will be able to do.

HANDS-ON EXERCISE 2

You Don't Have to Be an Artist

Objective: Insert clip art into a presentation, then use various tools on the Drawing and Drawing+ toolbars to modify the clip art. Use Figure 3.5 as a guide in the exercise.

STEP 1: Create the Title Slide

- Create a new presentation:
  - If necessary, start PowerPoint. Click the option button to create a **Blank Presentation** as you have been doing throughout the text. Click **OK.** If necessary, click the **Maximize button** so that PowerPoint takes the entire desktop.
  - If PowerPoint is already started, pull down the **File menu** and click **New** (or click the **New button** on the Standard toolbar). If necessary, double click the **Blank Presentation icon** to display the New Presentation dialog box.
- You should see the New slide dialog box with the **AutoLayout** for the title slide already selected. Click **OK** to create the title slide. Click the placeholder for the title. Type **What You Can Do With Clip Art** as shown in Figure 3.5a.
- Click the placeholder for the subtitle. Enter your name.
- Click the **Save button** on the Standard toolbar. Save the presentation as **You Don't Have to Be an Artist** in the **Exploring PowerPoint folder.**

STEP 2: The Drawing+ Toolbar

- Click the **New Slide command button** at the right of the status bar to display the New Slide dialog box.
- Select (click) the **Title Only AutoLayout.** (This is AutoLayout number 11 and is the third layout in the third row.) Click **OK** to create the slide shown in Figure 3.5b.
- Point to the **Drawing toolbar** (or any other toolbar), then click the **right mouse button** to display the shortcut menu shown in Figure 3.5b. Click **Drawing+** to display this toolbar.

STEP 3: Add the Clip Art

- If necessary, click and drag the title bar of the Drawing+ toolbar to anchor it at the left side of the window.

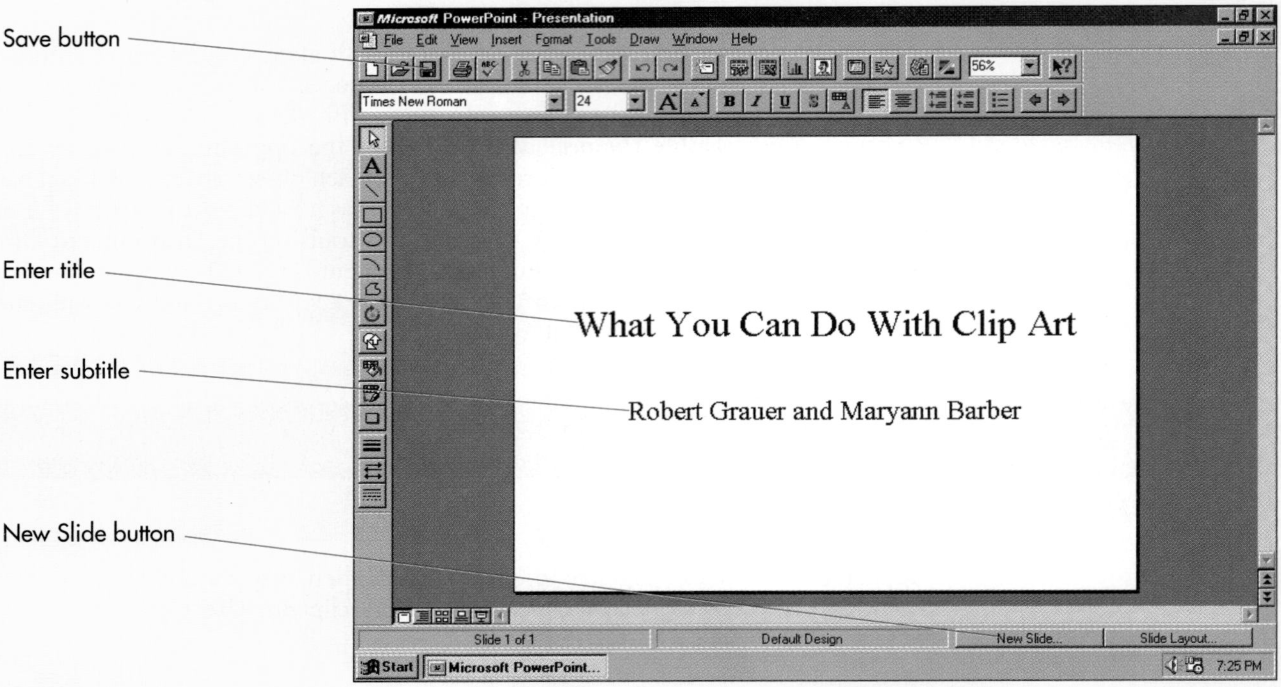
Save button
Enter title
Enter subtitle
New Slide button
Microsoft PowerPoint - Presentation
What You Can Do With Clip Art
Robert Grauer and Maryann Barber
Slide 1 of 1
Default Design
New Slide...
Slide Layout...

(a) Create the Title Slide (step 1)

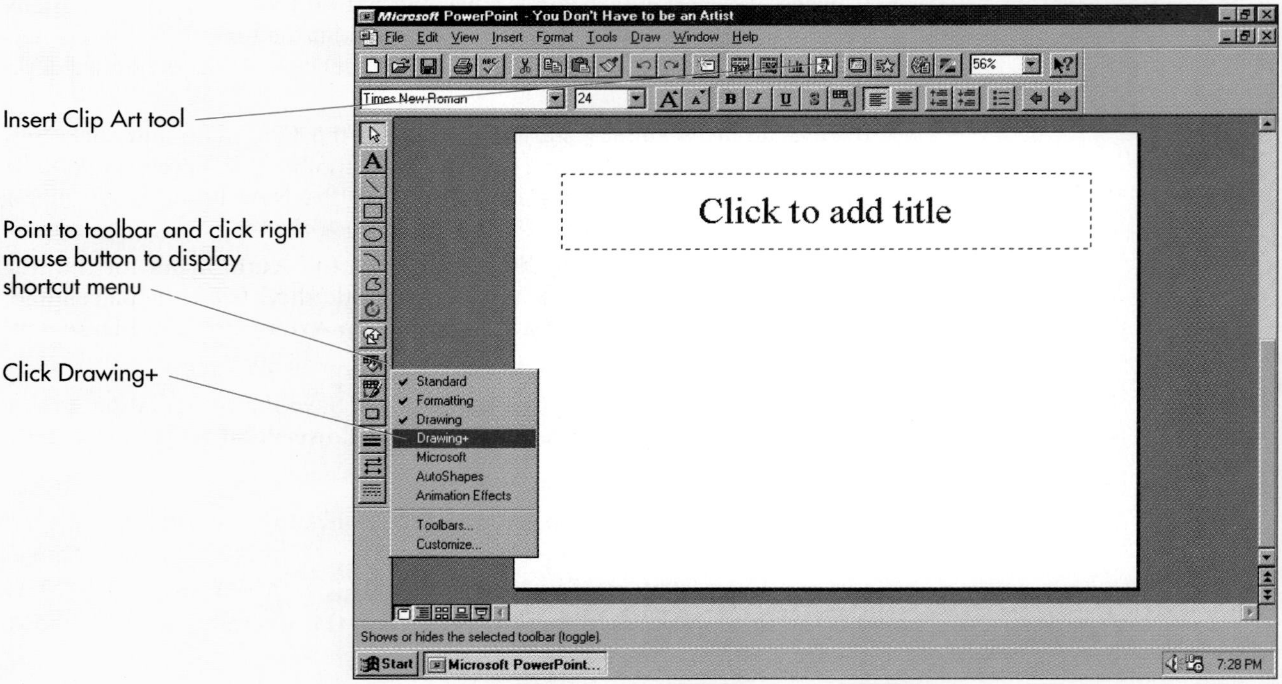
Insert Clip Art tool
Point to toolbar and click right mouse button to display shortcut menu
Click Drawing+
Microsoft PowerPoint - You Don't Have to be an Artist
Click to add title
Standard
Formatting
Drawing
Drawing+
Microsoft
AutoShapes
Animation Effects
Toolbars...
Customize...
Shows or hides the selected toolbar (toggle)

(b) The Drawing+ Toolbar (step 2)

FIGURE 3.5 Hands-on Exercise 2

➤ Click the **Insert Clip Art button** on the Standard toolbar to display the dialog box in Figure 3.5c. Select the **Cartoons category** (scrolling through the categories if required).

➤ Click the **down arrow** to scroll through the available cartoons until you can select the cartoon of the duck smashing the PC. Click **Insert** to insert the clip art onto the slide.

➤ Click the **placeholder** for the title. Type **The Original Clip Art** as the title of the slide. Save the presentation.

THE RECOLOR COMMAND

The Recolor command modifies an embedded object by substituting one color for another. Point to the embedded object, click the right mouse button to display a shortcut menu, then click the Recolor command to display the Recolor dialog box. Choose an existing (original) color, then click the associated down arrow to choose a new color. Change as many colors as you like, then click the OK command button to exit the command and return to the presentation. (The Recolor command is not available after an object has been ungrouped.)

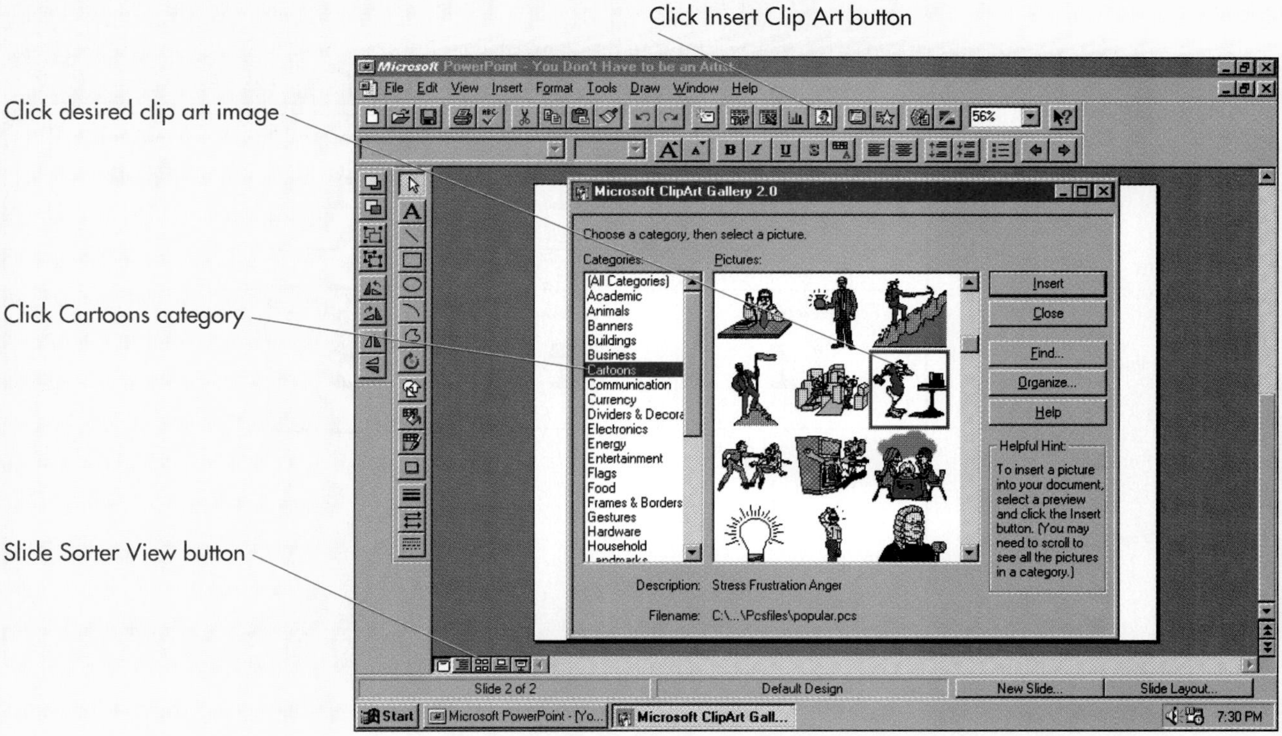
Click Insert Clip Art button
Click desired clip art image
Click Cartoons category
Slide Sorter View button
Microsoft ClipArt Gallery 2.0
Choose a category, then select a picture.
Categories:
Pictures:
Insert
Close
Find...
Organize...
Help
Helpful Hint:
To insert a picture into your document, select a preview and click the Insert button. (You may need to scroll to see all the pictures in a category.)
Description: Stress Frustration Anger
Filename: C:\...\Pcsfiles\popular.pcs
Slide 2 of 2
Default Design
New Slide...
Slide Layout...
7:30 PM

(c) Add the Clip Art (step 3)

FIGURE 3.5 Hands-on Exercise 2 (continued)

STEP 4: Copy the Slide

- Click the **Slide Sorter View button** on the status bar to change to the view in Figure 3.5d. Slide 2, the slide with the duck is selected.
- Click the **Copy button** on the Standard toolbar to copy the slide to the clipboard.
- Click the **Paste button** on the Standard toolbar to paste the contents of the clipboard into the presentation, which creates a new slide (slide 3) identical to slide 2.
- Click the **Paste button** four additional times so that you wind up with seven slides in all, as shown in Figure 3.5d.
- Save the presentation.

TOOL TIPS

Point to any button on any toolbar, and PowerPoint displays the name of the toolbar button, which is also indicative of its function. If pointing to a button has no effect, pull down the View menu, click Toolbars, and check the box to Show Tool Tips.

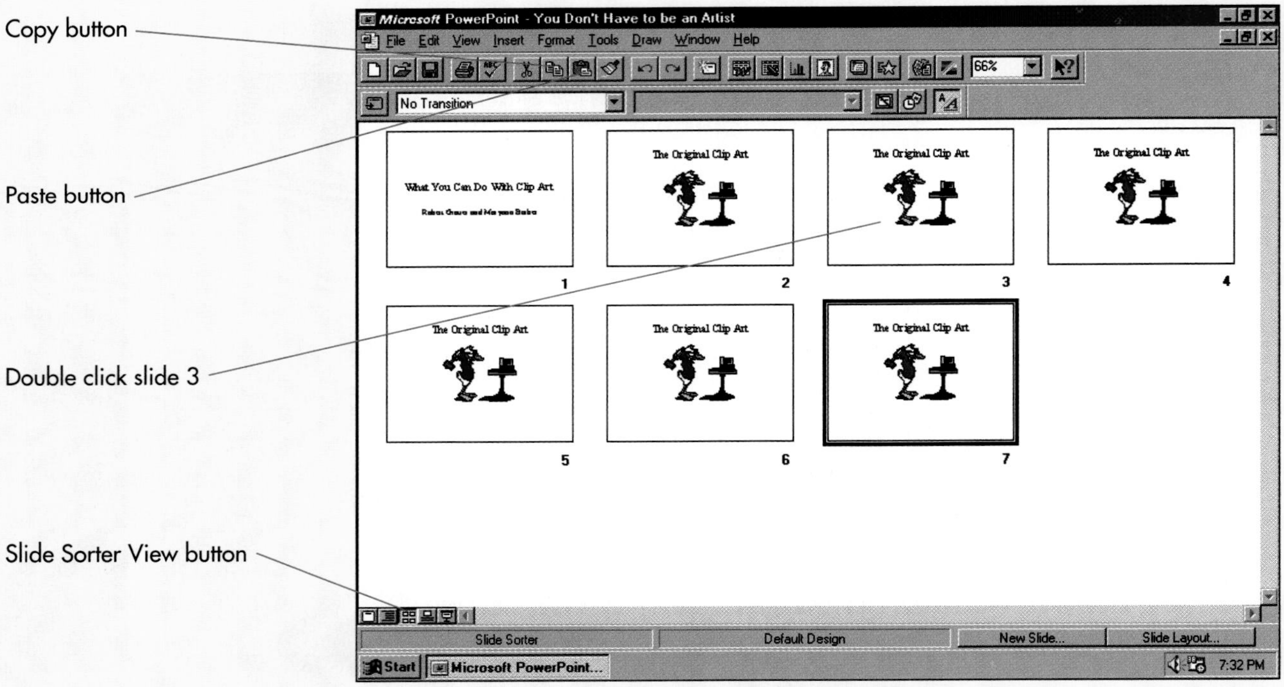

Copy button
Paste button
Double click slide 3
Slide Sorter View button
Microsoft PowerPoint - You Don't Have to be an Artist
File Edit View Insert Format Tools Draw Window Help
66%
No Transition
What You Can Do With Clip Art
The Original Clip Art
1
2
3
4
5
6
7
Slide Sorter
Default Design
New Slide...
Slide Layout...
Start
Microsoft PowerPoint...
7:32 PM

(d) Copy the Slide (step 4)

FIGURE 3.5 Hands-on Exercise 2 (continued)

STEP 5: Flip Vertically

- Double click **slide 3** to simultaneously select the slide and change to the Slide view, as shown in Figure 3.5e. The status bar should indicate that slide 3 is the current slide.
- Click and drag to select the text of the slide title, then type **Flip Vertically** as the new title.
- Click anywhere on the clip art to select the entire image. You should see eight sizing handles around the image as shown in the figure.
- Pull down the **Draw menu** and click **Ungroup,** or click the **Disassemble Picture (Ungroup) button** on the Drawing+ toolbar.
- You will see the dialog box in Figure 3.5e. Click **OK** to convert the object to a PowerPoint image, allowing you to use the PowerPoint tools to edit the image.
- You should see two sets of sizing handles: one set surrounding the duck, and the other set around the computer and the table.
- Click outside the selected area, then click anywhere on the duck to select just the duck.
- Click the **Flip Vertical button** on the Drawing+ toolbar. The duck is now upside down.
- Save the presentation.

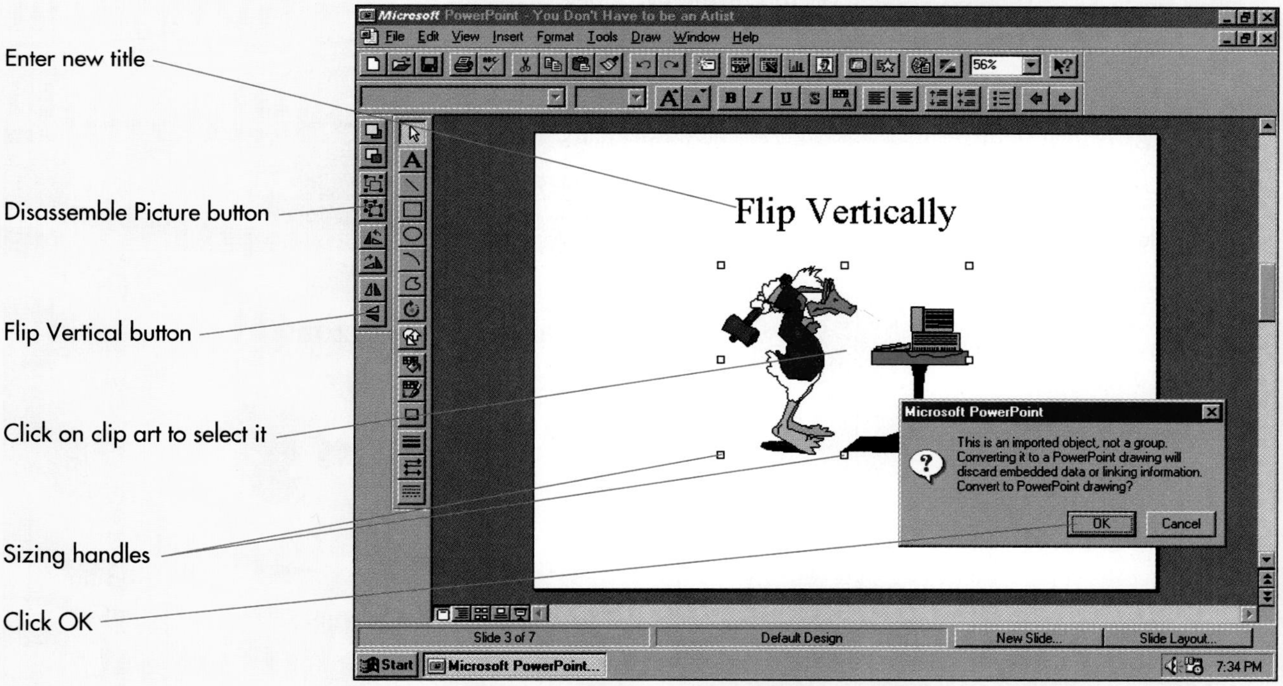

Enter new title
Disassemble Picture button
Flip Vertical button
Click on clip art to select it
Sizing handles
Click OK
Microsoft PowerPoint - You Don't Have to be an Artist
File Edit View Insert Format Tools Draw Window Help
Flip Vertically
Microsoft PowerPoint
This is an imported object, not a group. Converting it to a PowerPoint drawing will discard embedded data or linking information. Convert to PowerPoint drawing?
OK
Cancel
Slide 3 of 7
Default Design
New Slide...
Slide Layout...
Start
Microsoft PowerPoint...
7:34 PM

(e) The Ungroup Command (step 5)

FIGURE 3.5 Hands-on Exercise 2 (continued)

FLIP AND ROTATE

You can rotate an object 90 degrees to the left or right, or you can flip an object on its vertical or horizontal axis. If you are unable to use these tools, it is because the object is not a PowerPoint object. Just select the object, ungroup it, then regroup it. The object is transformed into a PowerPoint object, which can then be rotated or flipped.

STEP 6: Copy and Flip Horizontally

- Press the **PgDn key** (or click the **Next Slide button** at the bottom of the scroll bar) to move to slide 4. (You can also drag the scroll box (slide elevator) on the vertical scroll bar to move to slide 4.)
- Click and drag to select the slide title, then type **Copy and Flip Horizontally** as the new title as shown in Figure 3.5f.
- Click the clip art to select it, then drag the clip art to the left edge of the slide. Ungroup the duck and the computer as in step 5.
- Click outside the selected objects. Select just the duck. Click the **Copy button** on the Standard toolbar (which copies the duck to the clipboard).
- Click the **Paste button** on the Standard toolbar. You should see a second duck on top of the first duck.

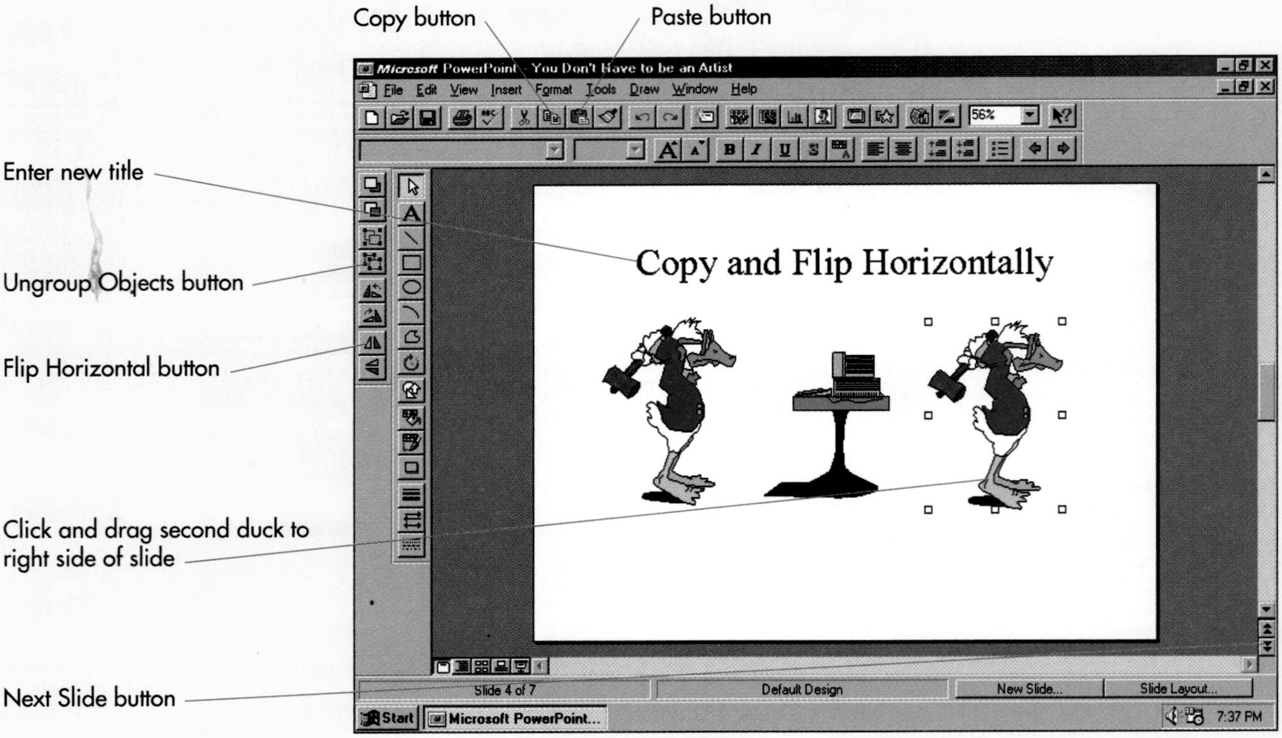

Copy button
Paste button
Enter new title
Ungroup Objects button
Flip Horizontal button
Click and drag second duck to right side of slide
Next Slide button
Microsoft PowerPoint - You Don't Have to be an Artist
File Edit View Insert Format Tools Draw Window Help
56%
Copy and Flip Horizontally
Slide 4 of 7
Default Design
New Slide...
Slide Layout...
Start
Microsoft PowerPoint...
7:37 PM

(f) Copy and Flip Horizontally (step 6)

FIGURE 3.5 Hands-on Exercise 2 (continued)

- ➤ Click and drag the second duck past the computer all the way to the right of the slide as shown in Figure 3.5f. Click the **Flip Horizontal button** to turn the duck around. Move the table and/or the ducks to adjust the spacing as desired.
- ➤ Save the presentation.

> **ALIGNING OBJECTS**
>
> You can improve the appearance of any slide by precisely aligning the objects it contains. Press and hold the Shift key to select the objects you want to align. Pull down the Draw menu, click Align, then choose the alignment you want (lefts, centers, rights, tops, middles, or bottoms) from the cascade menu.

STEP 7: Change Colors

- ➤ Press the **PgDn key** to move to slide 5. Click and drag to select the text of the slide title, then type **Change Colors** as the new title as shown in Figure 3.5g.
- ➤ Repeat the actions from the previous step to copy the duck and flip him horizontally:
  - Click and drag the clip art to the left side of the slide, then **ungroup** the duck and the computer.

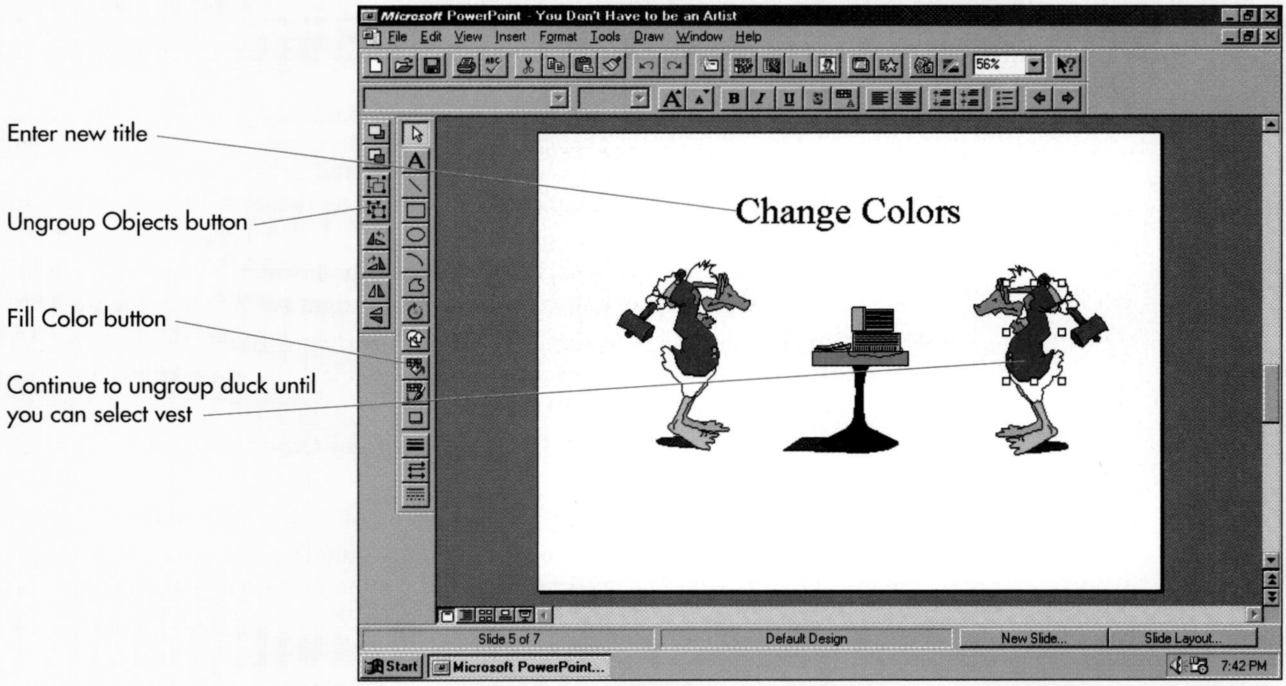

Enter new title
Ungroup Objects button
Fill Color button
Continue to ungroup duck until you can select vest
Microsoft PowerPoint - You Don't Have to be an Artist
File Edit View Insert Format Tools Draw Window Help
56%
Change Colors
Slide 5 of 7
Default Design
New Slide...
Slide Layout...
Start
Microsoft PowerPoint...
7:42 PM

(g) Change Colors (step 7)

FIGURE 3.5 Hands-on Exercise 2 (continued)

- Click outside the selected area to deselect both objects. Select the duck, click the **Copy button,** click the **Paste button,** then drag the second duck to the right of the computer.
- Click the **Flip Horizontal** button to turn the duck around.

➤ Check that the duck on the right is still selected, then click the **Ungroup Objects button** to ungroup the objects that make up this duck and his hammer. The duck is now a separate object; the hammer and shadow are a second object.

➤ Click outside the selected objects, then click the duck. Click the **Ungroup Objects button** to ungroup the objects that make up the duck.

➤ Continue to ungroup the duck until you have separated his vest from his tie. Click outside the selected objects, then click the **duck's vest** to select just the vest as shown in Figure 3.5g.

➤ Click the **Fill Color button** to produce the available fill colors. Click **Green** to change the vest to green. Repeat these steps to change the costume of the other duck to a black vest with a blue tie.

➤ Save the presentation.

FILL, LINE, AND SHADOW

All drawn objects have attributes (characteristics) that determine the appearance of the object. To change an attribute, select the object, then click the appropriate tool on the Drawing+ toolbar. You can apply a shadow. You can change the style of the exterior line and/or the color of the line. You can also change the interior (fill) color of the object and/or the fill pattern.

STEP 8: Ungroup and Resize

➤ Press the **PgDn key** to move to slide 6. Click and drag to select the text of the slide title, then type **Ungroup and Resize** as the new title as shown in Figure 3.5h.

➤ Check that the title is still selected. Pull down the **Format menu.** Click **Alignment.** Click **Right** to move the slide title to the right as shown in Figure 3.5h.

➤ Ungroup the duck and computer as you have been doing throughout the exercise. Click outside the selected areas, then select the duck. Click and drag the duck to the upper left part of the slide.

➤ Click the computer and table. Click the **Ungroup Objects button** to separate these items.

➤ Click outside the selected items, then click and drag the table under the duck.

➤ Click the computer. Drag a **corner handle** to increase the size of the computer, then click and drag to position the computer closer to the duck.

➤ Save the presentation.

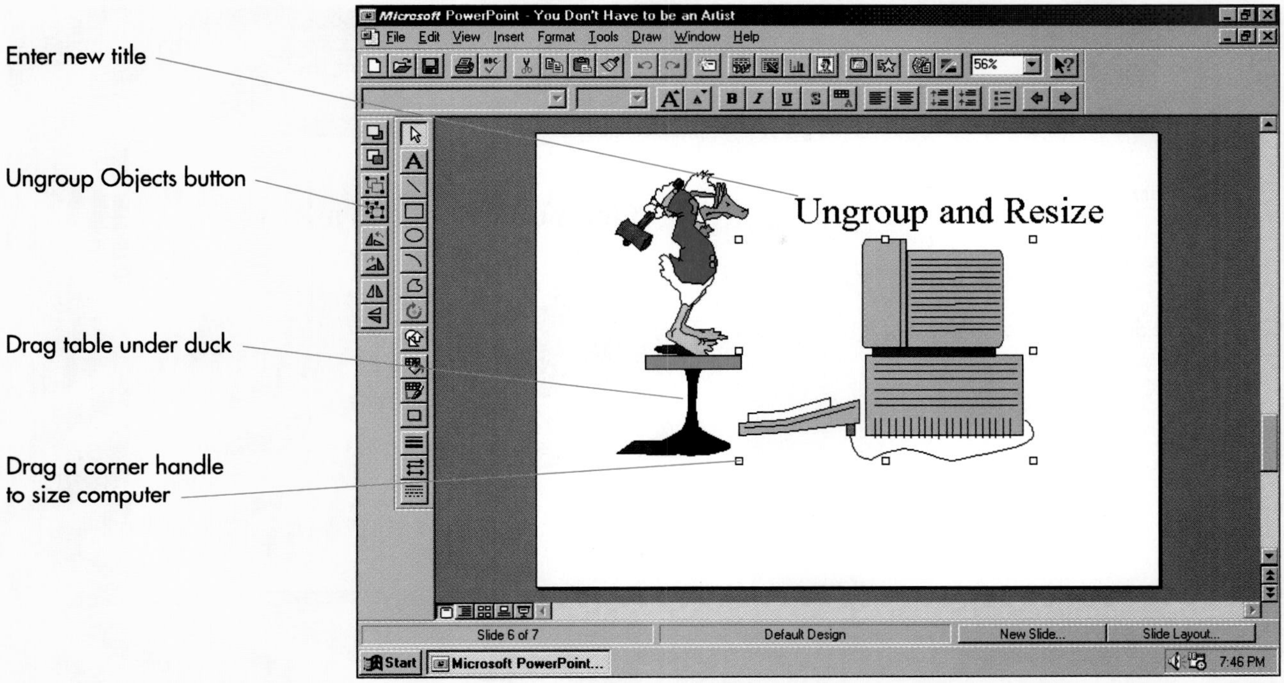
Enter new title
Ungroup Objects button
Drag table under duck
Drag a corner handle to size computer
Microsoft PowerPoint - You Don't Have to be an Artist
File Edit View Insert Format Tools Draw Window Help
Ungroup and Resize
Slide 6 of 7
Default Design
New Slide...
Slide Layout...
Start
Microsoft PowerPoint...
7:46 PM

(h) Ungroup and Resize (step 8)

FIGURE 3.5 Hands-on Exercise 2 (continued)

PICK UP THE MOUSE

You always seem to run out of room on your real desk, just when you need to move the mouse a little further. The solution is to pick up the mouse and move it closer to you—the pointer will stay in its present position on the screen, but when you put the mouse down, you will have more room on your desk in which to work.

STEP 9: The Duplicate Command

- Press the **PgDn key** to move to slide 7. Click and drag to select the slide title, then type **Get Your Ducks in a Row** as the new title as shown in Figure 3.5i.
- Click and drag the clip art to the left side of the slide, then **ungroup** the duck and the computer. Click outside the selection to deselect both items, then click and drag the computer and table to the right of the slide.
- Select the duck. Pull down the **Edit menu** and click **Duplicate** (a combination of the Copy and Paste commands). You will see a second duck to the right of the first. Drag the second duck to the right until the ducks are separated as shown in Figure 3.5i.
- Pull down the **Edit menu** a second time and click **Duplicate Again.** A third duck will appear. (The distance between the second and third ducks is equal to the distance between the first and second ducks.)

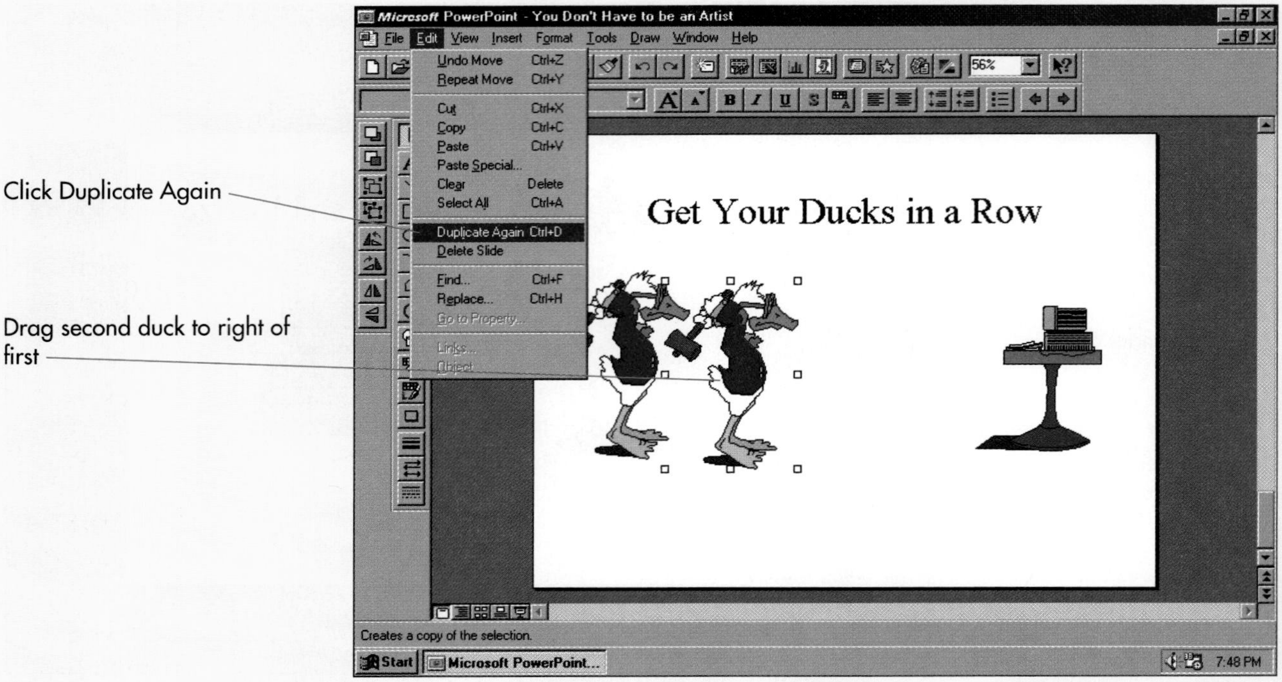
Click Duplicate Again
Drag second duck to right of first
Microsoft PowerPoint - You Don't Have to be an Artist
File Edit View Insert Format Tools Draw Window Help
Undo Move Ctrl+Z
Repeat Move Ctrl+Y
Cut Ctrl+X
Copy Ctrl+C
Paste Ctrl+V
Paste Special...
Clear Delete
Select All Ctrl+A
Duplicate Again Ctrl+D
Delete Slide
Find... Ctrl+F
Replace... Ctrl+H
Go to Property...
Links...
Object
56%
Get Your Ducks in a Row
Creates a copy of the selection.
Start
Microsoft PowerPoint...
7:48 PM

(i) The Duplicate Command (step 9)

FIGURE 3.5 Hands-on Exercise 2 (continued)

- Execute the **Duplicate Again** command a second time to create the fourth and final duck. Change the vest colors as you see fit.
- Save the presentation.

STEP 10: Print the Audience Handouts

- Pull down the **File menu.** Click **Slide Setup.** If necessary, click the **Portrait option button** to change the orientation for the Notes, Handouts, and Outline. Click **OK.**
- Pull down the **File menu.** Click **Print** to produce the Print dialog box. Click the **arrow** in the Print What drop-down list box. Click **Handouts (2 slides per page).**
- Check that the **All option button** is selected. Check the box to **Frame Slides.** Click **OK** to print the handouts.
- Save the presentation. Exit PowerPoint if you do not want to continue with the next exercise at this time.

OBJECT LINKING AND EMBEDDING

OLE

One of the primary advantages of the Windows environment is the ability to create a ***compound document*** containing data from multiple applications. This is accomplished through ***Object Linking and Embedding*** (OLE, pronounced "oh-lay") and it enables you to insert data (objects) from other applications into a PowerPoint presentation. You have, in fact, used OLE every time you inserted a clip art object into a presentation. You used it again at the beginning of this chapter to insert a graph created with the Microsoft Graph application. The next several pages describe other types of objects you can use to enhance a presentation.

In actuality, linking and embedding are two different techniques. The essential difference between the two is that embedding places the object into the presentation, whereas linking does not. In other words, an ***embedded object*** is stored within the presentation, and the presentation, in turn, becomes the only user (container) of that object. A ***linked object,*** on the other hand, is stored in its own file, and the presentation is one of many potential containers of that object. The presentation does not contain the object per se, but only a representation of the object as well as a pointer (link) to the file containing the object (the source document). The advantage of linking is that the presentation is updated automatically if the object is changed in the source document.

The choice between linking and embedding depends on how the object will be used. Linking is preferable if the object is likely to change and your presentation requires the latest version. Linking should also be used when the same object is placed in many documents, so that any change to the object has to be made in only one place (the source document). Embedding should be used if you need to take the presentation with you—for example, if you intend to show the presentation on a different computer.

The easiest way to link or embed an object is through the appropriate AutoLayout as shown in Figure 3.6. Choose the AutoLayout for an Object slide as shown in Figure 3.6a, then double click the object placeholder to produce the Insert Object dialog box in Figure 3.6b. The object types displayed within the dialog box depend on the applications that are installed on your system.

The option buttons to create a new object or to create the object from a file are mutually exclusive in that you choose one or the other. If you embed an object, you can choose either option. If you link, however, you must choose the Create from File option because a linked object has to exist in its own file. This in turn produces the dialog box in Figure 3.6c, in which you must enter the source file name as well as check the box to create a link. The example links the Excel workbook, Grade Book in the Exploring Excel folder, to the PowerPoint presentation and is illustrated in the next hands-on exercise.

WordArt

Microsoft WordArt is a separate application included with Microsoft Office that enables you to add special effects to text, then embed the text as an object into a presentation. WordArt is called from within PowerPoint by choosing the AutoLayout for an object slide, double clicking the object placeholder, and selecting WordArt object.

WordArt is intuitive and easy to use. In essence, you enter the text in the dialog box of Figure 3.7a, then choose a shape for the text from among the selections shown in Figure 3.7b. You can create special effects by choosing one of several different shadows as shown in Figure 3.7c. You can use any TrueType font installed on your system, and you can change the color and/or patterns of the WordArt object. Figure 3.7d shows the completed WordArt object.

Organization Charts

Microsoft Organization Chart is yet another application included with Microsoft Office; it enables you to create an organization chart and embed it into a presentation. You start the application by choosing the AutoLayout containing an organization chart or by creating an object slide and choosing Microsoft Organization Chart as the object.

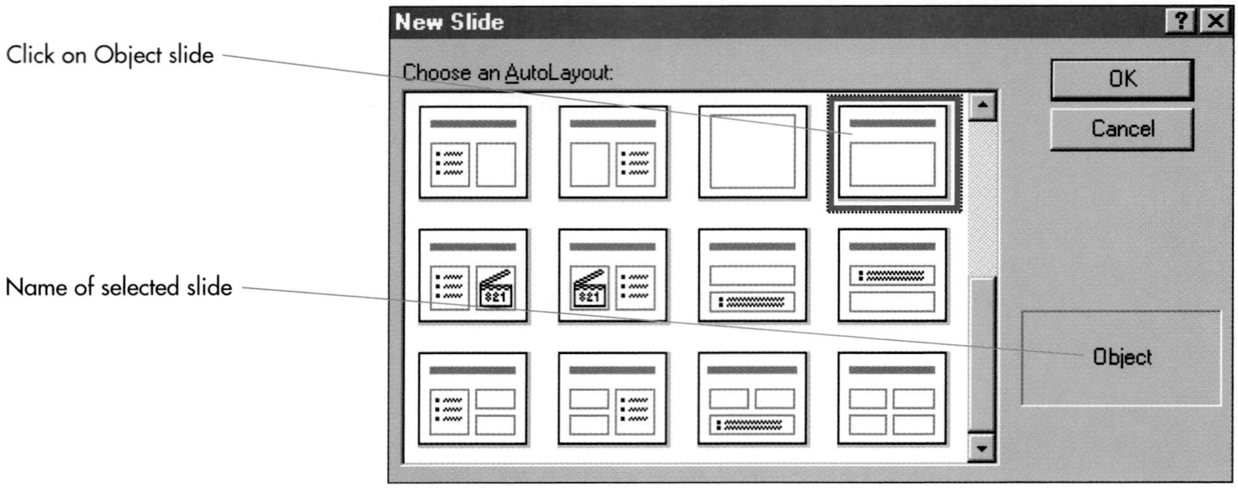
Click on Object slide
Name of selected slide
New Slide
Choose an AutoLayout:
OK
Cancel
Object

(a) The AutoLayout

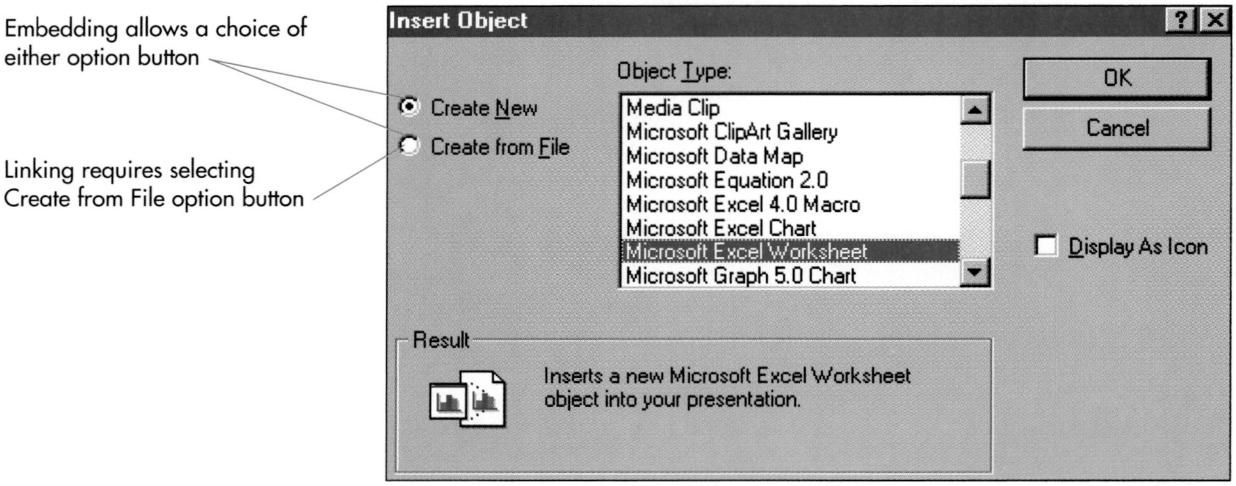
Embedding allows a choice of either option button
Linking requires selecting Create from File option button
Insert Object
Create New
Create from File
Object Type:
Media Clip
Microsoft ClipArt Gallery
Microsoft Data Map
Microsoft Equation 2.0
Microsoft Excel 4.0 Macro
Microsoft Excel Chart
Microsoft Excel Worksheet
Microsoft Graph 5.0 Chart
OK
Cancel
Display As Icon
Result
Inserts a new Microsoft Excel Worksheet object into your presentation.

(b) Insert Object Dialog Box

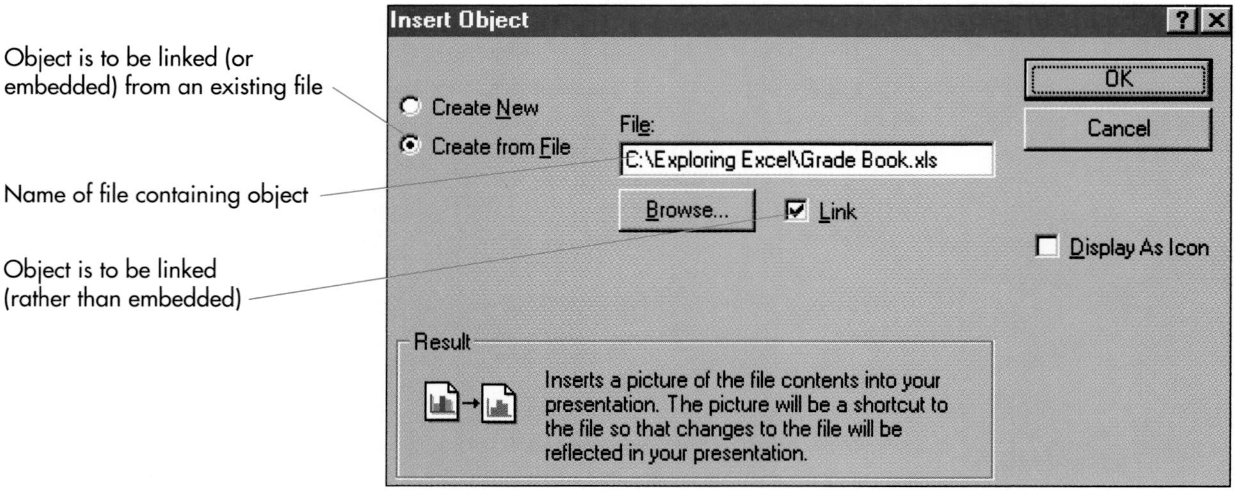
Object is to be linked (or embedded) from an existing file
Name of file containing object
Object is to be linked (rather than embedded)
Insert Object
Create New
Create from File
File:
C:\Exploring Excel\Grade Book.xls
Browse...
Link
OK
Cancel
Display As Icon
Result
Inserts a picture of the file contents into your presentation. The picture will be a shortcut to the file so that changes to the file will be reflected in your presentation.

(c) Create the Link

FIGURE 3.6 Object Linking and Embedding

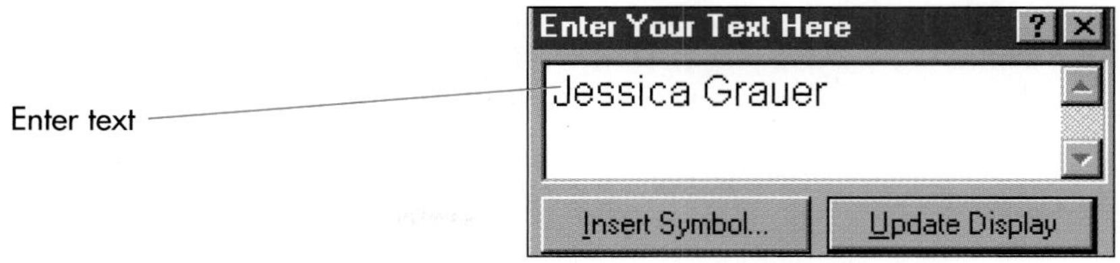

Enter Your Text Here
Jessica Grauer
Enter text
Insert Symbol...
Update Display

(a) Enter Text

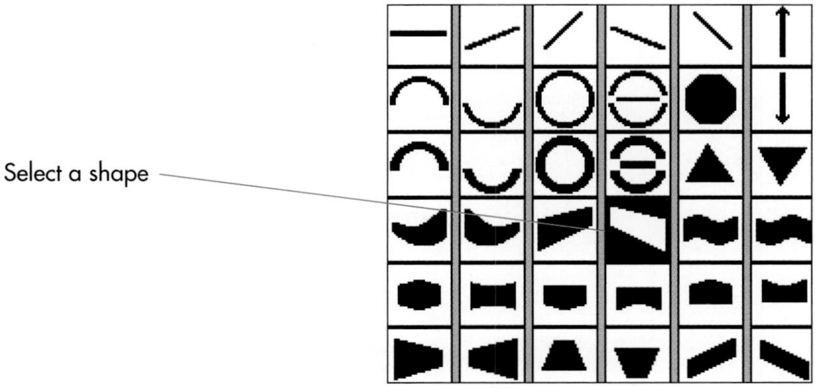

Select a shape

(b) Text Shapes

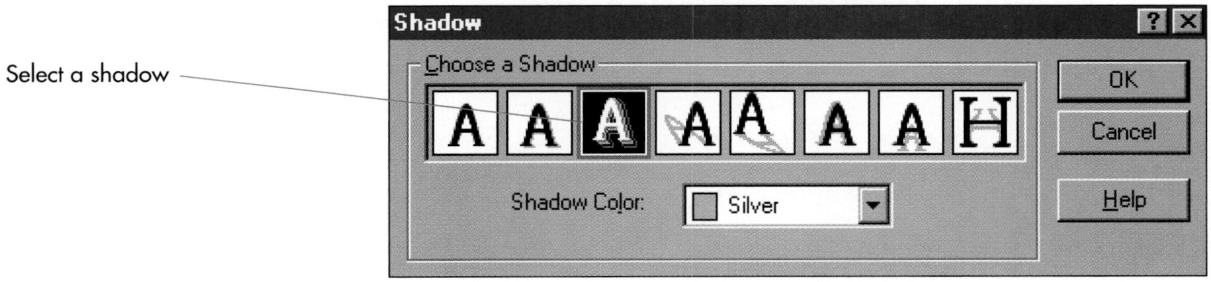

Shadow
Choose a Shadow
Select a shadow
Shadow Color:
Silver
OK
Cancel
Help

(c) Shadows

Jessica Grauer

(d) Completed Text

FIGURE 3.7 WordArt

A partially completed organization chart is shown in Figure 3.8. To add additional boxes, you just click the appropriate command button at the top of the window. The coworker buttons create a box on the same level to the left or right of the current box. The subordinate command button creates a box under the current box, while the manager button creates a box above the current box. To delete a box, select the box, then press the Del key.

You can change the design of the connecting lines and/or the boxes in the chart, as well as their color. You can also change the font and/or alignment of the text within the individual boxes. Microsoft Organization Chart is illustrated in the hands-on exercise that follows shortly.

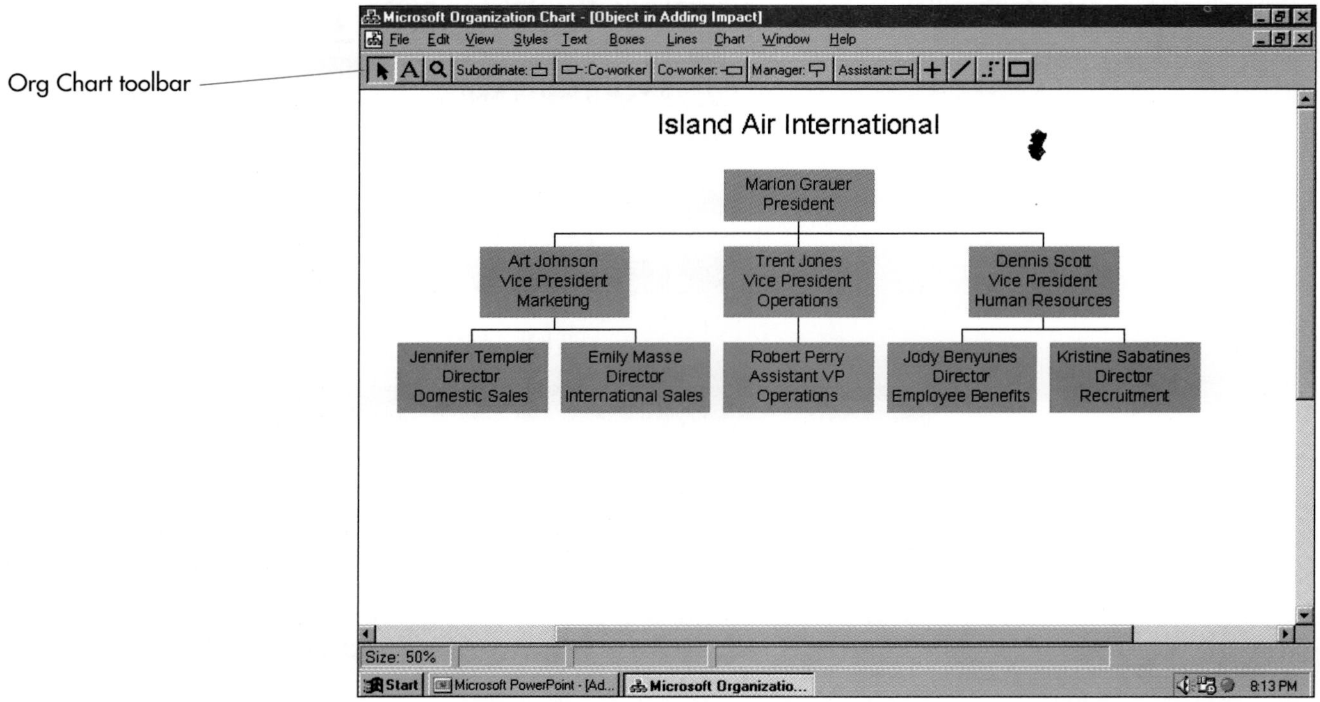

Org Chart toolbar
Microsoft Organization Chart - [Object in Adding Impact]
File Edit View Styles Text Boxes Lines Chart Window Help
Subordinate: Co-worker Co-worker: Manager: Assistant:
Island Air International
Marion Grauer President
Art Johnson Vice President Marketing
Trent Jones Vice President Operations
Dennis Scott Vice President Human Resources
Jennifer Templer Director Domestic Sales
Emily Masse Director International Sales
Robert Perry Assistant VP Operations
Jody Benyunes Director Employee Benefits
Kristine Sabatines Director Recruitment
Size: 50%
Start Microsoft PowerPoint - [Ad... Microsoft Organizatio...
8:13 PM

FIGURE 3.8 Organization Chart

Sound

Sound can be linked or embedded into a presentation just like any other object. Realize, however, that sound requires additional hardware, namely a sound card and speakers, and we urge you to include these options on any machine you buy. (Sound may not be available in a laboratory setting for obvious reasons.)

Sounds exist as separate files that are inserted into a presentation through the Insert Object command as illustrated in the following hands-on exercise. Additional information about the different types of sound files is found in Appendix B, Introduction to Multimedia.

HANDS-ON EXERCISE 3

Adding Impact through Object Linking and Embedding

Objective: To link an Excel worksheet to a PowerPoint presentation; to embed an organization chart, a WordArt object, and a sound file into a PowerPoint presentation. Use Figure 3.9 as a guide in doing the exercise. Completion of the exercise requires that Microsoft Excel be installed on your system.

STEP 1: Create the Title Slide

- Create a new presentation:
  - If necessary, start PowerPoint. Click the option button to create a **Blank Presentation,** then click **OK.** If necessary, click the **Maximize button** so that PowerPoint takes the entire desktop.
  - If PowerPoint is already started, pull down the **File menu** and click **New** (or click the **New button** on the Standard toolbar). If necessary, double click the **Blank Presentation icon** to display the New Presentation dialog box.
- You should see the New slide dialog box with the AutoLayout for the title slide already selected. Click **OK** to create the title slide. Click the placeholder for the title and enter **Adding Impact** as the title of the presentation. Click the placeholder for the subtitle. Enter your name.
- Click the **Save button** on the Standard toolbar. Save the presentation as **Adding Impact** in the **Exploring PowerPoint folder.**

STEP 2: Add an Object Slide

- Click the **New Slide button** on the status bar to add a second slide. You should see the New Slide dialog box. Click the **down arrow** and scroll through the available slide layouts until you can select the **Object slide** (AutoLayout number 16). Click **OK.**
- You should see the slide in Figure 3.9a.

THE AUTOLAYOUTS ARE NUMBERED

Each of the 24 AutoLayouts has an assigned number, corresponding to its position within the New Slide dialog box. (The layouts are numbered consecutively from left to right and top to bottom.) The number can be used as a shortcut to select the AutoLayout in lieu of clicking; type 2, for example, to select a bulleted list (the second slide in row 1). Other frequently used AutoLayouts include a title slide (number 1), a graph and title (number 8), an organization chart and title (number 7), an object and title (number 16), and a blank slide (number 12).

STEP 3: Insert the Excel Worksheet

- Double click the **placeholder** to add an object, producing the Insert Object dialog box. Scroll through the **Object Type** list box until you can select **Microsoft Excel Worksheet.** Then:

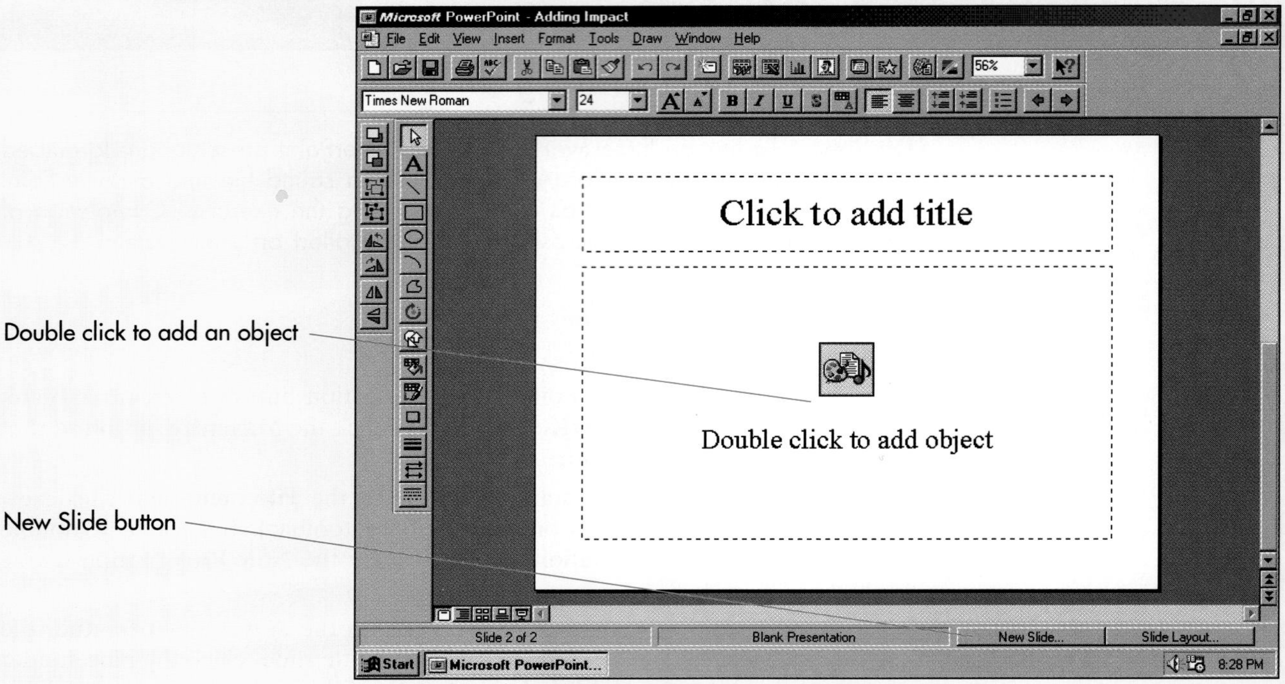
Double click to add an object
New Slide button
Microsoft PowerPoint - Adding Impact
File Edit View Insert Format Tools Draw Window Help
Times New Roman
24
56%
Click to add title
Double click to add object
Slide 2 of 2
Blank Presentation
New Slide...
Slide Layout...
Start
Microsoft PowerPoint...
8:28 PM

(a) Add an Object Slide (step 2)

FIGURE 3.9 Hands-on Exercise 3

- Click the option button for **Create from File** to produce the dialog box in Figure 3.9b.
- Click the **Browse button** to display the Browse dialog box. Click the **down arrow** on the Look In list box and select the **Exploring PowerPoint folder** (which contains the Excel workbook you are looking for).
- Select the **Grade Book workbook** from within the Exploring PowerPoint folder. Click **OK** to close the Browse dialog box.

LINKING VERSUS EMBEDDING

Linking is very different from embedding as it provides a dynamic connection between the source and container (destination) documents. A linked object (e.g., an Excel worksheet) is tied to the container document (e.g., a PowerPoint presentation) in such a way that any changes to the source file are automatically reflected in the container document. Linking is especially useful when the same object is inserted in multiple documents, as changes to the object are made in only one place (in the source file). A linked object must be saved as a separate file. An embedded object, on the other hand, is inserted directly into a source document and need not exist in its own file.

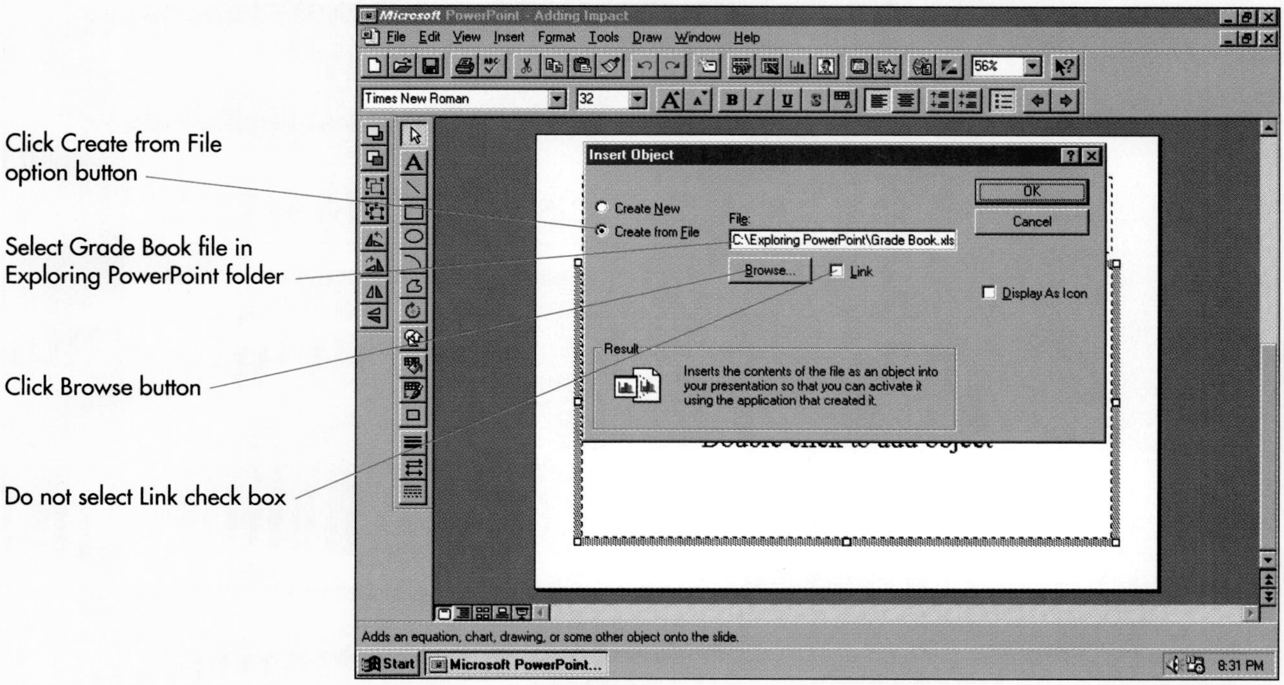
Click Create from File option button
Select Grade Book file in Exploring PowerPoint folder
Click Browse button
Do not select Link check box
Microsoft PowerPoint - Adding Impact
File Edit View Insert Format Tools Draw Window Help
Times New Roman
32
56%
Insert Object
Create New
Create from File
File:
C:\Exploring PowerPoint\Grade Book.xls
Browse...
Link
OK
Cancel
Display As Icon
Result
Inserts the contents of the file as an object into your presentation so that you can activate it using the application that created it.
Adds an equation, chart, drawing, or some other object onto the slide.
Start
Microsoft PowerPoint...
8:31 PM

(b) Select the Object (step 3)

FIGURE 3.9 Hands-on Exercise 3 (continued)

- If necessary, clear the Link check box as we want to embed (rather than link) the worksheet into the presentation. Click **OK** to insert the worksheet into the presentation. (This may take a moment, depending on the speed of your system.)

➤ Save the presentation.

STEP 4: Move and Size the Worksheet

➤ You should see the worksheet in Figure 3.9c. The sizing handles indicate that the worksheet is currently selected and can be moved and sized like any other Windows object.

➤ Click anywhere outside the worksheet to deselect it. The sizing handles disappear.

➤ Click the **title placeholder** and type **CIS120 Grade Book** as the title of the slide.

➤ Save the presentation.

IN-PLACE EDITING

In-place editing enables you to double click an Excel worksheet in order to edit the object. You remain in PowerPoint, but the toolbar and pull-down menus are those of Excel. The File and Window menus are exceptions, however, and contain PowerPoint commands to save the presentation and/or view multiple presentations.

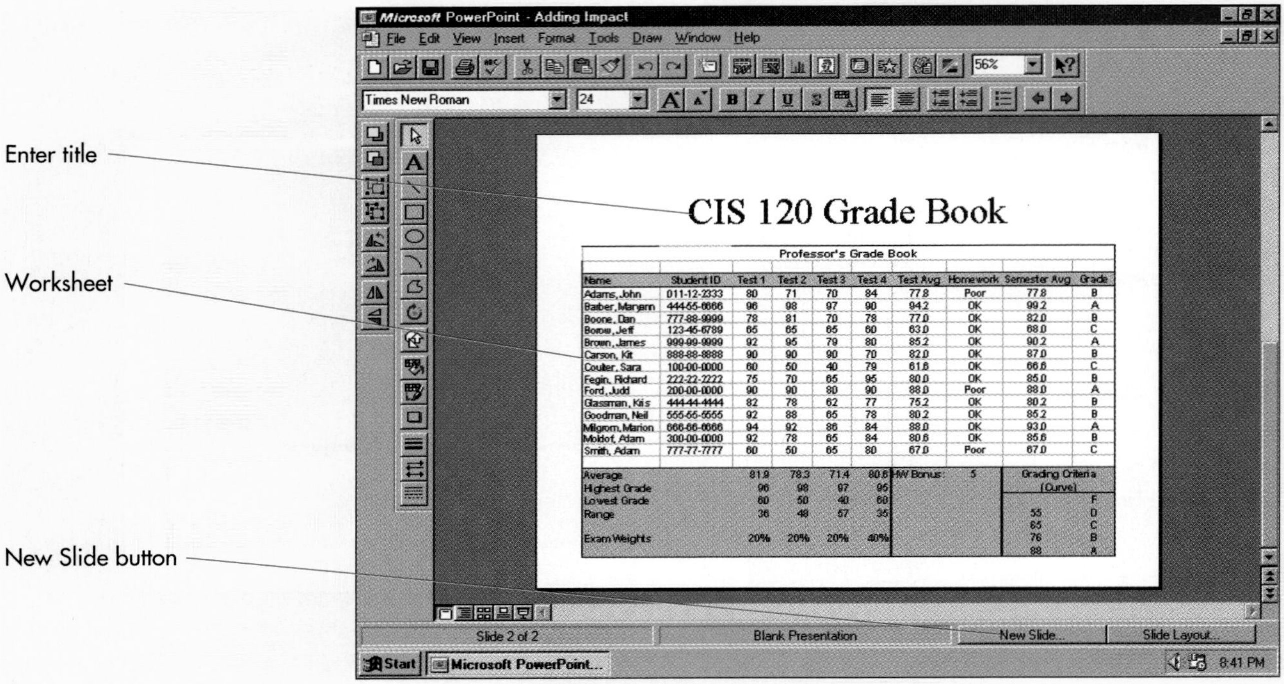
Enter title
Worksheet
New Slide button
Microsoft PowerPoint - Adding Impact
File Edit View Insert Format Tools Draw Window Help
Times New Roman
24
56%
CIS 120 Grade Book
Professor's Grade Book
Slide 2 of 2
Blank Presentation
New Slide...
Slide Layout...
Start
Microsoft PowerPoint...
8:41 PM

(c) Complete the Slide (step 4)

FIGURE 3.9 Hands-on Exercise 3 (continued)

STEP 5: Add the Organization Chart

➤ Click the **New Slide button** on the status bar. Click the AutoLayout for an **Organization chart** (or just type the number **7,** which is the number of the desired layout). Click **OK** to add the slide, then double click the placeholder to add the organization chart.

➤ You should see a window titled **Microsoft Organization Chart** open within the PowerPoint window, as shown in Figure 3.9d. Click the **Maximize button** of the Microsoft Organization Chart window.

➤ The text in the first box is already selected. Type your name and press **enter** to move to the second line. Type **President** for your title.

➤ Click in the first box in the second row. Enter the name of a friend as Vice President of Marketing. (Press **enter** to move to a second line.) Add two additional friends as Vice Presidents of Operations and Human Resources.

STEP 6: Complete the Organization Chart

➤ You can add detail to the chart by entering additional boxes for subordinates or coworkers. Enter the subordinates as shown in Figure 3.9e:

- To add a subordinate, click the subordinate button on the Organization Chart toolbar, then click the box under which the subordinate is to appear.
- To add a coworker, manager, or assistant, follow the same procedure as for a subordinate.
- To enter a person's name and title in an existing box, click in the box, then enter the text. Press the **enter key** to go from line to line.
- To delete a box, click in the box to select it, then press the **Del key.**

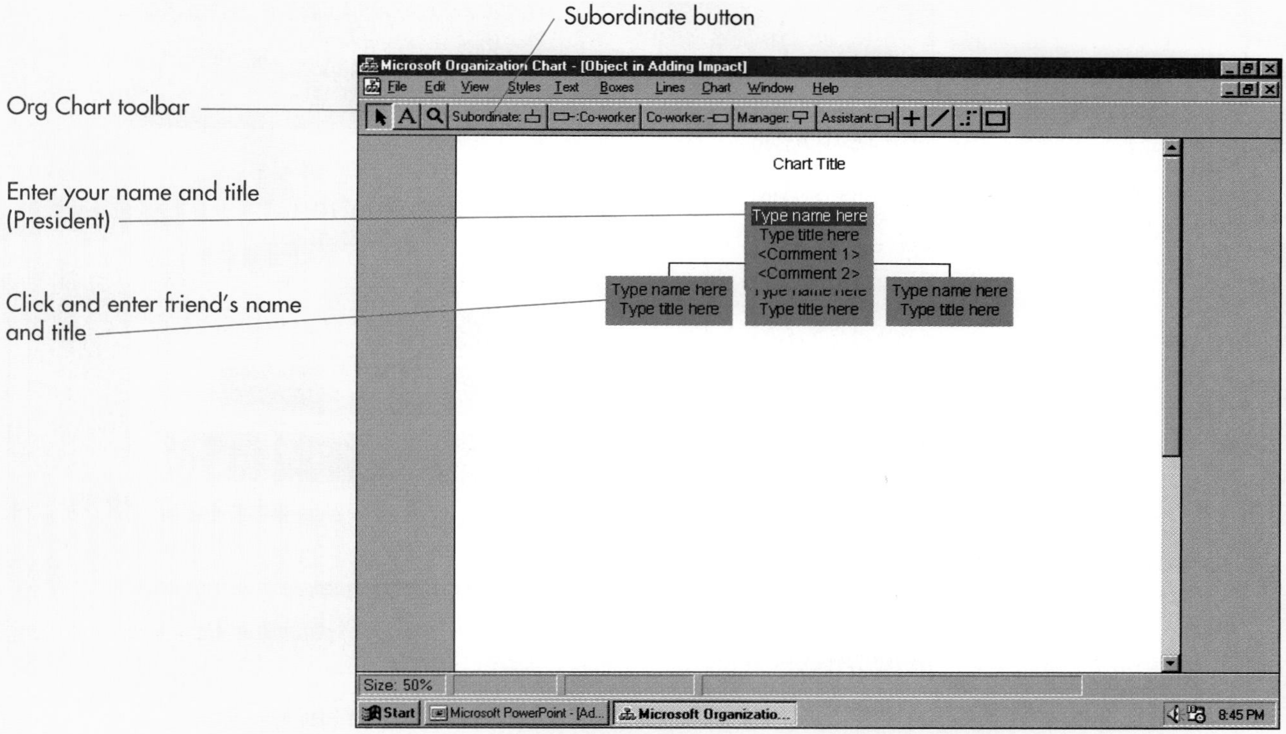

Subordinate button
Org Chart toolbar
Enter your name and title (President)
Click and enter friend's name and title
Microsoft Organization Chart - [Object in Adding Impact]
File Edit View Styles Text Boxes Lines Chart Window Help
Subordinate: Co-worker Co-worker: Manager: Assistant:
Chart Title
Type name here
Type title here
<Comment 1>
<Comment 2>
Type name here
Type title here
Type name here
Type title here
Size: 50%
Start
Microsoft PowerPoint - [Ad...
Microsoft Organizatio...
8:45 PM

(d) Create the Organization Chart (step 5)

FIGURE 3.9 Hands-on Exercise 3 (continued)

- Pull down the **File menu.** Click **Exit and Return to Adding Impact** (the name of the presentation). Click **Yes** when asked whether to update the object. You should see an organization chart similar to the one in Figure 3.9e.
- Click the placeholder for the slide title and enter the title of your organization.
- Save the presentation.

SELECT, THEN DO

You can change the appearance of the various boxes within an organization chart by selecting the box, then executing the appropriate formatting command. It's generally best, however, to retain a uniform appearance for the chart as a whole by formatting the entire chart at one time. Thus, to select multiple boxes, press and hold the Shift key as you click each box in succession, or press Ctrl+A to select all of the boxes at the same time. Pull down the Boxes menu, then select the command to change the border style, border color, or border line style. To change the line color, style, or thickness, select all of the lines (pull down the Edit menu, click Select, and click Connecting lines), then choose the desired commands from the Lines menu.

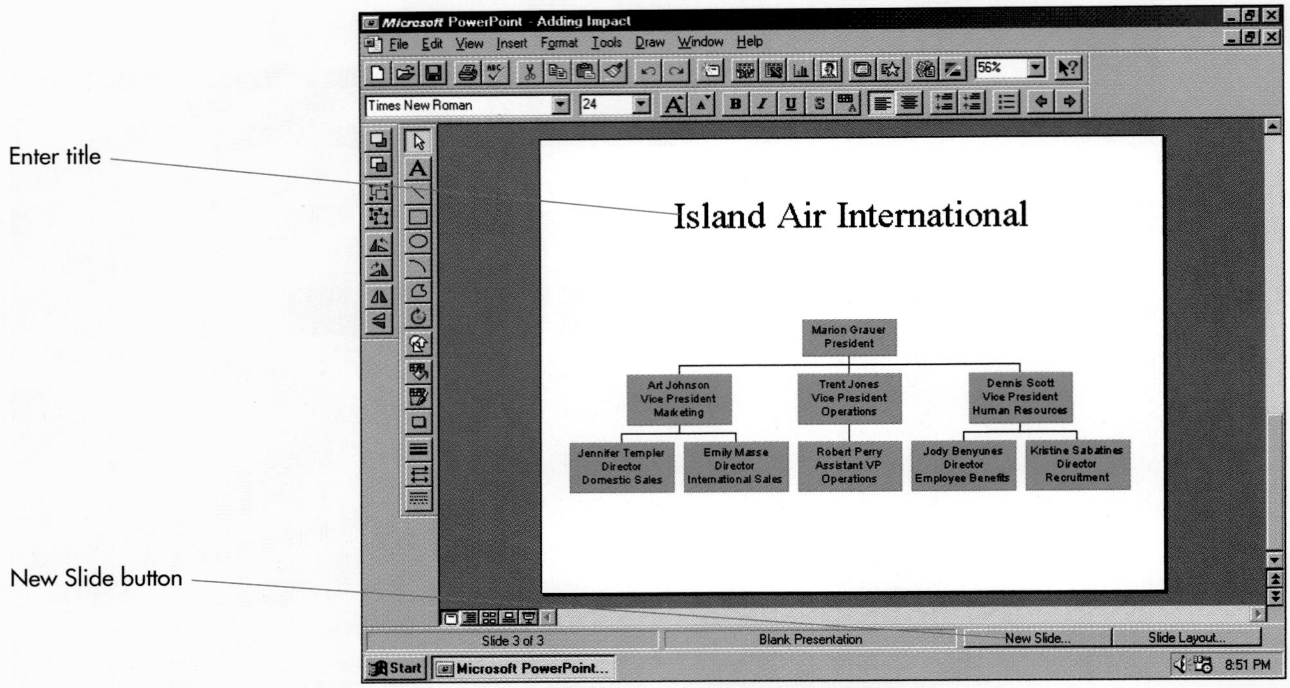

Enter title
New Slide button
Microsoft PowerPoint - Adding Impact
File Edit View Insert Format Tools Draw Window Help
Island Air International
Marion Grauer
President
Art Johnson
Vice President
Marketing
Trent Jones
Vice President
Operations
Dennis Scott
Vice President
Human Resources
Jennifer Templer
Director
Domestic Sales
Emily Masse
Director
International Sales
Robert Perry
Assistant VP
Operations
Jody Benyunes
Director
Employee Benefits
Kristine Sabatines
Director
Recruitment
Slide 3 of 3
Blank Presentation
New Slide...
Slide Layout...
Start
Microsoft PowerPoint...
8:51 PM

(e) The Completed Organization Chart (step 6)

FIGURE 3.9 Hands-on Exercise 3 (continued)

STEP 7: Clip Art and AutoShapes

➤ Click the **New Slide button** on the status bar, then do one of the following:

- Click **AutoLayout Number 11** (Title only), click **OK** to add the slide to the presentation, then click the **Insert Clip Art button** on the Standard toolbar to display the ClipArt Gallery dialog box, *or*
- Click **AutoLayout Number 16** (Object), click **OK** to add the slide to the presentation, then double click the placeholder to add the object. Choose **Microsoft ClipArt Gallery** from the list of available objects to display the ClipArt Gallery dialog box.

➤ Choose an appropriate clip art image. Click **Insert,** then move and size the clip art so that it is positioned as shown in Figure 3.9f. Click in the title placeholder, then enter **Clip Art and AutoShapes** as the title for this slide.

➤ Click the **AutoShapes button** on the Drawing toolbar to display the AutoShapes toolbar. Select (click) the **Balloon tool,** then click and drag on the slide where you want the balloon to go. Release the mouse.

➤ The balloon should be selected automatically with the sizing handles displayed:

- Type **I can do this!** as the caption. (You must enter the text when the balloon is selected.)
- If necessary, click and drag the balloon to adjust its size or position.
- To change the Fill color or Line color, click the appropriate tool on the Drawing toolbar, then select one of the displayed colors.

➤ Click outside the balloon to deselect it.

➤ Save the presentation. Close the AutoShapes toolbar.

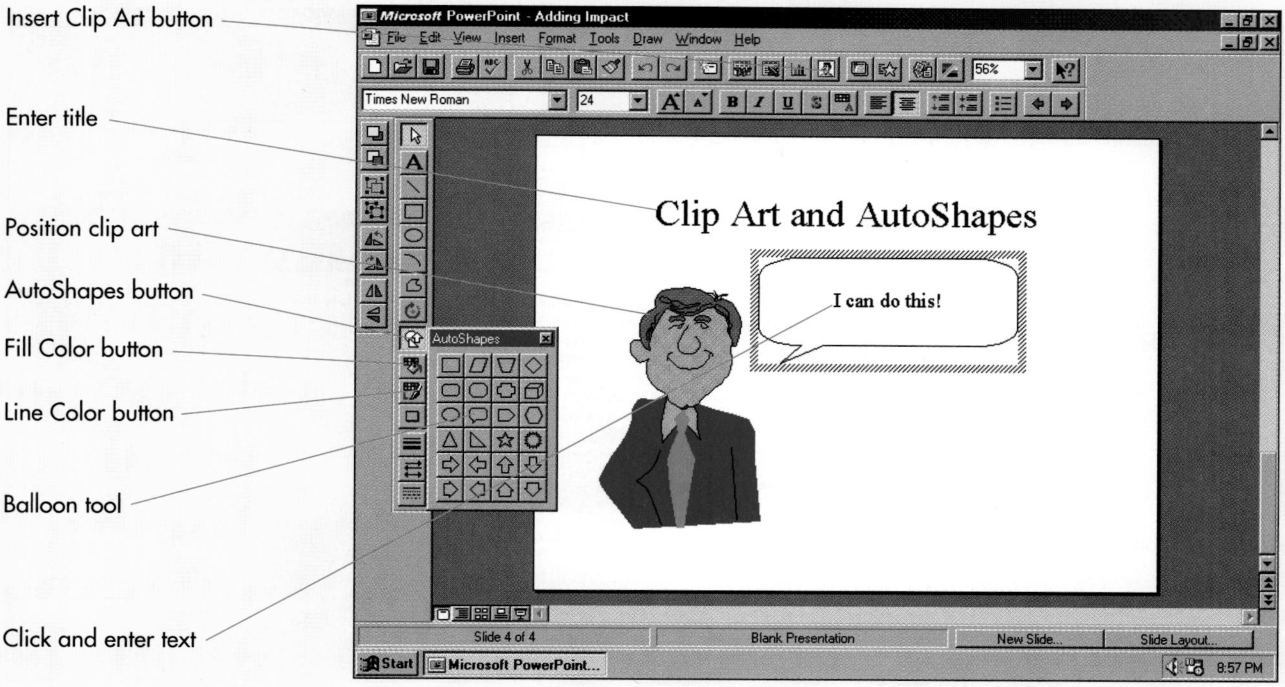
Insert Clip Art button
Enter title
Position clip art
AutoShapes button
Fill Color button
Line Color button
Balloon tool
Click and enter text
Microsoft PowerPoint - Adding Impact
Clip Art and AutoShapes
I can do this!
AutoShapes
Slide 4 of 4
Blank Presentation
New Slide...
Slide Layout...
Start
Microsoft PowerPoint...
8:57 PM

(f) Clip Art and AutoShapes (step 7)

FIGURE 3.9 Hands-on Exercise 3 (continued)

AUTOSHAPES

An AutoShape is a predefined shape that is drawn automatically when you select its icon from the AutoShapes toolbar, then click and drag in the slide. (To display the AutoShapes toolbar, click the AutoShape tool on the Drawing toolbar.) To place text inside an AutoShape, select the shape and start typing. You can also change the fill color or line thickness by selecting the shape, then clicking the appropriate button on the Drawing toolbar. See practice exercise 3 at the end of the chapter for additional information.

STEP 8: Insert a Slide

- Click the **Slide Sorter View button** above the status bar to change to the Slide Sorter view. Click the last slide (the one with the clip art that you just created) to position yourself at the point within the presentation where you want to add a slide. (The new slide will be inserted after the selected slide.)
- Pull down the **Insert menu** and click **Slides from File** to display the Insert File dialog box shown in Figure 3.9g.
- Select (click) the **My Chart presentation** (that you created in the first hands-on exercise), then click the **Insert button** to insert the slide(s) from that presentation into the current presentation. The graph from the first exercise has been inserted as the fifth slide in this presentation.

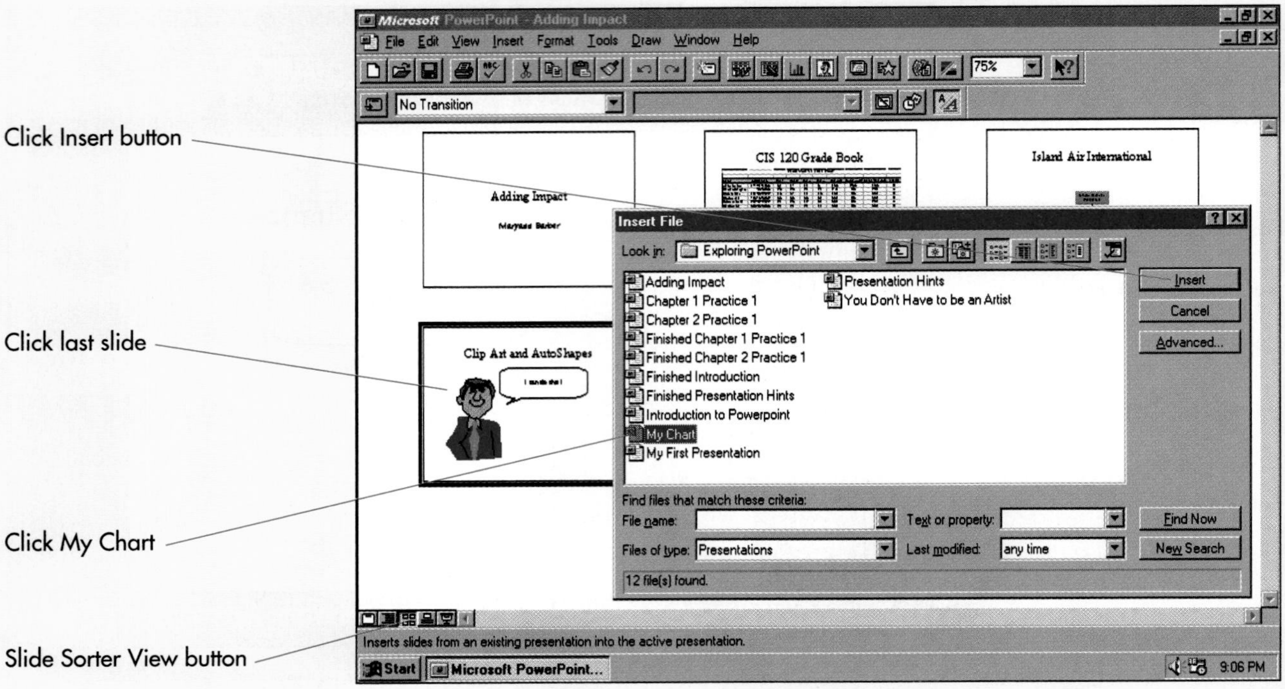

Click Insert button
Click last slide
Click My Chart
Slide Sorter View button
Microsoft PowerPoint - Adding Impact
File Edit View Insert Format Tools Draw Window Help
No Transition
Adding Impact
CIS 120 Grade Book
Island Air International
Clip Art and AutoShapes
Insert File
Look in: Exploring PowerPoint
Adding Impact
Chapter 1 Practice 1
Chapter 2 Practice 1
Finished Chapter 1 Practice 1
Finished Chapter 2 Practice 1
Finished Introduction
Finished Presentation Hints
Introduction to Powerpoint
My Chart
My First Presentation
Presentation Hints
You Don't Have to be an Artist
Insert
Cancel
Advanced...
Find files that match these criteria:
File name:
Text or property:
Find Now
Files of type: Presentations
Last modified: any time
New Search
12 file(s) found.
Inserts slides from an existing presentation into the active presentation.
Start
Microsoft PowerPoint...
9:06 PM

(g) Insert a Slide (step 8)

FIGURE 3.9 Hands-on Exercise 3 (continued)

USE WHAT YOU HAVE

You work hard to develop individual slides and thus you may find it useful to reuse a slide from one presentation to the next. Change to the Slide Sorter view in the current presentation, then click on the slide after which you want to insert a slide(s) from another presentation. Pull down the Insert menu, click the Slides from File command, then specify the presentation containing the slide(s) you want. The command is limited, however, in that it inserts every slide, and hence you may have to delete unwanted slides after they have been inserted. Press and hold the Shift key to select any slides you do not want, then press the Del key to delete those slides.

STEP 9: WordArt

- Click the slide containing the chart, then click the **New Slide button** on the status bar. Click the AutoLayout for a **blank slide** (or type **12** as the number of the desired layout). Click **OK** to add the slide.
- Change to the **Slide view.** Pull down the **Insert menu** and click **Object** to produce the Insert Object dialog box. Scroll until you can select **Microsoft WordArt 2.0** from the Object Type list box.
- Click the **Create New option button,** then click **OK.** You should see a screen similar to Figure 3.9h. Type **The End** in the Enter Your Text dialog box. Click the **Update Display command button.**

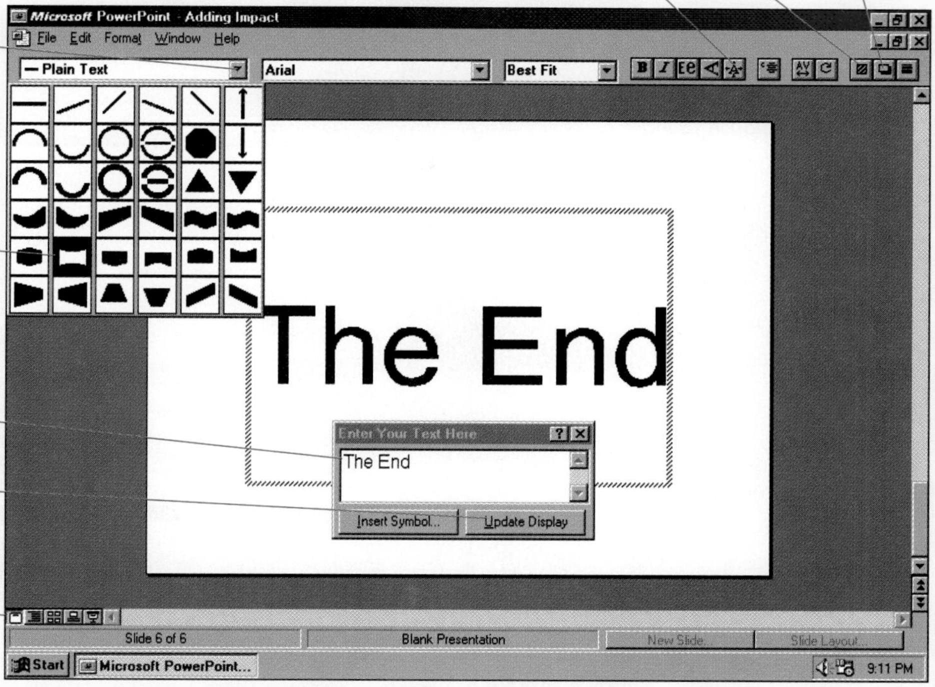

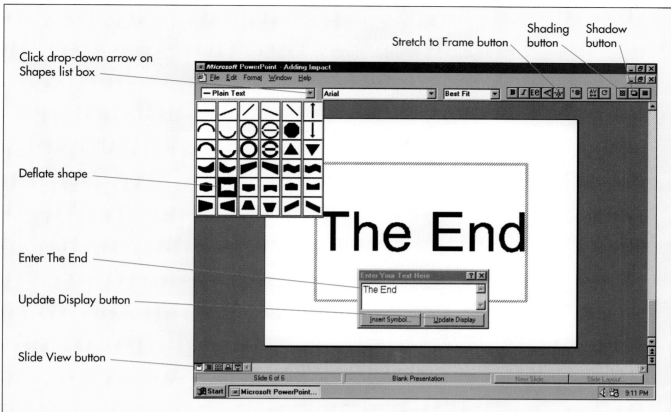

Click drop-down arrow on Shapes list box
Deflate shape
Enter The End
Update Display button
Slide View button
Stretch to Frame button
Shading button
Shadow button
Microsoft PowerPoint - Adding Impact
File Edit Format Window Help
Plain Text
Arial
Best Fit
The End
Enter Your Text Here
The End
Insert Symbol...
Update Display
Slide 6 of 6
Blank Presentation
New Slide...
Slide Layout...
Start
Microsoft PowerPoint...
9:11 PM

(h) WordArt (step 8)

FIGURE 3.9 Hands-on Exercise 3 (continued)

- Click the **drop-down arrow** on the Shapes list box and click **Deflate shape.** The shape of the text changes to match the shape chosen. Click the **Stretch to Frame button** on the WordArt toolbar so that the text will always fill the frame, regardless of the size of the frame.
- You can experiment with other effects to enhance the WordArt image. Click the **Shadow button** to add a shadow to the text and/or change the color of the shadow. Click the **Shading button** and change the **Foreground color** to **red.**
- Click outside the WordArt to deselect it and return to the PowerPoint presentation. The WordArt object should be selected with the sizing handles displayed. Click and drag a corner to enlarge the WordArt object so that it fills almost the entire slide.
- Save the presentation.

STEP 9: Sound (requires a sound card)

- Pull down the **Insert Menu.** Click **Sound** to display the Insert Sound dialog box in Figure 3.9i. If necessary, change to the **Exploring PowerPoint folder,** then double click the **Applause sound file** to insert the sound object into the presentation.
- A tiny microphone appears in the middle of the slide to indicate that the sound file has been embedded on the slide. Point to the microphone and click the **right mouse button** to display a shortcut menu, then click **Play Wave Sound Object** to play the sound and hear the applause.
- Save the presentation.

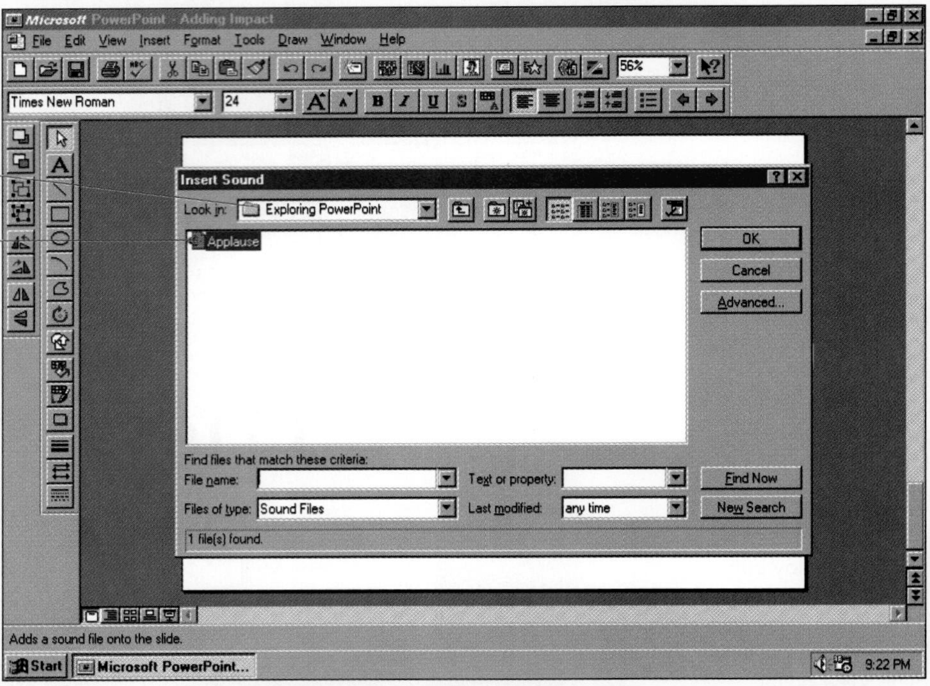
Select Exploring PowerPoint folder
Double click Applause sound file
Microsoft PowerPoint - Adding Impact
File Edit View Insert Format Tools Draw Window Help
Times New Roman
24
Insert Sound
Look in: Exploring PowerPoint
Applause
OK
Cancel
Advanced...
Find files that match these criteria:
File name:
Text or property:
Find Now
Files of type: Sound Files
Last modified: any time
New Search
1 file(s) found.
Adds a sound file onto the slide.
Start
Microsoft PowerPoint...
9:22 PM

(i) Insert a Sound (step 9)

FIGURE 3.9 Hands-on Exercise 3 (continued)

> **THE WINDOWS 95 FIND COMMAND**
>
> We supplied the sound of applause, but you are likely to have many other sound files on your system, any one of which can be embedded into a presentation. The easiest way to locate these files is through the Windows 95 Find command. Click the Start button, click (or point to) the Find command, then click Files or Folders to display the Find dialog box. Enter *.wav (the "wav" indicates a sound file) in the Named text box and My Computer in the Look In box. Click Find Now. Use the right mouse button to click and drag a file from the Find Files window onto your presentation, release the mouse, then click the Copy Here command to embed the sound onto the slide.

STEP 10: Animation Settings

- ➤ Click and drag the sound icon to the upper right portion of the slide as shown in Figure 3.9j.
- ➤ Point to the icon, click the **right mouse button** to display a shortcut menu, then click **Animation Settings** to display the Animation Settings dialog box in Figure 3.9j.
- ➤ Click the **drop-down arrow** on the Play Options list box and click **Play.** Click the **More command button** to display the More Play Options dialog box.

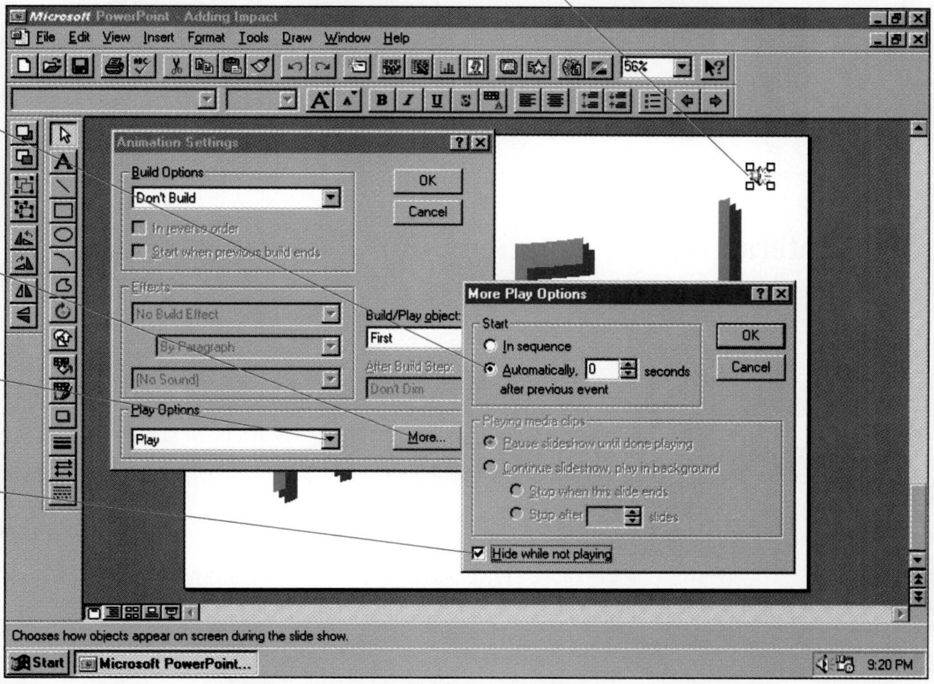
Click and drag sound file icon to upper-right corner
Click to play sound automatically after 0 seconds
Click More button
Click drop-down arrow and select Play
Select Hide while not playing

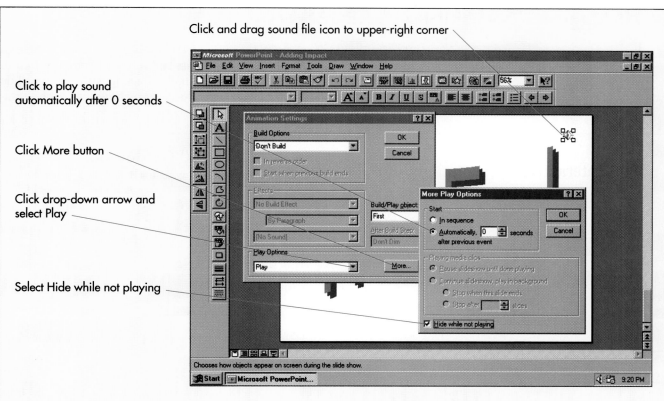

(j) Animation Settings (step 10)

FIGURE 3.9 Hands-on Exercise 3 (continued)

- Click the option button to play the sound automatically (after 0 seconds). Check the box to **Hide** the icon while not playing. Click **OK** to close the More Play Options dialog box. Click **OK** to close the Animation Settings dialog box.
- Save the presentation.

STEP 11: Applause, Applause

- Press **Ctrl+Home** to move to the first slide in the presentation, then click the **Slide Show button** to view the presentation.
- Click the **left mouse button** (or press the **PgDn key**) to move from slide to slide until you come to the end of the presentation. The applause you hear on the last slide is for your efforts in this exercise.
- Click the mouse a final time to return to the Slide view. Exit PowerPoint if you do not want to continue with the next exercise at this time.

BRANCHING WITHIN A PRESENTATION

The most effective public speakers are sensitive to their audiences and are able to adapt their presentations to specific situations. Thus far all of the presentations in our text have been designed to be viewed sequentially, starting with the first slide and ending with the last slide. Figure 3.10 introduces ***branching*** into a presenta-

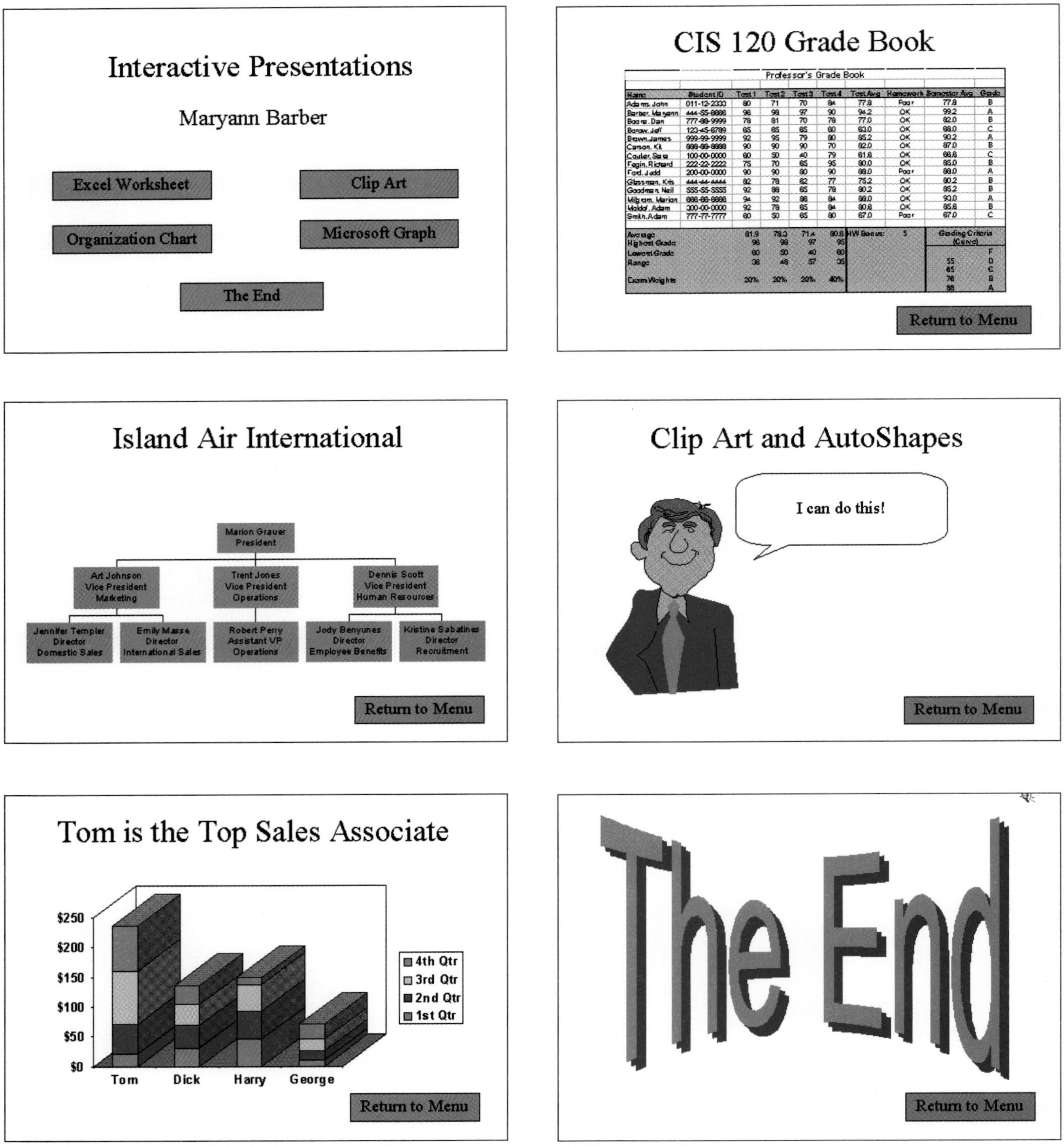

Interactive Presentations
Maryann Barber
Excel Worksheet
Clip Art
Organization Chart
Microsoft Graph
The End
CIS 120 Grade Book
Professor's Grade Book
Return to Menu
Island Air International
Marion Grauer President
Art Johnson Vice President Marketing
Trent Jones Vice President Operations
Dennis Scott Vice President Human Resources
Jennifer Templer Director Domestic Sales
Emily Masse Director International Sales
Robert Perry Assistant VP Operations
Jody Benyunes Director Employee Benefits
Kristine Sabatines Director Recruitment
Return to Menu
Clip Art and AutoShapes
I can do this!
Return to Menu
Tom is the Top Sales Associate
$250
$200
$150
$100
$50
$0
Tom
Dick
Harry
George
4th Qtr
3rd Qtr
2nd Qtr
1st Qtr
Return to Menu
The End
Return to Menu

FIGURE 3.10 Branching within a Presentation

tion by placing buttons onto a slide that enable you to move nonsequentially through a presentation.

Figure 3.10 shows a slightly modified version of the presentation created in the previous hands-on exercise. The title slide has been modified to include five command buttons, each of which branches to a specific slide in the presentation. Click any of these buttons during the slide show, and you are transferred immediately to that slide. Click the "Return to Menu" button on any of the remaining slides, and you go back to the first slide in the presentation.

You are under no obligation to use the command buttons and can still move through the presentation sequentially by clicking the left mouse button (or pressing the PgDn key) to move to the next sequential slide. The command buttons are created through the ***Interactive Settings command*** in the Tools menu as demonstrated in the next hands-on exercise.

THE SLIDE NAVIGATOR

The Slide Navigator provides an alternate way to branch to various slides during a presentation. It is always accessible to the presenter regardless of whether or not branching has been built in. The disadvantage is that the Navigator is not intuitive to the novice, it lists every slide in a presentation (there may be many), and further, it requires additional mouse clicks when compared to predefined command buttons. See online Help for additional information.

HANDS-ON EXERCISE 4

Branching within a Presentation

Objective: To use the Interactive Settings command to enable branching within a presentation. Use Figure 3.11 as a guide in doing the exercise.

STEP 1: Create the Title Slide

- Open the **Adding Impact presentation** from the previous exercise.
- Click and drag to select the title of the presentation, then change the title to **Interactive Presentations.**
- Click the border of the title placeholder, then click and drag the border to move it the top of the slide as shown in Figure 3.11a.
- Click the **placeholder** containing your name, then click and drag that placeholder toward the top of the slide so that it is under the title.
- Pull down the **File menu,** click the **Save As command,** then save the presentation as **Interactive Presentations.**

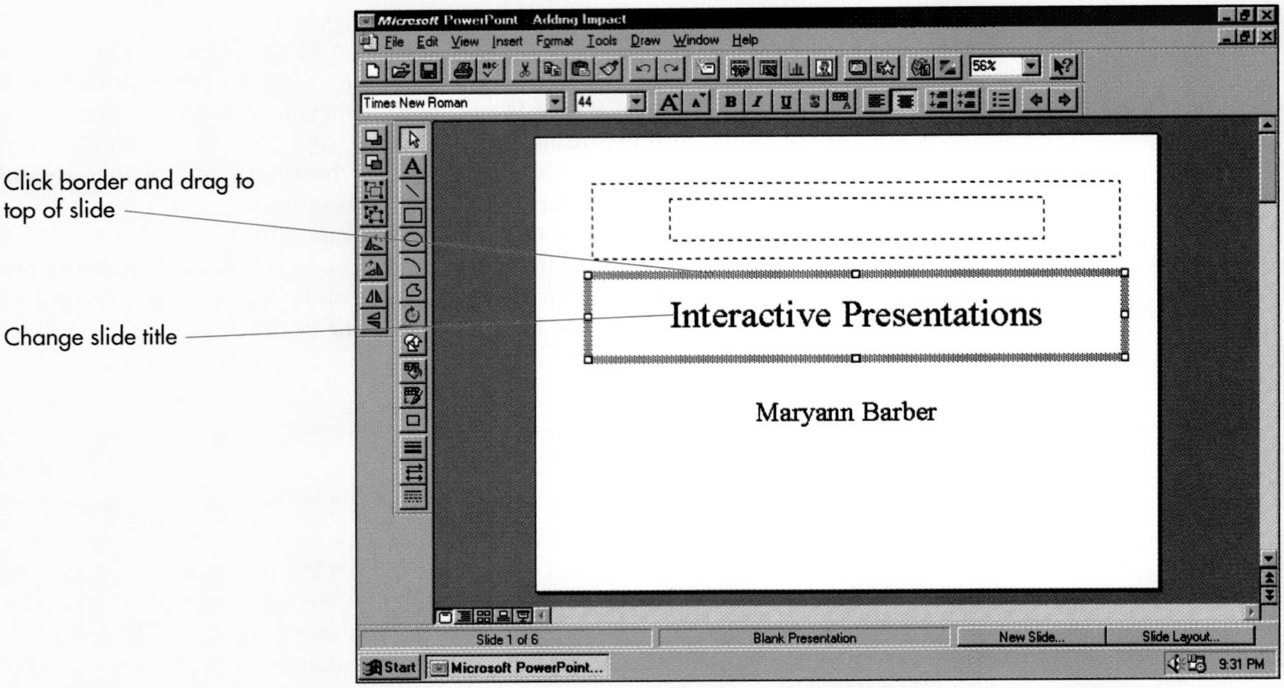

Click border and drag to top of slide
Change slide title
Microsoft PowerPoint - Adding Impact
File Edit View Insert Format Tools Draw Window Help
Times New Roman
44
56%
Interactive Presentations
Maryann Barber
Slide 1 of 6
Blank Presentation
New Slide...
Slide Layout...
Start
Microsoft PowerPoint...
9:31 PM

(a) Create the Title (step 1)

FIGURE 3.11 Hands-on Exercise 4

THE SAVE AS COMMAND

The Save As command saves a presentation under a different name, and is useful when you want to retain a copy of the original presentation prior to making any changes. The original (unmodified) presentation is kept on disk under its original name. A second copy of the presentation is saved under a new name and remains in memory. All subsequent editing is done on the new presentation.

STEP 2: Create the First Button (menu option)

- Click the **Text tool** on the Drawing toolbar, then click and drag in the slide where you want the first button to go. Release the mouse to create the button.
- Enter **Excel Worksheet** as the name of the first menu option as shown in Figure 3.11b.
- Click the **Center Alignment button** on the Formatting toolbar to center the text within the button.
- Click the **Line Style button** on the Drawing toolbar to display the available line styles as shown in Figure 3.11b. Click the second style to display a border around the button.
- Click the **Fill Color button** on the Drawing toolbar. Click **Green** as the color of the button.
- Save the presentation.

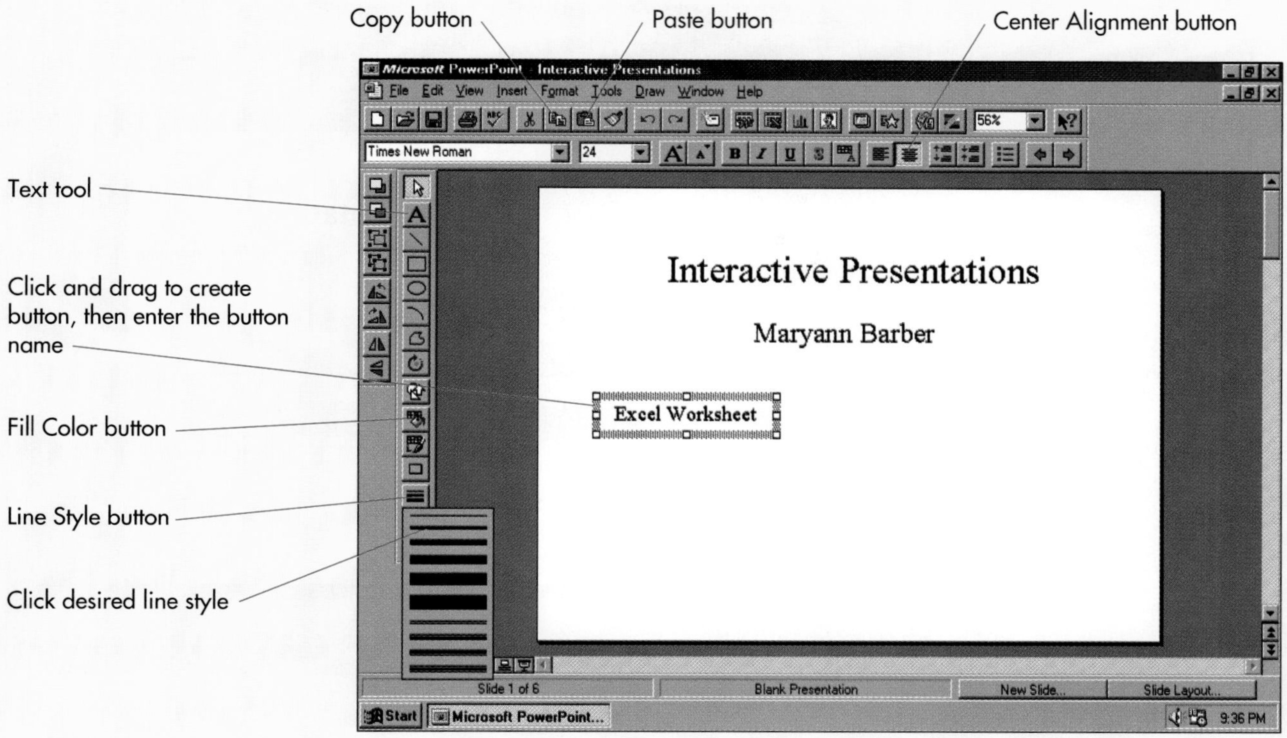

Copy button
Paste button
Center Alignment button
Text tool
Click and drag to create button, then enter the button name
Fill Color button
Line Style button
Click desired line style
Microsoft PowerPoint - Interactive Presentations
File Edit View Insert Format Tools Draw Window Help
Times New Roman
24
56%
Interactive Presentations
Maryann Barber
Excel Worksheet
Slide 1 of 6
Blank Presentation
New Slide...
Slide Layout...
Start
Microsoft PowerPoint...
9:36 PM

(b) Create the First Menu Option (step 2)

FIGURE 3.11 Hands-on Exercise 4 (continued)

STEP 3: Create the Other Buttons

- Select (click) the button you just created, then click the **Copy button** on the Standard toolbar to copy the button to the clipboard.
- Click the **Paste button,** then click and drag the copied button to the right of the original button. (Do not worry about the alignment or position of the two buttons.) You now have two Excel Worksheet buttons.
- Click in the second (copied) button, then change the text to **Clip Art.**
- Paste the button three more times, then move the buttons and change the names as shown in Figure 3.11c.
- Click the **Excel Worksheet button.** Press and hold the **Shift key** as you click the **Organization Chart button** to select both buttons.
- Pull down the **Draw menu.** Click the **Align command,** then click **Lefts** from the cascaded menu as shown in Figure 3.11c. The selected buttons should be aligned on their left side.
- Align the **Microsoft Graph** and **Clip Art buttons** by selecting the buttons two at a time and aligning them on their right side.
- Save the presentation.

STEP 4: Create the Branch

- Click outside all five buttons, then click the **Excel Worksheet button** to select just this button.

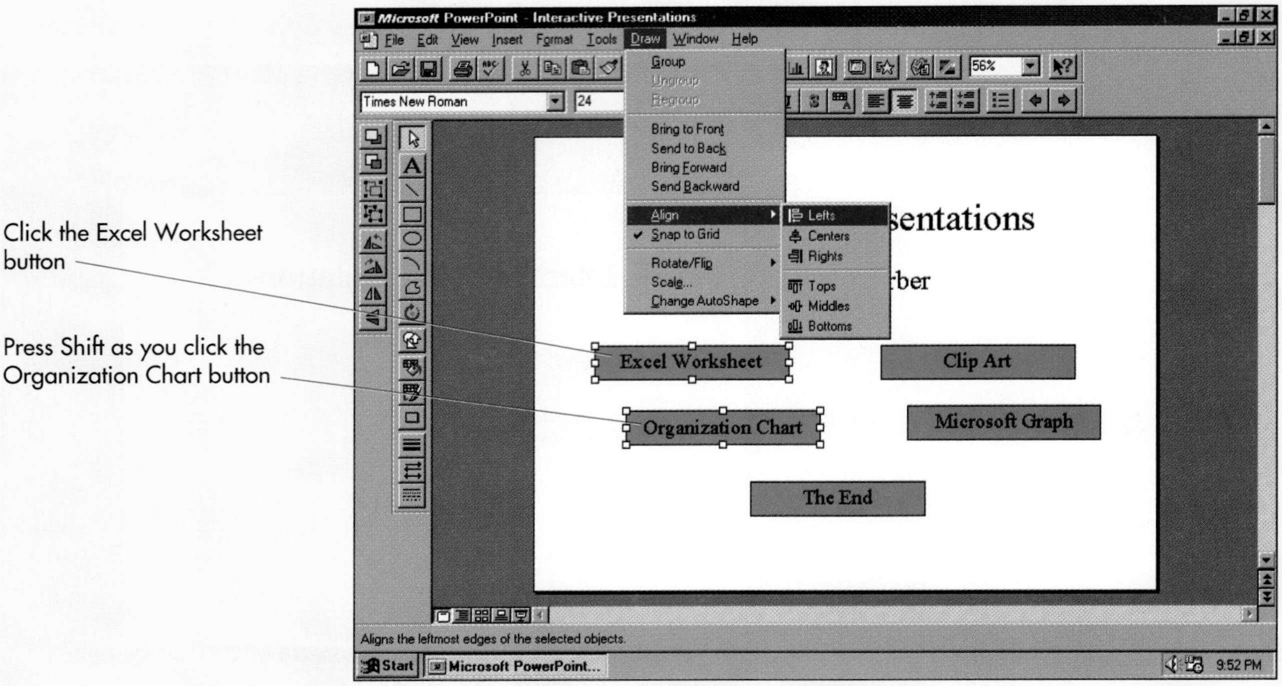
Click the Excel Worksheet button
Press Shift as you click the Organization Chart button
Microsoft PowerPoint - Interactive Presentations
File Edit View Insert Format Tools Draw Window Help
Group
Ungroup
Regroup
Bring to Front
Send to Back
Bring Forward
Send Backward
Align
Snap to Grid
Rotate/Flip
Scale...
Change AutoShape
Lefts
Centers
Rights
Tops
Middles
Bottoms
Excel Worksheet
Clip Art
Organization Chart
Microsoft Graph
The End
Aligns the leftmost edges of the selected objects.
Start
Microsoft PowerPoint...
9:52 PM

(c) Create the Other Buttons (step 3)

FIGURE 3.11 Hands-on Exercise 4 (continued)

- Pull down the **Tools menu.** Click **Interactive Settings** to display the Interactive Settings dialog box, then click the **Go to option button** as shown in Figure 3.11d.
- Click the **drop-down arrow** in the Slides list box, click **Slide . . .** from the displayed list of available slides to display the Go To Slide dialog box shown in the figure. Select slide 2 (CIS120 Grade Book) as shown in Figure 3.11d. Click **OK.** Click **OK** a second time.

STEP 5: Create the Return Branch

- Press the **PgDn key** to move to slide number 2 (the slide containing the Excel worksheet).
- Create a **Return to Menu** button in the lower-right corner of this slide, as shown in Figure 3.11e. (You may need to size and/or move the worksheet before creating the button.)
  - Click the **Text tool** on the Drawing toolbar, then click and drag in the slide where you want the button to go. Release the mouse and enter **Return to Menu** as the name of the button.
  - Click the **Center Alignment button** on the Formatting toolbar to center the text within the button. Click the **Line Style** and **Fill Color buttons** on the Drawing toolbar to format the button as we did in step 2. (Choose any line style and fill color.)
- Pull down the **Tools menu,** click **Interactive Settings** to display the Interactive Settings dialog box, then click the **Go to option button.** Click the **drop-down arrow** in the Slides list box, click **Slide . . .** from the displayed list, select

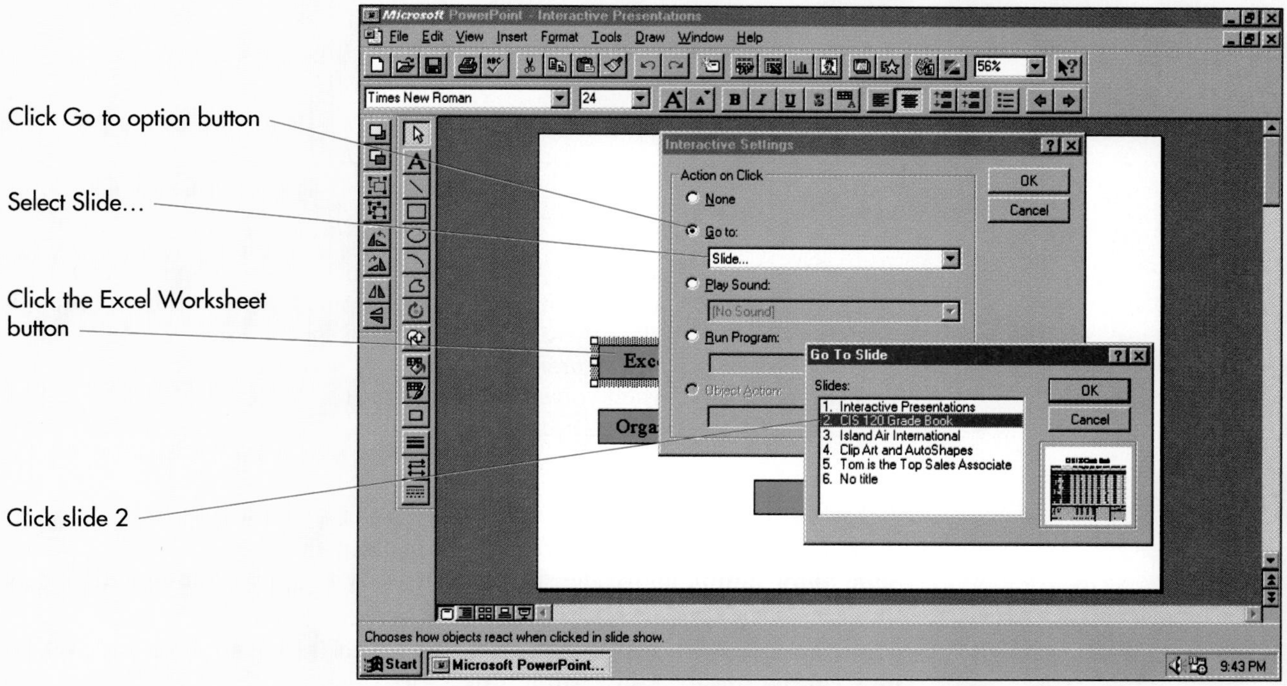
Click Go to option button
Select Slide...
Click the Excel Worksheet button
Click slide 2

(d) Create the Branch (step 4)

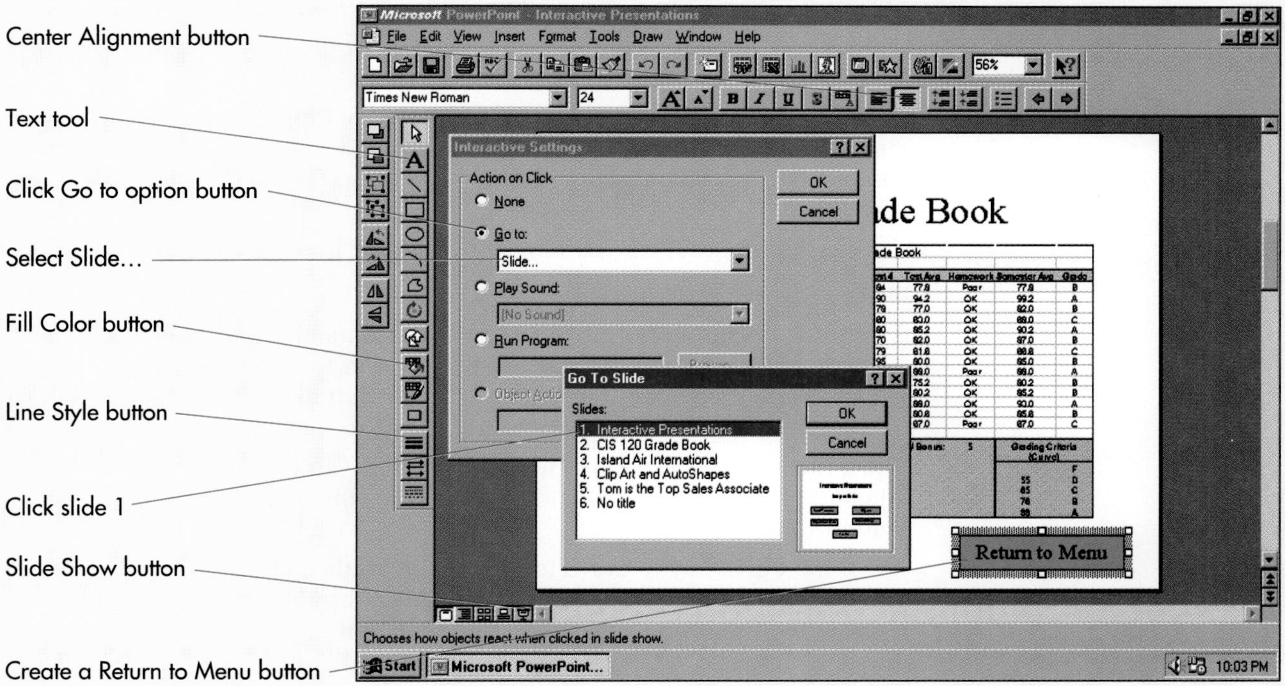
Center Alignment button
Text tool
Click Go to option button
Select Slide...
Fill Color button
Line Style button
Click slide 1
Slide Show button
Create a Return to Menu button

(e) Create the Return Branch (step 5)

FIGURE 3.11 Hands-on Exercise 4 (continued)

the title slide (**Interactive Presentations**) from the list of available slides, then click **OK.** Click **OK** to close the Interactive Settings dialog box.

➤ Save the presentation.

THE SLIDE ELEVATOR

PowerPoint uses the scroll box (common to all Windows applications) in the vertical scroll bar as an elevator to move up and down within the presentation. Click and drag the elevator to go to a specific slide; as you drag, you will see a Scroll Tip indicating the slide you are about to display. Release the mouse when you see the number (title) of the slide you want.

STEP 6: Test the Branching

➤ Press **Ctrl+Home** to return to the first slide in the presentation. Click the **Slide Show button** above the status bar to view the presentation and display the title slide.

➤ Click the **Excel Worksheet button** to branch to this slide. Click the **Return to Menu button** to return to the title slide. Click the **Excel Worksheet button** a second time to return to this slide.

➤ Press **Esc** to end the slide show and return to the Slide view.

STEP 7: Create Branches for the Remaining Buttons

➤ Press **Ctrl+Home** to return to the title slide in the presentation, then select (click) the **Organization Chart button.**

➤ Pull down the **Tools menu,** click **Interactive Settings,** then click the **Go to option button.** Click the **down arrow** in the Slides list box, and select slide 3 (**Island Air International**) to create the branch. Click **OK.** Click **OK** a second time.

➤ Create the branches for the remaining buttons in similar fashion.

STEP 8: Create the Remaining Return Buttons

➤ Press the **PgDn key** to move to the slide containing the Excel worksheet. Click the border of the **Return to Menu button** to select the button and display the sizing handles, then click the **Copy button** on the Standard toolbar to copy the button (including the branching) to the clipboard.

➤ Press the **PgDn key** to move to the next slide. Click the **Paste button** on the Standard toolbar to paste the contents of the clipboard (the Return to Menu button) onto this slide.

➤ Press the **PgDn key** to move to the next slide, then click the **Paste button** to paste the button onto this slide as well. Paste the **Return to Menu** button on each of the remaining slides in the presentation.

➤ Click the **Slide Sorter button** to change to the slide view to see the entire presentation as shown in Figure 3.11f.

- The title slide contains five buttons, one for each slide in the presentation.
- Each of the remaining slides contains a return button that branches back to the title slide.

➤ Save the presentation.

Individual slides have Return to Menu buttons

Slide Sorter View button

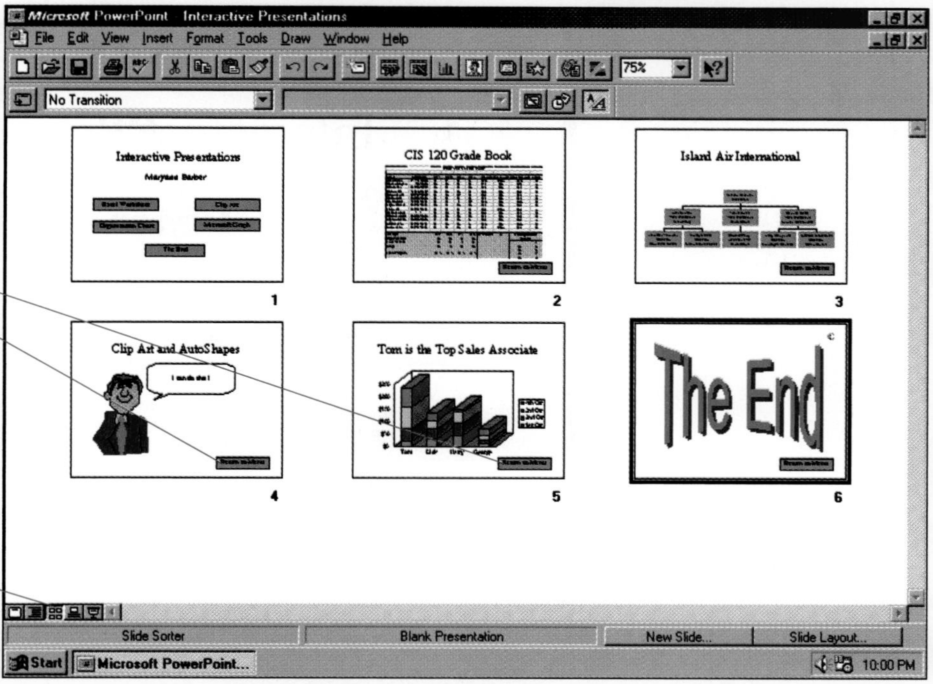

Microsoft PowerPoint Interactive Presentations
File Edit View Insert Format Tools Draw Window Help
No Transition
Interactive Presentations
CIS 120 Grade Book
Island Air International
Clip Art and AutoShapes
Tom is the Top Sales Associate
The End
Slide Sorter
Blank Presentation
New Slide...
Slide Layout...
Start
Microsoft PowerPoint...
10:00 PM

(f) Create the Remaining Buttons (step 8)

FIGURE 3.11 Hands-on Exercise 4 (continued)

CUT, COPY, AND PASTE

Ctrl+X, Ctrl+C, and **Ctrl+V** are shortcuts to cut, copy, and paste, respectively, and apply to all applications in the Office suite as well as to Windows applications in general. (The shortcuts are easier to remember when you realize that the operative letters—X, C, and V—are next to each other at the bottom left side of the keyboard.) You can also use the Cut, Copy, and Paste buttons on the Standard toolbar.

STEP 9: Show Time

- Press **Ctrl+Home** to move to the beginning of the presentation, then click the **Slide Show button** to view the presentation. The title slide is displayed on your monitor as shown in Figure 3.11g.
- You can branch to any slide in the presentation by clicking the appropriate command button on the title slide. You can return to the title slide at any time by clicking the **Return to Menu button** that is present on every slide except the title slide.
- You can also view the presentation in sequence by clicking the **left mouse button** (or by pressing the **PgDn key**) to move from one slide to the next.
- Go through the presentation (in any sequence) to review the material from the chapter. Click the **left mouse button** at the end of the presentation or press the **Esc key** to return to the Slide view.

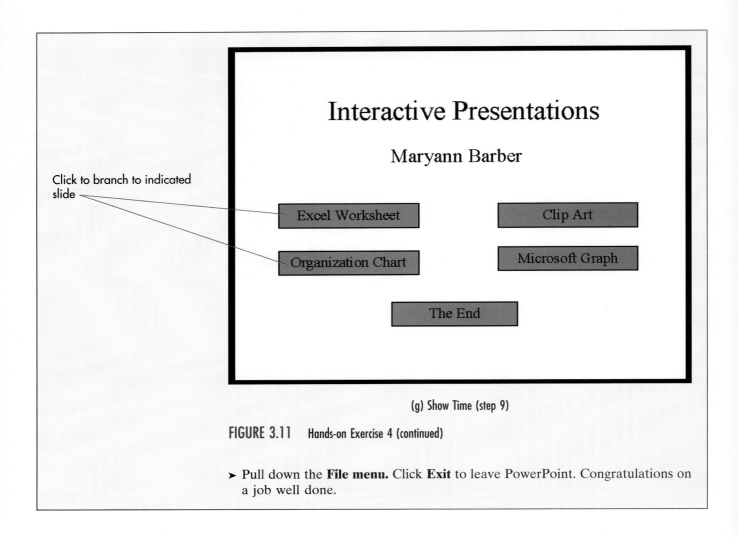

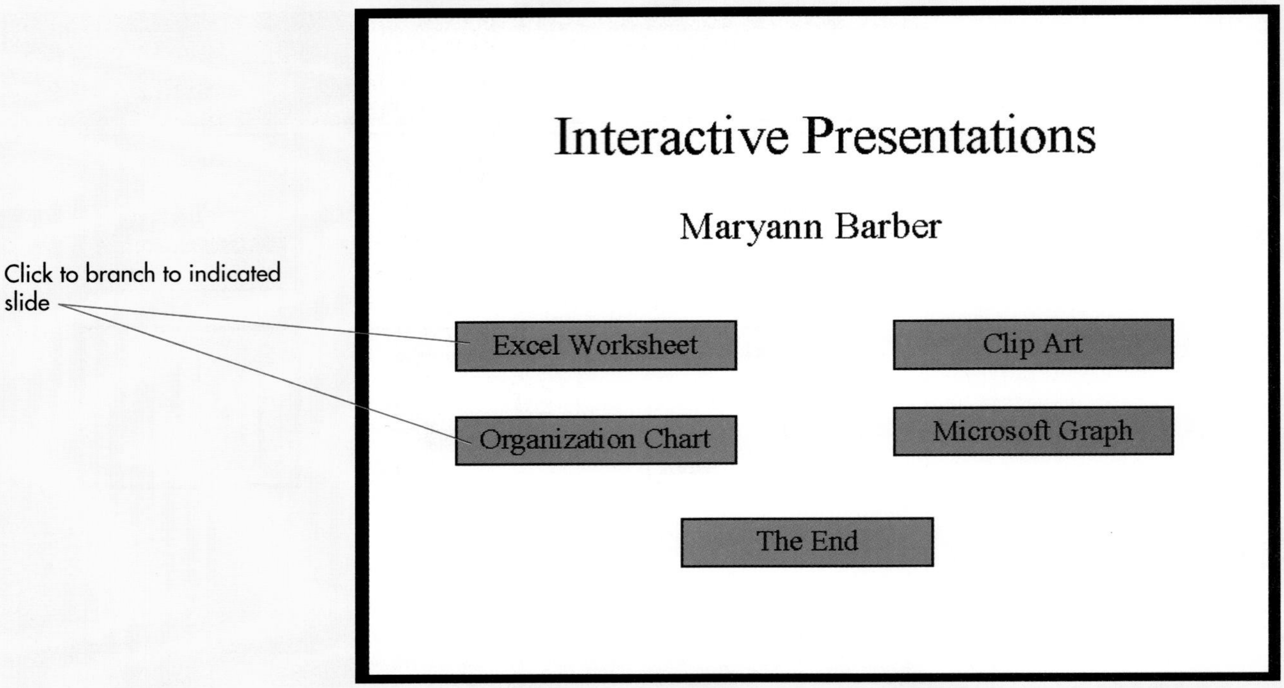
Interactive Presentations
Maryann Barber
Click to branch to indicated slide
Excel Worksheet
Clip Art
Organization Chart
Microsoft Graph
The End

(g) Show Time (step 9)

FIGURE 3.11 Hands-on Exercise 4 (continued)

➤ Pull down the **File menu.** Click **Exit** to leave PowerPoint. Congratulations on a job well done.

SUMMARY

Microsoft Graph has many of the same commands and capabilities as the charting component of Microsoft Excel. After a graph has been inserted into a presentation, it becomes an embedded object that retains its connection to Microsoft Graph. Thus, you can double click the graph to restart Microsoft Graph and edit the graph. You can also click the graph to select it as an object on a PowerPoint slide, then move or size the graph just as you would any other Windows object.

A clip art image consists of a series of lines and shapes, each of which is considered an object in and of itself. The Group command combines individual objects so that you can work with them at the same time. The Ungroup command does the opposite and breaks up an object into smaller objects so you can work with the smaller objects individually.

Object Linking and Embedding (OLE) enables you to link or embed information (objects) created in other applications. The choice between linking and embedding depends on how the object will be used. Linking is preferable if the object is likely to change and your presentation requires the latest version, or when the same object is shared among many users. Embedding should be used if you plan to show the presentation on a different computer from the one used to create the presentation.

Microsoft WordArt enables you to add special effects to text, then embed the text object into a presentation. WordArt is called from within PowerPoint by choosing the AutoLayout for an Object slide, double clicking the object placeholder, and selecting a WordArt object.

Microsoft Organization Chart enables you to create an organization chart and embed it into a presentation. The application is called from within PowerPoint by choosing the AutoLayout containing an organization chart or by creating an object slide and choosing Microsoft Organization Chart as the object type.

PowerPoint enables you to embed a sound file or a video clip (a movie) as an object into a presentation. Movies do not require additional hardware. Sound requires a sound board and speakers.

The Interactive Settings command introduces branching into a presentation by placing command buttons onto a slide that let you to move directly to a specific slide.

KEY WORDS AND CONCEPTS

AutoShape
AutoShapes toolbar
Branching
Category names
Compound document
Data points
Data series
Datasheet
Drawing toolbar
Drawing+ toolbar
Embedded object
Group command
Interactive Settings command
In-place editing
Linked object
Microsoft Graph
Microsoft Organization Chart
Microsoft WordArt
Object
Object Linking and Embedding
Recolor command
Sound
Ungroup command

MULTIPLE CHOICE

1. What happens if you click the Datasheet button on the Microsoft Graph toolbar twice in a row?
   (a) The datasheet is closed (hidden)
   (b) The datasheet is opened (displayed)
   (c) The datasheet is in the same status (either opened or closed) as it was before it was clicked
   (d) Impossible to determine

2. Which of the following is true of data series that are plotted in rows?
   (a) The first row in the datasheet contains the category names for the X axis
   (b) The first column in the datasheet contains the legend
   (c) Both (a) and (b)
   (d) Neither (a) nor (b)

3. Which of the following is true of data series that are plotted in columns?
   (a) The first column in the datasheet contains the category names for the X axis
   (b) The first row in the datasheet contains the legend
   (c) Both (a) and (b)
   (d) Neither (a) nor (b)
4. What happens if you select a slide in the Slide Sorter view, click the Copy button, then click the Paste button twice in a row?
   (a) You have made one additional copy of the slide
   (b) You have made two additional copies of the slide
   (c) You have made three additional copies of the slide
   (d) The situation is impossible because you cannot execute the Paste command twice in a row
5. How do you size an object so that it maintains the original proportion between height and width?
   (a) Drag a sizing handle on the left or right side of the object to change its width, then drag a sizing handle on the top or bottom edge to change the height
   (b) Drag a sizing handle on any of the corners
   (c) Both (a) and (b)
   (d) Neither (a) nor (b)
6. What happens if you select an object, then click the Flip Vertical button twice in a row?
   (a) The object has been rotated 90 degrees
   (b) The object has been rotated 180 degrees (turned upside down)
   (c) The object has been rotated 270 degrees
   (d) The object has been rotated 360 degrees and is in the same position as when you started
7. What is the difference between clicking and double clicking an embedded object?
   (a) Clicking selects the object; double clicking starts the application that created the object
   (b) Double clicking selects the object; clicking starts the application that create the object
   (c) Clicking changes to the Slide Sorter view; double clicking changes to the Outline view
   (d) Double clicking changes to the Slide Sorter view; clicking changes to the Outline view
8. Under which circumstances would you choose linking over embedding?
   (a) When the same object is referenced in many different documents
   (b) When an object is constantly changing and you need the latest version
   (c) Both (a) and (b)
   (d) Neither (a) nor (b)
9. Under which circumstances would you choose embedding over linking?
   (a) When you need to show a presentation on a different computer
   (b) When the same object is referenced in many different documents
   (c) Both (a) and (b)
   (d) Neither (a) nor (b)

10. Which of the following can be created as an embedded object?
   (a) A graph created by Microsoft Graph
   (b) Text created by Microsoft WordArt
   (c) Clip art or WordArt
   (d) All of the above

11. Which of the following is true regarding the sequence of slides in a slide show?
   (a) The slides in a presentation must be viewed sequentially, starting with the first slide and ending with the last slide
   (b) The next slide in a presentation is displayed by clicking the left mouse button or by pressing the PgDn key
   (c) Both (a) and (b)
   (d) Neither (a) nor (b)

12. How do you insert clip art onto an existing slide?
   (a) Pull down the Insert menu, click Object, then choose Microsoft ClipArt Gallery from the list of available objects
   (b) Click the Insert Clip Art button on the Standard toolbar
   (c) Pull down the Insert menu and click the Clip Art command
   (d) All of the above

13. How do you create a new slide containing a graph?
   (a) Create a blank slide, then pull down the Insert menu and click the Microsoft Graph command
   (b) Create a blank slide, then click the Insert Graph button on the Standard toolbar
   (c) Click the New Slide button, select an AutoLayout containing a graph, then double click the placeholder for the graph in the Slide view
   (d) All of the above

14. What happens if you select an object, click the Copy command, move to a new slide, and click the Paste command?
   (a) Nothing because you cannot copy and paste an object on two different slides
   (b) The selected object has been moved from the first slide to the second slide
   (c) The selected object has been copied from the first slide to the second slide
   (d) The selected object has been copied from the first slide to the second slide, and in addition, remains on the clipboard from where it can be pasted onto another slide

15. What happens if you select an object, click the Cut command, move to a new slide, and click the Paste command?
   (a) Nothing because you cannot copy and paste an object on two different slides
   (b) The selected object has been moved from the first slide to the second slide
   (c) The selected object has been copied from the first slide to the second slide
   (d) The selected object has been copied from the first slide to the second slide, and in addition, remains on the clipboard from where it can be pasted onto another slide

ANSWERS

1. c
2. c
3. c
4. b
5. b
6. d
7. a
8. c
9. a
10. d
11. b
12. d
13. d
14. d
15. b

EXPLORING MICROSOFT POWERPOINT 7.0

1. Use Figure 3.12 to match each action with its result. A given action may be used more than once or not at all.

Action		**Result**
a. Click at 1	____	Suppress the display of the datasheet
b. Click at 2	____	Change the data series to columns
c. Click at 3	____	Change the format of the chart to stacked column
d. Click at 4	____	Return to PowerPoint
e. Click at 5	____	Suppress the display of the legend
f. Click at 6		
g. Click at 7 and enter the new city		

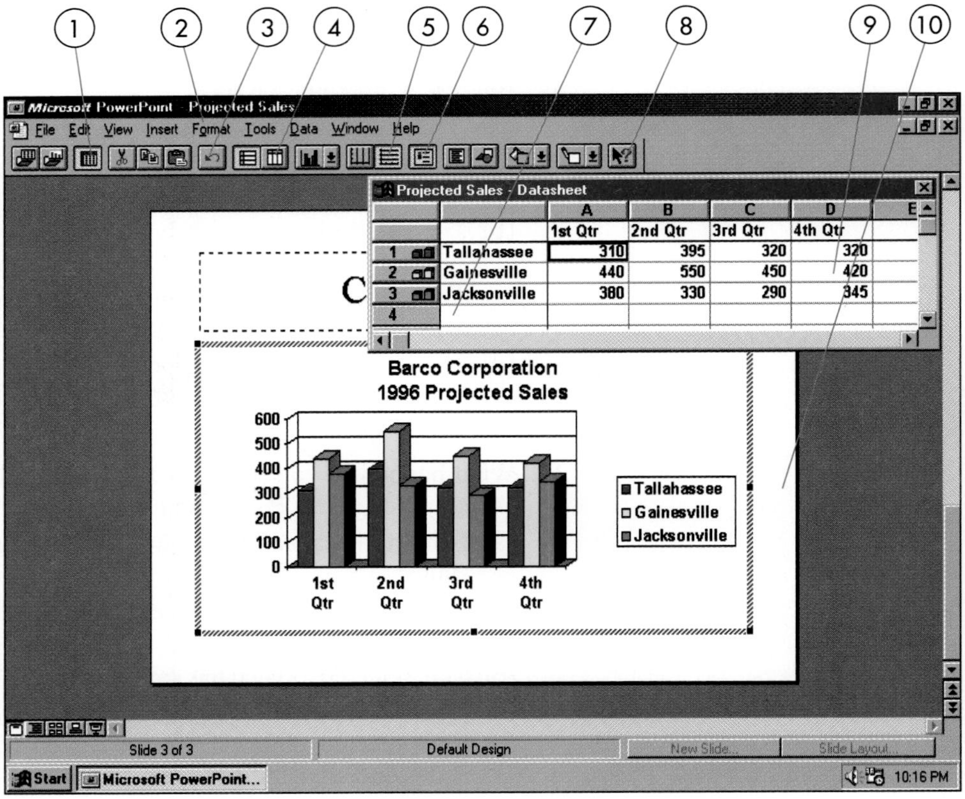

1
2
3
4
5
6
7
8
9
10
Microsoft PowerPoint - Projected Sales
File Edit View Insert Format Tools Data Window Help
Projected Sales - Datasheet
A B C D E
1st Qtr 2nd Qtr 3rd Qtr 4th Qtr
1 Tallahassee 310 395 320 320
2 Gainesville 440 550 450 420
3 Jacksonville 380 330 290 345
4
Barco Corporation
1996 Projected Sales
600
500
400
300
200
100
0
1st Qtr
2nd Qtr
3rd Qtr
4th Qtr
Tallahassee
Gainesville
Jacksonville
Slide 3 of 3
Default Design
New Slide...
Slide Layout...
Start
Microsoft PowerPoint...
10:16 PM

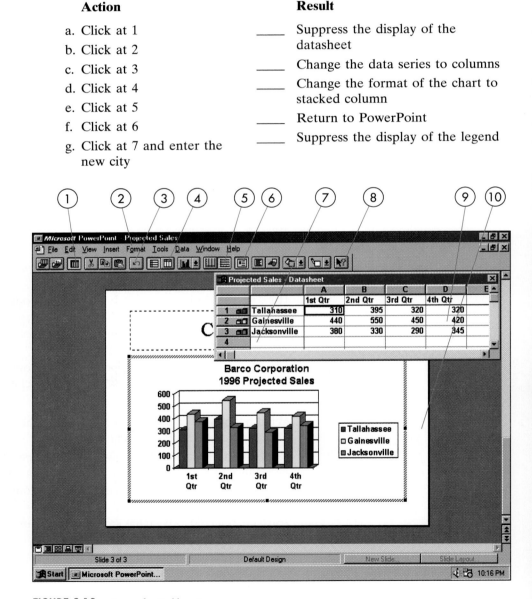

FIGURE 3.12 Screen for Problem 1

h. Click at 8
i. Click at 9 and enter the new data
j. Click at 10

____ Change Gainesville's 4th Quarter sales
____ Undo the last action taken
____ Add a new series for Orlando
____ Toggle the horizontal gridlines off
____ Access online Help

2. Answer the following with respect to Figure 3.13:

a. What is the name of the presentation containing the slide in Figure 3.13?
b. Which toolbars are currently displayed?
c. How many objects are displayed on the slide? How many different types of objects? Which object (if any) is currently selected?
d. What would happen if you pointed to the selected object and clicked the right mouse button? If you pressed the Delete key?
e. What is the difference between clicking and double clicking the WordArt object? How would you change the text on the slide to "CIS120"?

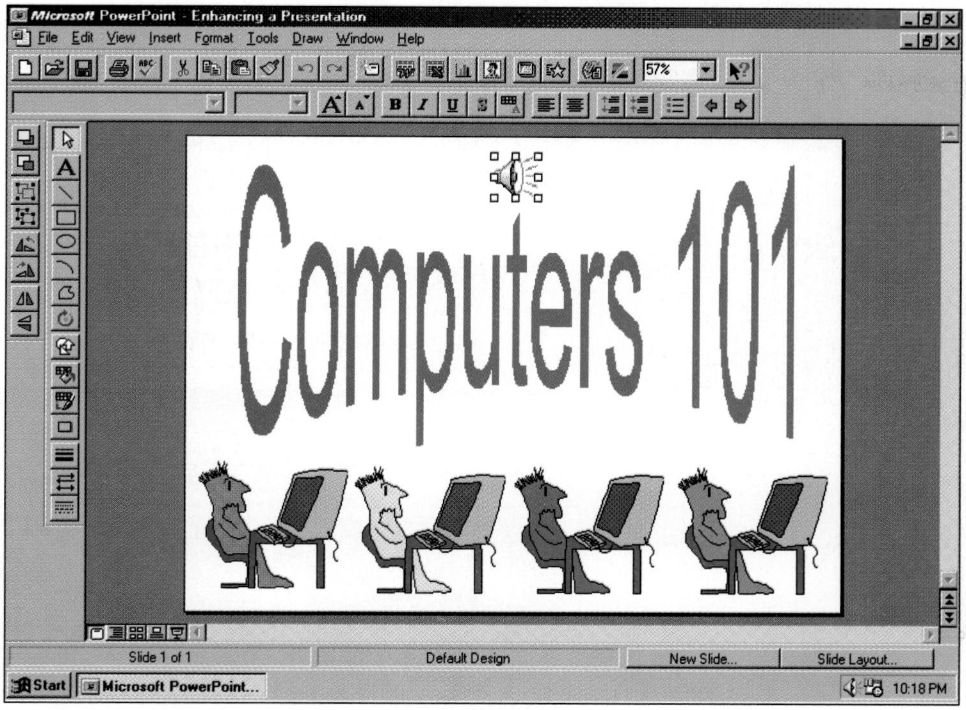

Microsoft PowerPoint - Enhancing a Presentation
File Edit View Insert Format Tools Draw Window Help
57%
Computers 101
Slide 1 of 1
Default Design
New Slide...
Slide Layout...
Start
Microsoft PowerPoint...
10:18 PM

FIGURE 3.13 Screen for Problem 2

3. Answer the following with respect to Figure 3.14.

a. What is the name of the folder that is displayed in the figure?
b. Which view is used to display the files within the folder? What other views are available? How do you change the view?
c. How many objects are in the folder? What is the total amount of space taken by all of the objects?
d. How could you determine the file size of Beethoven's 5th Symphony? How could you play the file?
e. Why are there two different types of icons within the folder? (Hint: see Appendix B, Introduction to Multimedia.)

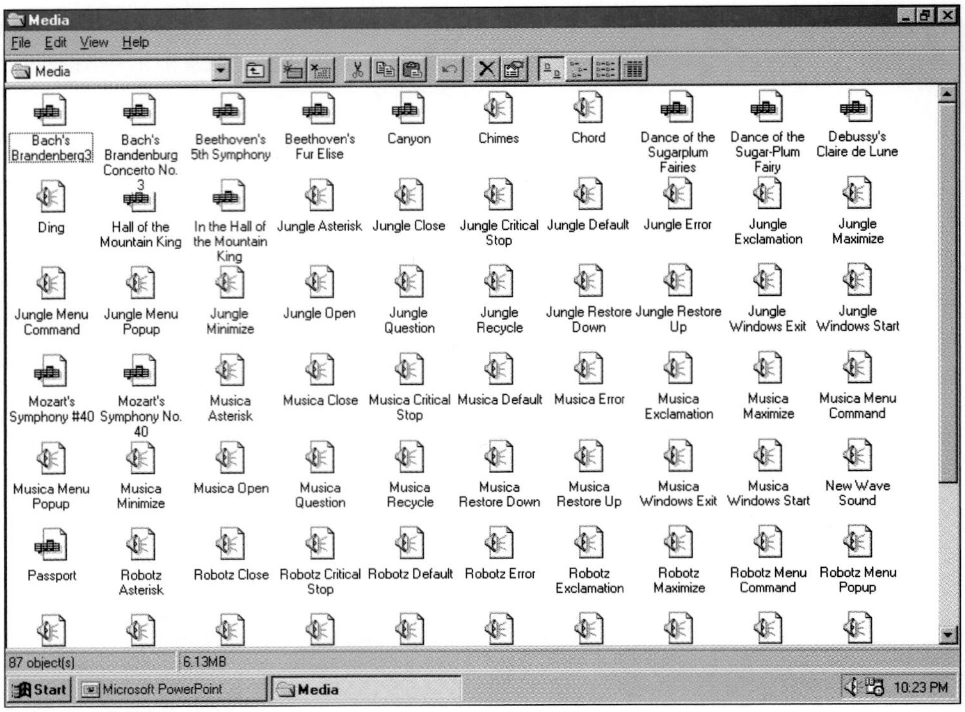
Media
File Edit View Help
Media
Bach's Brandenberg3
Bach's Brandenburg Concerto No. 3
Beethoven's 5th Symphony
Beethoven's Fur Elise
Canyon
Chimes
Chord
Dance of the Sugarplum Fairies
Dance of the Sugar-Plum Fairy
Debussy's Claire de Lune
Ding
Hall of the Mountain King
In the Hall of the Mountain King
Jungle Asterisk
Jungle Close
Jungle Critical Stop
Jungle Default
Jungle Error
Jungle Exclamation
Jungle Maximize
Jungle Menu Command
Jungle Menu Popup
Jungle Minimize
Jungle Open
Jungle Question
Jungle Recycle
Jungle Restore Down
Jungle Restore Up
Jungle Windows Exit
Jungle Windows Start
Mozart's Symphony #40
Mozart's Symphony No. 40
Musica Asterisk
Musica Close
Musica Critical Stop
Musica Default
Musica Error
Musica Exclamation
Musica Maximize
Musica Menu Command
Musica Menu Popup
Musica Minimize
Musica Open
Musica Question
Musica Recycle
Musica Restore Down
Musica Restore Up
Musica Windows Exit
Musica Windows Start
New Wave Sound
Passport
Robotz Asterisk
Robotz Close
Robotz Critical Stop
Robotz Default
Robotz Error
Robotz Exclamation
Robotz Maximize
Robotz Menu Command
Robotz Menu Popup
87 object(s)
6.13MB
Start
Microsoft PowerPoint
Media
10:23 PM

FIGURE 3.14 Screen for Problem 3

4. Answer the following with respect to Figure 3.15. (The presentation in Figure 3.15 is found in the Valupack\Audio\Cambium folder on the CD version of Microsoft Office.)

   a. What is the name of the presentation displayed in Figure 3.15? What is the significance of the words "Read Only" in the title bar?

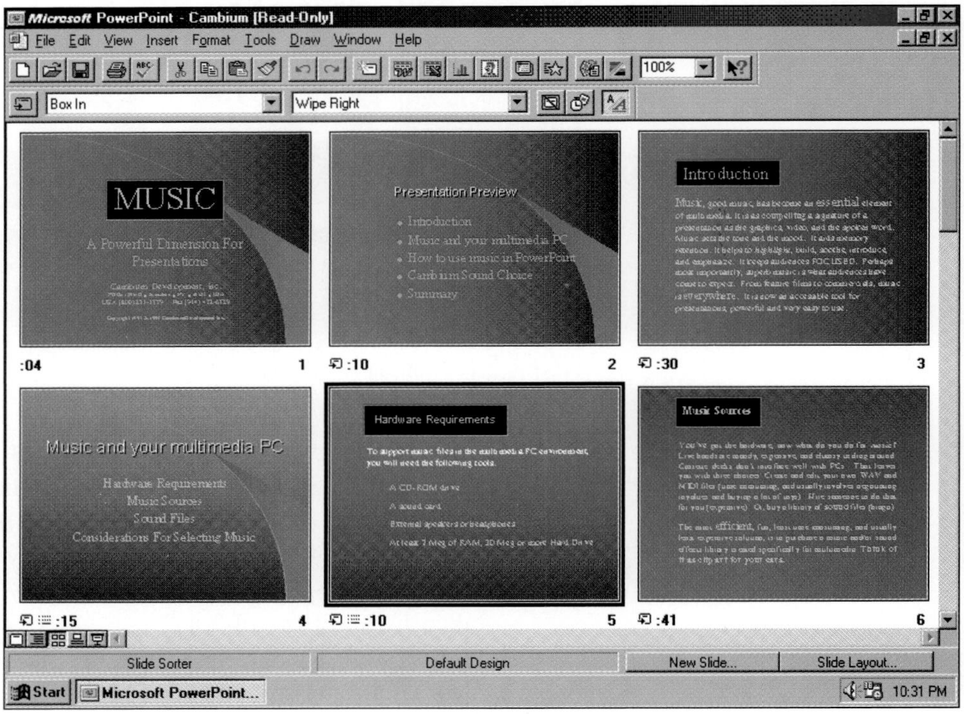
Microsoft PowerPoint - Cambium [Read-Only]
File Edit View Insert Format Tools Draw Window Help
100%
Box In
Wipe Right
MUSIC
A Powerful Dimension For Presentations
:04
1
Presentation Preview
Introduction
Music and your multimedia PC
How to use music in PowerPoint
Cambium Sound Choice
Summary
:10
2
Introduction
:30
3
Music and your multimedia PC
Hardware Requirements
Music Sources
Sound Files
Considerations For Selecting Music
:15
4
Hardware Requirements
A CD-ROM drive
A sound card
External speakers or headphones
:10
5
Music Sources
:41
6
Slide Sorter
Default Design
New Slide...
Slide Layout...
Start
Microsoft PowerPoint...
10:31 PM

FIGURE 3.15 Screen for Problem 4

b. Which slide is currently selected? What transition effect (if any) is operative for this slide? What build effect (if any) is operative for this slide?
c. What happens if you click the selected slide? What happens if you double click the selected slide?
d. What happens if you click slide 2, then click the tiny slide icon below the slide?
e. What is the significance of the numbers that appear under each of the slides?

PRACTICE WITH MICROSOFT POWERPOINT 7.0

1. Microsoft WordArt is an ideal tool to create the title slide of a presentation, as can be seen from Figure 3.16. Open the Adding Impact presentation created in the third hands-on exercise and do the following:

a. Switch to the Slide Sorter view. Select the Title Slide, then press the Del key to delete the slide.
b. Click the New Slide button on the status bar to insert a new slide. Choose AutoLayout 12 for a blank slide. Click OK.
c. Double click the new slide to change to the Slide view. Pull down the Insert menu and click Object to produce the Insert Object dialog box.
d. Scroll until you can select Microsoft WordArt 2.0. Click the Create New option button, then click OK.
e. You're on your own. Duplicate our slide or, better yet, create your own. Let's see how creative you can be and how much impact you can add.

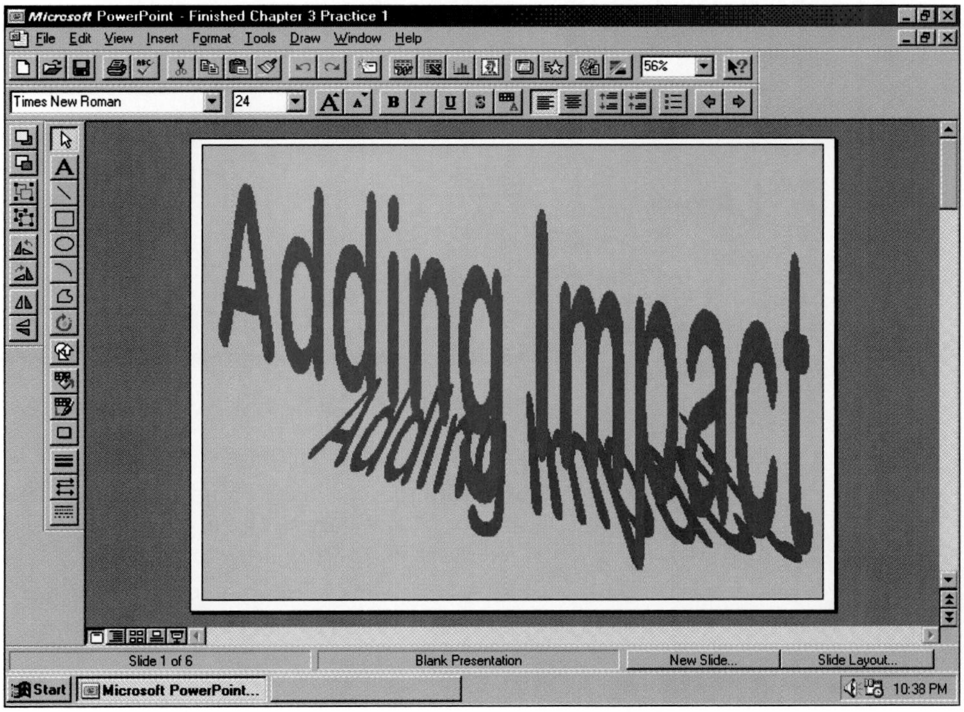
Microsoft PowerPoint - Finished Chapter 3 Practice 1
File Edit View Insert Format Tools Draw Window Help
56%
Times New Roman
24
Adding Impact
Adding Impact
Slide 1 of 6
Blank Presentation
New Slide...
Slide Layout...
Start
Microsoft PowerPoint...
10:38 PM

FIGURE 3.16 Screen for Practice Exercise 1

2. Microsoft Organization Chart offers considerable flexibility in the appearance of an organization chart as shown by the chart in Figure 3.17. You can change the line thickness, style, or color for the boxes or connecting lines. You can change the shape of a border and/or add a shadow effect. You can change the font and/or color of text within a box.

   All of these changes are done within the context of *select-then-do;* that is, you select the box (or boxes) for which the change is to apply, then you execute the appropriate command. (To select multiple boxes, press and hold the Shift key as you click additional boxes. You can also use the Select commands in the Edit menu.) Open the Adding Impact presentation created in the third hands-on exercise and do the following:

   a. Switch to the Slide Sorter view. Select the slide with the organization chart.
   b. Double click the slide to change to the Slide view. Double click the Organization Chart to edit the chart so that it matches Figure 3.17.
   c. Change the box and/or line style as you see fit.
   d. Print a full-page version of the revised slide and submit it to your instructor as proof you did the exercise.

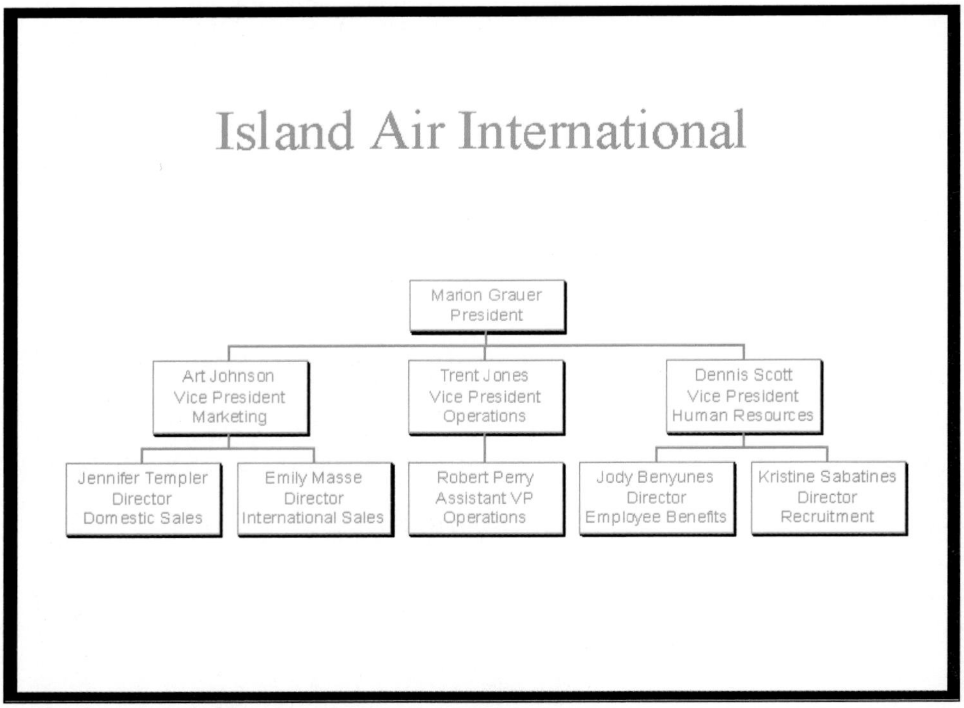
Island Air International
Marion Grauer
President
Art Johnson
Vice President
Marketing
Trent Jones
Vice President
Operations
Dennis Scott
Vice President
Human Resources
Jennifer Templer
Director
Domestic Sales
Emily Masse
Director
International Sales
Robert Perry
Assistant VP
Operations
Jody Benyunes
Director
Employee Benefits
Kristine Sabatines
Director
Recruitment

FIGURE 3.17 Screen for Practice Exercise 2

3. Exploring AutoShapes: Figure 3.18 displays a single slide containing a variety of AutoShapes. Open the presentation created in the third hands-on exercise and do the following:

   a. Add a blank slide immediately before the last slide.
   b. Click the AutoShapes tool on the Drawing toolbar to display the AutoShapes toolbar.

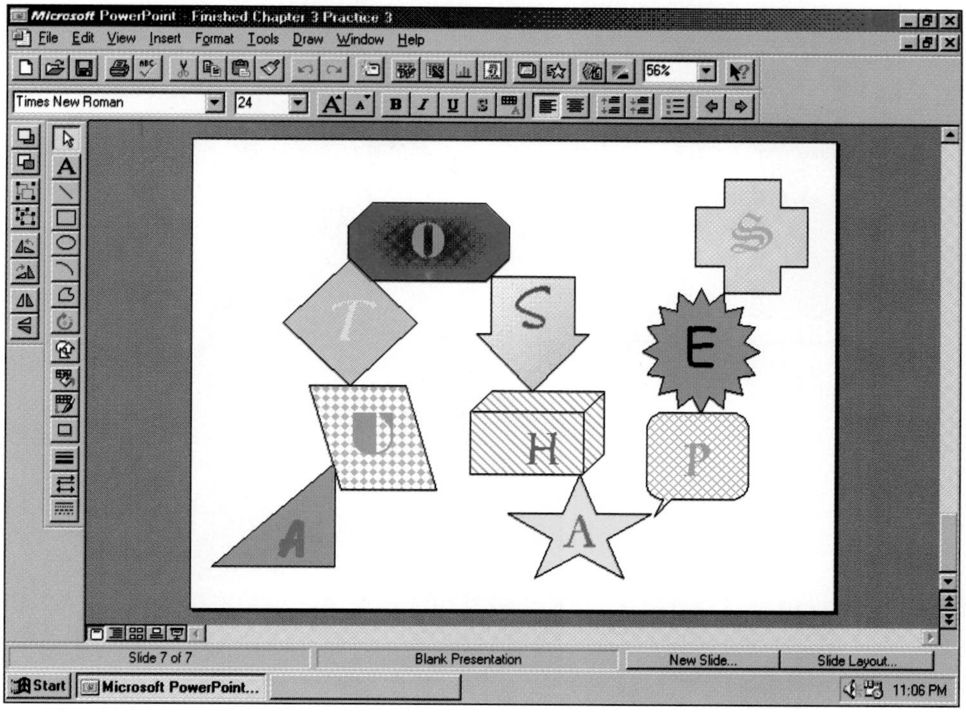
Microsoft PowerPoint - Finished Chapter 3 Practice 3
File Edit View Insert Format Tools Draw Window Help
56%
Times New Roman
24
O
S
T
S
E
U
H
P
A
A
Slide 7 of 7
Blank Presentation
New Slide...
Slide Layout...
Start
Microsoft PowerPoint...
11:06 PM

FIGURE 3.18 Screen for Practice Exercise 3

c. Point to an AutoShape, then click and drag in the slide to create the shape on the slide. (You can press and hold the Shift key as you drag for special effects; for example, press and hold the Shift key as you drag the ellipse or rectangle tool to draw a circle or square, respectively. You can also use the Shift key in conjunction with the Line tool to draw a perfect horizontal or vertical line, or a line at a 45-degree angle.)

d. To place text inside a shape, select the shape and start typing.

e. To change the fill color or line thickness, select the shape, then click the appropriate button on the Drawing toolbar.

f. Use these techniques to duplicate Figure 3.18, or better yet, create your own design. Add your name to the completed slide and submit it to your instructor.

4. Figure 3.19 shows two additional examples of what you can do with clip art. The smaller slide on the edge of the page contains the original clip art image. The full-size slide shows the modified slide and is the objective of the exercise. To create Figure 3.19a:

a. Create a blank slide in any presentation. Click the Insert Clip Art button on the Standard toolbar to open the ClipArt Gallery. Add the Worried image from the Cartoons category.

b. Select the clip art image and move it to the right side of the slide. Click the Copy and Paste buttons on the Standard toolbar to copy the image, then drag the copied image to the left side of the slide.

c. Point to the image on the left (it has not yet been flipped), click the right mouse button to display a shortcut menu, then click the Recolor command to produce the Recolor Picture dialog box. Click the check box for an original color (e.g., blue), then click the down arrow next to the corresponding new color to choose a different color (e.g., green). Click OK to

What should we do?

(a) Clip Art 1

There's Good News ...
And Bad News

(b) Clip Art 2

FIGURE 3.19 Screen for Practice Exercise 4

implement the recoloring. Repeat these steps to change the hair coloring of the gentleman on the right. (You need not follow our color scheme exactly.)

d. Select the image on the left, recolor the image, then ungroup and regroup the clip art to convert it to a PowerPoint object. Click the Flip Horizontal button to reverse the image.
e. Click and drag the Rectangle tool to draw a rectangle under our puzzled friends. Do not be concerned if the rectangle is on top of the men and you cannot see their elbows. Check that the rectangle is still selected, then click the Fill Color button on the Drawing+ toolbar to change the color of the rectangle to brown. You can also change the texture (fill color).
f. Click outside the rectangle to deselect it. Press and hold the Shift key to select both of the men, then click the Bring Forward button on the Drawing+ toolbar.
g. Add the AutoShape with the indicated text. Add your name to the slide.

To create Figure 3.19b:

h. Create a blank slide in any presentation. Click the Insert Clip Art button on the Standard toolbar to open the ClipArt Gallery. Add the Information Newspaper image from the Cartoons category.
i. Click and drag the image to size and position it as shown in Figure 3.19b.
j. Copy the clip art image, then click and drag the copied image so that the figures are separated from one another.
k. Ungroup all of the elements in the copied image. Select just the smile, then flip and resize the smile to change it to a frown. (This takes a little practice.)
l. Use the Fill Color tool on the Drawing toolbar to recolor the clothing.
m. Click and drag the Text tool on the Drawing toolbar to create the first text box, then type *There's Good News* in the text box. Be sure the text is still selected, then change the font, size, and color as you see fit.
n. Repeat the previous steps to create the second text box. Print both slides and submit them to your instructor.

CASE STUDIES

The Federal Budget

The federal government spends billions more than it takes in. In fiscal year 1993, for example, government expenditures totaled $1,408 billion versus income of only $1,154 billion leaving a deficit of $254 billion. Thirty-one percent of the income came from Social Security and Medicare taxes, 36% from personal income taxes, 8% from corporate income taxes, and 7% from excise, estate, and other miscellaneous taxes. The remaining 18% was borrowed.

Social Security and Medicare accounted for 35% of the expenditures and the defense budget another 24%. Social programs including Medicaid and aid to dependent children totaled 17%. Community development (consisting of agricultural, educational, environmental, economic, and space programs) totaled 8% of the budget. Interest on the national debt amounted to 14%. The cost of law enforcement and government itself accounted for the final 2%.

Use the information contained within this problem to create a presentation that shows the distribution of income and expenditures. Do some independent research and obtain data on the budget, the deficit, and the national debt for the years 1945, 1967, and 1980. The numbers may surprise you; for example, how does the interest expense for the current year compare to the total budget in 1967 (at the height of the Viet Nam War)? to the total budget in 1945 (at the end of World War II)? Create additional graphs to reflect your findings, then write your representative in Congress. We are in trouble!

Before and After

As you already know, PowerPoint provides a set of drawing tools to develop virtually any type of illustration. Even if you are not artistic, you can use these tools to modify existing clip art and thus create new and very different illustrations. All it takes is a little imagination and a sense of what can be done. Choose any clip art image(s), then modify that image(s) to create an entirely different effect. Present your results in a three-slide presentation consisting of a title slide, a "before slide" showing the original image(s), and an "after slide" showing the modifications. Print the audience handouts for your presentation, three slides per page, and be sure to check the box to frame the slides. Ask your instructor to hold a class contest in which the class votes to determine the most creative application.

Photographs versus Clip Art

The right clip art can enhance a presentation, but there are times when clip art just won't do. It may be too juvenile or simply inappropriate. Photographs offer an alternative and are inserted into a presentation through the Insert Picture command. Once inserted into a presentation, photographs can be moved or sized just like any other Windows object. The CD-ROM version of Microsoft Office contains a Valuepack with a series of photographs from two different vendors. We invite you to explore these photographs, then report back to the class on their quality and cost.

Our Last Case

Once again we refer you to the Valuepack on the CD-ROM version of Microsoft Office to view a 45-slide presentation that introduces (and reviews) the major features in PowerPoint. The presentation is called "QuikPrev" (for quick preview) and is found in the PPQPREV folder within the Valuepack folder on the CD-ROM. It is a multimedia presentation that incorporates music, video, as well as the various other objects discussed in this chapter. Sit back, relax, and enjoy the show.

A

APPENDIX A: TOOLBARS

OVERVIEW

PowerPoint has nine predefined toolbars, which provide access to commonly used commands. The toolbars are displayed in Figure A.1 and are listed here for convenience. They are the Animation Effects, AutoShapes, Drawing, Drawing+, Formatting, Microsoft, Outlining, Slide Sorter, and Standard toolbars. When you first start PowerPoint, the Standard and Formatting toolbars are displayed immediately below the menu bar, and the Drawing toolbar is displayed along the left edge of the window. The Outlining and Slide Sorter toolbars are displayed automatically when you switch to the Outline and Slide Sorter views, respectively. The Animation Effects, AutoShape, Drawing+, and Microsoft toolbars are available for use as needed.

In addition to the PowerPoint predefined toolbars, Microsoft Graph, Microsoft WordArt, and Microsoft Organization Chart display application-specific toolbars when the applications are open. These toolbars are shown in Figure A.2.

The buttons on the toolbars are intended to be indicative of their functions. Clicking the Print button, for example (the fourth button from the left on the Standard toolbar), executes the Print command. If you are unsure of the purpose of any toolbar button, point to it, and a ToolTip will appear that displays its name.

You can display multiple toolbars at one time, move them to new locations on the screen, customize their appearance, or suppress their display.

- To display or hide a toolbar, pull down the View menu and click the Toolbars command. Select (deselect) the toolbar(s) that you want to display (hide). The selected toolbar(s) will be displayed in the same position as when last displayed. You may also point to any toolbar and click with the right mouse button to bring up a shortcut menu, after which you can select the toolbar to be displayed (hidden).

- To change the size of the buttons, display them in monochrome rather than color, or suppress the display of the ToolTips, pull down the View menu, click Toolbars, and then select (deselect) the appropriate check box. Alternatively, you can click on any toolbar with the right mouse button, select Toolbars, and then select (deselect) the appropriate check box.
- Toolbars may be either docked (along the edge of the window) or left floating (in their own window). A toolbar moved to the edge of the window will dock along that edge. A toolbar moved anywhere else in the window will float in its own window. Docked toolbars are one tool wide (high), whereas floating toolbars can be resized by clicking and dragging a border or corner as you would with any other window.
    - To move a docked toolbar, click anywhere in the gray background area and drag the toolbar to its new location.
    - To move a floating toolbar, drag its title bar to its new location.
- To customize one or more toolbars, display the toolbar(s) on the screen. Then pull down the View menu, click Toolbars, and click the Customize command button. Alternatively, you can click on any toolbar with the right mouse button, and then select Customize from the shortcut menu.
    - To move a button, drag the button to its new location on that toolbar or any other displayed toolbar.
    - To copy a button, press the Ctrl key as you drag the button to its new location on that toolbar or any other displayed toolbar.
    - To delete a button, drag the button off the toolbar and release the mouse button.
    - To add a button, select the category from the Categories list box and then drag the button to the desired location on the toolbar. (To see a description of a tool's function prior to adding it to a toolbar, click the tool in the Customize dialog box and read the displayed description.)
    - To restore a predefined toolbar to its default appearance, pull down the View menu, click Toolbars, select (highlight) the desired toolbar, and click the Reset command button.
- Buttons can also be moved, copied, or deleted without displaying the Customize dialog box.
    - To move a button, press the Alt key as you drag the button to the new location.
    - To copy a button, press the Alt and Ctrl keys as you drag the button to the new location.
    - To delete a button, press the Alt key as you drag the button off the toolbar.
- To create your own toolbar, pull down the View menu, click Toolbar, and click the New command button. Alternatively, you can click on any toolbar with the right mouse button, select Toolbars from the shortcut menu, and then click the New command button.
    - Enter a name for the toolbar in the dialog box that follows. The name can be any length and can contain spaces.
    - The new toolbar will appear at the top left of the screen. Initially it will be big enough to hold only one button. Add, move, and delete buttons following the same procedures as outlined above. The toolbar will automatically size itself as new buttons are added and deleted.
    - To delete a custom toolbar, pull down the View menu, click Toolbars, and make sure that the custom toolbar to be deleted is the only one selected

(highlighted). Click the Delete command button. Prior to closing the dialog box, you can undelete the toolbar by clicking the Undelete button. Once you have exited the dialog box, however, the custom toolbar cannot be undeleted. (Note that a predefined toolbar cannot be deleted.)

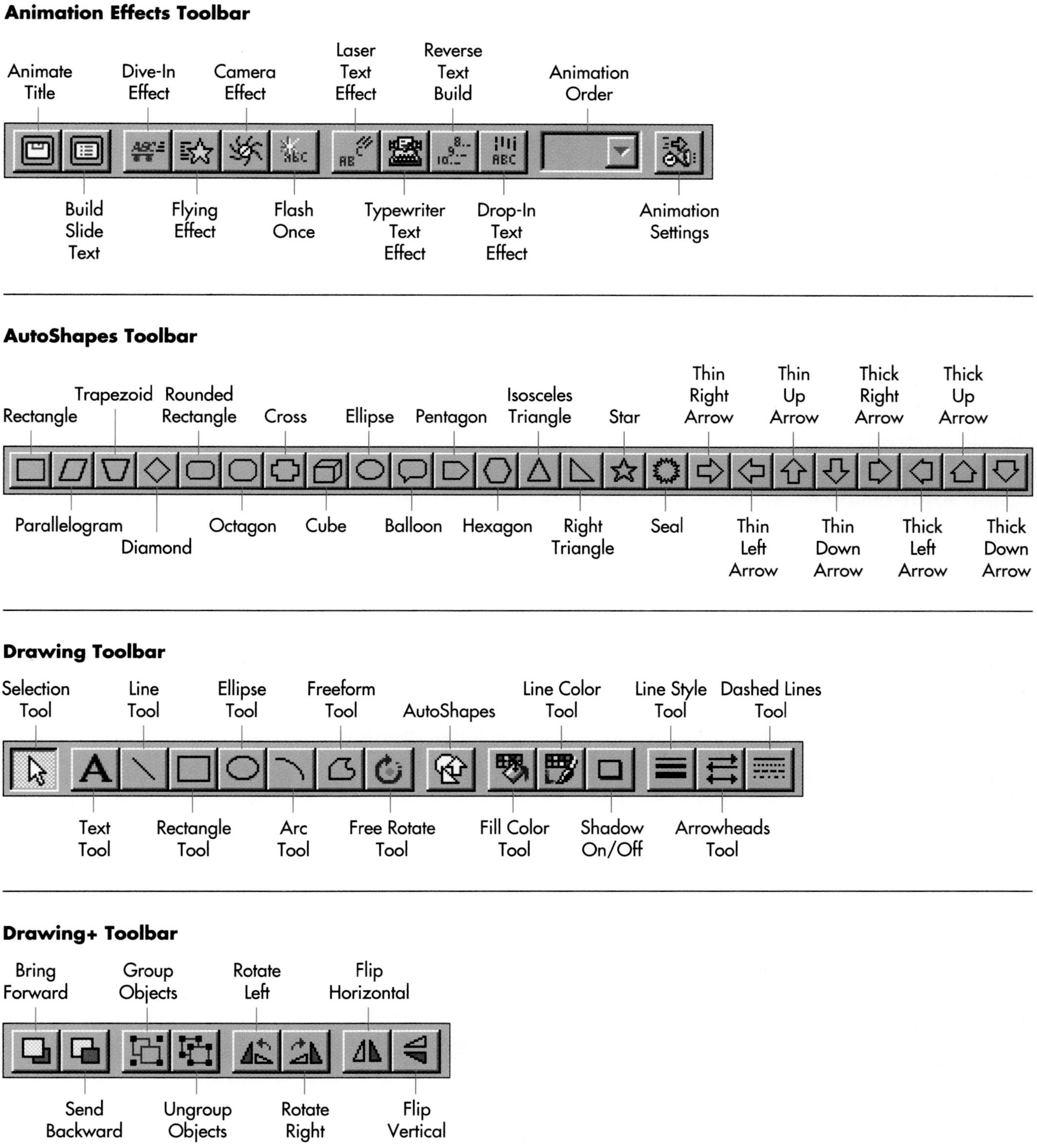

Animation Effects Toolbar
Animate Title
Dive-In Effect
Camera Effect
Laser Text Effect
Reverse Text Build
Animation Order
Build Slide Text
Flying Effect
Flash Once
Typewriter Text Effect
Drop-In Text Effect
Animation Settings
AutoShapes Toolbar
Rectangle
Trapezoid
Rounded Rectangle
Cross
Ellipse
Pentagon
Isosceles Triangle
Star
Thin Right Arrow
Thin Up Arrow
Thick Right Arrow
Thick Up Arrow
Parallelogram
Diamond
Octagon
Cube
Balloon
Hexagon
Right Triangle
Seal
Thin Left Arrow
Thin Down Arrow
Thick Left Arrow
Thick Down Arrow
Drawing Toolbar
Selection Tool
Line Tool
Ellipse Tool
Freeform Tool
AutoShapes
Line Color Tool
Line Style Tool
Dashed Lines Tool
Text Tool
Rectangle Tool
Arc Tool
Free Rotate Tool
Fill Color Tool
Shadow On/Off
Arrowheads Tool
Drawing+ Toolbar
Bring Forward
Group Objects
Rotate Left
Flip Horizontal
Send Backward
Ungroup Objects
Rotate Right
Flip Vertical

FIGURE A.1 PowerPoint Toolbars

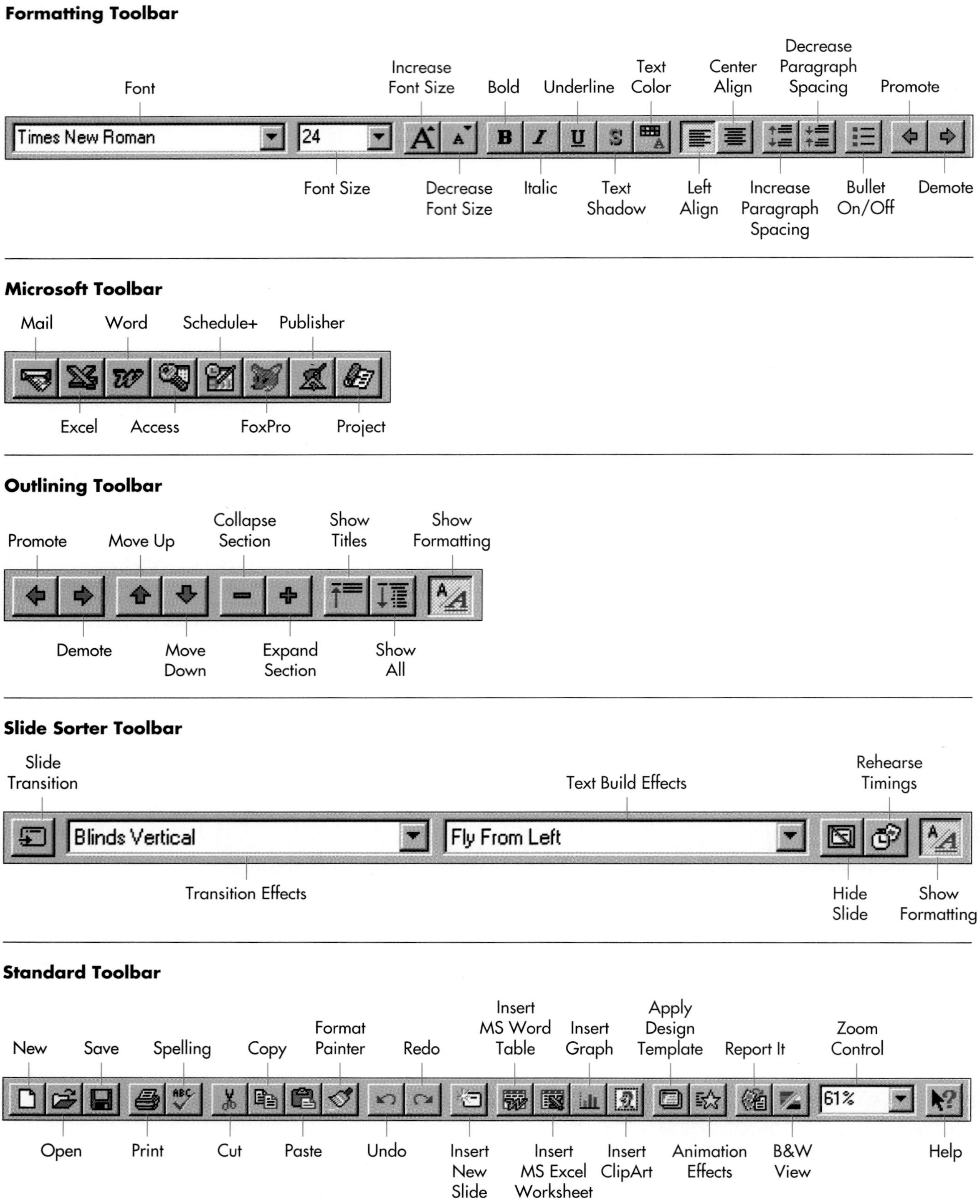
Formatting Toolbar
Font
Increase Font Size
Bold
Underline
Text Color
Center Align
Decrease Paragraph Spacing
Promote
Times New Roman
24
Font Size
Decrease Font Size
Italic
Text Shadow
Left Align
Increase Paragraph Spacing
Bullet On/Off
Demote
Microsoft Toolbar
Mail
Word
Schedule+
Publisher
Excel
Access
FoxPro
Project
Outlining Toolbar
Promote
Move Up
Collapse Section
Show Titles
Show Formatting
Demote
Move Down
Expand Section
Show All
Slide Sorter Toolbar
Slide Transition
Text Build Effects
Rehearse Timings
Blinds Vertical
Fly From Left
Transition Effects
Hide Slide
Show Formatting
Standard Toolbar
New
Save
Spelling
Copy
Format Painter
Redo
Insert MS Word Table
Insert Graph
Apply Design Template
Report It
Zoom Control
61%
Open
Print
Cut
Paste
Undo
Insert New Slide
Insert MS Excel Worksheet
Insert ClipArt
Animation Effects
B&W View
Help

FIGURE A.1 PowerPoint Toolbars (continued)

Microsoft Graph

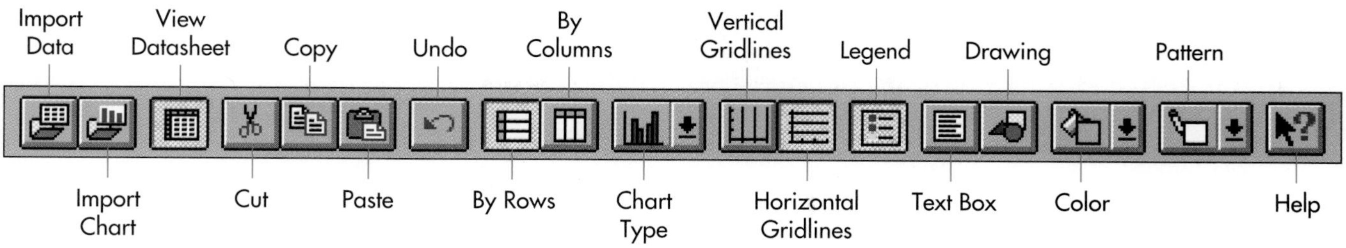
Import Data
View Datasheet
Copy
Undo
By Columns
Vertical Gridlines
Legend
Drawing
Pattern
Import Chart
Cut
Paste
By Rows
Chart Type
Horizontal Gridlines
Text Box
Color
Help

Microsoft Organization Chart

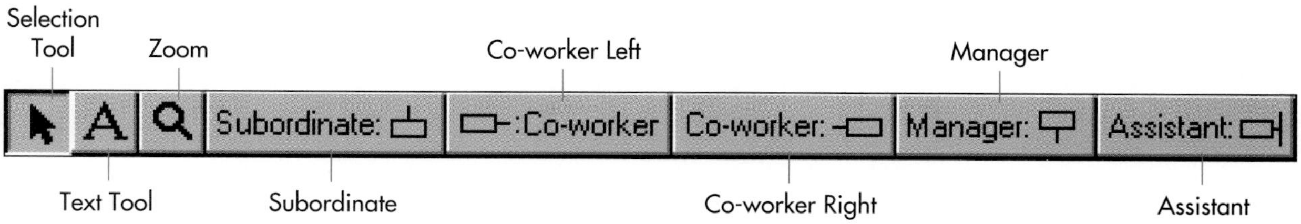
Selection Tool
Zoom
Co-worker Left
Manager
Subordinate:
:Co-worker
Co-worker:
Manager:
Assistant:
Text Tool
Subordinate
Co-worker Right
Assistant

Microsoft WordArt

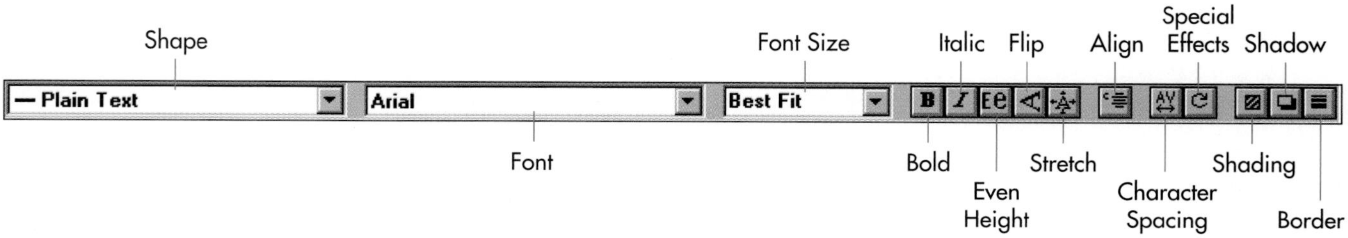
Shape
Font Size
Italic
Flip
Align
Special Effects
Shadow
Plain Text
Arial
Best Fit
Font
Bold
Even Height
Stretch
Character Spacing
Shading
Border

FIGURE A.2 Toolbars from Supplementary Applications

B

APPENDIX B: INTRODUCTION TO MULTIMEDIA

OVERVIEW

Multimedia combines the text and graphics capability of the PC with high-quality sound and video. The combination of different media, under the control of the PC, has opened up a new world of education and entertainment. This appendix introduces you to the basics of multimedia and shows you how to incorporate sound and video into a PowerPoint presentation.

We begin with a brief discussion of the hardware requirements needed to run multimedia applications. We explain the different file types that are associated with multimedia and discuss the support that is built into Windows 95. We also describe the royalty-free multimedia files that are available on the PowerPoint (or Office Professional) CD-ROM.

The appendix also contains two hands-on exercises that let you apply the conceptual material. The first exercise is independent of PowerPoint and has you experiment with various sound and video files to better acquaint you with the capabilities of multimedia. The second exercise shows you how to create your own multimedia presentation.

THE MULTIMEDIA COMPUTER

Multimedia is possible only because of recent advances in technology that include faster microprocessors, CD-ROM, and sophisticated sound and video boards. But how fast a microprocessor do you really need? What type of CD-ROM and sound card should you consider? The answers are critical to both the consumer and the developer. The consumer wants a system that is capable of running "typical" multimedia applications. The developer, on the other hand, wants to appeal to the widest possible audience and must write an application so that it runs on the "typical" configuration.

To guide developers, and to let the public know the specific hardware needed, the ***Multimedia PC Marketing Council (MPC)*** was established to determine the suggested minimum specification for a multimedia computer. Three standards have been published to date—***MPC-1, MPC-2,*** and ***MPC-3,*** in 1991, 1993, and 1995, respectively, as shown in Figure B.1. Implicit within each standard is the requirement that the system retail for less than $2,000. If your budget can afford it, you may want to go beyond the MPC-3 configuration (to a faster microprocessor, more memory, and a larger hard drive), but you should not consider a system with less capability. And don't forget to include speakers to amplify the sound, a microphone if you want to record your own sounds, and a joystick for games.

THE MULTIMEDIA UPGRADE

Computer magazines are filled with advertisements for multimedia upgrades—kits that contain a sound card and CD-ROM; but are they worth the investment? If your existing system meets our other minimum requirements—a 486/66 processor, 8MB of RAM, and a 350MB disk—by all means upgrade. If, on the other hand, you re lacking one or more of these components, you are better off waiting until you are ready to replace the entire system. And one final piece of advice if you do decide to upgrade. Installing a CD-ROM and sound card on an existing system is not easy! Purchase the hardware at a local store and have a professional install it for you.

	MPC-1 (1991)	**MPC-2 (1993)**	**MPC-3 (1995)**
CPU	80386 16MHz	80486SX 25MHz	75MHz Pentium
RAM	2MB	4MB	8MB
Disk capacity	30MB	160MB	540MB
Sound card	8 bit	8 bit	16 bit with multivoice internal synthesizer
CD-ROM	Single speed	Double speed	Quadruple speed
Video system	VGA (640 × 480)	SVGA (800 × 600)	30 frames/second at 320 × 240 pixels

FIGURE B.1 The Multimedia PC

THE BASICS OF MULTIMEDIA

A few years ago multimedia was an extra. Today it is a virtual standard, and everyone has a favorite multimedia application. But did you ever stop to think of how the application was created? Or of the large number of individual files that are needed for the sound and visual effects that are at the heart of the application? In this section we look at the individual components, the sound and video files, that comprise a multimedia application.

Sound

The sound you hear from your PC is the result of a sound file (stored on disk or a CD-ROM) being played through the sound card in your system. There are, however, two very different types of sound files: a WAV file and a MIDI file. Each is discussed in turn.

A ***WAV file*** is a digitized recording of an actual sound (a voice, music, or special effects). It is created by a chip in the sound card that converts a recorded sound (e.g., your voice by way of a microphone) into a file on disk. The sound card divides the sound wave into tiny segments (known as samples) and stores each sample as a binary number. The quality of the sound is determined by two factors—the sampling rate and the resolution of each sample. The higher each of these values, the better the quality, and the larger the corresponding file.

The ***sampling rate*** (or frequency) is the number of samples per second and is expressed in KHz (thousands of samples per second). The higher the sampling rate, the more accurately the sound will be represented in the wave file. Common sampling rates are 11KHz, 22KHz, and 44KHz. The ***resolution*** is the number of bits (binary digits) used to store each sample. The more bits, the better. The first sound cards provided for only eight bits and are obsolete. Sixteen bits are standard in today's environment.

WAV files, even those that last only a few seconds, grow large very quickly. Eight-bit sound, for example, at a sampling rate of 11KHz (11,000 samples a second), requires approximately 11KB of disk space per second. Thirty seconds of sound at this sampling rate will take some 330KB. If you improve the quality by using a 16-bit sound card, and by doubling the sampling rate to 22KHz, the same 30 seconds of sound will consume 1.3MB, or almost an entire high-density floppy disk!

A ***MIDI file*** (Musical Instrument Digital Interface) is very different from a WAV file and is used only to create music. It does not store an actual sound (as does a WAV file), but rather the instructions to create that sound. In other words, a MIDI file is the electronic equivalent of sheet music. The advantage of a MIDI file is that it is much more compact than a WAV file because it stores instructions to create the sound rather than the actual sound.

Video

An ***AVI*** (Audio-Video Interleaved) ***file*** is the Microsoft standard for a digital video (i.e., a multimedia) file. It takes approximately 4.5MB to store one second of *uncompressed* color video in the AVI format. That may sound unbelievable, but you can verify the number with a little arithmetic.

A single VGA screen contains approximately 300,000 (640 × 480) pixels, each of which requires (at least) one byte of storage to store the color associated with that pixel. Allocating one byte (or 8 bits) per pixel yields only 256 (or 2^8) different colors. It is more common, therefore, to define color palettes based on two or even three bytes per pixel, which yield 65,536 (2^{16}) and 16,777,216 (2^{24}) colors, respectively. The more colors you have, the better the picture, but the larger the file.

In addition, to fool the eye and create the effect of motion, the screen must display at least 15 screens (frames) a second. If we multiply 300,000 bytes per frame, times 15 frames per second, we arrive at the earlier number of 4.5MB of data for each second of video. Storage requirements of this magnitude are clearly prohibitive in that an entire 640MB CD would hold less than three minutes of video. And even if storage capacity were not a problem, it's simply not possible for a CD-ROM to deliver almost 5MB of data per second to the PC. Clearly, something has to be done.

Full-motion video is made possible in two ways: by reducing the size of the window in which the video clip is displayed, and through ***file compression.*** Think, for a moment, of the video clips you have seen (or consider the SIDEWALK.AVI file in Figure B.2) and realize that they are displayed in a window that is 320 × 240, or one quarter of a VGA screen. The smaller window immediately reduces the storage by a factor of four.

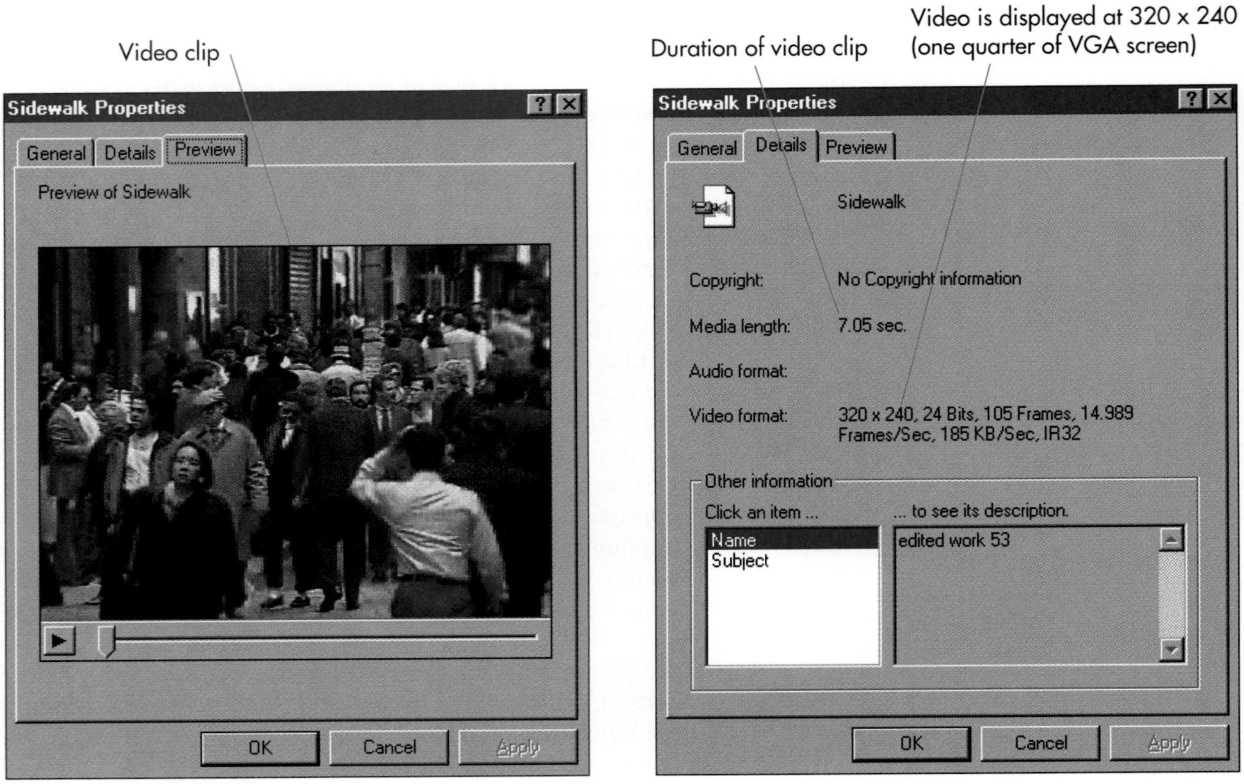
Video clip
Sidewalk Properties
General
Details
Preview
Preview of Sidewalk
OK
Cancel
Apply
Duration of video clip
Video is displayed at 320 x 240 (one quarter of VGA screen)
Sidewalk Properties
General
Details
Preview
Sidewalk
Copyright:
No Copyright information
Media length:
7.05 sec.
Audio format:
Video format:
320 x 240, 24 Bits, 105 Frames, 14.989 Frames/Sec, 185 KB/Sec, IR32
Other information
Click an item ...
... to see its description.
Name
Subject
edited work 53
OK
Cancel
Apply

(a) Preview

(b) Details

FIGURE B.2 A Video Clip

Even more significant than a reduced window is the availability of sophisticated compression-decompression algorithms, which dramatically reduce the storage requirements. In essence, these algorithms do not store every pixel in every frame, but only information about how pixels change from frame to frame. The details of file compression are not important at this time. What is important is that you appreciate the enormous amount of data that is required for multimedia applications.

Realize, too, that even with the smaller window and file compression, AVI files are still inordinately large. The seven-second movie clip in Figure B.2, for example, requires 1.3MB, or almost an entire high-density floppy disk. Nevertheless, compare this requirement to our earlier calculations, which showed that an uncompressed video running on a VGA screen would take approximately 4.5MB per second!

THE AVI (AUDIO-VIDEO INTERLEAVED) STANDARD

The AVI format was introduced in 1992 and specified a standard video clip of 160 × 120 pixels, or one sixteenth of a VGA screen. The tiny screen was not overly impressive to the public at large, but it represented a significant technical achievement. Improved technology such as the local bus, quad speed CD-ROM, better compression algorithms, and faster microprocessors have resulted in today's standard clip of 320 × 240, or one quarter of a VGA screen.

Windows 95 Support

Windows 95 includes the necessary software (in the form of accessories) to play various types of multimedia files. The tools can be accessed from the Start button or through shortcuts in the Multimedia folder shown in Figure B.3a. The appropriate accessory is also opened automatically when you double click the corresponding media file type.

The ***CD Player*** enables you to play audio CDs in a CD-ROM drive while you work on your PC. The controls on the Windows CD player look just like those on a regular CD player. It also has many of the same features, such as random play, and a programmable playback order.

The ***Media Player*** lets you play audio, video, or animation files. ***Volume Control*** enables you to control the volume and/or balance of your sound card.

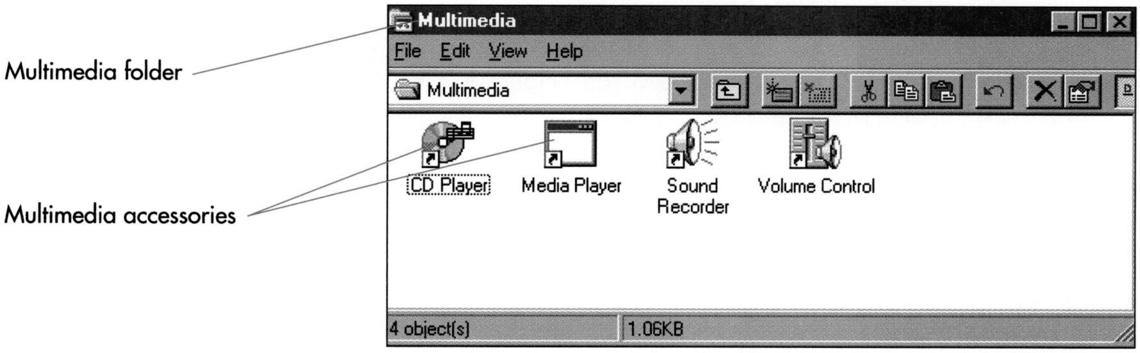
Multimedia folder
Multimedia accessories
Multimedia
File Edit View Help
Multimedia
CD Player
Media Player
Sound Recorder
Volume Control
4 object(s)
1.06KB

(a) Multimedia Tools

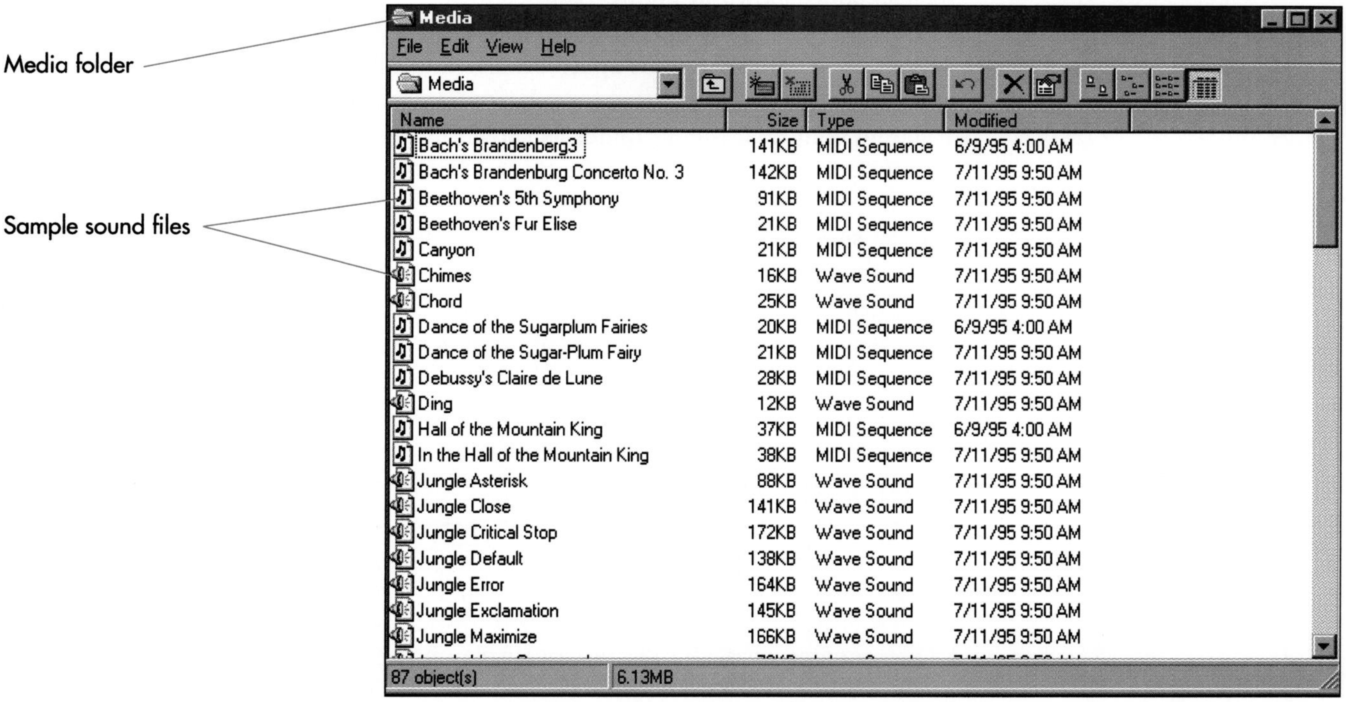
Media folder
Sample sound files
Media
File Edit View Help
Media
Name
Size
Type
Modified
Bach's Brandenberg3 141KB MIDI Sequence 6/9/95 4:00 AM
Bach's Brandenburg Concerto No. 3 142KB MIDI Sequence 7/11/95 9:50 AM
Beethoven's 5th Symphony 91KB MIDI Sequence 7/11/95 9:50 AM
Beethoven's Fur Elise 21KB MIDI Sequence 7/11/95 9:50 AM
Canyon 21KB MIDI Sequence 7/11/95 9:50 AM
Chimes 16KB Wave Sound 7/11/95 9:50 AM
Chord 25KB Wave Sound 7/11/95 9:50 AM
Dance of the Sugarplum Fairies 20KB MIDI Sequence 6/9/95 4:00 AM
Dance of the Sugar-Plum Fairy 21KB MIDI Sequence 7/11/95 9:50 AM
Debussy's Claire de Lune 28KB MIDI Sequence 7/11/95 9:50 AM
Ding 12KB Wave Sound 7/11/95 9:50 AM
Hall of the Mountain King 37KB MIDI Sequence 6/9/95 4:00 AM
In the Hall of the Mountain King 38KB MIDI Sequence 7/11/95 9:50 AM
Jungle Asterisk 88KB Wave Sound 7/11/95 9:50 AM
Jungle Close 141KB Wave Sound 7/11/95 9:50 AM
Jungle Critical Stop 172KB Wave Sound 7/11/95 9:50 AM
Jungle Default 138KB Wave Sound 7/11/95 9:50 AM
Jungle Error 164KB Wave Sound 7/11/95 9:50 AM
Jungle Exclamation 145KB Wave Sound 7/11/95 9:50 AM
Jungle Maximize 166KB Wave Sound 7/11/95 9:50 AM
87 object(s)
6.13MB

(b) Media Files

FIGURE B.3 Multimedia Support

The ***Sound Recorder*** is used to record and play back a WAV file. Options within the Sound Recorder enable you to record at different qualities (e.g., CD or radio). You can also add special effects to a recorded sound, such as an echo, or you can speed up or slow down the recording. You can even play it backwards.

In addition to the multimedia accessories, Windows also provides sample files on which you can experiment. The files are stored in the ***Media folder,*** as shown in Figure B.3b. The exercise that follows has you locate the Media folder on your system, then use the Windows accessories to play various files in the folder.

HANDS-ON EXERCISE 1

Introduction to Multimedia

Objective: Use the Windows 95 Find command to locate and demonstrate WAV, MIDI, and AVI files. The exercise requires a sound card but can be done without a CD-ROM. Use Figure B.4 as a guide in the exercise.

STEP 1: The Find Command

➤ Click the **Start Button** on the Windows 95 taskbar. Click (or point to) the **Find command,** then click **Files or Folders** to display the dialog box in Figure B.4a. (No files will be listed since the search has not yet taken place, and the Media folder will not be displayed.) The size and/or position of the dialog box may be different from the one in the figure.

➤ Type **Media** (the folder you are searching for) in the Named text box. Click the **drop-down arrow** in the Look in list box. Click **My Computer** to search all of the drives on your system. Be sure the **Include subfolders** box is checked as shown in Figure B.4a.

➤ Click the **Find Now button** to begin the search, then watch the status bar as Windows searches for the specified files and folders.

➤ The results of the search are displayed within the Find Files dialog box and should contain a Media folder as shown in Figure B.4a. (Your view may be different from ours.) If you do not see the folder, check the search parameters:

- Be sure that you spelled **Media** correctly and that you are looking in **My Computer.**
- Click the **Date Modified tab.** Click the **All Files option button.**
- Click the **Advanced tab.** Be sure that **All Files and Folders** is specified in the Of Type list box and that the Containing text box is clear.

ORDINARY FILES

A multimedia file is just like any other file with respect to ordinary file operations. Point to the file (in My Computer or the Windows Explorer), then click the right mouse button to display a menu to cut or copy the file, rename or delete the file, or display its properties. You can also use the right mouse button to click and drag the file to a different drive or folder or create a shortcut on the desktop.

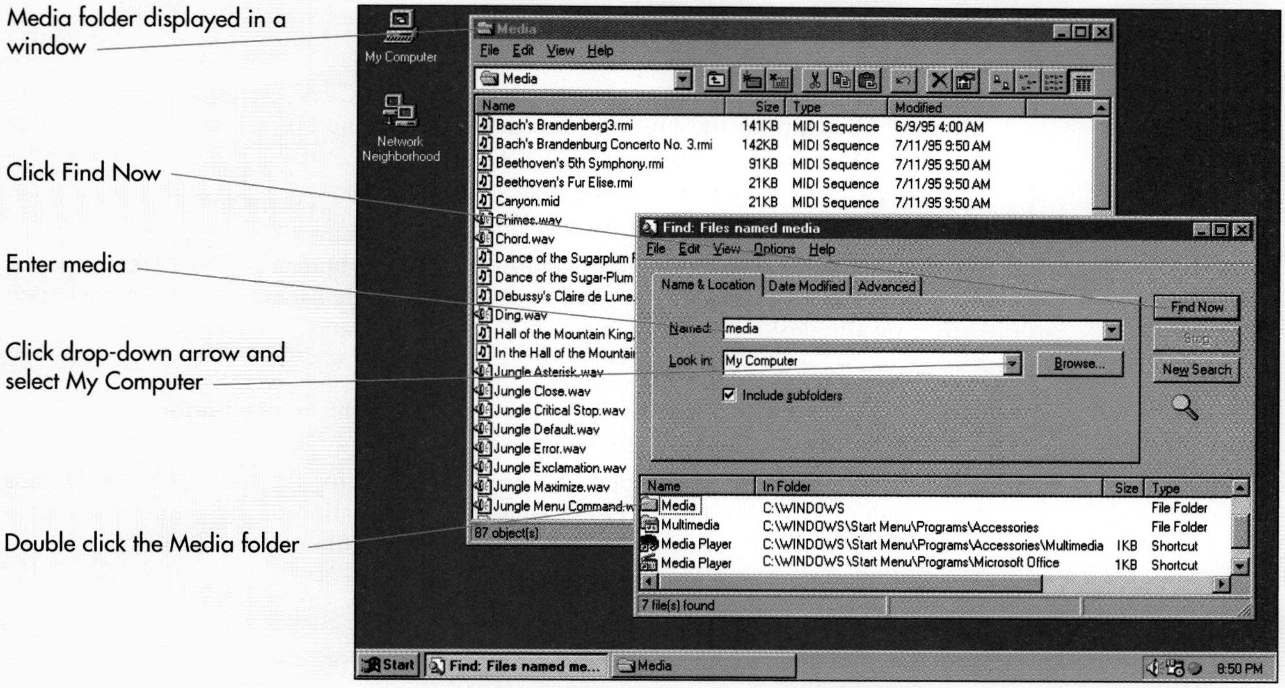
Media folder displayed in a window
Click Find Now
Enter media
Click drop-down arrow and select My Computer
Double click the Media folder

(a) Find the Media Folder (steps 1 & 2)

FIGURE B.4 Hands-on Exercise 1

- Pull down the **Options menu** and verify that the Case Sensitive option is off (i.e., that the option does not have a check).
- Click the **Find Now button** to repeat the search with these parameters.

➤ If you still do not see a Media folder, ask your instructor about reinstalling the multimedia component in Windows 95.

STEP 2: The Media Folder

➤ Double click the **Media folder** to open a window for this folder as shown in Figure B.4a. The size and position of your window may be different from ours.

FILE EXTENSIONS

Long-time DOS users will recognize the three-character extension at the end of a file name, which indicates the file type. The extensions are displayed or hidden according to an option set in the View menu in My Computer or the Windows Explorer. Windows 95 maintains the file extension for compatibility, and in addition, displays an icon next to the file name to indicate the file type. The icons are more easily recognized in the Large Icons view, as opposed to the Details view. Extensions of WAV and MID denote a wave form and MIDI file, respectively. An AVI (Audio-Video Interleaved) file is the Microsoft standard for a multimedia file with video and sound.

➤ To display the Details view and the file extensions within that view:

- Pull down the **View menu.** Click **Details.**
- Pull down the **View menu** a second time. Click **Options,** then click the **View tab** in the Options dialog box. Clear the box (if necessary) to **Hide MS-DOS file extensions.** Click **OK.**

➤ The view in your Media window should match Figure B.4a. You may, however, see a different number of objects.

➤ Click anywhere in the **Find window** (or click its button on the Taskbar). Click the **Close button** in this window so that only the Media folder remains open on the desktop.

STEP 3: WAV Files

➤ Point to the **Chord.wav** file, then click the **right mouse button** to display a menu with commands pertaining to the selected file.

➤ Click **Properties** to display the property sheet for the file. Click the **Details tab** as shown in Figure B.4b. Note that the duration of the sound (the media length) is just a little over one second, yet the file requires 25KB of storage.

➤ Close the Properties dialog box.

➤ Play the sound:

- Double click the icon next to the file name, or
- Right click the file, then click the **Play command.** The Sound Recorder will appear on the screen as the sound is played.
- If necessary, close the Sound Recorder after the sound has finished playing.

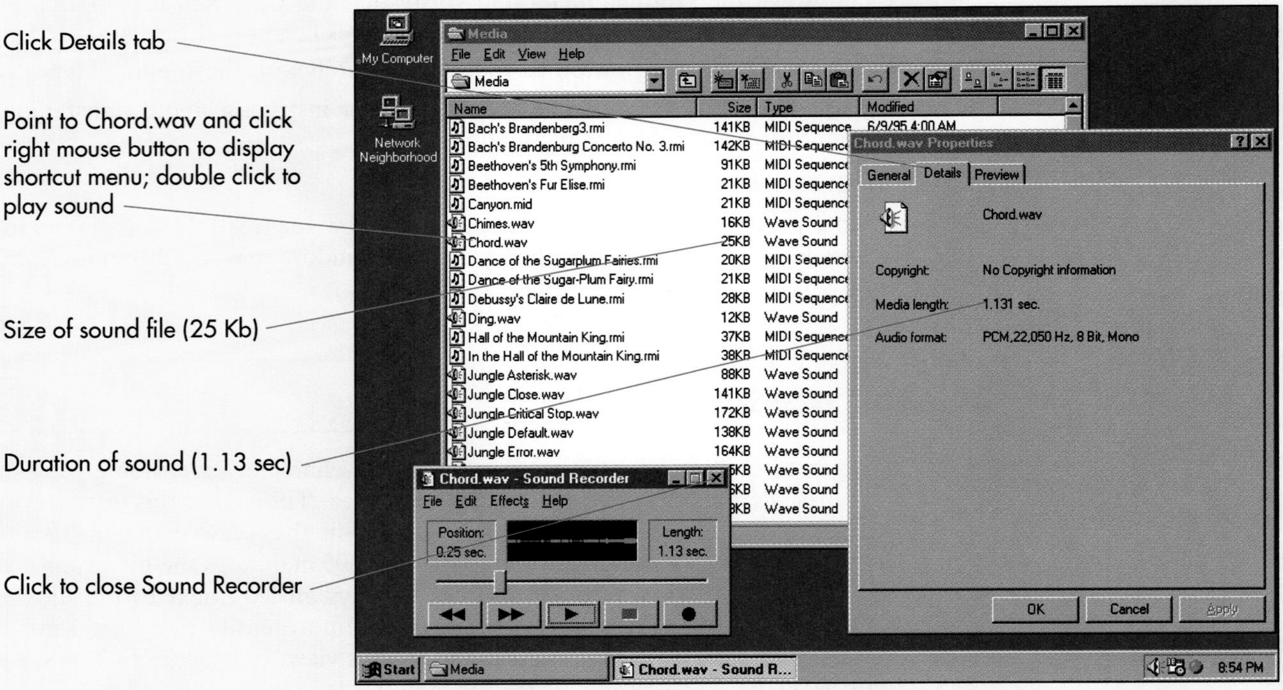
Click Details tab
Point to Chord.wav and click right mouse button to display shortcut menu; double click to play sound
Size of sound file (25 Kb)
Duration of sound (1.13 sec)
Click to close Sound Recorder
My Computer
Network Neighborhood
Media
File Edit View Help
Name
Size
Type
Modified
Chord.wav Properties
General
Details
Preview
Chord.wav
Copyright:
No Copyright information
Media length:
1.131 sec.
Audio format:
PCM,22,050 Hz, 8 Bit, Mono
OK
Cancel
Apply
Chord.wav - Sound Recorder
File Edit Effects Help
Position:
0.25 sec.
Length:
1.13 sec.
Start
Chord.wav - Sound R...
8:54 PM

(b) WAV Files (step 3)

FIGURE B.4 Hands-on Exercise 1 (continued)

➤ Double click the other WAV files to play the other sound files. If necessary, close the Sound Recorder after playing each sound.

RECORD YOUR OWN WAV FILES

You can record your own WAV files (then link or embed those files in a PowerPoint presentation), provided you have a microphone. To create a new sound (WAV) file, right click in the folder that is to contain the file, click New, then click Wave Sound to specify the type of object you want to create. Change the default file name, then double click the file to open the Sound Recorder. Click the Record button to start recording and the Stop button when you have finished. Click the Play button to hear the recorded sound. Close the Sound Recorder, then use the Insert Sound command in PowerPoint to insert your new sound into a presentation.

STEP 4: MIDI Files

➤ Play either the **Canyon.mid** or the **Passport.mid** file:

- Double click the icon next to the file name, or
- Right click the file to select the file and display a menu. Click **Play.**

➤ The Media Player will appear on the screen as shown in Figure B.4c. Unlike the WAV files, which last but a second, the MIDI files are musical compositions that last two minutes each.

➤ Experiment with the controls on the Media Player:

- Click the **Pause button** to suspend playing.
- Click the **Play button** (which appears after you click the Pause button) to resume playing.
- Click the **Stop button** to stop playing.
- Click the **Rewind button** to return to the beginning of the recording.

➤ Close the Media Player when you are finished listening. Close the Media window.

WAV FILES VERSUS MIDI FILES

A WAV file stores an actual sound, whereas a MIDI file stores the instructions to create the sound. Because a WAV file stores a recorded sound, it can represent any type of sound—a voice, music, or special effects. A MIDI file can store only music. WAV files, even those that last only a few seconds, are very large because the sound is sampled thousands of times a second to create the file. MIDI files, however, are much more compact because they store the instructions to create the sound rather than the sound itself.

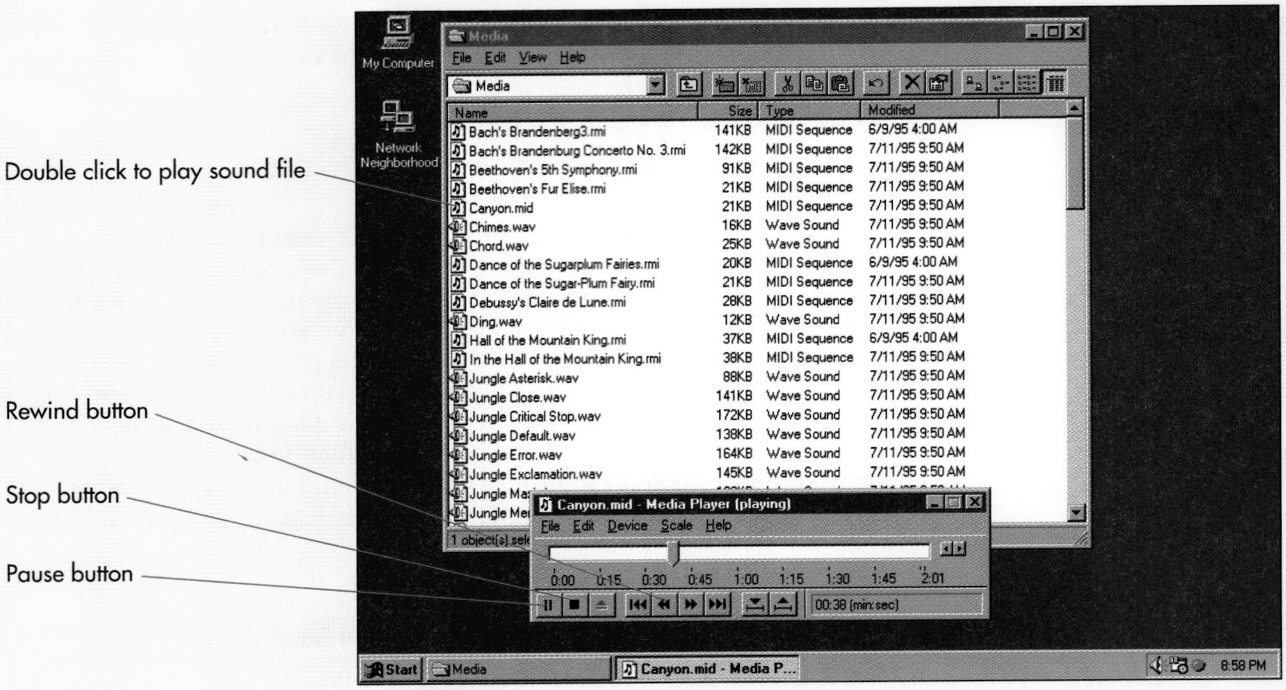
Double click to play sound file
Rewind button
Stop button
Pause button
Media
Canyon.mid - Media Player (playing)

(c) MIDI Files (step 4)

FIGURE B.4 Hands-on Exercise 1 (continued)

STEP 5: Video Clips

- Click the **Start button** on the Windows 95 taskbar. Click (or point to) the **Find command,** then click **Files or Folders** to display the dialog box in Figure B.4d.
  - Place the PowerPoint or Office Professional CD in the CD-ROM drive, as the best AVI files, for purposes of demonstration, are found on this CD. (You can still do the exercise if you don't have the CD.)
  - Enter ***.avi** (the type of file you are searching for) in the Named text box. Click the **drop-down arrow** in the Look in list box and select **My Computer** (to search drive C and the CD-ROM).
  - Be sure the **include subfolders** box is checked.
  - Click the **Find Now button** to begin the search, then watch the status bar as Windows searches for the specified files and folders.
- The results of the search are displayed within the Find Files dialog box and should contain multiple AVI files. If you do not see any files at all, check the search parameters, then repeat the search.
- Select (click) a video clip (e.g., Sidewalk.avi in Figure B.4d), click the **right mouse button** to display a shortcut menu, then click **Play** to view the video clip (or double click the file name).
- View as many video clips as you like, then close the Find Files dialog box when you are finished.
- Exit Windows if you do not want to continue with the next exercise at this time.

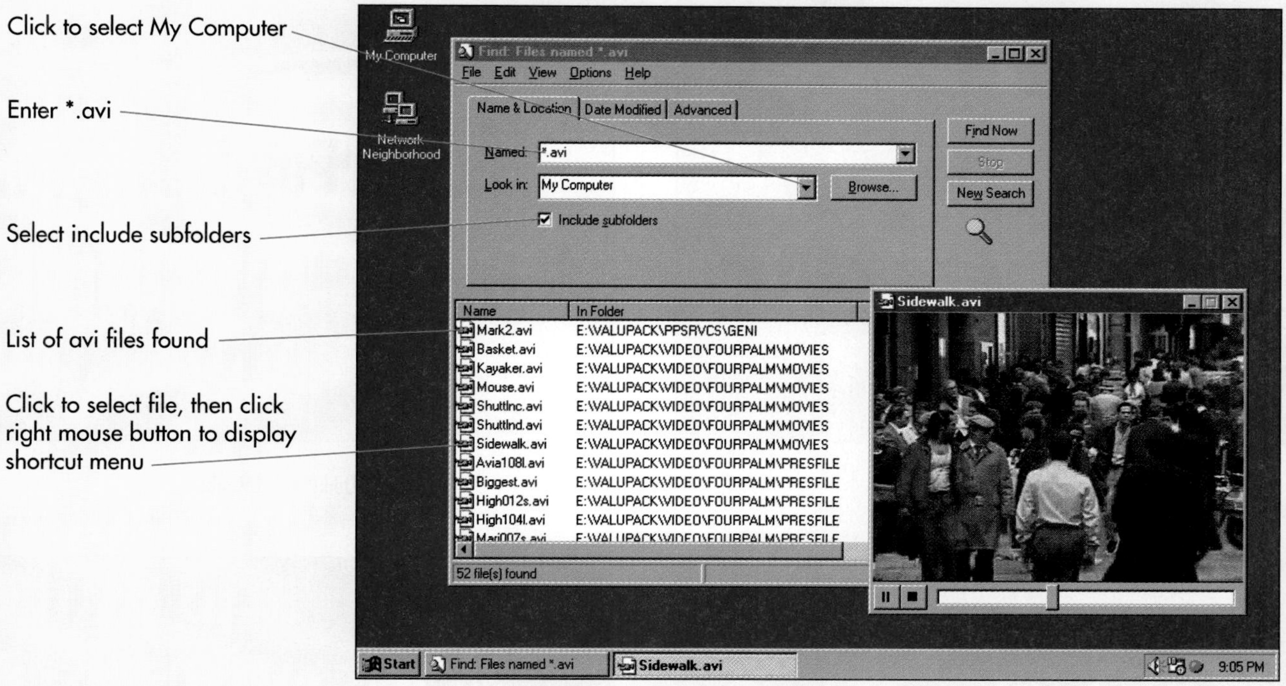
Click to select My Computer
Enter *.avi
Select include subfolders
List of avi files found
Click to select file, then click right mouse button to display shortcut menu
My Computer
Network Neighborhood
Find: Files named *.avi
File Edit View Options Help
Name & Location
Date Modified
Advanced
Named: *.avi
Look in: My Computer
Browse...
Include subfolders
Find Now
Stop
New Search
Name
In Folder
Mark2.avi E:\VALUPACK\PPSRVCS\GENI
Basket.avi E:\VALUPACK\VIDEO\FOURPALM\MOVIES
Kayaker.avi E:\VALUPACK\VIDEO\FOURPALM\MOVIES
Mouse.avi E:\VALUPACK\VIDEO\FOURPALM\MOVIES
Shuttlnc.avi E:\VALUPACK\VIDEO\FOURPALM\MOVIES
Shuttlnd.avi E:\VALUPACK\VIDEO\FOURPALM\MOVIES
Sidewalk.avi E:\VALUPACK\VIDEO\FOURPALM\MOVIES
Avia108l.avi E:\VALUPACK\VIDEO\FOURPALM\PRESFILE
Biggest.avi E:\VALUPACK\VIDEO\FOURPALM\PRESFILE
High012s.avi E:\VALUPACK\VIDEO\FOURPALM\PRESFILE
High104l.avi E:\VALUPACK\VIDEO\FOURPALM\PRESFILE
52 file(s) found
Sidewalk.avi
Start
Find: Files named *.avi
Sidewalk.avi
9:05 PM

(d) Video Clips (step 4)

FIGURE B.4 Hands-on Exercise 1 (continued)

MULTIMEDIA PRESENTATIONS

The exercise just completed had you explore the elements of multimedia and experiment with individual files. You learned about the different types of sound files and saw the impact of a video clip. The effectiveness of multimedia, however, depends on integrating the various elements into a cohesive unit.

Perhaps the best way to explore the potential of multimedia is to view professional presentations such as those in Figure B.5. These presentations in Figures B.5a, B.5b, and B.5c can be found on the ***PowerPoint Multimedia CD*** and are interesting for two reasons. First, they show what can be done in PowerPoint by an individual knowledgeable in the basics of multimedia. Second, they acquaint you with some of the resources on the CD and tell you how to acquire royalty-free multimedia for inclusion in your own presentation.

THE VALUE PACK

Both the PowerPoint Multimedia and the Office Professional CDs contain a variety of professionally created multimedia presentations. Use the Windows 95 Find command to search for all PowerPoint presentations (files with a PPT extension), then view the presentations that are of interest to you. You will find information from companies offering audio and video files. You will also find additional resources on the CD (e.g., clip art and additional templates) that you can use in your presentations.

Ever Feel Like You're
Talking to a Brick Wall?
© 1995 Four Palms, Inc.

(a) 4PALMS (7.3 Mb)

Welcome to
Microsoft
PowerPoint
95
Quick Preview
This Quick Preview will take about 5 minutes to complete.
Click at anytime to continue.

(b) QuikPrev (4.9 Mb)

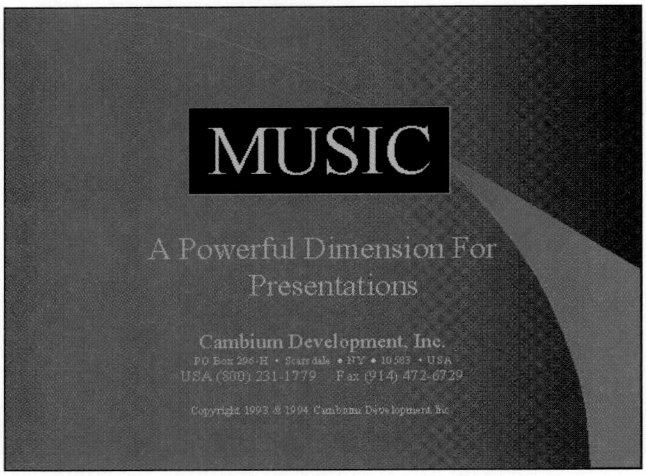

MUSIC
A Powerful Dimension For
Presentations
Cambium Development, Inc.
PO Box 296-H • Scarsdale • NY • 10583 • USA
USA (800) 231-1779 Fax (914) 472-6729

(c) Cambium (5.9 Mb)

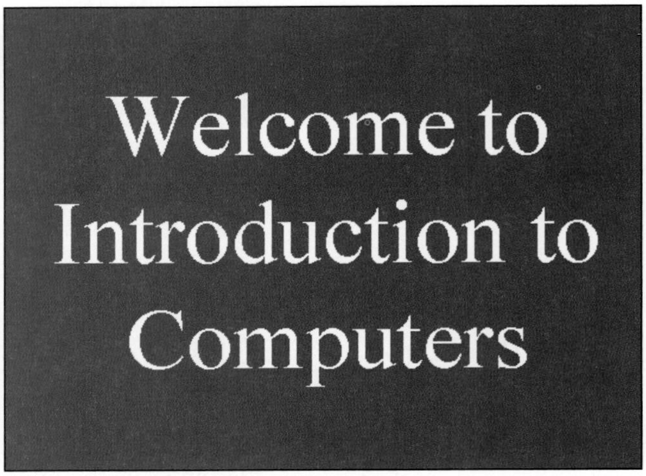

Welcome to
Introduction to
Computers

(d) Multimedia (278 Kb)

FIGURE B.5 Multimedia Presentations

A partially completed version of the presentation in Figure B.5d is found on the data disk and will be the basis of the next hands-on exercise in which you create your own multimedia presentation.

Implementation in PowerPoint

A multimedia presentation is a show, and like any show, it requires careful planning if it is to be successful. The actors in a show, or the objects on a PowerPoint slide, must be thoroughly scripted so that the performance is as effective as possible. Consider now Figure B.6, which contains one of the slides in the presentation you will create.

Figure B.6a contains the actual slide, whereas Figures B.6b and B.6c show the dialog boxes associated with two of the objects on the slide. The slide contains a total of nine objects (a single text box and eight students). Each of these objects is an "actor" in the presentation and requires instructions as to when to appear on stage and how to make that entrance.

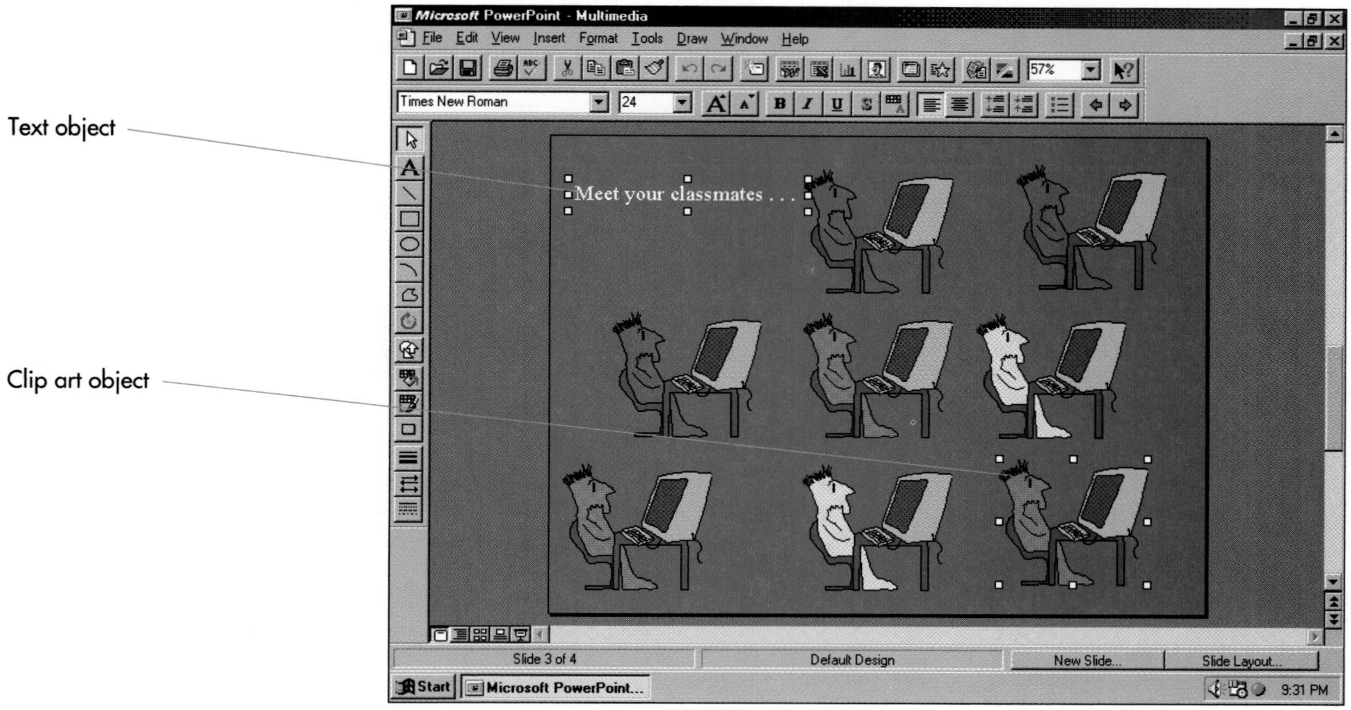
Text object
Clip art object
Microsoft PowerPoint - Multimedia
File Edit View Insert Format Tools Draw Window Help
Times New Roman
24
57%
Meet your classmates . . .
Slide 3 of 4
Default Design
New Slide...
Slide Layout...
Start
Microsoft PowerPoint...
9:31 PM

(a) The Slide

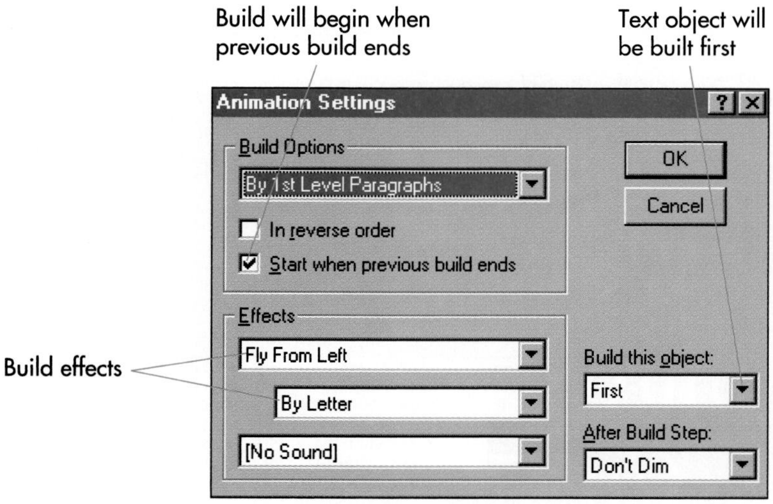
Build will begin when previous build ends
Text object will be built first
Build effects
Animation Settings
Build Options
By 1st Level Paragraphs
In reverse order
Start when previous build ends
Effects
Fly From Left
By Letter
[No Sound]
OK
Cancel
Build this object:
First
After Build Step:
Don't Dim

(b) Text Object

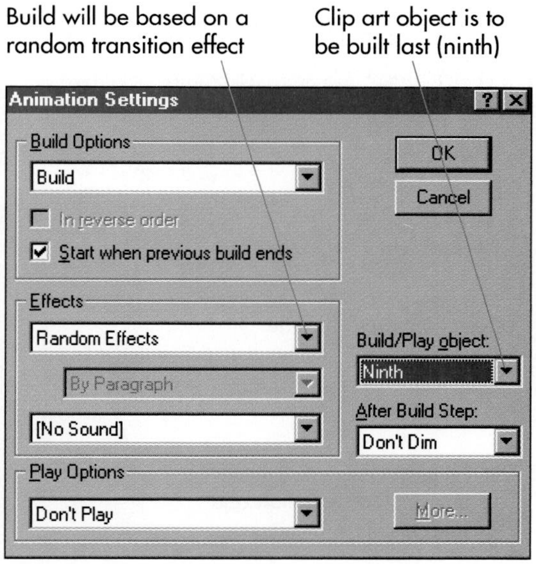
Build will be based on a random transition effect
Clip art object is to be built last (ninth)
Animation Settings
Build Options
Build
In reverse order
Start when previous build ends
Effects
Random Effects
By Paragraph
[No Sound]
Play Options
Don't Play
OK
Cancel
Build/Play object:
Ninth
After Build Step:
Don't Dim
More...

(c) Student

FIGURE B.6 Animation Settings

You, as director, have decided that the text box will fly in from the left of the slide and that this action will take place before any of the students appear. Once the text is displayed on screen, the students are to fly in from various directions, one student at a time, until all eight students are onstage. The ***Animation Settings command*** (in the Tools menu) is the means by which you convey these instructions to the object.

Figure B.6b displays the Animation Settings dialog box for the text. The text is to be built first, and the build is to begin as soon as the previous build ends (i.e., as soon as the slide appears and without the need to click the mouse.) The special effects call for the text to fly in from the left, letter by letter. Figure B.6c displays the instructions for the student in the lower-right corner of the slide, who is to appear last (the ninth object), and whose entrance will be based on a random transition effect. These instructions may sound complicated, but they work beautifully, as you will see in the next hands-on exercise.

HANDS-ON EXERCISE 2

Creating a Multimedia Presentation

Objective: Add music (a MIDI file) to the first slide of a presentation so that it plays continually throughout the presentation; use the Animation Settings command to control the appearance of objects on a slide. The exercise requires a sound card but can be done without a CD-ROM. Use Figure B.7 as a guide in the exercise.

STEP 1: Choose the Music

- Open the **Multimedia presentation** in the **Exploring PowerPoint folder** as shown in Figure B.7a.
- Click the **Start button** on the Windows 95 taskbar. Click (or point to) the **Find command,** then click **Files or Folders** to display the Find Files dialog

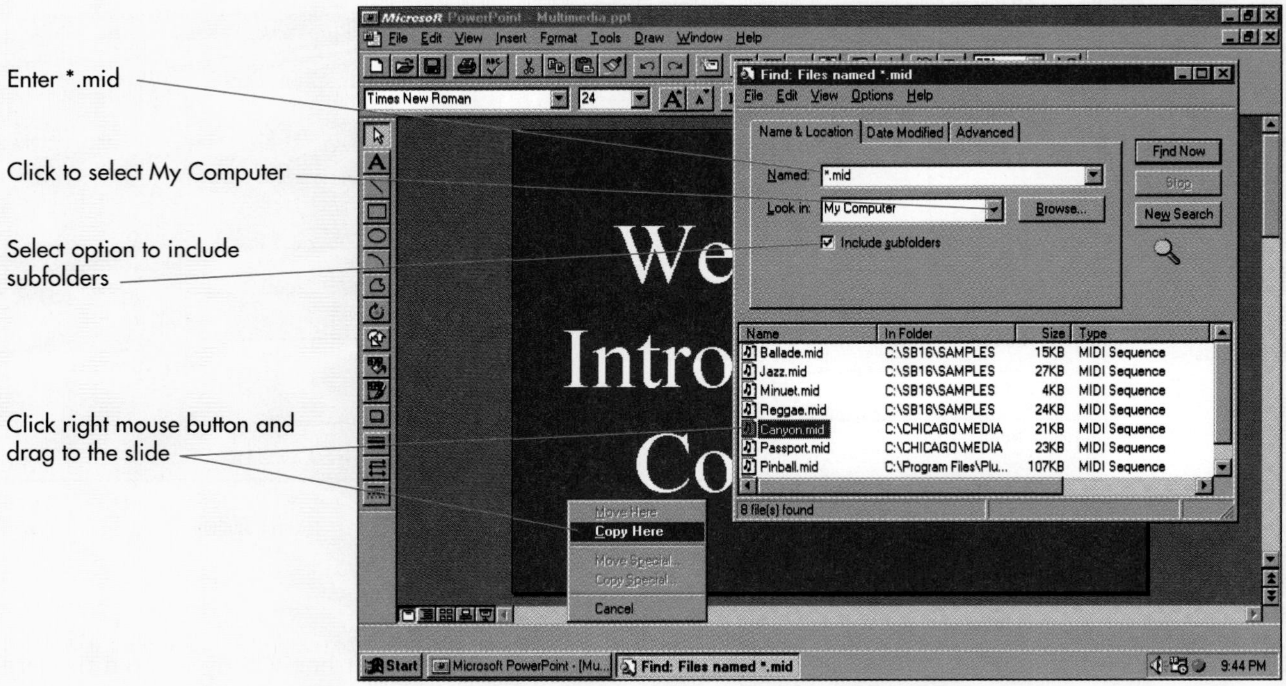

Enter *.mid
Click to select My Computer
Select option to include subfolders
Click right mouse button and drag to the slide
Find: Files named *.mid
Name & Location
Date Modified
Advanced
Named: *.mid
Look in: My Computer
Browse...
Include subfolders
Find Now
Stop
New Search
Ballade.mid
Jazz.mid
Minuet.mid
Reggae.mid
Canyon.mid
Passport.mid
Pinball.mid
8 file(s) found
Move Here
Copy Here
Move Special...
Copy Special...
Cancel
Start
Microsoft PowerPoint - [Mu...
Find: Files named *.mid
9:44 PM

(a) Add the Music (step 1)

FIGURE B.7 Hands-on Exercise 2

box. The size and/or position of the dialog [illegible]
in the figure:

- Enter ***.MID** (the type of file you are sear[illegible] box. Click the **drop-down arrow** in the Look in [illegible] **puter** (to search all drives on your system).
- Be sure the **include subfolders** box is checked.
- Click the **Find Now button** to begin the search, then [illegible] as Windows searches for the specified files and folders.

➤ The results of the search are displayed within the Find Files [illegible] should contain multiple files with the MID extension. If you do [illegible] files at all, check the search parameters, then repeat the search.

➤ Select (click) any file (e.g., Canyon.mid in Figure B.7a, click the **right** [illegible] **button** to display a shortcut menu, then click **Play** to hear the music. [illegible] the Media Player when you are finished listening. (You can click the **St**[illegible] **button** to stop playing.)

➤ Listen to as many files as you like, then choose the music you want to include. Point to the file you want, then click and drag the file icon with the **right mouse button** to the PowerPoint slide.

➤ Release the mouse to display the shortcut menu and click **Copy Here** to copy the sound object onto the PowerPoint slide. Close the Find Files dialog box.

ADDITIONAL TEMPLATES

The PowerPoint Multimedia (or Office Professional) CD contains 58 additional templates from which to choose. Pull down the Format menu and click the Apply Design Template command (or double click the Design Template portion of the status bar) to display the Apply Design Template dialog box. Click the drop-down arrow on the Look In list box, select the drive containing the CD-ROM, open the Valuepack folder, then open the Pptmpl folder to display the available templates.

STEP 2: Play Options

➤ The sound file should be selected. Pull down the **Tools menu** and click **Animation Settings** to display the Animation Settings dialog box as shown in Figure B.7b:

- Click the **drop-down arrow** on the Build Options list box and click **Build.**
- Check the box to **Start when previous build ends.**
- Click the **drop-down arrow** on the Play Options list box and click **Play.**

➤ Click the **More command button** to display the More Play Options dialog box.

- Click the option button to play **Automatically** (after 0 seconds).
- Click the option button to **Continue slide show, play in background.**
- Click the option button to **Stop after 4 slides** (click the **up arrow** to select 4 slides, the number of slides in the presentation).

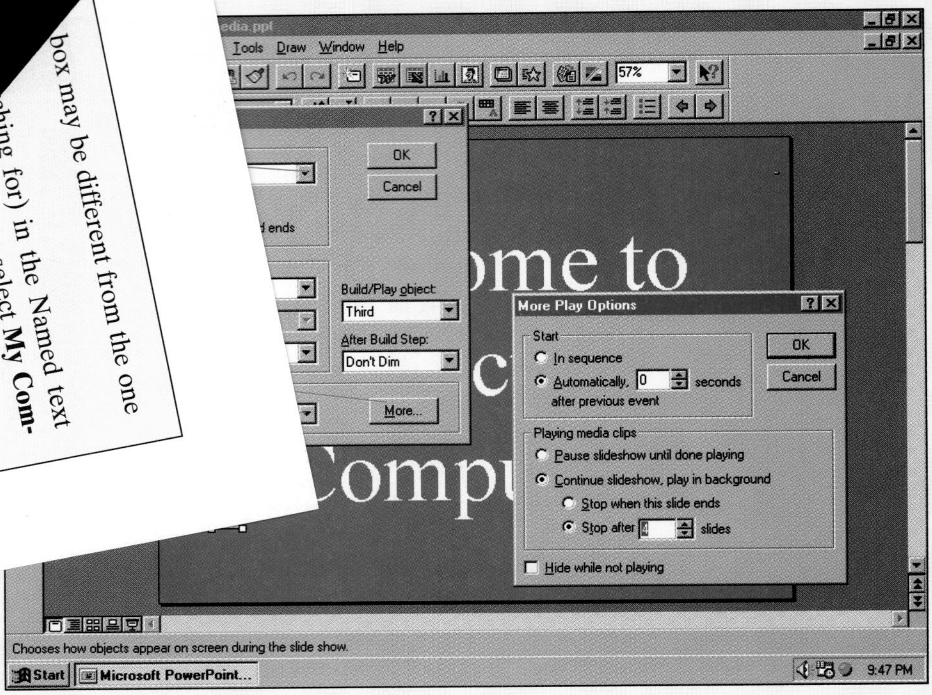
More Play Options
Start
In sequence
Automatically, 0 seconds after previous event
Playing media clips
Pause slideshow until done playing
Continue slideshow, play in background
Stop when this slide ends
Stop after 4 slides
Hide while not playing
OK
Cancel
Build/Play object:
Third
After Build Step:
Don't Dim
More...
Chooses how objects appear on screen during the slide show.
Start
Microsoft PowerPoint...
9:47 PM

(b) Set the Music (step 2)

FIGURE B.7 Hands-on Exercise 2 (continued)

- Verify that your settings match those in Figure B.7b. Click **OK** to close the More Play Options dialog box. Click **OK** to close the Animation Settings dialog box.
- Click the **Slide Show button** above the status bar. You should see the title slide and hear the music. Click the **Stop button** on the Media Player when it appears, then press **Esc** to stop the show in order to return to the Slide view and continue working.
- Click and drag a corner sizing handle to shrink the icon on the slide so that the Media Player will not be visible during the actual show.
- Save the presentation.

THE VOICE OVER

Use the Sound Recorder to create a voice-over narration that you can play during a self-running presentation. Music and/or narration are especially effective in stand-alone presentations such as those found in a kiosk or demonstration booth.

Click to select title of slide
Sound object
Slide Show button
Microsoft PowerPoint - Multimedia.ppt
File Edit View Insert Format Tools Draw Window Help
57%
Times New Roman
102
Welcome to
Introdu
Comp
Animation Settings
Build Options
By 1st Level Paragraphs
In reverse order
Start when previous build ends
OK
Cancel
Effects
Fly From Left
By Letter
[No Sound]
Build this object:
Second
After Build Step:
Don't Dim
Chooses how objects appear on screen during the slide show.
Start
Microsoft PowerPoint...
10:04 PM

(c) Complete the First Slide (step 3)

FIGURE B.7 Hands-on Exercise 2 (continued)

STEP 3: Animation Settings (the title slide)

- Click on the slide to select the title as shown in Figure B.7c. Pull down the **Tools menu** and click **Animation Settings** to display the Animation Settings dialog box:
  - Click the **drop-down arrow** on the Build Options list box and select **By 1st Level Paragraphs.**
  - Click the check box to **Start when previous build ends.**
  - Click the **drop-down arrow** on the Effects list boxes and select **Fly From Left** and **By Letter.**
  - Click the **drop-down arrow** on the Build this object list box and click **Second** (the letters are to appear after the music starts).
  - Verify that your settings match those in Figure B.7c, then click **OK** to close the Animation Settings dialog box.
- Click the **Slide Show button** above the status bar. This time you will not only hear the music, but you will also see the letters fly in from the left. Press the **Esc key,** after you see the title, to stop the music (the Media Player is hidden), then press the **Esc key** a second time to return to the Slide view and continue working.
- Save the presentation.

YOU'RE THE DIRECTOR

No one ever said that multimedia was quick or easy. Creating an effective presentation takes time, much more time than you might expect initially, as each slide has to be choreographed in detail. Think of yourself as the director who must tell the actors (the objects on a slide) when to come on stage and how to make their entrance. It takes patience and practice.

STEP 4: Animation Settings (the students)

- Use the **Slide Elevator** (or press the **PgDn key** twice) to select the third slide as shown in Figure B.7d.
- Click the **Slide Show button** to view this slide as it will appear in the slide show. There are no animation effects on the slide as it currently exists, and all of the students appear at the same time. Press **Esc** to return to the Slide view.
- Press and hold the **Shift key** as you click each of the eight students to select all of the students at one time as shown in Figure B.7d.
- Point to any selected student and click the **right mouse button** to display a shortcut menu, then click **Animation Settings** to display the Animation Settings dialog box. (The settings will be applied to all the selected objects.)

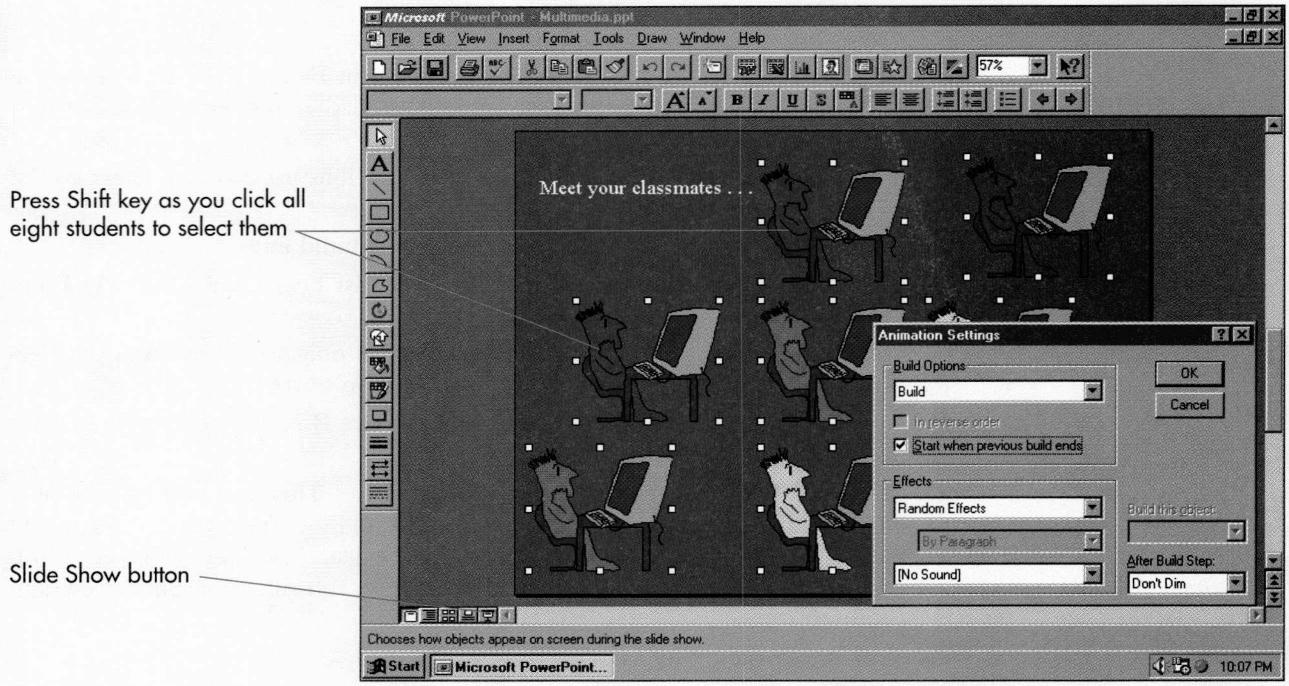
Press Shift key as you click all eight students to select them
Slide Show button
Microsoft PowerPoint - Multimedia.ppt
File Edit View Insert Format Tools Draw Window Help
57%
Meet your classmates . . .
Animation Settings
Build Options
Build
In reverse order
Start when previous build ends
OK
Cancel
Effects
Random Effects
By Paragraph
[No Sound]
Build this object:
After Build Step:
Don't Dim
Chooses how objects appear on screen during the slide show.
Start
Microsoft PowerPoint...
10:07 PM

(d) Animation Settings (step 4)

FIGURE B.7 Hands-on Exercise 2 (continued)

- Click the **drop-down arrow** on the Build Effects list box and click **Build.**
- Click the check box to **Start when previous build ends.**
- If necessary, click the **drop-down arrow** in the Effects list box and choose **Random Effects.**
- Click **OK** to accept the settings and close the Animation Settings dialog box.

➤ Point to the placeholder for Meet Your Classmates, click the **right mouse button** to display a shortcut menu, then click **Animation Settings:**

- Click the **drop-down arrow** on the Build Options list box and select **By 1st Level Paragraphs.**
- Click the check box to **Start when previous build ends.**
- Click the **drop-down arrow** on the Effects list boxes and select **Fly From Left** and **By Letter.**
- Click the **drop-down arrow** on the Build this object list box and click **First** (the letters are to appear before the students).
- Click **OK** to close the Animation Settings dialog box.

➤ Click the **Slide Show button** to view this slide with the animation effects you added. (The students appear by default in the order they were added to the slide when the slide was created initially.) Press **Esc** to return to the Slide view.

➤ Save the presentation.

THE ANIMATION EFFECTS TOOLBAR

The Animation Effects toolbar is the easiest way to change the order in which objects are built on a slide. Point to any visible toolbar, click the right mouse button, then click Animation Effects to display (hide) the toolbar. Select the object on the slide, click the drop-down arrow on the Animation Order list box, then choose the appropriate number (e.g., 1, if the object is to appear first).

STEP 5: Rehearse the Timings

➤ Press **Ctrl+Home** to return to the first slide. Pull down the **View menu** and click **Slide Show** to display the Slide Show dialog box. Click the option button to **Rehearse New Timings,** then click the **Show button.**

➤ The first slide appears in the Slide Show view, and the Rehearsal dialog box is displayed in the lower-right corner of the screen. Click the mouse to register the elapsed time and move to the next slide.

➤ The second slide in the presentation should appear as shown in Figure B.7e with the animation effects built in. The cumulative time appears on the left (00:01:10 seconds). The time for this specific slide (00:00:17 seconds) is shown at the right.

- Click the **Repeat button** to redo the timing for the slide. (You won't see the new timing until the slide concludes.)
- Click the **Pause button** to (temporarily) stop the clock. Click the Pause button a second time to resume the clock. (The music continues to play.)

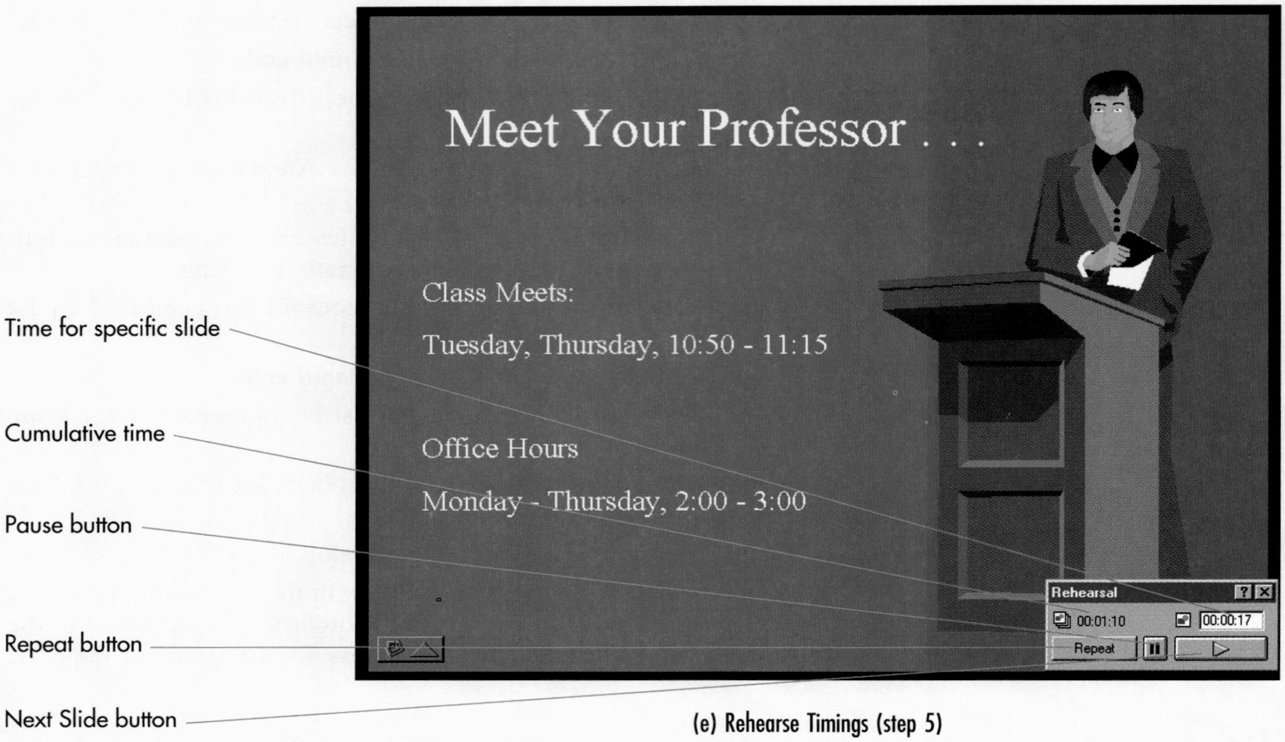
Meet Your Professor . . .
Class Meets:
Tuesday, Thursday, 10:50 - 11:15
Office Hours
Monday - Thursday, 2:00 - 3:00
Rehearsal
00:01:10
00:00:17
Repeat
Time for specific slide
Cumulative time
Pause button
Repeat button
Next Slide button

(e) Rehearse Timings (step 5)

FIGURE B.7 Hands-on Exercise 2 (continued)

- Click the **Next slide button** to record the timing and move to the next slide.
- Continue rehearsing the show until you reach the last slide (containing the PC and other equipment), then click on this last slide to end the presentation. Be sure to click the mouse to record the timing for the last slide.

➤ You should see a dialog box at the end of the presentation that indicates the total time of the slide show. Click **Yes** when asked whether you want to record the new timings.

➤ Save the presentation.

STEP 6: Slide Show Options

➤ You should be back in the Slide Sorter view as shown in Figure B.7f, with the timings recorded under each slide. Pull down the **View menu** and click **Slide Show** to display the Slide Show dialog box.

➤ Click the **All option button** under Slides, click the **Use Slide Timings option button** under Advance, and check the box to **Loop Continuously under Esc.**

➤ Click the **Show button,** then sit back and enjoy the show, which will cycle continually until you press the **Esc key.**

➤ End the show by clicking at the appropriate place in the last slide or by pressing the **Esc key.**

➤ Save the presentation. Exit PowerPoint. Welcome to Multimedia!!

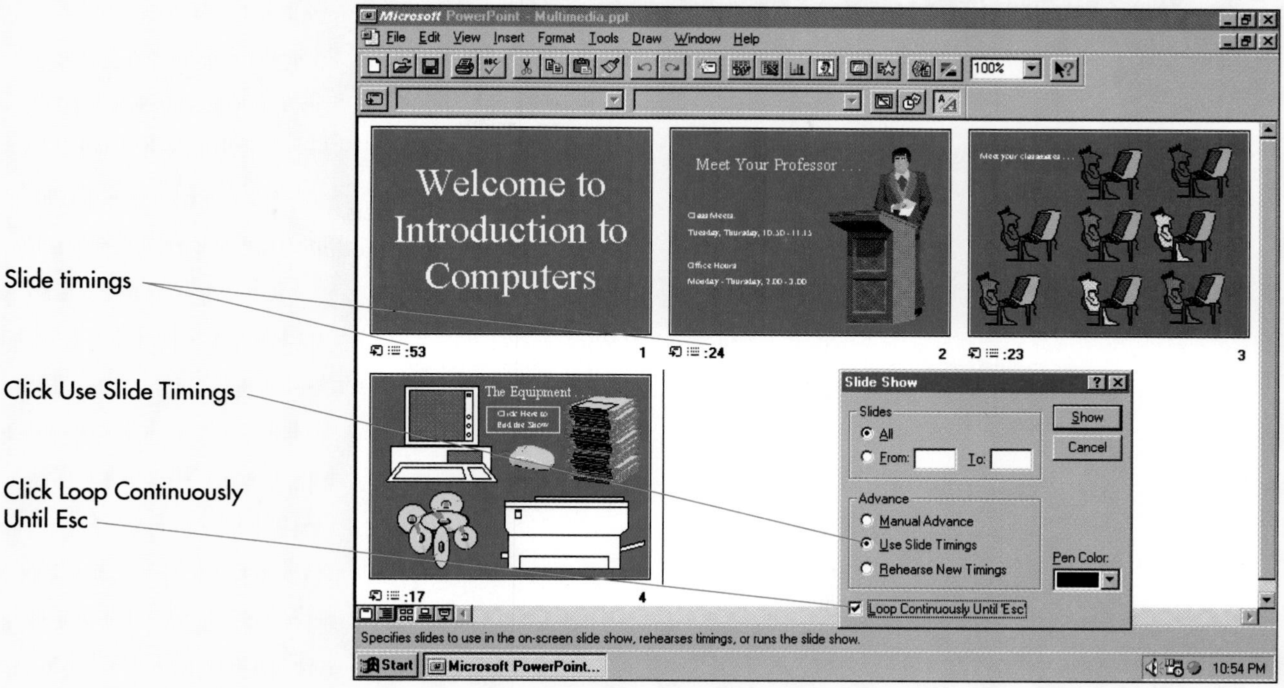
Slide timings
Click Use Slide Timings
Click Loop Continuously Until Esc
Microsoft PowerPoint - Multimedia.ppt
File Edit View Insert Format Tools Draw Window Help
Welcome to Introduction to Computers
Meet Your Professor . . .
The Equipment . . .
:53
:24
:23
:17
Slide Show
Slides
All
From:
To:
Show
Cancel
Advance
Manual Advance
Use Slide Timings
Rehearse New Timings
Pen Color:
Loop Continuously Until 'Esc'
Specifies slides to use in the on-screen slide show, rehearses timings, or runs the slide show.
Start
Microsoft PowerPoint...
10:54 PM

(f) Automate Timings (step 6)

FIGURE B.7 Hands-on Exercise 2 (continued)

SUMMARY

The Multimedia PC Marketing Council has established a minimum specification for a multimedia computer, which is intended to guide both the consumer and the developer. Three standards—MPC-1, MPC-2, and MPC-3—have been published to date.

There are two different types of sound files: WAV files and MIDI files. A WAV file records an actual sound and requires large amounts of disk space because the sound is sampled several thousand times a second to create the file. A MIDI file is much more compact than a WAV file because it stores the instructions to create the sound rather than the actual sound. A WAV file can represent any type of sound (a voice, music, or special effects) because it is a recorded sound. A MIDI file is the electronic equivalent of sheet music and can store only music.

An AVI (Audio-Video Interleaved) file is the Microsoft standard for a digital video (multimedia) file. AVI files are optimized to play at a resolution of 320 $\times$ 240 (one quarter of a VGA screen) to reduce the storage requirements.

Windows 95 provides the software tools necessary to play the different types of multimedia files. The accessories can be accessed through the Start button or through shortcuts in the Multimedia folder.

The slides in a multimedia production must be carefully scripted with respect to when and how each object is to appear. The Animation Settings command is the means by which the information is specified.

KEY WORDS AND CONCEPTS

- Animation Settings command
- AVI file
- CD player
- File compression
- Media folder
- Media Player
- MIDI file
- MPC-1
- MPC-2
- MPC-3
- Multimedia PC Marketing Council
- PowerPoint Multimedia CD
- Resolution
- Sampling rate
- Sound Recorder
- Volume control
- WAV file

PREREQUISITES: ESSENTIALS OF WINDOWS 95®

OBJECTIVES

After reading this appendix you will be able to:

1. Describe the objects on the Windows desktop; use the Start button to access the online help.
2. Explain the function of the minimize, maximize, restore, and close buttons; move and size a window.
3. Discuss the function of a dialog box; describe the different types of dialog boxes and the various ways in which information is supplied.
4. Format a floppy disk.
5. Use My Computer to locate a specific file or folder; describe the different views available for My Computer.
6. Describe how folders are used to organize a disk; create a new folder; copy and/or move a file from one folder to another.
7. Delete a file, then recover the deleted file from the Recycle Bin.
8. Describe the document orientation of Windows 95; use the New command to create a document without explicitly opening the associated application.
9. Explain the differences in browsing with My Computer versus browsing with the Windows Explorer.

OVERVIEW

Windows 95 is a computer program (actually many programs) that controls the operation of your computer and its peripherals. One of the most significant benefits of the Windows environment is the common user interface and consistent command structure that are imposed on every Windows application. Once you learn the basic concepts and techniques, you can apply that knowledge to every Windows application. This appendix teaches you those concepts so that you will be able to work productively in the Windows environment. It is written for you, the computer novice, and assumes no previous knowledge about a computer or about Windows. Our goal is to get you "up and running" as quickly as possible so that you can do the work you want to do.

We begin with an introduction to the Windows desktop, the graphical user interface that lets you work in intuitive fashion by pointing at icons and clicking the mouse. We show you how to use the online help facility to look up information when you need it. We identify the basic components of a window and describe how to execute commands and supply information through various types of dialog boxes.

The appendix also shows you how to manage the hundreds (indeed, thousands) of files that are stored on the typical system. We describe the use of My Computer to search the drives on your computer for a specific file or folder. (All files in Windows 95 are stored in folders, which are the electronic equivalent of manila folders in a filing cabinet.) We show you how to create a new folder and how to move or copy a file from one folder to another. We show you how to rename a file, how to delete a file, and how to recover a deleted file from the Recycle Bin.

All file operations are done through My Computer or through the more powerful Windows Explorer. My Computer is intuitive and geared for the novice, as it opens a new window for each folder you open. Explorer, on the other hand, is more sophisticated and provides a hierarchical view of the entire system in a single window. A beginner will prefer My Computer, whereas a more experienced user will most likely opt for the Explorer. This is the same sequence in which we present the material. We start with My Computer, then show you how to accomplish the same result more quickly through the Explorer.

THE DESKTOP

Windows 95 creates a working environment for your computer that parallels the working environment at home or in an office. You work at a desk. Windows operations take place on the ***desktop.***

There are physical objects on a desk such as folders, a dictionary, a calculator, or a phone. The computer equivalent of those objects appear as ***icons*** (pictorial symbols) on the desktop. Each object on a real desk has attributes (properties) such as size, weight, and color. In similar fashion, Windows assigns properties to every object on its desktop. And just as you can move the objects on a real desk, you can rearrange the objects on the Windows desktop.

Figure 1a displays the desktop when Windows is first installed on a new computer. This desktop has only a few objects and is similar to the desk in a new office, just after you move in. Figure 1b displays a different desktop, one with three open windows, and is similar to a desk during the middle of a working day. Do not be concerned if your Windows desktop is different from ours. Your real desk is arranged differently from those of your friends, and so your Windows desktop will also be different.

The simplicity of the desktop in Figure 1a helps you to focus on what's important. The ***Start button,*** as its name suggests, is where you begin. Click the Start button (mouse operations are explained in the next section) and you see a menu that provides access to any program (e.g., Microsoft Word or Microsoft Excel) on your computer. The Start button also gives you access to an online help facility that provides information about every aspect of Windows.

In addition to the Start button, the desktop in Figure 1a contains three objects, each of which has a special purpose. ***My Computer*** enables you to browse the disk drives (and optional CD-ROM drive) that are attached to your computer.

Double click to browse disk drives
Double click to access network drives
Double click to recover deleted files
Click here to begin
My Computer
Network Neighborhood
Recycle Bin
Start
12:56 PM

(a) New Desktop

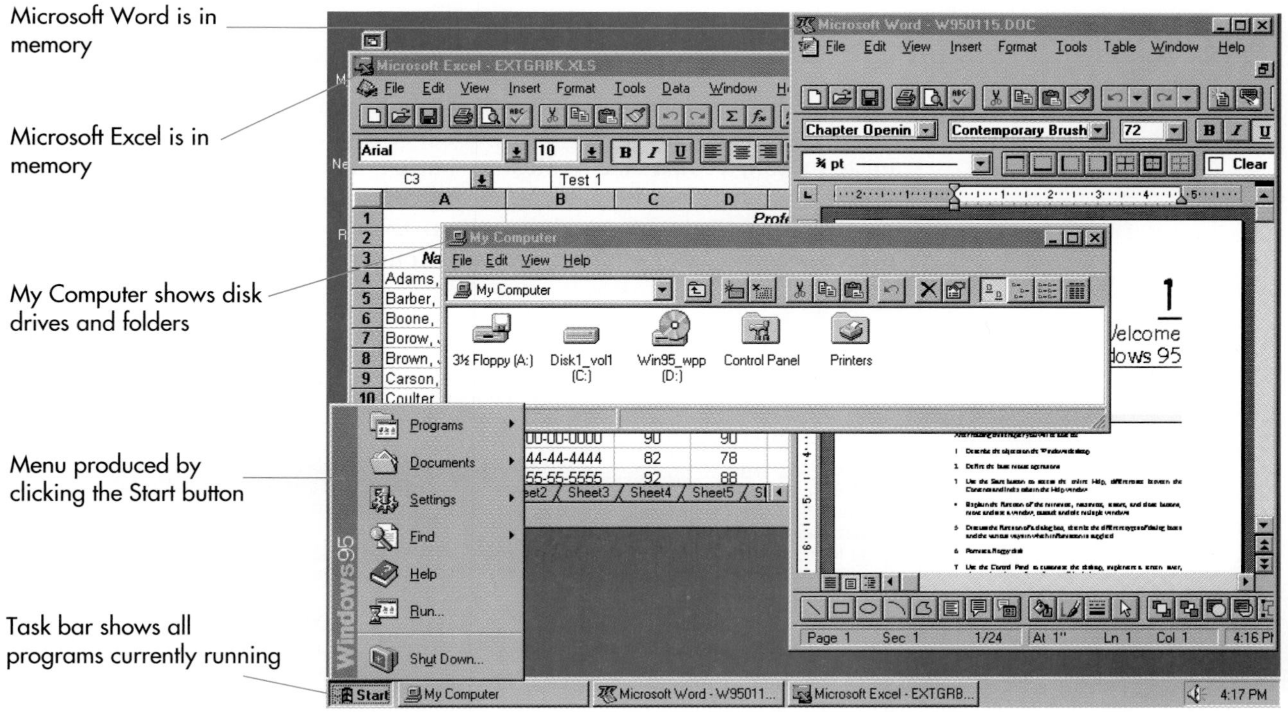
Microsoft Word is in memory
Microsoft Excel is in memory
My Computer shows disk drives and folders
Menu produced by clicking the Start button
Task bar shows all programs currently running
Microsoft Word - W950115.DOC
Microsoft Excel - EXTGRBK.XLS
My Computer
3½ Floppy (A:)
Disk1_vol1 (C:)
Win95_wpp (D:)
Control Panel
Printers
Programs
Documents
Settings
Find
Help
Run...
Shut Down...
Windows95
Start
4:17 PM

(b) A Working Desk

FIGURE 1 The Windows Desktop

Network Neighborhood extends your view of the computer to include the accessible drives on the network to which your machine is attached, if indeed it is part of a network. (You will not see this icon if you are not connected to a network.) The ***Recycle Bin*** lets you recover a file that was previously deleted and is illustrated in a hands-on exercise later in the appendix (see page 40).

Each object in Figure 1a contains additional objects that are displayed when you open (double click) the object. Double click My Computer in Figure 1a, for example, and you see the objects contained in the My Computer window of Figure 1b. Double click Network Neighborhood, and you will see all of the drives available on your network.

Two additional windows are open on the desktop in Figure 1b and correspond to programs that are currently in use. Each window has a title bar that displays the name of the program and the associated document. (The Start button was used to open each program, Microsoft Word and Microsoft Excel, in Figure 1b.) You can work in any window as long as you want, then switch to a different window. ***Multitasking,*** the ability to run several programs at the same time, is one of the major benefits of the Windows environment. It lets you run a word processor in one window, a spreadsheet in a second window, communicate online in a third window, run a game in a fourth window, and so on.

The ***taskbar*** at the bottom of the desktop shows all of the programs that are currently running (open in memory). It contains a button for each open program and lets you switch back and forth between those programs, by clicking the appropriate button. The taskbar in Figure 1a does not contain any buttons (other than the Start button) since there are no open applications. The taskbar in Figure 1b, however, contains three additional buttons, one for each open window.

ANATOMY OF A WINDOW

Figure 2 displays a typical window and labels its essential elements. Every window has the same components as every other window, which include a title bar, a Minimize button, a Maximize or Restore button, and a Close button. Other elements, that may or may not be present, include a horizontal and/or vertical scroll bar, a menu bar, a status bar, and a toolbar. Every window also contains additional objects (icons) that pertain specifically to the programs(s) or data associated with that window.

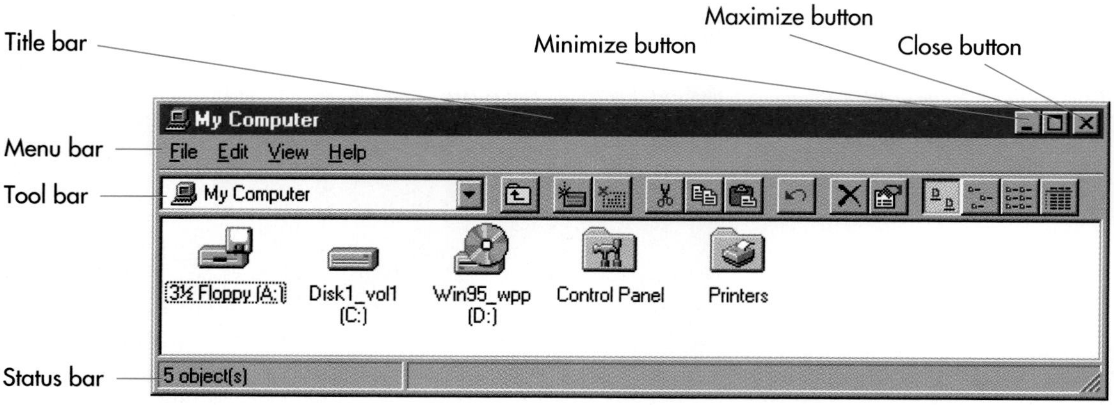
Title bar
Maximize button
Minimize button
Close button
My Computer
Menu bar
File Edit View Help
Tool bar
My Computer
3½ Floppy (A:)
Disk1_vol1 (C:)
Win95_wpp (D:)
Control Panel
Printers
Status bar
5 object(s)

FIGURE 2 Anatomy of a Window

The ***title bar*** appears at the top of the window and displays the name of the window—for example, My Computer in Figure 2. The icon at the extreme left of the title bar provides access to a control menu that lets you select operations relevant to the window. The ***Minimize button*** shrinks the window to a button on the taskbar. The ***Maximize button*** enlarges the window so that it takes up the entire desktop. The ***Restore button*** (which is not shown in Figure 2) appears instead of the Maximize button after a window has been maximized, and restores the window to its previous size. The ***Close button*** closes the window and removes it from the desktop.

The ***menu bar*** appears immediately below the title bar and provides access to pull-down menus as discussed in the next section. A ***toolbar*** appears below the menu bar and lets you execute a command by clicking an icon, as opposed to pulling down a menu. The ***status bar*** is found at the bottom of the window and displays information about the window as a whole or about a selected object within a window.

A ***vertical (horizontal) scroll bar*** appears at the right (bottom) border of a window when its contents are not completely visible and provides access to the unseen areas. Scroll bars do not appear in Figure 2 since all five objects in the window are visible.

MY COMPUTER

My Computer lets you browse the disk drives (and CD-ROM) on your system. It is present on every desktop, but the contents depend on the specific configuration. Our system, for example, has one floppy drive, one hard disk, and a CD-ROM, each of which is represented by an icon within the My Computer window. My Computer is discussed in greater detail later in this appendix, beginning on page 19.

Moving and Sizing a Window

Any window can be sized or moved on the desktop through appropriate actions with the mouse. To ***size a window,*** point to any border (the mouse pointer changes to a double arrow), then drag the border in the direction you want to go: inward to shrink the window or outward to enlarge it. You can also drag a corner (instead of a border) to change both dimensions at the same time. To ***move a window*** while retaining its current size, click and drag the title bar to a new position on the desktop.

Pull-down Menus

The menu bar provides access to ***pull-down menus*** that enable you to execute commands within an application (program). A pull-down menu is accessed by clicking the menu name or by pressing the Alt key plus the underlined letter in the menu name; for example, press Alt+V to pull down the View menu. Three pull-down menus associated with My Computer are shown in Figure 3.

The commands within a menu are executed by clicking the command once the menu has been pulled down, or by typing the underlined letter (for example, C to execute the Close command in the File menu). Alternatively, you can bypass the menu entirely if you know the equivalent keystrokes shown to the right of the command in the menu (e.g., Ctrl+X, Ctrl+C, or Ctrl+V to cut, copy, or paste as

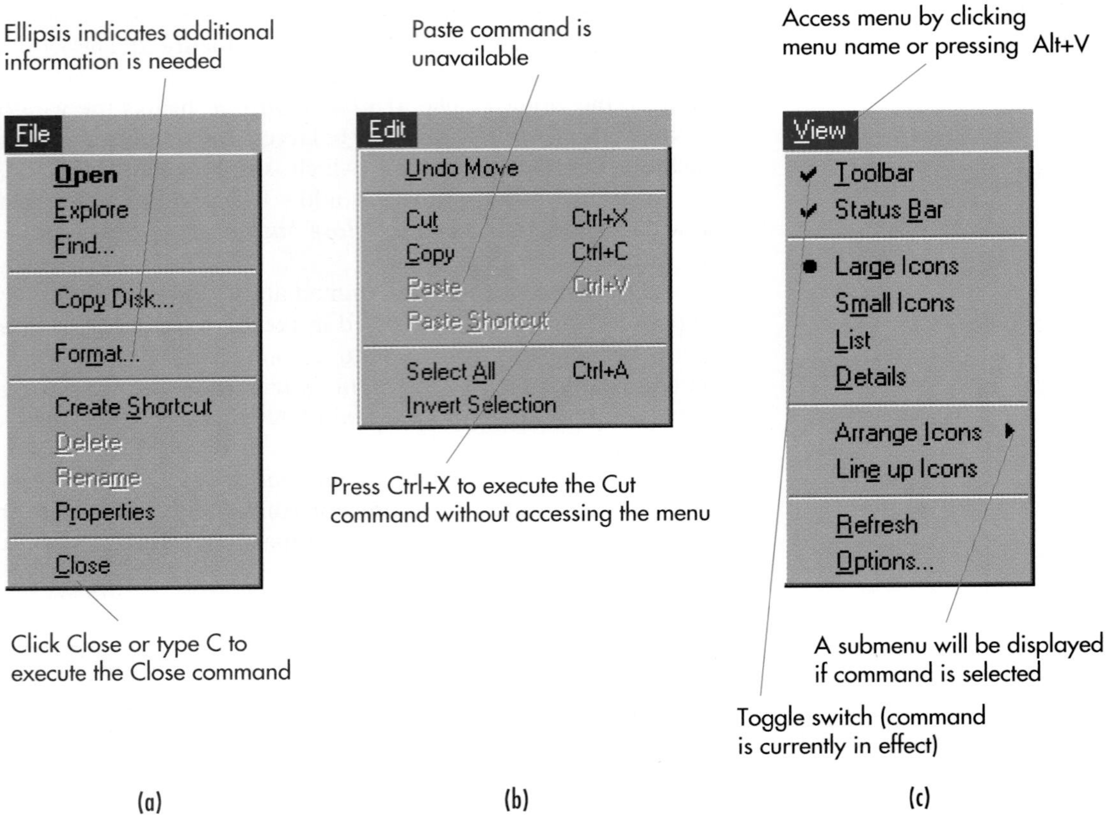

Ellipsis indicates additional information is needed
File
Open
Explore
Find...
Copy Disk...
Format...
Create Shortcut
Delete
Rename
Properties
Close
Click Close or type C to execute the Close command
Paste command is unavailable
Edit
Undo Move
Cut Ctrl+X
Copy Ctrl+C
Paste Ctrl+V
Paste Shortcut
Select All Ctrl+A
Invert Selection
Press Ctrl+X to execute the Cut command without accessing the menu
Access menu by clicking menu name or pressing Alt+V
View
Toolbar
Status Bar
Large Icons
Small Icons
List
Details
Arrange Icons
Line up Icons
Refresh
Options...
A submenu will be displayed if command is selected
Toggle switch (command is currently in effect)
(a)
(b)
(c)

FIGURE 3 Pull-down Menus

shown within the Edit menu). A ***dimmed command*** (e.g., the Paste command in the Edit menu) means the command is not currently executable, and that some additional action has to be taken for the command to become available.

An ***ellipsis*** (. . .) following a command indicates that additional information is required to execute the command; for example, selection of the Format command in the File menu requires the user to specify additional information about the formatting process. This information is entered into a dialog box (discussed in the next section), which appears immediately after the command has been selected.

A check next to a command indicates a toggle switch, whereby the command is either on or off. There is a check next to the Toolbar command in the View menu of Figure 3, which means the command is in effect (and thus the toolbar will be displayed). Click the Toolbar command and the check disappears, which suppresses the display of the toolbar. Click the command a second time, the check reappears, as does the toolbar in the associated window.

An arrowhead after a command (e.g., the Arrange Icons command in the View menu) indicates a ***submenu*** will follow with additional menu options.

Dialog Boxes

A ***dialog box*** appears when additional information is needed to execute a command. The Format command, for example, requires information about which drive to format and the type of formatting desired.

Option (radio) buttons indicate mutually exclusive choices, one of which must be chosen; for example, one of three Format Type options in Figure 4a. Click a button to select an option, which automatically deselects the previously selected option.

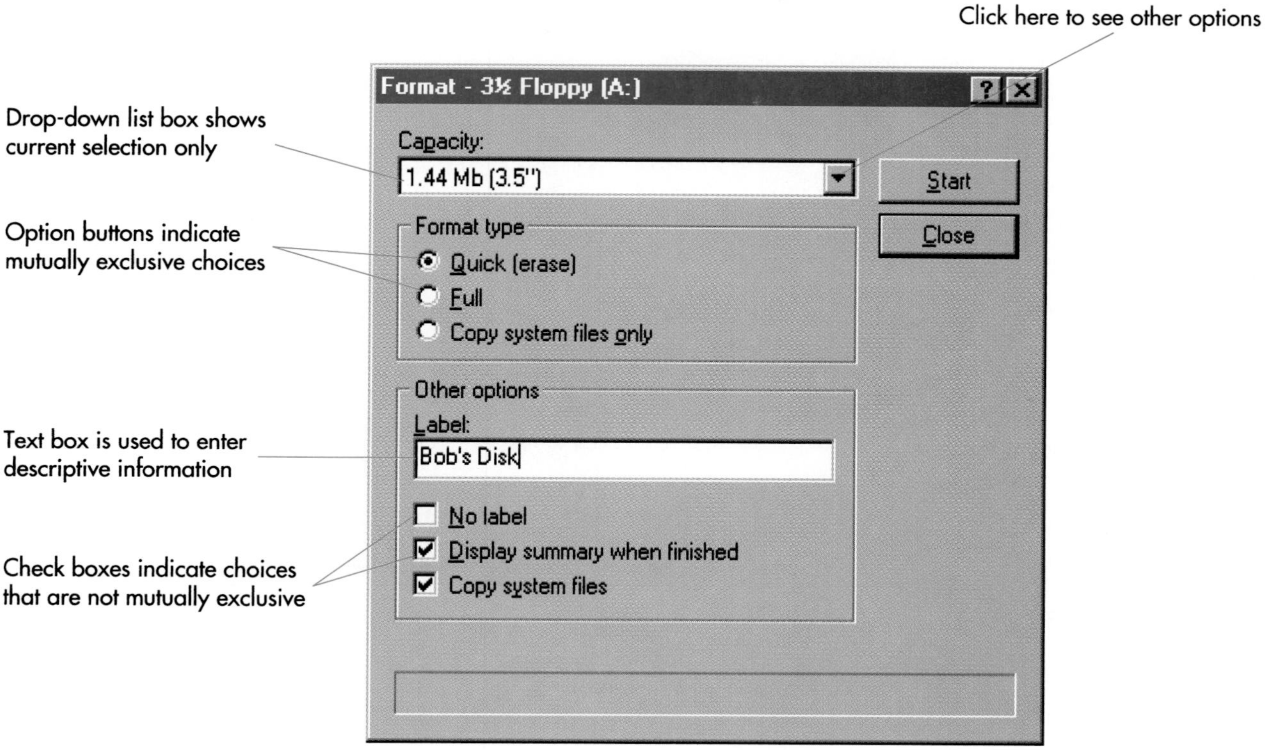

Click here to see other options
Drop-down list box shows current selection only
Option buttons indicate mutually exclusive choices
Text box is used to enter descriptive information
Check boxes indicate choices that are not mutually exclusive
Format - 3½ Floppy (A:)
Capacity:
1.44 Mb (3.5")
Start
Close
Format type
Quick (erase)
Full
Copy system files only
Other options
Label:
Bob's Disk
No label
Display summary when finished
Copy system files

(a) Option Boxes and Check Boxes

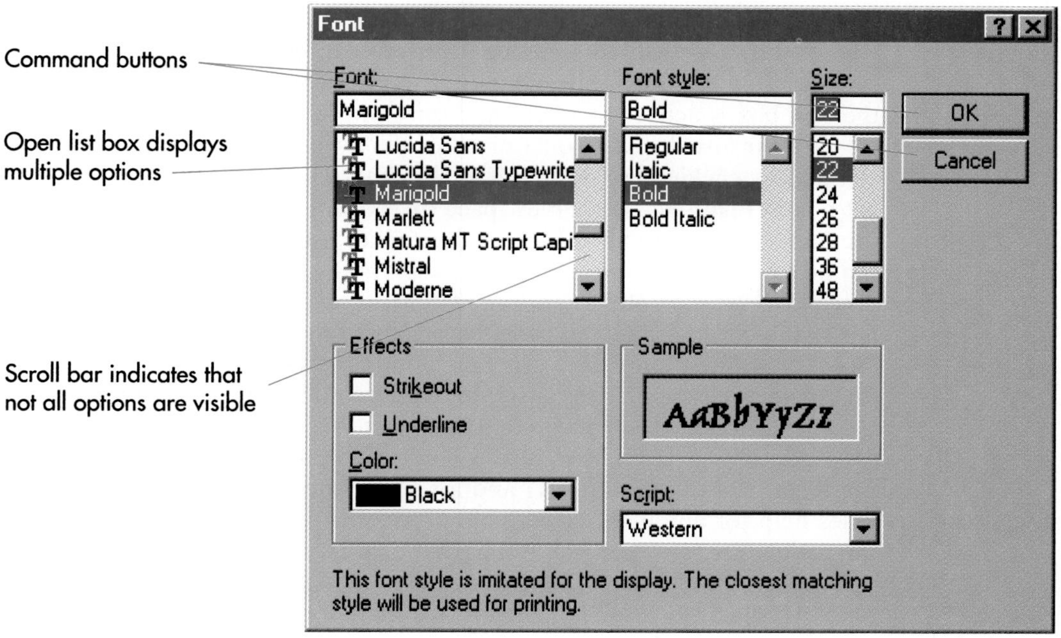

Command buttons
Open list box displays multiple options
Scroll bar indicates that not all options are visible
Font
Font:
Marigold
Lucida Sans
Lucida Sans Typewrite
Marigold
Marlett
Matura MT Script Capi
Mistral
Moderne
Font style:
Bold
Regular
Italic
Bold
Bold Italic
Size:
22
20
22
24
26
28
36
48
OK
Cancel
Effects
Strikeout
Underline
Color:
Black
Sample
AaBbYyZz
Script:
Western
This font style is imitated for the display. The closest matching style will be used for printing.

(b) List Boxes

FIGURE 4 Dialog Boxes

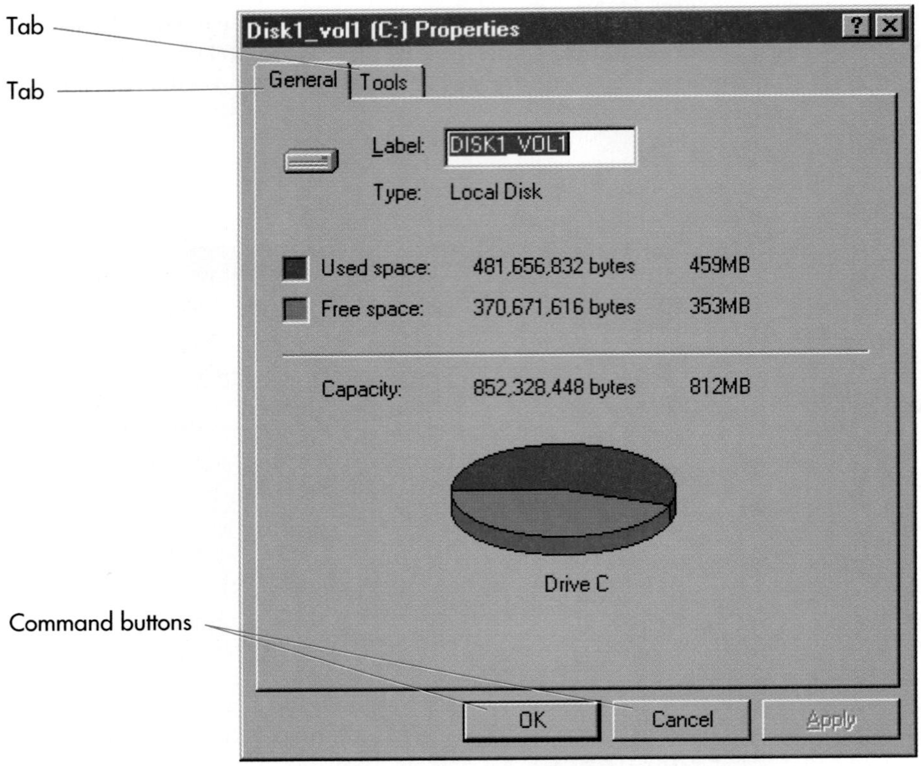
Tab
Tab
Command buttons
Disk1_vol1 (C:) Properties
General
Tools
Label:
DISK1_VOL1
Type:
Local Disk
Used space:
481,656,832 bytes
459MB
Free space:
370,671,616 bytes
353MB
Capacity:
852,328,448 bytes
812MB
Drive C
OK
Cancel
Apply

(c) Tabbed Dialog Box

FIGURE 4 Dialog Boxes (continued)

Check boxes are used instead of option buttons if the choices are not mutually exclusive or if an option is not required. Multiple boxes can be checked as in Figure 4a, or no boxes may be checked as in Figure 4b. Individual options are selected (cleared) by clicking on the appropriate check box.

A ***text box*** is used to enter descriptive information, such as Bob's Disk in Figure 4a. A flashing vertical bar (an I-beam) appears within the text box (when the text box is active) to mark the insertion point for the text you will enter.

A ***list box*** displays some or all of the available choices, any one of which is selected by clicking the desired item. A ***drop-down list box,*** such as the Capacity list box in Figure 4a, conserves space by showing only the current selection. Click the arrow of a drop-down list box to produce a list of available options. An ***open list box,*** such as those in Figure 4b, displays the choices without having to click a down arrow. (A scroll bar appears within an open list box if not all of the choices are visible at one time and provides access to the hidden choices.)

A ***tabbed dialog box*** provides multiple sets of options. The dialog box in Figure 4c, for example, has two tabs, each with its own set of options. Click either tab (the General tab is currently selected) to display the associated options.

All dialog boxes have a title bar, which contains a What's This button (in the form of a question mark) and a Close button. The ***What's This button*** provides help for any item in the dialog box; click the button, then click the item in the dialog box for which you want additional information. The Close button at the right of the title bar closes the dialog box.

All dialog boxes also contain one or more ***command buttons,*** the function of which is generally apparent from the button's name. The Start button, in Figure 4a, for example, initiates the formatting process. The OK Command button in

Figure 4b accepts the settings and closes the dialog box. The Cancel button does just the opposite, and ignores (cancels) the settings, then closes the dialog box without further action.

ONLINE HELP

Windows 95 has an extensive ***online help*** facility that contains information about virtually every topic in Windows. We believe that the best time to learn about help is as you begin your study of Windows. Help is available at any time, and is accessed most easily by clicking the ***Help command*** in the Start menu, which produces the help window in Figure 5.

The ***Contents tab*** in Figure 5a is similar to the table of contents in an ordinary book. The major topics are represented by books, each of which can be opened to display additional topics. Each open book will eventually display one or more specific topics, which may be viewed and/or printed to provide the indicated information.

The ***Index tab*** in Figure 5b is analogous to the index of an ordinary book. Type the first several letters of the topic to look up, click the topic when it appears in the window, then click the Display button to view the descriptive information as shown in Figure 5c. The help information is task-specific and describes how to accomplish the desired task.

You can print the contents of the Help windows in Figures 5a and 5b by clicking the Print command button at the bottom of a window. You can also print the contents of the display window in Figure 5c by right clicking in the window, then clicking the Print topic command from the shortcut menu.

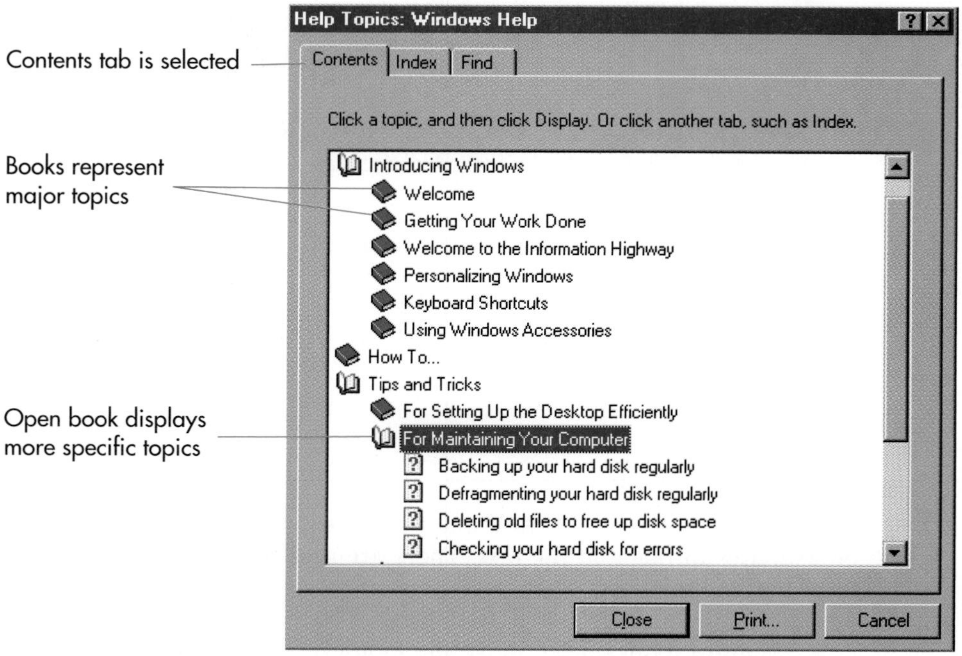

Contents tab is selected
Books represent major topics
Open book displays more specific topics
Help Topics: Windows Help
Contents
Index
Find
Click a topic, and then click Display. Or click another tab, such as Index.
Introducing Windows
Welcome
Getting Your Work Done
Welcome to the Information Highway
Personalizing Windows
Keyboard Shortcuts
Using Windows Accessories
How To...
Tips and Tricks
For Setting Up the Desktop Efficiently
For Maintaining Your Computer
Backing up your hard disk regularly
Defragmenting your hard disk regularly
Deleting old files to free up disk space
Checking your hard disk for errors
Close
Print...
Cancel

(a) Contents Tab

FIGURE 5 Online Help

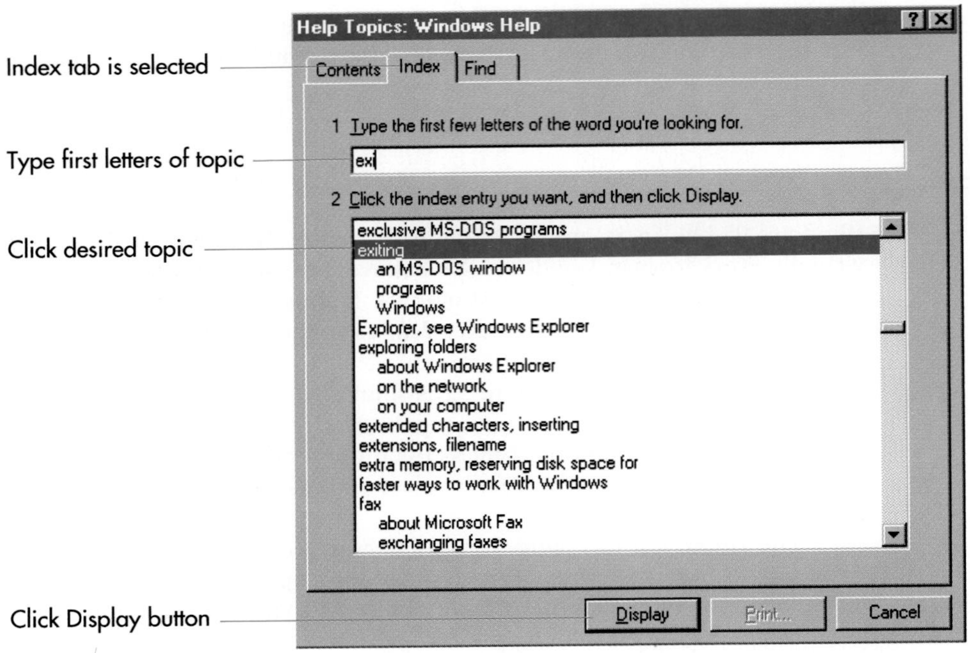
Help Topics: Windows Help
Index tab is selected
Contents
Index
Find
1 Type the first few letters of the word you're looking for.
Type first letters of topic
exi
2 Click the index entry you want, and then click Display.
Click desired topic
exclusive MS-DOS programs
exiting
an MS-DOS window
programs
Windows
Explorer, see Windows Explorer
exploring folders
about Windows Explorer
on the network
on your computer
extended characters, inserting
extensions, filename
extra memory, reserving disk space for
faster ways to work with Windows
fax
about Microsoft Fax
exchanging faxes
Click Display button
Display
Print...
Cancel

(b) Index Tab

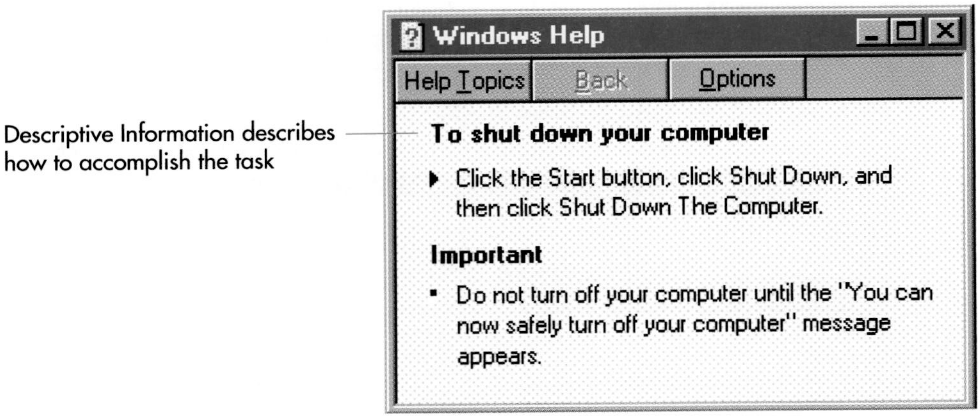
Windows Help
Help Topics
Back
Options
Descriptive Information describes how to accomplish the task
To shut down your computer
Click the Start button, click Shut Down, and then click Shut Down The Computer.
Important
Do not turn off your computer until the "You can now safely turn off your computer" message appears.

(c) Help Display

FIGURE 5 Online Help (continued)

THE MOUSE

The mouse is indispensable to Windows and is referenced continually in the hands-on exercises throughout the text. There are four basic operations with which you must become familiar:

- To ***point*** to an object, move the mouse pointer onto the object.
- To ***click*** an object, point to it, then press and release the left mouse button; to ***right click*** an object, point to the object, then press and release the right mouse button.

- To ***double click*** an object, point to it, then quickly click the left button twice in succession.
- To ***drag*** an object, move the pointer to the object, then press and hold the left button while you move the mouse to a new position.

The mouse is a pointing device—move the mouse on your desk and the ***mouse pointer,*** typically a small arrowhead, moves on the monitor. The mouse pointer assumes different shapes according to the location of the pointer or the nature of the current action—for example, a double arrow when you change the size of a window, an I-beam to insert text, a hand to jump from one help topic to the next, or a circle with a line through it to indicate that an attempted action is invalid.

The mouse pointer will also change to an hourglass to indicate that Windows is processing your last command, and that no further commands may be issued until the action is completed. The more powerful your computer, the less frequently the hourglass will appear; and conversely, the less powerful your system, the more you see the hourglass.

The Mouse versus the Keyboard

Almost every command in Windows can be executed in different ways, using either the mouse or the keyboard. Most people start with the mouse but add keyboard shortcuts as they become more proficient. There is no right or wrong technique, just different techniques, and the one you choose depends entirely on personal preference in a specific situation. If, for example, your hands are already on the keyboard, it is faster to use the keyboard equivalent. Other times, your hand will be on the mouse and that will be the fastest way. Toolbars provide still other ways to execute common commands.

In the beginning you may wonder why there are so many different ways to do the same thing, but you will eventually recognize the many options as part of Windows' charm. It is not necessary to memorize anything, nor should you even try; just be flexible and willing to experiment. The more you practice, the faster all of this will become second nature to you.

FORMATTING A DISK

All disks have to be formatted before they can hold data. The formatting process divides a disk into concentric circles called tracks, then further divides each track into sectors. You don't have to worry about formatting a hard disk, as that is done at the factory prior to the machine being sold. You do, however, have to format a floppy disk in order for Windows to read from and write to the disk. The procedure to format a floppy disk is described in step 6 of the following exercise.

FORMATTING A DISK

You must format a floppy disk at its rated capacity or else you may be unable to read the disk. There are two types of 3½-inch disks, double-density (720KB) and high-density (1.44MB). The easiest way to determine the type of disk is to look at the disk itself for the labels DD or HD, for double- and high-density, respectively. You can also check the number of square holes in the disk; a double-density disk has one, a high-density has two.

LEARNING BY DOING

Learning is best accomplished by doing, and so we come to the first of four exercises in this appendix. The exercises enable you to apply the concepts you have learned, then extend those concepts to further exploration on your own.

Our first exercise welcomes you to Windows 95, shows you how to open, move, and size a window on the desktop, and how to format a floppy disk.

HANDS-ON EXERCISE 1

Welcome to Windows 95

Objective: To turn on the computer and start Windows 95; to use the help facility and explore the topic "Ten Minutes to Using Windows"; to open, move, and size a window; to format a floppy disk. Use Figure 6 as a guide in the exercise.

STEP 1: Turn the Computer On

- The floppy drive should be empty prior to starting your machine. This ensures that the system starts by reading files from the hard disk (which contains the Windows files), as opposed to a floppy disk (which does not).
- The number and location of the on/off switches depend on the nature and manufacturer of the devices connected to the computer. The easiest possible setup is when all components of the system are plugged into a surge protector, in which case only a single switch has to be turned on. In any event:
  - Turn on the monitor if it has a separate switch.
  - Turn on the printer if it has a separate switch.
  - Turn on the power switch of the system unit.
- Your system will take a minute or so to get started, after which you should see the desktop in Figure 6a (the Start menu is *not* yet visible). Do not be concerned if the appearance of your desktop is different from ours.
- You may (or may not) see the Welcome message in Figure 6a. All of the command buttons are interesting and merit further exploration, which we will do at a later time. But for now, we ask that you click the **Close button** if you see the Welcome message.
- Click the **Start button** to display the Start menu. Again, do not be concerned if your start menu is different from ours, or if your icons are smaller (or larger) than ours.
- Click the **Help command** as shown in Figure 6a.

MASTER THE MOUSE

Moving the mouse pointer is easy, but it takes practice to move it to an exact position on the screen. If you're having trouble, be sure the mouse is perpendicular to the system unit. Move the mouse to the left or right, and the mouse pointer moves left or right on the screen. Move the mouse forward or back, and the pointer moves up or down.

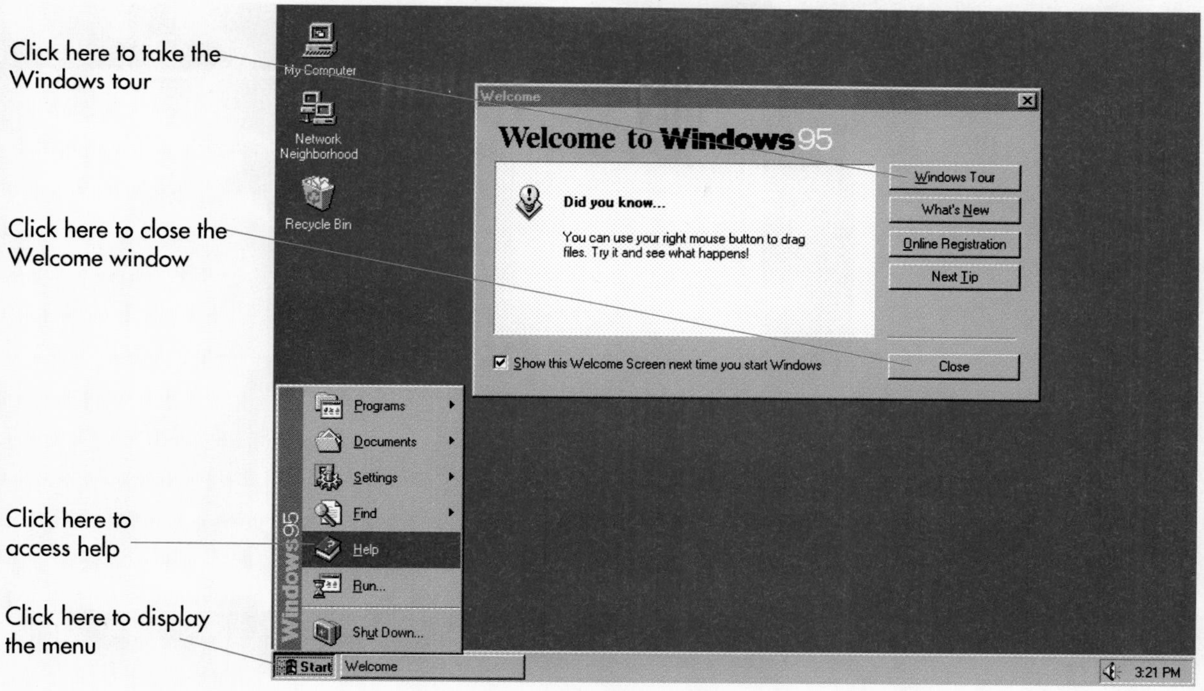
Click here to take the Windows tour
Click here to close the Welcome window
Click here to access help
Click here to display the menu
My Computer
Network Neighborhood
Recycle Bin
Welcome
Welcome to Windows95
Did you know...
You can use your right mouse button to drag files. Try it and see what happens!
Windows Tour
What's New
Online Registration
Next Tip
Show this Welcome Screen next time you start Windows
Close
Programs
Documents
Settings
Find
Help
Run...
Shut Down...
Windows95
Start
3:21 PM

(a) Welcome to Windows 95 (step 1)

FIGURE 6 Hands-on Exercise 1

STEP 2: Ten Minutes to Windows

- If necessary, click the **Contents tab** in the Help Topics dialog box. All of the books on your screen will be closed.
- Click the topic **Ten Minutes to Using Windows,** then click the **Display button** to begin the Windows tour. (You can double click the topic to avoid having to click the Display button.)
- You should see the menu in Figure 6b. Click the **Book icon** next to Using Help to learn about the help facility.
- Follow the instructions provided by Windows until you complete the session on help. Click the **Exit button** at the upper right of the screen, then click the **Exit Tour button** to return to the desktop and continue with the exercise.

DOUBLE CLICKING FOR BEGINNERS

If you are having trouble double clicking, it is because you are not clicking quickly enough, or more likely, because you are moving the mouse (however slightly) between clicks. Relax, hold the mouse firmly on your desk, and try again.

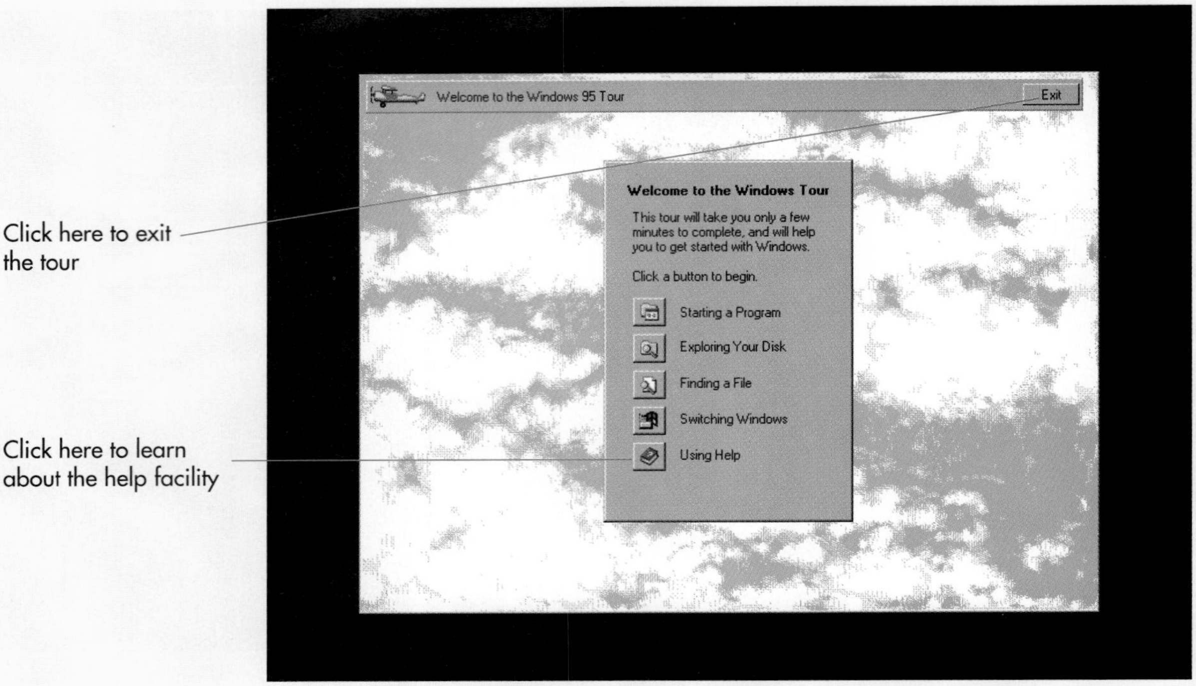
Click here to exit the tour
Click here to learn about the help facility
Welcome to the Windows 95 Tour
Exit
Welcome to the Windows Tour
This tour will take you only a few minutes to complete, and will help you to get started with Windows.
Click a button to begin.
Starting a Program
Exploring Your Disk
Finding a File
Switching Windows
Using Help

(b) Windows 95 Tour (step 2)

FIGURE 6 Hands-on Exercise 1 (continued)

STEP 3: Open My Computer

- Point to the **My Computer icon,** click the **right mouse button,** then click the **Open command** from the shortcut menu. (Alternatively, you can double click the **icon** to open it directly.)
- My Computer will open into a window as shown in Figure 6c. (The menus are not yet visible.) Do not be concerned if the contents of your window or its size and position on the desktop are different from ours.
- Pull down the **View menu** (point to the menu and click) as shown in Figure 6c. Make or verify the following selections. (You have to pull down the menu each time you choose a different command.)
  - The **Toolbar command** should be checked. The Toolbar command functions as a toggle switch. Click the command and the toolbar is displayed; click the command a second time and the toolbar disappears.)
  - The **Status Bar command** should be checked. The Status Bar command also functions as a toggle switch.
  - **Large Icons** should be selected.
- Pull down the **View menu** a final time. Click the **Arrange Icons command** and (if necessary) click the **AutoArrange command** so that a check appears. Click outside the menu (or press the **Esc key**) if the command is already checked.

Drag the title bar to move the window (when menu is closed)

Click and drag a border to size the window (when menu is closed)

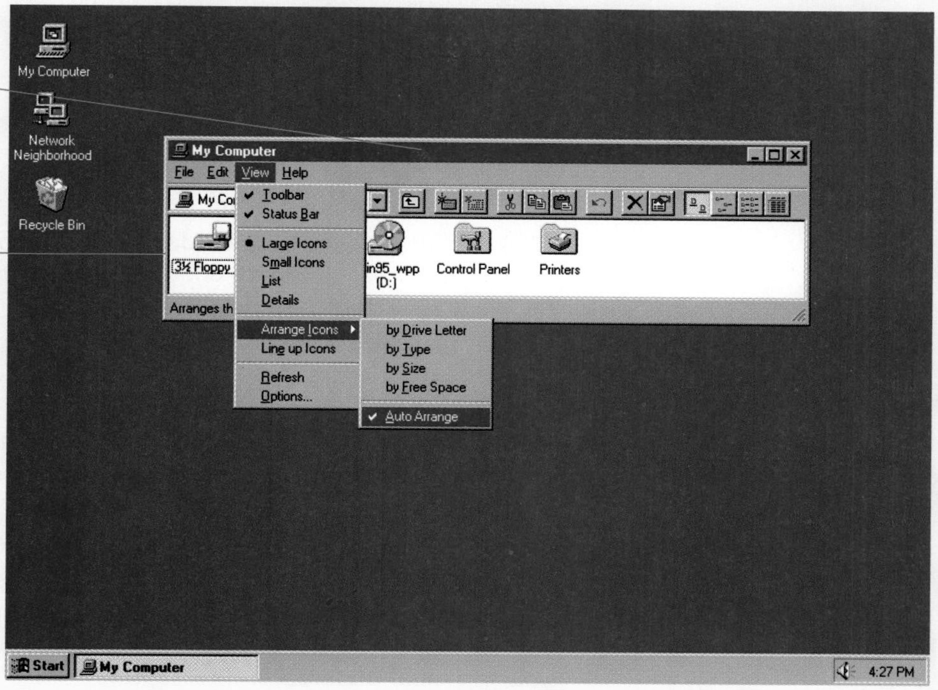

My Computer
Network Neighborhood
Recycle Bin
My Computer
File Edit View Help
Toolbar
Status Bar
Large Icons
Small Icons
List
Details
Arrange Icons
Line up Icons
Refresh
Options...
by Drive Letter
by Type
by Size
by Free Space
Auto Arrange
3½ Floppy
in95_wpp (D:)
Control Panel
Printers
Arranges th
Start
My Computer
4:27 PM

(c) My Computer (step 3)

FIGURE 6 Hands-on Exercise 1 (continued)

> **TOOLTIPS**
>
> Point to any button on the toolbar, and Windows displays the name of the button, which is indicative of its function. Point to the clock at the extreme right of the taskbar, and you will see a ToolTip with today's date. Point to the Start button, and you will see a ToolTip telling you to click here to begin.

STEP 4: Move and Size the Window

➤ Move and size the My Computer window on your desk to match the display in Figure 6c. (Press **Esc** to close the open menus.)
  - Click the **Restore button** (which appears only if the window has been maximized) or else you will not be able to move and size the window.
  - To change the width or height of the window, click and drag a border (the mouse pointer changes to a double arrow) in the direction you want to go; drag the border inward to shrink the window or outward to enlarge it.
  - To change the width and height at the same time, click and drag a corner rather than a border.
  - To change the position of the window, click and drag the title bar.

➤ Click the **Maximize button** so that the window expands to fill the entire screen. Click the **Restore button** (which replaces the Maximize button and is not shown in Figure 6c) to return the window to its previous size.

- Click the **Minimize button** to shrink the My Computer window to a button on the taskbar. My Computer is still open and remains active in memory.
- Click the **My Computer button** on the taskbar to reopen the window.

STEP 5: Scrolling

- Pull down the **View menu** and click **Details** (or click the **Details button** on the toolbar). You are now in the Details view as shown in Figure 6d.
- Click and drag the bottom border of the window inward so that you see the vertical scroll bar in Figure 6d. The scroll bar indicates that the contents of the window are not completely visible.
  - Click the **down arrow** on the scroll bar. The top line (for drive A) disappears from view, and a new line containing the Control Panel comes into view.
  - Click the **down arrow** a second time, which brings the Printers folder into view at the bottom of the window as the icon for drive C scrolls off the screen.
- Click the **Small Icons button** on the toolbar. Size the window so that the scroll bar disappears when the contents of the window become completely visible.
- Click the **Details button** on the toolbar. The scroll bar returns because you can no longer see the complete contents. Move and/or size the window to your personal preference.

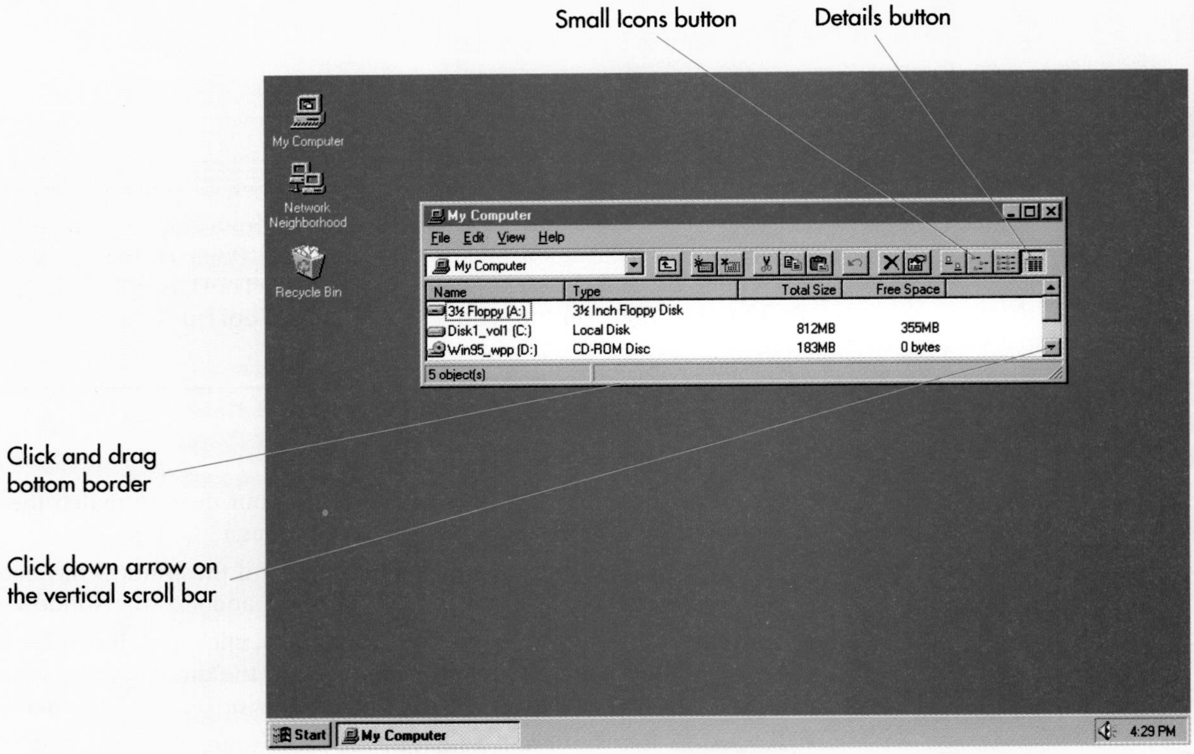

Small Icons button
Details button
Click and drag bottom border
Click down arrow on the vertical scroll bar
My Computer
Network Neighborhood
Recycle Bin
My Computer
File Edit View Help
Name
Type
Total Size
Free Space
3½ Floppy (A:)
3½ Inch Floppy Disk
Disk1_vol1 (C:)
Local Disk
812MB
355MB
Win95_wpp (D:)
CD-ROM Disc
183MB
0 bytes
5 object(s)
Start
4:29 PM

(d) Scrolling (step 5)

FIGURE 6 Hands-on Exercise 1 (continued)

THE DETAILS VIEW

The Details view provides information about each object in a folder—for example, the capacity (total size) and amount of free space on a disk. To switch to the Details view, pull down the View menu and click Details. You can also click the Details button on the toolbar, provided the toolbar is displayed.

STEP 6: Format a Floppy Disk

- ➤ Click the **icon** for **drive A.** Pull down the **File menu** and click **Format.**
- ➤ You will see the dialog box in Figure 6e. Move the dialog box by clicking and dragging its **title bar** so that your screen matches ours.
- ➤ Click the **What's This button** (the mouse pointer changes to a question mark). Click the **Full option button** (under Format type) for an explanation. Click anywhere in the dialog box to close the popup window.
- ➤ Set the formatting parameters as shown in Figure 6e:
  - Set the **Capacity** to match the floppy disk you purchased (see boxed tip on page 11).
  - Click the **Full option button** to choose a full format. This option is well worth the extra time as it ensures the integrity of your disk.

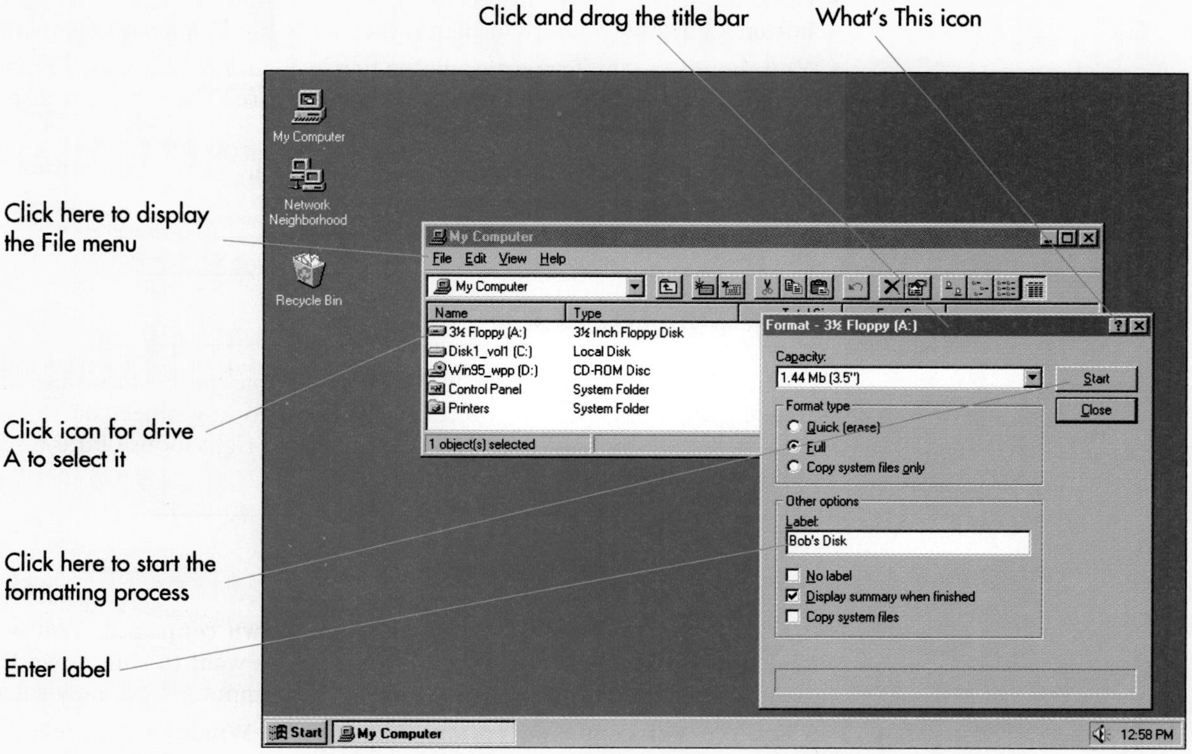

Click and drag the title bar
What's This icon
Click here to display the File menu
Click icon for drive A to select it
Click here to start the formatting process
Enter label
My Computer
Network Neighborhood
Recycle Bin
File Edit View Help
Name
Type
3½ Floppy (A:)
3½ Inch Floppy Disk
Disk1_vol1 (C:)
Local Disk
Win95_wpp (D:)
CD-ROM Disc
Control Panel
System Folder
Printers
System Folder
1 object(s) selected
Format - 3½ Floppy (A:)
Capacity:
1.44 Mb (3.5")
Start
Close
Format type
Quick (erase)
Full
Copy system files only
Other options
Label:
Bob's Disk
No label
Display summary when finished
Copy system files
Start
My Computer
12:58 PM

(e) Format a Floppy Disk (step 6)

FIGURE 6 Hands-on Exercise 1 (continued)

- Click the **Label text box** if it's empty, or click and drag over the existing label if there is an entry. Enter a new label such as **Bob's Disk** as shown in Figure 6e.

➤ Click the **Start command button** to begin the formatting operation. This will take about a minute, and you can see the progress of the formatting process at the bottom of the dialog box.

➤ After the formatting process is complete, you will see an informational dialog box with the results of the formatting operation. Read the information, then click the **Close command button** to close the informational dialog box.

➤ Click the **Close button** to close the Format dialog box.

WHAT'S THIS?

The What's This button (a question mark) appears in the title bar of almost every dialog box. Click the question mark, then click the item you want information about, which then appears in a popup window. To print the contents of the popup window, click the right mouse button inside the window, and click Print Topic. Click outside the popup window to close the window and continue working.

STEP 7: Disk Properties

➤ Click the **drive A icon** in the My Computer window, click the **right mouse button** to display a shortcut menu, then click the **Properties command.**

➤ You should see the Properties dialog box in Figure 6f although you may have to move and size the window to match our figure. The pie chart displays the percentage of free and unused space.

➤ Click **OK** to close the Properties dialog box. Click the **Close button** to close My Computer.

PROPERTIES EVERYWHERE

Windows assigns ***properties*** to every object on the desktop and stores those properties with the object itself. Point to any object on the desktop, including the desktop itself, then click the right mouse button to display the property sheet for that object.

STEP 8: Exit Windows

➤ Click the **Start button,** then click the **Shut Down command.** You will see a dialog box asking whether you're sure that you want to shut down the computer. (The option button to shut down the computer is already selected.)

➤ Click the **Yes command button,** then wait as Windows gets ready to shut down your system. Wait until you see another screen indicating that it is OK to turn off the computer.

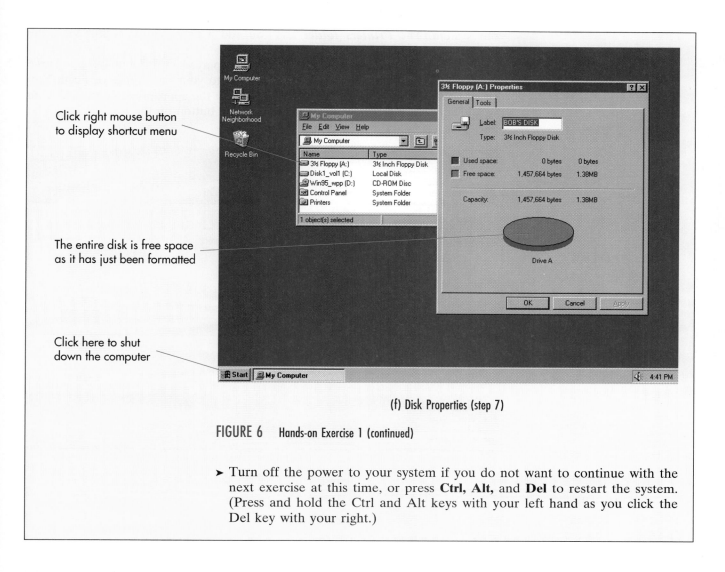

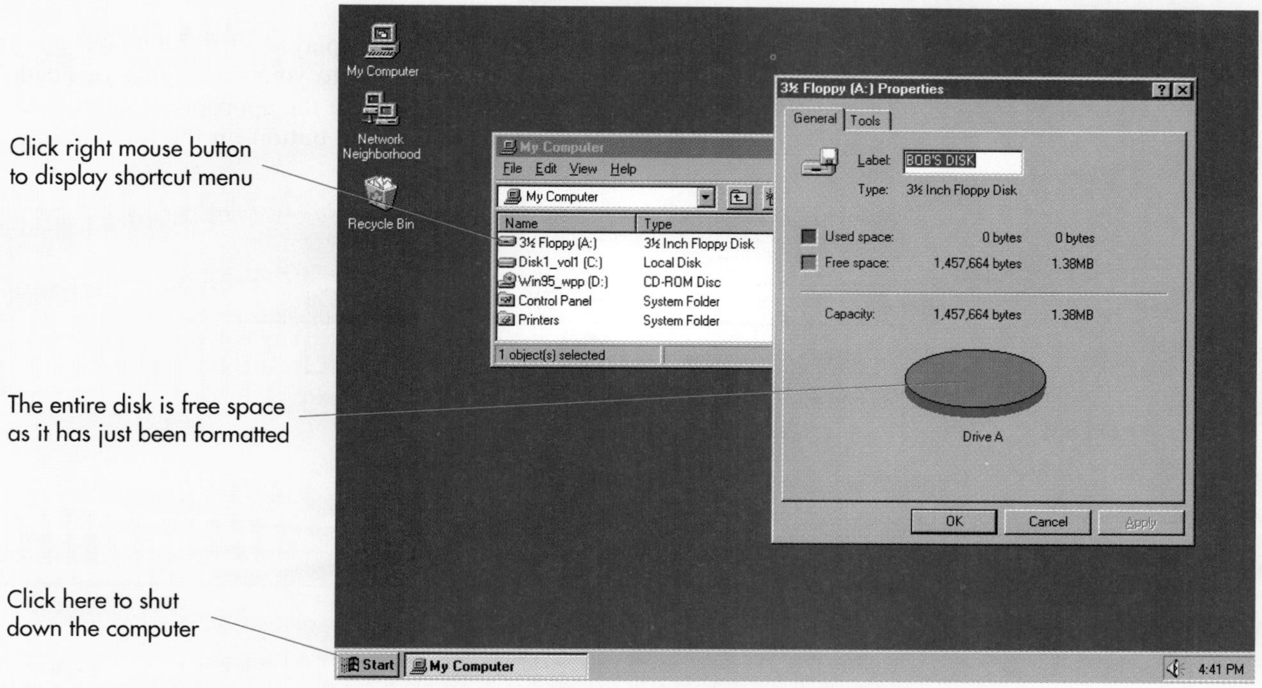
Click right mouse button to display shortcut menu
The entire disk is free space as it has just been formatted
Click here to shut down the computer
My Computer
Network Neighborhood
Recycle Bin
My Computer
File Edit View Help
My Computer
Name
Type
3½ Floppy (A:)
3½ Inch Floppy Disk
Disk1_vol1 (C:)
Local Disk
Win95_wpp (D:)
CD-ROM Disc
Control Panel
System Folder
Printers
System Folder
1 object(s) selected
3½ Floppy (A:) Properties
General
Tools
Label: BOB'S DISK
Type: 3½ Inch Floppy Disk
Used space: 0 bytes 0 bytes
Free space: 1,457,664 bytes 1.38MB
Capacity: 1,457,664 bytes 1.38MB
Drive A
OK
Cancel
Apply
Start
My Computer
4:41 PM

(f) Disk Properties (step 7)

FIGURE 6 Hands-on Exercise 1 (continued)

➤ Turn off the power to your system if you do not want to continue with the next exercise at this time, or press **Ctrl, Alt,** and **Del** to restart the system. (Press and hold the Ctrl and Alt keys with your left hand as you click the Del key with your right.)

MY COMPUTER

My Computer enables you to browse all of the drives (floppy disks, hard disks, and CD-ROM drive) that are attached to your computer. It is present on every desktop, but its contents will vary, depending on the specific configuration. Our system, for example, has one floppy drive, one hard disk, and a CD-ROM as shown in Figure 7. Each drive is represented by an icon and is assigned a letter.

The first (often only) floppy drive is designated as drive A, regardless of whether it is a 3½-inch drive or the older, and now nearly obsolete, 5¼-inch drive. A second floppy drive, if it exists, is drive B. Our system contains a single 3½ floppy drive (note the icon in Figure 7a) and is typical of systems purchased in today's environment.

The first (often only) hard disk on a system is always drive C, whether or not there are one or two floppy drives. A system with one floppy drive and one hard disk (today's most common configuration) will contain icons for drive A and drive C. Additional hard drives (if any) and/or the CD-ROM are labeled from D on.

In addition to an icon for each drive on your system, My Computer contains two other folders. (Folders are discussed in the next section.) The ***Control Panel*** enables you to configure (set up) all of the devices (mouse, sound, and so on) on your system. The ***Printers folder*** lets you add a new printer and/or view the progress of a printed document.

The contents of My Computer can be displayed in different views (Large Icons, Small Icons, Details, and List) according to your preference or need. You can switch from one view to the next by choosing the appropriate command from the View menu or by clicking the corresponding button on the toolbar.

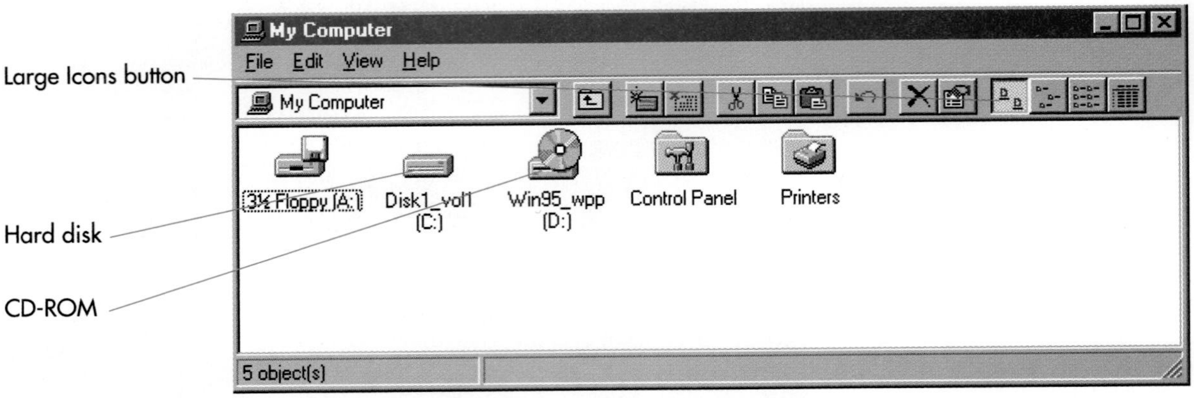

Large Icons button
Hard disk
CD-ROM
My Computer
File Edit View Help
My Computer
3½ Floppy (A:)
Disk1_vol1 (C:)
Win95_wpp (D:)
Control Panel
Printers
5 object(s)

(a) Large Icons

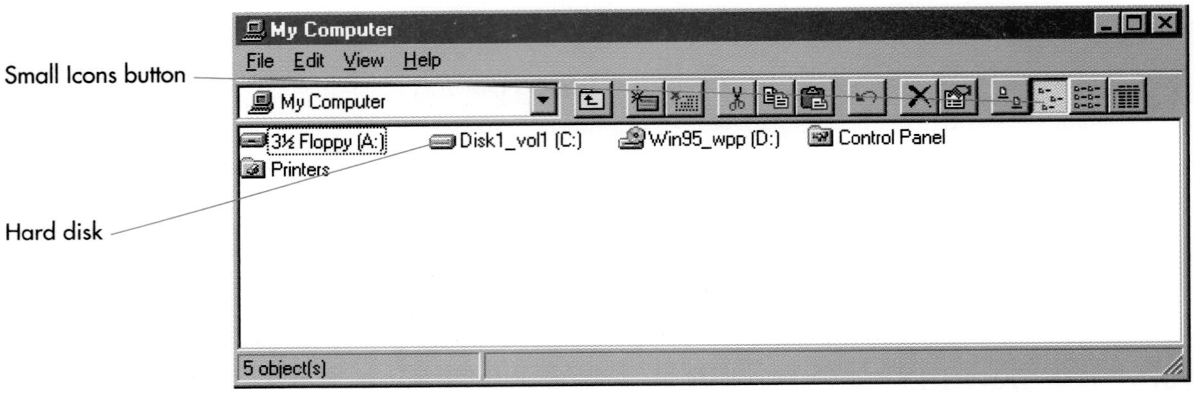

Small Icons button
Hard disk
My Computer
File Edit View Help
My Computer
3½ Floppy (A:)
Disk1_vol1 (C:)
Win95_wpp (D:)
Control Panel
Printers
5 object(s)

(b) Small Icons

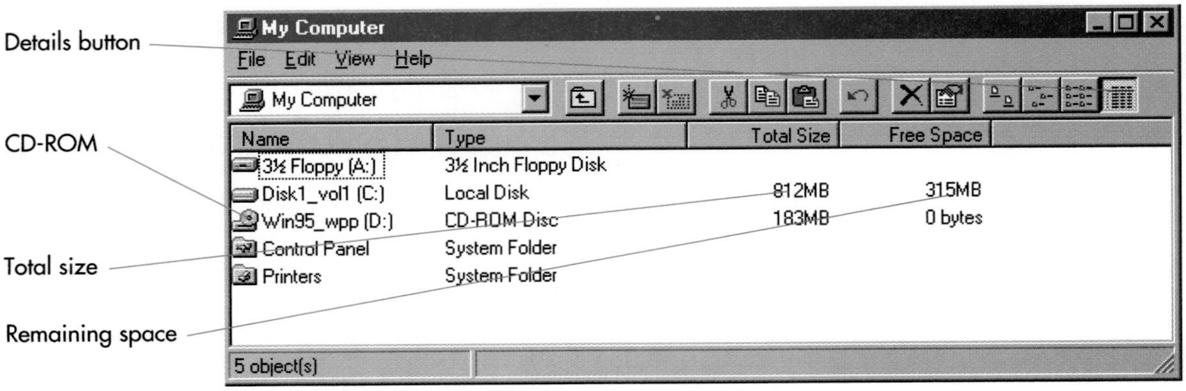

Details button
CD-ROM
Total size
Remaining space
My Computer
File Edit View Help
My Computer
Name
Type
Total Size
Free Space
3½ Floppy (A:)
3½ Inch Floppy Disk
Disk1_vol1 (C:)
Local Disk
812MB
315MB
Win95_wpp (D:)
CD-ROM Disc
183MB
0 bytes
Control Panel
System Folder
Printers
System Folder
5 object(s)

(c) Details View

FIGURE 7 My Computer

The ***Large Icons view*** and ***Small Icons view*** in Figures 7a and 7b, respectively, display each object as a large or small icon. The choice between the two depends on your personal preference. You might, for example, choose large icons if there are only a few objects in the window. Small icons would be preferable if there were many objects and you wanted to see them all. The ***Details view*** in Figure 7c displays additional information about each object. You see the type of object, the total size of the disk, and the remaining space on the disk. (A List view is also available and displays the objects with small icons but without the file details.)

FILES AND FOLDERS

A ***file*** is any data or set of instructions that have been given a name and stored on disk. There are, in general, two types of files, program files and data files. Microsoft Word and Microsoft Excel are program files. The documents and spreadsheets created by these programs are data files. A ***program file*** is executable because it contains instructions that tell the computer what to do. A ***data file*** is not executable and can be used only in conjunction with a specific program.

A file must have a name by which it can be identified. The file name can contain up to 255 characters and may include spaces and other punctuation. (This is very different from the rules that existed under MS-DOS that limited file names to eight characters followed by an optional three-character extension.) Long file names permit descriptive entries such as, *Term Paper for Western Civilization* (as opposed to a more cryptic *TPWCIV* that would be required under MS-DOS).

Files are stored in ***folders*** to better organize the hundreds (often thousands) of files on a hard disk. A Windows folder is similar in concept to a manila folder in a filing cabinet and contains one or more documents (files) that are somehow related to each other. An office worker stores his or her documents in manila folders. In Windows, you store your data files (documents) in electronic folders on disk.

Folders are the key to the Windows storage system. You can create any number of folders to hold your work just as you can place any number of manila folders into a filing cabinet. You can create one folder for your word processing documents and a different folder for your spreadsheets. Alternatively, you can create a folder to hold all of your work for a specific class, which may contain a combination of word processing documents and spreadsheets. The choice is entirely up to you, and you can use any system that makes sense to you. Anything at all can go into a folder—program files, data files, even other folders.

Figure 8 displays two different views of a folder containing six documents. The name of the folder (Homework) appears in the title bar next to the icon of an open folder. The Minimize, Maximize, and Close buttons appear at the right of the title bar. A toolbar appears below the menu bar in each view.

The Details view in Figure 8a displays the name of each file in the folder (note the descriptive file name), the file size, the type of file, and the date and time the file was last modified. Figure 8b shows the Large Icons view, which displays only the file name and an icon representing the application that created the file. The choice between views depends on your personal preference. (A Small Icons view and List view are also available.)

File Type

Every data file has a specific ***file type*** that is determined by the application that created the file initially. One way to recognize the file type is to examine the Type column in the Details view as shown in Figure 8a. The History Term Paper, for

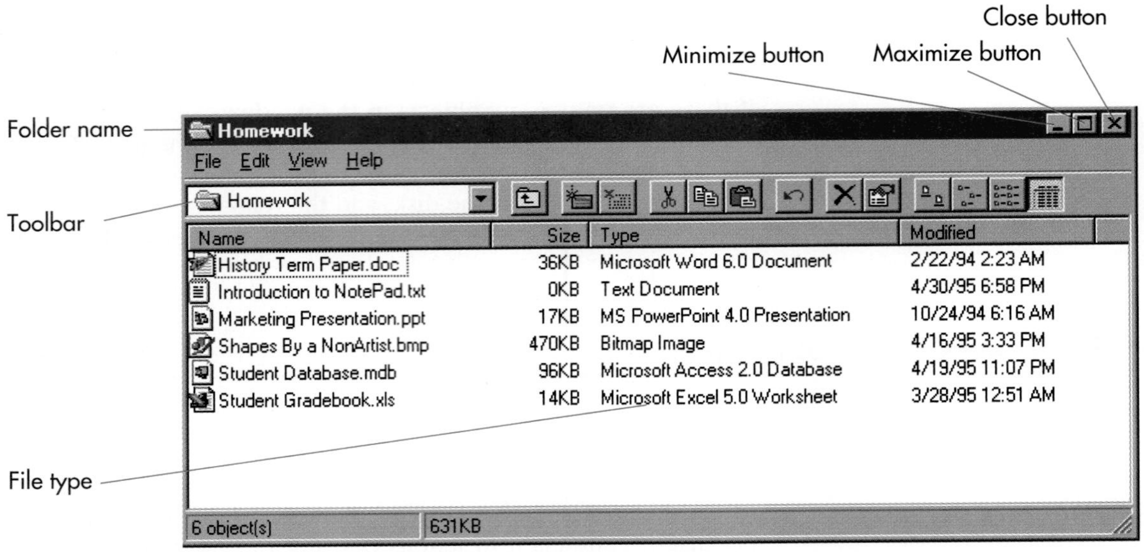
Close button
Minimize button
Maximize button
Folder name
Homework
File Edit View Help
Toolbar
Homework
Name
Size
Type
Modified
History Term Paper.doc
36KB
Microsoft Word 6.0 Document
2/22/94 2:23 AM
Introduction to NotePad.txt
0KB
Text Document
4/30/95 6:58 PM
Marketing Presentation.ppt
17KB
MS PowerPoint 4.0 Presentation
10/24/94 6:16 AM
Shapes By a NonArtist.bmp
470KB
Bitmap Image
4/16/95 3:33 PM
Student Database.mdb
96KB
Microsoft Access 2.0 Database
4/19/95 11:07 PM
Student Gradebook.xls
14KB
Microsoft Excel 5.0 Worksheet
3/28/95 12:51 AM
File type
6 object(s)
631KB

(a) Details View

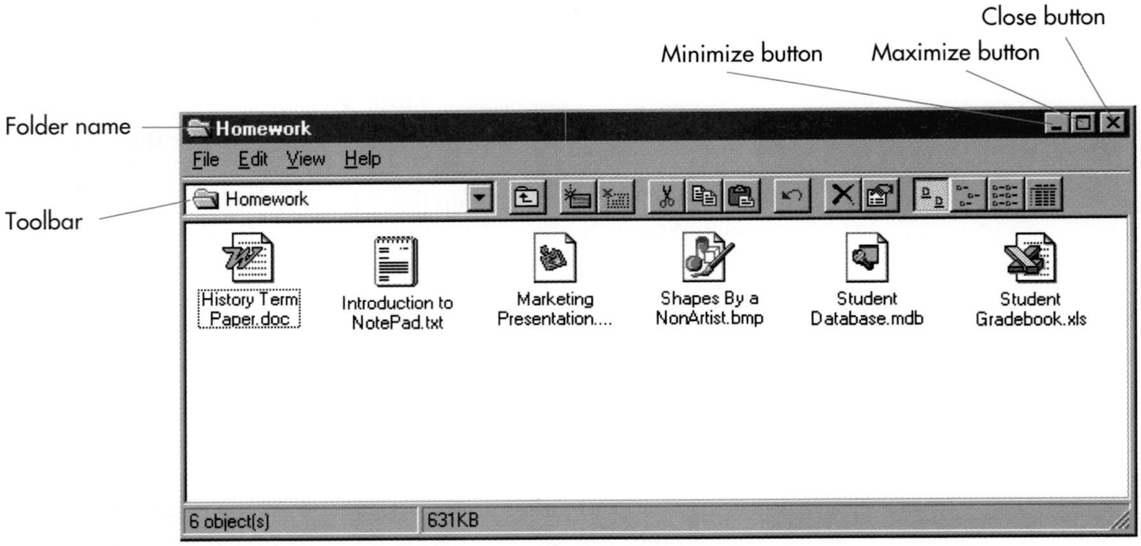
Close button
Minimize button
Maximize button
Folder name
Homework
File Edit View Help
Toolbar
Homework
History Term Paper.doc
Introduction to NotePad.txt
Marketing Presentation....
Shapes By a NonArtist.bmp
Student Database.mdb
Student Gradebook.xls
6 object(s)
631KB

(b) Large Icons View

FIGURE 8 The Homework Folder

example, is a Microsoft Word 6.0 document, and the Student Gradebook is an Excel 5.0 workbook.

You can also determine the file type (or associated application) from any view (not just the Details view) by examining the application icon displayed next to the file name. Look carefully at the icon next to the History Term Paper in Figure 8a, for example, and you will recognize the icon for Microsoft Word. The application icon is recognized more easily in the Large Icons view in Figure 8b.

Still another way to determine the file type is through the three-character extension displayed after the file name. (A period separates the file name from the extension.) Each application has a specific extension, which is automatically assigned to the file name when the file is created. DOC and XLS, for example, are the extensions for Microsoft Word and Excel, respectively. The extension may be suppressed or displayed according to an option in the View menu of My Computer. See step 2 of the hands-on exercise on page 25.

Browsing My Computer

You need to be able to locate a folder and/or its documents quickly so that you can retrieve the documents and go to work. There are several ways to do this, the easiest of which is to browse My Computer. Assume, for example, that you are looking for the Homework folder in Figure 9 in order to work on your term paper for history. Figure 9 shows how easy it is to locate the Homework folder.

You would start by double clicking the My Computer icon on the desktop. This opens the My Computer window and displays all of the drives on your system. Next you would double click the icon for drive C because this is the drive that contains the folder you are looking for. This opens a second window, which displays all of the folders on drive C. And finally you would double click the icon for the Homework folder to open a third window containing the documents in the Homework folder. Once you are in the Homework folder, you would double click the icon of any existing document (which starts the associated application and opens the document), enabling you to begin work.

LEARNING BY DOING

The following exercise has you create a new folder on drive C, then create various files in that folder. The files are created using Notepad and Paint, two accessories that are included in Windows 95. We chose to create the files using these

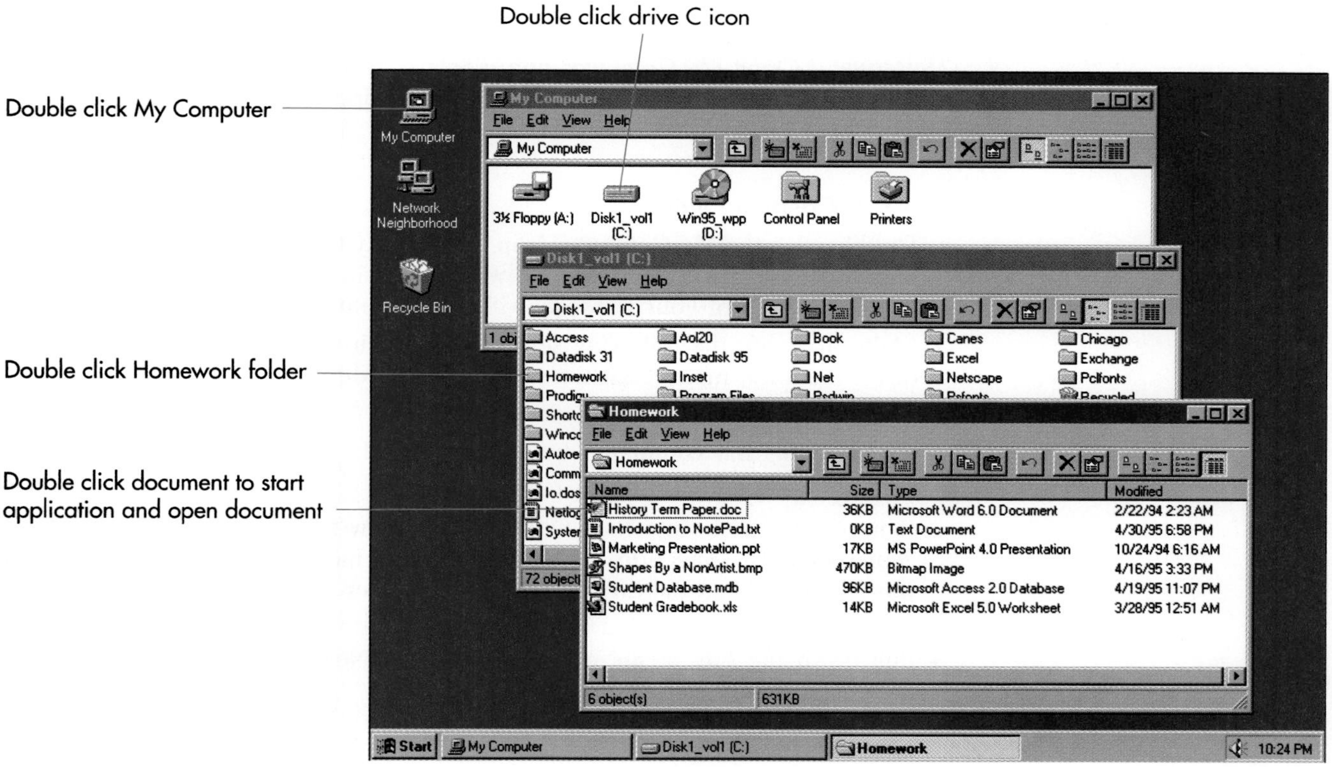

Double click drive C icon
Double click My Computer
Double click Homework folder
Double click document to start application and open document
My Computer
Network Neighborhood
Recycle Bin
File Edit View Help
3½ Floppy (A:)
Disk1_vol1 (C:)
Win95_wpp (D:)
Control Panel
Printers
Disk1_vol1 (C:)
Access
Aol20
Book
Canes
Chicago
Datadisk 31
Datadisk 95
Dos
Excel
Exchange
Homework
Inset
Net
Netscape
Pcfonts
Homework
Name
Size
Type
Modified
History Term Paper.doc
36KB
Microsoft Word 6.0 Document
2/22/94 2:23 AM
Introduction to NotePad.txt
0KB
Text Document
4/30/95 6:58 PM
Marketing Presentation.ppt
17KB
MS PowerPoint 4.0 Presentation
10/24/94 6:16 AM
Shapes By a NonArtist.bmp
470KB
Bitmap Image
4/16/95 3:33 PM
Student Database.mdb
96KB
Microsoft Access 2.0 Database
4/19/95 11:07 PM
Student Gradebook.xls
14KB
Microsoft Excel 5.0 Worksheet
3/28/95 12:51 AM
6 object(s)
631KB
Start
10:24 PM

FIGURE 9 Browsing My Computer

simple accessories, rather than more powerful applications such as Word or Excel, because we wanted to create the files quickly and easily. We also wanted to avoid reliance on specific applications that are not part of Windows 95. The emphasis throughout this appendix is the ability to manipulate files within the Windows environment after they have been created.

The exercise also illustrates the document orientation of Windows 95, which enables you to think in terms of the document rather than the application that created it. You simply point to an open folder, click the right mouse button to display a shortcut menu, then select the ***New command.*** You will be presented with a list of objects (file types) that are recognized by Windows 95 because the associated applications have been previously installed. Choose the file type that you want, and the associated application will be opened automatically. (See step 4 in the following hands-on exercise.)

THE NOTEPAD ACCESSORY

The Notepad accessory is ideal to create "quick and dirty" files that require no formatting and that are smaller than 64K. Notepad opens and saves files in ASCII (text) format only. Use a different editor, e.g., the WordPad accessory or a full-fledged word processor such as Microsoft Word, to create larger files or files that require formatting.

HANDS-ON EXERCISE 2

My Computer

Objective: Open My Computer and create a new folder on drive C. Use the New command to create a Notepad document and a Paint drawing. Use Figure 10 as a guide in the exercise.

STEP 1: Create a Folder

- Double click the **My Computer icon** to open My Computer. Double click the **icon** for **drive C** to open a second window as shown in Figure 10a. The size and/or position of your windows will be different from ours.
- Make or verify the following selections in each window. (You have to pull down the View menu each time you choose a different command.)
  - The **Toolbar command** should be checked.
  - The **Status Bar command** should be checked.
  - **Large Icons** should be selected.
- If necessary, click anywhere within the window for drive C to make it the active window. (The title bar reflects the internal label of your disk, which was assigned when the disk was formatted. Your label will be different from ours.)
- Pull down the **File menu,** click (or point to) **New** to display the submenu, then click **Folder** as shown in Figure 10a.

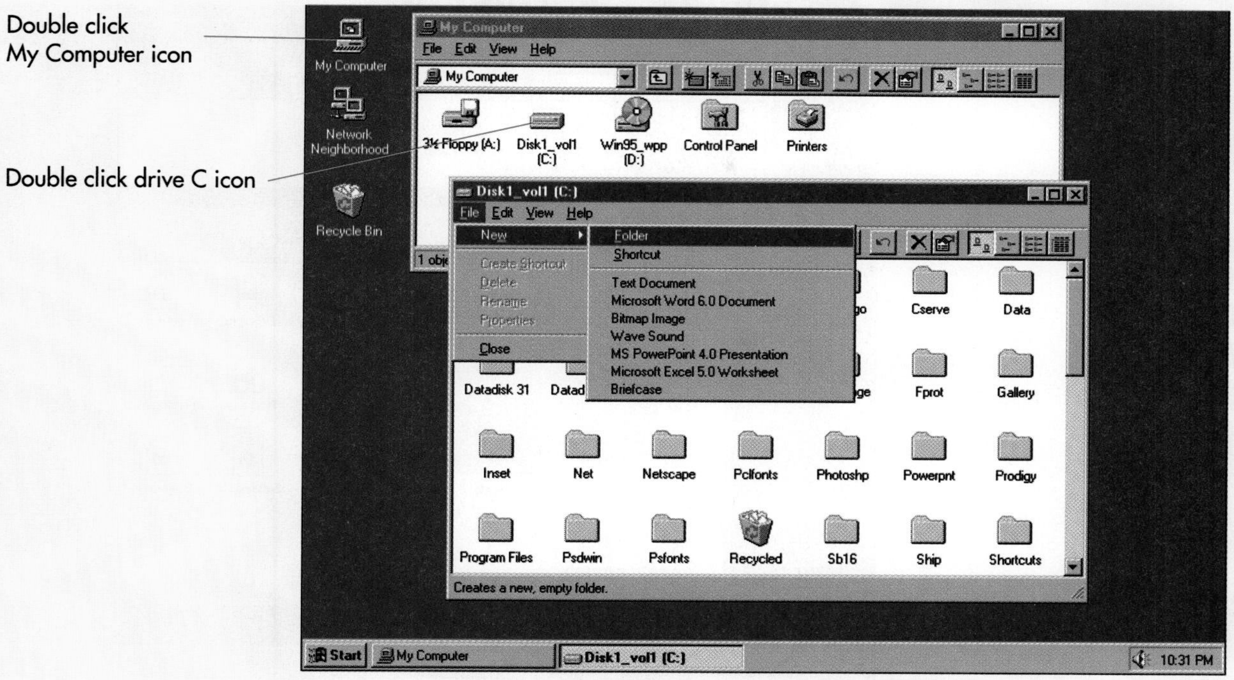
Double click
My Computer icon
Double click drive C icon
My Computer
File Edit View Help
3½ Floppy (A:)
Disk1_vol1 (C:)
Win95_wpp (D:)
Control Panel
Printers
Disk1_vol1 (C:)
New
Create Shortcut
Delete
Rename
Properties
Close
Folder
Shortcut
Text Document
Microsoft Word 6.0 Document
Bitmap Image
Wave Sound
MS PowerPoint 4.0 Presentation
Microsoft Excel 5.0 Worksheet
Briefcase
Cserve
Data
Datadisk 31
Fprot
Gallery
Inset
Net
Netscape
Pclfonts
Photoshp
Powerpnt
Prodigy
Program Files
Psdwin
Psfonts
Recycled
Sb16
Ship
Shortcuts
Creates a new, empty folder.
Network Neighborhood
Recycle Bin
Start
10:31 PM

(a) Create a Folder (step 1)

FIGURE 10 Hands-on Exercise 2

> **HOMEWORK FOLDER ALREADY EXISTS**
>
> If you are working on a LAN with other students, you may see the error message "Cannot Rename New Folder. A folder with the name you specified already exists." This means that another student has already created the homework folder on this machine, and hence you must delete that student's folder in order to create a homework folder of your own. Press Esc (or click OK) to close the Error Renaming File dialog box. Press Esc a second time to deselect the folder name (homework). Select (click) the existing homework folder and press the Del key, then create a homework folder of your own.

STEP 2: The View Menu

- A new folder has been created within the window for drive C with the name of the folder (New Folder) highlighted. Type **Homework** to change the name of the folder as shown in Figure 10b. Press **enter.**
- Pull down the **View menu** and click the **Arrange Icons command.** Click **By Name** to arrange the folders alphabetically within the window for drive C.
- Pull down the **View menu** a second time. Click **Options,** then click the **View tab** in the Options dialog box. Check the box (if necessary) to **Hide MS-DOS file extensions.** Click **OK.**

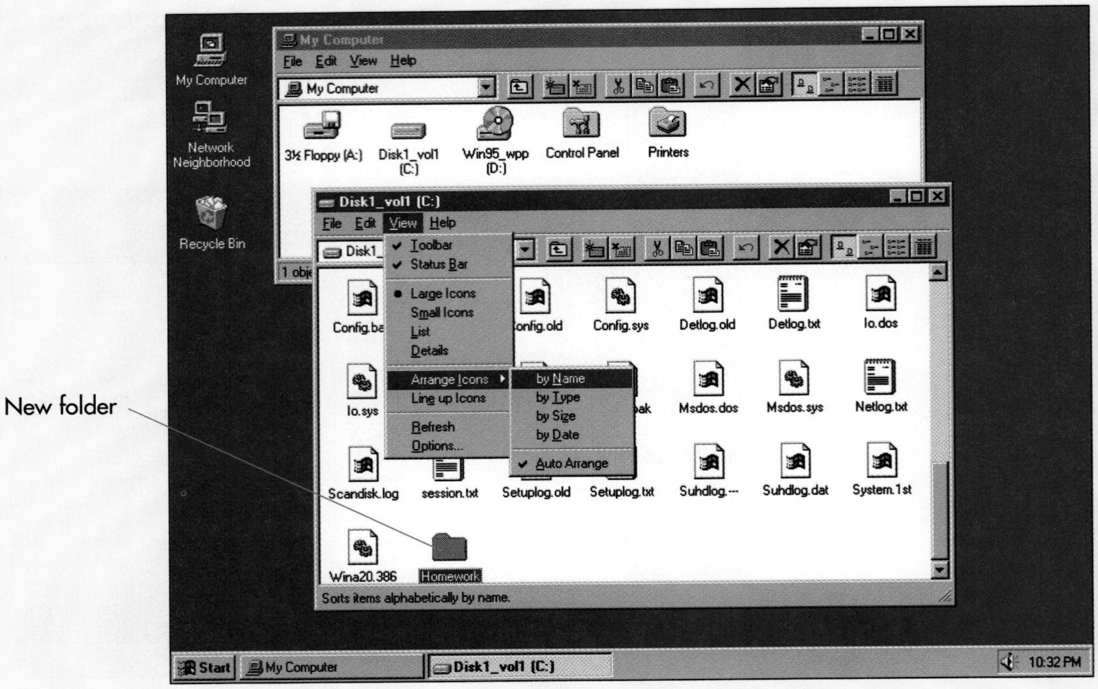
New folder
My Computer
Network Neighborhood
Recycle Bin
My Computer
File Edit View Help
My Computer
3½ Floppy (A:)
Disk1_vol1 (C:)
Win95_wpp (D:)
Control Panel
Printers
Disk1_vol1 (C:)
File Edit View Help
Toolbar
Status Bar
Large Icons
Small Icons
List
Details
Arrange Icons
Line up Icons
Refresh
Options...
by Name
by Type
by Size
by Date
Auto Arrange
Config.old
Config.sys
Detlog.old
Detlog.txt
Io.dos
Io.sys
Msdos.dos
Msdos.sys
Netlog.txt
Scandisk.log
session.txt
Setuplog.old
Setuplog.txt
Suhdlog.---
Suhdlog.dat
System.1st
Wina20.386
Homework
Sorts items alphabetically by name.
Start
My Computer
Disk1_vol1 (C:)
10:32 PM

(b) View Menu (step 2)

FIGURE 10 Hands-on Exercise 2 (continued)

RENAME COMMAND

Point to a file or a folder, then click the right mouse button to display a menu with commands pertaining to the object. Click the Rename command. The name of the file or folder will be highlighted with the insertion point (a flashing vertical line) positioned at the end of the name. Type a new name—for example, Homework—to replace the selected name, or click anywhere within the name to change the insertion point and edit the name.

STEP 3: Open the Homework Folder

- Click the **Homework folder** to select it. Pull down the **File menu** and click **Open** (or double click the **folder** without pulling down the menu) to open the Homework folder.
- The Homework folder opens into a window as shown in Figure 10c. The window is empty because the folder does not contain any documents. If necessary, pull down the **View menu** and check the **Toolbar command** to display the toolbar.
- **Right click** a blank position on the taskbar to display the menu in Figure 10c. Click **Tile Vertically** to tile the three open windows.

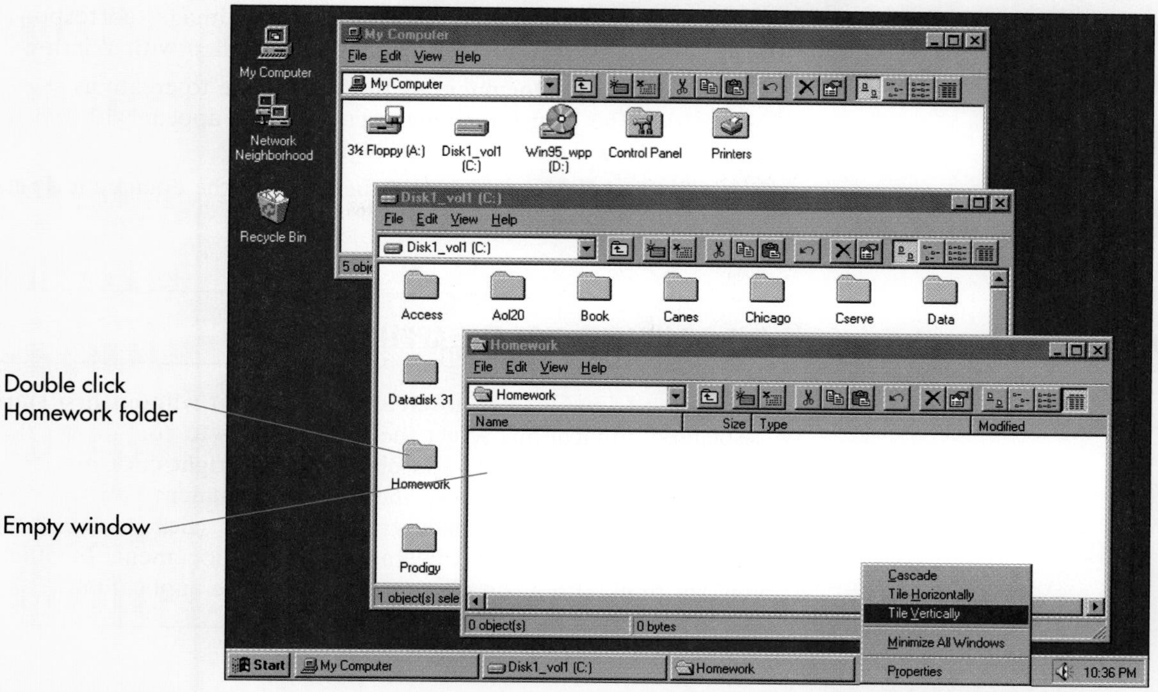
Double click Homework folder
Empty window
My Computer
Network Neighborhood
Recycle Bin
File Edit View Help
3½ Floppy (A:)
Disk1_vol1 (C:)
Win95_wpp (D:)
Control Panel
Printers
Disk1_vol1 (C:)
Access
Aol20
Book
Canes
Chicago
Cserve
Data
Datadisk 31
Homework
Prodigy
Name
Size
Type
Modified
0 object(s)
0 bytes
Cascade
Tile Horizontally
Tile Vertically
Minimize All Windows
Properties
Start
10:36 PM

(c) Open the Homework Folder (step 3)

FIGURE 10 Hands-on Exercise 2 (continued)

THE RIGHT MOUSE BUTTON

The right mouse button is the fastest way to change the properties of any object on the desktop or even the desktop itself. Point to a blank area on the desktop, click the right mouse button, then click Properties in the shortcut menu to display the dialog box (property sheet) for the desktop. In similar fashion, you can right click the taskbar to change its properties. You can also right click any icon on the desktop or any icon in a window.

STEP 4: The New Command

- The windows on your desktop should be tiled vertically as shown in Figure 10d. Click in the **Homework window.** The title bar for the Homework window should be highlighted, indicating that this is the active window.
- Pull down the **File menu** (or point to an empty area in the window and click the right mouse button).
- Click (or point to) the **New command** to display a submenu. The document types depend on the installed applications:
  - You may (or may not) see Microsoft Word Document or Microsoft Excel Worksheet, depending on whether or not you have installed these applications.

- You will see Text Document and Bitmap Image, corresponding to the Notepad and Paint accessories that are installed with Windows 95.

➤ Select (click) **Text Document** as the type of file to create as shown below in Figure 10d. The icon for a new document will appear with the name of the document, New Text Document, highlighted.

➤ Type **Files and Folders** to change the name of the document. Press the **enter** key.

THE DOCUMENT, NOT THE APPLICATION

Windows 95 enables you to create a document without first starting the associated application. Select the folder that is to contain the document, pull down the File menu, and click New (or right click an empty space within a folder), then choose the type of document you want to create. Once the document has been created, double click its icon to load the associated application and begin editing the document. In other words, you can think about the document and not the application.

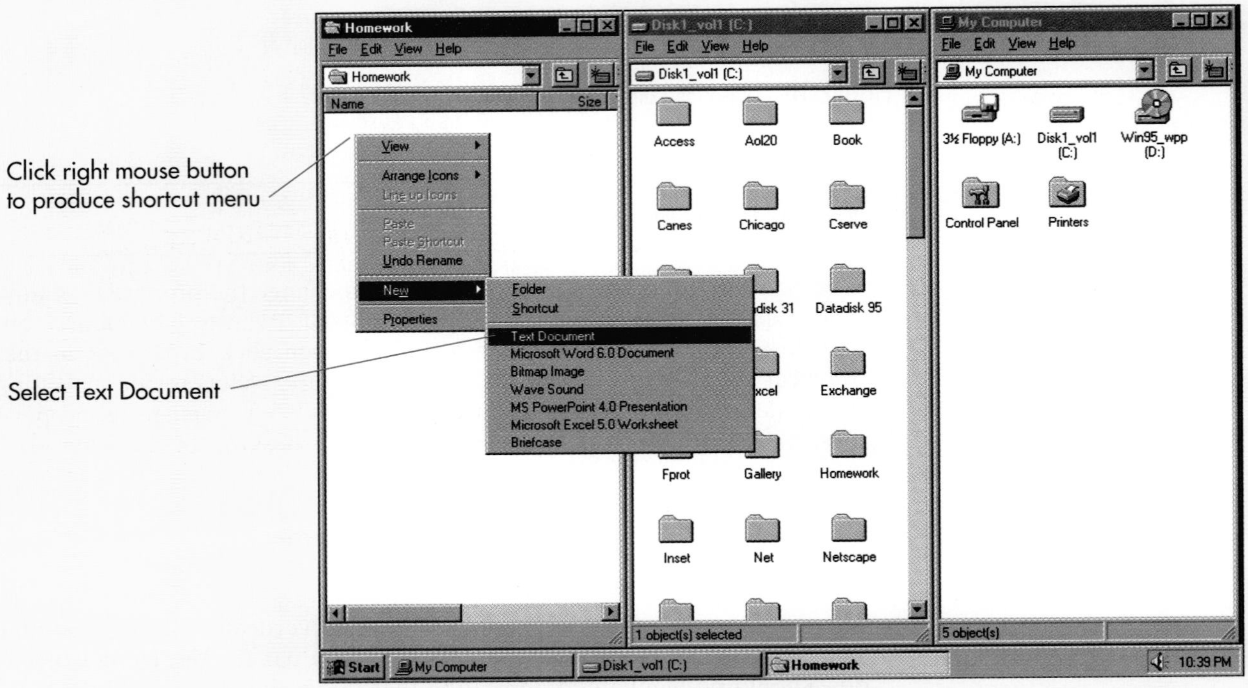

Click right mouse button to produce shortcut menu
Select Text Document
Homework
File Edit View Help
Name
Size
View
Arrange Icons
Line up Icons
Paste
Paste Shortcut
Undo Rename
New
Properties
Folder
Shortcut
Text Document
Microsoft Word 6.0 Document
Bitmap Image
Wave Sound
MS PowerPoint 4.0 Presentation
Microsoft Excel 5.0 Worksheet
Briefcase
Disk1_vol1 (C:)
Access
Aol20
Book
Canes
Chicago
Cserve
Datadisk 95
Exchange
Fprot
Gallery
Homework
Inset
Net
Netscape
1 object(s) selected
My Computer
3½ Floppy (A:)
Disk1_vol1 (C:)
Win95_wpp (D:)
Control Panel
Printers
5 object(s)
Start
10:39 PM

(d) The New Command (step 4)

FIGURE 10 Hands-on Exercise 2 (continued)

STEP 5: Create the Document

- If necessary, pull down the **View menu** and change to the **Large Icons view** so that the view in your Homework folder matches the view in Figure 10e.
- Select (click) the **Files and Folders document.** Pull down the **File menu.** Click **Open** (or double click the **Files and Folders icon** without pulling down the File menu) to load Notepad and open a Notepad window. The window is empty because the text of the document has not yet been entered.
- Pull down the **Edit menu:**
  - If there is no check mark next to Word Wrap, click the **Word Wrap** command to enable this feature.
  - If there is a check mark next to Word Wrap, click outside the menu to close the menu without changing any settings.
- Type the text of the document as shown in Figure 10e. Type just as you would on a regular typewriter with one exception—press the enter key only at the end of a paragraph, not at the end of every line. Since word wrap is in effect, Notepad will automatically start a new line when the word you are typing does not fit at the end of the current line.
- Pull down the **File menu** and click **Save** to save the document when you are finished.
- Click the **Close button** to close the Notepad accessory.

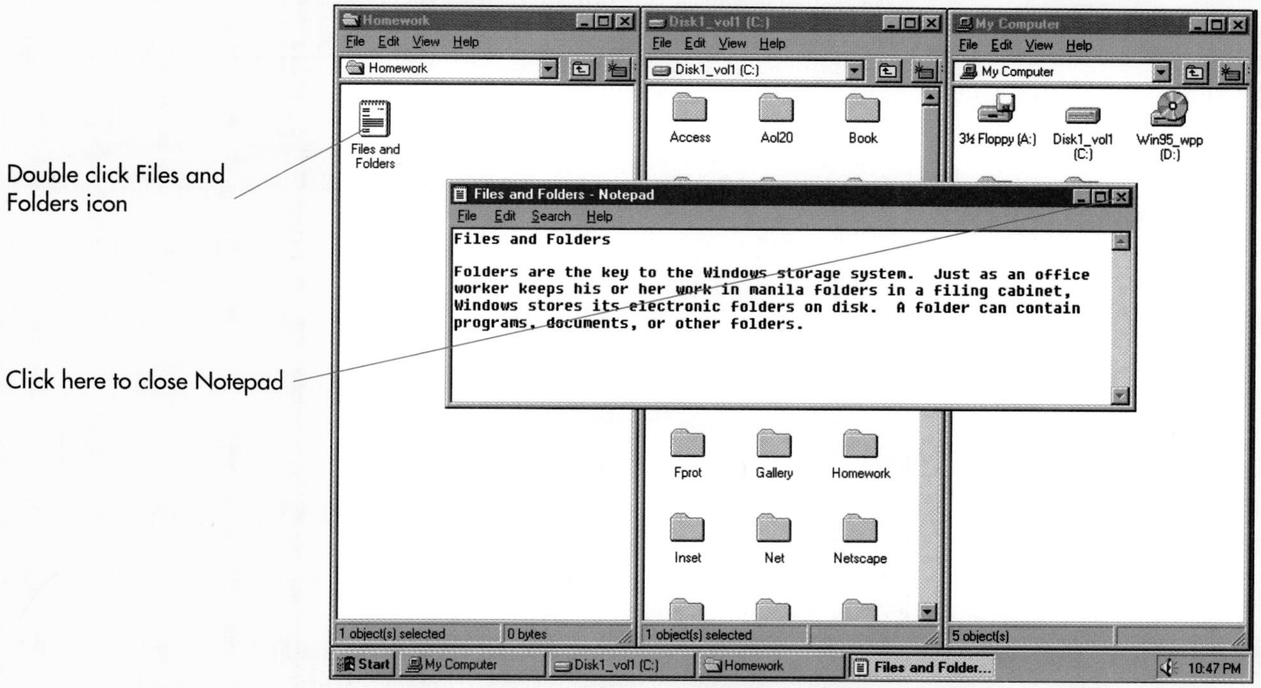
Double click Files and Folders icon
Click here to close Notepad
Homework
Disk1_vol1 (C:)
My Computer
Files and Folders
Access
Aol20
Book
3½ Floppy (A:)
Disk1_vol1 (C:)
Win95_wpp (D:)
Files and Folders - Notepad
File Edit Search Help
Files and Folders
Folders are the key to the Windows storage system. Just as an office worker keeps his or her work in manila folders in a filing cabinet, Windows stores its electronic folders on disk. A folder can contain programs, documents, or other folders.
Fprot
Gallery
Homework
Inset
Net
Netscape
1 object(s) selected
0 bytes
5 object(s)
Start
Files and Folder...
10:47 PM

(e) Create the Document (step 5)

FIGURE 10 Hands-on Exercise 2 (continued)

FILE EXTENSIONS

Long-time DOS users will recognize a three-character extension at the end of a file name to indicate the file type; for example, TXT to indicate a text (ASCII) file. The extensions are displayed or hidden according to the option you establish through the View menu of My Computer. Open My Computer, pull down the View menu, and click the Options command. Click the View tab, then check (clear) the box to hide (show) MS-DOS file extensions. Click OK.

STEP 6: Create a Drawing

- **Right click** within the Homework folder, click the **New command,** then click **Bitmap Image** as the type of file to create. The icon for a new drawing will appear with the name of the drawing (New Bitmap Image) highlighted.
- Type **Rectangles** to change the name of the drawing. Press **enter.**
- Pull down the **File menu** and click **Open** (or double click the **Rectangles icon** without pulling down the menu) to open a Paint window. The window is empty because the drawing has not yet been created.
- Click the **Maximize button** (if necessary) so that the window takes the entire desktop. Create a drawing of various rectangles as shown in Figure 10f.
- To draw a rectangle:
  - Select (click) the rectangle tool.

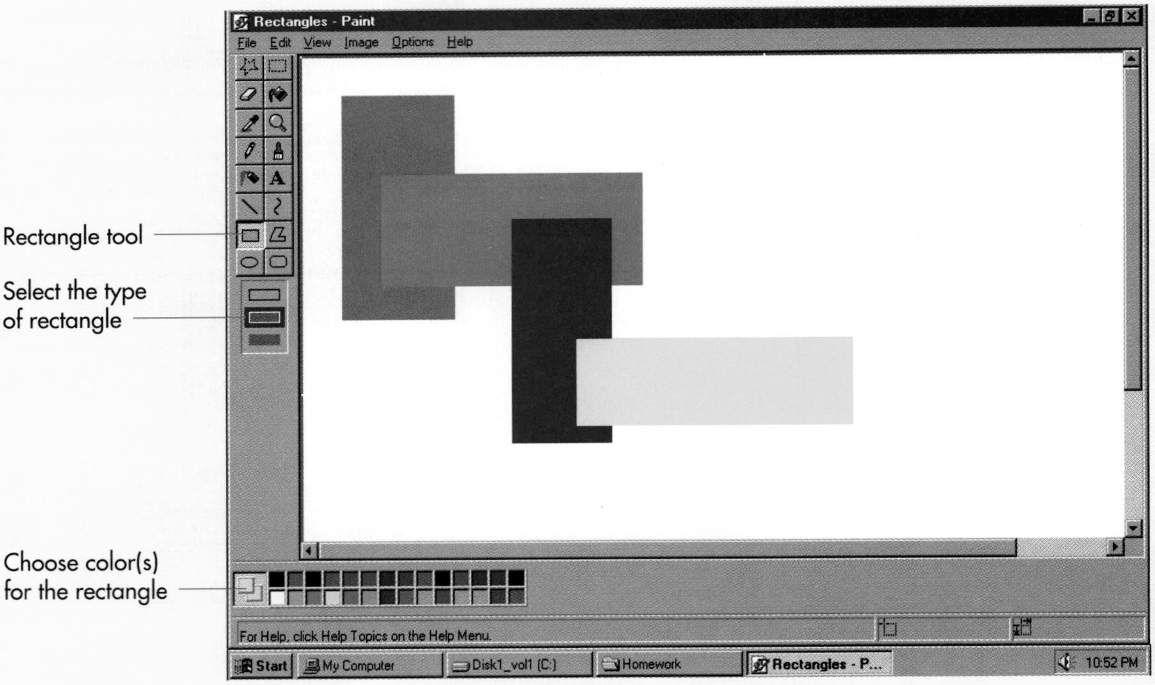

Rectangle tool
Select the type of rectangle
Choose color(s) for the rectangle
Rectangles - Paint
File Edit View Image Options Help
For Help, click Help Topics on the Help Menu.
Start
My Computer
Disk1_vol1 (C:)
Homework
Rectangles - P...
10:52 PM

(f) Create the Drawing (step 6)

FIGURE 10 Hands-on Exercise 2 (continued)

- Select (click) the type of rectangle you want (a border only, a filled rectangle with a border, or a filled rectangle with no border).
- Select (click) the colors for the border and fill using the left and right mouse button, respectively.
- Click in the drawing area, then click and drag to create the rectangle.

➤ Pull down the **File menu** and click **Save As** to produce the Save As dialog box. Change the file type to **16-Color Bitmap** (from the default 256-color bitmap) to create a smaller file and conserve space on the floppy disk.

➤ Click **Save.** Click **Yes** to replace the file.

➤ Click the **Close button** to close Paint when you have finished the drawing.

THE PAINT ACCESSORY

The Paint accessory enables you to create simple or (depending on your ability) elaborate drawings. There is a sense of familiarity to the application since it follows the common user interface and consistent command structure common to all Windows applications. The Open, Save, and Print commands, for example, are found in the File menu. The Cut, Copy, Paste, and Undo commands are in the Edit menu. There is also a Help menu, which explains the various Paint commands and which functions identically to the Help menu in all Windows applications.

STEP 7: Edit the Document

➤ Double click the **Files and Folders icon** to reopen the document in a Notepad window. Pull down the **Edit menu** and toggle **Word Wrap on.** Press **Ctrl+End** to move to the end of the document.

➤ Add the additional text as shown in Figure 10g. Do *not* save the document at this time.

➤ Click the **Close button** to exit Notepad. You will see the informational message in Figure 10g, which indicates you have forgotten to save the changes. Click **Yes** to save the changes and exit.

DOS NOTATION

The visually oriented storage system within Windows 95 makes it easy to identify folders and the documents within those folders. DOS, however, was not so simple and used a text-based notation to indicate the drive, folder, and file. For example, C:\HOMEWORK\FILES AND FOLDERS specifies the file FILES AND FOLDERS, in the HOMEWORK folder, on drive C.

STEP 8: Change the View

➤ Right click an empty space on the taskbar, then click the **Tile Horizontally command** to tile the windows as shown in Figure 10h. (The order of your windows may be different from ours.)

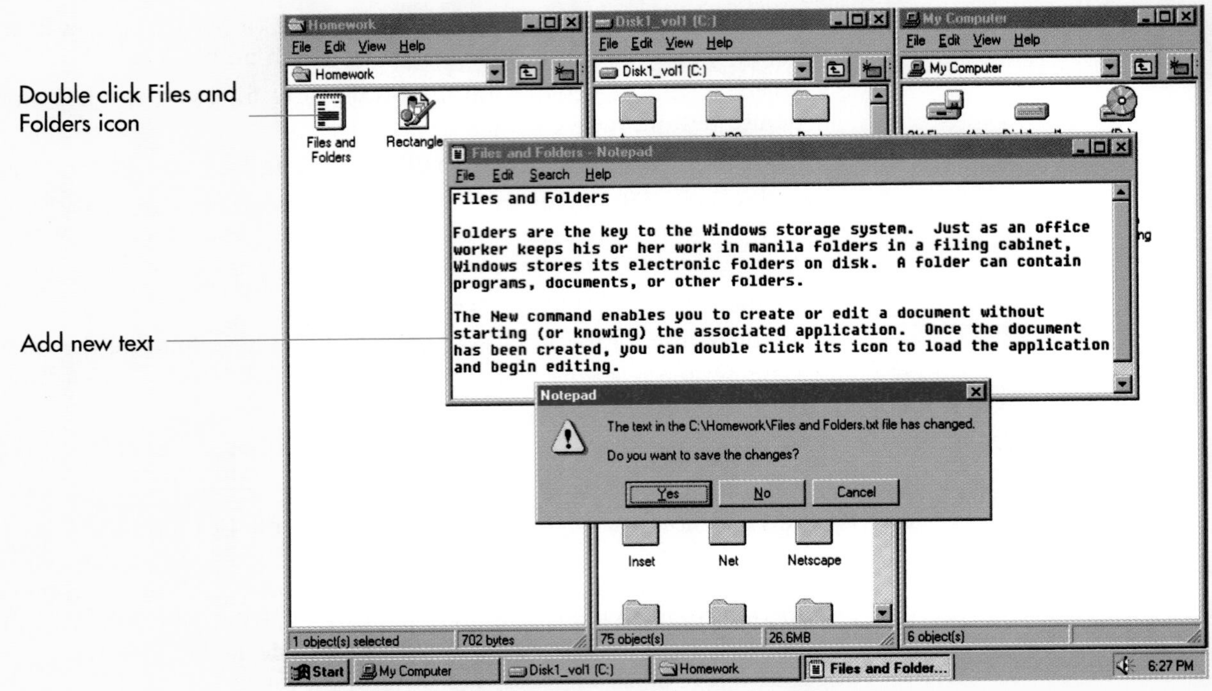
Double click Files and Folders icon
Add new text
Homework
File Edit View Help
Files and Folders
Rectangle
Disk1_vol1 (C:)
My Computer
Files and Folders - Notepad
File Edit Search Help
Files and Folders
Folders are the key to the Windows storage system. Just as an office worker keeps his or her work in manila folders in a filing cabinet, Windows stores its electronic folders on disk. A folder can contain programs, documents, or other folders.
The New command enables you to create or edit a document without starting (or knowing) the associated application. Once the document has been created, you can double click its icon to load the application and begin editing.
Notepad
The text in the C:\Homework\Files and Folders.txt file has changed.
Do you want to save the changes?
Yes
No
Cancel
Inset
Net
Netscape
1 object(s) selected
702 bytes
75 object(s)
26.6MB
6 object(s)
Start
My Computer
Disk1_vol1 (C:)
Homework
Files and Folder...
6:27 PM

(g) Edit the Document (step 7)

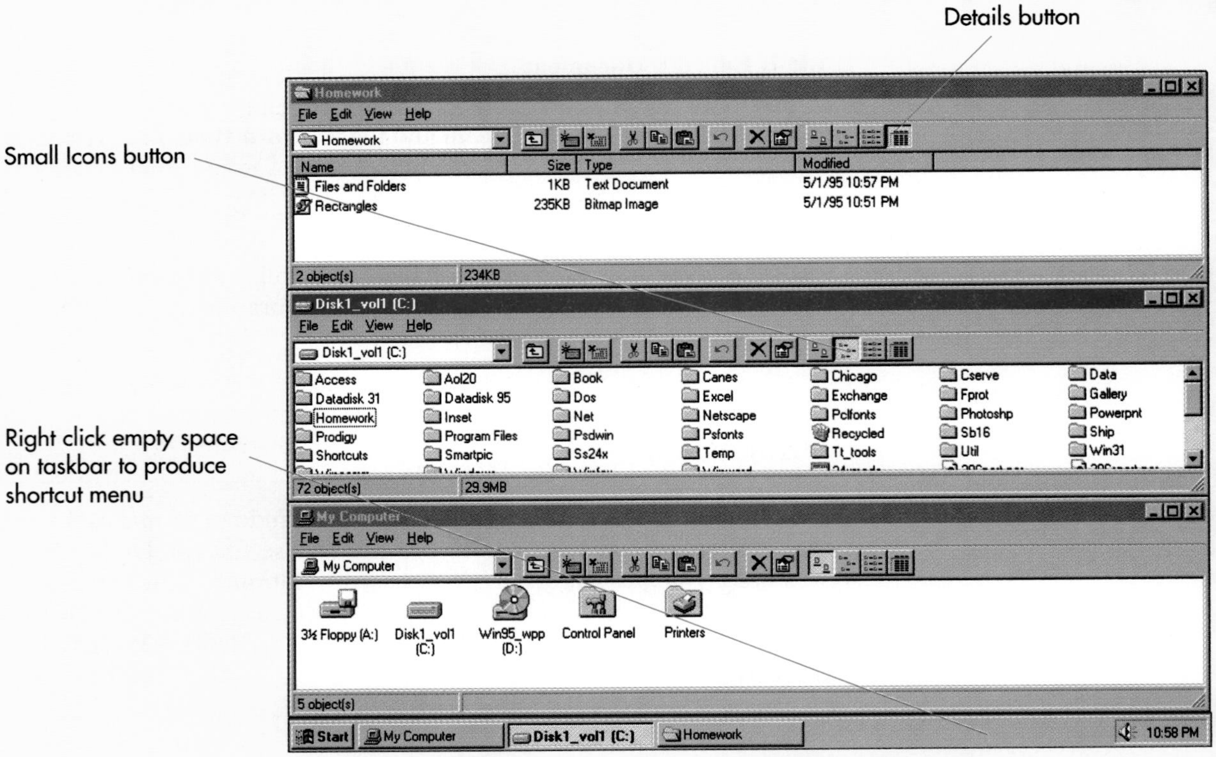
Details button
Small Icons button
Right click empty space on taskbar to produce shortcut menu
Homework
File Edit View Help
Name
Size
Type
Modified
Files and Folders
1KB
Text Document
5/1/95 10:57 PM
Rectangles
235KB
Bitmap Image
5/1/95 10:51 PM
2 object(s)
234KB
Disk1_vol1 (C:)
Access
Datadisk 31
Homework
Prodigy
Shortcuts
Aol20
Datadisk 95
Inset
Program Files
Smartpic
Book
Dos
Net
Psdwin
Ss24x
Canes
Excel
Netscape
Psfonts
Temp
Chicago
Exchange
Pclfonts
Recycled
Tt_tools
Cserve
Fprot
Photoshp
Sb16
Util
Data
Gallery
Powerpnt
Ship
Win31
72 object(s)
29.9MB
My Computer
3½ Floppy (A:)
Disk1_vol1 (C:)
Win95_wpp (D:)
Control Panel
Printers
5 object(s)
Start
My Computer
Disk1_vol1 (C:)
Homework
10:58 PM

(h) Change the View (step 7)

FIGURE 10 Hands-on Exercise 2 (continued)

➤ Click in the window for the **Homework folder,** then click the **Details button** on the toolbar to display the details view.

➤ Press the **F5 key** to refresh the window and update the file properties (the file size, type, and the date and time of the last modification).

➤ Click in the window for drive C, then click the **List view** or **Small Icons button** on the toolbar to display small icons as shown in Figure 10h.

STEP 9: Continue with the Next Exercise

➤ You have created a folder and several documents on drive C that you will need in the next exercise. Hence, if you are working at school and cannot be guaranteed the same machine the next time you enter the lab, it is important that you continue with the next exercise at this time. Otherwise, you will have to re-create all of the files in this exercise.

FILE OPERATIONS

The exercise just completed had you create a folder and place documents in that folder. As you continue to work on the computer, you will create additional folders, as well as files within those folders. Learning how to manage those files is one of the most important skills you can acquire. This section describes the different types of file operations that you will perform on a daily basis.

Moving and Copying a File

There are two basic ways to move or copy a file from one location to another. You can use the ***Cut, Copy,*** and ***Paste commands,*** or you can simply drag and drop the files from one location to the other. Both techniques require you to open the disk or folder containing the source file (the file you are moving or copying) in order to select the file you will move or copy. This is typically done by opening successive windows through My Computer.

Assume, for example, that you want to copy a file from the Homework folder on drive C to a floppy disk in drive A. You would begin by double clicking the My Computer icon to open the My Computer window. Then you would double click the icon for drive C because that is the drive containing the file you want to copy. And then you would double click the icon for the Homework folder (opening a third window) because that is the folder containing the file to be copied.

To copy the file (after the Homework folder has been opened), select the file by clicking its icon, then drag the icon to the drive A icon in the My Computer window. (Alternatively, you could select the file, pull down the Edit menu, and click the Copy command, then click the icon for drive A, pull down the Edit menu, and click the Paste command.) It sounds complicated, but it's not and you will get a chance to practice in the hands-on exercise.

Backup

It's not a question of if it will happen, but when—hard disks die, files are lost, or viruses may infect a system. It has happened to us and it will happen to you, but you can prepare for the inevitable by creating adequate ***backup*** *before* the problem occurs. The essence of a backup strategy is to decide which files to back up, how often to do the backup, and where to keep the backup. Once you decide on a strategy, follow it, and follow it faithfully!

Our strategy is very simple—back up what you can't afford to lose, do so on a daily basis, and store the backup away from your computer. You need not copy every file, every day. Instead copy just the files that changed during the current session. Realize, too, that it is much more important to back up your data files, rather than your program files. You can always reinstall the application from the original disks, or if necessary, go to the vendor for another copy of an application. You, however, are the only one who has a copy of the term paper that is due tomorrow.

Deleting Files

The ***Delete command*** deletes (removes) a file from a disk. If, however, the file was deleted from a hard disk, it is not really gone, but moved instead to the Recycle Bin from where it can be subsequently recovered.

The ***Recycle Bin*** is a special folder that contains all of the files that were previously deleted from any hard disk on your system. Think of the Recycle Bin as similar to the wastebasket in your room. You throw out (delete) a report by tossing it into a wastebasket. The report is gone (deleted) from your desk, but you can still get it back by taking it out of the wastebasket as long as the basket wasn't emptied. The Recycle Bin works the same way. Files are not deleted from the hard disk per se, but are moved instead to the Recycle Bin from where they can be recovered. The Recycle Bin should be emptied periodically, however, or else you will run out of space on the disk. Once a file is removed from the Recycle Bin, it can no longer be recovered.

WRITE-PROTECT YOUR BACKUP DISKS

You can write-protect a floppy disk to ensure that its contents are not accidentally altered or erased. A 3½-inch disk is write-protected by sliding the built-in tab so that the write-protect notch is open. The disk is write-enabled when the notch is covered. The procedure is reversed for a 5¼-inch disk; that is, the disk is write-protected when the notch is covered and write-enabled when the notch is open.

HANDS-ON EXERCISE 3

File Operations

Objective: Copy a file from drive C to drive A, and from drive A back to drive C. Delete a file from drive C, then restore the file using the Recycle Bin. Demonstrate the effects of write-protecting a disk. Use Figure 11 as a guide in the exercise.

STEP 1: Open the Homework Folder

➤ Double click the **icon** for **My Computer** to open My Computer. Double click the **icon** for **drive C** to open a second window showing the contents of drive C. Double click the **Homework folder** to open a third window showing the contents of the Homework folder.

- ➤ Right click the taskbar to tile the windows vertically as shown in Figure 11a. Your windows may appear in a different order from those in the figure.
- ➤ Make or verify the following selections in each window. (You have to pull down the View menu each time you choose a different command.)
  - The **Toolbar command** should be checked.
  - The **Status Bar command** should be checked.
  - Choose the **Details view** in the Homework window and the **Large Icons view** in the other windows.
- ➤ Pull down the **View menu** in any open window. Click **Options,** then click the **View tab** in the Options dialog box. Check the box (if necessary) to **Hide MS-DOS file extensions.** Click **OK** to exit the dialog box.

QUICK VIEW

If you forget what is in a particular document, you can use the Quick View command to preview the document without having to open it. Select (click) the file you want to preview, then pull down the File menu and click Quick View (or right click the file and select the Quick View command) to display the file in a preview window. If you decide to edit the file, pull down the File menu and click Open File for Editing; otherwise click the Close button to close the preview window.

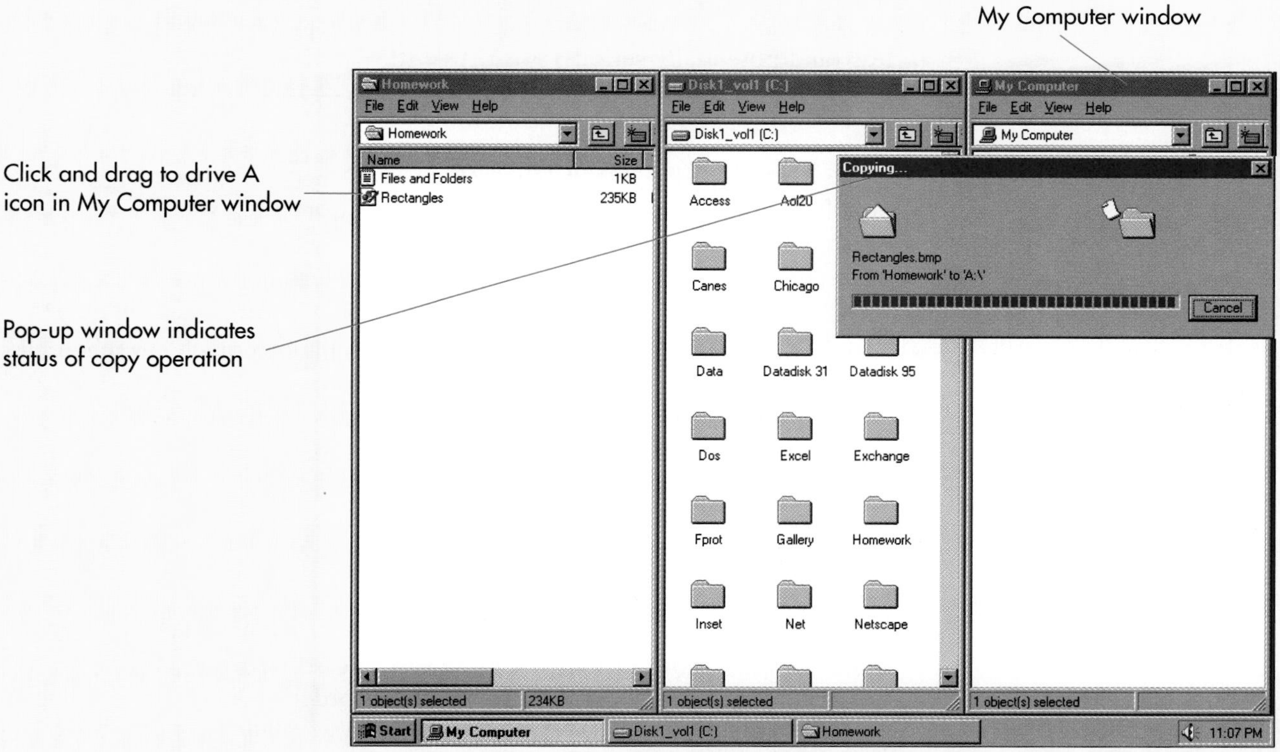
My Computer window
Click and drag to drive A icon in My Computer window
Pop-up window indicates status of copy operation
Homework
File Edit View Help
Name
Size
Files and Folders
1KB
Rectangles
235KB
Disk1_vol1 (C:)
Access
Aol20
Canes
Chicago
Data
Datadisk 31
Datadisk 95
Dos
Excel
Exchange
Fprot
Gallery
Homework
Inset
Net
Netscape
My Computer
Copying...
Rectangles.bmp
From 'Homework' to 'A:\'
Cancel
1 object(s) selected
234KB
Start
11:07 PM

(a) Copy to Drive A (step 1)

FIGURE 11 Hands-on Exercise 3

STEP 2: Backup the Homework Folder

➤ Place a freshly formatted disk in drive A. Be sure that the disk is not write-protected or else you will not be able to copy files to the disk.

➤ Click and drag the icon for the **Rectangles file** from the Homework folder to the icon for **drive A** in the My Computer window.

- You will see the ⃠ symbol as you drag the file until you reach a suitable destination (e.g., until you point to the icon for drive A). The ⃠ symbol will change to a plus sign when the icon for drive A is highlighted, indicating that the file can be copied successfully.
- Release the mouse to complete the copy operation. You will see a popup window as shown in Figure 11a, indicating the progress of the copy operation. This takes several seconds since Rectangles is a large file (235KB).

➤ Click and drag the icon for the **Files and Folders file** from the Homework folder to the icon for drive A. You may or may not see a popup window showing the copy operation since the file is small (1KB) and copies quickly.

USE THE RIGHT MOUSE BUTTON TO MOVE OR COPY A FILE

The result of dragging a file with the left mouse button depends on whether the source and destination folders are on the same or different drives. Dragging a file to a folder on a different drive copies the file. Dragging the file to a folder on the same drive moves the file. If you find this hard to remember, and most people do, click and drag with the right mouse button to produce a shortcut menu asking whether you want to copy or move the file. This simple tip can save you from making a careless (and potentially serious) error. Use it!

STEP 3: View the Contents of Drive A

➤ Double click the **icon** for **drive A** in the My Computer window to open a fourth window.

➤ Right click a blank area on the taskbar. Tile the windows vertically or horizontally (it doesn't matter which) to display the windows as in Figure 11b.

➤ Click in the window for drive A. If necessary, pull down the **View menu,** display the toolbar, and change to the **Details view.**

➤ Compare the file details for each file in the Homework folder and drive A; the details are identical, reflecting the fact that the files have been copied.

CHANGE THE COLUMN WIDTH

Drag the right border of a column heading to the right (left) to increase (decrease) the width of the column in order to see more (less) information in that column. Double click the right border of a column heading to automatically adjust the column width to accommodate the widest entry in that column.

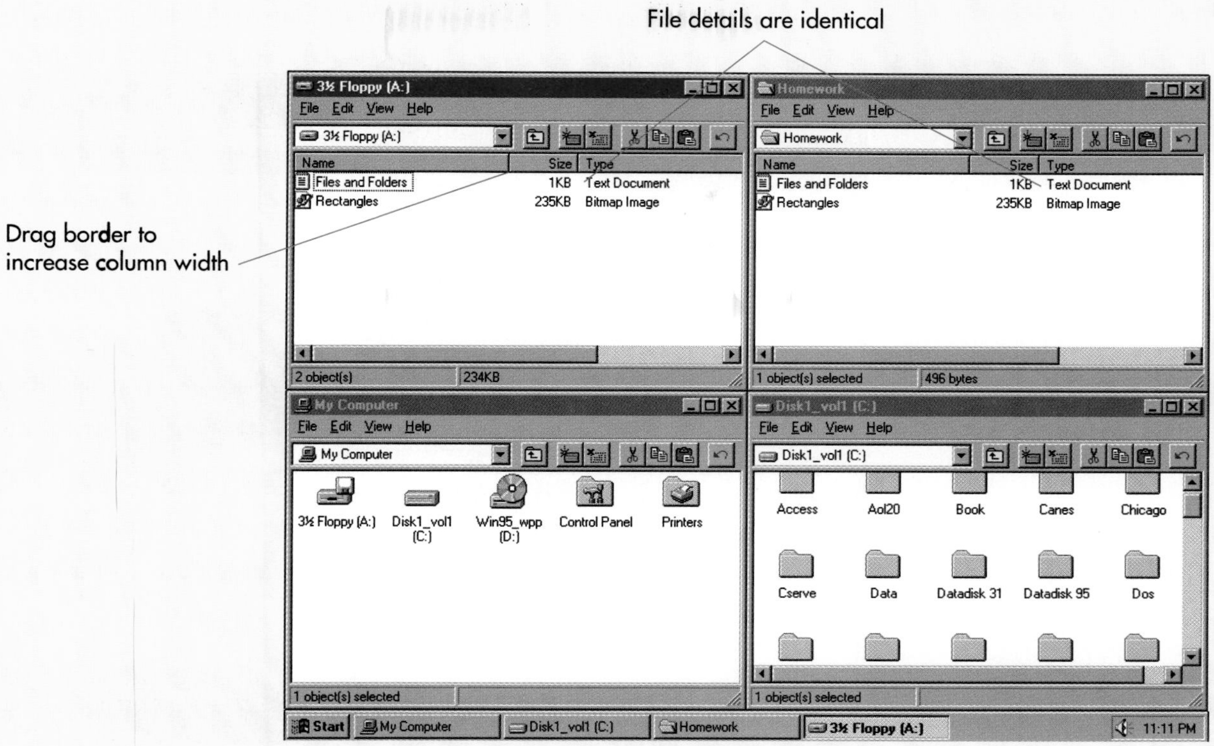
File details are identical
Drag border to
increase column width
3½ Floppy (A:)
File Edit View Help
Name
Size
Type
Files and Folders
1KB
Text Document
Rectangles
235KB
Bitmap Image
2 object(s)
234KB
Homework
1 object(s) selected
496 bytes
My Computer
3½ Floppy (A:)
Disk1_vol1 (C:)
Win95_wpp (D:)
Control Panel
Printers
Access
Aol20
Book
Canes
Chicago
Cserve
Data
Datadisk 31
Datadisk 95
Dos
Start
11:11 PM

(b) View the Contents of Drive A (step 3)

FIGURE 11 Hands-on Exercise 3 (continued)

STEP 4: Delete a File

- Select (click) the **Files and Folders icon** in the Homework folder. Pull down the **File menu.** Click **Delete.**
- You will see the dialog box in Figure 11c, asking whether you want to delete the file. Click **Yes** to delete the file.
- Right click the **Rectangles icon** in the Homework folder to display a shortcut menu. Click **Delete.**
- Click **Yes** when asked whether to delete the Rectangles file. The Homework folder is now empty.

THE UNDO COMMAND

The Undo command pertains not just to application programs such as Notepad or Paint, but to file operations as well. It will, for example, undelete a file if it is executed immediately after the Delete command. Pull down the Edit menu and click Undo to reverse (undo) the last command. Some operations cannot be undone (in which case the command will be dimmed out), but Undo is always worth a try.

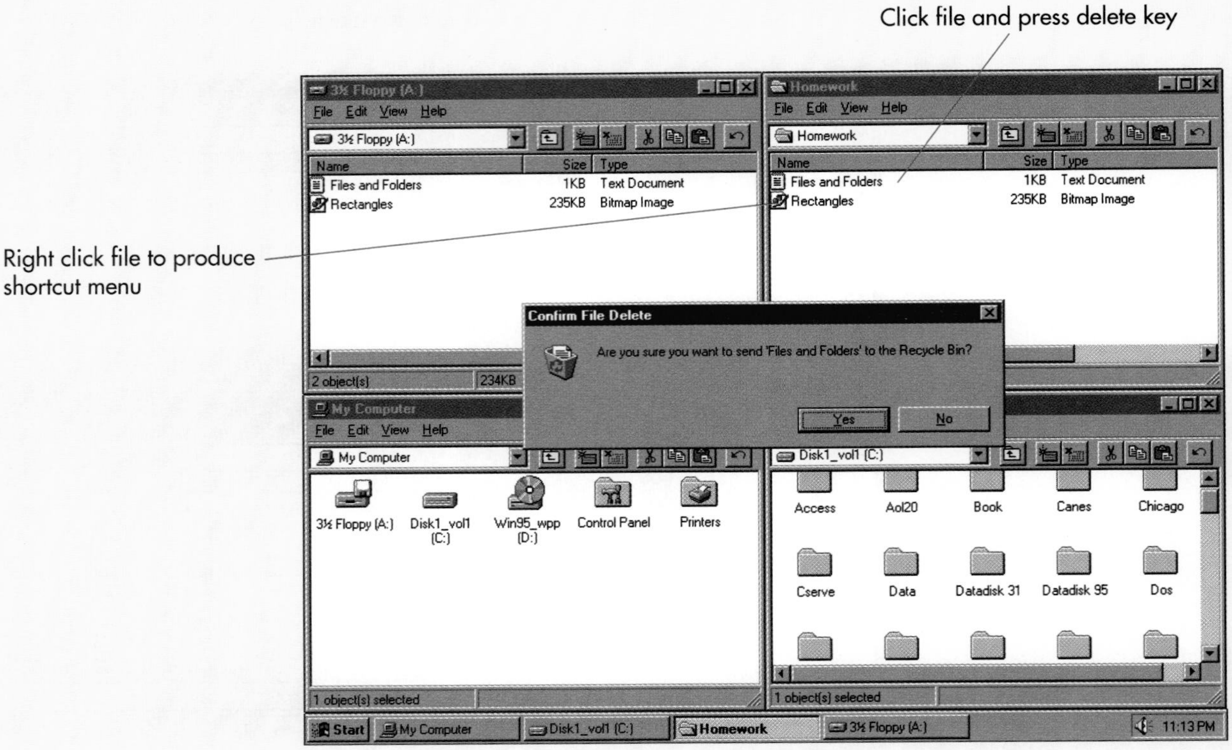

Click file and press delete key
Right click file to produce shortcut menu
3½ Floppy (A:)
File Edit View Help
Name
Size
Type
Files and Folders
1KB
Text Document
Rectangles
235KB
Bitmap Image
Homework
Confirm File Delete
Are you sure you want to send 'Files and Folders' to the Recycle Bin?
Yes
No
My Computer
Disk1_vol1 (C:)
Win95_wpp (D:)
Control Panel
Printers
Access
Aol20
Book
Canes
Chicago
Cserve
Data
Datadisk 31
Datadisk 95
Dos
1 object(s) selected
Start
11:13 PM

(c) Delete a File (step 4)

FIGURE 11 Hands-on Exercise 3 (continued)

STEP 5: Copy from Drive A to Drive C

➤ The backup you did in step 2 enables you to copy (restore) the Files and Folders file from drive A to drive C. You can do this in one of two ways:
  - Select (click) the **Files and Folders icon** in the window for drive A. Pull down the **Edit menu.** Click **Copy.** Click in the **Homework folder.** Pull down the **Edit menu.** Click **Paste** as shown in Figure 11d.
  - Click and drag the **icon** for the **Files and Folders file** from drive A to the Homework folder.

➤ Either way, you will see a popup window showing the Files and Folders file being copied from drive A to drive C.

➤ Use whichever technique you prefer to copy the Rectangles file from drive A to drive C.

BACK UP IMPORTANT FILES

We cannot overemphasize the importance of adequate backup and urge you to copy your data files to floppy disks and store those disks away from your computer. It takes only a few minutes, but you will thank us, when (not if) you lose an important file and wish you had another copy.

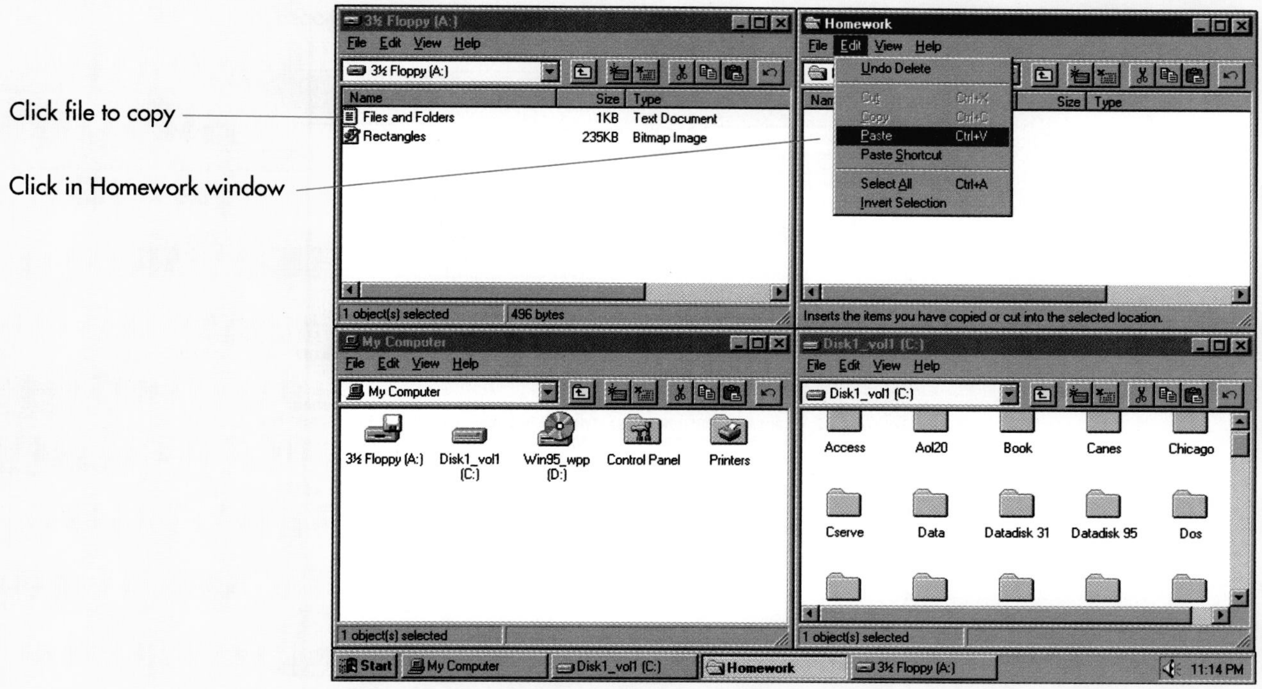
Click file to copy
Click in Homework window
3½ Floppy (A:)
File Edit View Help
Name Size Type
Files and Folders 1KB Text Document
Rectangles 235KB Bitmap Image
1 object(s) selected 496 bytes
Homework
Undo Delete
Cut Ctrl+X
Copy Ctrl+C
Paste Ctrl+V
Paste Shortcut
Select All Ctrl+A
Invert Selection
Inserts the items you have copied or cut into the selected location.
My Computer
3½ Floppy (A:)
Disk1_vol1 (C:)
Win95_wpp (D:)
Control Panel
Printers
1 object(s) selected
Disk1_vol1 (C:)
Access
Aol20
Book
Canes
Chicago
Cserve
Data
Datadisk 31
Datadisk 95
Dos
1 object(s) selected
Start
Homework
11:14 PM

(d) Copy to Drive C (step 5)

FIGURE 11 Hands-on Exercise 3 (continued)

STEP 6: Modify a File

- Double click the **Files and Folders icon** in the Homework folder to reopen the file as shown in Figure 11e. Pull down the **Edit menu** and toggle **Word Wrap on.**
- Press **Ctrl+End** to move to the end of the document. Add the paragraph shown in Figure 11e.
- Pull down the **File menu** and click **Save** to save the modified file. Click the **Close button** to close the file.
- The Files and Folders document has been modified and should once again be backed up to drive A. Click and drag the **icon** for **Files and Folders** from the Homework folder to the drive A window.
- You will see a message indicating that the folder (drive A) already contains a file called Files and Folders (which was previously copied in step 2) and asking whether you want to replace the existing file with the new file. Click **Yes.**

THE SEND TO COMMAND

The Send To command is an alternative way to copy a file to a floppy disk and has the advantage that the floppy disk icon need not be visible. Select (click) the file to copy, then pull down the File menu (or simply right click the file). Click the Send To command, then select the appropriate floppy drive from the resulting submenu.

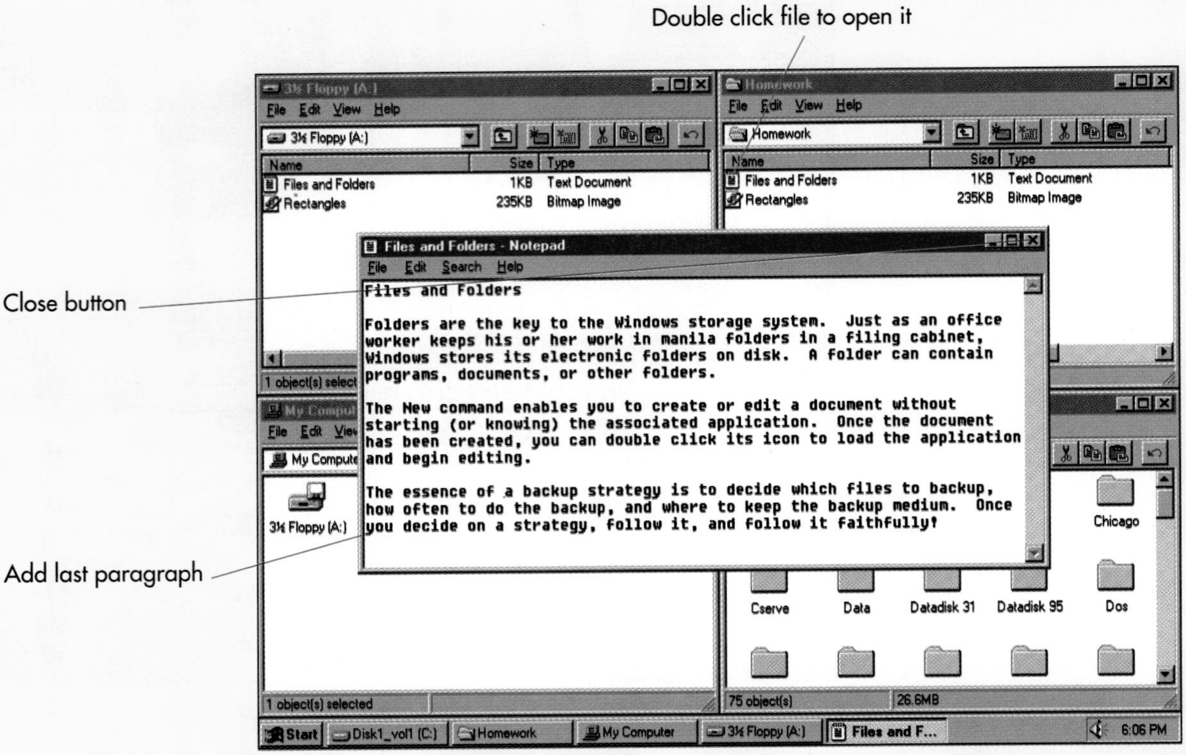
Double click file to open it
Close button
Add last paragraph
Files and Folders - Notepad
Files and Folders
Folders are the key to the Windows storage system. Just as an office worker keeps his or her work in manila folders in a filing cabinet, Windows stores its electronic folders on disk. A folder can contain programs, documents, or other folders.
The New command enables you to create or edit a document without starting (or knowing) the associated application. Once the document has been created, you can double click its icon to load the application and begin editing.
The essence of a backup strategy is to decide which files to backup, how often to do the backup, and where to keep the backup medium. Once you decide on a strategy, follow it, and follow it faithfully!

(e) Modify the File (step 6)

FIGURE 11 Hands-on Exercise 3 (continued)

STEP 7: Write-protect a Disk

- You can write-protect a floppy disk so that its contents cannot be changed; that is, existing files cannot be modified or erased nor can new files be added.
- Remove the floppy disk from drive A and follow the appropriate procedure:
  - To write-protect a 3½ disk, move the built-in tab so that the write-protect notch is open.
  - To write-protect a 5¼ disk, cover the write-protect notch with a piece of opaque tape.
- Return the write-protected disk to the floppy drive.
- Click the **icon** for the **Rectangles file** on drive A, then press the **Del key** to delete the file.
- You will see a warning message asking whether you are sure you want to delete the file. Click **Yes.**
- You will see the error message in Figure 11f, indicating that the file cannot be deleted because the disk is write-protected. Click **OK.**
- Remove the write-protection by reversing the procedure you followed earlier. Select the **Rectangles file** a second time and delete the file. Click **Yes** in response to the confirmation message, after which the file will be deleted from drive A.
- You have just deleted the Rectangles file, but we want it back on drive A for the next exercise. Accordingly, click and drag the **Rectangles icon** in the Homework folder to the icon for **drive A** in the My Computer window.

Click file to delete, press Del key

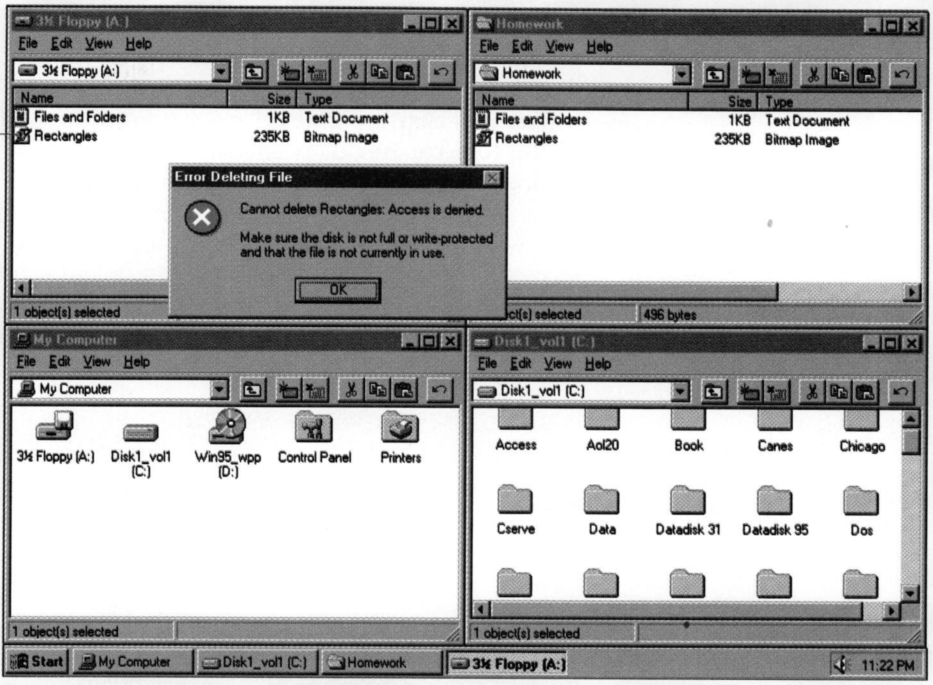

3½ Floppy (A:)
File Edit View Help
Name
Size
Type
Files and Folders
1KB
Text Document
Rectangles
235KB
Bitmap Image
Error Deleting File
Cannot delete Rectangles: Access is denied.
Make sure the disk is not full or write-protected and that the file is not currently in use.
OK
1 object(s) selected
Homework
496 bytes
My Computer
3½ Floppy (A:)
Disk1_vol1 (C:)
Win95_wpp (D:)
Control Panel
Printers
Access
Aol20
Book
Canes
Chicago
Cserve
Data
Datadisk 31
Datadisk 95
Dos
Start
11:22 PM

(f) Write-Protect a Disk (step 7)

FIGURE 11 Hands-on Exercise 3 (continued)

➤ Click the **Close button** in the window for drive A.

STEP 8: The Recycle Bin

➤ Select (click) the **Files and Folders icon** in the Homework folder. Pull down the **File menu** and click **Delete.** Click **Yes** in the dialog box asking whether you want to delete the file.

➤ To restore a file, you need to open the Recycle Bin:

- Double click the **Recycle Bin icon** if you can see the icon on the desktop *or*
- Double click the **Recycled icon** within the window for drive C. (You may have to scroll in order to see the icon.)

➤ Right click a blank area on the taskbar, then tile the open windows as shown in Figure 11g. The position of your windows may be different from ours. The view in the Recycle Bin may also be different.

➤ Your Recycle Bin contains all files that have been previously deleted from drive C, and hence you may see a different number of files than those displayed in Figure 11g.

➤ Scroll until you can select the (most recent) **Files and Folders icon.** Pull down the **File menu** and click the **Restore command.** The Files and Folders file is returned to the Homework folder.

EMPTY THE RECYCLE BIN

All files that are deleted from a hard drive are automatically moved to the Recycle Bin. This enables you to restore (undelete) a file, but it also prevents you from recovering the space taken up by those files. Accordingly, you should periodically delete files from the Recycle Bin or otherwise you will find yourself running out of space on your hard disk. Be careful, though, because once you delete a file from the Recycle Bin, it is gone for good!

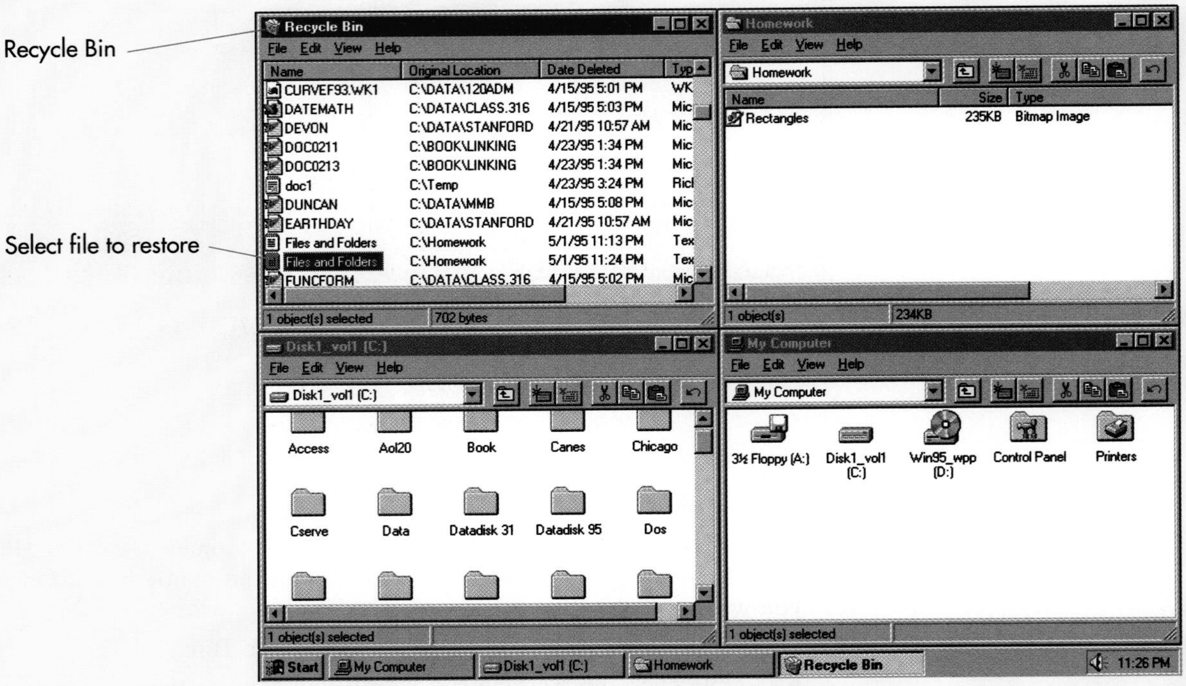

Recycle Bin
Select file to restore

(g) The Recycle Bin (step 8)

FIGURE 11 Hands-on Exercise 3 (continued)

STEP 9: Exit Windows

- Click the **Close button** in each of the four open windows (the Recycle Bin, My Computer, drive C, and Homework) to close each window.
- Exit Windows if you do not want to continue with the next exercise.

WINDOWS EXPLORER

The ***Windows Explorer*** enables you to browse through all of the drives, folders, and files on your system. It does not do anything that could not be accomplished through successive windows via My Computer. The Explorer does, however, let you perform a given task more quickly, and for that reason is preferred by more experienced users.

Assume, for example, that you are taking five classes this semester, and that you are using the computer in each course. You've created a separate folder to hold the work for each class and have stored the contents of all five folders on a single floppy disk. Assume further that you need to retrieve your third English assignment so that you can modify the assignment.

You can use My Computer to browse the system as shown in Figure 12a. You would start by opening My Computer, double clicking the icon for drive A to open a second window, then double clicking the icon for the English folder to display its documents. The process is intuitive, but it can quickly lead to a desktop cluttered with open windows. And what if you next needed to work on a paper for Art History? That would require you to open the Art History folder, which produces yet another open window on the desktop.

The Explorer window in Figure 12b offers a more sophisticated way to browse the system as it shows the hierarchy of folders as well as the contents of the selected folder. The Explorer window is divided into two panes. The left pane contains a tree diagram of the entire system, showing all drives and optionally the folders in each drive. One (and only one) object is always selected in the left pane, and its contents are displayed automatically in the right pane.

Look carefully at the tree diagram in Figure 12b and note that the English folder is currently selected. The icon for the selected folder is an open folder to differentiate it from the other folders, which are closed and are not currently selected. The right pane displays the contents of the selected folder (English in Figure 12b) and is seen to contain three documents, Assignments 1, 2, and 3. The right pane is displayed in the Details view, but could just as easily have been displayed in another view (e.g., Large or Small Icons) by clicking the appropriate button on the toolbar.

As indicated, only one folder can be selected (open) at a time in the left pane, and its contents are displayed in the right pane. To see the contents of a different folder (e.g., Accounting), you would select (click) the Accounting folder, which will automatically close the English folder.

The tree diagram in the left pane displays the drives and their folders in hierarchical fashion. The desktop is always at the top of the hierarchy and contains My Computer, which in turn contains various drives, each of which contains folders, which in turn contain documents and/or additional folders. Each object may be expanded or collapsed to display or hide its subordinates.

Look again at the icon next to My Computer in Figure 12b, and you see a minus sign indicating that My Computer has been expanded to show the various drives on the system. There is also a minus sign next to the icon for drive A to indicate that it too has been expanded to show the folders on the disk. Note, however, the plus sign next to drives C and D, indicating that these parts of the tree are currently collapsed and thus their subordinates are not visible.

A folder may contain additional folders, and thus individual folders may also be expanded or collapsed. The minus sign to the left of the Finance folder in Figure 12b, for example, shows that the folder has been expanded and contains two additional folders, for Assignments and Spreadsheets, respectively. The plus sign next to the Accounting folder, however, indicates the opposite; that is, the folder is collapsed and its folders are not currently visible. A folder with neither a plus or minus sign, such as Art History or Marketing, means that the folder does not contain additional folders and cannot be expanded or collapsed.

The advantage of the Windows Explorer over My Computer is the uncluttered screen and ease with which you switch from one folder to the next. If, for example, you wanted to see the contents of the Art History folder, all you would do would be to click its icon in the left pane, which automatically changes the right pane to show the documents in Art History. The Explorer also makes it easy to move or copy a file from one folder or drive to another as you will see in the hands-on exercise that follows shortly.

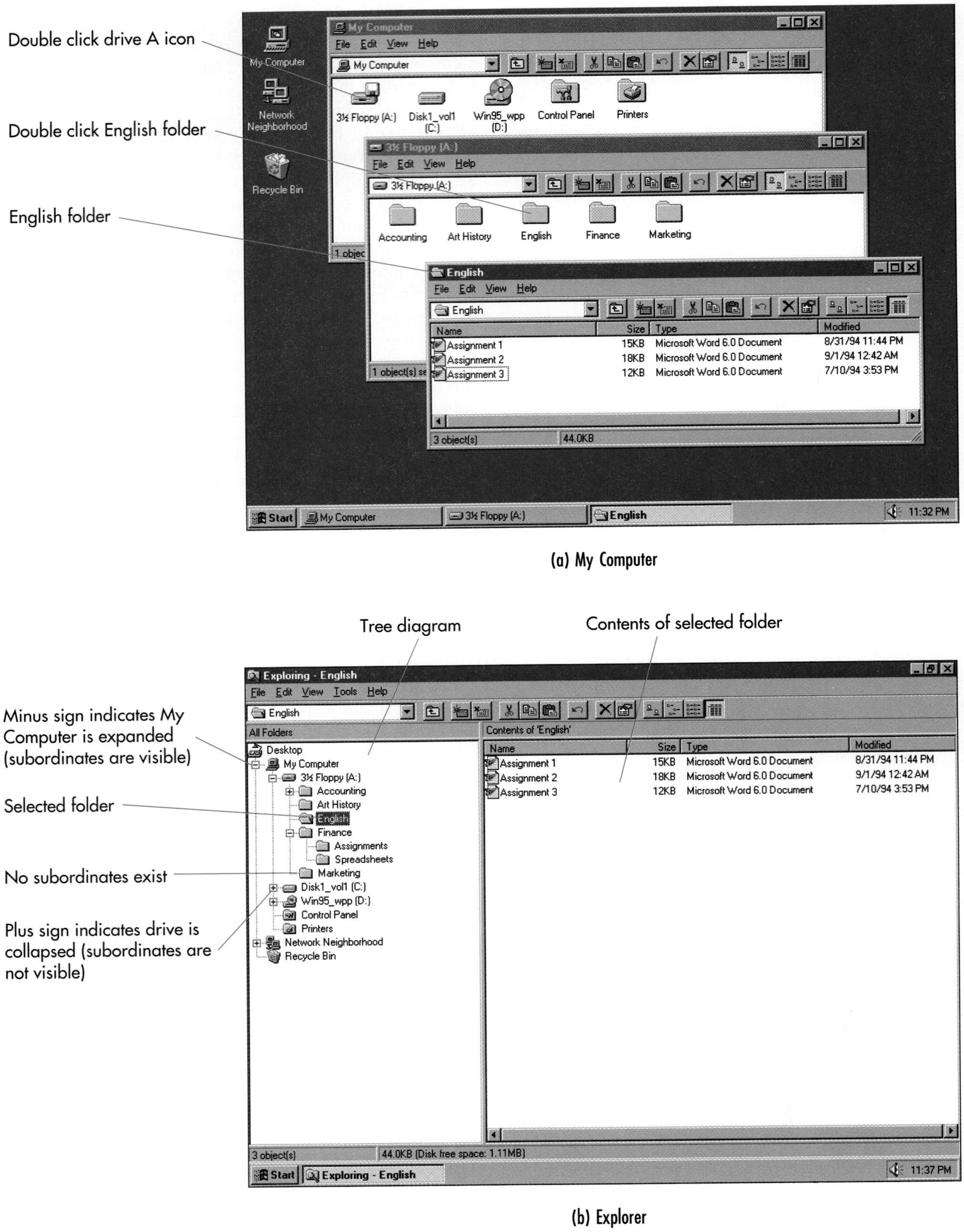

Double click drive A icon
Double click English folder
English folder
My Computer
File Edit View Help
3½ Floppy (A:)
Disk1_vol1 (C:)
Win95_wpp (D:)
Control Panel
Printers
Accounting
Art History
English
Finance
Marketing
Name Size Type Modified
Assignment 1 15KB Microsoft Word 6.0 Document 8/31/94 11:44 PM
Assignment 2 18KB Microsoft Word 6.0 Document 9/1/94 12:42 AM
Assignment 3 12KB Microsoft Word 6.0 Document 7/10/94 3:53 PM
3 object(s) 44.0KB
Start
11:32 PM
(a) My Computer
Tree diagram
Contents of selected folder
Minus sign indicates My Computer is expanded (subordinates are visible)
Selected folder
No subordinates exist
Plus sign indicates drive is collapsed (subordinates are not visible)
Exploring - English
File Edit View Tools Help
All Folders
Contents of 'English'
Desktop
My Computer
3½ Floppy (A:)
Accounting
Art History
English
Finance
Assignments
Spreadsheets
Marketing
Disk1_vol1 (C:)
Win95_wpp (D:)
Control Panel
Printers
Network Neighborhood
Recycle Bin
3 object(s)
44.0KB (Disk free space: 1.11MB)
11:37 PM
(b) Explorer

FIGURE 12 Browsing a System

ORGANIZE YOUR WORK

A folder may contain anything at all—program files, document files, or even other folders. Organize your folders in ways that make sense to you such as a separate folder for every class you are taking. You can also create folders within a folder; for example, a correspondence folder may contain two folders of its own, one for business correspondence and one for personal letters.

LEARN BY DOING

The Explorer is especially useful for moving or copying files from one folder or drive to another. You simply open the folder that contains the file, use the scroll bar in the left pane (if necessary) so that the destination folder is visible, then drag the file from the right pane to the destination folder. The Explorer is a powerful tool, but it takes practice to master.

The next exercise illustrates the procedure for moving and copying files and uses the floppy disk from the previous exercise. The disk already contains two files—one Notepad document and one Paint drawing. The exercise has you create an additional document of each type so that there are a total of four files on the floppy disk. You then create two folders on the floppy disk, one for drawings and one for documents, and move the respective files into each folder. And finally, you copy the contents of each folder from drive A to a different folder on drive C. By the end of the exercise you will have had considerable practice in both moving and copying files.

HANDS-ON EXERCISE 4

Windows Explorer

Objective: Use the Windows Explorer to copy and move a file from one folder to another. Use Figure 13 as a guide in the exercise.

STEP 1: Open the Windows Explorer

- Click the **Start button.** Click (or point to) the **Programs command** to display the Programs menu. Click **Windows Explorer.**
- Click the **Maximize button** so that the Explorer takes the entire desktop as shown in Figure 13a. Do not be concerned if your screen is different from ours.
- Make or verify the following selections using the **View menu.** (You have to pull down the View menu each time you choose a different command.)
  - The **Toolbar command** should be checked.
  - The **Status Bar command** should be checked.
  - The **Details view** should be selected.
- Pull down the **View menu** a second time. Click **Options,** then click the **View tab** in the Options dialog box. Check the box (if necessary) to **Hide MS-DOS file extensions.** Click **OK.**

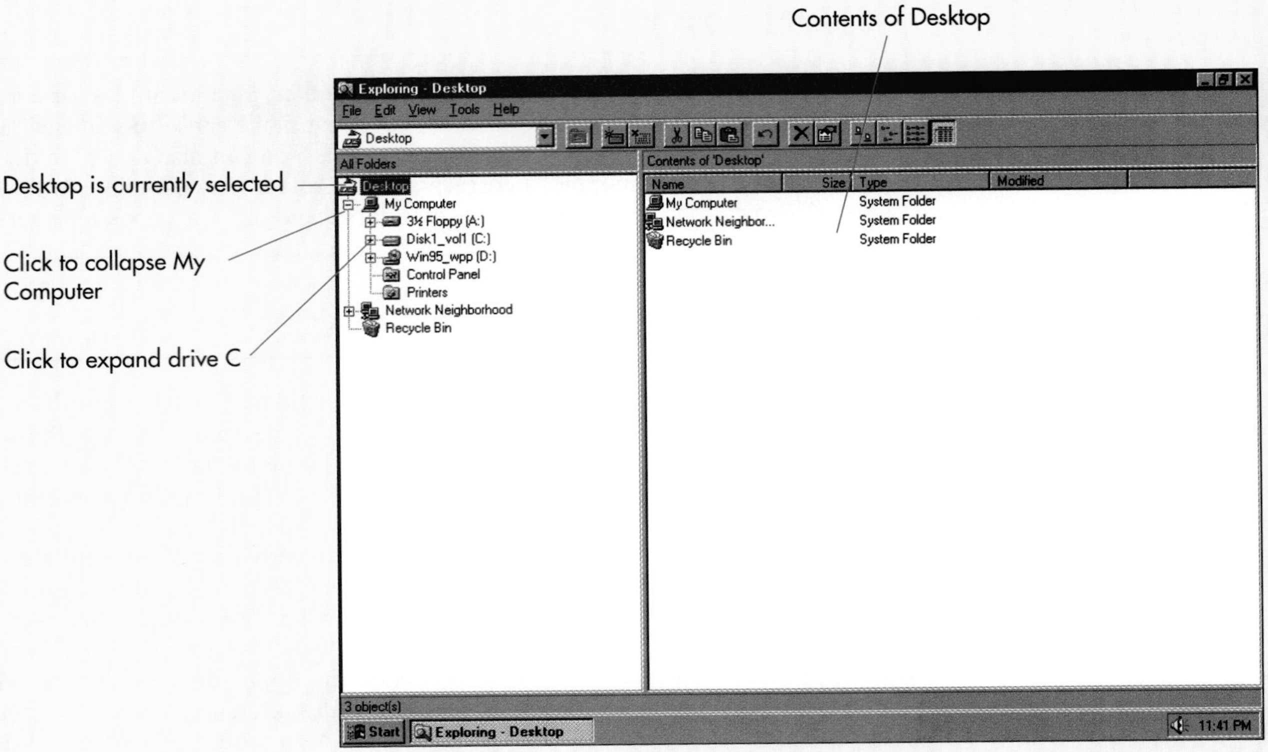
Contents of Desktop
Desktop is currently selected
Click to collapse My Computer
Click to expand drive C
Exploring - Desktop
File Edit View Tools Help
Desktop
All Folders
Contents of 'Desktop'
Desktop
My Computer
3½ Floppy (A:)
Disk1_vol1 (C:)
Win95_wpp (D:)
Control Panel
Printers
Network Neighborhood
Recycle Bin
Name
Size
Type
Modified
My Computer
Network Neighbor...
Recycle Bin
System Folder
System Folder
System Folder
3 object(s)
Start
Exploring - Desktop
11:41 PM

(a) Open the Windows Explorer (step 1)

FIGURE 13 Hands-on Exercise 4

STEP 2: Collapse and Expand My Computer

- Click (select) the **Desktop icon** in the left pane to display the contents of the desktop in the right pane. Our desktop contains only the icons for My Computer, Network Neighborhood, and the Recycle Bin. Your desktop may have different icons.
- Toggle back and forth between expanding and collapsing My Computer by clicking the plus or minus sign that appears next to the icon for My Computer. Clicking the plus sign expands My Computer, after which a minus sign is displayed. Clicking the minus sign collapses My Computer and changes to a plus sign. End with My Computer expanded and the **minus sign** displayed as shown in Figure 13a.
- Place the disk from the previous exercise in drive A. Expand and collapse each drive within My Computer. (Drive A does not have any folders at this time, and hence will have neither a plus nor a minus sign.)
- End with a **plus sign** next to drive C so that the hard drive is collapsed as shown in Figure 13a. (The contents of My Computer will depend on your particular configuration.)

STEP 3: Create a Notepad Document

- Click the **icon** for **drive A** in the left pane to view the contents of the disk in the right pane. You should see the Files and Folders and Rectangles files that were created in the previous exercise.
- Pull down the **File menu.** Click (or point to) **New** to display the submenu. Click **Text Document** as the type of file to create.

- The icon for a new document will appear with the name of the document (New Text Document) highlighted. Type **About Explorer** to change the name of the document. Press **enter.** Double click the **file icon** to open the Notepad accessory and create the document.
- Move and/or size the Notepad window to your preference. You can also maximize the window so that you have more room in which to work.
- Pull down the **Edit menu** and toggle **Word Wrap** on. Enter the text of the document as shown in Figure 13b.
- Pull down the **File menu** and click **Save** to save the document when you are finished. Click the **Close button** to close Notepad and return to the Explorer.

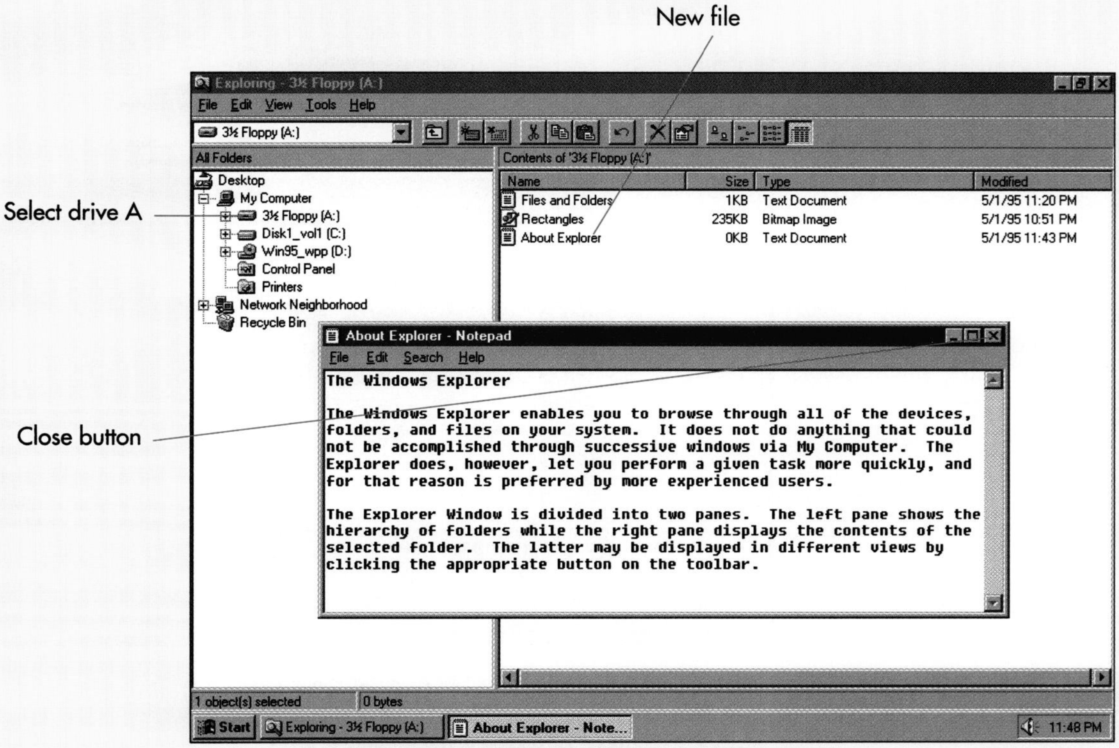
New file
Select drive A
Close button
Exploring - 3½ Floppy (A:)
File Edit View Tools Help
3½ Floppy (A:)
All Folders
Contents of '3½ Floppy (A:)'
Desktop
My Computer
3½ Floppy (A:)
Disk1_vol1 (C:)
Win95_wpp (D:)
Control Panel
Printers
Network Neighborhood
Recycle Bin
Name
Size
Type
Modified
Files and Folders
1KB
Text Document
5/1/95 11:20 PM
Rectangles
235KB
Bitmap Image
5/1/95 10:51 PM
About Explorer
0KB
Text Document
5/1/95 11:43 PM
About Explorer - Notepad
File Edit Search Help
The Windows Explorer
The Windows Explorer enables you to browse through all of the devices, folders, and files on your system. It does not do anything that could not be accomplished through successive windows via My Computer. The Explorer does, however, let you perform a given task more quickly, and for that reason is preferred by more experienced users.
The Explorer Window is divided into two panes. The left pane shows the hierarchy of folders while the right pane displays the contents of the selected folder. The latter may be displayed in different views by clicking the appropriate button on the toolbar.
1 object(s) selected
0 bytes
Start
Exploring - 3½ Floppy (A:)
About Explorer - Note...
11:48 PM

(b) Create a NotePad Document (step 3)

FIGURE 13 Hands-on Exercise 4 (continued)

STEP 4: Create a Paint Drawing

- Click the **icon** for **drive A** in the Explorer window, then pull down the **File menu.** (Alternatively, you can click the **right mouse button** in the right pane of the Explorer window when drive A is selected in the left pane.)
- Click (or point to) the **New command** to display the submenu. Click **Bitmap Image** as the type of file to create.
- The icon for a new drawing will appear with the name of the file (New Bitmap Image) highlighted. Type **Circles** to change the name of the file. Press **enter.** Double click the **file icon** to open the Paint accessory and create the drawing.
- Move and/or size the Paint window to your preference. You can also maximize the window so that you have more room in which to work.

- Create a simple drawing consisting of various circles and ellipses as shown in Figure 13c.
- Pull down the **File menu.** Click **Save As** to produce the Save As dialog box. Change the file type to **16-Color Bitmap** (from the default 256-color bitmap) to create a smaller file and conserve space on the floppy disk. Click **Save.** Click **Yes** to replace the file.
- Click the **Close button** to close Paint and return to the Explorer.

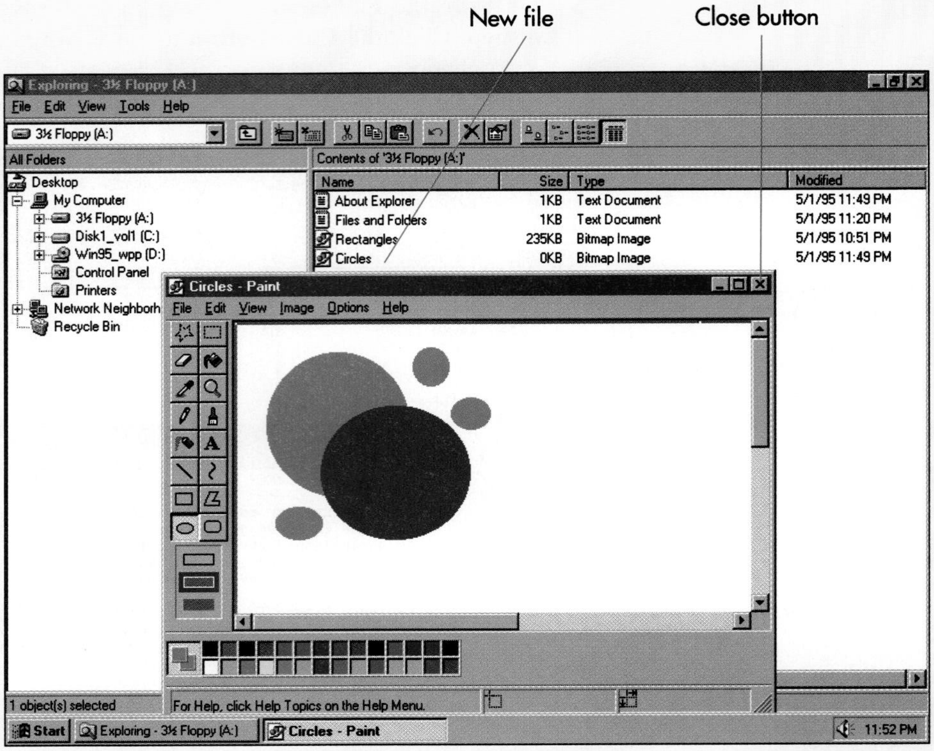

New file
Close button
Exploring - 3½ Floppy (A:)
File Edit View Tools Help
3½ Floppy (A:)
All Folders
Contents of '3½ Floppy (A:)'
Desktop
My Computer
3½ Floppy (A:)
Disk1_vol1 (C:)
Win95_wpp (D:)
Control Panel
Printers
Network Neighborh
Recycle Bin
Name
Size
Type
Modified
About Explorer
1KB
Text Document
5/1/95 11:49 PM
Files and Folders
1KB
Text Document
5/1/95 11:20 PM
Rectangles
235KB
Bitmap Image
5/1/95 10:51 PM
Circles
0KB
Bitmap Image
5/1/95 11:49 PM
Circles - Paint
File Edit View Image Options Help
1 object(s) selected
For Help, click Help Topics on the Help Menu.
Start
Exploring - 3½ Floppy (A:)
Circles - Paint
11:52 PM

(c) Create a Drawing (step 4)

FIGURE 13 Hands-on Exercise 4 (continued)

STEP 5: Create the Folders

- If necessary, click the **icon** for **drive A** in the left pane of the Explorer window. Drive A should contain four files as shown in Figure 13d (the folders have not yet been created).
- Pull down the **File menu,** click (or point to) the **New command,** then click **Folder** as the type of object to create.
- The icon for a new folder will appear with the name of the folder (New Folder) highlighted. Type **Documents** to change the name of the folder. Press **enter.**
- Click the **icon** for **drive A** in the left pane. Pull down the **File menu.** Click (or point to) the **New command.** Click **Folder** as the type of object to create.
- The icon for a new folder will appear with the name of the folder (New Folder) highlighted. Type **Drawings** to change the name of the folder. Press **enter.** The right pane should now contain four documents and two folders.

- Pull down the **View menu.** Click (or point to) the **Arrange Icons command** to display a submenu, then click the **By Name command.**
- Click the **plus sign** next to drive A to expand the drive. Your screen should match Figure 13d:
  - The left pane shows the subordinate folders on drive A.
  - The right pane displays the contents of drive A (the selected object in the left pane). The folders are shown first and appear in alphabetical order. The document names are displayed after the folders and are also in alphabetical order.

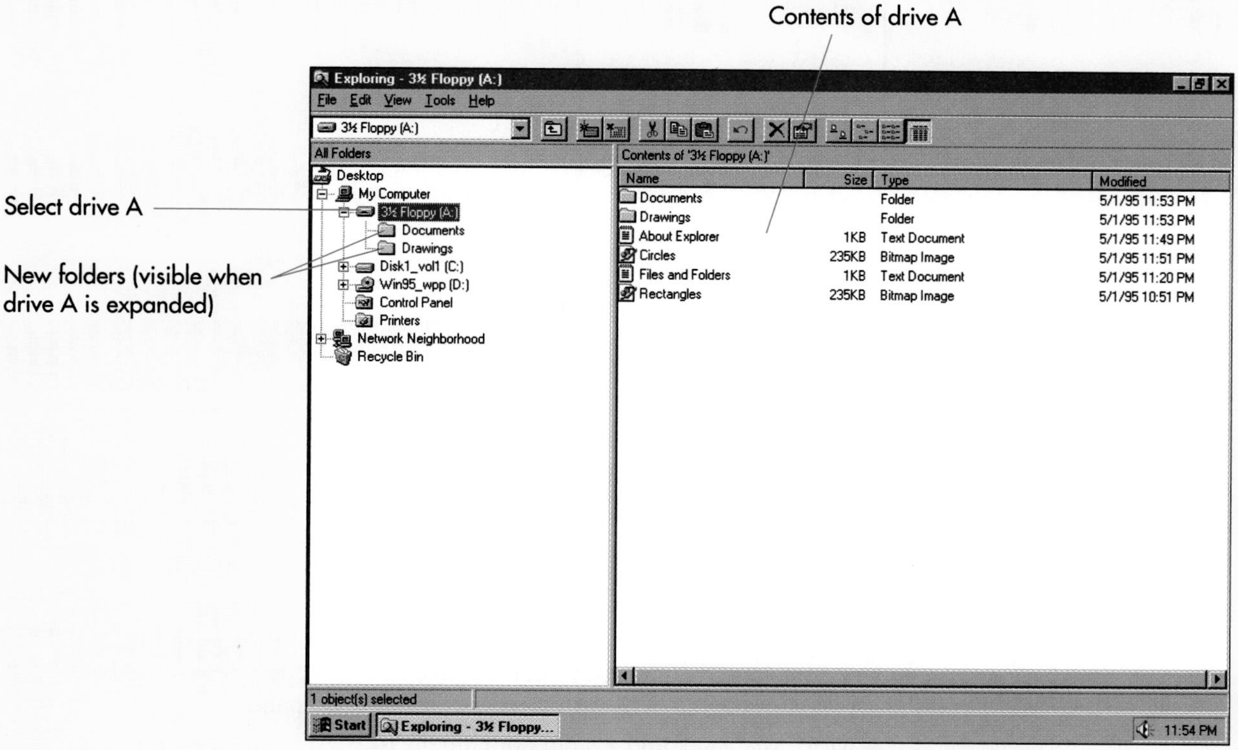

Contents of drive A
Select drive A
New folders (visible when drive A is expanded)
Exploring - 3½ Floppy (A:)
File Edit View Tools Help
3½ Floppy (A:)
All Folders
Contents of '3½ Floppy (A:)'
Desktop
My Computer
3½ Floppy (A:)
Documents
Drawings
Disk1_vol1 (C:)
Win95_wpp (D:)
Control Panel
Printers
Network Neighborhood
Recycle Bin
Name Size Type Modified
Documents Folder 5/1/95 11:53 PM
Drawings Folder 5/1/95 11:53 PM
About Explorer 1KB Text Document 5/1/95 11:49 PM
Circles 235KB Bitmap Image 5/1/95 11:51 PM
Files and Folders 1KB Text Document 5/1/95 11:20 PM
Rectangles 235KB Bitmap Image 5/1/95 10:51 PM
1 object(s) selected
Start
Exploring - 3½ Floppy...
11:54 PM

(d) Create the Folders (step 5)

FIGURE 13 Hands-on Exercise 4 (continued)

STEP 6: Move the Files

- This step has you move the Notepad documents and Paint drawings to the Documents and Drawings folders, respectively.
- To move the About Explorer document:
  - Point to the **icon** for **About Explorer** in the right pane. Use the **right mouse button** to click and drag the icon to the Documents folder in the left pane.
  - Release the mouse to display the menu shown in Figure 13e. Click **Move Here** to move the file. A popup window will appear briefly as the file is being moved.

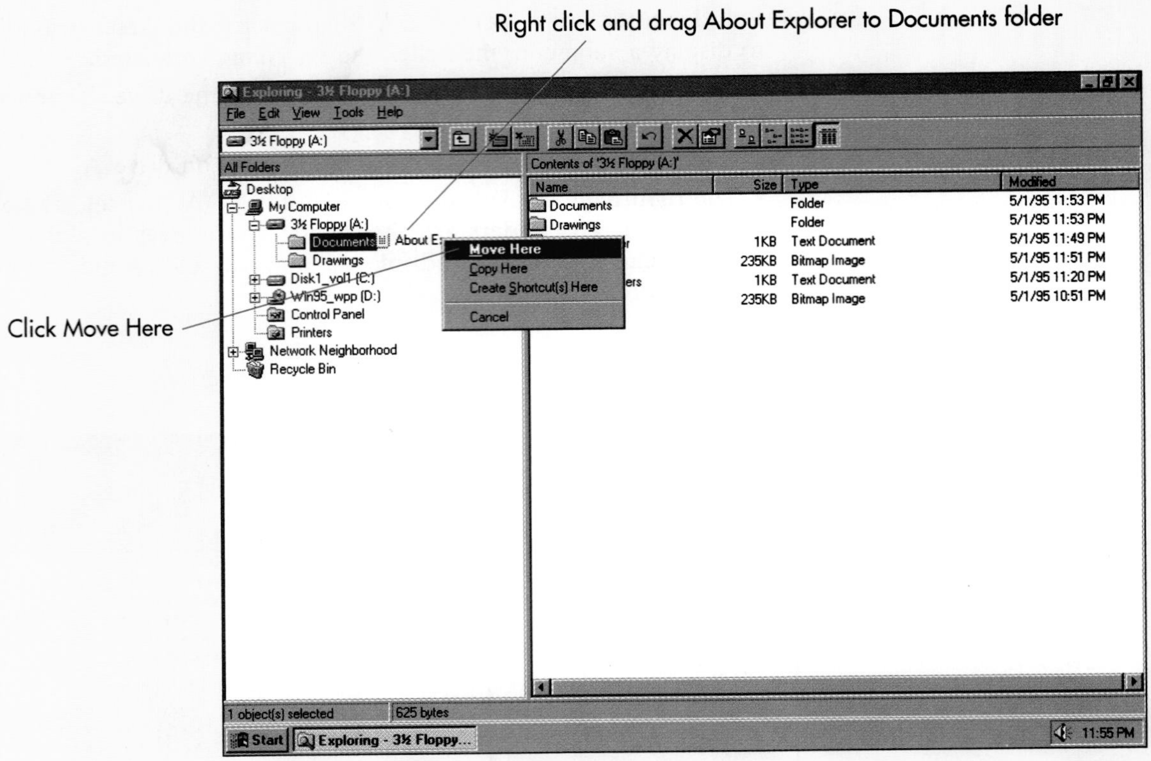

Right click and drag About Explorer to Documents folder
Click Move Here
Exploring - 3½ Floppy (A:)
Move Here
Copy Here
Create Shortcut(s) Here
Cancel

(e) Move the Files (step 6)

FIGURE 13 Hands-on Exercise 4 (continued)

- To prove that the file has been moved, you can view the contents of the Documents folder:
  - Click the **Documents folder** in the left pane to select the folder. The icon for the Documents folder changes to an open folder and its contents (About Explorer) are displayed in the right pane.
- Move the Files and Folders document to the Documents folder:
  - Click the **icon** for **drive A** to select the drive and display its contents.
  - Point to the **icon** for **Files and Folders.** Use the **right mouse button** to click and drag the icon to the Documents folder in the left pane.
  - Release the mouse to display a menu. Click **Move Here** to move the file.
- Use the **right mouse button** to move the Circles and Rectangles files to the Drawings folder.

STEP 7: Copy the Contents of the Documents Folder

- This step has you copy the contents of the Documents folder on drive A to the Homework folder on drive C. Click (select) the **Documents folder** on drive A to open the folder and display its contents as shown in Figure 13f.
- Click the **plus sign** next to the icon for drive C to expand the drive and display its folders. You should see the Homework folder that was created in the first exercise. Do *not* click the folder on drive C as the Documents folder on drive A is to remain open.

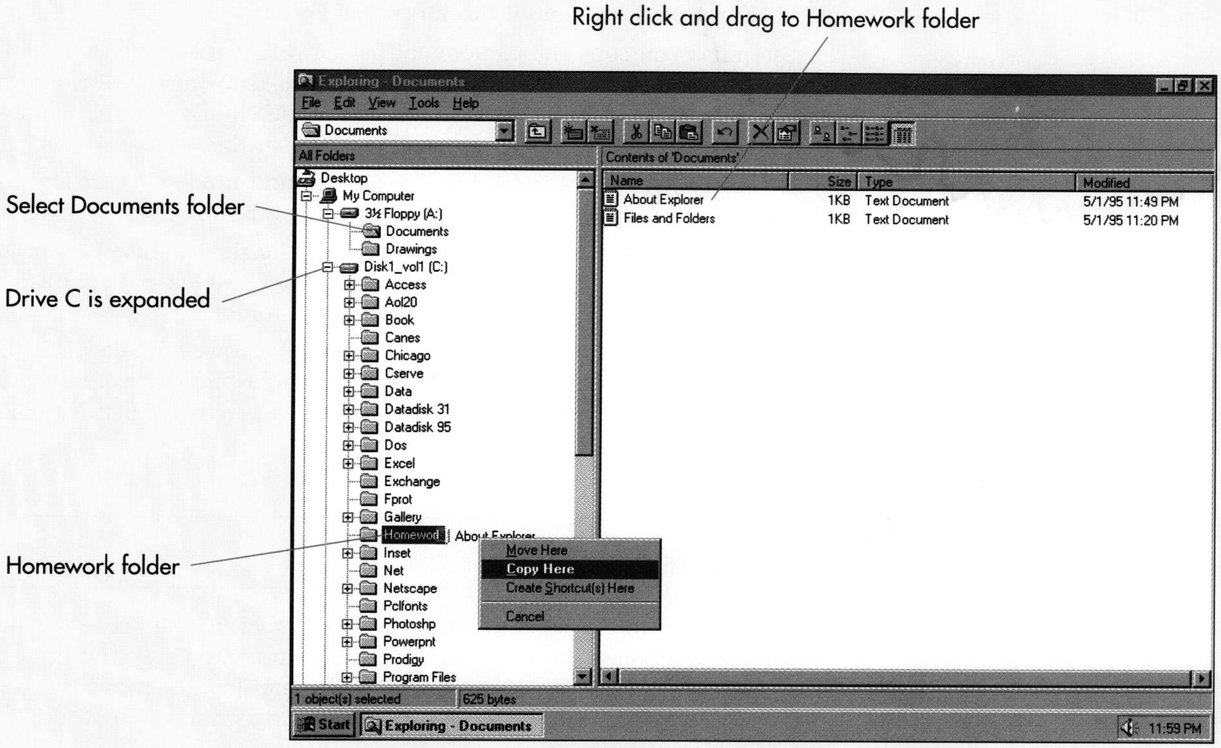
Right click and drag to Homework folder
Select Documents folder
Drive C is expanded
Homework folder
Exploring - Documents
File Edit View Tools Help
Documents
All Folders
Contents of 'Documents'
Desktop
My Computer
3½ Floppy (A:)
Documents
Drawings
Disk1_vol1 (C:)
Access
Aol20
Book
Canes
Chicago
Cserve
Data
Datadisk 31
Datadisk 95
Dos
Excel
Exchange
Fprot
Gallery
Homework
Inset
Net
Netscape
Pclfonts
Photoshp
Powerpnt
Prodigy
Program Files
Name
Size
Type
Modified
About Explorer
1KB
Text Document
5/1/95 11:49 PM
Files and Folders
1KB
Text Document
5/1/95 11:20 PM
Move Here
Copy Here
Create Shortcut(s) Here
Cancel
1 object(s) selected
625 bytes
Start
Exploring - Documents
11:59 PM

(f) Copy to Drive C (step 7)

FIGURE 13 Hands-on Exercise 4 (continued)

- Point to the **About Explorer file** (in the Documents folder on drive A). Use the **right mouse button** to click and drag the icon to the Homework folder on drive C. Release the mouse. Click **Copy Here** to copy the file to the Homework folder.
- Point to the **Files and Folders file** (in the Documents folder on drive A). Use the **right mouse button** to click and drag the icon to the Homework folder on drive C. Release the mouse. Click **Copy Here.**
- You will see a dialog box asking whether you want to replace the Files and Folders file that is already in the Homework folder (from the previous hands-on exercise). Click **No** since the files are the same.

OPEN FOLDERS QUICKLY

Click in the left pane of the Explorer window, then type any letter to select (open) the first folder whose name begins with that letter. If you type two letters in quick succession—for example, W and O—you will open the first folder beginning with the letters W and O. Pausing between the letters—that is, typing W, then leisurely typing O—will open a folder beginning with W, then open a second folder (while closing the first) whose name begins with O.

STEP 8: Copy the Contents of the Drawings Folder

- This step has you copy the contents of the Drawings folder on drive A to the Homework folder on drive C. Click (select) the **Drawings folder** on drive A to open the folder and display its contents. You should see the Circles and Rectangles files that were moved to this folder in the previous step.
- Click the **icon** for the **Circles file,** then press and hold the **Ctrl key** as you click the **icon** for the **Rectangles file** to select both files.
- Point to either of the selected files, then click the **right mouse button** as you drag both files to the Homework folder on drive C. Release the mouse. Click **Copy Here** to copy the files to the Homework folder.
- Explorer will begin to copy both files. You will, however, see a dialog box asking whether you want to replace the Rectangles file that is already in the Homework folder (from the previous hands-on exercise). Click **No** since the files are the same.

SELECT MULTIPLE FILES

You can perform the same operation on multiple files at the same time by selecting the files prior to executing the command. Press and hold the Ctrl key as you click the icon of each additional file you want to select. If the files are adjacent to one another, click the icon of the first file, then press and hold the Shift key as you click the icon of the last file.

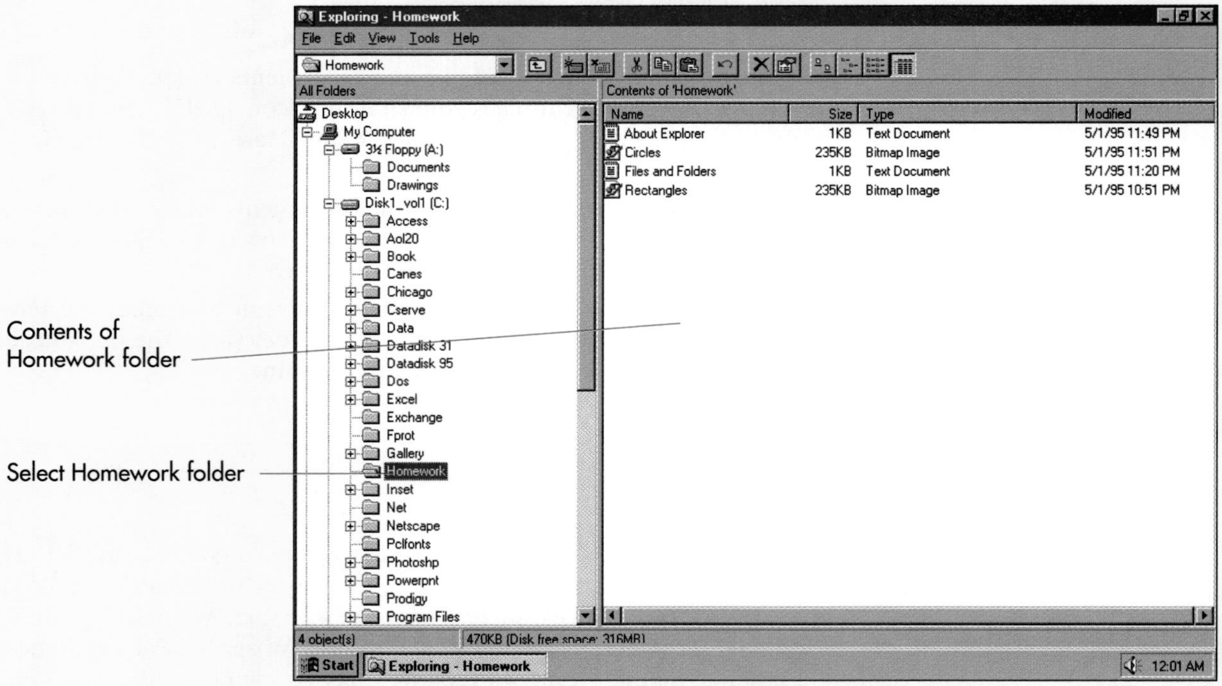

Contents of Homework folder
Select Homework folder
Exploring - Homework
File Edit View Tools Help
Homework
All Folders
Contents of 'Homework'
Desktop
My Computer
3½ Floppy (A:)
Documents
Drawings
Disk1_vol1 (C:)
Access
Aol20
Book
Canes
Chicago
Cserve
Data
Datadisk 31
Datadisk 95
Dos
Excel
Exchange
Fprot
Gallery
Homework
Inset
Net
Netscape
Pclfonts
Photoshp
Powerpnt
Prodigy
Program Files
Name
Size
Type
Modified
About Explorer
1KB
Text Document
5/1/95 11:49 PM
Circles
235KB
Bitmap Image
5/1/95 11:51 PM
Files and Folders
1KB
Text Document
5/1/95 11:20 PM
Rectangles
235KB
Bitmap Image
5/1/95 10:51 PM
4 object(s)
Start
Exploring - Homework
12:01 AM

(g) Check Your Work (step 9)

FIGURE 13 Hands-on Exercise 4 (continued)

STEP 9: Check Your Work

- Select (click) the **Homework folder** on drive C to display its contents.
- The icon changes to an open folder, and you should see the four files in Figure 13g.
- Please delete the Homework folder from drive C if you are working in a lab where other students have access to this machine. Select (click) the **Homework folder** and press the **Del key.** Click **Yes** when asked whether to delete the folder.
- Click the **Close button** to close Explorer. Click the **Start button.** Click the **Shut Down** command to exit Windows.

SUMMARY

All Windows operations take place on the desktop. The Start button, as its name suggests, is where you begin. Online help is accessed by clicking the Help command from the Start button. The mouse is essential to Windows and has four basic actions: pointing, clicking (with the left or right button), double clicking, and dragging. The mouse pointer assumes different shapes according to the nature of the current action.

Every window contains the same basic elements, which include a title bar, a Minimize button, a Maximize or Restore button, and a Close button. Other elements that may be present include a menu bar, vertical and/or horizontal scroll bars, a status bar, and a toolbar. All windows may be moved and sized.

A dialog box supplies information needed to execute a command. Option buttons indicate mutually exclusive choices, one of which must be chosen. Check boxes are used if the choices are not mutually exclusive or if an option is not required. A text box supplies descriptive information. A (drop-down or open) list box displays multiple choices, any of which may be selected. A tabbed dialog box provides access to multiple sets of options.

The first (often only) floppy drive on a system is designated as drive A. The first (often only) hard disk is drive C regardless of whether there are one or two floppy drives. Additional hard drives and/or the CD-ROM drive are labeled from D on.

A file name can contain up to 255 characters in length and may include spaces and other punctuation. Files are stored in folders to better organize the hundreds (or thousands) of files on a disk. A folder may contain program files, data files, and/or other folders.

The most basic way to locate a specific file or folder is to use My Computer, which opens a new window for each successive folder. The Windows Explorer is a more sophisticated tool that displays a hierarchical view of the entire system in a single window.

The Delete command deletes (removes) a file from a disk. If, however, the file was deleted from a hard disk, it is not really gone, but moved instead to the Recycle Bin from where it can be subsequently recovered.

The result of dragging a file icon from one folder to another depends on whether the folders are on the same or different drives. Dragging the file to a folder on the same drive moves the file. Dragging the file to a folder on a different drive copies the file. It's easier, therefore, to click and drag with the right mouse button to produce a menu from which you can select the operation.

KEY WORDS AND CONCEPTS

Backup
Check box
Click
Close button
Command button
Contents tab
Control Panel
Copy command
Cut command
Data file
Delete command
Desktop
Details view
Dialog box
Dimmed command
Double click
Drag
Drop-down list box
Ellipsis
File
File type
Folder
Help command
Horizontal scroll bar
Icons
Index tab
Large Icons view
List box
Maximize button
Menu bar
Minimize button
Mouse pointer
Move a window
My Computer
Network Neighborhood
New command
Online help
Open list box
Option buttons
Paste command
Point
Printers folder
Program file
Properties
Pull-down menu
Recycle Bin
Rename command
Restore button
Right click
Size a window
Small Icons View
Start button
Status bar
Submenu
Tabbed dialog box
Taskbar
Text box
Title bar
Toolbar
Vertical scroll bar
What's This button
Windows Explorer
Windows 95

INDEX

A

B

C

D